# Living Out Loud

D0084396

*Living Out Loud: An Introduction to LGBTQ History, Society, and Culture* offe[rs] students an evidence-based foundation in the interdisciplinary field of LGBTQ Studies. Chapters on history, diversity, dating/relationships, education, sexual health, and globalization reflect current research and thinking in the social sciences, humanities, and sciences. Coverage of current events and recommendations for additional readings, videos, and web resources help students apply the contents in their lives, making *Living Out Loud* the perfect core text for LGBTQ+ Studies (and similar) courses.

**Michael J. Murphy**, PhD, is Associate Professor of Gender and Sexuality Studies at the University of Illinois Springfield, where he has taught since 2009. He holds degrees in the history of art, and women's/gender/sexuality studies, from the University of Iowa and Washington University in St. Louis. Since 2005 he has taught numerous courses in women's/gender studies, critical men's/masculinity studies, and LGBTQ+/sexuality studies. He is the author of many encyclopedia and journal articles, and other publications including *Activities for Teaching Gender and Sexuality in the University Classroom*, Michael J. Murphy and Elizabeth Ribarsky, eds. (Lanham, MD: Rowman & Littlefield Education, 2013). He lives with his husband in St. Louis, Missouri.

**Brytton Bjorngaard** is an Assistant Professor of Digital Media at the University of Illinois Springfield. She holds an MFA in Graphic Design from Iowa State University and a BA in Graphic Design from Saint Mary's University of Minnesota. She is a freelance graphic designer, working primarily for non-profit organizations in the Springfield, Illinois area, including the Enos Park Neighborhood Improvement Association, Springfield Art Association, Shelterbelt Press, and Compass for Kids.

"Clear explanations of central concepts, a wide range of disciplinary approaches, and a commitment to critical analysis make this a superb choice for Introduction to LGBTQ or Sexuality Studies courses! The chapters are comprehensive and the approach innovative. Frank discussions of sexual behavior, attention to intersectionality, and a superb discussion of the politics of globalization make this text stand out."

—Andrea Friedman, Professor, History and Women, Gender, and Sexuality Studies, Washington University in St. Louis

"I am grateful to be alive during this part of the r/evolution when scholars are explaining LGBTQ Studies' foundation for the next generation. Thank you Murphy and Bjorngaard for lovingly collecting and explaining the data that makes our stories real."

—Loraine Hutchins, co-editor, *Bi Any Other Name*; co-founder BiNet USA

"This wide-ranging, college-level, introduction to LGBTQ+ Studies fills a pressing need for just such a volume. Avoiding jargon, the authors summarize debates in history, health, politics, sociology, and literature, and welcome students to the whole, fascinating world of sexuality and gender studies."

—Jonathan Ned Katz, Codirector, OutHistory.org

"I was excited to first hear of a narrative textbook as an introduction to LGBTQ+ Studies. After reading *Living Out Loud*, I'm just as enthusiastic about how relatable and approachable this work is in reaching the ever-evolving target of LGBTQ+ cultural competency. I look forward to quoting and sharing this book in both my professional life and in my advocacy."

—Jaimie Hileman, Executive Director, Trans Education Service

# Living Out Loud

## An Introduction to LGBTQ History, Society, and Culture

Edited by Michael J. Murphy with
Brytton Bjorngaard

Routledge
Taylor & Francis Group

NEW YORK AND LONDON

First published 2019
by Routledge
711 Third Avenue, New York, NY 10017

and by Routledge
2 Park Square, Milton Park, Abingdon, Oxon, OX14 4RN

*Routledge is an imprint of the Taylor & Francis Group, an informa business*

© 2019 Michael J. Murphy

The right of Michael J. Murphy to be identified as the author
of the editorial material, and of the authors for their individual
chapters, has been asserted in accordance with sections 77 and 78
of the Copyright, Designs and Patents Act 1988.

All rights reserved. No part of this book may be reprinted or
reproduced or utilised in any form or by any electronic, mechanical,
or other means, now known or hereafter invented, including
photocopying and recording, or in any information storage or
retrieval system, without permission in writing from the author.

*Trademark notice*: Product or corporate names may be trademarks
or registered trademarks, and are used only for identification and
explanation without intent to infringe.

*Library of Congress Cataloging-in-Publication Data*
Names: Murphy, Michael J. (Writer on gender studies), editor. |
    Bjorngaard, Brytton, editor.
Title: Living out loud : an introduction to LGBTQ history,
    society, and culture / edited by Michael Murphy with Brytton
    Bjorngaard.
Description: New York, NY : Routledge, 2018. | Includes
    bibliographical references and index.
Identifiers: LCCN 2017052690 (print) | LCCN 2017055677
    (ebook) | ISBN 9781315640228 (Master Ebook) | ISBN
    9781317276371 (Wed pdf) | ISBN 9781317276364 ( ePub) |
    ISBN 9781317276364 (mobipocket) | ISBN 9781138191914
    (hardback : alk. paper) | ISBN 9781138191921 (pbk. : alk. paper)
Subjects: LCSH: Gays—History. | Sexual minorities—History.
Classification: LCC HQ76.25 (ebook) | LCC HQ76.25 .L526
    2018 (print) | DDC 306.76/6—dc23
LC record available at https://lccn.loc.gov/2017052690


ISBN: 978-1-138-19191-4 (hbk)
ISBN: 978-1-138-19192-1 (pbk)
ISBN: 978-1-315-64022-8 (ebk)


Typeset in Bembo
by Swales & Willis Ltd, Exeter, Devon, UK

# Dedication

This book is dedicated to the memory of all those killed the night of June 12, 2016 at Pulse nightclub (Orlando, Florida) in the largest act of gun violence against LGBTQ+ people in U.S. history. We will remember!

Stanley Almodovar III, 23
Amanda L. Alvear, 25
Oscar A. Aracena Montero, 26
Rodolfo Ayala Ayala, 33
Antonio Davon Brown, 29
Darryl Roman Burt II, 29
Angel Candelario-Padro, 28
Juan Chavez Martinez, 25
Luis Daniel Conde, 39
Cory James Connell, 21
Tevin Eugene Crosby, 25
Deonka Deidra Drayton, 32
Simón Adrian Carrillo Fernández, 31
Leroy Valentin Fernandez, 25
Mercedez Marisol Flores, 26
Peter Ommy Gonzalez Cruz, 22
Juan Ramon Guerrero, 22
Paul Terrell Henry, 41
Frank Hernandez, 27
Miguel Angel Honorato, 30
Javier Jorge Reyes, 40
Jason Benjamin Josaphat, 19
Eddie Jamoldroy Justice, 30
Anthony Luis Laureano Disla, 25
Christopher Andrew Leinonen, 32

Alejandro Barrios Martinez, 21
Brenda Marquez McCool, 49
Gilberto R. Silva Menendez, 25
Kimberly Jean Morris, 37
Akyra Monet Murray, 18
Luis Omar Ocasio Capo, 20
Geraldo A. Ortiz Jimenez, 25
Eric Ivan Ortiz-Rivera, 36
Joel Rayon Paniagua, 32
Jean Carlos Mendez Perez, 35
Enrique L. Rios, Jr., 25
Jean Carlos Nieves Rodríguez, 27
Xavier Emmanuel Serrano-Rosado, 35
Christopher Joseph Sanfeliz, 24
Yilmary Rodríguez Solivan, 24
Edward Sotomayor Jr., 34
Shane Evan Tomlinson, 33
Martin Benitez Torres, 33
Jonathan A. Camuy Vega, 24
Juan Pablo Rivera Velázquez, 37
Luis Sergio Vielma, 22
Franky Jimmy DeJesus Velázquez, 50
Luis Daniel Wilson-Leon, 37
Jerald Arthur Wright, 31

and

Maureen "Mo" Costello and all the staff at MoKaBe's Coffee House (St. Louis, Missouri). For over 20 years, MoKaBe's has been the *de facto* LGBTQIA community center, and ground zero for social justice activism, in St. Louis. It's also where much of this book was written and edited;

and

My long-suffering husband, David Ridder, whose "real job" allows me to engage in intellectual peregrinations that sometimes result in books (like the one you hold in your hand).

# Brief Contents

# Detailed Contents

# Preface

*Living Out Loud: An Introduction to LGBTQ History, Society, and Culture* is the first narrative textbook designed to support college-level *Introduction to LGBTQ Studies* (and similar) courses. Students enrolled in such courses are typically sophomores and juniors, with a range of motivations, interest levels, educational preparation, and academic majors. They may identify (or be on the way to identifying) as lesbian, gay, bisexual, transgender, queer/questioning, intersex or other types of gender and sexual minorities (LGBTQ+). Or they may have LGBTQ+ friends or family members who they wish to better support through learning more about their lives, experiences, issues, and accomplishments.

Accordingly, *Living Out Loud* takes an introductory approach that assumes little prior knowledge about LGBTQ+ topics. Unlike many text readers or collections of conference papers in this subject area, which can employ advanced concepts and vocabularies, *Living Out Loud* offers an accessible, student-friendly text with content, tone, language, and design that is appropriate for lower- and mid-level college and university students. It introduces students to foundational topics, concepts, terms, and debates in the rapidly expanding field of interdisciplinary LGBTQ+ Studies.

*Living Out Loud* has been sized so that it may serve as a sole course text or, if supplemented with articles or monographs, can provide the backbone of a more customized course. The book is divided into nine chapters focused on a discrete disciplinary or on interdisciplinary areas of academic study. Care has been taken to include entire chapters or chapter sections from the humanities, sciences, and social sciences. The book is unique in its inclusion of chapters on LGBTQ+ Sexual Behavior and Sexual Health; Literature and Visual Art; Education; Relationships; and, Globalization. Chapter authors have been mindful to address LGBTQ+ racial and ethnic diversity, and better integrate bisexual and transgender people, topics, experiences, and themes.

To engage today's students, each chapter is illustrated with a range of charts, tables, graphs, infographics, and photographs. Focus boxes—by guest and main chapter authors—expand each chapter's scope in new and interesting directions. Each chapter concludes with a list of recommended readings, films/videos, and Internet resources. The goal is to introduce students to the exciting field of LGBTQ Studies and provide a broad, multi-disciplinary foundation for subsequent, more-advanced academic work.

## TO THE STUDENT

The book you hold in your hands is the product of three years of research and writing; over a decade of study and teaching about LGBTQ+ history, culture, and society; and a lifetime of being a gay man. Most people who know me would probably describe me as a talker (when I graduated high school, my best friend gave me a mug depicting three yaks and the words "Yak! Yak! Yak!"). But my experience of growing up gay in the 1970s and 1980s was one of overwhelming, stifling silence. Homosexuality was rarely depicted in the media, and then not positively, and hardly mentioned in polite society. I came out in the early 1980s, when the scale of the HIV/AIDS epidemic was just beginning to be understood and gay men were often vilified by conservative political, religious, and social "leaders."

At that time, information about gays and lesbians was hard to come by. The Internet hadn't been invented and the public library had nothing on the shelves. Desperate to acquire an understanding of feelings I barely knew how to name, I remember sneaking looks at the few books in the sexualities section of the local mall's bookstore. My main sources of education on how to be gay were barely older lesbians and gay men who mentored me in what it meant to live a productive, useful, and (occasionally) fabulous gay life. I learned about gay sex— not in a sex-ed class—but from pornography, sexual partners, and HIV/AIDS prevention campaigns. (Given the haphazard state of that education and the decade in which I came out, I count myself very lucky to be alive.) In college, I never had the opportunity to take one of the newly created courses on gay and lesbian art, history, film, and literature, and in graduate school some professors actively discouraged me from focusing on this subject for my doctoral research.

When I eventually had the opportunity to offer LGBTQ-themed courses as a university professor, I came to realize that some things had gotten better, while other things had stayed the same. Despite the advent of the Internet and a wealth of resources to support LGBTQ+ people, we were still missing from the content of most students' high school and college courses. New social media platforms on the Internet and smartphones made it easier to connect with sexual and romantic partners, but abstinence-only sex "education" programs that never mentioned same-sex sexual behavior or STI prevention left LGBTQ+ young people vulnerable to exploitation, violence, and disease.

In some ways the social, cultural, and legal climate for LGBTQ+ people has improved dramatically. But we still confront issues such as: lack of legal recognition for the full diversity of LGBTQ+ families and relationships; the new politics of HIV/AIDS ("barebacking," PrEP, sero-sorting, etc.); discrimination in housing, employment, and public accommodation; the epidemic of violence against transwomen of color; lack of access to medically necessary healthcare for most transgender people; the continuing invisibility of bisexuals in LGBTQ+ social, cultural, and political spaces; and emergent issues affecting LGBTQ+ youth and elders such as suicide, homelessness, substance abuse, sex trafficking, lack of culturally competent healthcare, and the lifetime effects of legalized discrimination, bigotry, and inequality.

I launched this book project so that today's LGBTQ+ and allied college students would have a resource that I never had. The content has been driven by the question: *What have we learned from a generation of academic research about LGBTQ+ history, society and culture?* If this book in any way helps young LGBTQ+ students better understand themselves, their history, their culture, and their lives—and feel more empowered to live their lives out loud—I will deem it a success.

Over my many years of teaching, students have strengthened my thinking about most of the topics covered by this book. I'm happy to hear your thoughts and feedback. Contact me at LivingOutLoud2018@gmail.com.

## A Note on Language

Words and language are a form of power. They are how we describe the world around us; they are also how we organize that world and give it meaning. Therefore, words need to be used with care when talking about historically marginalized groups such as lesbian, gay, bisexual, transgender, and queer people.

Throughout this book, the various authors use terms (such as gay, gay and lesbian, LGBT, LGBTQ, LGBTQIA) to describe gender and sexual minorities in the United States and around the world. The exact make-up of the initialism LGBTQ is the subject of ongoing and often-contentious debate among the very people the term aims to describe. The argument often boils down to practicality vs. inclusion.

Some argue that every conceivable sexual and gender minority be represented in the initialism using the first letter of their group's name. This has resulted in an initialism as long as LGBTQQIAAP. However accurate, such lengthy initialisms can raise practical and stylistic issues of pronounceability, readability, and word-count limits in academic publishing. Others prefer a single word or short term (i.e. gay, queer, or gay and lesbian) or a standardized initialism (i.e. LGBT). However, not including every letter can be viewed as a form of erasure of some people's experiences and existence. Commonly left out are bisexuals, queers, and intersex and transgender people.

Moreover, use of initialisms such as LGBT or LGBTQ can be fundamentally inaccurate, especially when describing a group or event that was exclusively (or properly named) gay or lesbian (i.e. Gay Activists Alliance; Lesbian Avengers). The automatic inclusion of bisexual and transgender people (in initialisms such as LGBT and LGBTQ) can have the effect of erasing bisexuals, queers, and transgender people—by inaccurately conflating their experiences with those of lesbians and gay men.

As editor of this project, I decided early on to not dictate language use to the contributors. Rather, I insisted that authors be self-conscious, intentional, and accurate in how they used terms like LGBTQ. In a number of places in the following text it was simply not appropriate nor accurate to use this generic abbreviation to describe people, events, or experiences addressed by the authors.

Also challenging: the academic research on which much of this book relies is not always clear, consistent, accurate, or inclusive in its use of identity terms. The fact remains, bisexuals and transgender people have not and are not systematically included in research on LGBT people. Throughout the book, I've asked chapter authors to not exceed or expand on terms used by their research sources—if a study did not include bisexual or transgender people, then we should not pretend that it did—and to point out the gaps in knowledge such oversights or intentional inclusions create. We cannot develop appropriate and inclusive laws, social services, and public policies without more complete and accurate information about LGBTQ+ people in all their diversity.

For all these reasons, terms to describe gender and sexual minorities will vary in usage throughout the book and within each chapter and focus box. As you read I ask that you give each author the benefit of the doubt, understanding that the demands of book publishing and the limitations of research sources, as much as author or editor preferences, can influence which words are used. Rather than a sign of scholarly error or inconsistency, I've chosen to view the argument over the "correct" initialism and the proliferation of terms to describe gender and sexuality as a sign of the vibrancy, creativity, and dynamism of gender and sexual minority people. This book is not the final word so long as we continue creating new words to describe our identities, experiences, and communities.

## TO THE INSTRUCTOR

*Living Out Loud* was conceived as a core textbook to support introductory LGBTQ-themed courses at college and university levels (such as "Intro to LGBTQ Studies" or similar). Students bring a range of motivations, experiences, and identities to such classes and they may only be able to take one course on these themes while in college. Therefore, the text assumes little prior knowledge while also aiming for university-level terminology and conceptual vocabulary. It was envisioned as a core textbook but has been sized to allow for the assignment of supplemental readings, such as journal articles and monographs. Because the intended audience is primarily students enrolled in U.S. colleges and universities, the text focuses for the most part on the United States, but global differences and globalization/transnational issues are addressed where appropriate—and is the focus of Chapter 9 in its entirety.

Our overarching goal has been to summarize in a readable text what we have learned through academic research about LGBTQ+ history, culture, and society. Although the chapters are evidence based, we have tried to avoid cumbersome citation styles that interrupt the prose with numerous references to source material. Citations are typically grouped at the end of sentences, paragraphs, or sections. Citations are meant to be indicative not exhaustive. We have also aimed to improve readability and create interest by regularly interrupting the main text with focus boxes, images, charts, tables, and graphs. Another important goal was better coverage of racial and ethnic diversity, and more inclusion of bisexuals and transgender people. At the outset I decided I did not want the text to isolate or "silo" specific identities into separate chapters, and therefore encouraged all authors to integrate bisexual and transgender themes with gay and lesbian themes. The lack of research data on bisexuals and transgender people made this a challenge for some of the topics included.

Chapters are arranged in an order that makes sense for my *Intro to LGBTQ Studies* class. Because I find students better understand contemporary social and cultural issues with the benefit of some historical perspective, I always begin with a unit on LGBTQ history (Ch. 1: Histories). However, depending on the experience and makeup of your class, it may also make sense to start your course with a presentation of fundamental terms and basic sociological information (Ch. 2: Diversities). The middle chapters of the book are grouped with a focus on individual life (such as dating, sexual behavior, and relationships), institutional life (education, politics), and cultural production/representation (popular culture, literature, visual arts). These chapters build on the content and vocabulary introduced in the first two chapters of the book. In my experience, discussion of global and transnational topics (Ch. 9: Globalization/Transnationalism) is best addressed after establishing a foundation of basic terms and concepts, and other social and cultural content. However, chapters are written in such a way that should allow for assignment in whatever order makes sense for your students, course, and institution.

Every chapter concludes with a carefully curated list of additional readings, films/videos, and websites, where students can learn more about each chapter's topic. The bias in selection has been toward education rather than entertainment but, of course, the two are not easily separated. Nevertheless, non-fiction readings and documentary films/videos predominate. Internet sources were selected for both relevance and persistence—this book will be in print for several years (hopefully) and we chose web resources for both their relevance and likely continued existence.

There is always material that could (and should) be included in a text such as this, and not every reader will agree with what we have chosen to include. As you and your students use this book, I welcome your thoughts, feedback, and suggestions for future editions of the text.

Contact me at LivingOutLoud2018@gmail.com.

Michael J. Murphy
St. Louis, Missouri
October 2017

# Acknowledgments

Brytton Bjorngaard would like to thank:

-my colleague, Michael Murphy, for inviting me to join this profound project and giving me a place to put my background in copyright to good use alongside my design skills . . . and for giving me a project that makes my search history far more interesting;

-my parents, for their support. They always say, "Really? Another project on top of everything you already do . . ." but saw the value in this and didn't say it. And listened to me rattle off STD statistics at the holiday dinner table without complaint.

Michael Murphy would like to thank:

-my colleague Brytton Bjorngaard for her unfailing good humor and endless good advice about graphic design, copyright practices, and expertise securing image reproduction rights. Her charts, tables, graphs, illustrations, and infographics make the text more interesting and attractive to read;

-Routledge/Taylor & Francis editorial and production staff: acquisitions editor Samantha Barbaro, and editorial assistants Margaret Moore, Athena Bryan, and Erik Zimmerman;

-Tommy Thompson, for his timely research assistance;

-named and anonymous reviewers of the book proposal and chapter drafts. Matt Swango (St. Louis Effort for AIDS), Eli Green (Widener University), and Loraine Hutchins offered numerous specific recommendations that made the text stronger and more inclusive;

-members of the "Teaching College Sexualities," "QSTDY-L," and "SEX-NET" listservs for their many suggestions;

-Amy Cislo, Susan Stiritz, Beth Ribarsky, Jo Ellen and Eugene Potchen-Webb, Monte Abbott, Tiffani Saunders, Missy Thibodeaux-Thompson, Angela Miller, Elizabeth Childs, Akiko Tsuchida, and Linda Nicholson for many conversations about gender, sexuality, and activism over the years. Special thanks to Andrea Friedman who first reviewed the book proposal and encouraged me to pursue the project;

–members and supporters of the Metro Trans Umbrella Group (St. Louis) for their many kind, patient, and generous conversations about how to better incorporate transgender people and their experiences into the text, especially Sayer Johnson, Jaimie Hileman, Elaine Brune, and Jarek Steele;

–various libraries, archives, and museums that provided help with research, articles, and images for the book. We are especially indebted to contributors to the Wikimedia Commons project, without which the book would be significantly diminished visually;

–students in all my women's, gender, and sexuality studies courses over the years for help sharpening my thinking and broadening my knowledge on LGBTQIA, gender, and sexuality topics.

# CHAPTER 1
# Out of the Past
## *Histories*

*Christianne Anastasia Gadd*

*Laurie Casagrande*, National Coming Out Day Poster, "Unfortunately, History Has Set the Record a Little Too Straight," *1988. Source: Laurie Casagrande. Image courtesy of Syracuse Cultural Workers.*

October 11, 1988, marked the first observance of National Coming Out Day in the United States. Jean O'Leary and Robert Eichberg, two activists for lesbian and gay rights, hoped this occasion would increase awareness of the lesbian, gay, bisexual, and transgender people in their lives and communities. To promote National Coming Out Day, Minnesota's Gay and Lesbian Community Action Council published a poster that read "Unfortunately, History Has Set the Record a Little Too Straight." Below the title were ten photos of well-known public figures of the past—including the Renaissance artist Michelangelo, writers Walt Whitman, James Baldwin, and Willa Cather, and former First Lady Eleanor Roosevelt—who had been involved in same-sex romantic or sexual relationships at some point in their lives. Though the admirable goal of the poster was to challenge the assumption that only heterosexual people had made important contributions to society, for viewers aware that the concepts of heterosexuality and homosexuality were relatively modern inventions, it also raised some questions about the artist's effort to reclaim LGBT history. Was it accurate, let alone desirable, to describe historic figures, or anyone in the past, using present-day terminology and understandings of sexual identity that these individuals themselves might have found foreign, or that they might have rejected?

This example illustrates one of the primary challenges facing historians of sexuality. How do we understand manifestations of same-sex love and sexuality in different cultures and across different eras? Some historians argue that same-sex desire has existed throughout history and in a number of cultures; in other words, that there have always been individuals whose primary romantic attachments and sexual attractions have been with others of the same sex. Historians who take this approach, called *essentialism*, tend to emphasize the similarities between past and present manifestations of same-sex love and sexuality. From the essentialist perspective, the homosexual is a distinctive type of person whose history can be traced back to the earliest civilizations.

Other historians, using an approach called *social construction*, argue that the meanings of same-sex romantic and sexual relationships are determined by the unique time and place in which they occur, as well as by the social status (determined, in part, by a person's race, age, gender, and class) of those who engage in them. From this perspective, a sexual act between an older, wealthy, married, male "citizen" and a young, unmarried, male slave in ancient Greece would have a significantly different social meaning than the same sexual act between two wealthy adult "citizens." Similarly, a romantic relationship between two middle-class, unmarried, African-American women in the nineteenth century United States would have had a different social meaning than a romance between two working-class, married, white women in Ireland in the same time period. Social constructionists argue that modern-day concepts and terminology of sexuality cannot be used to "accurately position people who lived in different circumstances" and that the term "homosexual" is particularly problematic when applied to individuals who lived in non-Western, pre-twentieth century societies (Eaklor, 2008, 8). While both perspectives have their merits and flaws, a social constructionist approach allows historians to explore how understandings of same-sex romance and sexuality have changed over time, and to investigate what these changes tell us about the ways in which different societies have viewed sexuality.

Since the 1970s historians and other scholars have amassed a mountain of evidence demonstrating that same-sex attraction and sexual behaviors, and a wide variety of gender expressions and identities, have been practiced throughout time and across cultures. However, in the interests of space, this chapter provides a general overview of these practices in what is today the United States, noting both the similarities and differences between their manifestations and the ways in which they were understood.

The terminology of sexual identity is also a point of contention among scholars of the past. As the example at the beginning of this chapter illustrates, historians have struggled with the impulse to use words like gay, lesbian, bisexual, or transgender to describe individuals who might not have known, understood, or embraced these words or concepts. While some argue that such terminology is useful to construct a linear history of LGBT people's existence throughout human history, others believe that use of these words glosses over the historically and culturally specific meanings of same-sex sexual behavior and sexual and gender identities. To address this issue, this chapter endeavors to describe same-sex sexual behavior and same-sex romantic or affectionate relationships using the terminology appropriate to each culture or era discussed. The terms gay, lesbian, bisexual or transgender are largely reserved for descriptions of post-nineteenth century individuals and/or societies shown by the historical record to have understood and used these terms themselves.

## EARLY AMERICA

### Gender and Sexuality among Native Americans

Though the cultures which flourished in North America prior to the arrival of European explorers and settlers varied considerably, same-sex sexual acts took place in many of them, carrying with them different social meanings. Heterosexual marriage—monogamous or polygamous—was usually part of Native American tribal norms, and an individual's gender dictated their roles within the tribe. While their roles were in some ways complementary, men and women had often very separate lives, with clearly defined responsibilities falling to each group.

One of the challenges facing historians who study sexual practices among the indigenous people of the Americas, and in particular Native Americans, is that much of the documentation that exists was created by European—and later American—explorers and colonizers. These outsiders interpreted what they observed through their own particular set of beliefs and social values, which doubtless influenced the accounts they produced.

To European colonizers, the most noteworthy thing about Native American gender expression and/or sexual practice was the presence of what has often been called persons of a "third" gender. Spanish and French explorers who encountered Native American societies regularly noted the appearance of individuals who did not appear to be conventionally male nor female. A sixteenth-century visitor to California wrote of seeing several Native American men in "women's apparel," and a Spanish explorer, who lived in captivity among

UNITED STATES
Native American Great Plains tribes viewed gender on a spectrum from male to female, including transgender and intersex persons who were considered to have special spiritual significance.

PORTUGAL
16th-19th Century:
In Lisbon, communities of men and women were known to have same-sex relationships, and were targeted by the Inquisition.

ITALY
15th-17th Century:
During the early Renaissance, "masculine love" was a term used to describe male homosexual orientation (also used in France and England). Michelangelo described same-sex love in his poems, although these references were later edited out. Ancient marble statues unearthed in Rome depicting intersex people inspired a number of Renaissance artists.

# SEXUAL ORIENTATION AND GENDER IDENTITY THROUGHOUT HISTORY

Lesbian, gay, bisexual, transgender, intersex and related identities have been present in various forms throughout history. All cultures have included, with varying degrees of acceptance, individuals who practice same-sex relations as well as those whose gender, gender identity and gender expression challenge prevailing norms, and many cultures still do.

MEXICO
In the Mayan culture of the Yucatan Peninsula, sexual relations between men were accepted as part of the social structure. Other indigenous peoples in the region have similar traditions.

NIGERIA
Among the Igbo people of Nigeria (and parts of Benin), a married woman with independent wealth may choose to separate from her husband and marry one or more women.

SOUTH AFRICA
16th - 20th century:
Wealthy and powerful women, could – even if already married to a man – marry other women, and having many wives was seen as a reflection of prosperity.

KENYA
Among the Nandi, women may marry other wome[n]
The older generally takes on a traditionally male re[le]
and is considered a "female husband". The young[er]
may become pregnant by a man but the legal and so[cial]
'father' of the children will be the female husban[d]

ANGOLA
16th - 17th century:
Some communities openly accepted homosexuality, cross-dressing and other behaviour blurring the lines of gender stereotypes.

DEM. REP. OF CONGO
16th - 17th century:
Men who acted and dressed in a manner considered feminine and women who acted and dressed in a manner considered masculine, were identified as kitesha.

EGYPT
24th century B[C]
The ancient Egyptian royal servants Niankhkhnum a[nd]
Khnumhotep are believed to be among the first record[ed]
same-sex couple in history, as reflected by the drawin[gs]
in their tom[b]

*Sexual Orientation and Gender Identity throughout History. Source: UN OHCHR and UN Free & Equal campaign.*

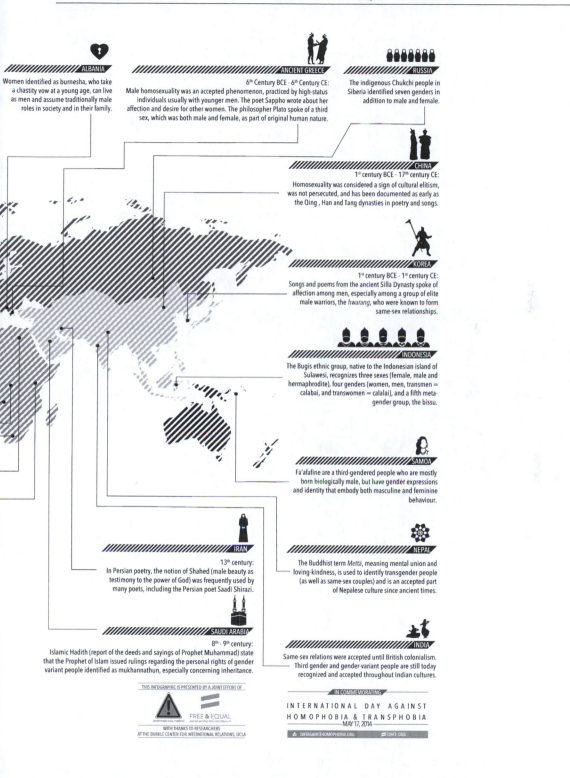

**ALBANIA**

Women identified as burnesha, who take a chastity vow at a young age, can live as men and assume traditionally male roles in society and in their family.

**ANCIENT GREECE**

6th Century BCE - 6th Century CE: Male homosexuality was an accepted phenomenon, practiced by high-status individuals usually with younger men. The poet Sappho wrote about her affection and desire for other women. The philosopher Plato spoke of a third sex, which was both male and female, as part of original human nature.

**RUSSIA**

The indigenous Chukchi people in Siberia identified seven genders in addition to male and female.

**CHINA**

1st century BCE - 17th century CE: Homosexuality was considered a sign of cultural elitism, was not persecuted, and has been documented as early as the Qing , Han and Tang dynasties in poetry and songs.

**KOREA**

1st century BCE - 1st century CE: Songs and poems from the ancient Silla Dynasty spoke of affection among men, especially among a group of elite male warriors, the hwarang, who were known to form same-sex relationships.

**INDONESIA**

The Bugis ethnic group, native to the Indonesian island of Sulawesi, recognizes three sexes (female, male and hermaphrodite), four genders (women, men, transmen = calabai, and transwomen = calalai), and a fifth meta-gender group, the bissu.

**SAMOA**

Fa'afafine are a third-gendered people who are mostly born biologically male, but have gender expressions and identity that embody both masculine and feminine behaviour.

**IRAN**

13th century: In Persian poetry, the notion of Shahed (male beauty as testimony to the power of God) was frequently used by many poets, including the Persian poet Saadi Shirazi.

**NEPAL**

The Buddhist term Mettā, meaning mental union and loving-kindness, is used to identify transgender people (as well as same-sex couples) and is an accepted part of Nepalese culture since ancient times.

**SAUDI ARABIA**

8th - 9th century: Islamic Hadith (report of the deeds and sayings of Prophet Muhammad) state that the Prophet of Islam issued rulings regarding the personal rights of gender variant people identified as mukhannathun, especially concerning inheritance.

**INDIA**

Same-sex relations were accepted until British colonialism. Third gender and gender-variant people are still today recognized and accepted throughout Indian cultures.

THIS INFOGRAPHIC IS PRESENTED BY A JOINT EFFORT OF

FREE & EQUAL

WITH THANKS TO RESEARCHERS AT THE BURKLE CENTER FOR INTERNTIONAL RELATIONS, UCLA

IN COMMEMORATING

INTERNATIONAL DAY AGAINST HOMOPHOBIA & TRANSPHOBIA
MAY 17, 2014

DAYAGAINSTHOMOPHOBIA.ORG     UNFE.ORG

a tribe of Native Americans in Florida, claimed to have seen two men married to each other; that he described one of these men as wearing women's apparel and performing the tasks typically associated with women suggests that what he observed was not the marriage of two men, but the marriage of a man to an individual whose gender was neither male nor female (Gutiérrez, 2010, 21). Similar observations appear in other Europeans' travelogues. One French missionary struggled to reconcile his observations of the Illinois tribe with his binary understanding of gender, writing that some of the tribe's men, "while still young, assume the garb of women, and retain it throughout their lives . . . they never marry and glory in demeaning themselves to do everything that the women do" (Miller, 1995, 29). But, he noted, these individuals also played other social roles not typically associated with their tribe's women. The missionary's understanding of gender prevented him from considering the possibility of these individuals occupying another gender role altogether.

The term early eighteenth-century explorers' accounts commonly used for such individuals was *berdache*, which came from the Arabic and Persian terms for a younger male partner in a same-sex sexual act. In addition to wrongly associating homosexuality with gender identity, this term incorrectly implied that the individual thus described did not conform to gender norms, which was not the case. European observers simply did not comprehend that these individuals occupied an acknowledged gender category within the context of their tribes. Native Americans would not have used the word *berdache* to describe themselves. There were a few different terms used by Native American tribes to describe those individuals whose gender was something other than fully man or woman, including the Navajo *nadle*, the Arapaho

*John K. Hillers (American, 1843–1925),* We'wha, *a Zuni* lhamana *(two-spirit person) weaving (ca. 1871–1907). Source: U.S. National Archives and Records Administration, Wash., D.C. Image courtesy of Wikimedia Commons.*

*haxu'xan,* and the Lakota *winkte*. Over 150 tribes have been documented to have roles like these, and, in recent years, Native Americans have advocated for the use of the term "two-spirit," instead of *berdache*, in anthropological and historical surveys of Native American cultures (Fur, 2007).

As with gender, Europeans' attitudes toward, and definitions of, same-sex sexual activity were also often at odds with those of Native American societies. Colonizers attempted to enforce their own visions of morality on Native Americans in a variety of ways, including through the policing of their sexual practices. For example, a 1731 case in New Mexico involved a Spanish landowner who claimed to have caught two men from the Pueblo tribe in a sexual act on his land. He reported the men to local Spanish authorities and they were put on trial. While eventually convicted and sentenced to whipping and temporary banishment, they only avoided capital punishment due to their legal defender's claim that the landowner had misinterpreted the situation he encountered. (He asserted that the Pueblo men had been attired in skimpy, though culturally and seasonally appropriate, attire, but the landowner's lack of familiarity with Pueblo clothing conventions led him to believe he had discovered the men in a state of undress). Colonizers' attempts to curtail both Native American same-sex sexual practices and two-spirit gender presentation continued through the eighteenth century and were subsequently taken up and continued by the U.S. government—under the guise of Native American "assimilation" efforts—into the twentieth century (Miller, 1995).

## American Colonies

Even though the word Puritan is often used as shorthand for sexually repressed, the Europeans (some of whom were indeed Puritans) who settled the land they called New England thought often and deeply about sexual activity. The fragile new society's existence relied on reproduction, so men and women were encouraged to marry early and to bear as many children as possible, and people were discouraged from living alone (D'Emilio and Freedman, 1997). Puritans, accordingly, saw non-procreative sexual behavior as a significant threat to their way of life.

Legal and religious authorities in colonial New England saw themselves as responsible for maintaining the unity and well-being of their communities, and sought to minimize dissent and disruption. There were strict codes of punishment for all types of transgressions that threatened community stability, including offenses of a sexual nature. Sexual sins were classified as either natural or unnatural, with the former category covering masturbation, incest, and heterosexual fornication or adultery. Unnatural sins contravened the "natural order," defined by Scripture, and were broadly characterized by the "going after [of] strange flesh," as in bestiality and same-sex sexual activity (Godbeer, 2007, 95).

Punishments for sexual conduct outside the bounds of heterosexual marriage included fines or whipping. Those who publicly confessed and accepted their punishment usually were fully accepted back into the community, though harsher punishments—such as permanent banishment or death—could be levied against individuals who persistently engaged in non-heterosexual sexual practices without expressing remorse or compensating those they had wronged. Laws regarding sodomy (an act of non-procreative penetration by a man) often prescribed the death penalty as punishment; for example, the 1647 charter of Rhode Island mandated "death without remedy" as the punishment for sodomy, defined by the document as "a vile affection, whereby men . . . leave the natural use of woman and burn in their lusts toward one another" (Crompton, 1976, 281). However, this most extreme penalty was only rarely applied. Same-sex sexual practices between women are mentioned far less frequently in legal records than those between men, but evidence suggests that they were punished largely by whipping (D'Emilio and Freedman, 1997).

Colonial authorities' responses to sexual sins were predicated on a religious belief that all humans were innately flawed and prone to sin, and thus punishments were based on people's acts rather than their identities. Sometimes the penalties meted out to those convicted of same-sex sexual transgressions differed considerably from those prescribed in the law. For example, in 1677 Nicholas Sension appeared before a Connecticut court to answer to a charge of "sodomy," a crime whose definitions varied in some respects but which was commonly construed by colonial authorities as involving two individuals of the same sex (usually men; the historical record contains only two instances where women were punished for sexual acts with each other) (Godbeer, 2007). Sension had been confronted, 30 years earlier, by colonial authorities after several men had complained about his unwanted sexual advances, but had not been charged with a crime. At this trial, more than a dozen of Sension's male neighbors testified that they had either experienced or had heard about his sexual advances toward other men, including the initial complainant—Sension's indentured servant, Nathaniel Pond—and another man who said he had witnessed Sension and Pond having sex. Despite this testimony Sension received a sentence far lighter than the capital punishment mandated for sodomy. His entire estate was placed in bond to ensure his future good behavior and, if he refrained from additional offenses, would revert to his family upon his death (D'Emilio and Freedman, 1997). The court's leniency may have been because the prosecution lacked insufficient proof of sodomy, and Sension could therefore only be charged with "attempted sodomy," a lesser crime that didn't warrant capital punishment. It is also likely related to the fact that Sension, an affluent and well-liked member of his community, had primarily attempted or committed same-sex sex acts with younger men of lower social status.

A similar case from the colonial era, involving a Baptist minister whose "inward disposition" to make sexual advances toward younger male community members, likewise resulted in a sentence far less severe than the capital penalty mandated for sodomy. In both cases, the accused men's behavior contravened sexual norms while still upholding social hierarchies of power. While Governor William Bradford, along with other colonial leaders, firmly believed that "one wicked person [might] infect many," the authorities' pragmatic responses to these two cases were likely undergirded by a belief that social stability would be more endangered by the severe punishment of high-status sexual "offenders" than by the sexual offenses themselves (Godbeer, 2007). Although capital punishment was mandated for sodomy, only five of the 162 instances of punishment by death in the seventeenth-century colonies were meted out for same-sex sexual offenses (Paternoster, 1991). This suggests that the light sentences given to Sension and other high-status colonists charged with same-sex sexual offenses may have been the rule rather than the exception.

It is difficult to discern how frequently American colonists were prosecuted for illegal same-sex sexual behavior. Court records tended to refer euphemistically to such acts—for example, stating that a group of youths "committed much wickedness in a filthy corrupting way with one another" rather than specifying the acts involved. Also, the enforcement of social and sexual norms in the New England colonies differed from that of the middle and southern colonies—areas that today comprise states like Pennsylvania,

Virginia, the Carolinas, and Georgia. The northern colonies were fundamentally religious projects with Puritanism at the very core of their social structures. In the middle and southern colonies, by contrast, economic objectives trumped spiritual concerns, meaning that comparatively less time was devoted to policing individuals' sexual behavior.

Though social and sexual norms differed among the American colonies, these fledgling seventeenth- and eighteenth-century communities shared the belief that a clear and permanent distinction between men and women was necessary for social stability. Many colonial leaders issued proscriptions against dressing in clothing associated with the opposite sex, and the historical record contains numerous instances of colonists being accused of this transgression. These include a 1652 case against a Massachusetts man for "putting on woemen's apparell and goeinge about from house to house in the nighte" and two cases, in 1677 and 1692, against a woman for wearing men's clothing. These crimes "[confounded] the course of nature," thereby posing an existential threat to the colonies' survival. Massachusetts' 1696 law specifically forbidding colonists' cross-gender dress indicates both the seriousness with which colonial authorities regarded this offense and its commonplace nature (Reis, 2009).

Prohibitions against cross-gender dressing were often, though not always, unrelated to colonial concerns about same-sex sexual activity. Certainly, some colonists expressed concern that individuals who dressed as the opposite gender might be trying to "deceive" others into same-sex sexual activity, but the majority of cases in which colonists were charged with gender-inappropriate dress do not reflect this concern.

The issue of sexual deception was more commonly raised in colonial cases involving individuals who might today identify as intersex—that is, individuals whose genitals differed from female or male norms. One well-documented case in 1629 involved Thomasine Hall, a Virginia colonist who did not have a conventionally "female" appearance but dressed in women's clothing. Community members had forcibly examined Hall's genitalia and determined Hall to be male, and thereby guilty of cross-gender dressing. Hall, however, explained to the court that her genitals possessed both male and female characteristics; she testified that she perceived herself as female, and that, therefore, she was not guilty of cross-dressing (Brown, 1996).

The threat to social stability posed by a person of indeterminate gender was underscored by Hall's own testimony. Hall reported that she lived as a woman through their early 20s but later adopted a more masculine appearance and joined the army, before returning to civilian life to live as a woman. Colonial authorities felt the need to categorize Hall as either female or male, to prevent other colonists from unwittingly engaging with Hall in same-sex sexual behavior. Unable to make such a determination based on Hall's genitalia and self-description, the court arrived at a solution which required Hall to wear men's clothing along with the apron and head covering typical of a woman. This unusual attire marked Hall as neither fully male nor fully female and, by so doing, suggested that Hall was off-limits, sexually, to other Virginians, as neither men nor women could be fully sure that sex with Hall would not be a same-sex act (Reis, 2009).

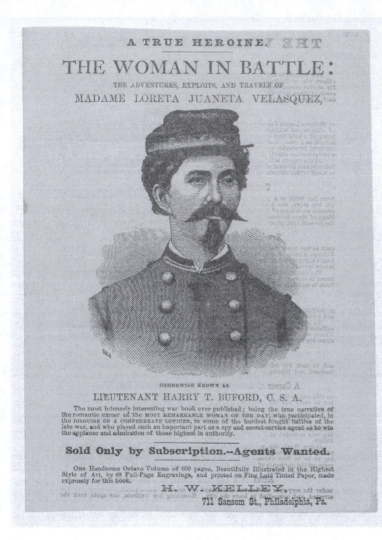

A TRUE HEROINE.

# THE WOMAN IN BATTLE:

THE ADVENTURES, EXPLOITS, AND TRAVELS OF
MADAME LORETA JUANETA VELASQUEZ,

OTHERWISE KNOWN AS
LIEUTENANT HARRY T. BUFORD, C. S. A.

The most intensely interesting war book ever published; being the true narrative of the romantic career of the MOST REMARKABLE WOMAN OF THE DAY; who participated, in the disguise of A CONFEDERATE OFFICER, in some of the hardest-fought battles of the late war, and who played such an important part as a spy and secret-service agent as to win the applause and admiration of those highest in authority.

### Sold Only by Subscription.--Agents Wanted.

One Handsome Octavo Volume of 600 pages, Beautifully Illustrated in the Highest Style of Art, by 48 Full-Page Engravings, and printed on Fine Laid Tinted Paper, made expressly for this book.

H. W. KELLEY,
711 Sansom St., Philadelphia, Pa.

*Broadside advertising the memoirs of Loreta Janeta Velazquez, a Cuban woman who dressed and fought as a male Confederate officer in the U.S. Civil War (ca. 1876). Source: Duke University Libraries, Digital Collections.*

# THE NINETEENTH CENTURY

## Gender Ideologies

Beliefs about gender and sexual behavior in the nineteenth-century United States were, in many respects, different from those of the colonial era, and their formation was influenced by new economic developments and technological advances. The factories that sprang up across the northeast during the early 1800s, along with new technologies that made agriculture and trade less labor-intensive, challenged the centrality of the family unit to the country's economy. Children were increasingly viewed as financial burdens rather than economic assets, and white middle-class married couples—first in the northeast, and later in other regions—began to intentionally limit the number of children they had. As scholars have noted, this tendency led to a gradual social acceptance of non-procreative sexual acts (at least those which took place between married couples); this change in attitude effectively, if not intentionally, undercut one of the previous centuries' primary arguments against same-sex sex (Rupp, 1999).

Whereas in earlier decades, both men's and women's labor were seen as essential to a family's economic survival, the white middle-class beliefs about gender that emerged in the nineteenth century now associated work, and public life, exclusively with men. Women, on the other hand, were associated with leisure, family, and the home. White middle-class men were expected to venture into the "public" sphere to fulfill their economic, social, and political responsibilities, but this exposed them to moral temptations and corroded their sensibilities. Women were expected to provide male breadwinners with peaceful homes where, under the uncorrupted influence of their wives and daughters, they could be morally rehabilitated. Prior to marriage, due to these beliefs about gender, most middle-class white men and women circulated in largely sex-segregated spheres of work and leisure.

This binary model required a rethinking of previous eras' sexual ideologies. In the past, Western society had considered women's interest in sex to equal—and sometimes to exceed—men's interest. But now that white middle-class women were expected to serve as paragons of virtue in their families and communities, women began to be portrayed as almost wholly disinterested in sex. The "true woman" was to be "passionless" and her disinterest in sex was expected to help her husband keep his supposedly voracious sexual appetite in check. It is important to remember, however, that beliefs are not the same as behaviors, and while heterosexual marriage was seen as the only appropriate sexual outlet for virtuous middle-class white men and women, this did not prevent extramarital or non-heterosexual sex from occurring, particularly among the Americans excluded from the white middle-class group among whom this belief was most popular. There were also unintended corollary effects from this ideology; one historian has observed that "ironically, the ideology of profound sexual difference, in conjunction with economic and social sex segregation, also encouraged same-sex love and sexuality" (Rupp, 1999).

## Romantic Friendships

Diaries, letters, and other historical documents from the era before the Civil War period suggest a widespread acceptance by white middle-class Americans of physical and emotional intimacy between friends of the same sex. Henry David Thoreau's essay "Friendship" (1907) paid tribute to the strong bonds of love, loyalty, and affection that could arise between two friends who truly understood each other. Because the differences between men's and women's natures prevented them from developing such an understanding, Thoreau wrote, the development of such an ideal friendship was "more rare between the sexes than between two of the same sex" (Kaplan, 1997, 203).

White middle-class men and women expressed their affection for their close friends both discursively (in writing) and demonstratively (through behavior). Whether shared in sentimental letters to each other, detailed in impassioned diary or journal entries, or shown through tender physical gestures, the mutual love of "romantic friends" was socially affirmed. The relationships themselves were lauded for encouraging noble behavior such as loyalty, devotion, and selflessness. There were, to be sure, certain limits on romantic friendships but these were vague, shifting, and dependent upon the age, race, gender, and social class of the participants.

Romantic friendships between women are also well-documented, due in part to the preservation of letters and journals from white middle-class women who later gained renown for their achievements in artistic and professional fields. For example, writer and women's rights advocate Margaret Fuller confided in her journal about a woman she loved "passionately," writing that "her face was always gleaming before me; her voice was echoing in my ear; all poetic thoughts clustered round the dear image. This love was for me a key which unlocked many a treasure which I still possess" (Faderman, 1981). Poet Emily Dickinson's letters to her sister-in-law, Susan Gilbert express similarly warm sentiments:

"Susie, will you . . . come home next Saturday, and be my own again, and kiss me as you used to? . . . I cannot wait, feel that now I must have you—that the expectation once more to see your face again, makes me feel hot and feverish" (Faderman, 1981). Some women outside of the white middle class also left records of their romantic friendships; two African-American women in Connecticut—one a schoolteacher, one a domestic servant—corresponded at length about their love and desire for each other. "How I did miss you last night . . . no kisses is like youres [sic] . . . You are the first girl that I ever *love* so and you are the last one . . . what a pleasure it would be to me to address you *My Husband*" (Hansen, 1995, 162). In each of these cases, there is no evidence to suggest that any of the women involved felt that their romantic feelings were morally or socially questionable (though one of the mothers of the African-American domestic servant did caution her daughter to downplay her feelings for her female friend, at least in front of potential male suitors).

*Frances Shimer and Cindarella Gregory founded Shimer College (Chicago, IL) in 1860. Their relationship was described as "passionate." Source: Northern Illinois University Archives, Shimer College Collection. Image courtesy of Wikimedia Commons.*

Romantic friendships between white middle-class men of this era are less well-documented than those of women, but the historical record indicates that they were as socially accepted as women's romantic friendships, and even merited special praise for their ability to encourage the "natural" male entrepreneurial drive and to stoke men's inherent desire to achieve economic prosperity. Among the male romantic friendships studied by historians, perhaps the most well-known is that of Abraham Lincoln and Joshua Speed. The two men were both unmarried and in their late 20s when they first met in Springfield, Illinois, and quickly decided to share Speed's small living space (and sole double bed) above the general store that he owned. While they parted ways nearly four years later, Speed and Lincoln continued to correspond until Lincoln's death, and many of the letters discovered by historians express the warm, loving sentiments common to romantic friendships. In one, Lincoln notes that Speed sent him a violet; in another, he writes, "I shall be very lonesome without you" (Basler, 2001, 141).

No matter how intense the bonds between romantic friends, these same-sex relationships were expected to precede—not to delay or impede—marriage to an opposite-sex spouse. Letters between Lincoln and Speed suggest that they, like other romantic friend pairs, struggled with this social expectation. Speed figured prominently in Lincoln's courtship of Mary Todd, encouraging his diffident friend to pursue the relationship even as he agreed that it might prove a less fulfilling union than the one they shared, Lincoln reciprocated when Speed expressed some reluctance about his pending nuptials, writing sympathetically, "I now have no doubt that it is the peculiar misfortune of both you and me to dream dreams of Elysium far exceeding all that anything earthly can realize. Far short of your dreams as you may be, no woman could do more to realize them than that same black-eyed Fanny" (Basler, 2001, 143). Both men were acutely aware that marriage was part of the social contract for white middle-class men, and encouraged each other to honor that obligation in spite of the reservations each expressed.

Romantic friendships were most common among white, middle-class Americans who lived in the country's northeast region, but also occurred when working-class people lived in isolation from the opposite sex in settings like the military, the prison system, or in the mining towns of the American West. It is clear from the narratives and autobiographies published by formerly enslaved men and women that emotionally intense same-sex relationships provided daily emotional and practical support. Frederick Douglass, in his well-known autobiography, reminisced about the "ardent friendship" of his "brother slaves" and noted that "I never loved, esteemed, or confided in men more than I did in these" (Lussana, 2016, 1).

It is difficult to say if, or how many, romantic friendships had a physical erotic or sexual component. In some cases, the evidence seems clear. For instance, letters from one upper-class white man in the South to another refer admiringly to the recipient's "long fleshen pole—the exquisite touches of which I often had the honor of feeling" and describe the joys of male-male anal sex (Duberman, 1990, 155). Similarly, in a letter to her romantic friend (a schoolteacher), a young domestic servant in Connecticut implies that their relationship included a physical component. She promises that she won't let any of her close friends at boarding school touch her breasts, or at least one of them, writing, "I shall try to keep your [favored] one always for you" (Hansen, 1995, 160). However, not all historical documents testifying to the existence of romantic friendships contains evidence of physical or (what would be understood today as) sexual contact. This makes it difficult to say for certain whether such relationships can be appropriately viewed as forerunners of same-sex sex, romantic, and sexual relationships in later periods.

## Education and the New Woman

In the later years of the nineteenth century, a new model of white, middle-class womanhood emerged in the United States. This "New Woman" was characterized as white, well-off, and college-educated; she largely rejected the expectations of "true womanhood," actively pursued her rights, asserted her independence, and worked to improve her society (Smith-Rosenberg, 1989). As one historian describes it, the emergence of the New Woman was the result of "the growth of the feminist, abolitionist, and temperance movements, which awakened women politically; widening educational opportunities; and an expanding middle class, which held out more possibilities of economic independence to women" (Miller, 1995, 55).

Many of these New Women chose not to marry, and some—although not all—had long-term same-sex relationships in which they shared their personal and professional lives with other women from similar backgrounds. The term "Boston marriage" was used to describe these partnerships, which were primarily a phenomenon of the white upper and middle classes. Social attitudes toward such relationships were mixed, as they prevented women from fulfilling their highest social obligation: to marry and bear children. There is little evidence to suggest that social ambivalence toward Boston marriages was based on an understanding of them as sexually "deviant" in any way.

Some of the most visible examples of these lifelong partnerships between women come from academia. Neither M. Carey Thomas, the president of Bryn Mawr College, nor Mount Holyoke College president Mary Wooley made any efforts to hide the fact that they had chosen to spend their lives with a female companion. At Mount Holyoke, students and faculty alike were apparently aware that Wooley and her partner made a point of seeing each other every evening to kiss good night and thus could not have been surprised when Wooley's partner moved into the President's house to live with her. Through to the end of the nineteenth century such partnerships were generally considered in much the same way "romantic friendships" had been earlier: loving, supportive, and mutually ennobling (Faderman, 1981).

## Sex-Segregated Societies in the American West

The mining camps and cowboy towns of the nineteenth-century American West were predominantly male enclaves, a fact that might have subconsciously attracted men whose sexual desires were male-directed (Miller, 1995). The hard work of miners and cowboys could be made considerably easier by the assistance of a trusted sidekick, and partnerships that began in a professional context frequently turned into close friendships nurtured in the hours away from work. The strength of the emotional bonds between these male pairs is suggested by the grief expressed when death separated them; a 1915 poem written by a ranch hand mourned the passing of his friend and acknowledged that "We loved each other in the way men do / and never spoke about it, Al and me. / But we both knowed, and knowin' it so true / Was more than any woman's kiss could be" (Williams, 1986, 158). More dramatically, one miner took his own life following his partner's death, leaving a note that simply explained, "I can't live without Cy" (Rupp, 1999, 55).

Evidence suggests that same-sex sexual activity was a regular feature within these mostly male social environments. One cowboy reported that "sodomy" (in this context meaning anal sex between men) was a "popular method" of sexual release preferred by a "majority" of the men who lived at a logging camp he visited. During his visit, he recalls, "I was initiated into the discomforts, adjustments, and ecstasies of this form of sexual activity." Another observer of cowboy life described the progression of physical relationships between cowboys and their sidekicks, writing that their initial efforts were made "gingerly," but "as bashfulness waned [and] good will matured, they'd graduate to the ecstatically comforting" (Williams, 1986, 159). It is difficult, due to lack of documentation, to determine if the men who engaged in same-sex sex in these contexts saw male sexual partners as inferior—but acceptable—alternatives to the female sexual partners largely unavailable in frontier societies. Likewise, it is hard to know if they considered the physical or emotional aspects of their same-sex partnerships to have any relationship to their sexual practices outside of these contexts.

Other same-sex sexual subcultures on the frontier included those that emerged in brothels, where some of the women who made their living selling sex to men often forged romantic and sexual relationships with each other. On occasion, female patrons, dressed as men, visited the brothels too (Johnson, 2000). Additionally, records

*'Stag' cowboy dance (ca. 1870s?) Miners, ranchers, farmers, and cowboys on the American frontier often spent their work and leisure time solely with other men, which could lead to same-sex romantic and sexual relationships.*

from the largely sex-segregated nineteenth-century Mormon community in Utah suggest that some of the male-male missionary pairs assigned to evangelize across the country developed intimate and affectionate attachments to each other that outlasted their two-year terms of service. Moreover, some of the most notable figures in late-nineteenth and early-twentieth century Mormon culture—including the male director of the famed Mormon Tabernacle Choir and the female president of the Mormons' children's program—shared their homes and personal lives with members of the same sex. In keeping with the dictates of the Mormon religion, however, these lasting and committed relationships coexisted, rather than supplanted, heterosexual ties. The choir director, for example, "lived with a succession of what the Mormon publication *Juvenile Instructor* termed his 'numerous boys,' most of whom also married but remained close" to him, while the female administrator developed so close a bond with one of her husband's other wives that the two women ended up living together, while their husband moved out to live elsewhere (Rupp, 1999).

In the nineteenth century, sex-segregated communities formed in the cities and on the frontier, enabling the formation of a variety of emotionally—and sometimes physically—intimate same-sex relationships. As the twentieth century dawned these sex-segregated spheres would break down, bringing in new beliefs about same-sex sexual desire and behavior (Rupp, 1999).

## THE EARLY TWENTIETH CENTURY

### The Origins and Influence of Sexology

In the United States the emergence of a consumer society around the turn of the twentieth century brought discussions of sexuality and sexual expression into the public sphere. The new concepts of heterosexuality and homosexuality were used to describe specific types of individuals, marking a shift away from earlier eras' focus on acts, rather than identities. These concepts had their origins in the late nineteenth century, when a new field of medical and psychological study called sexology began to examine what drove people to engage in certain varieties of non-procreative sexual behavior, specifically same-sex sexual behavior (Rupp, 1999). Their work would come to influence the ways in which Western cultures understood both same-sex and opposite-sex sexual desire.

The earliest sexological works to consider the origins of same-sex sexual desires focused on "inversion," which was defined as a person "thinking, acting, and feeling in total violation of one's expected gender" (Rupp, 1999). For example, a pamphlet published in 1868 by a German lawyer named Karl Heinrich Ulrichs suggested that men who desired sex with other men possessed female souls, while women who pursued same-sex sex had male souls (Ulrichs, 1994). The discord between the gender of a person's soul and one's physical body was evident not only by the desire for same-sex sex, but by acting or dressing in ways that differed from social expectations. The kind of same-sex-desiring man Ulrichs described as an "urning" would display feminine mannerisms, while the same-sex-desiring female "urningin" would act in a masculine way. While it would be easy for modern-day readers to see problems with this model's confusion between gender, sexual orientation, and personality traits, its insistence that same-sex sexual attraction was an inborn trait made it a useful tool in arguing against criminal penalties for same-sex sexual activity. Ulrichs was himself part of a group of Germans who advocated for the decriminalization of same-sex sex. One of his colleagues in this effort was Karl-Maria Kertbeny, in whose 1869 publication the German word for homosexual (and, later, for heterosexual) first appeared.

In 1886 German psychiatrist Richard von Krafft-Ebing published *Psychopathia Sexualis*, a lengthy work containing over 200 case studies illustrating different varieties of sexual behavior. In his discussion of same-sex-attracted individuals, he took care to highlight the extent to which their self-presentation, personalities, and mannerisms deviated from gender norms—a true female homosexual, he suggested, had "of the feminine qualities only the genital organs; thought, sentiment, action, even external appearance are those of a man" (Rupp, 1999, 80). The concept of homosexuality as a kind of gender inversion spread across the Western world in the late nineteenth century, and was introduced in the United States in 1892 by a Chicago doctor who used the term "homosexual" to describe individuals whose "general mental state is that of the opposite sex" (Rupp, 1999, 80).

In the first few decades of the twentieth century, however, the notion that gender inversion was the driving factor behind same-sex attraction gradually faded as sexologists and psychologists came to view same-sex sexual object choice "as the defining characteristic of a new category of 'homosexuals'" (Rupp, 1999). In other words, sexologists no longer saw an individual's same-sex sexual desire as a symptom of an underlying problem with their gender. Instead, they came to view same-sex desire as a fundamental "problem" itself. British sexologist Havelock Ellis affirmed in 1913 that people who desired same-sex sex might retain "all the other impulses and tastes . . . of the sex to which the person by anatomical configuration belongs"; and Austrian psychiatrist Sigmund Freud claimed that "complete masculinity" was not incompatible with male same-sex sexual desire. It is important to note, however, that these experts had trouble reconciling women's same-sex sexual desires within this model and continued to hunt for telltale signs of "masculinity" in the self-presentation or mannerisms of same-sex-attracted women (Rupp, 1999).

While nineteenth-century experts had conjectured about the physiological causes of same-sex sexual desire, the spread of Freud's theories in the early twentieth century "gave an enormous boost to the idea that social factors were at work in producing same-sex desire" (Rupp, 1999). Freud theorized that a person's sexuality developed via a complex psychological process of identifying with or against one's mother and father. Heterosexuality was viewed as the outcome of a "normal" sexual identity development process; homosexuality and bisexuality showed that the sexual identity development process had been arrested or "perverted." As his ideas were popularized—albeit in watered-down form—through the popular press, people began to understand same-sex sexual desire as a socially influenced, rather than biologically based, phenomenon.

These new understandings had important ramifications for efforts to gain social acceptance of same-sex-attraction. The model that claimed same-sex desire was the result of an inborn condition or trait suggested that there was little use in trying to prevent, or punish, this natural deviation. If, on the other hand, same-sex sexual desire was created by social factors, then it was incumbent on society to prevent these social factors from wreaking havoc on the process of "normal" sexual identity development.

It is also important to understand that the extent to which individuals adopted the new theories and terminology of same-sex desire varied considerably. While some people, like historian F. O. Matthiessen, felt relief when he read one sexologist's explanation of same-sex desire, others, such as the poet Walt Whitman, steadfastly rejected the implication that his love for male comrades had any relation to the models of inversion or homosexuality (Rupp, 1999). Many same-sex attracted individuals would not have had access to the academic and professional realms in which such theories were discussed; others may have felt that the models were too broad as they completely ignored the contextual distinctions that were central to earlier models of sexuality. Still others may have rejected these models' conflation of same-sex romantic and emotional intimacy with "perverse" sexual desires. This might have motivated some of the public statements, against too-intimate friendships between college girls, made in the twentieth century by academic women who had felt no need to hide their same-sex partnerships just a few decades earlier.

Regardless, in the few decades before and after 1900, there were a number of, sometimes contradictory, medical, scientific, and psychological theories aimed at explaining (what today is understood as) "sexuality" or "sexual orientation." Although primarily an elite discourse of "experts," these theories gradually permeated popular discourse, and some same-sex attracted and gender non-conforming individuals began to adopt the concepts and terminology of these theories to describe their attractions and desires. But, starting in the 1920s and 1930s, the terms homosexuality and heterosexuality, and the idea that sexuality was primarily about one's sexual object choice, became more widely adopted and employed to described same-sex and different-sex attraction (Rupp, 1999).

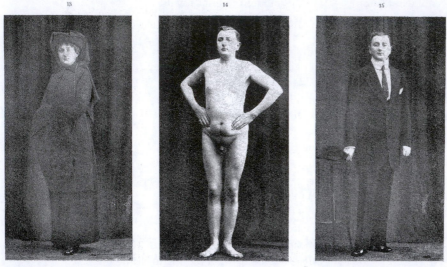

Feminismus beim Manne (vgl. S. 145)                                                    Tafel V.

13                                    14                                    15

Der Fall stellt eine der häufigen Verbindungen von Androgynie, Transvestitismus und Homosexualität dar. Die Androgynie (Bild 14) tritt besonders in der Becken-, Brust- und Kehlkopfbildung, sowie im Gesichtsausdruck, Gestik und Mimik des 30jährigen Patienten zutage. Bild 13 zeigt ihn, wie er bei der Kriegsmusterung erschien. Er trägt Trauer, weil seine Mutter gestorben ist; ein Zeichen, wie ernst er seinen Transvestitismus nimmt. Dem weiblichen Geschlecht gegenüber besteht völlige Indifferenz, dagegen reagiert er auf männliche Personen positiv lustbetont.

Hirschfeld, Sexualpathologie. II.                                    A. Marcus & E. Webers Verlag, Bonn.

*European and American sexologists often intermingled concepts that researchers and LGBTQ+ people today separate, such as "gender expression," "gender identity," and "sexual orientation." This image of an "androgynous, cross-dressing homosexual," appeared in prominent German sexologist Magnus Hirschfeld's book* Sexual Pathology *(Bonn, 1921). Source: Wellcome Collection (London) #L0025695/CC BY 4.0 license. Image courtesy of Wikimedia Commons.*

## Developing Communities

At the same time that sexologists were formulating new theories to explain same-sex desire, same-sex attracted individuals and communities were increasingly evident in Europe and the United States. The 1895 trial of Oscar Wilde in England for sodomy and gross indecency was covered in sensationalistic detail by American newspapers; that his sexual crimes were well-known to the American public is clear from the estimated 900 church sermons preached against him between 1895 and 1900 (Miller, 1995). A Chicago physician had remarked in 1889 on the ubiquity of same-sex-attracted individuals, writing that "there is in every community of any size a colony of sexual perverts; they are usually known to each other, are likely to congregate together" (Terry, 1999, 74). One American correspondent explained to English sexologist Havelock Ellis in the early twentieth century that "the world of sexual inverts is, indeed, a large one in any American city . . . it is a community distinctly organized—words, customs, traditions of its own; and every city has numerous meeting places" (Eaklor, 2008). The majority of these urban subcultures involved men. Due to social customs and fewer economic opportunities, many women simply did not have the ability to live an independent life free from the supervision of fathers, husbands, or family.

New York City's well-documented same-sex subcultures fostered a variety of sexual relationships between men of all classes. Hotels, parks, cafeterias, rooming houses, and private clubs were all sites where same-sex-attracted men could mingle. Within this metropolitan subculture a man's gender expression and sex-role preferences played a greater part in determining his gender and sexual identity than did his sexual desire for other men. Conventionally masculine men who took the active (or penetrating) role in a same-sex sexual act were considered "normal," relative to other types of men who might be called "fairies," "faggots," or "queens" (all of which were terms referring to men who took the passive/penetrated sexual role and were feminine-acting and -appearing). Class-based differences played a role in this subculture, with "normal" working-class men displaying a greater tolerance of "fairies" than did the middle-class "queers" who disdained the fairies' effeminacy. These gender-based distinctions between same-sex attracted men largely faded by the end of the 1930s, when the word gay came into broader use as a synonym for homosexual (Eaklor, 2008). This change marked a "transition from a world divided into 'fairies' and 'men' on the basis of gender persona to one divided into 'homosexuals' and 'heterosexuals' on the basis of sexual object choice" (Chauncey, 1994, 358).

*"But this is exclusively a woman's hotel!"*
*"Well!"*

*Early-twentieth century urban gay men distinguished effeminate homosexuals ("fairies" or "pansies") from more masculine (or "normal") men who nevertheless might engage in homosexual sex. This cartoon may indicate continued belief that homosexuality resulted from gender "inversion"—the idea that homosexual men were women in male bodies— even as inversion theory was being replaced by sexual object choice (or sexual orientation) theory. Source: Illustration by Ken Browne, published in Broadway Brevities (New York), Vol. III, No. 7, (December 14, 1931).*

## Harlem and African-American Same-Sex Sexual Culture

The predominantly middle-class, African-American community of Harlem in New York City emerged in the early 1920s as a result of the mass migration of African-Americans from the South to urban areas in the North. Many of its residents saw themselves as what W. E. B. DuBois had called "New Negroes." They were educated, worldly, proud of their black identity, and insistent upon their equality with white Americans. The residents and habitués of the neighborhood were responsible for an astonishing amount of cultural production during this period, which became known as the Harlem Renaissance.

Black writers, singers, artists, and actors rubbed shoulders in a variety of Harlem's social outlets, joined by middle-class whites who flocked to the neighborhood not just for its parties and performances, but for its relatively laissez-faire attitude toward sex. Harlem's vibrant nightlife included popular commercial events like masquerade balls, which tacitly permitted guests to dress in drag, and cabaret shows featuring vocalists whose lyrics often explicitly referred to same-sex desire. But many community establishments enforced gender and sexual norms to avoid attracting the attention of New York City police vice squads. This tendency, coupled with the economic struggles faced by many Harlem residents, spurred the development of alternative social outlets. Much of the socializing between same-sex-attracted individuals occurred behind closed doors in "buffet flats" (apartments whose owners rented out rooms by the hour or the evening) or private homes at "rent parties" where Harlem residents attempted to offset the high cost of urban living by opening their doors to a diverse crowd of guests, eager to enjoy bootleg alcohol, music, and dancing with the partners of their choice.

*Bisexual blues singer of the Harlem Renaissance, Bessie Smith (1894–1937) in 1936. Photo by Carl Van Vechten. Source: Library of Congress, Prints & Photographs Division, Carl Van Vechten Collection. Image courtesy of Wikimedia Commons.*

Some of the best-known figures of the Harlem Renaissance—including writers Angelina Weld Grimké, Claude McKay, Alice Dunbar-Nelson, and Countee Cullen, as well as blues singers like Ma Rainey and Bessie Smith—were open about their sexual attraction to both men and women. While "sissy men" and "bulldagger" women were fixtures of the Harlem community, the neighborhood was not totally free from homophobia. African-American churches were prominent in community life, and some of their leaders strongly objected to the community's tolerance of gender transgression and sexual freedom. Reverend Adam Clayton Powell, Sr., gave fiery sermons about the evils of "perversion" and "degenerates," and Reverend Frederick Asbury Cullen (father of gay poet Countee Cullen) exhorted his followers, particularly black men, to hew closely to a narrow definition of masculinity and manliness, and to quash any desires which might lead them astray. But these screeds were, at best, a muted counterpoint to the rest of Harlem's culture, in which masculine women, feminine men, and same-sex love and desire were regular topics of music, literature, and art.

## Cultural Anxiety About Women's Same-Sex Sexuality

There was a general shift during the 1920s and into the 1930s to policing sexual "deviance" and a focus on the pathologization of homosexuality and gender variance, while medical, social, and legal proscriptions also increased in the 1930s. Though researchers like Magnus Hirschfeld in Germany and Harry Benjamin in the US attempted to push back against this, the prevailing ethos was one of intolerance toward those who flouted sexual or gender conventions.

During this time a general consensus emerged to acknowledge that "normal" middle-class white women, like men, experienced sexual urges, and women's sexuality became the subject of enhanced scrutiny. This scrutiny was driven, in part, by social anxiety about the rapid social gains made by women in the post-war years, including the achievement of women's suffrage, public debates over birth control, and growing acceptance of young middle-class women's employment outside of the home. Critics feared that the growing independence of young middle-class white women would cause them to postpone, or avoid altogether, heterosexual marriage and childbearing. They found this possibility particularly troubling because many of the immigrants arriving in the US belonged to cultures which encouraged women to have as many children as possible; to their eyes, young white women who preferred to delay, or limit, their childbearing were contributing to white Americans' "race suicide."

As a result of these fears women's colleges, where growing numbers of young middle-class women enrolled, became the targets of conservative ire. The *New York Times* reported in 1910 that "the gravest charge that is made against girls' colleges [is that] they turn the minds of their students away from the normal, natural, interests of womankind." Critics characterized women's colleges as places which endangered women's healthy heterosexual development, in part because many female faculty members were unmarried and cohabitated with other female faculty members, and in part because the same-sex environment virtually forced young women to direct their nascent sexual desires toward each other. While this fear was far from new—as early as the 1870s doctors like J. G. Holland had cautioned parents against letting their daughters attend women's colleges—it had been revitalized by the growing bodies of work in sexology and psychology that suggested young women's "natural" sexual desires could be easily warped by prolonged exposure to all-female environments, and the "unnatural" older women who populated them.

The intense "romantic friendships" between young middle-class women that were widely accepted in the nineteenth century, had been increasingly regarded with suspicion since the early decades of the twentieth century. Since many of these romantic friendships developed in the single-sex environment of the women's college, the institutions themselves were assailed as virtual hotbeds of sexual perversion, as were their faculty and students. Popular magazines like the *Ladies Home Journal* counseled young women to avoid "crushes" or friendships that were "far too intimate" as they were "seldom anything but harmful to those who indulge[d]" in them, and *Harper's Bazaar* warned parents of college-bound daughters that "one-tenth" of the college women who had "crushes" on fellow female students were "moral degenerates."

Toward the end of the decade same-sex relationships between women drew a great deal attention because of the 1927 stage production of *The Captive* in New York City and the 1928 publication of Radclyffe Hall's book, *The Well of Loneliness*.

TRUE TOWEL TALES: No. 6 ... AS TOLD US BY A SOLDIER

*Illustration as described by the soldier*

**BUNA BATHTUB**

"We came across this Buna village," says a private in the army, "and down on the beach was a canoe that the natives had no use for. It was full of rainwater and we were dirty. The natives thought we were wacky — but whatta bath, brother, *whatta bath!*"

A fresh-water bath is a welcome novelty sometimes to our men who are battle-hot and swamp-dirty. But they do have towels — and they're grateful for 'em! Good towels, too. Many are Cannons — brisk, efficient, hard-working — the kind you're proud to own as standard home equipment. We all need towels — but *they* need them more. That's why there aren't as many here at home. The best reason in the world for us to take especial care of those we have!

CANNON

*Cannon Towels*

CANNON SHEETS          CANNON HOSIERY

**Millions of Cannon Towels**

are now going to the Armed Forces. So you may find a smaller selection in the stores — fewer styles and a limited variety of colors. But the durable Cannon quality, the hardy quality that will see you through, remains the same. When the war is over, Cannon will again present the newest styles in the most charming colors. For free booklet, "How to Make Your Towels Last Longer," write to Cannon Mills, Inc., 70 Worth Street, New York 13, N. Y.

**For Victory—Buy U. S. War Bonds!**

HOW TO MAKE YOUR TOWELS LAST LONGER AND "STAY DURABLE FOR THE DURATION"

Launder before they become too soiled
Fluff-dry terry towels — never iron
If loops are snagged — cut off, never pull
Mend selvage and other breaks immediately
Buy good-quality towels — always the best economy

*Advertising during World Wars I and II, like this 1944 ad for Cannon Towels, often unintentionally revealed how the sex-segregated environment of war provided opportunities for homoerotic and gender-expansive play. (Illustration by James Bingham for advertising agency N. W. Ayers.)*

Both the play and novel focused on same-sex love and desire between women, and both were the subject of censorship efforts by government officials concerned about their ability to corrupt their audiences— especially women. *The Well of Loneliness*, a semi-autobiographical tale of a self-identified female "invert" named Stephen Gordon and her ill-fated same-sex love affair, was ruled "obscene" upon its initial publication in England, and subsequently banned; in the US it was subjected to a similar trial, but a New York court found that its literary merit and relatively chaste depiction of the "delicate social problem" of homosexuality elevated it above mere pornography. *The Captive*, described in the *New York Times* as a "tragedy" about "a young woman, well-bred and of good family, who falls into a twisted relationship with another woman," was performed 160 times before the New York City District Attorney, bowing to pressure from moral crusaders, ordered its cast arrested and the production shut down. The state's public obscenity code was changed, shortly after the show was shuttered, to ban the performance of plays "depicting or dealing with the subject of sex degeneracy, or sex perversion." The widespread publicity surrounding these works' legal battles, in conjunction with popular discourse about the perils of women's romantic friendships and women's colleges, virtually ensured that most Americans in the 1920s were aware of the "problem" of female homosexuality.

## THE MID TWENTIETH CENTURY

### World War II

Following the United States' entry into World War II, vast numbers of young American men and women were eager to do their part in supporting their country's efforts. Young men enlisted in various branches of the military, while women joined auxiliary organizations or took jobs in military manufacturing. In many cases, these young Americans had to relocate to urban centers of war-related manufacturing or to military installations on the East and West Coasts, leaving their hometowns and families behind. Thrown into an unfamiliar setting alongside peers from all walks of life, many of these young Americans discovered, or began to explore, their same-sex sexual desires in homosocial environments, which proved, at least in wartime, relatively tolerant of such behavior.

While the U.S. military had always considered sodomy to be a criminal offense, and could ask recruits whether they had had homosexual feelings or experiences, only during World War II did the military ask potential enlistees if they were homosexuals. This question reflected an evolution in the military's perspective; now, as historian Allan Bérubé observed, it saw "the homosexual as a personality type unfit for military service and combat." But this question was far from being a true bar to military service for same-sex-attracted men. In fact, the historical record shows that many men learned they were gay only *after* they entered the military, where they were exposed to both a potential gay subculture and overtly hostile joking about homosexuality. Being perceived by their peers as gay was, in general, not particularly problematic for soldiers, but being caught in same-sex sexual activity could result in severe punishment and possibly dishonorable discharge. Having "HS" to indicate "homosexual" stamped on military discharge papers disqualified veterans from receiving benefits and often prevented them from getting a civil service job (Bérubé, 1990).

In contrast to the enlistment process for men, women interested in joining a military auxiliary organization like the Women's Army Corps (WACs) or the Navy's WAVES (Women Accepted for Volunteer Emergency Service) faced somewhat more restrictive application criteria—they could not be married or pregnant—but were not explicitly asked about their sexual orientation during enlistment. This could be because the military viewed male homosexuals' supposed "effeminacy" as incompatible with men's military duties, while some of the "masculine" characteristics popularly associated with female homosexuals were desirable in female military recruits. Women who moved to work at defense jobs discovered communities of other women, some of whom—the "gay girls"—were interested in same-sex sexual relationships. According to witnesses sent to investigate a mothers' complaint about the Women's Auxiliary Corps training camp being "full of homosexuals and sex-maniacs," some of these women had short hair and appeared "mannish" (Bérubé, 1990, 256). But since the WAC officers were more concerned with keeping their ranks full, they largely disregarded such complaints or conducted only cursory investigations before reporting that they had found nothing alarming.

When the war drew to a close, many men and women stayed in the cities where they had worked or served. Along the West Coast, especially, former service members and war workers who had discovered or embraced their same-sex sexual desires established social enclaves within these cities. These enclaves were the buds from which larger gay and lesbian urban communities (sometimes referred to as gay ghettoes) would bloom in subsequent decades, but their development was arrested by the virulent homophobia that suffused mainstream American culture in the post-war period and through the 1950s.

During wartime the need for laborers to perform "men's" jobs while much of the male workforce was engaged in military activities had required the expansion of women's gender roles. Many women had relished the feeling of independence and sense of community that their war work had conferred, but after the war they found themselves under severe social pressure to return to more "feminine" pursuits like marriage, childrearing, and housekeeping. Women who resisted these pressures, along with many women's military auxiliary groups, quickly found themselves the targets of scrutiny for their perceived failure to conform to the expectations of "normal," heterosexual womanhood. The military, which had often turned a blind eye to homosexuality in its ranks during the war, embarked on an intensive investigation into the matter in the late 1940s. About 1,000 men and women were discharged on charges of homosexuality in the waning years of the decade—a number that would more than double in the 1950s as Americans began to view homosexuality not only as a moral failing or a sickness but also as a threat to national security (Bérubé, 1990). As Americans watched the growing populations in Communist countries, it became even more imperative to reproduce and maintain the American populace; if heterosexuality was seen as central to national purpose during a Cold War with the Soviet Union, homosexuality came to be seen as sick, criminal, and downright un-American.

## Christine Jorgensen, Harry Benjamin, and WPATH

Christine Jorgensen was the first U.S. transgender woman to become widely known for having sexual reassignment surgery (also called gender confirmation or gender affirmation surgery). Born George William Jorgensen, Jr. (1926–1989), Christine Jorgensen grew up in New York City and served in the U.S. Army during World War II. In 1951 and 1952 Jorgensen underwent hormone therapy and surgeries in Denmark and the US to reconstruct her genitals and feminize other parts of her body. Newspapers declared Jorgensen's the "first sex change operation," however similar surgeries were first performed in 1920s and 1930s Germany under the supervision of Dr. Magnus Hirschfeld of the Institute for Sex Research. Jorgensen became an instant nationwide celebrity and she became the subject of dozens of sensationalized tabloid magazine stories, an autobiographical book, musical recordings, and even a Hollywood movie. She parlayed her celebrity into work as an actress, nightclub singer, recording artist, and lecturer, and was a vocal advocate for transgender rights

Although the 1950s and 1960s were often bleak decades for LGBTQ+ people, Jorgensen's gender transition appears to have been celebrated because it did not challenge the strict gender binary that was promoted during these decades. Before her transition Jorgensen was a paragon of masculinity: handsome, white, middle-class, a military veteran. Some of those same traits and characteristics allowed her to embody ideal femininity after her gender transition. As was expected of heterosexual women, Jorgensen attempted to marry a man—twice—but was denied a marriage license because her birth certificate listed her as male. Even though she transitioned from one gender to another, that transition did not fundamentally undermine the era's belief that gender was binary in form.

One of Jorgensen's later surgeries in the US was overseen by endocrinologist Dr. Harry Benjamin. Benjamin was born and educated in Germany where he met Magnus Hirschfeld. He

*Christine Jorgensen (January 1954). Source: Photo by Maurice Seymour, New York. Image courtesy of Wikimedia Commons.*

later practiced in New York and San Francisco, where he specialized in gender transition-related medical care for patients that, today, would be described as transgender. His 1966 book *The Transsexual Phenomenon* was the first significant effort to describe best practices for the medical care of transgender patients.

The wealthy industrialist Reed Erickson sought treatment from Benjamin in the early 1960s and eventually funded the Harry Benjamin Foundation, which led to the creation of The Harry Benjamin International Gender Dysphoria Association (HBIGDA). Erickson and HBIGDA did pioneering research and educational work on transgender people and issues. In 2007 HBIGDA formally changed its name to The World Professional Association for Transgender Health, which produces and distributes the *WPATH Standards of Care for the Health of Transsexual, Transgender, and Gender Nonconforming People*—a milestone document guiding medical care for transgender people worldwide (Meyerowitz, 2004; Stryker, 2008).

*Michael J. Murphy*

## The Homophile Movement

The same era which saw the lives of gay, lesbian, and bisexual Americans grow overcast by a cloud of cultural paranoia and suspicion also saw the emergence

*Bayard Rustin, a black gay man, organized the 1963 March on Washington where Martin Luther King, Jr. gave his famous "I Have a Dream" speech. Source: Photo by Orlando Fernandez. Courtesy of the Library of Congress, Prints & Photographs Division and Wikimedia Commons.*

of the country's first organized movement to advocate for their civil rights. The homophile movement, as it was known, grew out of a social network of men and women who met in the gay and lesbian enclaves that had increased in size after World War II.

Many of these organizations avoided identifying themselves as "homosexual" groups in an effort to avoid that term's negative and medicalized implications. Additionally, many of them chose deliberately innocuous names, avoiding anything that might make the aims of the group obvious to outsiders. In 1950 Harry Hay, Rudi Gernreich, and three other Los Angeles-area gay men, held the first meeting of the Mattachine Society, a "service and welfare organization devoted to the protection and improvement of Society's Androgynous Minority" (Roscoe and Hay, 1996). The group was named for a French medieval performer who only appeared in public while masked, similar to the way that many homosexuals in the 1950s felt the need to assume a "mask" while in public. A few years later Del Martin, Phyllis Lyon, and six other women in San Francisco founded the Daughters of Bilitis, which took its name from a fictional female character alleged to have been the lover of the Greek poet Sappho. While their group was initially social in nature, it quickly developed a more activist orientation and became the first exclusively lesbian homophile group in the country.

One of the primary goals of homophile groups was to provide a safe social environment and they insisted on discretion in order to protect their members' safety. Because bars and clubs that solicited (or merely tolerated) openly homosexual or gender variant patrons were frequently raided by the police, and patrons who were arrested risked being exposed as homosexuals, homophiles' meetings were usually held in private homes. They were open only to existing members and their invited guests, and members were expected to adhere in public to gender-normative dress codes that required men to wear suits and women to wear dresses (Hillman, 2011). During this era, to have been identified as a homosexual put an individual at risk of losing their job, being evicted from their home, losing custody of their children, or being forced to undergo psychological treatment, so avoiding detection by hostile observers was of paramount importance to the continued functioning of these groups (Bernstein, 1997).

The homophile groups did far more than just socialize, though; they published newsletters and pamphlets (and later magazines) filled with personal advice and important information related to discrimination in housing, in the workplace, and in the courts (Gallo, 2006). In general, most homophile groups shared a similar strategic plan to achieve social acceptance for homosexuals, which was to emphasize the extent to which many homosexuals' lives and values aligned with mainstream American norms (thereby minimizing, though still affirming, homosexuals' sexual difference from that mainstream). To this end, they focused a great deal of their efforts on outreach to the medical and psychological communities, hoping that their demonstration of "normalcy" in almost all regards would persuade professionals in those fields to advocate for the social and legal tolerance of homosexuals.

When members of homophile groups engaged in public outreach—speaking on panels to medical professionals or publishing pamphlets or magazines—they frequently assumed pseudonyms or altered their appearance to avoid negative repercussions. Though today we might think of such measures as emblematic of paranoia, the fears of lesbian, gay, bisexual and transgender Americans were well-founded. In Boise, Idaho, in 1955 police whipped the city into a frenzy looking for a suspected "homosexual ring," interviewing 1,500 Boise residents to gather the names of "suspected homosexuals," and eventually arresting 16 men on a variety of sex-related charges; many of these men lost their jobs, homes, and families as a result (Miller, 2002, 50). In Florida, a decade-long effort to purge homosexuals from the ranks of the state's educational institutions began in 1956; through tactics of intimidation, harassment, innuendo, and interrogation, dozens of educators were stripped of their professional credentials and sometimes turned out of their communities (Graves, 2009). Also during this decade a number of individuals harassed by the federal government for their suspected homosexuality committed suicide (Johnson, 2004a).

*Barbara Gittings and other homophile activists picket the White House in 1965. Source: Photo by Kay Tobin Lahusen. Courtesy of New York Public Library Manuscripts and Archives Division and Wikimedia Commons.*

The lingering history of sexual inversion and its entanglement of sexuality with gender identity and expression became unpleasant, both politically and personally, to many of those focused on moving through specific channels to achieve tolerance. Even as homophile organizations coalesced, the overwhelming cultural pressure toward normative sexuality influenced people from a wide variety of backgrounds. In 1952 the famous blues singer and "male impersonator" Gladys Bentley published an essay in the African-American magazine *Ebony* renouncing her past. Entitled "I Am a Woman Again," the article explained how "female hormone injections" and the loving tenderness of a recently acquired husband had helped Bentley, known in the 1920s, 1930s, and 1940s for her masculine appearance and same-sex love affairs, escape from "the no-man's land which exists between the boundaries of the two sexes" and to move "back toward the path of normalcy"

(Garber, 1998, 58). As evidenced by this high-profile example, and by the nascent homophile movement, being "normal" was both socially and politically expedient for many people with same-sex desires or non-normative gender expression, as prevailing social attitudes remained intolerant of deviations from the norm as the 1950s went on.

## THE 1960s: CIVIL RIGHTS, WOMEN'S LIBERATION, AND GAY LIBERATION

The history of the United States in the 1960s is marked by movements for social change. The black civil rights movement of the 1950s continued its work, as the second-wave feminist movement began to coalesce, and students and political activists united in their opposition to the Vietnam War. Overlooked in many popular histories of this era is the emergence of the Gay Liberation movement, which both succeeded and opposed the homophile movement that began in the 1950s.

The homophile organizations founded in the 1950s grew in size and number in the 1960s, with affiliate chapters of the Mattachine Society and the Daughters of Bilitis—along with smaller independent groups—popping up across the country. As the membership and leadership of these groups changed over time their perspectives on homosexuality and their approach to achieving social tolerance gradually shifted. Whereas some early homophile activists accepted the pathologization of homosexuality but argued for tolerance in spite of it, later homophile leaders rejected the notion that homosexuality was an illness or disorder of any type. Similarly, the early homophiles' emphasis on discretion was replaced with an insistence on visibility. In 1965, for instance, homophiles formed picket lines at the White House, at the United Nations, and at Philadelphia's Independence Hall to protest anti-gay policies or to promote gay rights.

*The Stonewall Inn, Greenwich Village (New York City), 1969. Source: Photo by Diana Davies. Courtesy of New York Public Library, Digital Collections and Wikimedia Commons.*

In June 1969 a commonplace occurrence turned into an extraordinary situation when police raided the Stonewall Inn, a predominantly male gay bar in New York City's Greenwich Village. While all bars with gay, lesbian, bisexual, or transgender clientele knew they could be raided at any time by police looking for patrons violating laws against cross-dressing, public indecency, or "lewd" behavior, and while most patrons arrested in such raids tended to take a cooperative stance in hopes that the charges would be resolved quietly, on this particular evening that acquiescent attitude evaporated. Ejected patrons, passersby, and neighborhood locals began to congregate outside of the Stonewall, jeering and throwing bottles and bricks at police as they herded arrested bar-goers into their police vehicles. The police barricaded themselves inside the bar until backup arrived to help disperse the crowd of about 1,000 rioters. Because the riot was reported in the local press, including radio and television outlets, there was a significant surge in attendance at the bar the following night. Over the next five days there were more skirmishes with police, but patrons and their supporters also engaged in public displays of same-sex affection; they chanted, sang songs, and gave speeches. While the Stonewall Inn's regular clientele was mostly made up of gay men, the protests included transgender women, lesbians, and drag queens. This rare moment of unity did not start the late twentieth-century movement for LGBT civil rights, but it did serve to channel the pent-up frustrations of persecuted sexual and gender minorities in an explicitly activist direction.

## Why Stonewall?

The 1969 Stonewall Riots (sometimes also called the Stonewall Uprising or just Stonewall) is often described as the start of the LGBTQ rights movement. There's no doubt Stonewall was a significant event, however it was far from the first example of direct, collective, militant LGBTQ resistance against oppressive police treatment in U.S. history.

In May 1959 a group of transgender women and gay men pelted police officers with donuts and coffee cups to protest police harassment at Cooper Do-Nuts in Los Angeles. The police arrested a number of protesters but they were able to escape police custody (Faderman & Timmons, 2006). In August 1966, a group of 50—60 customers, including many drag queens and sex workers, pushed back against police brutality by overturning tables, throwing dishes, and smashing windows at Compton's Cafeteria in the Tenderloin District of San Francisco. During the riot, a newspaper stand was burned, a police car was vandalized, and police were beaten with purses and high-heeled shoes (Stryker, 2008). In the early morning of January 1, 1967, 12 undercover police officers infiltrated the Black Cat Tavern in the Silver Lake neighborhood of Los Angeles, California. They started beating and arresting patrons for same-sex behavior (kissing) and cross-dressing—both of which were illegal at the time. The commotion expanded to involve another bar across the street where the police beat the bar's owner, bartenders, and patrons. On February 11, 1967, the newly formed group PRIDE (Personal Rights in Defense and Education) organized a demonstration against the raids, attended by over 200 people. It marks the first known time the word Pride was used in connection with lesbian or gay identity. The newsletter of PRIDE, *The Los Angeles Advocate*, first published in 1967, would become *The Advocate*, an award-winning national lesbian and gay newsmagazine, still in print today. In August 1968 a similar raid of The Patch bar in Wilmington, California, was actively resisted and transformed into a political rally for gay rights (Faderman & Timmons, 2006).

*(continued)*

*(continued)*

Despite these, and other, earlier examples of LGBTQ resistance, the Stonewall riots have become iconic because they occurred in a major metropolitan area with a critical mass of lesbian and gay people who worked to memorialize and commemorate the events of June 1969. Although Chicago, San Francisco, and Los Angeles all hosted gay rights marches in June 1970, lesbian and gay activists in New York City actively sought to link the June 1970 Christopher Street Liberation Day parade to earlier activism by homophile organizations. The annual repetition of this parade on the anniversary of the Stonewall riots, helped cement Stonewall as *the* watershed moment in gay rights history (Armstrong & Crage, 2006).

*Michael J. Murphy*

## THE 1970s

### Identity, Rights, and Activism

In the 1970s conflicts between activists from the homophile movement and gay liberation activists became visible. Militant, openly gay, and often gender non-conforming, many members of the latter group aligned themselves with the Gay Liberation Front (GLF), an organization whose broad platform inveighed against racism, capitalism, sexism, heterosexism, and other forms of social oppression. This was not surprising, as many of those involved in the gay rights movement had cut their teeth, as activists, in the black civil rights movement—some alongside or in the anti-Vietnam War protests of the "New Left." When the GLF found itself torn by internal struggles over which aspects of its program deserved the majority of its attention, a group of former GLF members broke away to form their own group called the Gay Activists Alliance (GAA), a single-issue organization dedicated to securing "basic human rights, dignity, and freedom for all gay people."

The GLF insisted that the oppression of gay people was just one facet of an inherently discriminatory capitalist social system that had to be dismantled. However, the rights-based approaches taken by groups like GAA focused less on working against, and more on working within, this system. Though their aims were more moderate than GLF's, the GAA's tactics were nonetheless radical; they were best known for public actions, known as zaps, that were designed to draw the public's attention to LGBT issues. Some of these zaps were held at television studios that had produced anti-gay programs, at businesses with anti-gay employment policies, and at the homes or workplaces of public figures and politicians who made anti-gay statements, and the media coverage these bold actions received ensured that their impact was felt well beyond the city in which they took place.

Conflicts within and between post-Stonewall gay activism and organizations highlighted some of the differences within the LGBT community. Not only did people disagree over how radical the movement should be, they also argued over who belonged in it. Clashes between gay men and lesbians were especially frequent in the 1970s, as many lesbians felt that their interests were better represented by women's liberation and feminist groups than by male-dominated gay liberation and gay activist organizations. Bisexual people faced mistrust and questioning about their sexuality from both heterosexuals and homosexuals. Transgender individuals, particularly transgender women, butted heads with radical feminists and lesbian separatists, who largely refused to accept transgender women as "real" women. Other clashes arose from the overwhelming whiteness of both gay-focused and feminist-oriented organizations, and people of color broke away to form new groups that acknowledged, instead of minimizing, the intersections between race, gender, and sexuality.

Gay and lesbian activists in the 1970s continued the early efforts of the homophile movement to educate psychological and medical professionals in the hopes of ending the social stigma that resulted from the notion that homosexuality was an illness or disorder. In 1970 members of the GAA and GLF picketed the annual meeting of the American Psychiatric Association (APA) to protest the continued pathologization of homosexuality, and in 1972 Barbara Gittings and Franklin Kameny organized a panel on homosexuality called "Psychiatry: Friend or Foe to Homosexuals?" Their panelists included a practicing psychiatrist, billed as Dr. H. Anonymous, who wore a mask and spoke through a device that disguised his voice—precautions necessary, he explained, to prevent his professional work from being discredited. Following the panel, the APA began debating the removal of homosexuality from its official list of mental disorders. In 1975 the APA affirmed its belief that homosexuality "implies no impairment in judgement, stability, reliability, or general social and vocational capabilities" and offered its support for "civil rights legislation at the local, and state and federal level that would offer citizens who engage in acts of homosexuality the same protections now guaranteed to others" on the basis of race, creed, and color.

*Barbara Gittings, Franklin Kameny, and "Dr. Henry Anonymous" (Dr. John E. Fryer) at the annual meeting of the American Psychiatric Association (1972). Source: Photo by Kay Tobin Lahusen. Courtesy of New York Public Library, Digital Collections and Wikimedia Commons.*

In much the same way that activists had ultimately achieved their goal by working with, rather than against, the APA, some activists in the 1970s sought to win legal protections and rights for homosexual people by working within the political realm. In 1975 the ban on employing gay men and lesbians in the federal government was finally lifted as the U.S. Civil Service Commission removed references to "sexual perversion" in its regulations (Braukman, 2004). While some lesbian, gay, and bisexual politicians had held office prior to the 1970s, none were open about their sexuality at the time of their election. In 1974 Kathy Kozachenko was the first openly lesbian candidate to run for political office, winning a seat on the Ann Arbor, Michigan, city council. The same year, in Massachusetts, Elaine Noble became the first openly lesbian candidate elected to a state legislature. And in 1977 Harvey Milk won a seat on the San Francisco Board of Supervisors, becoming the first openly gay person elected to public office in the state of California. Milk's term was cut short when he was assassinated by a disgruntled former city employee in 1978, but he remains one of the best-known examples of the first generation of openly gay politicians.

## THE 1970s: GAY CULTURES AND COMMUNITIES

Across the United States an institutionalized and public, lesbian and gay (and, to a lesser extent, transgender and bisexual) life developed and flourished during the 1970s. Though the majority of the communities around which this public life centered were urban, in more rural areas, too, groups of likeminded individuals laid claim to neighborhoods and carved out enclaves of their own. Some of most common, and arguably some of the most significant, fixtures within these communities centered on sexual orientation included bars, bookstores, and bathhouses. Each of these spaces enabled same-sex-attracted individuals to forge social and sexual connections with one another in a much more open manner than would have been possible elsewhere.

Many of these communities also created their own newspapers, which allowed readers to encounter relevant news that the mainstream media often eschewed, in addition to beckoning isolated LGBT people toward the communities for which they were written. At least 50 different lesbian- or gay-focused newspapers and journals were published throughout the 1970s, the better-lived counterparts of countless others that existed only briefly (Downs, 2016). These publications allowed readers to see themselves as part of a larger national coalition of lesbian, gay and bisexual people, at the same time they encouraged them to take part in creating and sustaining the communities they lived in or near.

In addition to the bars, bookstores, and bathhouses, LGBT Americans created other outlets for socializing and support in the 1970s, including their own churches and religious auxiliary organizations. The Metropolitan Community Church, or MCC, was founded in 1968 by Pentecostal minister Reverend Troy Perry as an explicitly affirming institution for lesbian, gay, bisexual, and transgender Christians, and had established dozens of branches across the country by the mid-1970s; Jewish LGBT people could worship in the country's first gay synagogue, founded in Los Angeles in 1972; while Roman Catholics and Episcopalians could join faith-based groups like Dignity or Integrity, respectively (Eaklor, 2008). The movement for LGBT religious inclusion was strong enough that, in 1971, over 70 participants from 11 denominations participated in the first-ever Conference on Religion and the Homosexual (Comstock, 1996). No longer willing to tolerate being shunned by religious institutions, gay, lesbian, bisexual, and transgender individuals asserted their equal rights to worship.

Even as gay activists made progress toward securing legal protections against discrimination, a cultural backlash was brewing. In 1977, for example, minor celebrity and outspoken Christian Anita Bryant spearheaded a campaign called Save Our Children, which successfully sought to repeal a Dade County, Florida, ordinance that prohibited discrimination in housing, employment, and public accommodation based on sexual orientation. Similar successful campaigns were carried out in 1979 in Minnesota, Kansas, and Oregon. In 1978 legislators in California introduced Proposition 6, also called the Briggs Initiative, a law which would have prevented any openly homosexual person from working in the state's public schools. Activists started a campaign called No on 6, which urged gay and lesbian people to speak openly and publicly about the harm that the proposed law would cause them. Republican and Democratic politicians also spoke out against the proposition, including then-president Jimmy Carter and future president Ronald Reagan. While the Briggs Initiative was ultimately defeated, the cycle of progress and backlash in relation to LGBT rights would continue for decades to come.

## THE 1980s: ACTIVISM, AIDS, AND ANGER

As the new decade dawned, the LGBT community seemed well-positioned to continue the progress it had made in earlier decades. In late 1979 approximately 75,000 people had participated in the first National March on Washington for Lesbian and Gay Rights, and six months later the Democrats became the first major political party to include gay rights in the party platform they announced at their National Convention. Mainstream media representation of lesbian and gay characters was increasing in frequency and improving in quality, and vibrant communities centered on non-heterosexual identities—and especially gay male identities—flourished in major cities across the country. People who lived outside of these urban enclaves could still establish a sense of identity and community by reading any one of the dozens of gay publications that had enjoyed national circulation since the 1970s.

At the same time, however, the country's politics were moving in a more conservative direction, due to factors both foreign (political instability in the Middle East and in Latin America; an antagonistic relationship with the powerful Soviet Union) and domestic (a sluggish economy; and growing resentment of the efforts of women and people of color to achieve parity with white men in employment and education). As the United States hewed more closely to the traditional social values championed by newly elected President Ronald

*Lesbian & Gay Caucus member holds a sign that reads "Black Lesbian Feminist" at the 1980 Democratic National Convention at Madison Square Garden in New York City (August 11–14, 1980). Source: Photo by Allen G. Shores. Courtesy of ONE National Gay and Lesbian Archives, USC.*

Reagan and a new wave of conservative political activists, the LGBT community became the target of political and cultural rhetoric that characterized not just homosexuality, but homosexuals, as threatening to the country's well-being.

## The Queer T-shirt

Since the 1970s some LGBTQ people have used t-shirts as a vehicle for political activism and personal expression. T-shirts were cheap, readily available, and carried an aura of working class and youthful rebellion starting in the 1950s. In that decade, t-shirts became fashionable as stand-alone garments, as opposed to being worn mostly as undershirts. After Stonewall some lesbians, gay men, and bisexuals began using the inexpensive t-shirts to express personal and political views, and make LGBTQ lives publicly visible.

In 1970, for example, lesbian activists, angry at National Organization of Women (NOW) President Betty Freidan's dismissal of lesbians in the women's movement as a "lavender menace," staged a demonstration at a major NOW conference in New York. The fiery activists took control of the event's main stage and protested over the microphone while wearing t-shirts with the phrase "Lavender Menace" printed across their chests (Katz, 2014). Forty-six years later, in 2016, administrators of Sierra High School in central California sent 16-year-old Taylor Victor home after she showed up to school wearing a t-shirt that read "Nobody Knows I'm a Lesbian" (Branson-Potts, 2016).

But not all lesbian and gay activists used overtly political symbols or messages on their t-shirts; some were more covert and hidden. At the 1982 Gay and Lesbian Pride celebration in Washington, D.C., marchers for the Virginia-based organization Blue Ridge Lambda Alliance wore t-shirts with the Greek letter lambda (λ) and the initials BRLA. Unlike the rainbow Pride flag, the lambda symbol was not well known as a symbol of the gay and lesbian rights movement, thus the t-shirt did little to communicate the wearer's involvement in LGBTQ causes. At similar gay pride celebrations in the 1980s, however, marchers wore t-shirts with provocative slogans like "We're Here, We're Queer, Get Used To It," which more clearly communicated the wearer's sexual orientation (Penney, 2013). Words and images on some t-shirts were less confrontational, for example, promoting a community picnic, bowling tournament, or HIV/AIDS awareness. Others could, and often did, risk harm. Those who wore such t-shirts risked a range of persecution, from loss of a job to physical violence.

Whatever words or images were used, LGBTQ activists' creative use of the humble t-shirt speaks of a collective need to be visible and recognized, even in times and places where that was risky or even dangerous.

*Eric Nolan Gonzaba*

## The AIDS Crisis

Recent research into the origins of AIDS suggests that HIV (the human immunodeficiency virus, which develops into AIDS) arrived in New York, by way of Haiti, by the early 1970s, and had spread across the country by the middle of the decade. Because HIV can remain in the body for years before an individual develops AIDS, it is possible for infected individuals to unwittingly spread the virus to others through the transmission of bodily fluids. While a few patients in the US, Sweden, Haiti, and Tanzania had sought medical treatment for symptoms of immunodeficiency in 1978, medical professionals did not draw connections between these unusual cases. But, in July 1981, the *New York Times* published an article entitled "Rare Cancer Seen in 41 Homosexuals," which reported on a recent spate of diagnoses of young gay men in New York and San Francisco with Kaposi's Sarcoma (KS), a type of cancer that characteristically affected men over 50 and was rarely fatal. The article noted that many of the men diagnosed with KS frequently engaged in sexual encounters with many different partners and suggested that the spate of cases might also be related to patients' reported use of recreational drugs thought to enhance their sexual experiences, and assured readers that "there was no apparent danger to nonhomosexuals from contagion." By May of the following year the *Times* reported that at least 335 people, primarily gay men, had been diagnosed with a "serious disorder of the immune system" that caused KS and made them susceptible to a host of other rare cancers and infections, including pneumonia; one-third of them had already died. Researchers initially referred to the condition as GRID (gay- related immunodeficiency), but as it became clear that Americans from all walks of life were at risk of contracting the illness, the disease was dubbed AIDS (acquired immunodeficiency syndrome).

Media coverage of AIDS increased the visibility of the gay community—primarily of gay men—while also constructing a particular set of stereotypes. Because much of this coverage was and has been about gay men, and specifically about gay white men, it reinforced the mainstream idea of gayness as both white and male. Some scholars suggest that the tragedy of the AIDS epidemic "forced many mainstream institutions into sustained negotiation with the gay and lesbian community," resulting in lasting connections that helped gay activists gain ground on other issues (D'Emilio and Freedman, 1997).

At the same time, media coverage often suggested that gay men were promiscuous, prone to anonymous sex, diseased, possibly drug-addicted, morally corrupt, and therefore deserving of the disease. Positioning gay men as the "carriers" of this terrible virus meant that they—and gayness itself—was perceived as a threat to "innocent" heterosexuals. This "threat" was in part related to the transmission of HIV via blood transfusions, and in part due to concerns about whether seemingly heterosexual men might have had same-sex encounters.

By 1986, the first time President Reagan mentioned AIDS in a public speech, over 16,000 Americans had died of complications of the disease. Many

LGBT people had, from the outset, tried to deal with the crisis internally; friends, family, and people with no overt connection to the LGBT community also tried to help. As early as 1982 activists in San Francisco and New York founded community groups that disseminated information on safer sex and provided people with AIDS with crisis counseling, legal aid, and referrals to social and medical services. While many of the leaders of these groups were gay men, lesbians increasingly assumed the burden of work as their male counterparts grew too ill to participate. By the mid-1980s frustration with the slow responses of government agencies and the pharmaceutical industry reached a boiling point. One outlet for this rage was the AIDS Coalition to Unleash Power (ACT UP), created in 1987 by some former members of Gay Men's Health Crisis (GMHC), a New York City-based AIDS service organization. ACT UP was a political action group, rather than a support group. It held highly visible, often shocking, public demonstrations (such as die-ins, a macabre take on the sit-in protest) to demand that the government increase funding for research on AIDS and that pharmaceutical companies make treatment accessible and affordable. In some cases these targeted actions achieved concrete goals—for example, when the manufacturer of the first FDA-approved drug for HIV lowered the cost of the medication by 20% in response to sustained protests by ACT UP—and, taken as a whole, made clear the fact that—even in the midst of its decimation by a deadly epidemic—the nation's LGBT community would no longer be shamed into silence or invisibility.

*ACT UP Los Angeles protest against lack of research on alternative medications to treat HIV/AIDS, including Compound Q (Los Angeles, CA, 1989). Source: Courtesy ONE National Gay and Lesbian Archives, USC, ACT UP/Los Angeles Records.*

Although much of the LGBT community's focus remained fixed on AIDS throughout the 1980s, other concerns demanded its attention. The so-called Religious Right, a coordinated network of Republican politicians, Christian religious leaders, and conservative public figures, emerged in the early years of the decade and used a variety of tools— the ballot box, the pulpit, and the mass media—to discourage what it saw as the United States' departure from its "traditional" social and religious values. The Religious Right's worldview held that the US would receive divine retribution if it permitted its people to embrace "ungodly" beliefs or behaviors, which included feminism, social liberalism, and homosexuality. Thus, feminist women, political liberals, lesbians, and gay men were viewed as placing the country at risk of obliteration by natural disasters, wars, or epidemics of disease. Accordingly, politicians and activists affiliated with the Religious Right attempted to dismantle legal protections for LGBT people, produced virulently anti-gay videos, books, and pamphlets, and lobbied for extreme measures, such as forcibly quarantining or tattooing people with AIDS, or simply "exterminating" homosexuals.

In the face of this adversity, the LGBT community persevered. In 1987 the Second National March on Washington for Lesbian and Gay Rights drew more than half a million people to the capital for six days of activism and community. During the days leading up to the march, the NAMES Project AIDS Memorial Quilt was first publicly displayed on the National Mall. Conceived as a memorial project by Cleve Jones, one of Harvey Milk's political mentees, each panel of the quilt had been created in memory of an individual who had died of the disease. Attendees had much to protest since the last March on Washington, including the 1982 decision by the U.S. military that "homosexuality was incompatible with military service" and that homosexual service members would be discharged, and the 1986 Supreme Court decision, *Bowers v. Hardwick*, which upheld Texas' sodomy laws that criminalized consensual same-sex behavior, even in the privacy of one's home. It was also a time for collective mourning and a moment of rejuvenation, when the incandescent anger and determination of groups like ACT UP inspired attendees to return to their hometowns and join or start local LGBT groups with similar aims. The energy concentrated in Washington, D.C., before and during the March diffused across the country and powered the continued efforts of the LGBT community to obtain the rights, respect, and recognition they demanded.

## The Women's Music Movement

Beginning in the early 1970s, the women's music movement created a unique platform for lesbian visibility and activism. Concerts, album releases, and women's music festivals boldly named lesbian issues and relationships in every musical style, mobilizing audiences toward political action. In an era informed by radical feminism, before social media, women's music supporters made concert events into community celebrations of lesbian lives, paving the way for the mainstream success of Melissa Etheridge and the Indigo Girls in the 1990s. Offering an alternative to bar culture, concerts filled the lesbian calendar year-round for almost 40 years.

Women's music of the 1970s drew on older blues music traditions and shared many elements with folk-rock and Civil Rights Movement freedom songs, but added new feminist content (Davis, 1998; Faderman, 1991). An early recording featured the Chicago and New Haven Women's Liberation Rock Bands on the 1972 album *Mountain Moving Day*. Maxine Feldman's 1972 anthem "Angry Atthis," and Alix Dobkin's 1973 album *Lavender Jane Loves Women* followed. In 1973 Olivia Records became America's first lesbian-owned recording company. Its first artist was Meg Christian, whose 1974 album *I Know You Know* raised funds for Cris Williamson's best-selling

*(continued)*

*(continued)*

1975 release, *The Changer and the Changed*. These and other artists delighted fans with titles like "Sweet Darling Woman," "Leaping Lesbians" and "Ode to a Gym Teacher," and Olivia's 1977 album *Lesbian Concentrate* directly challenged the antigay initiative led in Florida by Anita Bryant (Morris, 1999). Performer Holly Near's company Redwood Records introduced audiences to songs with intersectional politics, featuring ensemble groups like Sweet Honey in the Rock. (Near, 1990). Distribution companies Ladyslipper and Goldenrod, still active today, delivered albums and cassettes to fans.

National concert tours brought lesbian–identified artists to audiences in small towns and, by the mid-1970s, women's music festivals drew thousands of participants. Beginning with the National Women's Music Festival, produced by Kristin Lems on the campus of the University of Illinois in 1974, dozens of four-day events met regularly in retreats from Alaska to Mississippi. Festivals on public land, such as Sisterfire in Washington, D.C., included men and transwomen. The largest outdoor event, the Michigan Womyn's Music Festival, hosted women-only festivals on 650 acres of private land. Impacting American lesbian activism for 40 years (1976–2015), Michigan's producer Lisa Vogel endured boycotts and threats of violence while inspiring a huge following. It ended after its 40th anniversary festival in 2015.

Today, artists from the women's music movement continue to tour and perform for both mixed and majority-lesbian audiences. Ongoing productions include the National Women's Music Festival, the Ohio Lesbian Festival, and Olivia Travel's year-round women's music cruises. The material legacies of bygone concerts and festivals (women's music albums and CDs, t-shirts, art, posters, photographs, and producers' notes) are now archived in the Sophia Smith collection at Smith College, the Lesbian Herstory Archives in Brooklyn, and at Radcliffe College's Schlesinger Library.

*Bonnie J. Morris*

## THE 1990s

LGBT activists in the 1990s pushed boldly ahead toward full citizenship in the face of conservative rhetoric that echoed the same anti-LGBT arguments made in the previous decades. In the legal arena some hard-fought battles were won and others lost. In addition to these legal advances, one of the biggest achievements of this era was the attainment of unprecedented visibility for LGBT individuals in American popular culture.

### Legal Battles: Marriage, Discrimination, Hate Crimes

In the courts, one of the major battles of the 1990s was fought over allowing lesbian, gay, and bisexual individuals to serve in the armed forces. President William J. Clinton, elected in 1992, had hoped to remove the World War II-era policies that mandated discharge for homosexual service members, but faced significant resistance from the military and from social and political conservatives. As a compromise, in 1994 the military adopted a new policy called Don't Ask, Don't Tell, Don't Pursue, Don't Harass (commonly referred to simply as Don't Ask, Don't Tell). Military officials were expected to curtail their efforts to identify and discharge homosexuals in exchange for lesbian, gay, and bisexual service members not disclosing their sexual orientation. While some viewed this policy as a step in the right direction, others were disheartened by their failure to convince Americans that being gay, lesbian, or bisexual was no bar to a successful military career. This policy remained in place until 2011, when the Department of Defense finally determined that integrating openly gay, lesbian, and bisexual people into the armed forces would cause little or no disruption to the military's day-to-day operations.

Other battles were waged over the legal recognition of same-sex partnerships. Cases in Hawaii (1991) and Vermont (1996) were among the first to challenge the constitutionality of denying same-sex couples marriage licenses. Though the plaintiffs in these cases were not successful, some incremental positive changes were achieved. In 1999 Vermont introduced same-sex civil unions, which conferred the rights of marriage (but only within its state). In response to these efforts, Republican opponents in Congress mustered support for a 1996 measure known as the Defense of Marriage Act (DOMA), which defined federal marriage as between a man and a woman, and which allowed states to refuse to recognize same-sex marriages from other states (Eaklor, 2008). On the same day DOMA was passed, Congress rejected the Employment Non-Discrimination Act, which would have made it illegal to discriminate on the grounds of sexual orientation against applicants in hiring decisions. A 1998 Executive Order signed by President Clinton achieved some of the same aims; it prohibited sexual orientation-based discrimination within the federal government.

An additional legal achievement for LGBT activists in the 1990s was the inclusion of sexual orientation as a category covered by federal definitions of hate crimes. This decade brought heightened public awareness of the violence faced by LGBT people as a result of two separate murders. The first, in 1994, involved a transgender man known as Brandon Teena, who was slain by two male acquaintances; one week earlier, the same acquaintances had sexually assaulted Teena after discovering he was not biologically male. Teena's story was the basis for a book, a documentary, and for the award-winning independent film *Boys Don't Cry* (1999). The second highly publicized murder occurred in Laramie, Wyoming, in 1998; gay college student Matthew Shepard was brutally beaten and left for dead by two men who'd gained his confidence by posing as gay themselves. The story received significant coverage from the mainstream media and became the basis for a play, *The Laramie Project*, which was based on interviews with city residents and later made into a cable-TV film. These cases were instrumental in helping non-LGBT Americans understand the dangers faced by LGBT people every day as a mere fact of their existence.

## LGBT Cultural Landmarks

Following the death of American multi-millionaire Malcom Forbes in 1990, conservative cultural and political figures came out to pay their respects. Observing this with dismay, Michelangelo Signorile wrote a feature story for the LGBT publication *OutWeek* called "The Other Side of Malcom Forbes." The story revealed a facet of Forbes' life that he'd attempted to keep quiet—according to Signorile and his sources, the deceased had been "as queer as a three dollar bill." This was the decade's first high-profile instance of outing, or disclosing the sexual orientation of another person without their consent. The mainstream American press weighed in on whether or not such behavior was ethical—most seemed to consider it in poor taste, or verging on libel or slander—but Signorile and other LGBT activists insisted that it was necessary. Signorile wrote, "For the sake of posterity, the truth must be told. One of the most influential men in America died . . . and he was gay. And that must be recorded." Moreover, he argued, outing famous and beloved American figures sent "a clear message to the American public that we are everywhere." His defense of outing echoed the arguments made by activists in the 1970s, who had argued that public visibility was key to the achievement of LGBT equality.

Visibility was also enhanced by increasing representation in American entertainment culture of openly LGBT celebrities. Throughout the 1990s some of the country's most popular television sitcoms and soap operas had incorporated characters identified as lesbian, gay, or bisexual (transgender individuals were only infrequently included), and programs like *Ellen* (1997) and *Will and Grace* (1998) featured such individuals in starring roles. Additionally, the number of athletes, public figures, and politicians who came out as gay, lesbian, bisexual, or transgender in this period made growing numbers of Americans aware that the community was, in fact, "everywhere." Reflecting this awareness, in 1995 Bill Clinton became the first U.S. President to appoint one of his staff members as a liaison to the LGBT community; two years earlier, he had become the first sitting President to host leaders of LGBT-oriented organizations and political action committees at a meeting in the White House.

## 2000–PRESENT

Progress toward LGBT equality has been made at a rapid pace following the dawn of a new millennium, though the community has faced substantial challenges from within and without. In 2000, nearly 200,000 people converged on Washington, D.C. for the Millennium March for Equality, an event organized by leaders of some of the country's most powerful and wealthy LGBT advocacy organizations. Many within the LGBT community objected to the event's focus on equality, rather than rights, and argued that leadership was wrongheadedly focused on achieving their aims through a program of LGBT assimilation. One lesbian publication chastised organizers for this approach, cautioning that LGBT people would not "be protected for looking 'just like them'" or "made safe by throwing overboard all the tacky, unacceptable queers who might offend" mainstream, heterosexual Americans (Eaklor, 2008). The diverging approaches and aims of grassroots and corporate LGBT activists continues to create tension in the community to this day.

## Public History

Though sites with significance to the LGBT community have been included in the National Register of Historic Places and on the roster of National Historic Landmarks since the 1966 Historic Preservation Act was adopted, "their connections to LGBT heritage almost always went undocumented in inventory-nomination forms and the subject went unmentioned—or was referred to only in euphemisms—when visitors toured places open to the public" (Springate, 2016).

*Sylvia Rivera Way street sign, Greenwich Village, New York City. Rivera (1951–2002) was a veteran of the Stonewall uprising and a longtime transgender rights activist. Source: Photo by Gotty/ own work, Public Domain. Image courtesy of Wikimedia Commons.*

As public support for LGBT civil rights has increased in the United States, alongside a growing body of scholarship on LGBT history, it is now more possible than ever to document and demonstrate the significance of "lavender landmarks." By identifying, marking, and publicizing significant sites like hotels, bars, hospitals, community centers, government agencies, parks, and private residences, activists have helped to make visible parts of the historical record that were long overlooked. The Washington, D.C., home of early gay activist Franklin Kameny, who coined the popular Gay Liberation slogan "Gay is Good!" and the Chicago home where Henry Gerber drew up plans for the country's first chartered organization for homosexual rights, are two such sites to recently join the National Register of Historic Places, and in 2016 the Stonewall Inn was designated by President Barack Obama as a National Historic Monument.

In the political realm, some of the greatest strides toward equal rights for LGBT Americans were made during the two-term presidency of Barack Obama. In addition to overseeing the repeal of Don't Ask, Don't Tell, President Obama publicly affirmed his support for LGBT people and issues in a way no previous president had done. Following the 2014 Supreme Court decision,

*Poster remembering transgender lives lost to violence, Transgender Day of Remembrance, Washington D.C. (Nov. 20, 2014). Source: Photo by Ted Eytan/ CC BY-SA 2.0 license. Image courtesy of Wikimedia Commons.*

which overturned the Defense of Marriage Act and legalized same-sex marriage in all 50 states, the White House was lit up in the colors of the rainbow Pride flag associated with the LGBT community and the President hosted a celebration in the Rose Garden.

In spite of the significant advances lesbian, gay, bisexual, and transgender Americans have seen over the last decade, much work remains to be done. The Employment Non-Discrimination Act still has not been passed by Congress, imperiling LGBT individuals' professional success. Many states have refused to adopt non-discrimination ordinances, or have flatly declined to include sexual orientation or gender identity in existing policies. Transgender individuals, in particular, still must contend with local and state laws that prevent them from changing government identification documents, and prohibit them from using sex-segregated facilities like restrooms and locker rooms; additionally, transgender women of color are disproportionately targeted, around the world, in anti-LGBT hate crimes; every year since 1998 the Transgender Day of Remembrance has been observed on November 20 to honor the memory of those lost to violence (GLAAD, 2016b).

Perhaps the largest question facing the LGBT community now is about the limits of inclusivity and group cohesion. As its designation has grown, over time, from gay and lesbian to LGBT, present efforts to expand the acronym to include people who identify as queer, questioning, intersex, asexual, or pansexual. Some question whether all these individuals truly share the same values or hope for the same goals, while others suggest that creating a broad coalition of marginalized individuals is essential to protect some of its hard-won social and legal achievements. As long as LGBTQ people can continue to find common cause, and to work together to achieve a more equitable society for individuals who are anything other than cisgender heterosexuals, the progress it has made over the past half-century portends its future success.

## Learn More

### Readings

Bérubé, A. (1990). *Coming out under fire: The history of gay men and women in World War Two*. New York: Free Press.

Chauncey, G. (1994). *Gay New York: Gender, urban culture, and the makings of the gay male world, 1890–1940*. New York: Basic.

D'Emilio, J. (1983). *Sexual politics, sexual communities: The making of a homosexual minority in the United States, 1940–1970*. Chicago, IL: University of Chicago.

Eaklor, V. (2008). *Queer America: A GLBT history of the twentieth century*. Westport, CT: Greenwood.

Faderman, L. (1991). *Odd girls and twilight lovers: A history of lesbian life in 20th century America*. New York, NY: Columbian University.

Johnson, D. K. (2004a) *The lavender scare: The Cold War persecution of gays and lesbians in the federal government*. Chicago: University of Chicago.

Katz, J. N. (1992). *Gay American history: Lesbians and gay men in the U.S.A.* New York: Plume.

Katz, J. N. (1995). *The invention of heterosexuality*. New York, NY: Dutton.

Meyerowitz, J. (2004). *How sex changed: A history of transsexuality in the United States*. Cambridge, MA: Harvard University.

Reis, E. (2009). *Bodies in doubt: An American history of intersex*. Baltimore: Johns Hopkins University.

Rupp, L. (1999). *A desired past: A short history of same-sex love in America*. Chicago: University of Chicago.

Stein, M. (2012). *Rethinking the gay and lesbian movement*. New York: Routledge.

Stryker, S. (2008). *Transgender history*. Seattle, WA: Seal.

## *Film/Video*

Baus, J. (Producer), Hunt, D. (Producer/Project Coordinator), & Scagliotti, J. (Director). (1999). *After Stonewall* [Motion picture]. United States: First Run.

Beauchemin, M. (Director), Levy, L. (Director) & Vogel, G. (Director). (1990). *Two-spirit people* [Motion picture]. United States: Frameline.

Cantillon, J. (2013). *The other side: A queer history's last call* [Documentary film]. United States: Ross.

Davis, K., & Heilbroner, D. (Producers). (2010). *The American experience: Stonewall uprising*. [DVD] United States: PBS.

Dupre, J. (Producer), & McKenna, C. (Producer). (2004). *Out of the past: The struggle for gay and lesbian rights in America* [Motion picture]. United States: Zeitgeist.

Epstein, R. (Director), & Schmiechen, R. (Producer). (1984). *The times of Harvey Milk* [Motion picture]. United States: Black Sands.

France, D. (Director). (2012). *How to survive a plague*. [Motion picture]. United States: Public Square.

Hubbard, J. (Director). (2012). *United in anger: A history of ACT-UP*. [Motion picture]. New York, NY: United in Anger.

Kates, N. (Director/Producer), & Singer, B. (Director/Producer). (2002). *Brother outsider: The life of Bayard Rustin* [Motion picture]. United States: California Newsreel.

Rosenberg, R. (Co-Director/Producer), Scagliotti, J. (Producer), Schiller & G. (Director/Producer). (1984). *Before Stonewall* [Motion picture]. United States: First Run.

Silverman, V., & Stryker, S. (Directors). (2005). *Screaming queens: The riot at Compton's Cafeteria* [DVD]. San Francisco: Frameline.

Weissman, D., & Weber, B. (Directors). (2012). *We were here: The AIDS years in San Francisco* [DVD]. United States: Weissman Projects.

## *Internet*

ACT UP Oral History Project: www.actuporalhistory.org

A Brief History of the Bisexual Movement: www.binetusa.org/bihistory.htm

GLBT Historical Society (San Francisco): www.glbthistory.org/

Lesbian Herstory Archives: www.lesbianherstoryarchives.org/

New York Public Library—Gay and Lesbian Collections & AIDS/HIV Collections: www.nypl.org/about/divisions/manuscripts-division/aids-hiv-collections

NOTCHES—(re)marks on the history of sexuality: notchesblog.com/

OutHistory.org: www.outhistory.org

People with a History: An Online Guide to Lesbian, Gay, Bisexual, and Trans* History: sourcebooks.web.fordham.edu/pwh/

The Library of Congress—LGBTQ+ Studies Research Guide: www.loc.gov/rr/main/lgbtq/lgbtqgeneralguide/index.html

# CHAPTER 2
# Same Difference
## *Diversities*

*Michael J. Murphy*

*Marchers with rainbow flags at WorldPride parade, London (June 27, 2015). Source: Photo by Bikeworldtravel, courtesy of Shutterstock.*

I n the month of June, to coincide with LGBTQ+ Pride events and the anniversary of Stonewall, homes, businesses, and government buildings around the world will display a flag with horizontal stripes, each of a different color: red, orange, yellow, green, blue, and purple. The Pride Flag (as it's often called) was created in 1978 by Gilbert Baker, a San Francisco artist, responding to a local activist's call for a community symbol. Baker's original flag had eight stripes: pink, red, orange, yellow, green, blue, indigo, and violet. According to Baker these colors represented (respectively) the concepts of sexuality, life, healing, sun, nature, art, harmony, and spirit. Baker dyed and sewed the first flag himself but when he approached a commercial flag company about mass-producing his flag he learned that hot pink was not a commercially available color, so he reduced the flag to seven stripes. Baker's rainbow scheme was adopted by the San Francisco Pride Parade Committee in 1979 but, wanting to display the colors evenly along the Pride Parade route, they dispensed with the indigo stripe. The resulting six stripe flag is the one flown today and recognized by the International Congress of Flag Makers. In June 2015, the Museum of Modern Art in New York City added the Pride flag to its design collection (Antonelli & Fisher, 2015).

Today the Pride Flag is closely identified with the LGBTQ+ community as a symbol of both unity and diversity. And that diversity extends beyond the symbolism of the six colors of the flag. Derivatives of the standard Pride Flag have been created to represent many LGBTQ+ groups, events, and subcultures (or "tribes") including bisexual and transgender people, African Americans, bears, the leather community, pansexuals, and genderqueers (Anderson, 1993). In June 2017, to much controversy, the City of Philadelphia debuted a modified Pride Flag with black and brown stripes added, to better recognize LGBTQ+ people of color (Abad-Santos, 2017). Diversity within unity; change over time: the Pride Flag is a near perfect metaphor for the LGBTQ+ community, perhaps explaining its adoption as a symbol globally.

Use of symbols like the Pride Flag and terms like LGBTQ+ can obscure important differences and distinctions between lesbian, gay, bisexual, transgender, and queer people, making it seem as if all LGBTQ+ people's experiences are the same. However, individual LGBTQ+ people are as diverse as any other large population group in the human family. Key to understanding this diversity are differences in biological sex, gender, and sexual orientation. Moreover, each of these major distinctions is cross-cut by differences in race, ethnicity, class, age, and geography. This chapter explains some of these differences, to show what connects LGBTQ+ people as a community and what distinguishes its various sub-groups and individuals.

## THE BIG THREE: SEX, GENDER, SEXUAL ORIENTATION

### Sex

One of the major distinctions within the LGBTQ+ community is along the lines of biological sex. Although the word sex is commonly used interchangeably with the word gender, or used to describe sexual behavior (i.e. having sex), in this chapter the word sex is used to refer to biological and physiological aspects of the body—a person's femaleness or maleness (or some combination of these). (The term gender is defined and discussed below.) Differences in biological sex can be one of the ways that lesbians and bisexual women distinguish themselves from gay and bisexual men (and the kinds of people to whom they are romantically and sexually attracted). And it is also key to understanding the experiences of intersex and transgender people.

If asked, many people might say that genes or genitals determine a person's biological sex, however sex also encompasses hormones, internal reproductive anatomy, brain anatomy, and secondary sex characteristics. Although some cultures, now and in the past, recognize three (or more) sex categories, contemporary Western societies generally recognize only two sexes: female and male. Nevertheless, the notion that sex is binary (having only two, mutually exclusive, positions) is not supported by scientific research on what are called sex differences. In fact, all humans combine elements of biological sex—like genes and hormones—that are commonly thought of as solely female or male. To understand this, it can be helpful to review typical human sexual development from conception to puberty, with an eye to both differences and similarities between "the sexes" (Birke, 1992; Blackless et al., 2000; Fausto-Sterling, 2000).

### Typical Sexual Development

Human sexual development begins with the combination of genetic material from both biological parents during conception. Each cell in the human body contains 23 pairs of chromosomes, for a total of 46. (A chromosome is a tightly wound bundle of genetic material called DNA [deoxyribonucleic acid]. A discrete section of DNA is often called a gene.) One pair of chromosomes—the sex chromosomes—plays a big role in determining a person's biological sex. Under a microscope, the sex chromosomes look a little like the letters X and Y. In most cells of a genetic female, there are two X sex chromosomes; in most cells of a genetic male, there is one X and one Y sex chromosome. However, sperm and egg cells are different from other cells in that they only have 23 chromosomes. Sperm and eggs are produced through a process of cellular division called meiosis, when

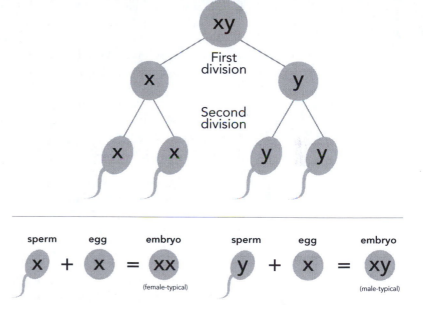

*Meiosis & Conception: Production of sperm and egg cells happens through a process of cellular division called meiosis. When a sperm and egg meet at the moment of conception, a zygote results.*

a normal cell—having 46 chromosomes—divides, with half the original cell's 46 chromosomes going to each of two new egg or sperm cells. Because typical female cells have two X sex chromosomes, each egg produced through meiosis will have one X sex chromosome. Similarly, because typical male cells have one X and one Y sex chromosome, each sperm produced through meiosis will have either one X or one Y sex chromosome (Birke, 1992; Johnson, 2004b).

At conception, when an egg combines with a sperm, chromosomes carried by the egg and sperm merge so that the fertilized egg—called a zygote—has a total of 46 chromosomes. If a sperm with an X sex chromosome fertilizes the egg (which always contains an X sex chromosome), then the resulting zygote will be genetically female (XX). If a sperm with a Y sex chromosome fertilizes the egg, then the zygote will be genetically male (XY). Although it might seem that the sperm determines the zygote's genetic sex, the unique chemical environment of the female reproductive tract and substances released by the egg can affect which sperm reaches the egg and, hence, the genetic sex of the resulting zygote (Angier, 1999). After conception, throughout the various stages of development in the womb and after birth, every cell (except egg and sperm cells) in a person's body carries the same combination of X and/or Y sex chromosomes as the combination at conception.

Before the sixth week of pregnancy, during which time the developing offspring is called an embryo, the internal and external anatomy of genetically female (XX) and genetically male (XY) embryos are virtually indistinguishable. The internal reproductive organs of both consist of two primitive gonads and two sets of tube-like ducts: the Wolffian and Müllerian ducts. And the area where the external genitalia—labia, penis, testicles—will develop is not obviously female or male in form or appearance. At this stage, the developing embryo is often described as sexually "bi-potential" or "indifferent," meaning it could develop sexual and reproductive anatomy that is typically female or typically male (regardless of its cellular genetics) (Birke, 1992; Fausto-Sterling, 2000).

Around the sixth week of pregnancy, a specific gene on the Y chromosome of genetically male (XY) embryos, working together with other genes, signals the primitive gonads to develop into testes (also called testicles) (Fausto-Sterling, 2012). The testes then begin synthesizing a group of hormones called androgens, which include testosterone and Müllerian inhibiting substance. These hormones cause the embryo's external genital area to develop into a penis and scrotum. They also cause the Wolffian ducts to develop into the epididymis and vas deferens, the structures that will (in adult males) convey sperm from the testicles through the urethra and out through the penis during ejaculation (see: sexual anatomy figures in Chapter 3). Müllerian inhibiting substance prevents further development of the Müllerian ducts, though these undeveloped structures will remain present for the rest of a genetic male's life (Birke, 1992; Fausto-Sterling, 2000). This exposure to androgens in the womb also seems to have an effect on the structure and function of the genetically male embryo's brain, perhaps helping explain certain behavioral and cognitive differences later in life (Birke, 1992).

Less is known for certain about the anatomical development of the genetically female (XX) fetus, reflecting a longstanding bias toward male bodies in scientific research. Although it has long been argued that all fetuses are anatomically female by default, and that no genetic or hormonal triggers are required for the development of female reproductive organs, recent research suggests that the complex interaction of several genes signals the development of the primitive gonads into ovaries and the formation of external female genitals (Angier, 1999; Fausto-Sterling, 2012). The hormone estrogen, produced both by the mother and the XX fetus' developing ovaries, causes the Müllerian ducts to develop female-typical anatomy including fallopian tubes, uterus and cervix. Estrogen also causes the development of female genitals, including the labia and clitoris. Absent the stimulus provided by a spike in testosterone (from testes in genetically XY fetuses), the Wolffian ducts do not develop, but will remain present throughout a genetic-female's life (Birke, 1992; Fausto-Sterling, 2000).

Although an infant's *primary* sex characteristics—genetics, genitalia, internal reproductive organs—are typically present at birth, estrogen and androgen hormone spikes during puberty cause the development of *secondary*

## Born This Way?

The presence of same-sex attracted and gender-variant people throughout history and in every known culture raises the question: Was Lady Gaga right? Are LGBTQ people "born this way?" Since the early 1990s researchers have attempted to discover the causes of sexual orientation by looking at a range of genetic, hormonal, anatomical, and physiognomic evidence. Today, there is an emerging consensus among research scientists that there is likely some kind of biological contribution to sexual orientation and gender identity, but that social, cultural, and environmental contexts may affect the shape or form they take. Gender identity and sexual orientation are likely the result of complex, dynamic interactions between biological and socio-cultural factors, rather than either of these alone.

Some of the earliest scientific research found significantly higher numbers of gay men among identical and fraternal twins. (Twins are genetically very similar.) They also found that gay men were more common on the mother's side of families. Both findings suggest there may be a genetic or inherited component to sexual orientation. Other research has found that the higher number of older brothers a man has, the more likely he is to be gay. Each older brother increases by one third a boy's chances of growing up to be gay. Scientists have suggested that this may be caused by the mother's immune system response to carrying a male fetus during pregnancy. With each subsequent pregnancy, her immune system reacts to the fetus like it would to an allergen or "foreign body." How this maternal response might affect her son's sexual orientation later in life is not fully understood.

*(continued)*

*(continued)*

A small amount of research has found some gay men's brain anatomy to be more similar to heterosexual women's than to other men's. Some researchers have observed other physical differences between gay and lesbians, and heterosexuals: finger-length ratios; fingerprint and hair-growth patterns; right or left handedness; facial appearance; and so on. Many of these kinds of traits are determined by fetal hormone exposure during gestation suggesting that the environment in the womb may influence later romantic attraction and sexual orientation (Bailey et al., 2016; LeVay, 2016). More recently, scientists have begun to build on research into the biology of sexual orientation to consider the causes of transgender identity. Although not far advanced, such research suggests that genetics and/or fetal hormone exposure may shape gender identity, not just sexual orientation (Erickson-Schroth, 2013).

There are a number of concerns with this research. First, most of the research has been conducted on gay men. Lesbians and all bisexuals are rarely the focus of similar scientific research. Even with such a narrow focus, research findings are more suggestive than conclusive. Not *all* identical or fraternal twins share the same sexual orientation; not *all* men with older brothers identify as gay; and so on. Also, much of the research reinforces the idea that sex, gender, and sexual orientation are binary (cisgender or transgender; homosexual or heterosexual, etc.) Findings about gay men are often compared to those for heterosexual women; data on lesbians likened to heterosexual men; and so on. The possibility that sex, gender, and sexual orientation exist on a gradient or spectrum, or is changeable over time (sexual fluidity), has not often been raised among scientists studying the "cause" of sexual orientation (Diamond, 2008).

Also, for many biological differences it can be difficult to know if a particular sexual orientation or gender identity is a *cause* or an *effect*. For example, is it small differences in brain structures that cause a certain sexual orientation or gender identity? Or, is it a lifetime of behaving or identifying as queer, gay, or trans that causes differences in brain structures? Bodies, like genders and sexualities, are not fixed or static—they shift and change over an individual's lifetime. Yet, many legal arguments for LGBTQ civil rights are based on the idea that gender identity and sexual orientation are innate and immutable, rather than chosen or changeable. If gender identity and sexual orientation come to be understood as fluid, what happens to rights based on LGBTQ immutability (Diamond & Rosky, 2016)? Finally, all scientific research occurs within larger social and political contexts, and these have not always been hospitable to gender and sexual minorities. Some have expressed fears that if the "cause" of minority gender or sexual identities is found, then repressive social, political, or religious forces will attempt to impose a "cure," with devastating consequences for LGBTQ people (Fausto-Sterling, 2012; Jordan-Young, 2010).

sex characteristics. Genetic females and males both experience a growth in height; increase in muscle and bone mass; changes to shape of body and face; changes in skin texture and secretions; and, appearance of pubic, underarm, and other body hair. In most genetic females, a complicated interaction of several glands causes first menstruation around ages 9–12. The breasts will often increase in size, skin soften, face become rounder, and an increase of fat around the hips and buttocks can cause a widening of the hips (compared to the waist). At puberty most genetic males will experience an increase in muscle mass, growth in size of penis and testicles, deepening of the voice, appearance of a beard and (sometimes) chest hair, growth in size of the Adam's apple, thickening of the bone above the eyebrows (the brow ridge), squaring of the face and jaw, and growth of shoulders wider than hips. Although the body keeps changing over the course of our lives, by the end of the teenage years the body's primary and secondary sex characteristics are generally fully developed (Birke, 1992; Carroll, 2016; Corinna, 2016; Renzetti, Curran, & Maier, 2012).

### Blurring the Binary: The Sex Continuum

At birth, a newborn that has followed a typical developmental path will be assigned to one of two sex and gender categories, usually based solely on the shape and appearance of its genitals. Those having female-typical genitals—a vagina, labia, clitoris—will usually be assigned female and called girls. Those with male-typical genitals—a penis, testicles—will be assigned male and called boys. But as the above description of typical development implies, sex is comprised of more than genitals. Biologist Anne Fausto-Sterling has argued that sex is made up of several different components: genetics/chromosomes, anatomy, physiology, hormones, and morphology (bodily form or shape). The assignment of newborns to a sex and gender category assumes that all the other components of their sex are congruent, and consistent with genital appearance. Yet, as the above description of typical sexual development suggests every human's biological sex is a combination of traits and characteristics that are often thought of as belonging to only one sex (Fausto-Sterling, 1993, 2000, 2012).

All humans are the result of genetic material—sex chromosomes—contributed by their biological mother and father when sperm and egg unite at conception. Also, anatomically, everyone carries traces of sexual bi–potentiality for their entire lives, in the form of the undeveloped Wolffian or Müllerian ducts. Hormonally, everyone produces "male" and "female" hormones (estrogens and androgens [including testosterone]). Both genetic males and genetic females have both types of hormones, but in differing amounts at different stages of their lives. In the womb, testosterone produced by the genetic male's testes must first be converted into estrogen before it has any effect on the fetus' developing brain. At puberty, estrogen is essential to genetic females' sexual development and the regulation of the reproductive system. But in genetic males it is essential to the maturation of sperm in the testes, is highly concentrated in semen, and may affect the libido (sex drive). As genetic males age, testosterone levels typically decline, which allows estrogen to have a more pronounced effect on metabolic processes and physical traits: lower energy, increased abdominal fat, lower libido, loss of muscle mass, enlarged breasts (gynecomastia), and sexual dysfunction (Birke, 1992; Fine, 2010).

Regarding other physical and psychological "sex differences," a great deal of research has shown that "the sexes" are more alike than they are different. For some physical traits, like height, there is as much as an 80% overlap between females and males. Widely reported and often-repeated sex differences in cognitive abilities are very inconsistently supported by the research and there is considerable overlap in female and male scores. And many average differences between the sexes are socially produced and culturally exaggerated. Also, many of the physical traits we associate with each sex—like muscularity, fat distribution, physical endurance—are highly susceptible to physical training. When women's and men's physical activities are similar, many physical differences between "the sexes," such as muscular strength and bone density, shrink or disappear altogether (Birke, 1992; Fine, 2010).

Even physical traits that seem to offer indisputable proof of a person's sex (such as genetics and genitals) do not enable the sorting of humans into mutually exclusive female or male groups. Although typical sexual development usually produces a genetically female (XX) or genetically male (XY) fetus, not all sexual development follows a typical path. Sometimes during meiosis an egg or sperm is produced with no sex chromosomes, two Xs, two Ys, or both an X and a Y. When an anomalous sperm or egg joins with a typical sperm or egg the resulting zygote may contain a fewer or greater number of sex chromosomes than is typical. Some of these anomalous sex chromosome combinations can cause serious developmental and health problems. Sex chromosome combinations that cause Turner (XO) or Klinefelter (XXY) syndrome, for example, can bring an individual to the attention of a physician, whereupon the genetic anomaly is detected. In other cases, anomalous sex chromosome combinations cause no physical symptoms or health effects and go undetected for life (Birke, 1992; Fausto-Sterling, 2000).

Although commonly the sole basis for sex and gender assignment at birth—especially when the sex of the fetus is not known prior to birth—genitals can vary widely in size, shape, color and appearance. Moreover, it is estimated that one in 2,000 live births cannot be easily assigned to one of the two major sex categories based on genital appearance. A variety of genetic, hormonal, and environmental conditions during pregnancy can lead to such "ambiguous genitals": genetic (XX) females born with a clitoris deemed "too large" or labia that resemble a scrotum; and genetic (XY) males born with a "micropenis" or an incompletely formed scrotum or penis (Blackless et al., 2000; Fausto-Sterling, 1993, 2000).

Although some variations in sexual development can require immediate life-saving medical care, atypical or "ambiguous" genitals do not necessarily represent a medical emergency. Rather, such births pose a social and cultural crisis for societies that only recognize the existence of two sexes (female and male) and that base a person's social role, opportunities, and status on their sex. They also pose a challenge in societies that think of sexuality in terms of attraction or behavior between "same" or "different" sexes (i.e. homosexuality, heterosexuality, etc.) The very existence of ambiguous sexual anatomies, as well as the wide variance of genital size/shape/appearance among female- and male-typical individuals, suggests that the most accurate model for thinking about human biological sex may not be a binary but a spectrum or continuum. A binary model of sex implies that there are only two sexes and de-emphasizes differences within each sex category, suggesting that all males are similar in their sexual development and that they are radically different from all females (who are also sexually similar to each other). A sexual spectrum or continuum model might resemble a barbell, with large numbers of individuals clustered into female- and male-typical groups at each end, with a small, but significant, number of people arrayed at various points in between—depending on the sexual trait or characteristic being represented by the model (anatomy, genetics, hormone profiles, etc.) Even though it better represents what research has uncovered about human biological sex, a sexual continuum model can be threatening to those whose identities, desires, or social status are grounded in the belief that sex differences are binary in form (Fausto-Sterling, 1993; Kessler, 1998; Roughgarden, 2013).

For these reasons, newborns with "ambiguous genitalia" may be operated on soon after birth to create genitals that appear more typically female or male. However, due to limitations in medical technology, it is much easier to create a vaginal orifice than an organ that looks and functions like a penis (that developed in the womb and during puberty). Thus, infants with "ambiguous genitalia" are often assigned female and undergo surgery to create a vulva and vagina, regardless of their other sex traits (i.e. hormone profile, brain anatomy, sex chromosomes, internal reproductive organs, etc.) For genetically male (XY) infants, born with an incompletely formed penis (or one so "small" that doctors doubt it will ever allow for penetrative sexual intercourse) surgery entails removal of the penis and testes and creation of a vagina and labia using penile and scrotal skin. Genetically female (XX) infants, born with a clitoris deemed "too large" will often undergo surgery that amputates the clitoris or reduces it size. Infant genital surgeries can cause pain, damage nerves, and dull skin sensitivity, affecting the ability to experience sexual pleasure (Kessler, 1998; Fausto-Sterling, 2000). It is important to remember that it is only in societies that have advanced medical technologies and where infants are born in a medical context (such as a hospital) that newborns with "ambiguous genitalia" may be subject to surgery that modifies their genitals to "clarify" their sex. Such surgeries have become very controversial in recent years and many activists, biomedical ethicists, and human rights organizations have opposed them on human rights grounds. They argue that, except in cases of true medical emergency, any genital surgery be postponed until an intersex person is old enough to participate in medical decision-making about their own body (Chase, 1998; Dreger, 1998; HRW, 2017).

## LGBTQQIAPXYZ . . . what?

The initialism LGBTQ+ (or LGBT, LGBTQIA, LGBTQIA, etc.) is often used as shorthand to describe sexual and gender minorities as a group. (An initialism is an abbreviation formed of initial letters where each letter is pronounced separately [e.g. ACLU]). Which letters and identities are included and what each letter means is the subject of much debate but these are some generally accepted definitions:

**L is for Lesbian**, a female-bodied or woman-identified person whose romantic or sexual attraction or behavior is primarily oriented toward other woman-identified or female-bodied people. L comes first to counteract the tendency of men to come first in androcentric and patriarchal societies.

**G is for Gay**, a male-bodied or man-identified person whose romantic or sexual attraction or behavior is primarily oriented toward other male-bodied or man-identified people. Gay is sometimes used as shorthand for all sexual minorities, although this can be controversial because it obscures differences between lesbian, gay, and bisexual people.

**B is for Bisexual**, a person of any sex or gender having the capacity for romantic or sexual attraction or behavior with more than one gender.

**T is for Transgender and Transsexual.** Transgender can be used as both an umbrella term to describe anyone who expresses gender in socially unexpected or atypical ways, or more narrowly to describe those whose gender identity does not correspond to the sex or gender they were assigned at birth. Transsexual is an older term that refers to a person who has surgically modified their body to better align with their gender identity.

**Q is for Queer and Questioning.** Queer is a difficult-to-define word which may be used by gender and sexual minorities who reject or do not easily fit into one of the other categories listed here. It implies a sexual or gender identity, gender expression, sexual practice, or political position, at odds with social norms for sex, gender, and sexual orientation. Queer was once a derogatory term for homosexuals and should be used with care. Questioning refers to someone struggling with their sexual or gender identity and/or has not yet decided where, how, or if they fit on the LGBTQ+ spectrum.

**I is for Intersex**, a person whose sexual development results in physical sexual characteristics (most often genitals and reproductive organs but also hormones and genetics) that do not allow them to be easily labeled female or male at birth (though some intersex conditions are not discovered until puberty or adulthood).

**A is for Ally, Asexual, Agender, and Aromantic.** An Ally is a cisgender and/or heterosexual person who affirms and supports LGBTQ+ people, communities, and civil rights. Asexual people experience low or no sexual attraction to others. Agender people reject the gender categories of woman and man, and present as an indeterminate gender. Aromantic people do not experience romantic attraction to others.

**P is for Pansexual and Polyamorous.** Pansexuals are romantically or sexually attracted to a range of sexes or genders. Polyamorous refers to someone who has sexual or romantic relationships with more than one partner at a time, with the knowledge and consent of all involved.

### Intersex

Until recently, the term hermaphrodite was used to describe a person having both female and male sex organs (internal and/or external) (Dreger, 2000). But, starting in the 1990s, when activists and scholars started to question the ethics of genital surgery on infants, the term intersex began to be preferred. Intersex is now used to describe those whose bodies combine sex traits and characteristics that are considered typical for males or females, including genitals, gonads (testes, ovaries), or chromosomes (Chase, 1998). In medical contexts, intersex conditions are sometimes called Disorders of Sexual Development (DSD), however some intersex people object to this term because it implies that being intersex is a "disorder" that requires "fixing" with medical treatment. Some have suggested the term Differences (or Variations, or Divergences) in Sexual Development instead. Such language better reflects the fact that intersex conditions are but one of many naturally occurring variations in human sexual development (Reis, 2007; Roughgarden, 2013).

Even though all humans combine female-typical and male-typical sexual traits, the term intersex is usually reserved for those with the most pronounced or obvious natural variations in sexual development. It has been estimated that about 2% of the human population, or about 150 million people across the world, is intersex. Due to enormous global disparities in healthcare, and the fact that most babies are not born in hospitals, many intersex conditions are never identified, recorded, or reported to researchers or scientists—especially if they involve only genetics, hormones, or internal organs (Blackless et al., 2000; Fausto-Sterling, 2000). Intersex people are often included under the LGBTQ+ umbrella along with others who blur the sex or gender binary, such as gender non-binary and transgender people (see box: Causes of Intersex Conditions). Some research has found that some intersex people exhibit more gender variant behavior or same-sex attraction than the general population. However, intersex conditions do not necessarily influence an intersex person's gender identity, how they express or present their identity to the world, or their sexual attractions, desires, fantasies, or behaviors (Fausto-Sterling, 2012; Jordan-Young, 2010).

---

## Causes of Intersex Conditions

Intersex conditions may have several different causes. Common causes include:

Congenital Adrenal Hyperplasia (CAH): a genetically female (XX) infant is born with female-typical gonads (ovaries) but external anatomy that is typical for genetically male (XY) newborns. CAH is caused by an excess of androgen hormones during fetal development that "masculinize" the external anatomy. CAH occurs in 1 in 20,000 births.

Androgen Insensitivity Syndrome (AIS): a genetically male (XY) infant is born with partially or incompletely formed male-typical or female-typical genitals. AIS is a genetic condition that causes the developing fetus to not respond to androgen hormones produced by its own adrenal glands during fetal development. As a result, its genitals are not "masculinized" during fetal development. AIS occurs in 1 in 20,000 births.

5-α Reductase Deficiency (5-ARD): a genetically male (XY) infant is born with internal male anatomy but genitals that appear female-typical. Though they may be raised as girls, at puberty, most go on to develop male-typical genitals and live as men. 5-ARD is caused by a deficiency in an enzyme (5-α reductase) needed to turn the weaker hormone testosterone (secreted by the fetal adrenal glands) into a stronger one: dihydrotestosterone (DHT). 5-ARD is most commonly found in small, isolated populations.

Klinefelter Syndrome (KS): the fetus is genetically male but inherits an extra X sex chromosome from either the mother or father. Their genetic profile, or karyotype, is usually described as XXY. At birth the testes and penis are small and at puberty they may develop female-typical secondary sex characteristics: breasts, little body hair, wider hips, narrower shoulders, etc. As adults, their semen contains no sperm. KS occurs in 1 in 1,000 births (Fausto-Sterling, 1999).

## Gender

Biological sex might seem to be one of the most fundamental distinctions between humans, helping explain numerous differences between females and males. It would also seem to explain certain groupings within the LGBTQ+ community differentiating, for example, lesbians/bisexual women and gay/bisexual men. But, if everyone is a mix of sexual traits, such seemingly obvious distinctions on the basis of sex become harder to make. Moreover, the experiences of transgender and queer people, and other kinds of social groupings within the LGBTQ+ community, are not so easily explained by sex differences. To understand these, we need a working understanding of the concept of gender and how it differs from biological sex.

In general, the term gender refers to the social, cultural, and psychological (rather than the biological) aspects of being a woman or man. However, gender is not just a personal trait or characteristic. It is a complex, dynamic, and interactive social system that operates at the individual, interpersonal, and institutional level. The gender system is complex because it has many aspects and operates at many levels. It is dynamic because it is constantly changing, albeit slowly. It is interactive because the various parts of the system interact with each other, and every member of society interacts with the gender system at all times, even if they are not aware they are doing so. As a system, gender is upheld and maintained by the beliefs and actions of every member of a society, and all members of that society are impacted by gender (Johnson, 2005; Lorber, 1995).

At the individual level, gender takes the form of gender identity, and gender expression or gender presentation. "Gender identity" refers to the subjective or internal sense of one's gender, usually as a girl/woman, boy/man, or something in between, or altogether different. Gender identity does not always correspond to a person's biological sex or the gender they were labeled with at birth. The source of gender identity is not entirely clear but there seem to be biological, socio-cultural, and environmental factors affecting how a person comes to identify as a particular gender (Erickson-Schroth, 2013). "Gender expression" (sometimes used interchangeably with the term gender presentation) refers to the way an individual's gender identity is communicated to society through speech, body language, clothing, hair, make-up, jewelry, etc. Gender expression may also involve temporary or permanent changes to the body, such as tattoos, piercings, cosmetic surgery, and physical size or shape due to dieting or exercise. Importantly, gender expression implies that outward signs of gender correspond to an internal or subjective gender identity (i.e. a person's exterior expresses their interior). Gender presentation is therefore a useful term to describe outward gender cues that may be temporary, performative, or self-consciously adopted, but don't necessarily express an internal gender identity. An example might be a person who cross-dresses for Hallowe'en. Although their costume "presents" a particular gender to society, it does not necessarily correspond to their internal gender identity. Thus, gender expression is a form of gender presentation, but gender presentation does not always express one's gender identity.

At the interpersonal level, gender operates through gender inference and gender attribution. As people move through society they infer other people's membership in a gender category based on their gender presentation and attribute a specific gender to them (Kessler & McKenna, 1978). Research by child psychologists has found that newborns do not possess the ability to infer and attribute gender to others, but small children acquire this social skill quite early in life, probably by observing and imitating the behavior of older children and adults (Fausto-Sterling, 2012; Fine, 2010). Those who are not easily categorized as women or men on the basis of their gender expression/presentation can endure responses ranging from curiosity to extreme physical violence (Perry, 2001; Wilchins & Taylor, 2006). These kinds of reactions suggest the importance of unambiguous membership in one of the socially provided gender categories (usually girl/woman or boy/man) for the day-to-day functioning of society at every level. If gender were superficial or unimportant, reactions to gender ambiguity and gender transgressions would not be so extreme (Lorber, 1995).

Gender also operates within social institutions: schools, families, workplaces, the military, religious organizations, and so on. These institutions reflect,

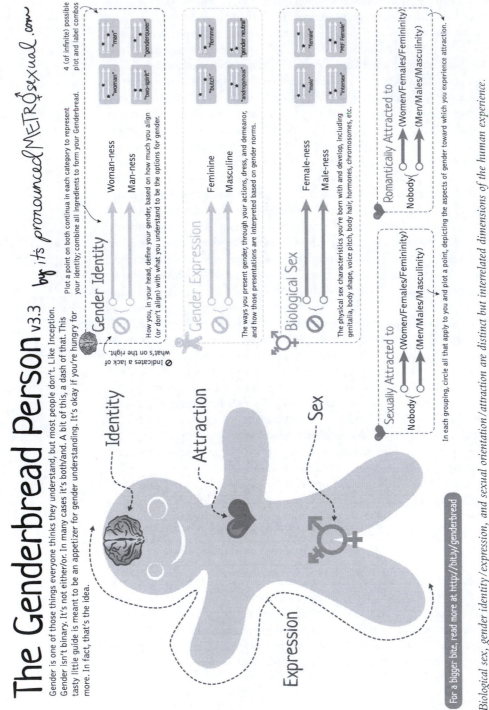

# The Genderbread Person v3.3

by it's *pronounced* METR♂sexual .com

Gender is one of those things everyone thinks they understand, but most people don't. Like Inception. Gender isn't binary. It's not either/or. In many cases it's both/and. A bit of this, a dash of that. This tasty little guide is meant to be an appetizer for gender understanding. It's okay if you're hungry for more. In fact, that's the idea.

Identity

Attraction

Sex

Expression

⊘ Indicates a lack of what's on the right.

## Gender Identity

Woman-ness

Man-ness

How you, in your head, define your gender, based on how much you align (or don't align) with what you understand to be the options for gender.

## Gender Expression

Feminine

Masculine

The ways you present gender, through your actions, dress, and demeanor, and how those presentations are interpreted based on gender norms.

## Biological Sex

Female-ness

Male-ness

The physical sex characteristics you're born with and develop, including genitalia, body shape, body hair, voice pitch, hormones, chromosomes, etc.

Plot a point on both continua in each category to represent your identity; combine all ingredients to form your Genderbread.

4 (of infinite) possible plot and label combos

"woman"   "man"

"two-spirit"   "genderqueer"

"butch"   "femme"

"androgynous"   "gender neutral"

"male"   "female"

"intersex"   "MtF Female"

### Sexually Attracted to

Nobody { (Women/Females/Femininity)
(Men/Males/Masculinity)

### Romantically Attracted to

Nobody { (Women/Females/Femininity)
(Men/Males/Masculinity)

In each grouping, circle all that apply to you and plot a point, depicting the aspects of gender toward which you experience attraction.

For a bigger bite, read more at http://bit.ly/genderbread

*Biological sex, gender identity/expression, and sexual orientation/attraction are distinct but interrelated dimensions of the human experience.*
*Source: Sam Killerman.*

communicate, and reinforce society's beliefs or "norms" about gender identities, expressions/presentations, behaviors, and interactions. They also sort and segregate, distribute goods and resources, and allocate rights, privileges, benefits, and responsibilities to individuals based upon their gender. Gender norms are ubiquitous and pervasive. Like the proverbial goldfish (that does not know the water is wet), many people are not even aware gender norms exist. Gender-based thinking, behavior, and treatment may be unnoticeable, especially to those who fully conform to society's gender norms. Those whose gender presentation approximates what is socially expected for a person of their biological sex are deemed gender normative, and those who do not may be described by a variety of terms including gender transgressive, gender non-conforming, gender variant, gender expansive, transgender, and genderqueer (more on these terms below).

Gender norms are communicated through forms of culture like language, clothing, music, theatre, literature, and the mass media. Gender norms shape everyone's thinking about what it means to be a girl/woman or a boy/man, how a person in one of those two categories is expected to feel, think, act, and behave, and the consequences of failing to conform to these expectations. Gender norms also contribute to average gender differences in: types and levels of education; career paths and achievement; health; life expectancy; income and wealth; and access to opportunities and resources. They also often help reinforce a hierarchy or difference in power between existing gender categories. In many societies throughout history the boy/man gender category has been granted more power, privilege, and status than the girl/woman category. The term patriarchy describes societies organized to benefit and advantage those in the boy/man gender category, who are almost always biological males. But the rights, benefits, and privileges individual boys/men enjoy in patriarchal societies are also influenced by other aspects of identity such as gender expression/presentation, sexual orientation, race/ethnicity, social class, and physical ability (Johnson, 2005; Lorber, 1995).

Finally, although sex is not the same as gender, it is important to acknowledge that each is rarely experienced without the other in day-to-day life, especially at individual and interpersonal levels. While it can be useful to think about sex and gender as distinct dimensions of human experience, some aspects of biological sex can contribute to some aspects of gender (and vice versa). For example, secondary sex characteristics—including height, chest size, hip-to-shoulder width ratio, muscle mass, fat distribution, body hair, facial shape, etc.—may be used to infer a person's biological sex and gender identity, and attribute to them membership in a specific gender category. Of course, none of those sex characteristics is conclusive evidence of a person's biological sex and many are alterable through diet, exercise, grooming, wardrobe, and medical treatments such as hormone therapy and surgery. Such alterations to biological sex are often driven by gendered social norms that dictate what women and men are "supposed" to look and act like, suggesting how gender can shape or influence biological sex (Birke, 1992; Fausto-Sterling, 2012).

### Gender and LGBTQ+ People

Gender—especially gender identity and gender presentation—plays an important role in many LGBTQ+ people's personal style and forms the basis of many

LGBTQ+ subcultures. LGBTQ+ people are socialized into one of the gender categories provided by their society. Some fully embrace and identify with the gender category to which they were assigned at birth. Their gender presentation may make them indistinguishable from everyone else. However, others may present gender in ways that are atypical or socially unacceptable for someone of their sex. An example would be those gay or bisexual men whose mannerisms, speech patterns, or personal style are considered more "feminine" or "effeminate" than expected for men (Bergling, 2001). Or, those lesbians or bisexual women who similarly express their gender in ways that are considered "too masculine" for women (Halberstam, 1998). As discussed more fully below, transgender people may or may not present gender in ways that are typical or expected for someone of their sex. And some who identify as queer may intentionally present or express gender in a way that undermines social norms and expectations about the presumed connection between gender and biological sex (Wilchins, 2011). Although LGBTQ+ people exhibit a wide range of gender, an atypical gender presentation is a common device to imply a character's homosexuality in film, television, and other forms of popular culture. Such stereotypes both reflect and shape everyday tendencies to infer and attribute a person's sexual orientation based on their gender presentation (Walters, 2003).

Some research has shown that "gender non-conformity" during childhood is a strong predictor of adult bisexuality or homosexuality. ("Gender non-conformity" is a highly controversial term; more neutral or affirming language might be gender expansive or gender variant behavior.) In this research, which mostly studied young boys, gender non-conformity usually refers to cross-gender behavior. In other words, behavior that is typical for the "other" sex: little boys who behave in ways that are typical for little girls. However, the connection

## The "Bear" Community

The "bear" community and self-identified bears are a subset of gay men that emerged in the 1980s when gay male popular culture (film, magazines, porn) idealized young, smooth, hairless bodies (Wright, 1997). By contrast, the bear community caters to gay men who are (or are attracted to) physically larger, older, and hirsute gay men. During the subsequent 30 years, the bear community developed distinct languages, subtypes, social spaces, and popular/material culture.

The bear community is known for creating inclusive and welcoming spaces for those who do not resemble (or are not attracted to) the body type—young, lean, muscular, hairless—that continues to be prevalent in gay male social spaces and popular culture. While the bear community includes a wide variety of body types, bears tend to favor a hyper-masculine gender presentation manifest through facial hair, larger body size, and a preference for working-class clothing (Manley, Levitt, & Mosher, 2007). But bears may also employ both masculine *and* feminine body language, patterns of speech, and gestures. Additionally, the bear community uses an animal-themed nomenclature to differentiate different "types" of bears: an "otter" is a lean, but hairy man; a young hairy man is a "cub;" older bears with graying hair are termed "polar bears;" and, bears of East-Asian ancestry are described as "panda bears."

Over time, the bear community has developed its own distinct style and culture (Mann, 2010). There are numerous bear spaces, from permanent locations like the Lonestar Saloon in San Francisco, to large events such as the annual Bear Week in Provincetown. There are also many types of bear media: a feature film series (the *Bear City* trilogy); a multi-season *YouTube* series (*Where the Bears Are*); erotic films and publications featuring bear body types; and dating/hook-up cell phone apps (such as *GROWLr*) and Internet sites (www.Bear411.com) dedicated to bears and their admirers. Finally, there are a wide variety of bear commodities ranging from t-shirts and jewelry to humor books and art. These various products serve to reproduce and solidify the boundaries of bear subculture.

*Shaun Edmonds*

between childhood gendered behavior and adult bisexuality or homosexuality is not straightforward. Not all adult bisexuals or homosexuals were "gender non-conforming" children, and not all "gender non-conforming" children grow up to identify as bisexual or homosexual. Moreover, not all transgender adults presented an atypical gender during childhood. It is not known if childhood "gender non-conformity" is evidence of an innate predisposition, the result of upbringing or environment, or some combination of the two (Bailey & Zucker, 1995; Jordan-Young, 2010; Savin-Williams, 1997).

Apart from cross-gender or "gender non-conforming" behavior, some LGBTQ+ people intentionally present an exaggerated version of the gender expected for their sex. Examples are "femme" or "lipstick" bisexual women's or lesbians' expressions of hyper-femininity using hairstyle, clothing, jewelry, and accessories (Munt & Smyth, 1998; Nestle, 1992). Some bisexual and gay men may present a rugged or hypermasculinity through similar means: clothing, hair, language, hobbies, and so on that the wider society deems masculine (Hennen, 2008). Finally, other LGBTQ+ people may simply downplay or "mute" all outward signs of feminine or masculine gender, presenting a more androgynous or gender-fluid style. Cross-gender, exaggerated gender, and muted gender presentations demonstrate that gender is not simply determined by one's biological sex but, rather, can offer an arena for play, experimentation, and personal or cultural expression (Bornstein & Bergman, 2010; Nestle, Howell, & Wilchins, 2002).

### Gender and LGBTQ+ Sexual Style

Less obvious aspects of gender expression may be sexual behavior and sexual style, and it is in these areas that some LGBTQ+ peoples' gender may be most transgressive. Recall that gender is personal, social, and cultural, and involves elements of identity, expression, and behavior. Thus, sexual behavior can be thought of as a form of gender presentation or expression. Moreover, many romantic and sexual behaviors are highly gendered. Who first expresses romantic interest or initiates sexual behavior, and who responds; who is more assertive during sexual activity and who is more passive; who assumes specific sexual roles or positions—these behaviors are often gendered feminine or masculine, and are expected of women or men, respectively. Gender norms help shape individual thinking about which sexual behaviors are expected, permitted, or prohibited for each sex or gender grouping in society: men are "supposed" to be sexually assertive and play the insertive role in sex; women are "supposed" to be sexually passive and play the receptive role; and so on. However, it is important to note that societal gender norms and expectations for sexual behavior may not be the same as individual sexual tastes, experiences, and histories. A person may identify as one gender, present as a different gender, and prefer gendered sexual behaviors that are (or are not) expected from a person of their sex, gender identity, or gender presentation (Schwartz & Rutter, 1998).

This difference—between societal norms and individual experiences—further demonstrates that biological sex and gender identity do not determine a person's sexual attractions, tastes, or behaviors. Moreover, because sexual behavior is a form of gender expression or presentation, same-sex romantic or sexual behavior can represent a form of gender-transgressive behavior in societies where heterosexuality is the privileged norm. Same-sex desire and sexual behavior can threaten or undermine heteronormative beliefs that everyone is "naturally" heterosexual, heterosexuality is the only desirable sexual orientation, and romantic attraction and sexual behavior are determined by an individual's biological sex. When lesbians or bisexual women engage in sexual behaviors that are gendered masculine, and gay or bisexual men engage in courting rituals that are gendered feminine, they demonstrate that gendered sexual and romantic behaviors are not necessarily linked to biological sex or gender identity. The challenges these sexual behaviors pose to gender norms in heteronormative societies helps explain why same-sex romantic and sexual behavior is often strongly prohibited and harshly punished (Ingraham, 2002; Sedgwick, 1990; Warner, 2000).

LGBTQ+ gender expression and presentation can provide a means to signal personal sexual style. Sexual style refers to individual tastes or preferences in types of sexual partners, sexual behaviors, or sexual roles, which is often communicated through gender expression (or personal style.) Some LGBTQ+ people express their sexual style through elements of their gender expression: hairstyle, clothing, jewelry, accessories, and body modification such as tattoos and piercings. Sexual stylization of the body has been one of the most creative and prolific areas of LGBTQ+ cultural production (think: fashion, piercings, etc.) and some of LGBTQ+ sexual styles carry highly specific, personal, shifting, or contested gendered meanings within discrete LGBTQ+ sexual subcultures. The gendering of sexual style in LGBTQ+ life is evident in slang terms, such as femme, butch, bottom, top, vers/versatile, daddy, boy/boi, masc (and many more), which are often used within LGBTQ+ social and cultural spaces, and romantic and sexual discourse (Baker, 2004). LGBTQ+ gendered sexual styles may be worn every day; worn only within LGBTQ+ social spaces such as bars, nightclubs, or at special events such as Pride parades or festivals; or only shared with romantic or sexual partners. As with gendered sexual behavior, gendered sexual styles may have little relationship to other aspects of a person's identity.

Gendered sexual style can also form the basis of some LGBTQ+ subcultures or tribes. In the mid-twentieth century, certain lesbian subcultures practiced "butch/femme" personal and partnership styles, in which one partner was more masculine in appearance while the other was more conventionally feminine (Kennedy & Davis, 1993). Although less formalized today, the terms butch and femme may still be used to describe relatively masculine or feminine lesbian or bisexual women. These terms may also be used by gay and bisexual men, but more to describe gender presentation that sexual style (Baker, 2004). Gendered sexual style also undergirds certain gay and bisexual male physical subtypes, such as "twinks," "otters," and "bears." Sometimes used derogatively, the term twink typically refers to young, fashionable gay men with slender or lightly muscled bodies and little body hair. They are presumed to be effeminate and prefer receptive roles in penetrative sexual behavior, but this may not always be the case (Baker, 2004). "Otter" is slang for a lean, hairy-bodied bisexual or gay man, and "bear" refers to physically larger, hairy-bodied gay or bisexual men (Wright, 1997). Members of the LGBTQ+ (and non-LGBTQ+) BDSM/Leather community may also signal their group membership, tastes in partners, and sex-role preferences through clothing, accessories, and sexual scenarios that can also be highly gendered (Bauer, 2014; Hale, 1997; Thompson, 1991). Each of these LGBTQ+ tribes has numerous subdivisions, and there are other major subtypes within the LGBTQ+ community—the existence, definition, and boundaries of which are often fluid and vigorously contested—but whose membership is often signaled through gendered sexual style.

## Transgender/Cisgender

While some bisexuals, lesbians, and gay men may not present or express gender in ways that society expects for someone of their biological sex, transgender people often experience a more profound conflict between their gender identity and their gender assignment at birth.

The terminology used to describe transgender people's lives and experiences is evolving and subject to much debate. Transgender is a slippery and complicated word that is difficult to define. Part of the challenge lies in the multiple meanings of the Latin prefix *trans-* which, when used before a noun (i.e. transnational, transcontinental, etc.), means across, beyond, through, or surpassing. Transgender, then, could be defined as the crossing of genders (or gender boundaries). Generally speaking, the word transgender is used to describe someone whose gender identity and gender presentation is not consistent with the gender they were labeled with or assigned at birth. The word is most commonly used as an adjective that modifies a noun (i.e. transgender healthcare). Terms such as "transgenderism," "transgendered," and "a transgender" are inaccurate usages; correct usage would be "transgender person/woman/man" or "transgender people/women/men" (GLAAD, 2016a; Stryker, 2008; Teich, 2012).

Some transgender people have a gender presentation that reflects their gender identity rather than their gender assignment at birth, and their gender presentation may or may not be the result of medical, surgical, or other forms of body modification. An example might be a newborn assigned at birth to the gender category boy (usually based on genital appearances) but who comes to feel that she identifies as a girl or woman (depending on age), and who may elect to express her gender in ways that are typical or expected of girls or women—through clothes, hair, mannerisms, preferred pronouns, body shape. Her awareness of incongruence between her gender identity and gender assignment might be evident in childhood or not until much later in her life. Her gender presentation may or may not involve body modification achieved through dieting, exercise, hormone therapy, or surgery. The term transgender describes a person's gender but says little about their biological sex, sexual orientation,

---

## Gender Affirming Pronouns

The idea that sex and gender are binary (despite evidence to the contrary) is perpetuated through many forms of cultural expression: clothing, architecture, literature, theatre, art, and language. In many languages, most nouns and pronouns are gendered either feminine or masculine. (Remember, nouns are words that refer to a person, place, or thing; pronouns are words that stand in for nouns mentioned earlier in a conversation or sentence.) In English, only certain pronouns are gendered, such as she, he, her, him, hers, his.

Gendered pronouns are one of the ways we attribute gender to others, often based on assumptions about their gender identity and biological sex. Referring to someone using gendered pronouns that do not match their gender identity can be meant (and felt) as an insult or slight. But for many transgender people, use of incorrect gendered pronouns can imply a lack of recognition of their authentic gendered selves.

Thus, many gender-inclusive groups now ask participants to provide their gender pronouns during introductions. Some transgender people simply ask that they be referred to by the gendered pronouns that match their gender identity (regardless of the gender they were labeled at birth or their current gender expression): she/her/hers or he/him/his. However, some genderqueer, non-binary, and "gender non-conforming" people object to the way such pronouns imply that sex and gender are binary, either female/feminine or male/masculine.

One popular alternative is to simply use the neutral pronouns they and their in place of she/her or he/his. Another system substitutes the pronoun zie where she/he would be used, and hir wherever her/him would be used. (Zie is pronounced like *zee* and hir is pronounced like *here*.) Instead of saying "She (or he) laughed," one would say, "Zie laughed." Instead of saying "Her (or his) eyes are blue," one would say, "Hir eyes are blue."

Gendered pronouns are embedded in habits of speech and thought, and it may take some effort to adapt. But using a person's preferred gender pronouns is a relatively simple way to support and affirm transgender, non-binary, and "gender non-conforming" people. Doing so shows respect for everyone's right to live and be treated as their authentic self.

romantic attraction, sexual behavior, or partner preferences. Transgender people may be female, male, or intersex; be romantically or sexually attracted to many different types of sexes or genders; have a range of sexual orientations; and, if sexually active, engage in a wide variety of sexual behaviors (or none at all) (Erickson-Schroth, 2014; GLAAD, 2016a; Stryker, 2008; Teich, 2012).

A related term to transgender is the word cisgender, which refers to a person whose gender identity and gender presentation is consistent with what society expects for the gender category to which they were assigned at birth. (The Latin prefix *cis-* denotes things that lie on the same side, while *trans-* implies a crossing of sides.) An example would be a person assigned to the gender category of girl at birth (typically based on genital appearance) and who identifies as a girl, and later as a woman, and has a gender presentation that is typical for girls and women in her society. Like transgender women, she also may or may not alter her body to better reflect her gender identity and meet societal expectations of those labeled girls or women (Stryker, 2008).

The terms transman and transwoman are sometimes also used to describe transgender people. Transmen are those who were assigned to the gender category girl at birth but identify, present, and choose to live socially as a boy or man. Transmasculine is an adjective sometimes used to describe transmen, as in "transmasculine activist." Transwomen are those who were assigned to the gender category boy at birth but identify, present, and choose to live socially as a girl or woman. Similarly, transfeminine is sometimes used to describe transwomen, as in "transfeminine writer." The abbreviations FtM (female-to-male) and MtF (male-to-female) are sometimes used to describe transgender people who have socially or medically transitioned to the gender that corresponds to their gender identity (rather than gender assignment at birth). Some transmen and transwomen who have transitioned to live fully in the gendered social category that matches their gender identity prefer to be described simply as women or men (Erickson-Schroth, 2014; GLAAD, 2016a).

The word transgender came into wider use in the 1990s because of activism for transgender rights and has come to replace earlier terms like cross-dresser and transvestite. Both these terms refer to someone who dresses in clothes of "the opposite sex"—itself a problematic concept. Cross-dressing (or transvestitism) is a legitimate social phenomenon, usually practiced by heterosexual men who experience erotic pleasure from dressing in feminine clothing. (Girls and women have, at times, had greater latitude to dress in "men's" clothes, and the terms cross-dressing and transvestite are not typically used to describe girls or women who dress as men) (Halberstam, 1998; Stryker, 2008; Teich 2012).

Transsexual is another older term, but still preferred by some transgender people, to describe those who have medically or surgically altered their bodies to be more consistent with their gender identities. Transsexual is not synonymous with transgender. Some people use transgender as an umbrella term to describe a wide variety of gender-variant or gender-expansive people, and transsexual to describe only those who have surgically altered their bodies. Others find the term transsexual problematic or even offensive (Stryker, 2008).

Transgender is also not the same as drag. The terms drag queen and drag king describe someone who temporarily dresses in (often-exaggerated) masculine or feminine attire usually for entertainment purposes, often in an LGBTQ+ bar or nightclub. The gender presentation of drag kings and queens—their drag persona—offers an arena for creative play and artistic expression, but typically does not correspond to the gender identity of the performer. Nevertheless, for some drag kings and queens, drag performances may offer one path into a transgender identity and gender transition to live full time in a different gender category than the one they were assigned at birth (Stryker, 2008).

Transgender people often report persistent, longtime feelings of belonging to a gender category other than the one they were assigned at birth. Living in a body that is inconsistent with their gender identity can be psychologically distressing, often motivating a choice to transition to live full time in a different gender. Some transgender people choose to alter the shape or form of their body to better align with their gender identity; others do not. Body modification can take the form of hormone therapy, plastic surgery to minimize/emphasize secondary sex characteristics (such as body hair and bone structure), breast reduction or enhancement ("top" surgery), and/or genital reconstruction ("bottom" surgery.) However, not all transgender people modify their bodies; not all bodily modification involves medical therapies; and body modification is not required to identify as transgender or live life full time in a gender category other than the one assigned at birth (Erickson-Schroth, 2014; Stryker, 2008; Teich, 2012; Tetzlaff, 2015).

Currently, transgender people seeking to medically modify their bodies may be required to first obtain a psychiatric diagnosis of Gender Dysphoria. Previously called Gender Identity Disorder, Gender Dysphoria is a persistent feeling of unhappiness or distress stemming from incongruence between one's biological sex, assigned gender, and gender identity (APA, 2013). The concept of Gender Dysphoria is highly controversial with some transgender people, who resent the implication that not identifying with their assigned gender is a form of mental illness requiring treatment. Obtaining a psychological diagnosis of Gender Dysphoria often requires long term psychotherapy and living full time for a year or more with a gender presentation consistent with gender identity (rather than gender assignment). Even then, many healthcare insurance plans do not cover medical care to transition, viewing it as "elective" or "cosmetic" (Erickson-Schroth, 2014; Stryker, 2008).

Many transgender people want nothing more than to present their gender in a way that is consistent both with their gender identity as a woman or a man and the societal expectations for that gender category (Green, J., 2004). However, some people covered by the broadest definition of transgender do not identify with or live socially as either women or men. The terms gender non-binary, gender expansive, gender variant, and genderqueer are sometimes used to describe such people. Gender non-binary (GNB) people may combine feminine and masculine aspects of gender (androgyny); have a neutral or non-existent gender identity (agender, non-gendered, genderfree, or neutrois); have multiple gender identities (bi-gender, tri-gender, pan-gender); have a gender identity or expression that varies over time (genderfluid); have a weak connection to a gender identity (demigender); or have a gender identity that only exists in their specific culture or society; or otherwise feel that their gender identity or expression is not fully feminine or masculine (Erickson-Schroth, 2014; GLAAD, 2016a; Stryker, 2008).

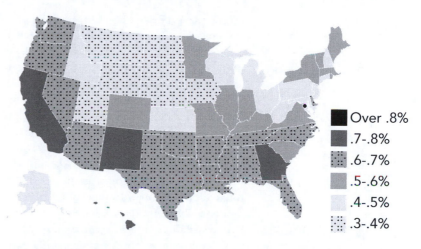

*Distribution of transgender people in the U.S. by state (2016). Hawai'i (.8%) and the District of Columbia (2.8%) have the highest estimated percentage of transgender residents; North Dakota (.3%) has the lowest. Source: Adapted from data collected by The Williams Institute.*

Gender non-binary people may or may not identify as transgender, depending on personal preference and their understanding of the meaning of that term. Some gender non-binary people express an androgynous gender; adopt a gender-neutral name (e.g., Chris); and employ gender-neutral titles and personal pronouns (i.e. Mx. instead of Mr. or Miss; personal pronouns they or sie instead of her or him). There is a lot of overlap between the terms non-binary and genderqueer, however, some do not like the negative historical connotations of the word queer and prefer the term non-binary. Other genderqueers embrace the confrontational nature of the word queer and view variant and expansive expressions of gender as a way to challenge the idea that there is only one "appropriate" gender for a particular sex (Bornstein & Bergman, 2010; GLAAD, 2016a; Nestle, Howell, & Wilchins, 2002).

Given the various meanings of the word transgender and the frequent absence of questions about gender identity and gender expression from many polls and surveys, it is difficult to say exactly how many transgender people live in the United States. In 2016 the Williams Institute estimated the adult transgender-identified population in the U.S. at .6% or 1.4 million individuals. Hawaii, California, Georgia, New Mexico, Texas, and Florida had the highest percentage (.7%–.8% for each state) of transgender people, while North Dakota, Iowa, Wyoming, Montana, and South Dakota had the lowest percentages (.3% for each state). Young adults (ages 18–24) were slightly more likely to identify as transgender than older adults, as were people of color, particularly within Latino groups (Gates, 2011; Flores et al., 2016).

## Sexual Orientation

The term sexual orientation typically describes the sex or gender of those to whom a person is romantically or sexually attracted, in relationship to their own sex or gender. (Although less precise, the term sexuality is sometimes used interchangeably with the term sexual orientation.) Everyday usage of the most common sexual orientation terms—bisexual, homosexual, heterosexual—can imply that sexual orientation is solely a personal trait or characteristic. However, sexual orientation also describes a social relationship (between a desiring person and those they desire). Researchers today understand sexual orientation to be made up of several components: attraction, arousal, behavior, fantasy, desire, and identity. These components can operate or be experienced independently. In other words, a person's sexual identity may not be consistent with their sexual attractions or sexual behaviors, especially over the course of their life (Bolin & Whelehan, 2009; Levay, 2016; Savin-Williams, 2009).

The dual meanings of the term sexual orientation (both an individual trait and a social relationship) reflect the origins of the concept among psychoanalysts and medical doctors in Europe and America in the late 1800s (Terry, 1999). However, this definition presents challenges when attempting to describe anyone with a shifting or ambiguous gender or sex: intersex, transgender/transsexual, androgynous, and genderqueer people. Does the sexual orientation of a transgender person change if they socially or medically transition to live in the gender category consistent with their gender identity (rather than the one they were assigned at birth)? Yes, according to the social relationship definition of sexual orientation, because their gender changed even though the sex/gender of the people they are sexually or romantically attracted to may not have. Even more complicating: some transgender people who elect to medically transition to a different gender report a change in the kinds of genders to which they are attracted. Prior to transition, they may have been attracted to males/men but after transition may find themselves attracted to females/women. This might be due to the effects of hormone therapy on brain anatomy and physiology, or the beneficial psychological effects of gender-affirming medical treatment allowing for a fuller exploration of sexual desires and attractions (Green, 2010; Hill-Meyer & Scarborough, 2014; Tetzlaff, 2015).

Moreover, while most people report that their sexual orientation is a stable part of their core personality, sexual orientation can shift or change over the course of a person's life. This phenomenon is sometimes referred to as sexual fluidity, and can involve a number of dimensions of sexual orientation: fantasy, desire, attraction, and identification. A heterosexual orientation appears to be the most stable over time, for both women and men. Gay men also report a relatively stable sexual orientation. However, lesbians, and bisexual women and men, more often report shifts in their sexual orientation, but the percentage experiencing sexual fluidity is still quite small. These differences might be explained by less social support for sexual minorities, especially bisexuals, or other, as yet unknown, causes. Importantly, sexual orientation does not appear to be changeable at will or through medical treatment or psychological counseling (APA Task Force on Appropriate Therapeutic Responses to Sexual Orientation, 2009; Diamond, 2008; Mock & Eibach, 2012).

To address some of these definitional problems, some sexuality researchers have begun to use sexual orientation terminology that is based solely on the types of people to whom a person is attracted. The term gynephilic is used to describe a person who is attracted to female or feminine people; the term androphilic refers to a person who is attracted to male or masculine people. Although these gender-based terms potentially avoid problems describing people who experience sexual fluidity, they can imply that lesbians and heterosexual men (and gay men and heterosexual women) have the same sexual orientation—the first group is gynephilic, the second is androphilic (Jordan-Young, 2010; LeVay, 2016). Moreover, these new terms are not very helpful for describing the sexual orientations of people who are attracted to a range of sexes or genders (i.e. bisexuals, pansexuals, etc.) For these and other reasons, the individual trait/social relationship terms for sexual orientation—bisexual, homosexual, heterosexual—remain the most commonly used, among both researchers and the general public.

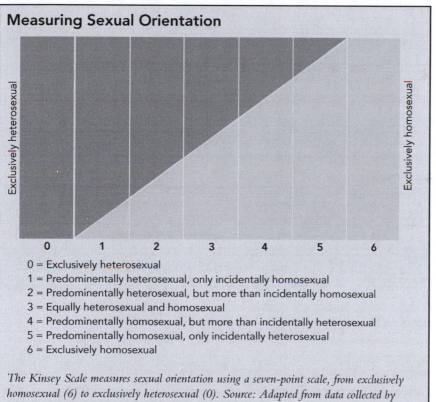

## Measuring Sexual Orientation

0 = Exclusively heterosexual
1 = Predominentally heterosexual, only incidentally homosexual
2 = Predominentally heterosexual, but more than incidentally homosexual
3 = Equally heterosexual and homosexual
4 = Predominentally homosexual, but more than incidentally heterosexual
5 = Predominentally homosexual, only incidentally heterosexual
6 = Exclusively homosexual

*The Kinsey Scale measures sexual orientation using a seven-point scale, from exclusively homosexual (6) to exclusively heterosexual (0). Source: Adapted from data collected by (Kinsey et al., 1948).*

Since the late-nineteenth century, there have been numerous attempts to create a scale (or instrument) that will measure human sexual orientation

*(continued)*

*(continued)*

and by one count there are now over 200 different such instruments (Davis, Yarber, & Bauserman, 1998).

Perhaps the most famous instrument is the Kinsey Scale, which measures sexual orientation on a seven-point scale, with a zero indicating exclusively heterosexual and a six being exclusively homosexual. Although simple to understand, the Kinsey Scale not only conflates the behavioral and psychological dimensions of sexuality, it also presents homosexuality and heterosexuality as mutually exclusive—if one is more homosexual, then one is less heterosexual, and so on. Finally, the Kinsey Scale does not account for changes in sexual behavior or desire over time, varying intensity of sexual attraction, or asexuality or pansexuality (Kinsey et al., 1948).

One scale that attempted to address issues with the Kinsey Scale was the Storms Sexual Orientation Graph. It built on developments in gender role theory in the 1970s which recognized that the kinds and degrees of gender and sexual attraction can vary independently and in intensity within a single person. Unlike the Kinsey Scale, the Storms Graph offered a true continuum that better captured experiences of bisexuality and asexuality. However, it was designed to measure sexual fantasy and does not capture the multiple dimensions of sexuality (behavior, identity, desire, etc.) or changes in sexuality over time (Storms, 1980).

An alternative, the Klein Sexual Orientation Grid (KSOG) recognized more sexual complexity. It acknowledged that sexuality consists of several dimensions that can operate independently and shift over the life course. It measured sexual orientation on a scale of one to seven for: past, present, and ideal future sexual attraction, behavior, and fantasies; emotional and social preferences; heterosexual/homosexual lifestyle; and self-identification (labeling). However, the KSOG is limited in that it: does not measure the age of sexual partners; does not distinguish between feelings of love and friendship; is vague about the meaning of frequency of sexual activity; and does not provide information about the respondents' gender (masculinity, femininity, androgynous, etc.) or the gender of those to whom they are attracted. It also requires respondents to make a trade-off between homosexuality and heterosexuality (Klein, Sepekoff, & Wolf, 1985; Sell, 1997).

## Homosexuality

The word homosexual is both a noun and adjective; that is, it indicates a type of person ("a homosexual") as well as a characteristic of a wide variety of other people, places, and things ("homosexual literature"). A homosexual is someone whose sexual attractions, desires, fantasies, and behaviors are exclusively or primarily oriented toward persons having a similar sex or gender: women who are sexually attracted to women; men who are sexually attracted to men. The term homosexual first appeared in German medical writing in the 1860s and in English in 1892, and for some the term still implies sickness or pathology (Katz, 1997; Terry, 1999). Therefore, outside scientific or academic contexts, the terms lesbian and gay are more commonly used. Lesbian is a term for a homosexual woman. It can be used as a noun ("a lesbian") or an adjective ("lesbian history"). The term gay is used both narrowly (to refer to homosexual men) and broadly (to mean all homosexuals, of any sex or gender). It is used more often as an adjective ("gay pride") and much less often as a noun ("a gay"; "the gays"), a usage many gays and lesbians find objectifying or offensive (GLAAD, 2016a).

Homosexual attraction, desire, and sexual behavior is found in most known societies, worldwide and throughout history, even in times and places where the word homosexual and the concept of homosexuality did not exist (Crompton, 2003; Greenberg, 1990; Rupp, 2001). Despite homophobic stereotypes of a "homosexual lifestyle," it can be as difficult to generalize about homosexuals as any other large, diverse population. Homosexuals are employed in all career fields; are found within all racial, ethnic, and other socio-economic groups; and live in cities, suburbs, and rural areas. They may be female, male, or intersex; identify as women, men, transgender (GNB), or some other gender; and exhibit a wide range of gender presentations depending on their sex, gender identity, personal taste/style, and social context. Despite popular myth and sensationalized news reports about "gaydar," it is not possible to determine if a person is homosexual from their physical appearance (Cox et al., 2016; France, 2007). Some homosexuals choose to style their lives and physical appearance per the prevailing tastes, preferences, and practices of one or more homosexual subcultures. They may identify or present themselves as a: twink or daddy; butch or femme; sporty or lipstick lesbian; leather dyke or leather daddy; bear, otter, twink, or pup—some or all of the time. Other homosexuals live lives and present their gender in ways that are indistinguishable from the wider population.

Given this diversity, knowing that a person is homosexual tells little about their sexual behavior, sex-role preferences, or tastes in sexual or romantic partners. Engaging in same-sex sexual behavior does not automatically make a person homosexual, nor does experiencing same-sex desire or attraction always lead to same-sex sexual behavior. Homosexual people are neither attracted to nor willing to have sex with anyone having a similar sex or gender (Bolin & Whelehan, 2009). Moreover, the term homosexual describes romantic or sexual relationships between adult (post-pubescent) individuals. Despite homophobic stereotypes of homosexuals as pedophiles or child sex abusers, the empirical research does not show that homosexuals sexually abuse children at higher rates than heterosexuals. And, given that over 90% of the population identifies as heterosexual, there are far more heterosexual than homosexual child sex abusers (Herek, n.d.)

Many surveys have been conducted to learn what percentage of the population is homosexual and the results vary depending on whether the survey asked about identification, attraction, or sexual behavior. However, there are some general trends in the data. The total percentage of lesbians and gays (in well-conducted surveys of a representative sample of the population) hovers around

| | Gay/Lesbian | Bisexual | Total |
|---|---|---|---|
| National Epidemiological Survey on Alcohol and Related Conditions, 2004-2005 | 1.0% | 0.7% | 1.7% |
| National Survey of Family Growth, 2006-2008 (Age 18-44) | 1.4% | 2.3% | 3.7% |
| General Social Survey, 2008 | 1.7% | 1.1% | 2.9% |
| California Health Interview Survey, 2009 | 1.8% | 1.4% | 3.2% |
| National Survey of Sexual Health and Behavior, 2009 | 2.5% | 3.1% | 5.6% |
| Canadian Community Health Survey, 2005 (Age 18-59) | 1.1% | 0.8% | 1.9% |
| Australian Longitudinal Study of Health and Relationships, 2005 | 0.9% | 1.2% | 2.1% |
| UK Integrated Household Survey, 2009-2010 | 1.0% | 0.5% | 1.5% |
| Norwegian Living Conditions Survey, 2010 | 0.7% | 0.5% | 1.2% |

*Various studies report similar percentages of adults who identify as lesbian/gay or bisexual. Studies report higher numbers for same-sex sexual behavior and sexual attraction. Source: Adapted from data collected by The Williams Institute.*

the low single digits, 3%–5%. More men identify as gay than women identify as lesbian, and more people report same-sex attractions and sexual behaviors than identify as gay or lesbian. Some surveys show that higher percentages of people of color (than Whites), and more younger people than older people, identify as gay or lesbian (Chandra, Copen & Mosher, 2013; Copen, Chandra, & Febo-Vazquez, 2016; Gates, 2017).

In 2011 the Williams Institute analyzed data from several surveys of sexual and gender minorities in the U.S. It estimated that 3.5% of the U.S. adult population—around 9 million people—identify as lesbian, gay, or bisexual. To put this in perspective, the number of Americans who identify as lesbian, gay, or bisexual is about the same as the population of the state of New Jersey or the countries of Sweden or Denmark. Although the percentage of the U.S. population identifying as lesbian, gay, or bisexual was quite small, an estimated 8% of those polled reported some lifetime experience with same-sex sexual behavior and 11% reported some lifetime same-sex attraction (Gates, 2011).

## Bisexuality

Bisexuality is the capacity for emotional, romantic, or sexual attraction to more than one sex or gender. Bisexuals can experience these attractions simultaneously or serially. That is, they might be attracted to those of a similar or different gender at the same time or in turn, at different points in their lives, and with different degrees of intensity. In recent years, several new terms have emerged with meanings similar to (or overlapping with) the term bisexual: queer, polysexual, pansexual, heteroflexible, homoflexible. Some prefer these terms because they do not imply that there are only two genders or that bisexuality is a midpoint between homosexuality and heterosexuality.

Despite stereotypes that bisexuals are just "confused" or "going through a phase," bisexuality is an authentic and distinct sexual orientation. Like all sexualities, bisexuality is comprised of sexual desires, fantasies, behaviors, and identity and these might not be congruent (line up) in a single individual. In other words, a person might experience sexual attraction toward or engage in sexual activity with people having a range of genders but never identify as bisexual. Likewise, knowing that someone identifies as bisexual does not necessarily indicate anything about their preferred or actual sexual behavior, partner or sex-role preferences, gender identification or presentation, or relationship status, or ability to commit to partners or relationships. Bisexuals may or may not participate in any LGBTQ+ subcultures or tribes, and they may express gender in ways that transgress or conform to societal expectations for their someone with their sex.

Sexual orientation is generally not a visible trait or characteristic and, because of this, bisexuals are often burdened by the unique experience of bi-erasure. If they are in a romantic or sexual relationship with someone deemed to be of the "same" sex, they are viewed as lesbian or gay; if they are in a relationship with someone deemed to be the "opposite" sex, they are deemed heterosexual. In both cases, their bisexuality may not be evident unless it is explicitly and repeatedly asserted. Because not all bisexuals are willing to continually "come out" as bisexual, their number can be underestimated. (Burleson, 2014; Eisner, 2013; Ka'ahumanu & Hutchins, 1991).

Research on the prevalence of bisexuality in humans has produced wildly varying numbers. Sigmund Freud, the founder of psychoanalysis, famously thought that everyone is born with the capacity for sexual attraction to either women or men, and it is through the process of psychosexual development that a person develops a heterosexual or, less often, a homosexual orientation (Freud & Strachey, [1905] 1975). Alfred Kinsey's research on sexual behavior in America found that 46% of the adult male population had engaged in sexual activity or had a sexual response to both females and males (Kinsey et al., 1948). Contemporary researchers have found large majorities (80%–90%) of self-identified lesbians and gay men have some lifetime experience with heterosexual sex, and significant numbers (8%–11%) of self-identified heterosexuals have experienced same-sex attraction or sexual behavior at some point in their lives (Copen, Chandra, & Febo-Vazquez, 2016; Herbenick et al., 2010).

Those surveys that ask about bisexual identification (rather than any lifetime same-sex attraction or behavior) typically find the number of bisexuals to be in the low single digits (2%–5%). Across a range of studies, more women than men, more people of color than Whites, and more younger than older people identify as bisexual. And the number of bisexuals is typically larger than the combined number of lesbians and gay men. A 2011 Williams Institute analysis found than 1.8% of adult Americans identified as bisexual (compared to 1.7% who identified as either lesbian or gay) (Gates, 2011, 2017; Gates & Newport, 2012). Surveys that include a wider range of sexual-orientation categories, such as "not strictly heterosexual" or "mostly heterosexual," yield significantly higher numbers (Savin-Williams & Vrangalova, 2013; Vrangalova & Savin-Williams, 2012). Using such expanded categories, a 2007 Cornell University survey of 20,000 people in 80 U.S. communities found that almost 15% of young women

*Marcher wearing "Bisexual Pride" t-shirt in Capital Pride Parade (Washington, D.C.) (June 7, 2014). Source: Photo by Tim Evanson/CC BY-SA 2.0 license. Image courtesy of Wikimedia Commons.*

and 6% of young men could be described as not-exclusively heterosexual or homosexual (Savin–Williams & Ream, 2007).

### Asexuality

Asexuality is the absence (or low level) of sexual attraction or desire for sexual activity. Unlike celibacy or sexual abstinence, asexuality is not a choice or a "phase," but a distinct sexual orientation (Brotto & Yule, 2016). Asexuals can have typical needs for physical and emotional intimacy, can experience sexual arousal and pleasure, and can form romantic relationships, but do not necessarily desire or frequently engage in sexual activity, alone or with others. Asexuals may be female, male, or intersex, and identify or present as cisgender, transgender, women, men, or some other gender. They may be romantically or affectionately oriented toward any or a range of genders. Some asexuals refer to themselves using the term ace or aces. Closely related terms are aromantic (a person who does not experience romantic attraction to others) and demisexual (those who only experience sexual attraction after forming strong emotional connections with partners) (Asexual Awareness Week, 2012; Bogaert, 2004; Prause & Graham, 2007).

Today, asexuality is receiving unprecedented visibility and attention from researchers, however it may not be a new phenomenon. About 1.5% of Alfred Kinsey's adult male interviewees had no "socio-sexual contact or relations" (Kinsey et al., 1948). More recent studies in the United Kingdom found that about 1% of the population had never felt sexual attraction to another person. More women than men (70% vs. 30%) identify as asexual to researchers (Bogaert, 2004).

## INTERSECTIONALITY: COMPLICATING THE BIG THREE

Biological sex, gender, and sexual orientation help account for a great deal of the diversity and social groupings within LGBTQ+ communities. But their meaning in the everyday lives of LGBTQ+ people is compounded by other major kinds and types of social difference, such as race, ethnicity, class, age, and geographic location. The intersection of these various kinds of social difference in an individual's life often determines their life chances—the quality and outcome of their life.

## Power: Privilege and Oppression

Sociologists often describe differences of power and status within social categories using the terms privilege and oppression. Privilege refers to unearned access to opportunities and rewards that are not the result of individual merit or personal accomplishments. Privilege is neither chosen nor earned; rather, it is conferred by society on the basis of certain arbitrary traits and characteristics, such as skin color, biological sex, sexual orientation, or gender expression. Often, those who enjoy the advantages of privilege are not aware that they benefit from it and may believe their life accomplishments are solely the result of individual effort, such as hard work and self-discipline. In the contemporary United States cisgender, heterosexual, White men enjoy unearned privileges based solely on those traits rather than on their individual merits or accomplishments. Unlike people of color, women, or LGBTQ+ people, such men may move through the world without being constantly reminded of their racial, gendered, or sexual status. Rather than always being referred to as "cisgender, heterosexual, White men" they are often simply referred to as "men"—the social standard or "norm" against which all other races, sexes, genders, and sexual orientations are measured and evaluated. The numerous social, cultural, and economic advantages, rewards, and opportunities conferred on such men—solely because they are cisgender, heterosexual, White, and male—constitutes a form of unearned privilege (McIntosh, 1988).

Conversely, the ever-present reminders of non-normative social status, and the unequal social, cultural, and economic resources that accompany them, is sometimes called oppression. Oppression is different from misery, suffering, or unhappiness. Rather, oppression is characterized by pervasive social systems that work together to limit or constrain individual choice and freedom, resulting in persistent patterns of social, cultural, and economic inequality. An example would be the history of forced segregation, criminalization of Black life, and inequalities of investment in jobs, education, social services, and infrastructure that have produced profound and lasting racial inequalities in many U.S. cities. Although a core American ideology is that success and failure is the result of individual effort, choice, and "merit," careful analysis has shown that persistent social inequalities in the United States—between Blacks and Whites, rich and poor, urban and rural, homosexuals and heterosexuals—are the result of social systems that confer advantage on some groups and disadvantage on others. Importantly, individuals may support or resist the social, cultural, economic, and historical systems that produce privilege and oppression, but those systems are larger than any individual action or belief. They constitute a set of rules that "order" society. So long as individuals follow the rules of the social systems that produce inequality, social inequality will result (Frye, 1983; Johnson, 2005).

Whether privileged or oppressed, no one experiences membership in the various categories of social difference one at a time. Rather, they simultaneously experience sex, gender, sexual orientation, race, class, ethnicity, geography, physical ability, and other traits and aspects of identity. Privilege or oppression stemming from membership in one social category can compound or contradict those conferred by membership in one (or more) other social categories. And advantages conferred by membership in a privileged social category may be used to mitigate disadvantages experienced due to membership in an oppressed social category. For example, White gay or bisexual men can experience privilege due to skin color or gender that may mitigate oppression experienced due to sexual orientation. The offsetting advantages of race and gender privilege conferred upon bisexual or gay White men might not be enjoyed by lesbian or bisexual women or LGBTQ+ people of color. The terms intersectional or intersectionality are often used to describe the complex interaction and experience of simultaneous membership in multiple social categories as they are experienced by individuals on a day-to-day basis (Crenshaw, 1991; Hankivsky, 2014; Newman, 2007).

Sexual orientation oppression and privilege operates through systems of heterosexism and homophobia. Heterosexism and heterosexist refer to a system of laws, rules, customs, beliefs, and practices that confer privilege on heterosexual people solely on the basis of their sexual orientation (Bullough, 2015; Newman, 2007). The term heteronormativity describes an outcome of heterosexism in which a heterosexual orientation is seen as desirable, positive, and a "default" or social "norm," while all other sexual orientations are viewed as undesirable, negative, and voluntary departures (or "deviance") from the social norm of heterosexuality (Warner, 1991). (Similarly, cis-sexism/cis-sexist describes a system that supports and perpetuates the idea that cisgender people represent a desirable social norm, while transgender, non-binary, and "gender non-conforming" people represent undesirable and abnormal social "deviants.") Heterosexism and cis-sexism represent forms of privilege and oppression because they operate through complex, pervasive, and often unrecognized social, cultural, and economic systems that are larger than any one person's actions or beliefs. They privilege cisgender and heterosexual people, and oppress gender and sexual minorities, solely on the basis of traits or characteristics—gender identity/expression and sexual orientation—that are experienced as fixed and innate, rather than on the basis of effort, achievement, or accomplishment. These forms of privilege and oppression are neither "earned" nor "deserved," but imposed on individuals based on arbitrary forms of naturally occurring human difference (Johnson, 2005).

An example of heterosexism at work are those discriminatory laws that long prevented same-sex couples from enjoying the rights, privileges, benefits, and responsibilities of government-recognized marriage. Until gay rights activists started to call for government marriage recognition, many people—of all sexual orientations—were unaware of the way marriage laws systematically advantaged different-sex couples and disadvantaged same-sex couples in the areas of tax, inheritance, insurance, parental rights, and retirement/government/military/employment benefits. The unearned advantages of marriage available to different-sex couples through government-recognized marriage, along with a lack of awareness that they were advantaged under law solely because of their different-sex status, represent forms of heterosexual privilege and homosexual oppression.

In this example, privilege (for heterosexual couples) and oppression (for same-sex couples wanting to marry) are the result of a legal system that produced inequality, not the ill will or harmful actions of any individual person. Marriage inequality resulted from law-abiding citizens following a long-accepted system of laws, customs, habits, and practices surrounding the institution of marriage in U.S. society. Government recognition of same-sex marriage was legalized in the United States by a U.S. Supreme Court decision in June 2015. Although actions by many individuals helped bring about this change, it was a court decision outlawing an oppressive system of laws, rules, and practices that ended governmental same-sex marriage discrimination. But even so, that decision only extended the benefits of marriage to certain kinds of relationships, while other kinds of relationships—including some LGBTQ+ relationships—still do not enjoy government recognition (Chauncey, 2009; Polikoff, 2008; Wolfson, 2007).

For LGBTQ+ people, oppression can also take the form of discriminatory acts that may be described as biphobia, homophobia, or transphobia. Homophobia refers to the irrational fear of homosexuality or negative attitudes or behavior toward homosexuals (Grimes, 2017; Obear, 1991). Homophobia can manifest through discriminatory rules and practices of social institutions (such as schools, governments, religions, and the military) and individual actions (such as use of harmful or hateful language, bullying, and physical violence). Internalized homophobia describes the phenomenon of LGBTQ+ people who hold negative stereotypes, beliefs, or attitudes toward other LGBTQ+ people, and that may or may not be manifest in harmful, discriminatory, or violent behavior (toward self or others). Transphobia and biphobia have similar meanings but refer to fear or negative behavior toward transgender or bisexual people. Importantly, perpetrators of anti-LGBTQ+ hate crimes often say their victims were chosen because they were perceived to not be presenting or expressing gender as expected for their biological sex (i.e. effeminate gay men, masculine lesbians). Media reports of homophobia and transphobia often focus on the psychology of individual perpetrators or characterize their actions as isolated events. A stereotype has emerged that perpetrators of anti-gay hate crimes are often homosexuals struggling with internalized homophobia. Indeed, some research has found that homophobic views are associated with suppressed or denied feelings of same-sex attraction or desire, conservative religious or political beliefs, traditional beliefs about gender roles, or authoritarian attitudes (Adams, Wright, & Lohr, 1996; Grey et al., 2013). However, such individualized explanations do not illuminate the broader cis-sexist and heterosexist systems, customs, practices, or histories within which transphobic and homophobic acts occur (Perry, 2001; Steinem, 1999 [2007]).

## Race and Ethnicity

In the United States, race and ethnicity are major categories of social difference that intersect with other major social categories in the lives of most every LGBTQ+ person. Many people believe that race is a fundamental form of difference within the human species that is primarily evident through skin color, facial shape, and other physical features. However, careful analysis has shown that race is neither a physical nor a biological phenomenon. Rather, race is a social construction that has emerged over centuries through laws, rules, customs, and practices that have produced within U.S. society racial differences and racialized social groupings with distinct social and cultural practices. Rather than a society organized according to fundamental or innate differences between "the races," U.S. law, society, and culture have actively worked to produce the very kinds of social, cultural, economic, and physical differences that are then used to justify unequal treatment (Omi & Winant, 2014). The term ethnicity refers to membership in a social group that has a common national ancestry or cultural tradition. Major racial and ethnic groups in the contemporary U.S. include African American (or Black), Asian American, Native American, European American (or Caucasian/White), and Hispanic/Latino. (The word "Hispanic" refers to those who trace their ancestry to countries in which Spanish is the primary language; "Latino" refers to people who trace their ancestry to Latin America [South America, Central America, Mexico, and parts of the Caribbean.]) Because cultural practices play such an important role in defining the boundaries of race and ethnicity, these social categories can overlap and often can be difficult to distinguish (Golash–Boza, 2016).

Just because race and ethnicity are social and cultural (rather than biological) in origin does not mean they are not real. Cultural ideas, beliefs, and patterns of thinking about race are pervasive in societies that distinguish people by race, but they can be hard to see, acknowledge, and resist. In the United States and Europe some of these ideas are legacies of slavery and colonialism and have persisted for centuries. Racial beliefs can affect access to power and opportunity, and the distribution of resources, which then produce disparities in education, employment, income, wealth, home ownership, arrest rates/incarceration, life expectancy, and physical and psychological well-being. This can happen through individual racism (acts that treat members of one racial group differently than others), or institutional (or structural) racism (when beliefs about one racial group's superiority are transformed into laws, groupings, or practices that disparately impact members of one racial group) (Golash–Boza, 2016). For example, when LGBTQ+ people of color are asked to provide more forms of identification (than Whites) to gain entrance to a gay bar, individual racism is at work (DeMarco, 1983). The underrepresentation of LGBTQ+ people of color in film and television (for example) is a form of institutional racism that reflects not just individual acts of discrimination but also a long history of racially discriminatory beliefs and practices about who should create and appear in popular cultural representations. Because membership in some racial and ethnic categories is empowering and enabling, while membership in others is stigmatizing and disabling, the effects of race and ethnicity in the lives of LGBTQ+ people can either increase or lessen the stigma associated with being a sexual or gender minority. Race and ethnicity influences who has access to

LGBTQ+ social spaces; whose concerns are prioritized in political activism; who is able to "speak for" or viewed as representative of LGBTQ+ people; and patterns of romantic and sexual desire and behavior.

| | Yes | No | Don't know/ Refused answer |
|---|---|---|---|
| Non-hispanic white | 3.2% | 93.9% | 2.8% |
| Black | 4.6% | 90.1% | 5.3% |
| Hispanic | 4.0% | 90.2% | 5.8% |
| Asian | 4.3% | 92.0% | 3.7% |

*Percentage of adults in U.S. who identify as LGBT (by race) (2017). Source: Adapted from data reported by Gallup.*

A 2012 Gallup poll found that higher percentages of people of color (than Whites) identify as LGBT. People of color make up a little over a quarter of the U.S. population (27%) but are about a third (33%) of LGBT-identified people (Gates & Newport, 2012). Similar trends were identified in a 2016 Gallup poll (Gates, 2017). Yet, because people of color comprise a minority of the overall population, they still find themselves in the minority in LGBTQ+ political organizations, social and cultural spaces, and media representations. As a result, LGBTQ+ people of color can be doubly marginalized and experience a sense of split identity: when they are among other LGBTQ+ people, they are seen as people of color; when they are in communities of color, they are seen as LGBTQ+.

Or they are "invisible." Although family, and racial and ethnic communities, can represent forms of support and understanding for LGBTQ+ people of color, stigmatization and homophobia can require them to suppress or hide the LGBTQ+ aspects of their identities. This may explain why national surveys find that, even though people of color comprise a large percentage of the LGBTQ+ community, African-American men are less likely than White or Latino men to identify as gay or bisexual, and African-American women and Latinas as less likely than White women to identify as bisexual or lesbian (Copen, Chandra, & Feb-Vazquez, 2016). Ironically, the "invisibility" or lack of recognition of LGBTQ+ people of color in racial/ethnic minority communities can contribute to the myth that homosexuality or gender variance is the product of Euro-American culture or a "White thing." In certain racial and ethnic communities of color, where having children and raising large families is viewed as a moral and ethical responsibility, identifying as lesbian or gay, or forming a same-sex relationship with the implications of childlessness, can be viewed as a form of betrayal of family and community (Conerly, 2000; Takagi, 1996).

Sadly, within LGBTQ+ communities, LGBTQ+ people of color can experience marginalization or outright discrimination that can leave them feeling like outsiders. For example, some research has shown that Latino gay men derive less psychological benefit than White gay men from disclosing their sexual orientation ("coming out") to friends and family members. Rather, Latino men's sexual orientation is often disclosed through subtle behaviors, such as repeatedly bringing a boyfriend or male partner to family gatherings (Villicana, Delucio, & Biernat, 2016). The emphasis on public visibility as an activist strategy within some White-dominated LGBTQ+ organizations can alienate those for whom coming out takes a less public or visible form. Also, in some community spaces, LGBTQ+ people of color may experience a "double burden of oppression"; being a member of an oppressed racial/ethnic group while also being asked to educate members of dominant groups about the history of racially/ethnically discriminatory social practices and structural barriers (Chung et al., 1994). As a result, LGBTQ+ people of color may struggle to forge a unified or hybrid identity that reflects their membership in racial, ethnic, sexual- and gender-minority social categories. This is made more difficult by the few social institutions or political organizations for people with multiple marginalized identities and the lack of role models, especially in popular culture and the media (Conerly, 2000; Leong, 1996).

LGBTQ+ people of color are also burdened by legacies of colonial-era thinking that intertwine racial and sexual stereotypes. Western images and writings about colonized peoples living in North Africa, the Middle East, South and East Asia, and the Americas has been described as "ambivalent" (Bhabha, 1984). This is reflected in myths about the sexuality of colonized people, who were often represented as both sexually passive and aggressive. In the Western colonial imagination, Black men were often characterized as both lazy servants and rapacious Mandingoes; East-Asian women were seen as either alluring courtesans or treacherous dragon ladies; East-Asian and Middle-Eastern men were simultaneously represented as sexless eunuchs, servile houseboys, and fearless warriors. These contradictory stereotypes allowed for flexibility in the exercise of colonial power over colonized people (Fung, 1991; Said, 1978).

## A Personal Reflection on the Rainbow Flag

I never cared for the rainbow flag. I saw it as too flashy. Having seen it mass-produced and put on everything from t-shirts to coffee cups, when I came to understand that rainbow flag represented the LGBT community, I avoided it. Growing up in Texas—biracial, queer, and a child of an immigrant—I attempted to blend in. Rainbows do the opposite of that. When I reached middle school, I realized something was different about me. The rainbow flag felt like a threat. If I wore or owned anything resembling a rainbow; I was in danger of being discovered. It would indicate to the world that I was the person I was trying so desperately not to be. The rainbow flag, the pride flag, seemed dangerous to a kid just trying to fly under the radar.

I knew the flag had a deeper meaning than decoration on drink koozies and dog collars, but I wasn't expecting it to be something that would resonate with me. It wasn't until I read an interview with creator Gilbert Baker, who passed away in May of 2017, about his flag that I began to have a better understanding. The pride flag first debuted in 1978 at the San Francisco Gay and Lesbian Pride Parade when Baker was asked to create a new symbol for the LGBT community. Before the rainbow flag, our community had the reclaimed pink triangle used by the Nazi Party to identify gay prisoners. Baker's vision was that the rainbow flag would serve as a beacon of hope and joy within the community, not from tragedy, but from life and pride. When asked why the colors of the rainbow, Baker had this to say, "The rainbow is a beautiful part of nature, all of the colors, and even the ones you can't see. So that fit us as a people because we are all of the colors" (Baker, 2012).

Thinking of the flag now as an out and proud queer transgender man, I realize that despite the fear I had of the flag growing up, it was *my* flag. I was that unseen color growing up, out of fear and denial I hid and tried to hide in the shadows. It is comforting to know for that scared closeted kid in Texas, the flag was meant for me. June, our Pride Month, is a perfect time to recognize what this symbol means. It is more than just cloth and stripes as Baker says but "an action." Take time to honor the late Gilbert Baker each time you look at those colors. As we raise our flags, sport our t-shirts, affix the rainbow bandanna on our dogs, know we do so as an action. An action that says we in the LGBT community are here.

We are strong. We are present. We are proud.

*Daniel B. Stewart*

Today, LGBTQ+ people of color often confront the legacy of colonial-era racial and sexual beliefs in LGBTQ+ social institutions and cultural representations. In the small amount of gay pornography produced featuring men of East-Asian ancestry, such men are overwhelmingly depicted as effeminate and cast in the role of receptive partners ("bottoms") in anal sex scenes (Fung, 1991). By contrast, Black men are typically represented as hyper-masculine sexual aggressors or dominant "tops," with an emphasis on the size of their genitals (Lick & Johnson, 2015). These pornographic fantasies intertwine race/ethnicity, gender presentation, and sexual behavior in ways that both reflect and shape the everyday experiences of bisexual and gay men of color. In gay bars, online dating forums, and Internet dating sites, some bisexual and gay men openly express their preference for sexual partners of color based on stereotypes about genital size and sex-role preferences. (Preferences against dating bisexual or gay men of color are also openly expressed in such spaces.) White bisexual and gay men who prefer partners of South- and East-Asian ancestry are often disparaged as "rice queens" or "curry queens," and some openly express their desires for stereotypically sensuous, physically graceful, and sexually submissive "gaysian" men (Roy, 1998; Tsang, 1994). In a dating scene that is dominated by White gay men, some bisexual and gay Asian men internalize negative stereotypes and adopt a passive, effeminate demeanor to attract the attention of White male sexual and romantic partners (Han, 2006). The pervasiveness of social and cultural sexual stereotypes about race and ethnicity can cause some LGBTQ+ people of color to doubt whether romantic and sexual partners are sincerely interested in them as unique individuals or only as objects or "fetishes" in some previously conceived racialized sexual fantasy. As a result, LGBTQ+ social and cultural spaces, such as gay bars and online dating venues, can offer opportunities to explore sexual freedom and produce painful encounters with racism—often at the same time.

Within some communities of color, same-sex relationships can conflict with the familial and domestic duties and responsibilities expected of all women and men. In the patriarchal and androcentric cultures of East and Southeast Asia, where Confucian and Buddhist traditions can be powerful, young men may be expected to live with parents until marriage, head their own households, and economically support elderly parents. Unmarried girls and young women, on the other hand, may be expected to assist their mothers in housework and elder care until they are married, when their domestic and elder-care responsibilities are transferred to their husband's household and his parents. There are similar gender-role expectations for marriage, reproduction, domestic work, and elder care in many Latin cultures. These cultural beliefs and practices can travel with Asian and Latin-American immigrants to the United States and can survive in communities of color for many generations. In light of these expectations, same-sex attractions or relationships may be rejected on moral or religious grounds, and may be viewed as a betrayal of cultural traditions and a shirking of duty to parents, family, and elders (Espin 1984; Thongthiraj, 1994). This may result in alienation from family, non-recognition of bisexual, lesbian, or gay identities, and unrelenting pressure to enter heterosexual marriage and fulfill gender-role expectations. This can be especially damaging because families and racial/ethnic minority communities offer a rare source of understanding and comfort for people of color living as minorities in discriminatory societies (Chung et al., 1994; Takagi, 1996).

LGBTQ+ people of color may also experience conflict due to different ideas about the relationship between gender, sexual behavior, and social status. For example, in certain parts of Latin America, the role one plays in penetrative sexual acts affects one's gendered social status more than the biological sex of one's sexual partners. (This contrasts with the Euro-American concept of sexual orientation, which views sexual attraction and sexual behavior as expressions of a core personality trait.) In sexual intercourse—same-sex and different-sex—the penetrator role is deemed to be masculine, active, and enjoys a higher social status, and the penetrated role is deemed to be feminine, passive, with a lower status. Therefore, in male same-sex encounters, males may be able to retain the high social status enjoyed by men as long as they only play the role of sexual penetrator. Males who are sexually penetrated by such men are relegated to a feminized, lower social status (akin to women) and can be referred to using language with negative or shameful connotations. Within this Latin American understanding of same-sex behavior, where sex-role preferences impact gendered social status, it would not necessarily be appropriate to describe all men who engage in sexual activity with other men as homosexual or gay, and many such men who only play the role of sexual penetrator also maintain primary sexual and romantic relationships with women. Due to this, the term Latin bisexuality is sometimes used to describe their sexual behavior (Almaguer, 1991; Kulick, 1997; Lancaster, 1988; Prieur, 1998).

Theoretically, phallocentric sex-gender systems, which conceptually link gender, social status, and penile penetration, make female same-sex sexual behavior culturally invisible in Latin America. However, because lesbianism and lesbian relationships can represent an escape from a patriarchal society's emphasis on heterosexual marriage, reproduction, and domestic responsibility to men in biological families, they can often be viewed as threatening to male-centered understandings of sexuality and prohibited or punished on the grounds of religion or morality (Espin, 1984).

The differing Latin American and Euro-American understandings of the relationship between gender, social status, and sex-role preferences may come into conflict when Euro-American sexual orientation concepts and terms (homosexual, lesbian, gay, etc.) are imported into Latin American countries through tourism and popular culture. In fact, today Euro-American and Latin American sex/gender systems co-exist in many Latin American countries. Moreover, Latin American understandings can travel with immigrants to the United States, where they may persist for generations. Their existence may help explain why some Latinos are less likely than Whites to identify as lesbian or gay—these Euro-American terms may not correspond to their understanding of same-sex attraction and/or sexual behavior (Kurtz, 1999; Prieur, 1998; Wright, 2000).

## Class

Although less frequently acknowledged than other major social categories, class (or socioeconomic status) has been an important force in LGBTQ+ lives—now and in the past. Despite this, LGBTQ+ social, cultural, and political efforts have not always prioritized issues of class—income inequality, affordable housing and healthcare, access to education, retirement security, and employment protections (Hussain, 1993).

Today, media depictions of the LGBTQ+ community convey an image of relative wealth, style, and luxury. This image originated in the early 1990s with a handful of gay-owned marketing companies that promoted the stereotype of highly educated, childless gays and lesbians, alienated from society and ignored by advertisers, but with high levels of disposable income. Since then, the size of the "pink dollar"—LGBTQ+ people's purchasing power—has been estimated at $300 billion to $800 billion annually (Witeck, 2013). However, these numbers are often based on unscientific surveys of subscribers to lifestyle magazines and mail order catalogs that over-sampled White, urban, gay men, who were more comfortable with openly identifying as gay. Marketers who believed the myth of gay affluence were inevitably disappointed when sales did not live up to projections, but anti-gay social forces readily embraced the myth since it seemed to prove that LGBTQ+ civil rights protections were unnecessary. More recently, a large amount of more careful research has revealed a more complicated picture of LGBTQ+ socio-economics (Lee Badgett, 1997; Chasin, 2000).

The National Gay and Lesbian Chamber of Commerce estimates there are 7.5 million LGBTQ+ workers in the U.S., in most every field of work and income levels (NGLCC, 2015). But the overall trend of numerous studies shows that, despite higher levels of education and longer work histories, gay men earn 10%–32% less than similarly qualified heterosexual men. While lesbians take home the same or more than heterosexual women, all women earn less than gay and straight men due to the gender wage gap (see below for more on this concept). Married heterosexual men receive the highest incomes, presumably due to the assumption that they have families to support and that their wives (if employed outside the home) will earn less than men for the same work. Married or partnered gay, lesbian, or bisexual workers, and married-heterosexual women, do not enjoy a similar "marriage premium" (Lee Badgett, 1997).

Surveys tend to lump bisexuals together with lesbians and gay men, but the little research that exists shows they earn less than lesbians, gay men, and heterosexuals (Lee Badgett, Durso, & Schneebaum, 2013; Pew Research Center, 2013). One study of Californian workers found bisexual men earned 10%–15% less, and bisexual women earned nearly 10% less, than heterosexual men (Carpenter, 2005). Another study found about 40% of bisexual women and men earn less than $25,000 per year (compared to 23%–30% of lesbians, gay men, and heterosexuals) (Gorman et al., 2015). The few studies on income of transgender people shows very high levels of un- and underemployment—twice the rate of the general population and as high as 60% in some studies. Transgender people of color experience under- and unemployment at four times the rate of the general population. (Grant et al., 2011). Although economic analyses do reveal the existence of some wealthy LGBTQ+ people, they appear no better off than their cisgender or heterosexual counterparts and are far fewer in number than popular stereotypes suggest (Lee Badgett et al., 2007).

These income disparities are caused by both workplace discrimination and occupational strategies that lead workers to self-select for lower-paying careers. Studies show that identifiably lesbian or gay job candidates receive fewer interviews and job offers than equally qualified heterosexuals. Once on the job, nearly 70% of LGB workers report discrimination in hiring, work assignments, promotion, and firing. In one 2011 study, 78% of transgender workers reported some form of workplace harassment or mistreatment, and 47% had been discriminated against in hiring, promotion, or retention (Lee Badgett et al., 2007; Sears & Mallory, 2011). As of late 2017, it was still legal in 29 states to refuse to hire or fire a worker solely based on sexual orientation. Gender identity and expression in the workplace is unprotected in 32 states (HRC, 2016b). LGBTQ+ workplace discrimination takes a toll on workers' mental and physical health, performance, and job satisfaction, and increases employer costs related to recruitment and retention, worker productivity, marketing, and litigation (Burns, 2012; Fidas & Cooper, 2014).

For these, and other, reasons as many as one third of LGBTQ+ workers elect to hide their gender identity or sexual orientation at work (Sears & Mallory, 2011). Some avoid specific jobs or workplaces that do not have a reputation as being supportive of LGBTQ+ employees and careers that require socializing outside of work (where same-sex partners or non-normative family structures might customarily be revealed to coworkers or supervisors). Others avoid career fields where it would be difficult to hide their gender or sexual status, or where the compensation and work culture penalties for being LGBTQ+ would be high. Instead, they seek out more accommodating employment, but pay a cost in lower salaries and benefits. Both lesbians and gay men take lower-paying jobs in the public sector or do social justice work for non-profit organizations out of a sense of responsibility or political commitment stemming from personal experiences with prejudice, discrimination, and harassment (Lee Badgett & King, 1997).

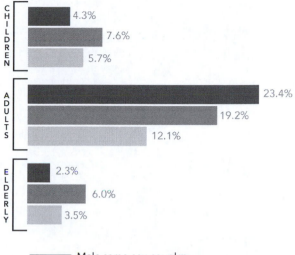

Male same-sex couples
Female same-sex couples
Different-sex married couples

*Poverty rates by age and family type (2014). Source: Adapted from data reported by the Center for American Progress and Movement Advancement Project.*

Some aspects of disparate LGBTQ+ incomes are explained by the gender wage gap. Many studies have shown that women receive only about 75% of the salary paid to similarly educated, trained, and qualified men. Moreover, career fields dominated by women (pink-collar jobs) tend to pay less than those dominated by men. Thus, gay men's lower incomes are partly explained by their overrepresentation in lower-paid, female-dominated careers (e.g. nursing, education, food service, personal care/services, social work, etc.) Likewise, lesbians' higher salaries may be explained by their disproportionate representation in higher paying fields (like banking, corporate law, and real estate) typically dominated by men. However, lesbians are also disproportionately employed in lower paying, but still male-dominated, blue-collar occupations (Lee Badgett & King, 1997; Lee Badgett et al., 2007).

Partly because of income and employment inequality, LGBTQ+ people experience higher rates of poverty than the general population. In large national surveys Americans who identify as LGBT report overall lower levels of education. Because educational attainment is associated with higher incomes, this can help explain higher rates of LGBTQ+ poverty (Gates & Newport, 2012). In 2013 approximately 30% of bisexual women and 25% of bisexual men lived in poverty (compared to 15% of heterosexual men and 21% of heterosexual women, and 20% of gay men and 23% of lesbians). Transgender people are nearly four times more likely to have extremely low (less than $10,000/year) household incomes. Children living in households headed by same-sex parents have twice the poverty rates of children in households headed by married heterosexual couples. A 2016 study found that more than a quarter of LGBT adults did not have enough money for food at some point during the previous year. A similar number participated in government food assistance (food stamp) programs. LGBTQ+ poverty follows broader social patterns. It is higher among unmarried individuals, women, families with children, people of color, and interracial

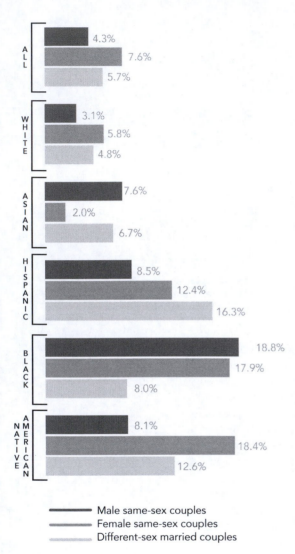

Male same-sex couples
Female same-sex couples
Different-sex married couples

*Adult poverty rates by family type and race/ethnicity (2014). Source: Adapted from data collected by the Center for American Progress and Movement Advancement Project.*

couples. Perhaps unsurprisingly, LGBTQ+ poverty has been found to be higher in states with anti–LGBTQ+ equality laws and such laws disproportionately affect the most vulnerable (Albelda et al., 2009; Lee Badgett, Durso, & Schneebaum, 2013; Brown, Romero, & Gates, 2016; CAP & MAP, 2014).

## Age

LGBTQ+ people portrayed in popular culture are overwhelmingly young but LGBTQ+ people can be any age and are well represented among middle-aged and elderly Americans. Yet, despite the dominance of youthful images in gay media, the unique issues confronting LGBTQ+ youth have only recently become better known and addressed. Although many LGBTQ+ adults report lifelong feelings of gender or sexual variance, they typically begin to be expressed during adolescence as part of the formation of an independent adult identity (Savin-Williams, 1998). However, many LGBTQ+ young people are financially and emotionally dependent on their parents and families of origin, often into their mid-twenties or later. For LGBTQ+ minors, parents can determine access to mental and physical healthcare, meaning that transgender youth may not have access to medically necessary treatments and all LGBTQ+ youth may be subjected to (often questionable) mental health "treatment" against their will (APA Task Force on Appropriate Therapeutic Responses to Sexual Orientation. 2009; Baum et al., n.d.).

Although the American Psychiatric Association removed homosexuality from its Diagnostic and Statistical Manual of Mental Disorders ("the DSM") in 1973, LGBTQ+ youth can still be diagnosed with a range of other mental health disorders. Even though there is no evidence that gender identity or sexual orientation can be changed voluntarily, or through counseling or therapy, some LGBTQ+ youth are forced to undergo harmful "reparative" therapy to change their gender presentation or sexual orientation, or confined in mental health institutions against their will (APA Task Force on Appropriate Therapeutic Responses to Sexual Orientation, 2009). Some parents send their LGBTQ+ children to overseas religious "residential treatment centers" for "behavior modification" where physical abuse and even deaths have been reported (Schlanger, 2014; Shapiro, 2015).

Where non-LGBTQ+ youth might be focused on being successful in school and how to pay for college, LGBTQ+ youth can be preoccupied with family rejection, school bullying, and fears of being outed. Peers, teachers, and school administrators can refuse to respect or may punish youths' transgender identity (Grant et al., 2011). LGBTQ+ youth are half as likely to report that they are happy and twice as likely to have experienced verbal and physical bullying at school, helping to explain why they are twice as likely to have experimented with drugs and alcohol, (HRC, n.d.). Sadly, LGBTQ+ youth are four times more likely than heterosexual peers to attempt suicide and their attempts are four to six times more likely to result in injury (CDC, 2011). Some research shows bisexual-identified and behaviorally bisexual youth have elevated rates of suicidal ideation and suicide attempts (MAP, 2016). Nearly half of transgender youth have contemplated suicide and a quarter has attempted it (Grossman & D'Augelli, 2007). All these statistics are higher for LGBTQ+ youth of color. Family rejection and lack of personal and community resources helps explain extremely high rates of homelessness among LGBTQ+ youth. A 2014 Urban Institute survey in six cities found that 10%–43% of homeless youth identify as LGBTQ+ or questioning. To survive, homeless LGBTQ+ youth often engage in drug or sex work, putting them at greater risk for addiction, violence, exploitation, and sexually transmitted infections (Cunningham et al., 2014).

As problems confronting LGBTQ+ youth became more widely known, some government agencies, charitable organizations, and national LGBTQ+ organizations have begun devoting more attention to their issues and concerns. The Matthew Shepard Foundation works to end anti-gay violence and hate crimes and The Trevor Project provides crisis intervention and suicide prevention resources to LGBTQ+ teens and young adults through its website and crisis hotline. Following a string of well-publicized LGBTQ+ youth suicides connected to school bullying in the 2010s, author Dan Savage and his husband Terry Miller founded the It Gets Better Project, aimed at helping LGBTQ+ youth envision a more positive future. Several states have enacted anti-bullying legislation but not all specifically name anti-gay bullying. The Gay, Lesbian, Straight Education Network works with students, teachers, school administrators, parents, and elected officials to help bring about a school environment that is supportive and affirming of all genders and sexual orientations. In 1996 a federal appeals court found that a school district can be held legally liable for ignoring anti-gay harassment. Subsequently, some LGBTQ+ students have won large legal settlements from school districts that failed to provide a safe educational environment (ACLU, 2012).

If popular culture stereotypes have obscured the complicated realities of LGBTQ+ youth, their elders are all but invisible. However, using 2010 U.S. census data, the Williams Institute estimated there are more than two million gay, lesbian, or bisexual Americans over the age of 55. These numbers are expected to double by 2030. The number of older transgender people is unknown (Gates, 2011). However, with the retirement of the Baby Boomer generation (born from 1945 to 1965) (with its significant number of LGBTQ+ people), more attention is now focused on LGBTQ+ elder and aging issues.

Although some anti-LGBTQ+ laws, policies, and attitudes are beginning to change, today's LGBTQ+ elders have lived most of their lives in a discriminatory social and cultural environment that leaves them fewer economic, social, and community resources in old age and retirement. Even if they are married, the historical lack of equal marriage recognition by the government can leave LGBTQ+ elders disadvantaged under Medicaid, Social Security, employer retirement plans, retiree health insurance benefits, estate and inheritance taxes, and veteran's benefits. Many live in poverty due to lower lifetime incomes, fewer retirement savings or pensions, lower rates of home ownership, unequal access to spousal retirement benefits, and less help from families and children. LGBTQ+ elders are also less likely to be married or partnered, and can also require specialized medical treatment due to HIV infection and hormones that may conflict with other medications. These issues are all compounded by racial, ethnic, wealth, and gender inequalities. For example, despite having longer work histories, elderly lesbians receive less income from Social Security and employer retirement plans and more from wages and public assistance programs. As a result, older lesbian couples are much more likely to live in poverty (Goldberg, 2009; SAGE & MAP, 2010). Transgender elders are chronically underserved and at heightened risk for maltreatment, discrimination, and homelessness, and experience physical and mental health disparities (NCTE, 2011).

Although anti-gay sentiment tends to be highest among the oldest members of the population, Baby Boomers lived part of their lives in the post-gay liberation era and have higher expectations for equal treatment. Nevertheless, many face prejudice and discrimination from the staff and residents of retirement homes and facilities, causing many to hide their identities or relationships. Elder-care professionals and facilities often lack cultural competency in the lives and experiences of LGBTQ+ people. This can contribute to higher rates of depression and loneliness, with negative physical health impacts for LGBTQ+ people in their care (Grossman, D'Augelli, & O'Connell, 2001). Laws outlawing discrimination in housing and public accommodations (which would benefit LGBTQ+ elders) exist in some states but there are currently no federal protections. One response has been the creation of senior centers, retirement homes, and low-income housing that specifically cater to the LGBTQ+ elderly. Such facilities have been established in several U.S. and European cities (Gross, 2007b; Lewis, 2014a). National LGBTQ+ rights and social service organizations have also begun to address LGBTQ+ aging issues by conducting research, lobbying public officials, and training eldercare professionals to offer LGBTQ-appropriate services (Choi & Meyer, 2016; SAGE & NCTE, 2012).

## Geography

Although popular representations often depict LGBTQ+ life as metropolitan, U.S. census data shows this to be an unsupported stereotype. Despite stereotypes of LGBTQ+ urbanity, the concentration of lesbians and gays in even the most stereotypically "gay" city is lower than media representations suggest. 2010 U.S. census data shows that major metropolitan areas often viewed as gay meccas have relatively small percentages of self-identified LGBTQ+ people: San Francisco (6.2%); Los Angeles (4.6%); Boston (4.8%); Portland (5.4%). More than 50% of self-identified LGBTQ+ Americans live in the South and

Midwest—regions of the country with the fewest large cities. Such areas are also home to large populations of African Americans and Latinos, with their share of LGBTQ+ people (Newport & Gates, 2015).

There can be little question that the population density of large metropolitan areas can lead to a critical mass of LGBTQ+ people able to create and support more organizations, services, institutions, and cultural opportunities, especially for

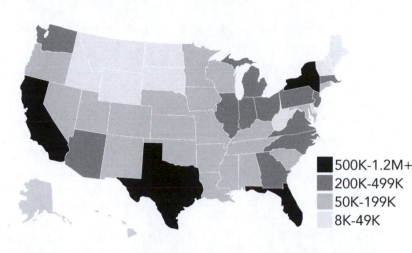

*Estimated LGBT population (by state) in U.S (2017). Source: Adapted from original with permission of Movement Advancement Project.*

transgender people, LGBTQ+ people of color, and those with specific tastes in sexual or romantic partners. Cities may also offer greater social diversity and tolerance of sexual diversity. Due to their large size, cities can also offer a degree of anonymity and freedom to craft a life free from family supervision and community surveillance. But urban anonymity can also produce feelings of isolation and loneliness. Opportunities for creating families of choice based on affection, affinity, or shared interests do not always replace the loss of birth families and community some LGBTQ+ people experience upon moving to a large city. Some research has suggested that, in order to make friends and forge new social connections, young gay and bisexual men who migrate to big cities can engage in more substance abuse and high-risk sexual behaviors (Pachankis, Eldahan, & Golub, 2016).

Although many large cities have well-known gay "ghettoes" and "gayborhoods," these are often the product of a gentrification that displaces low-income residents, who are also often people of color, which can contribute to race and class tensions (Knopp, 1997; Nero, 2005). High housing, and other, costs can prevent low-income LGBTQ+ people from fully participating in urban life. Moreover, gay enclaves provide convenient targets for violent homophobic and transphobic attacks. A politically influential gay community or well-known gay area of town does not always equate to protection against hate or violence. These examples demonstrate that urban gay enclaves based on minority gender or sexual identities are not insulated from larger social problems or conflicts (Taylor, 1997).

Despite media stereotypes and some well-publicized incidents of rural intolerance and homophobia, there is a long history of same-sex behavior and gender variance in the countryside. Same-sex sexual behavior and eroticized cross-dressing among frontiersmen, cowboys, ranchers, and prospectors is well known from the 1800s, and Alfred Kinsey's mid-twentieth century research found some of the highest rates of same-sex behavior in U.S. rural communities (Kinsey et al., 1948; Johnson, 2001). Kinsey seemed to argue that male homosexuality is tolerated in rural communities so long as the participants adhered to strict masculine gender norms. Others have shown that the kinds of masculine attire that are practical for performing farm work

| Rank | Urban Area | % LGBT |
|------|------------|--------|
| 1 | San Fran-Oakland-Hayward, CA | 6.2% |
| 2 | Portland-Vancouver-Hillsboro, OR-WA | 5.4% |
| 3 | Austin-Round Rock, TX | 5.3% |
| 4 | New Orleans-Metairie, LA | 5.1% |
| 5 | Seattle-Tacoma-Bellevue, WA | 4.8% |
| 6 | Boston-Cambridge-Newton, MA-NH | 4.8% |
| 7 | Salt Lake City, UT | 4.7% |
| 8 | Los Angeles-Long Beach-Anaheim, CA | 4.6% |
| 9 | Denver-Aurora-Lakewood, CO | 4.6% |
| 10 | Hartford-West Hartford-East Hartford, CT | 4.6% |
| 41 | Nashville-Davidson-Franklin, TN | 3.5% |
| 42 | Richmond, VA | 3.5% |
| 43 | Oklahoma City, OK | 3.5% |
| 44 | Houston-The Woodlands-Sugar Land, TX | 3.3% |
| 45 | Cincinnati, OH | 3.2% |
| 46 | Raleigh, NC | 3.2% |
| 47 | San Jose-Sunnyvale-Santa Clara, CA | 3.2% |
| 48 | Memphis, TN | 3.1% |
| 49 | Pittsburgh, PA | 3.0% |
| 50 | Birmingham-Hoover, AL | 2.6% |

*U.S. urban areas with the largest and smallest LGBT-identified populations (2012–14). Source: Adapted from data reported by Gallup.*

allowed gender-variant lesbians and bisexual women wider latitude to express a masculine gender or sexual style. As in other areas of LGBTQ+ life, in rural areas gender intersects with sexuality in ways that can both limit and expand the ability to live a full and authentic life (Kazyak, 2012; Marple, 2005).

Some LGBTQ+ people remain in rural areas to maintain close connections to families and communities of origin. There can be a kind of communal intimacy and mutual support in rural communities that can be difficult to establish for migrants to metropolitan areas. But this often requires careful management of gender presentation and sexual behavior. Female masculinity appears to be much more tolerated than male femininity, and it is not always interpreted as a sign of lesbianism. Perhaps due to the proximity to agricultural production and animal husbandry, there remains a strong rural emphasis on the reproductive nuclear family, often reinforced by the central role of religious organizations in community life. The smaller population of rural areas also means there may not be a critical mass of gender or sexual minorities who can create and sustain LGBTQ+ social institutions and cultural events (Cart & Stanley, 1999; Gottschalk & Newton, 2009; Oswald & Culton, 2003). Some evidence suggests that LGBTQ+ people living in states with the fewest large cities and least legal protections (the South, Midwest, and Mountain regions), are also where they fare the worst in terms of income, social acceptance, and health (Hasenbush et al., 2014). Thus, research on urban vs. rural LGBTQ+ well-being is mixed, suggesting that a variety of other factors are relevant to the quality of LGBTQ+ life than physical location (Wienke & Hill, 2013; Horvath et al., 2014).

Whatever the challenges, rural LGBTQ+ people have succeeded in forging some distinct rural cultures and communities. Beginning in 1979, the Radical Faeries organized rural gatherings of bisexual and gay men with the goal of creating an independent, anti-establishment, and spiritual queer community (Hennen, 2008). The "journal of record" for the Radical Faeries is *RFD: A Country Journal for Gay Men Everywhere* that publishes writings by and about rural gay life. Similarly inspired by 1960s countercultural movements, is the lesbian land (or Landdyke) movement that established rural female-only farms, music festivals, and living collectives. The goal was to create spaces outside of patriarchal culture's emphasis on female beauty ideals and to reinforce women's physical strength, independence, and self-sufficiency (Sandilands, 2002). Several publications supported rural lesbian and bisexual women's lives, including *Country Women*, *Amazon Quarterly*, and *Woman Spirit Magazine*.

In 1985 the International Gay Rodeo Association formed to sanction gay rodeos in Canada and the U.S. Gay rodeos spread appreciation for Western culture and the sport of rodeo, and raise money for charitable organizations (Le Coney & Trodd, 2009). Today, many small rural communities support LGBTQ+ bars that can be an oasis of LGBTQ+ life, often with lively drag communities and dating scenes. A new eco-queer movement is challenging heterocentric agricultural metaphors of production and re-production by attracting lesbians and gay men to rural areas to practice sustainable farming (Sbicca, 2012). Finally, there are significant overlaps between queer country/rural life and the aesthetics of the bisexual and gay male bear and related subcultures and personal styles, which celebrate a kind of rugged, out-doorsy masculinity stereotypically associated with rural communities (Wright, 1997).

## CONCLUSION

The image of the Pride Flag (that opened this chapter) is comprised of six horizontal stripes of equal length and width. Although the Pride Flag is a widely recognized symbol of both unity and diversity, it can also imply the absence of tensions and frictions between different parts of the LGBTQ+ community. This chapter has shown how commonly used terms like gender and sexual orientation are not easy to define and measure in a population. This can make it difficult to say exactly how many LGBTQ+ people exist in the world and to develop laws, policies, and programs to address the needs of this varied population. These important aspects of LGBTQ+ experience intersect with other social categories such as race, ethnicity, class, age, and geography. Together, membership in these various social categories uniquely impact LGBTQ+ individuals, affecting their well-being and ability to fully participate in the LGBTQ+ community.

## Learn More

*Readings*

Boykin, K. (Ed.). (2012). *For colored boys who have considered suicide when the rainbow is still not enough: Coming of age, coming out, and coming home*. New York, NY: Magnus.

Erickson-Schroth, L. (Ed.) (2014). *Trans bodies, trans selves: A resource for the transgender community*. Oxford, UK: Oxford University.

Fausto-Sterling, A. (2012). *Sex/gender: Biology in a social world*. New York, NY: Routledge.

Garbacik, J. (2013). *Gender & sexuality for beginners*. Danbury, CT: For Beginners.

Garber, M. (1995). *Vice versa: Bisexuality and the eroticism of everyday life*. New York, NY: Simon & Schuster.

Gluckman, A., & Reed, B. (Eds.) (1997). *Homo economics: Capitalism, community, and lesbian and gay life*. New York, NY: Routledge.

Gray, M. L., Johnson, C. R., & Gilley, B. J. (Eds.) (2016). *Queering the countryside: New frontiers in rural queer studies*. New York, NY: NYU.

Johnson, O. S. (2004). *The sexual spectrum: Exploring human diversity*. Vancouver, B.C.: Raincoast.

Knauer, N. (2016). *Gay and lesbian elders: History, law, and identity politics in the United States*. New York, NY: Routledge.

Leong, R. (Ed.) (1995). *Asian American sexualities: Dimensions of the gay and lesbian experience*. New York, NY: Routledge.

Ochs, R., & Rowley, S. E. (2005). *Getting bi: Voices of bisexuals around the world*. Boston, MA: Bisexual Resource Center.

Quesada, U., Gomez, L., & Vidal-Ortiz, S. (Eds.) (2015). *Queer brown voices: Personal narratives of Latina/o activism*. Austin, TX: University of Texas.

Ricketts, W. (Ed.) (2014). *Blue, too: More writing by (for or about) working class queers*. FourCats.

Rust, P. C. (Ed.). (2000). *Bisexuality in the United States: A social science reader*. New York, NY: Columbia University.

Singer, B., & Deschamps, D. (2017). *LGBTQ stats: Lesbian, gay, bisexual, transgender, and queer people by the numbers*. New York, NY: New Press.

## Film/Video

Barbosa, P., & Lenoir, G. (Directors). (2001). *De Colores: Lesbian and gay Latinos: Stories of strength, family and love* [DVD]. San Francisco: Woman Vision.

Baur, G. (Director). (2002). *Venus boyz* [DVD]. New York, NY: First Run.

Coal, C. (Director). (2008). *A place to live: The story of Triangle Square* [DVD]. United States: Bittersweet.

Davila, G. (Director). (2014). *Nancy from East Side Clover* [DVD]. United States: Film Bliss.

Dinco, D. (Director). (2011). *Homeboy* [DVD]. United States: Homeboy.

Ho, P., & Ku, A. (Directors). (2001). *Different shades of pink* [DVD]. San Francisco: Frameline.

Ingram, M. (Director). (2006). *Small town gay bar* [DVD]. United States: View Askew.

Ingram, M. (Director). (2010) *Bear nation: The bear movement in the gay community* [DVD]. United States: View Askew.

Intersex Society of North America. (2000). *Intersex: Redefining sex* [Motion picture]. Petaluma, CA: Intersex Society of North America.

Maddux, S. (Director). (2011). *Gen silent* [DVD]. United States: Interrobang!

McClodden, T. (Director). (2008). *Black/womyn: conversations with lesbians of African descent* [Documentary]. Harriet's Gun.

Mendez, J. (Director). (2012). *Gay Latino: Coming of age* [DVD]. United States: Evolutionary.

Mosbacher, D., & Reid, F. (Directors). (1996). *All God's children* [DVD]. United States: WomanVision.

Mossberg, J. (Director). (2013). *Out here* [DVD]. United States: Queer Farmer Film Project.

Peddle, E. D. (Director & Producer). (2005). *The aggressives* [DVD]. United States: 7thart.

Regan, M. (Director). (2001). *No dumb questions* [DVD] United States: Epiphany.

Riggs, M. (Director). (1989). *Tongues untied* [DVD]. San Francisco: Frameline.

Schermerhorn, C., & Cram, B. (Directors). (1997). *You don't know dick: Courageous hearts of transsexual men*. Berkeley, CA: University of California Extension Center for Media and Independent Learning.

Shavelson, L. (Director & Producer). (2015). *Three to infinity: Beyond two genders* [DVD]. United States: Photowords.

Symons, J. (Director). (1997). *Beauty before age* [DVD]. Blooming Grove, NY: New Day.
Ward, P. (Director). (2000). *Is it a boy or a girl?* [TV Documentary]. United States: Discovery Channel.
Ziegler, R. (Director). (2008). *Still black: A portrait of black transmen* [DVD]. United States: Still Black.

### Internet

Accord Alliance: www.accordalliance.org

American Institute of Bisexuality: www.bisexual.org

Asexual Visibility and Education Network (AVEN): www.asexuality.org

BiNet USA: www.binetusa.org

Bisexual Resource Center: www.biresource.net

Intersex Society of North America: www.isna.org

interACT: Advocates for Intersex Youth: interactadvocates.org

It Gets Better Project: www.itgetsbetter.org

Julia's Trans, Gender, Sexuality, & Activism Glossary: juliaserano.com terminology.html

Kinsey Institute: www.kinseyinstitute.org

National Center for Lesbian Rights: www.nclrights.org

National Center for Transgender Equality: www.transequality.org

National Queer API Alliance: www.nqapia.org

Services & Advocacy for Gay, Lesbian, Bisexual, & Transgender Elders (SAGE): www.sageusa.org

The Trevor Project: www.thetrevorproject.org

The Asexual Agenda: asexualagenda.wordpress.com

# CHAPTER 3
# Getting It On
## *Sexual Behavior and Sexual Health*

*Michael J. Murphy*

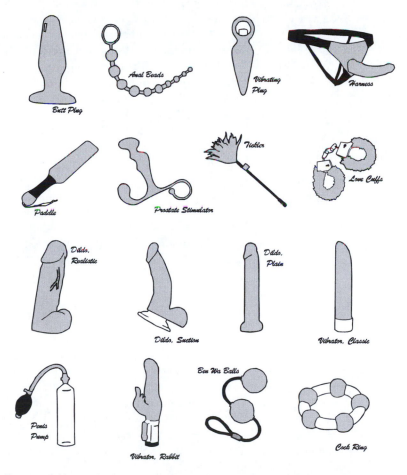

*A variety of "sex toys" are available to aid solo or partnered sexual activity. Source: Westminster Press, St. Louis, MO.*

Since 1997 the U.S. government has spent $1.5 billion on Abstinence-Only-Until-Marriage (AOUM; also called abstinence-only) sex education programs in the nation's schools. The explicit goal of these programs is to encourage young people to refrain from sexual activity until they are married. To receive federal funds, AOUM programs are required to emphasize: the social and economic benefits of sexual abstinence; marital monogamy and fidelity as a social norm; harm of childbirth out of wedlock; harm of sexual activity outside of marriage; techniques for rejecting sexual advances; and the need for economic self-sufficiency before having sex. Although abstinence from sexual intercourse is one of the many ways to avoid pregnancy and reduce exposure to sexually transmitted infections (STIs), an enormous amount of research—some by state and federal government agencies—has shown that abstinence-only sex education programs do not delay first sexual experience, reduce numbers of sexual partners, or reduce teen pregnancy (Trenholm et al., 2007). Youth exposed to such programs are just as likely to engage in risky sexual behavior and less likely to use condoms—to prevent pregnancy or protect against STIs. Although teen pregnancy rates have generally declined in the U.S. since 1991, states that emphasize abstinence most strongly in their sex education programs had higher rates of teen pregnancy than states that took a more comprehensive approach (Kost & Henshaw, 2013; Stanger-Hall & Hall, 2011).

Less often noted is the cisgender and heteronormative bias of these programs. Typically, they: assume all students are cisgender and heterosexual; present monogamous marriage as a universal goal; disparage non-traditional families; and treat same-sex sexual activity as a form of "experimentation." They do not acknowledge, much less affirm, diverse sexual orientations or gender identities, and some states mandate that non-heterosexual sexualities be presented in a negative light. They completely ignore the existence of transgender people. Despite the heavy burden of STIs among LGBTQ+ people, AOUM programs often do not provide complete or accurate information about the prevention, testing, and treatment of STIs. In fact, many programs omit basic information about condom use and STIs, and some deliberately misinform students about how HIV is transmitted and the effectiveness of condoms in preventing HIV infection (Bittner, 2012 cited in Pingel et al., 2013; Elia & Eliason, 2010; SIECUS, 2014).

In the absence of comprehensive, accurate, and affirming sex education in school, many LGBTQ+ young people learn about sex from their peers, the Internet, pornography, or through "trial and error" in their first sexual relationships (Arrington-Sanders et al., 2015; Kubicek et al., 2011; Pingel et al., 2013). However, the quality and accuracy of these sources can be unreliable, at best. Rarely do they help LGBTQ+ youth develop the knowledge base, communications skills, and sense of agency necessary to make healthy choices about sexual behavior. Nor do they convey a sense that sexual health is important for overall health and well-being. They can also leave LGBTQ+ young people vulnerable to sexual coercion and exploitation, sexual violence, and STIs that can affect their long-term health.

To help remedy this situation, this chapter presents basic information about sexual anatomy, sexual behavior, and sexual health, with an emphasis on LGBTQ+ people and experiences. The first section describes human sexual anatomy and common physical responses to sexual stimulation. The middle section discusses typical LGBTQ+ sexual behaviors and activities. The final section presents information about LGBTQ+ sexual health, with an emphasis on STIs, sexual risk, and strategies for healthier sex. Throughout the chapter, clinical and scientific terms for sexual anatomy and behavior are followed by lay terminology (slang) in parentheses. The initialism "LGBTQ+" is used to describe lesbians, gay men, bisexuals, transgender people, queers, and other gender and sexual minorities who use these and other identity labels. The chapter has two goals: to inform the general reader about the sexual behavior and sexual health of LGBTQ+ people, and to empower LGBTQ+ readers with the necessary information to make healthier sexual choices.

## SEXY BITS: SEXUAL ANATOMY

To understand LGBTQ+ sexual behavior and sexual health, it can be useful to have a basic understanding of human sexual anatomy and sexual response.[1] Often when such information is presented, the emphasis is on reproduction and sex differences in anatomy and physiology. Intentionally or not, this can give the impression that the "purpose" of sex is reproduction, although very little sexual activity results in pregnancy and childbirth (even when that is the goal). In fact, most sexually active adults spend a great deal of time and energy ensuring that sexual behavior does *not* result in pregnancy! Rather, most people engage in sexual activity to experience pleasure or feelings of intimacy with sexual partners (Schwartz & Rutter, 1998). An emphasis on anatomical sex differences can also reflect and reinforce binary thinking about sex and gender. It can imply that people who identify as, or are labeled, "female" or "male" have little in common anatomically or have dramatically difference experiences of sexual stimulation and pleasure. Current research simply does not support such thinking (Fausto-Sterling, 2012).

This section presents information about those body parts *typically* involved in sexual activity, with less emphasis on sex or gender differences. It is important to remember that "typical" is not the same as "universal." Not every (or even most) clitorises, penises, or anuses look or "work" the same way. An individual's sexual anatomy and physical response to sexual stimulation may differ from what is described and depicted in this section. Although there are some common patterns across all humans, individual anatomies can be influenced by genetics, hormones, environment, life experiences, and social and cultural context. Genitals and other sexual body parts may vary in size, shape and appearance due to intersex conditions, medical treatment (including surgery), injury or mutilation, age, piercing/tattooing, and other natural variations in human anatomy. They may vary in color from light pink to dark brown or purple. But even if all genitals looked the same, their appearance would tell us little about a person's gender identity, sexual orientation, or favorite/preferred sexual activities (and vice versa). Someone who identifies as male or a man may have a vagina and clitoris; a person with a feminine gender presentation may have a penis and testicles.

Just as sexual anatomy varies, so can sexual response. Individual responses to sexual stimulation can be affected by neurological differences, personal history, or memories of similar kinds of stimulation (as with sexual abuse and rape), and psychological state (such as feelings of fear or intimacy). Internalized social and cultural notions about which body parts are "sexual" or are appropriate for sexual activity can also affect whether we interpret a specific kind of touch as sexual. Finally, reducing "sex" to genital stimulation is a social and cultural, not biological, phenomenon. Many people derive sexual pleasure from stimulation and activities that do not involve the genitals. Anticipating, encountering, and accepting these differences in ourselves and our partners is part of what makes having sex interesting and enjoyable (Corinna, 2016).

## "How Does it Feel?": The Intersection of Sexuality and Disability

As a queer man with disabilities, I am always asked one question when it comes to my sexuality: "Can you have sex?" Every time I go online, go on a date, or try to hook up, this is the only thing guys seem to want to know about me. When they bring it up, they ask it with such confusion, trying to wrap their brains around the "how" of it all. Sex as a queer disabled man doesn't necessarily look the way we have come to expect, and while I can have sex, it goes so much deeper than the physical act. Let me tell you how sex, disability, and queerness feels.

When I am given the opportunity to be sexual with another person, I am flooded with emotions and feelings. I am really excited, because this means that a guy might actually consider me sexy and want to get naked with me. As we remove each other's clothes, and all of my scars, curves, and delicious deformities are there for him to see, I know that I must remember every taste, touch, and caress—I must enjoy every single second of this sex—because part of me fears that that at any moment my disability might become too much for him and he'll run for the door.

Also in that exact moment, I am reveling in the fact that I am naked because I want to be. Finally, my body is being explored out of desire and not duty. Every tingle, twinge, and touch is one of pure pleasure and not professional obligation. I am not being cleaned or cared for on someone else's clock, but rather I am connecting with a part of myself that makes me feel whole as a queer crippled man. This is the moment when my disability and my sexual identities merge, and I feel powerful because I get to show why my disability is one of the sexiest things I have to offer.

As the sexual tension resolves and our time comes to a close, I worry that I will have to ask him to help me put my clothes on, and that he will understand just how disabled I actually am, and never want to see me again.

> I feel scared and ashamed that I have to ask for help at all, and I get annoyed that other guys don't have to worry about this, while also trying to hold onto every morsel of this memory until the next time. The experience of sex, disability, and queerness means many different things to me. It is proof that I am a sexual being, and that my sex is real, valid, and important. It reminds me that I am a queer disabled man, and that I should be proud of that no matter what. Most importantly, each time I have sex, I learn that it is about the moments, not the mechanics.
>
> *Andrew Gurza*

## Brain, Nerves, Erogenous Zones

Regardless of the size, shape, and appearance of the genitals, the body's largest sex organ is the brain. Sexual arousal can begin with an exciting image or thought, a specific kind of touch, or feelings of intimacy or closeness to a partner—but these are all experienced in the brain. The brain is where we "feel" emotions, memories, sensations, pleasure, and pain. It is where we experience our sexual hopes, fears, history, expectations, and sense of ourselves as sexual beings.

The brain perceives and controls the body's organs through the central nervous system and a vast network of nerves with endings in all the body's organs, including the largest: the skin. However, the density of the skin's nerve endings varies significantly. The term erogenous zone describes areas of the skin that are dense with nerve endings and very sensitive to pleasure and pain. For many people these include the neck, lips, tongue, ears, fingers and palms, nipples, chest/chest wall, inner thigh, armpit, and genitals. And not all parts of the genitals are equally sensitive. Generally, the tip or end of the clitoris and penis is more sensitive than the shaft, and the first (or outer) third of the vagina and anus is more sensitive than further inside the body. Many erogenous zones are also mucous membranes; skin that secretes the sticky, slippery substance called mucus, and that line many bodily openings, such as the urethra, vagina, mouth, anus, and rectum. Some of these mucous membranes (such as those lining the vagina) may produce lubrication when sexually stimulated.

Whether alone or with a partner, sex always involves a dynamic, interactive relationship between the brain and the rest of the body, and not solely those parts commonly thought of as sexual, such as the genitals. When skin in an erogenous zone is stimulated (or we read an arousing text or view a sexy image), the stimulus is carried to the brain which, in turn, sends signals through the nervous system that cause changes in breathing, blood pressure, body temperature, and blood flow to the genital areas. Sexual pleasure, including orgasm, may be felt in the body but is experienced in the brain through the release of neurochemicals such as dopamine, oxytocin, and serotonin. However, stimulating skin in an erogenous zone does not always produce a pleasurable sensation in the brain.

Survivors of rape, sexual assault, or childhood sexual abuse may struggle to separate the stimulation of specific erogenous zones from past experiences of abuse or violence. Even though most people's anal region is dense with nerve endings, in many societies it is unacceptable for men to enjoy anal stimulation or penetration, and any touching in those areas may not be pleasurable. Many transgender people have negative feelings when body parts (that have been gendered in ways that do not align with their gender identity) are viewed, mentioned, or touched by sexual partners—even though those parts may be dense with nerve endings capable of providing pleasure (Bellwether, 2010; Green, 2010; Hill–Meyer & Scarborough, 2014).

Conversely, pleasure from erogenous zone stimulation may be heightened by erotically charged images and thoughts, memories of past sexual experiences, or a social/cultural context that tells us to interpret such stimulation as sexual. In cases of paralysis or spinal cord injury, the brain has even shown the ability to retrain itself to experience sexual pleasure, even orgasm, from stimulation of skin in areas not typically viewed as sexual (Doidge, 2007).

The unique character of each person's brain-body relationship helps explain individual differences in the kinds of images, thoughts, and activities that are sexually arousing, as well as preferred forms of sexual touch, and physical and emotional responses to sexual activity. This is one reason why sex is never just about sexual anatomy or physiology.

## Vulva: Vagina, Clitoris, Labia

People labeled female or girls at birth are often done so based on the appearance of external sexual anatomy, specifically the genitals. (However, not everyone who identifies as a girl, woman, or female has all or any of the anatomy described below.) Typical female external anatomy consists of inner and outer labia (lips), the clitoris (clit), the urethra (pee hole), and entrance to the vagina (cunt; pussy). Together this area of the body is called the vulva. The inner and outer labia are folds of skin extending the length of the vulva, from clitoris to perineum. The outer labia may be darker in color than surrounding skin and covered with pubic hair. The inner labia are smaller, more delicate folds of skin that merge together above the vagina and urethra, at the clitoris.

The clitoris is a wishbone-shaped organ that lies mostly inside the body. (Although the clitoris and penis are not the same organ, both develop *in utero* from the same fetal tissue and have similarly named parts and responses to sexual arousal.) The part of the clitoris that extends outside the body is called the glans clitoris. It is covered with a fold or "hood" of tissue that may retract from the glans during sexual arousal. The glans clitoris is densely packed with nerve endings and highly sensitive to touch. In some cultures, the clitoral shaft or hood are reduced in size or removed during puberty but most people born with a vulva have a clitoris and clitoral hood. The internal parts of the clitoris include the clitoral shaft, bulbs, and crura (or legs). The clitoral bulbs lie to either side of the vagina and the crura lie under the skin beneath the labia. The entire clitoris is formed of erectile tissue and is sensitive to both touch and pressure.

The vagina is a four- to six-inch-long tube of flexible muscular tissue that exits the body at the vulva and terminates inside the body at the cervix. The cervix is the entrance to the uterus, a grapefruit-sized organ in which a fetus is nurtured during pregnancy. At the end of the uterus opposite the cervix, the fallopian tubes connect to the ovaries, which are where ova (eggs) are stored. The upper (or inner) two-thirds of the vagina has little sensitivity to touch but the lower (or outer) third has many nerve endings and can be quite sensitive. Some people with vaginas experience pleasure from stimulation of the "G spot": an area of the vaginal wall located about a third of the way into the vagina and toward the abdomen. Depending on an individual's anatomy, touch in this area can stimulate a part of the clitoral system called the urethral sponge, which may also be responsible for producing some of the fluid during female ejaculation (Komisaruk, Beyer-Flores, & Whipple, 2006).

When sexually aroused, the brain directs blood vessels in the groin to slow the return of blood to the heart. As a result, the outer labia swell in size, the inner labia darken in color, and the clitoris fills with blood causing a stiffening (or erection) of the glans clitoris. The vaginal walls will thicken and begin to lubricate, and the entire vaginal canal will lengthen. Pressure from blood-filled organs surrounding the vagina will cause its outer third to tighten and the vaginal opening to become smaller.

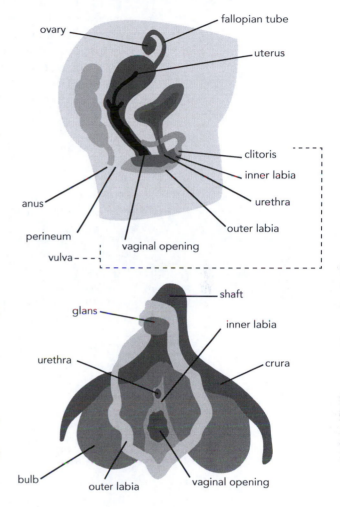

*Female-typical sexual anatomy (internal and external). Cutaway side view (top). Front close-up (bottom).*

Sexual arousal and excitement often culminates in orgasm. An orgasm is a brief, but intense and highly pleasurable, release of sexual tension involving involuntary contractions of genital (and other pelvic area) muscles and a release of neurochemicals in the brain creating a feeling of euphoria and well-being. In people with vulvas, pelvic muscles rhythmically contract causing a pleasurable sensation. There may also be uterine and anal muscular contractions. An orgasm typically consists of 8–15 pelvic muscular contractions at the rate of more than one per second. Orgasm is often accompanied by flushed skin, perspiration, fast breathing, hand/foot/buttock muscle spasms, vocal noises, and heightened blood pressure. Because most of the vagina is not highly sensitive, orgasms are thought to result primarily from clitoral stimulation—either from external stimulation of the glans clitoris, or of the clitoral crura through the vaginal wall (during vaginal penetration), or through the rectal wall (during anal penetration). Many (but not all) people with vulvas can experience multiple orgasms with little rest in between.

During orgasm, some people with vulvas also experience female ejaculation (squirting, gushing): expulsion of a small amount of clear fluid from the vagina and urethra. Female ejaculation is a poorly understood phenomenon but, unlike semen (which consists of fluid containing sperm), fluid involved in female ejaculation can include vaginal lubrication secreted during sexual arousal, personal lubricant used during sex, small amounts of dilute urine, and secretions of the Skene's and Bartholin's glands (which lie to either side of the vaginal opening) (Salama et al., 2015).

## Penis, Testicles, Prostate

Those labeled male or boys at birth are often done so based on external sexual anatomy, primarily the appearance of the genitals. (However, not everyone who identifies as a boy, man, or male has all or any of the anatomy described below.) Typical external male genitals consist of the penis (dick, cock) and testicles (balls, nuts). A penis is made up of three parts: the root, shaft, and head (or glans penis). The root of the penis extends inside the body for several inches and connects to muscles that assist in ejaculation and allow some voluntary movement of the penis. The shaft of the penis contains no bone or cartilage, but consists of three chambers of spongy tissue that, when filled with blood, create a penile erection (boner; hard-on).

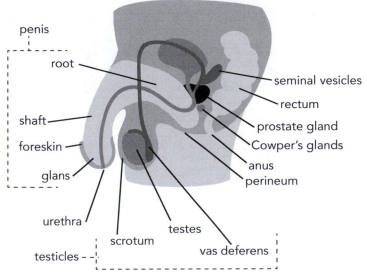

*Male-typical internal and external sexual anatomy, cutaway side view.*

The glans penis is packed with nerve endings and is one of the most sensitive parts of the penis. At the tip of the glans penis is the urethral opening (pee hole). The urethra is the tube through which urine (pee; piss) and semen (cum; jizz; spunk) exit the body. At birth, the glans penis is covered with a hood of soft tissue called a foreskin. In many parts of the world the foreskin is removed after birth in an operation called a circumcision. Multiple studies have found that human penises average three to four inches long when flaccid (not erect), five to six inches long and five inches in circumference when erect (Herbenick et al., 2014; Veale et al., 2015).

Hanging somewhat behind and below the penis, the testicles consist of a sack of skin called a scrotum that holds two egg-shaped, sperm-producing organs call testes. While the scrotum can be very sensitive to touch during sexual activity, strong pressure on the testes can cause intense pain or nausea. Starting at puberty, sperm are produced by the testicles at the rate of 300 million a day.

The vas deferens is an 18–inch long tube that connects the testicles to the seminal vesicles. Located behind the bladder, the seminal vesicles produce a fluid that nourishes the sperm. The vas deferens then passes through the prostate gland before merging with the urethra. The prostate is a walnut sized gland located at the base of the bladder. The bulbourethral (or Cowper's) glands are two pea-sized organs that lie at the root of the penis and are also connected to the vas deferens. After puberty, the Cowper's glands produce a clear, sticky pre-ejaculatory fluid (pre-cum) that lubricates and cleans the urethra prior to the passage of semen.

During sexual arousal, the brain constricts blood flow from the genitals back to the heart, resulting in erection of the penis and enlargement of the testicles. An erect penis may or may not differ dramatically in size from its flaccid state, and may stand out straight from the body or curve upward, downward, or to either side. When a penis is erect, the foreskin (if present) may retract completely behind the glans penis, but it can also cover all or part of the glans. After a sustained erection, the Cowper's glands will secrete a few drops of pre-ejaculatory fluid (pre-cum) that may seep from the urethral opening.

Similar to people with vulvas, people with a penis and testicles may experience orgasm after sustained sexual stimulation. Orgasm can result from focused stimulation of the penis and testicles and/or stimulation of the anus, rectum, and prostate gland. The intense feelings of pleasure and the rhythmic contractions of pelvic and anal muscles (described above) are often accompanied by ejaculation. Ejaculation is the release of semen (cum) from the body via the penile urethra. Just prior to ejaculation, the glans penis will swell in size and there are several brief contractions of the vas deferens, seminal vesicles, anal sphincter, and prostate gland. This moves sperm from the testicles, along with fluid from the seminal vesicles, prostate gland, and Cowper's glands, through the urethra and out of the tip of the penis.

During ejaculation, semen may ooze from the urethra or be propelled some distance. Each ejaculation produces about a teaspoon of semen, but this can vary by individual, age, time since last ejaculation, and level of sexual excitement. Some people with penises and testicles can experience multiple orgasms, but most require a brief rest period between orgasms during which it can difficult or impossible to have an erection or orgasm. During this period the glans penis can be highly sensitive to touch, the entire penis returns to its size when flaccid (soft), the testicles return to their normal size, and the scrotum lowers them away from the body (Carroll, 2016; Corinna, 2016).

## Anus, Rectum, Perianal Area

Even if they are not the focus of sexual activity, the nerves and muscles of the anus, rectum, and perianal area play a role in sexual pleasure and orgasm.

The anus (asshole) is the external opening of the intestinal tract. It is about an inch and half long and is comprised of two rings of muscle. The outer ring can be tightened and relaxed at will but the inner ring contracts involuntarily, before and after bowel movements. The anus leads into the rectum, an eight- to nine-inch-long tube of flexible tissue that forms the last section of the large intestine (or colon). Anal and rectal tissue is delicate and easily damaged during sexual activity and, unlike the vagina, does not self-lubricate when sexually stimulated.

The only access to the prostate gland (for those who have one) is via the rectum. It can be felt through the rectal lining, about three inches inside the anal opening, toward the abdomen. The patch of sensitive skin between the anus and the vulva (or the testicles) is called the perineum (taint). For people with vulvas, the perineal sponge is an area of nerves, blood vessels, and erectile tissue that lies inside the body, underneath the perineum. It is part of the clitoral system and during arousal swells with blood, causing pressure and tightening of the outer third of the vagina.

Sensations of pleasure from genital stimulation and orgasm often involve the muscles and nerves of the anal area. The anus and rectum are connected to the spinal cord by a branch of the pudendal nerve, which also connects the other genitals, bladder, prostate, penis, clitoris, and scrotum. The entire anal area is densely packed with nerve endings and highly sensitive to pressure and touch, but nerve endings are concentrated around the anus and the area of the rectum just inside the anal opening. The rectum is less sensitive to touch and more sensitive to pressure (Carroll, 2016; Corinna, 2016).

## Diverse Sexual Anatomies

While there are some common developmental patterns in human sexual anatomy, there is also great diversity within and between these patterns. Some intersex and transgender people may have atypical sexual anatomies, which may, in turn, affect their sexual behavior and sexual health.

### Intersex Anatomies

Intersex individuals are those who cannot be easily categorized as female or male based on criteria commonly used to determine one's sex (genetics, hormones, anatomy, physiology, etc.) (see Chapter 2 for more on intersex people). Some intersex conditions can affect the size, shape, and appearance of internal and external sexual and reproductive anatomy. At birth an intersex person may have genitals that differ in typical size (a "large" clitoris; a "small" penis, etc.). They may also have genitals that appear to combine typical female and male anatomy, such as labia that appear like a scrotum or a clitoris with a size or appearance closer to a small penis. These anatomical differences may persist into adulthood.

Treatments for some intersex conditions may also affect sexual anatomy. Some intersex infants undergo surgery to create genitals that conform to social expectations. Hormone therapy to ensure that the body develops in accordance with the assigned sex may affect their primary and secondary sex characteristics, including the size, shape, and appearance of the breasts and genitals. The wide variety of intersex conditions, unknown number of intersexed individuals, and lack of research on this population makes it difficult to know how their normal variations in sexual and reproductive anatomy affects their sexual behavior and sexual health (Chase, 1998; Fausto-Sterling, 2000).

### Transgender Anatomies

Unless a transgender person undergoes certain medical treatments, there is no reason to expect their genitals and other body parts will appear or function any differently than those of persons having a similar genetic or anatomical sex. However, genitals that do not correspond to a transgender person's gender identity can be the source of dysphoria—a general feeling of unease or anxiety about their body. An element of dysphoria may be discomfort with certain highly gendered sexual activities/positions or common medical or slang words for genitals and other body parts. For example, a female-to-male (FtM) transgender person may possess a vagina but may not enjoy being vaginally penetrated. This highly feminized sexual role can remind him that his sexual anatomy does not match his gender identity and can conflict with his self-image as a masculine man. Similarly, personal terms for body parts, like "front hole," "dicklit," and chest, may be preferred over medical terms such as vagina, clitoris, and breasts. Psychotherapy has the potential to mitigate body dysphoria, while medical treatment, including hormone therapy and gender affirmation surgery (sometimes also called sex reassignment surgery [SRS] or gender confirmation surgery), may bring the appearance and function of genitals and other body parts into closer alignment with a transgender person's gender identity and desired gender presentation.

Hormone treatment can have both subtle and pronounced effects on the anatomy, physiology, and brain chemistry of transgender people, potentially impacting sexual desire, patterns of arousal, and sexual function. Female-to-male transgender people (FtM; transmen) who undergo hormone therapy are typically prescribed testosterone (or, "T"), which is self-administered by injection. The effects of testosterone on genitals varies by individual but can include thinning of vaginal membranes and an increase in the size of the clitoris to 2–4 times its original size. During sexual arousal, the enlarged clitoris may become visibly erect and may become sufficiently large to allow for sexual penetration of partners. Testosterone may also increase desire for sex, patterns of sexual arousal, and the kinds of stimuli that are sexually arousing. Sexual arousal may be quicker and orgasms may be easier to achieve, but multiple orgasms may be more elusive.

Male-to-female transgender people (MtF; transwomen) who undergo hormone therapy are typically prescribed testosterone blockers and supplemental estrogen. Testosterone blockers prevent testosterone from affecting a variety of tissues and organs, potentially impacting sexual anatomy and sexual function.

Estrogen may stimulate breast or nipple growth, increase nipple sensitivity, and reduce sexual desire, semen production, and the size of external genitals. Erections may be fewer or no longer possible. For anyone on hormone treatment: some of the effects can be reversed; other effects—especially anatomical changes—may be irreversible.

Some transgender people have the desire and resources needed to bring their bodies into better alignment with their gender identity through surgery. Surgery to reduce or enlarge the chest (top surgery) may affect breast and nipple sensitivity, depending on the surgical technique used and whether underlying nerves are preserved. Surgery to alter the size, shape, or appearance of the genitals (bottom surgery) is very advanced and the best surgeons aim to produce genitals that are typical in appearance, allow for sexual intercourse, and provide sexual pleasure, including orgasm. Surgically constructed vaginas and clitorises typically allow for sexual penetration and orgasm, but constructed vaginas may not self-lubricate and will require the use of personal lubricant for penetration. Surgically constructed penises can allow for sexual penetration and can provide orgasm; however, they can only become erect using penile implants (such as flexible rods or inflatable chambers). The absence of sperm-producing testes and other internal male reproductive organs does not allow for ejaculation via the urethra (Bellwether, 2010; Green, 2010; Hill-Meyer & Scarborough, 2014; Tetzlaff, 2015).

No matter how genitals appear, function, or develop, it is important to remember that sexual stimulation is experienced in the brain. Sexual pleasure and orgasm can result from stimulation of many different parts of the body. For this reason, genitals that are altered by hormone therapy, created through surgery, or differ in some significant way from what is typical, can have the same capacity for sexual pleasure as those produced through more common developmental paths (*in utero*, at puberty, etc.). As with all the sexual anatomies discussed in this section, one cannot make assumptions about the gender identity, gender expression, sexual orientation, or sexual behavior of a person based solely on their sexual anatomy (Corinna, 2016).

## GETTING IT ON: SEXUAL BEHAVIOR

Popular culture is rife with inaccurate (and often homophobic) references to "gay sex." Yet, despite these stereotypes, there is no such thing. Like most adult humans, LGBTQ+ people engage in a wide variety of sexual behaviors, none of which are unique to LGBTQ+ people. Like their heterosexual and cisgender peers, LGBTQ+ sexual repertoires may include solo or partnered oral, anal, and vaginal sex; kissing, cuddling/hugging; and all over bodily contact or massage. They may also include sex toys, such as dildos and vibrators, personal lubricants, and a variety of safer-sex tools, such as condoms and dental dams (Newman, 2004; Rosenberger et al., 2011).

Like most people, LGBTQ+ peoples' sexual relationships can be very diverse. Some only have casual sexual encounters or a series of monogamous relationships; others only have sex with a single partner within a sexually exclusive or committed relationship; some have committed relationships that involve more than two partners; still others have "open" relationships where casual sexual encounters are permitted outside their primary relationship. Some LGBTQ+ people will experience some or all of these sexual relationships at some point in their adult lives. These sexual behaviors and sexual relationships are determined by the unique desires, tastes (or preferences), and anatomies of the participants (Bell, 1999).

Research consistently shows that many people who identify as heterosexual have some same-sex sexual experience in their lifetime, just as many who identify as bisexual, lesbian, or gay have some different-sex sexual experience during their lifetimes (Bailey et al., 2003; Herbenick et al., 2010). The 2011–2013 U.S. National Survey of Family Growth (NSFG) found that while about 7% of women identified as lesbian or bisexual and 4% of men identified as gay or bisexual, about 17% of women and 6% of men reported some same-sex sexual experience during their lifetimes. The NSFG also found about 90% of self-identified lesbian and bisexual women have some lifetime sexual experience with men, and 68% of self-identified gay and bisexual men have some lifetime sexual experience with women. Reports of lifetime same-sex sexual experiences were significantly lower for Latinas than for African-American and White women, and African-American men compared to Latino and White men (Copen, Chandra, & Febo-Vazquez, 2016). What these data do not show is that many people who prefer same-sex partners do not identify as gay, lesbian, bisexual, or queer, due to social stigma, internalized homophobia, or discomfort with these sexual identity labels (Silva, 2017; Ward, 2015).

This disconnect between sexual *identity* and sexual *behavior* has presented a challenge to public health workers seeking to reach populations at risk for STIs, especially those most heavily burdened by HIV/AIDS. To address this problem, terminology that focuses on sexual behavior (rather than sexual identity) began to be used starting in the early 1990s. Thus, the term "women who have sex with women" (or WSW) is often used to describe all women who engage in sexual activity with other women, regardless of how they identify. A similar meaning is implied by the term "men who have sex with men" (or MSM). Those who have sex with both men and women are described as "men who have sex with men and women" (MSMW) and "women who have sex with women and men" (WSWM). MSW or WSM are terms used to describe men who have sex with women and women who have sex with men.

Although such terms help shift the focus from identity to behavior, they may not be useful for describing some LGBTQ+ people's sexual behavior because they do not define what is meant by woman or man. By assuming congruence between gender expression, gender identity, and sexual anatomy, these terms aren't always useful for describing the sexual behavior of queer, transgender, or "gender non-conforming" people. They also risk erasing LGBTQ+ identities in research studies and public health outreach programs focused on sexual behavior and disease prevention and treatment (Young & Meyer, 2005). Despite these problems, in the discussion of sexual behavior that follows, behavior-based terms (WSW, etc.) will be used unless the sources of information specifically used more narrow identity-based terms (lesbian, gay, etc.).

Although there is comparatively little research on same-sex sexual behavior, we know much more about MSM than WSW—a fact reflected in the discussion that follows. Partly this is due to lack of government or other funding for large-scale studies of sexual behavior in the U.S. Funding that does exist, supports research on MSM and MSMW due to the disproportionate impact of HIV/AIDS and other STIs on these groups. And those few national surveys that collect data on sexual behavior, experiences, or attitudes often ignore gender and sexual minorities or report their experiences together with the larger population. Studies on the sexual behavior of transgender people and LGBTQ+ people of color are especially scarce, unless the focus is on STIs—which can create a false impression that these groups are somehow sexually "diseased" (Barton et al., 2016; Workowski & Bolan, 2015).

Finally, even large-scale studies of sexual behavior are limited by those who choose to participate. LGBTQ+ people represent relatively small percentages of the population and sometimes there are not enough participants in a study to allow researchers to draw scientifically valid conclusions about the larger LGBTQ+ population from only a few responses. Some researchers attempt to correct for this by conducting research in LGBTQ+ media or social spaces, such as online dating apps, gay bars, and Pride festivals. However, such studies can unintentionally exclude those who are not comfortable in, are excluded from, or do not have access to such spaces, or simply do not identify as LGBTQ+ (Durso & Gates, 2013). Recently, more inclusive surveys conducted by federal agencies and privately funded groups are beginning to help us better understand LGBTQ+ sexual behavior (Copen, Chandra, & Febo-Vazquez, 2011; Rosenberger et al., 2011; Schnarrs et al., 2012).

## Gay Male "Promiscuity"

One of the most pervasive stereotypes about gay male sexuality is that they are "promiscuous" (have a larger number of casual sexual partners). This term is often employed in homophobic religious and political rhetoric, or used to explain higher rates of STIs among men who have sex with men (Downs, 2016). However, the stereotype of gay male promiscuity is not supported by research.

Analysis of user profiles on the online dating website OkCupid.com, which has over four million users in Canada and the U.S., shows that both homosexual and heterosexual users report a median (50th percentile) of six lifetime sexual partners. In their OkCupid.com profiles, 45% of gay men say they've had five or fewer lifetime sexual partners (compared to 44% for heterosexual men) and 98% of gay men report 20 or fewer partners (compared to 99% for heterosexual men) (Rudder, 2014). Data from online dating sites may not be representative of the entire population because such sites cater to younger, tech savvy users looking for romantic and sexual partners. All research on lifetime number of sexual partners suffers from the difficulty of accurately recalling each sexual encounter, especially if they are numerous or occur over several decades. And respondents may under-report the numbers due to negative social attitudes about having large numbers of partners. Nevertheless, OkCupid.com's data are similar to findings in the more scientific and representative *General Social Survey* and the *National Survey of Family Growth* conducted by the U.S. government (Chandra et al., 2011).

It seems that most gay men have roughly the same number of lifetime sexual partners as most heterosexual men. But, a very small number of gay men do have comparatively large numbers of lifetime sexual partners. These few distort the "average" numbers of lifetime sexual partners often reported for all gay men. And though having many sexual partners is considered a risk factor for STIs (simply due to contact with more people with potentially more STI infections), STIs are spread by risky sexual behaviors with STI-infected partners—and it only takes one sexual encounter to spread or become infected with an STI.

## Non-Genital Intimacy

For many people the word sex implies sexual stimulation of the genitals, often meaning penetration of some bodily orifice (ex. anus, mouth, or vagina), usually by a penis. Such a narrow understanding of what constitutes sex has led to some serious misunderstandings about LGBTQ+ sex, especially that of lesbians and bisexual women. But LGBTQ+ sexual behavior often includes activities that do not involve genital contact: kissing, hugging, touching, rubbing, massage, and cuddling.

Sometimes these activities precede (foreplay) or follow (afterplay) genitally focused sexual activity. Other times, they are an expression of intimacy or sexual interest that occurs independent of penetrative or genitally focused sex. They may reflect: one or more partners' personal tastes; preference for non-penetrative sex; desire to express a wider range of physical intimacy; preference for safer-sex practices; an effort to avoid pregnancy; restrictions on other kinds of sexuality due to a partner's health or age; or other individual differences (Carroll, 2016; Cohen & Byers, 2014; Cohen, Byers, & Walsh, 2008).

Some research has shown that, compared to heterosexual women, lesbians and bisexual women typically engage in a wider range of sexual behaviors, more non-genital sexual behaviors, and for longer durations during each sexual encounter (Nichols, 2004). Romantic holding/cuddling and kissing on the mouth are also commonly reported in the sexual repertories of gay and bisexual men. Some limited research shows that bisexual men are less likely to engage in kissing and romantic holding than their gay male counterparts (Rosenberger et al., 2011).

Non-genital sexual behaviors carry very low risks for transmitting or acquiring STIs—if any participant is STI-infected—however, because they can involve skin-to-skin and mucous membrane contact, and shared body fluids

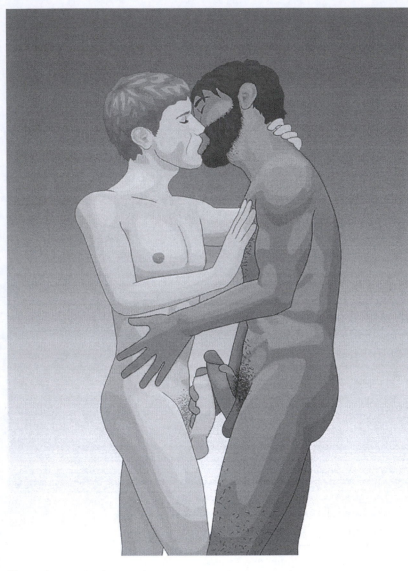

*Two males engaging in mutual masturbation. Source: Adapted from original by Seedfeeder/CC0 1.0 license. Original image courtesy of Wikimedia Commons.*

(such as saliva), they are not risk free. Although small amounts of HIV are present in saliva, open–mouth (French) kissing is considered a very low risk behavior for HIV infection but risk increases if there are sores or bleeding gums in the mouth (Carroll, 2016; Corinna, 2016).

## Masturbation: Solo and Partnered

Masturbation (jerking/whacking off; rubbing one out; polishing the pearl; petting the kitty) is the practice of touching or rubbing the genitals to produce sexual pleasure, usually to the point of orgasm. The word masturbation implies self-stimulation but mutual masturbation is when partners sexually stimulate each other, often simultaneously. Although often viewed with shame or embarrassment, masturbation is now considered beneficial to sexual health. It is how many people first become familiar with their unique sexual anatomy, preferred sexual touch, and capacity for sexual pleasure. It can also be a means for reducing stress and exploring sexual fantasies (Carroll, 2016; Corinna, 2016).

Masturbation commonly involves manual stimulation of the genitals and may involve stimulation of other erogenous zones, such as the chest, breasts, nipples, anus, and rectum. People with vulvas may masturbate using fingers, a dildo, or vibrator to stroke or rub the labia and clitoris, or penetrate the vagina. Those with a penis and testicles may masturbate by grasping the penis in a loose fist and repeatedly moving it the length of the penis. Those with an uncircumcised penis may also move their foreskin back and forth across the glans penis. No matter the shape of the genitals, masturbation may involve use of personal lubricants, erotica, or pornography (Carroll, 2016; Corinna, 2016; Moon & diamond, 2015; Silverstein & Picano, 2006).

Solo masturbation carries no STI risks, but partnered masturbation that involves contact with a partner's skin, mucous membranes, or body fluids (saliva, semen, pre-cum, vaginal fluids, rectal mucus, blood, etc.) does carry some STI risks if any participant is STI-infected. However, STI risk is low compared to penetrative oral, vaginal, or anal sex (Carroll, 2016; Corinna, 2016).

Although it is often represented as a source of shame or embarrassment, masturbation is a very common sexual activity. Of all Americans over age 14, 78% report having masturbated at some point in their lives, with highest percentages reported by men (over 90%) and women (around 80%) in their 20s and 30s (Herbenick et al., 2010). Some research has shown that over 90% of WSW have some lifetime experience with masturbation (O'Mara, 2012). Gay and bisexual men's rates of masturbation do not appear to differ from those of their heterosexual male counterparts, and 60%–70% of White and Latino gay and bisexual men report having engaged in masturbation during their most recent sexual encounter with a man (Rosenberger et al., 2011; Schnarrs et al., 2012). Transgender rates of masturbation are not known but comfort with the function and appearance of genitals can affect how, and how often, a person masturbates (Hill-Meyer & Scarborough, 2014).

## Oral Sex

Oral sex typically refers to the stimulation of a partner's genitals or other erogenous zones using the mouth, lips, teeth, or tongue, often aided by hands or fingers, potentially resulting in orgasm. The technical term for oral sex focused on the vulva, vagina, or clitoris is cunnilingus (eating out; muff diving). The term for oral sex focused on the penis or testicles is fellatio (blowjob; giving head; sucking off). Anilingus is the technical term for oral sex focused on the anus (rimming; rim job) (Carroll, 2016; Corinna, 2016).

Oral sex may be the sole activity, or one of several different activities, within a single sexual encounter. Oral sex can be pleasurable due to friction from mouthparts on sensitive skin, aided by lubrication from saliva. Individual preferences for giving or receiving oral sex vary and because sexual anatomies, preferred sexual touch, and the body's potential for sexual pleasure can vary, communication between sexual partners is key to pleasurable oral sex (Corinna, 2016; Moon & diamond, 2015; Silverstein & Picano, 2006).

Beyond pleasure, some practice oral sex to avoid pregnancy or reduce exposure to certain STIs. Oral sex carries higher risk for STIs—if any participant is STI-infected—because it can involve skin-to-skin and mucous membrane

contact, and shared body fluids (saliva, semen, "pre-cum," vaginal fluids, rectal mucus, menstrual fluid/blood, etc.). The types of STIs that may be transmitted vary depending on the body parts involved. Contact between the mucous membranes of the mouth and those of the penis, vagina, or anus carries risks for chlamydia, HPV, gonorrhea, syphilis, herpes. In addition, oral-anal contact can transmit Hepatitis A and B, Shigella, gonorrhea, and intestinal parasites. Most health experts agree that oral sex carries little or no risk for HIV infection, but risks increase if body fluids enter the mouth, or where mouth sores or bleeding gums are present (Carroll, 2016; Corinna, 2016).

*Two females engaging in oral sex (also known as "cunnilingus"). Source: Adapted from original by Seedfeeder/CC BY-SA 3.0 license. Original image courtesy of Wikimedia Commons.*

Oral sex is a very common sexual activity with large majorities—up to 90% for some age groups—of females and males reporting either giving or receiving oral sex in their lifetimes (Herbenick et al., 2010). Perhaps surprisingly, many self-identified lesbians and bisexual women (83%) and gay and bisexual men (63%) also report some lifetime experience with heterosexual oral sex (Copen, Chandra, & Febo-Vazquez, 2016). Regarding same-sex oral sex, roughly 2%–15% of U.S. women and men—regardless of how they identify sexually—report having given or received oral sex with a same-sex partner at some point in their lives (Herbenick et al., 2010). Rates of same-sex oral sex among African-American women (12%–13%) and Latinas (10%–12%) are lower than among White women. About 7% of African-American and 11%–13% of Latino men have given or received oral sex from another man (Dodge et al., 2010).

Numerous studies have shown that well over 90% of lesbians have some lifetime experience with oral sex with another woman (O'Mara, 2012). Among gay and bisexual men, oral sex is the most commonly reported sexual activity, with around 75% either giving or receiving oral sex during their most recent same-sex sexual encounter (Rosenberger et al., 2011; Schnarrs et al., 2012). Other studies have found that as many as 90% of MSM engaged in oral sex during their last sexual encounter (Taylor et al., 2012). As with masturbation, little is known about the rate or prevalence of oral sex among transgender people, but how and whether it is practiced is likely to be affected by individual and partner preferences, comfort with appearance and function of genitals and other erogenous zones, and (in cases of medically altered bodies) sensitivity of skin to sexual touch (Hill-Meyer & Scarborough, 2014).

## Vaginal Sex

Vaginal sex involves the stimulation or penetration of the vagina by a penis, fingers/hands, other body part, or object (like a sex toy, dildo or vibrator). It can also involve stimulation of the vulva, clitoris, and labia. Vaginal sex can occur in a wide variety of positions that allow contact with, or penetration of, a partner's vulva or vagina. For WSW, positions that allow vulva-to-vulva contact or rubbing of genitals on a partner's thigh is sometimes called tribadism or (more commonly) scissoring. The term fisting describes penetration of the vagina with all the fingers on one hand (but not usually an entire fist) (Carroll, 2016; Corinna, 2016; Moon & diamond, 2015).

A wide variety of dildos, vibrators, and other sex toys may also be used to penetrate the vagina during vaginal sex. Some of these resemble a penis; others are phallic shaped; while still others are designed to avoid any similarity to a penis. Some vibrators and dildos are designed to simultaneously stimulate the clitoris and penetrate the vagina, or penetrate the vagina and anus. Sex toy retailers sell leather, fabric, or rubber garments (strap-on; harness) that fit around the legs and/or waist, and hold a dildo or vibrator. This allows WSW to penetrate a partner's vagina with thrusts of the hips while leaving their hands free to support their weight or engage in other sexual activities. Pressure or friction from the base of the dildo or vibrator may also provide the harness-wearing partner pleasure during vaginal penetration (Moon & diamond, 2015; Newman, 2004).

The muscles that line the vaginal canal stretch to allow childbirth, thus the vagina can accommodate a hand, fist, large penis, or sex toy. Most vaginas are more resilient and less easily damaged by penetration than the anus and rectum, however FtM transgender people (transmen) who undergo hormone therapy can experience a thinning of the vaginal lining and loss of vaginal self-lubrication. When choosing sex toys, use common sense—avoid corners and sharp objects and use plenty of personal lubricant (Carroll, 2016; Corinna, 2016; Hill-Meyer & Scarborough, 2014).

Unlike the rectum, which is a much longer tube, the vagina is a "cul-de-sac" that terminates in the cervix (the entrance to the uterus). Depending on individual anatomy, longer sex toys/fingers/hands/penises may not fit entirely within a vagina, and not everyone with a vagina enjoys pressure on the cervix during penetration. Moreover, not everyone with a vagina enjoys vaginal penetration. FtM transgender people (transmen) who have not had gender confirmation (bottom) surgery may or may not engage in vaginal (or front hole) penetration if it contributes to body

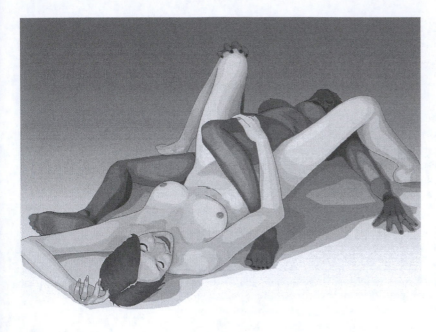

*Two females engaging in a type of vaginal sex called "scissoring." Source: Adapted from original by Seedfeeder/ CC BY-SA 3.0 license. Original image courtesy of Wikimedia Commons.*

dysmorphia or is physically painful (Hill–Meyer & Scarborough, 2014). As with other sexual activities, communication about preferred names for specific body parts, sexual touch, and activities is key to pleasurable vaginal penetration (Moon & diamond, 2014; Newman, 2004).

The labia and clitoris contain many nerve endings but there are comparatively few inside the vagina, and most people with vaginas cannot orgasm solely from vaginal penetration. Much of the pleasure of vaginal penetration seems to come from stimulation of the G spot and the internal parts of the clitoris—such as the clitoral bulbs and crura and the G spot—that surround the vagina. But for many, simultaneous clitoral stimulation, anal penetration, or stimulation of other body parts, such as chest or nipples, is often required for orgasm. Although many vaginas may self-lubricate when sexually aroused, some may require additional lubrication for pleasurable penetration and to reduce STI risks (Carroll, 2016; Corinna, 2016; Hill–Meyer & Scarborough, 2014).

Vaginal sex, especially without use of barriers (condoms, latex gloves, etc.), carries a high risk for many STIs, if any participant is STI-infected. Skin-to-skin and mucous membrane contact, and shared body fluids or sex toys, can allow gonorrhea, syphilis, HPV, herpes, and chlamydia to pass between partners. Body parts (hands, fingers, penis, clitoris) and shared sex toys (vibrators, dildos) that are used during vaginal sex may also pass STI-infected body fluids between partners. If a participant is HIV positive, penetrative vaginal sex carries a high risk for HIV transmission, especially if HIV-infected body fluids (saliva, semen, "pre-cum," vaginal fluids, rectal mucus, menstrual fluid/blood, etc.) are shared between partners. As with anal sex, insertive partners are less at risk for HIV infection than receptive partners. However, because vaginal tissue is usually not as easily damaged as anal or rectal tissue, the risks of HIV infection during vaginal sex are lower than for anal sex (Connell, 2016; Corinna, 2016; Deol & Heath-Toby, 2009; Dolan & Davis, 2010). Due to thinning of vaginal membranes caused by testosterone therapy, FtM transgender people (transmen) who assume a receptive role in vaginal sex (front hole penetration) can be at higher risk for acquiring STIs, especially HIV (Hill-Meyer & Scarborough, 2014; Kenagy & Hsieh, 2005). STI risks for MtF transgender people (transwomen) with surgically constructed vaginas who assume a receptive role in vaginal sex is not precisely known.

Vaginal sex is the most commonly reported sexual behavior. By their mid-to-late 20s, about 90% of men and women have had vaginal sex (Herbenick et al., 2010). Even many gay/bisexual men (64%) and lesbians/bisexual women (89%) report some lifetime experience with heterosexual vaginal sex (Copen, Chandra, & Febo-Vazquez, 2016). The lesbian culture website Autostraddle.com found that 97% of self-identified lesbian, bisexual, or queer women engaged in vaginal stimulation with fingers or hands during their last sexual encounter, but only about half engaged in vaginal penetration using a dildo, vibrator, or strap-on harness, and less than 20% engaged in vaginal fisting (Autostraddle.com, 2015). A study of partnered lesbian women in Canada and the U.S. found about a fifth engaged in vaginal sex weekly; 15% did so monthly; and 19% never did (Cohen & Byers, 2014). Other research has found that lesbians engage in manual vaginal stimulation, use dildos/vibrators, and experience vulva-to-vulva contact in well over half of their sexual encounters (Bailey et al., 2003; O'Mara, 2012).

## Anal Sex

Anal sex (fucking; being/getting fucked) is the stimulation or penetration of the anus and or rectum using fingers, hand, penis, clitoris, or sex toy such as a vibrator or dildo. Stimulation typically involves touching, massaging, and/or penetration of the anus into the rectum. Some people can orgasm solely from anal stimulation but most need some form of additional or simultaneous attention to the penis, clitoris, or other sensitive body parts. Anal sex may be practiced with penetration from behind when standing, lying on the stomach, lying on the side, or on hands-and-knees (doggy style). Face to face positions, with either partner on top, are also used. Different positions can offer different forms of pleasure depending on an individual's anatomy and preferences, so communication and some experimentation are often necessary for full enjoyment of anal sex (Carroll, 2016; Corinna, 2016; Moon & diamond, 2015; Silverstein & Picano, 2006).

A wide variety of intertwined individual, social, and cultural factors influence whether a person assumes the insertive (top) or receptive (bottom) role in anal sex. Some individuals have distinct sex-role preferences while others (versatiles) will perform either role, sometimes within a single sexual encounter with the same partner. Preferred sex role or position may also be influenced by prior experiences with anal sex, sexual identity, gender expression (with partners perceived to be more masculine playing top), relative genital size (for MSM), race/ethnicity, age, education, wealth, and employment status. Others may choose a certain role to reduce their or their partner's exposure to certain STIs, or because of the cultural significance attached to specific roles (with "tops" often viewed as more masculine, and "bottoms" often seen as more feminine) (Lick & Johnson, 2015; Sandfort & Dodge, 2008; Schnarrs et al., 2012; Zeglin, 2015).

*Two males engaging in anal sex. Source: Adapted from original by Seedfeeder/CC BY-SA 3.0 license. Original image courtesy of Wikimedia Commons.*

Although anal sex is often represented in popular culture as painful, undesirable, and even shameful or humiliating, it can be a source of pleasure for both receptive and insertive partners. Insertive partners may enjoy anal sex due to the friction and pressure applied to the penetrating body part by the receptive partner's anal sphincters and rectum. Even if the penetrating object is not a body part, insertive partners may find anal sex enjoyable simply from knowing their partner is enjoying being penetrated. Others find the act pleasurable because they perceive it as a form of (mutually consensual) dominance over their partners (Corinna, 2016; Moon & diamond, 2016; Silverstein & Picano, 2006).

Receptive partners may experience pleasure from anal sex due to the stimulation of nerve endings in the anus and rectum, and nearby muscles, nerves, and organs connected to the genitals. Receptive partners with prostate glands may find this sensitive organ stimulated during anal sex, depending on the penetrating organ or object, and the angle of penetration. Receptive partners with a clitoris may find that anal penetration also stimulates internal parts of the clitoris and clitoral system. For *all* receptive partners, anal sex can produce feelings of openness, loss of control, and vulnerability requiring trust in one's partner, which can contribute to feelings of intimacy during sex. Others enjoy feeling (consensually) dominated or subordinated by the insertive partner during anal sex, or experience pleasure solely from knowing that their partners experience pleasure in the act. For some people, the pleasure of anal sex may be enhanced by its reputation as a taboo or forbidden sexual activity (Corinna, 2016; Moon & diamond, 2016; Silverstein & Picano, 2006).

For the receptive partner, anal sex can be an uncomfortable or painful experience if not approached with knowledge, patience, and care. Oral-anal sex (anilingus; rimming) or massage using fingers or sex toys can temporarily stretch the anal sphincters to allow anal penetration. But, unlike most vaginas, the anus and rectum do not self-lubricate when sexually stimulated, so personal lubricant is often necessary for safe and pleasurable anal sex. Commercial personal lubricants can increase sensitivity and reduce friction (that can damage delicate anal and rectal tissues). Because oil-based lubricants may cause latex condoms, gloves, and dental dams to break, and silicone-based lubricants may damage silicone sex toys, water-based lubes are generally recommended for anal penetration. Although the rectum is flexible and can accommodate a large penis, sex toy, hand, or fist, the insertion of long or large objects should only be attempted with care and experience. To avoid an embarrassing emergency-room visit, use flexible, smooth-surfaced sex toys or other objects having a flared base, handle, or other design features that prevent complete insertion past the anal sphincters. Nothing with sharp points, edges, or corners should be inserted into the anus or rectum. Carefully trim fingernails or use latex gloves for anal play involving the fingers, hands, or fist. Flushing the rectum with warm water (an enema) can make anal sex more hygienic, less messy, and potentially reduce STI risk (Corinna, 2016; Moon & diamond, 2014; Newman, 2004).

To enhance pleasure and facilitate penetration, some people inhale liquid alkyl nitrites (poppers) during anal sex. Alkyl nitrites cause muscle tissue around blood vessels to relax, producing a drop in blood pressure and an increased heart rate as the heart pumps harder to re-supply blood to the brain and other organs. Alkyl nitrites users experience brief feelings of euphoria (a head rush or "high") and relaxation of anal sphincters, making anal penetration easier and less painful. However, if used in combination with some other drugs (including Viagra) alkyl nitrites can cause an unsafe drop in blood pressure. They may also damage eyesight and can cause feelings of detachment and lowered inhibitions associated with increased sexual risk-taking. Long a staple of gay male and dance club culture, poppers are illegal in many places but still sold in some bars, sex shops, and novelty stores as "deodorizers," "leather cleaners," or "aromas" (Colfax et al., 2001; Colfax et al., 2005; Silverstein & Picano, 2006).

Anal sex—especially penetrative anal sex without the use of barriers such as condoms, latex gloves, etc.—carries a high risk for most STIs, if any participant is STI-infected. Penetrative anal sex without condoms or other barriers (barebacking; breeding; seeding) increases risk, especially if body fluids such as blood, semen, or "pre-cum" are exchanged between partners. Skin-to-skin and mucous membrane contact allows gonorrhea, syphilis, HPV, herpes, and chlamydia to pass between partners. HIV-infected body fluids may also be passed between partners via shared sex toys. Contact between HIV-infected body fluids (semen, "pre-cum," or rectal mucus) and mucous membranes (of the anus, rectum, urethra, or foreskin lining) is the most common route of HIV infection among MSM. Even with careful preparation and use of lubricants, anal, rectal, and foreskin tissues are easily damaged during penetrative anal sex, and small tears can allow HIV-infected body fluids to enter a partner's bloodstream. Receptive partners in anal sex are at much greater risk for STI infection than insertive partners. However, insertive partners can become infected via contact between HIV-infected rectal mucus and the penile urethra, the lining of the foreskin (if uncircumcised), or the skin of the penis if it is damaged or broken (perhaps from extended sexual activity). The risk of HIV infection for insertive partners when the penetrating body part is a finger, hand, fist, clitoris, or other body part is unknown but is likely to be low unless cuts or broken skin are present (Carroll, 2016; Corinna, 2016; Deol & Heath-Toby, 2009; Wilton, 2012).

Although popular culture often represents anal sex as solely a "gay" sexual activity, research shows it to be much more widely practiced. About half of heterosexual women and men in the U.S. have engaged in some form of anal sex during their lifetime (Herbenick et al., 2010; McBride & Fortenberry, 2010). Little research has been conducted on anal sex among WSW, however it appears to be uncommon. One study of partnered lesbian women in Canada and the U.S. found that 7% engaged in anal stimulation or penetration at least once a week. Another 10% did so monthly and 70% did not at all (Cohen & Byers, 2014). Other research has found that only 16% of lesbians "sometimes" or "regularly" engaged in anal stimulation (O'Mara, 2012). Rates of anal sex among transgender women and men are not well understood.

Depending on age, 4%–11% of U.S. men report any lifetime experience receiving a penis in their anus, with highest rates reported by men ages 20–24 and 50–59 (Herbenick et al., 2010). About 7% of African-American men and 9% of Latino men report "bottoming" at some point in their lives (Dodge et al., 2010). Research focused on self-identified gay and bisexual men has found that three-fourths of self-identified gay men had some lifetime experience with anal sex, with equal percentages playing insertive and receptive roles (Underwood, 2003). Yet, even though large percentages of gay and bisexual men have some lifetime experience with anal sex, they seem to engage in this sexual activity much less frequently than stereotypes suggest. Insertive and receptive anal sex were some of the least common sexual behaviors reported by gay and bisexual men in their most recent same-sex sexual encounter. In that encounter, younger and gay men reported they were more likely to have taken the receptive position (bottomed) and older and bisexual men were more likely to have taken the insertive role (topped) (Dodge et al., 2013; Rosenberger et al., 2011; Schnarrs et al., 2012).

Hispanic and Black MSM are more likely than their White peers to have had anal sex during their last sexual encounter, however they also report less frequent anal sex overall and greater condom use during anal sex (Schnarrs et al., 2012; Taylor et al., 2012). Some research has found that Latino MSM's preferred sexual role is correlated with gender presentation, with the more masculine partner playing the insertive role and the more feminine assuming a receptive position. This gendered anal-sex role positioning, where penetrating is deemed masculine and honorable and being penetrated is deemed feminized and dishonorable, is most widely reported among MSM in Latin America and recent Latino immigrants to the U.S. (Gutmann & Vigoya, 2005; Kulick, 1997; Lancaster, 1988). However, other research focused on U.S. Latinos has found Latino MSM to be more sexually versatile, with anal-sex role position influenced by a wider range of sexual partners' traits. Older, employed, and better educated Latino MSM report more often playing the insertive role in anal sex, with their younger, under- or unemployed, and less educated partners more often taking the receptive position. This suggests that Latino MSM anal-sex role positioning may be less a matter of personal preference or gender presentation than it is about partners' relative social status, of which gender presentation is but one aspect (Carballo-Diéguez et al., 2004; Schnarrs et al., 2012).

## BDSM

The term BDSM is derived from three other terms: B&D (bondage and discipline); D&S (dominance and submission); and S&M (sadism and masochism). BDSM play may also be referred to as "kink/kinky," "leather," or "fetish" play. BDSM is practiced by a small minority people having a wide variety of sexes, genders, and sexual orientations—including cisgender and heterosexual people. Though there is a significant overlap between LGBTQ+ leather communities and BDSM enthusiasts, BDSM is not a solely LGBTQ+ activity. But because BDSM involves giving and receiving pleasure within a kind of social relationship that is not typically sanctioned in hetero-normative societies (such as temporary, negotiated, non-monogamous, non-procreative, etc.), BDSM can be considered a "queer" (or non-normative) sexual practice (Bauer, 2014; Corinna, 2016; Silverstein & Picano, 2006).

BDSM refers to the use of power, sensation, or specific objects or clothing (fetishes) to elicit erotic (sometimes sexual) pleasure and experience personal growth/self-knowledge, often through pain or discomfort. BDSM comprises a wide range of activities (called play) that take place within a ritualized context (a scene), the nature and boundaries of which are negotiated and agreed upon in advance by the participants. Scenes can involve cross-dressing, gender/power reversals, and temporary explorations of gender or sexual roles. They may also employ a variety of tools or implements, including rope, handcuffs, paddles, leather floggers/whips, mouth gags, nipple clamps, silk fabric, ice, hot wax, and feathers. A scene may or may not include activities typically regarded as sexual (such as genital stimulation, penetration, or orgasm). Rather, pleasure is derived from pain, restraint/confinement, extreme sensations, and temporary dominance over/submission to another (Corinna, 2016; Newman, 2004; Silverstein & Picano, 2006).

BDSM "power play" involves the consensual exchange of power between partners who assume roles: one role is dominant (a dom or top); and one is submissive (a sub or bottom). Doms accept power surrendered by a sub, guide BDSM play, and provide sensation, restraint/confinement, or activities that involve pain/discomfort. Subs follow a dom's direction, receive sensation/restraint/confinement, and surrender power to a dom. The temporary role played in a scene operates independent of the participants' sex, gender, or sexual orientation. Dom/sub roles are temporary and negotiated; they may be interchangeable (a switch), or a person may prefer/identify with the same (dom or sub) role in every scene.

BDSM "sensation play" uses tools or techniques to elicit erotic or sexual pleasure through extreme sensations, including cold, heat, tickling, and pain.

"Fetish play" can involve acting out fantasy scenarios using objects or garments that produce erotic or sexual feelings, including clothing (such as rubber or latex garments; military/professional uniforms), corsets, leather harnesses, stiletto heels, and so on. "Puppy play" is a BDSM role play activity in which a person dons a leather canine mask and assumes the demeanor of a playful puppy to release stress and embrace their animal instincts.

Subjecting someone to pain, confinement, or sexual contact without their express consent is potentially a crime—assault, kidnapping, etc. Thus, BDSM practitioners have adopted negotiated consent frameworks to guide BDSM play. Two common frameworks are "safe, sane, consensual" and "RACK" (Risk Aware Consensual Kink). In principle, participants in BDSM agree in advance on the nature of a scene and their individual boundaries, as well as a "safe" word that, when uttered, stops play immediately and without question. Practiced within a consent framework, BDSM can produce intense erotic experiences marked by care, mutual respect, and clear communication about desires and limits (Bauer, 2014; Corinna, 2016).

BDSM carries little STI risk unless there is sexual penetration (without barriers), piercing/blood play, or exchange of body fluids (Corinna, 2016). BDSM "kinksters" have established the vibrant online community FetLife where those interested in exploring BDSM play can learn about various practices, identities, and consent frameworks. BDSM clothing and accessories are sold at sex shops and via the Internet.

## Lesbian "Bed Death"

Lesbian "bed death" is a term often used to describe a decline in frequency of sexual activity in lesbian relationships over time. The concept originated from an early-1980s study that found lesbians had a lower sexual frequency than gay male and heterosexual couples (Blumstein & Schwartz, 1983). By the early 1990s the term lesbian "bed death" was widely used among researchers (and many lesbians) to explain any decline in frequency of sexual activity. One common explanation was that women (including lesbian women) had been socialized to be sexually inhibited and thus a relationship between two women increased the odds of low sexual frequency (Iasenza, 2002). Another theory held that lesbians had a lower libido because of internalized homophobia or stress due to being a sexual minority in a heterosexist society (Nichols, 2004).

Skeptical researchers began to question whether "sexual frequency" was the best measure of lesbian couples' sexual well-being. Moreover, some studies describing lesbian "bed death" defined "sex" as a genitally focused activity having the goal of orgasm. While it is true that heterosexual sex tends to be more focused on genital contact and orgasm, lesbians tend to have longer sexual encounters that involve the entire body not just the breasts or genitals. Their sexual encounters also do not always have orgasm as a primary goal (Iasenza, 2002; Nichols, 2004; O'Mara, 2012).

Using this broader definition of sex, researchers found lesbians to be more sexually arousable and sexually assertive, and more comfortable using erotic language than heterosexual women. They report less sexual dysfunction and higher levels of satisfaction with the quality of their sex lives (Iasenza, 2002). They also place a higher value on sexual reciprocity: giving and receiving pleasure by both partners. Though some research has found lesbians in long-term relationships experience a decrease in frequency of sexual activity, this seems to be related to a variety of issues and stressors: health issues related to age; the presence of children in the household; partner differences in levels of sexual desire; emotional and physical effects of medications; and the long-term effects of incest, rape, or sexual assault (Cohen & Byers, 2014; Iasenza, 2002; Nichols, 2005). But, overall, lesbian couples do not seem to experience a lower frequency of sexual activity than heterosexual women (Matthews, Tartaro, & Hughes, 2002), and lesbian relationships on average do not become asexual or platonic (Nichols, 2004).

## WRAP IT UP! SEXUAL HEALTH

### Sexually Transmitted Infections (STIs)

Sexually transmitted infections (STIs; sometimes also called sexually transmitted diseases [STDs]) result from contact with certain microorganisms—mainly parasites, bacteria, and viruses—that can infect the skin, mucus membranes, or body fluids. STIs are spread during sexual activity through physical contact or sharing body fluids with an STI-infected sexual partner. Regardless of the sexual activity, it is not possible for an STI to be transmitted or acquired during a sexual encounter if no STI microorganisms are present.

There are an estimated 20 million new STI infections each year in the United States, half of them among teens and young adults aged 15–24. The total number of new and existing STI infections in the U.S. is estimated at 110 million. The U.S. Centers for Disease Control and Prevention (CDC) estimates that half of all sexually active people will get an STI by age 25 (Barton et al., 2016; Satterwhite et al., 2013). The direct costs to the U.S. healthcare system of treating the eight most common STIs is estimated at nearly $16 billion (Owusu-Edusei et al., 2013).

Due to a variety of social, cultural, and behavioral factors, LGBTQ+ people are disproportionately affected by STIs. STI rates are generally lower among lesbians than bisexual or heterosexual women, but gay men's STI rates are generally higher than bisexual and heterosexual men's. MSM (including gay and bisexual men) account for much of recent increases in national STI infection rates (Barton et al., 2016; Jeffries, 2014). The rate and prevalence of most STIs among transgender people is not well understood, partly because nationally reported STI infection data does not distinguish between transgender and cisgender women and men. However, other research suggests that transgender people may be at high risk for certain STIs (such as HIV) but infection rates and risk factors are likely to differ for transgender women and transgender men (Grant et al., 2011; Stephens, Bernstein, & Philip, 2011; Workowski & Bolan, 2015). The following sections discuss those STIs that most impact LGBTQ+ people.

Despite being a risk group for many STIs, LGBTQ+ people (and everyone else) can enjoy a robust and satisfying sex life without ever acquiring an STI. It is important to remember: *identifying as LGBTQ+ is not itself a risk factor for STIs*. Rather, STIs are spread through specific behaviors that transmit STI micro-organisms between infected and uninfected sexual partners—no matter how those partners identify. Avoiding STIs requires: becoming informed about how STIs are spread; developing a personal strategy for managing STI risk (which may include safer-sex practices); getting regularly tested and asking partners to be tested; getting treated for any STIs; and communicating openly and honestly about STIs with potential sexual partners.

## Bacterial STIs

### Bacterial vaginosis

Bacterial vaginosis (BV) is a bacterial infection of the mucous membranes lining the vagina. It often has no symptoms but there may be itching, burning while urinating, a thin white or gray vaginal discharge, or a strong fishy odor. BV is the most common vaginal infection in sexually active women aged 15–44. It is estimated that as many as a third of U.S. cisgender women, and a quarter to half of all lesbians, have BV. Transgender men who have not surgically modified their genitals (bottom surgery) may also be susceptible to BV (Carroll, 2016; Corinna, 2016; Workowski & Bolan, 2015).

It is not known if sexual activity contributes to BV but researchers theorize that shared vaginal fluids might contribute to BV in WSW because infected partners often have the same bacterial strain. Having new or multiple sexual partners, sharing sex toys, and vaginal douching also seem to increase risk for BV. BV puts cisgender women at risk of developing pelvic inflammatory disease (PID), which can cause infertility, and contracting more serious STIs such as HIV, chlamydia, herpes, and gonorrhea. It can also cause early childbirth (Workowski & Bolan, 2015).

Testing for BV involves lab tests of samples of vaginal fluid, and treatment with prescription oral, gel, or cream antibiotics. Sometimes BV will go away without treatment. BV may be prevented by avoiding vaginal douching, limiting numbers of sexual partners, using condoms (or other barriers) for penetrative vaginal sex, and cleaning any shared sex toys that come into contact with vaginal fluids (Workowski & Bolan, 2015).

### Gonorrhea

Gonorrhea (the clap; the drip) is caused by the bacterium *Neisseria gonorrhoeae*. It can infect the warm, moist mucous membranes of the urethra, vagina, throat, and rectum. It is transmitted when sexual partners' mucous membranes come into contact during vaginal, anal, or oral sex—and one partner is infected with gonorrhea. It can also be passed from a gonorrhea-infected birth parent to an infant at birth. Gonorrhea often has no symptoms or may be mistaken for a bladder or vaginal infection. Symptoms may include a white, yellow, or green discharge from the vagina or penis, pain during urination, and painful testicles. Rectal gonorrheal infections can have no symptoms, or they can display discharge, itching, soreness, bleeding, or painful bowel movements. Gonorrhea infections of the throat may cause a sore throat or have no symptoms (Carroll, 2016; Corinna, 2016; Workowski & Bolan, 2015).

Although gonorrhea infection rates fell to historic lows in 2009, they have since increased. In 2015 nearly 400,000 new gonorrhea infections were reported in the U.S. (with an estimated 820,000 total infections). The rate of infection increased 13% between 2014 and 2015, with rates highest among teens and young adults (aged 15–29), Native Americans, Latinos, and African Americans (Barton et al., 2016). Although it is not commonly passed during sexual activity between women, WSW can still become infected with gonorrhea. MSM who engage in oral and anal sex are at higher risk for gonorrhea infections of the throat and rectum. Specific gonorrhea infection rates and risks are not known for transgender people but some research has found elevated rates of infection (ODPHP, 2010a; Workowski & Bolan, 2015).

Screening for gonorrhea involves laboratory tests of urine or fluid samples collected from the urethra, vagina, throat, or rectum. Treatment is usually with oral or injected antibiotics. Unfortunately, drug-resistant strains of gonorrhea bacteria have been detected so it is important to take all the prescribed medication and follow up with a health professional if symptoms continue or reappear (Workowski & Bolan, 2015).

If left untreated gonorrhea can cause PID (in people with uteruses) and a painful condition of the testicles that can lead to sterility (in people with penises and testicles). More rarely, gonorrhea can also spread to the joints or heart valves. Gonorrhea infection also increases the chances of getting or transmitting HIV (Barton et al., 2016).

### Syphilis

Syphilis is caused by the bacterium *Treponema pallidum*. Like gonorrhea it lives in the body's mucous membranes. It is transmitted through contact with a syphilis sore during vaginal, oral, or anal sex. Chancre sores are smooth, round, and usually painless. They can occur on the penis, vagina, anus, rectum, scrotum, lips, or mouth. Syphilis can also be transmitted to a fetus during pregnancy (Carroll, 2016; Corinna, 2016).

A syphilis infection may have no symptoms or symptoms that do not appear for years. During the primary stage, syphilis produces chancre sores, usually at the spot where the bacterium entered the body, and they usually appear 10–90 days after infection and last 3–6 weeks. Because sores can be hidden in the mouth, vagina, or rectum, it may not be obvious that a sexual partner has syphilis. If not

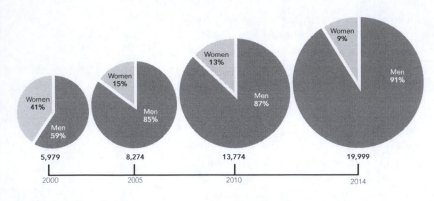

*Reported number of primary and secondary syphilis cases in the U.S. (2000–2014). Source: Adapted from original by U.S. Centers for Disease Control and Prevention.*

treated, syphilis progresses to secondary stage, characterized by skin rashes and mucous membrane lesions. Typically, the reddish rash does not itch, and can occur on the palms of hands or soles of feet. Other symptoms may include fever, swollen lymph nodes, sore throat, hair loss, headaches, weight loss, muscle aches, and fatigue. Without treatment, syphilis progresses to the latent and late states. During the latent (or hidden) stage, a person may have no symptoms for years. Late stage syphilis affects about 15% of untreated cases and can occur 10–30 years after infection. Late stage syphilis can damage the internal organs and nervous system, including the brain, heart, bones, and joints. Organ damage may be so severe that it causes death (Barton et al., 2016; Workowski & Bolan, 2015).

The rate of new syphilis infections in the U.S. reached a historic low in 2000–2001 but has increased nearly every year since. There was a 19% increase in new (primary and secondary) infections from 2014 to 2015, with nearly 24,000 new cases reported—the highest rate since 1994. A 2014–2015 increase in congenital syphilis infections (passed to an infant at birth) also suggests higher infection rates among women. Between 2000 and 2015 men, particularly MSM, accounted for most of the increase in infection rates. But in 2015 increased infection rates were found across all social groups, with highest rates among men aged 20–34, MSM, African Americans, Native Americans, and Latinos. Syphilis can be transmitted between WSW, and infection via oral sex has been reported, but this is rare. Specific syphilis infection rates and risks are not known for transgender people but some research has found elevated rates of infection (Barton et al., 2016; ODPHP, 2010a; Workowski & Bolan, 2015).

Increased national syphilis infection rates may be due to more comprehensive testing (which can detect syphilis before symptoms appear), and to less access to STI prevention education, testing, and treatment, due to deep budget cuts to public health department STI clinics and programs. Syphilis rates have risen more rapidly in states that have cut their budgets the most (Barton et al., 2016; Khazan & Berman, 2016).

Recent years have seen syphilis outbreaks in areas with large gay male populations (Chicago, Seattle, San Francisco, Southern California, Miami and New York City) and about half of MSM diagnosed with syphilis also test positive for HIV (Barton et al., 2016). Syphilis sores can bleed easily, making it easier for HIV to be transmitted between sexual partners.

Syphilis is diagnosed with a simple blood test and can be easily treated in its early stages with a single antibiotic injection. Latent-stage infections can require multiple weekly antibiotic injections (Workowski & Bolan, 2015).

### Chlamydia

Chlamydia is caused by the bacterium *Chlamydia trachomatis*. It is transmitted via the mouth, vagina, anus, or penis during vaginal, oral, or anal sex. It can also be passed from a chlamydia-infected birth parent to an infant during childbirth. Chlamydia is often called the "silent infection" because it may have no symptoms, but some common symptoms are abnormal vaginal or penile discharge, burning sensation during urination, or pain/swelling of the testicles. Rectal infections might cause pain, discharge, or bleeding, but infections of the throat typically do not have any symptoms. Symptoms may not appear until several weeks after infection. If left untreated, chlamydia can cause serious health problems, including PID. Chlamydia infection also increases the risk of acquiring HIV (Carroll, 2016; Corinna, 2016; Workowski & Bolan, 2015).

Chlamydia is the most frequently reported STI. In 2015 there were over 1.5 million new chlamydia infections reported in the U.S. and an estimated 2.86 million total infections. Numbers of new infections increased 6% from 2014 to 2015, with teens and young adults (aged 15–24), Native Americans, African Americans, and Latinos most affected. Chlamydia infection rates are twice as high among women than men, but rates among men have been climbing. Some of the increase is due to more comprehensive testing that better detects chlamydia infection in men. Chlamydia is common among MSM, with rectal and throat infection rates as high as 10% of MSM. Some research has found chlamydia infection rates to be slightly higher among WSW and WSWM, probably spread via oral sex, sexual activities that include vaginal penetration with fingers and hands, and shared sex toys (Singh, Fine, & Marrazzo, 2011). Specific chlamydia infection rates and risks are not known for transgender people but some research has found elevated infection rates (Barton et al., 2016; ODPHP, 2010a).

Chlamydia screening involves lab tests of urine, and throat, rectal, and vaginal fluids. Treatment is usually with oral antibiotics. Unless sexual partners are tested and treated, re-infection can occur (Workowski & Bolan, 2015).

## Viral STIs

### Hepatitis

Hepatitis is the name of a family of viral infections that damage the liver. Hepatitis A results from infection with the Hepatitis A virus, usually from ingesting fecal matter (shit; poop)—even in small amounts—found on objects, hands, food, drink, or through sexual contact with an infected person. It can be spread through direct oral-anal contact (anilingus; rimming) or contact with fingers or objects that contact the anus or rectum of infected persons. Symptoms can include nausea, diarrhea, fatigue, and abdominal pain (Carroll, 2016; CDC, 2016b; Corinna, 2016).

Hepatitis B results from infection with the Hepatitis B virus. It is spread via infected blood, semen, vaginal or other body fluids, usually at birth, or through sexual contact, or sharing drug needles. Symptoms can range from a mild illness (acute form) to a serious, lifelong illness (chronic form).

Hepatitis C is caused by the Hepatitis C virus and is usually transmitted through infected blood by sharing needles and IV drug equipment. It is not commonly transmitted through sexual activity (CDC, 2016b).

In 2014 the CDC estimated there were over 2,500 new Hepatitis A infections and over 18,100 new Hepatitis B infections in the U.S. The total number of Hepatitis B infections is estimated at over 400,000 but overall rates of Hepatitis A and B have declined since vaccines were introduced in the 1990s. In adults, about 10% of new Hepatitis A and 20% of new Hepatitis B cases occur in gay and bisexual men. While 25% of HIV-positive men also are infected with Hepatitis C (CDC, 2016b). Little research has been conducted on the prevalence of hepatitis among WSW (Barton et al., 2016). Some research has found elevated rates of Hepatitis B and C among transgender women, perhaps due to sharing IV needles used to inject hormones or cosmetic silicone (ODPHP, 2010a).

Hepatitis is diagnosed through laboratory blood tests. Mild forms of Hepatitis A and B are treated with rest, fluids, adequate nutrition, and anti-viral medications. Most people feel sick for a few months then start to feel better. Acute Hepatitis B usually clears up in less than six months, but the chronic form can cause serious liver disease that requires lifetime medical treatment. Hepatitis C can be treated with anti-viral medications. Vaccines for Hepatitis A and Hepatitis B are now routinely given to children. Currently, there is no vaccine for Hepatitis C but anti-viral drugs can reduce its health impact and potentially eliminate the infection altogether (Workowski & Bolan, 2015).

### Herpes

Herpes is a chronic, lifelong viral infection caused by two different viruses: Herpes simplex virus-1 (HSV-1) and Herpes simplex virus-2 (HSV-2). Cold sores around the mouth are caused by HSV-1, which is typically acquired non-sexually in childhood. HSV-2 causes most cases of anal and genital herpes, however HSV-1 can also be passed sexually and cause anal and genital symptoms. Most people with genital herpes have few if any symptoms, and may not even know they have the disease. The main symptom is small, red, painful blisters at the infection site. They appear 2–12 days after infection and can take two to four weeks to heal. When they break they ooze a yellowish fluid. Sometimes an outbreak of herpes blisters is accompanied by flu-like symptoms (fever, body aches, swollen lymph nodes, headache). Repeat blister outbreaks are common, especially in the first year after infection, but gradually reduce in number and severity over time (Barton et al., 2016; Carroll, 2016; Corinna, 2016).

Herpes can be transmitted during oral, vaginal, or anal sex through contact with a herpes blister, or body fluids such as saliva, semen, and vaginal and rectal mucus. It can also be transmitted through non-sexual contact with a herpes blister. However, it is not necessary for a blister to be present to transmit the virus. Herpes is most contagious at the beginning of an outbreak, even before symptoms appear. Broken herpes blisters bleed easily, which can increase the risk of transmitting or acquiring HIV from sexual partners (Barton et al., 2016; Carroll, 2016; Corinna, 2016).

Genital herpes is common in the United States, although infection rates appear to be in decline. The CDC estimates there were 776,000 new herpes infections in 2013, with over 24 million total infections. Although the overall infection rate is about one in six Americans, rates are significantly higher (one in two) among African Americans and lower among Whites and Latinos. Herpes is more easily transmitted from men to women than women to men, but women are twice as likely as men to be infected (Barton et al., 2016).

There do not appear to be significant differences in rates of HSV-2 in MSM or MSW (Xu, Sternberg, & Markowitz, 2010a). Although some research has shown slightly higher rates of HSV-2 among women who have had female sexual partners, other research has found lower rates among women who self-identify as lesbian or bisexual. Genital transmission of HSV-2 between WSW is possible but difficult, but WSW and WSWM who engage in oral sex may be at higher risk for oral-genital transmission of HSV-1 (Marrazzo, Stine, & Wald, 2003; Workowski & Bolan, 2015; Xu, Sternberg, & Markowitz, 2010b). Herpes infection rates among transgender people is not well understood, however transgender women (who have not undergone gender affirmation surgery) may be at risk for penile transmission/acquisition of herpes (ODPHP, 2010a; Workowski & Bolan, 2015).

Genital herpes is diagnosed through a simple blood test, or lab tests of fluid from a suspected herpes blister. Currently there is no cure for herpes (HSV-1 or HSV-2) but research to produce a vaccine is ongoing. Although barriers (condoms, latex gloves, dental dams) can help prevent the spread of herpes, only covered areas of skin are protected. Oral antiviral medication can reduce the amount of herpes virus in the blood, prevent or shorten outbreaks of herpes blisters, and reduce likelihood of transmitting the virus to sexual partners. Regular testing and use of antiviral medications by those infected are key to reducing sexual transmission of herpes (Workowski & Bolan, 2015).

### Human Papillomavirus (HPV)

HPV is a group of over 40 viruses that can be transmitted via the genitals, mouth, throat, and anus during vaginal, oral, or anal sex. It also can be transmitted through skin-to-skin contact during sexual activity or via shared sex toys, even if there are no visible signs or symptoms. Some HPV viruses cause approximately 90% of anal and genital warts, other types account for approximately 70% of cervical cancer, and still others are responsible for some kinds of throat, penis, rectal, and anal cancer. Anal/genital warts are soft, fleshy bumps that can appear in the vagina, on the vulva, on the shaft of the penis, or around the anus (Barton et al., 2016; Carroll, 2016; Corinna, 2016).

Nearly all sexually active people will get HPV during their lifetime and most will not know they have it. By some estimates HPV is the most common STI in the United States. The CDC estimates there are over 14 million new HPV infections every year, and 79 million Americans living with HPV (Barton et al., 2016). Genital HPV infection is common among WSW and is likely to be transmitted sexually between female partners (Marrazzo et al., 1998). The prevalence of HPV among transgender people is not known but some research has elevated infection rates (ODPHP, 2010a). Sexually active young men are much more likely to be infected with HPV and some studies have found the types of HPV that cause anal cancer in half of MSM (which is four times the rate in MSW) (Machalek et al., 2012; Nyitray et al., 2011). HPV-related anal cancer risk and occurrence is much higher in MSM, especially those who engage in unprotected receptive anal sex (bottoming), and increased risk of throat cancer may be connected to oral sex in MSM (Glick et al., 2013; Goldstone et al., 2011; Palefsky, 2010).

Health professionals can screen for HPV by visually inspecting for genital warts and testing for HPV-related cancers by taking samples of cells from the cervix, anus, rectum, throat, and/or penis. Such cells can be tested for HPV using a DNA test. Cervical tests (also called Pap smears) are part of routine gynecological exams, which should be done annually for anyone with a vagina, uterus, and cervix—no matter how they identify. However, tests for throat, penile, and rectal HPV-related cancers are not typically performed. Anyone who engages in receptive vaginal, anal, or oral sex should discuss their sexual histories with a health professional and undergo the appropriate HPV testing. There is no treatment for HPV, but in most people HPV is cleared from the immune system within two years of infection. Those with compromised immune systems, as with HIV infection, may be less able to clear HPV from their systems. HPV-caused anal/genital warts can be removed by a health professional or treated with a prescription cream. Treatment for HPV-related cancers—which can be life-threatening—may require chemotherapy, radiation, or surgery (Carroll, 2016; Workowski & Bolan, 2015).

Because HPV is spread primarily through skin-to-skin contact, dental dams and condoms provide only limited protection. However, there are vaccines for the types of HPV that cause cervical and anal cancer, and genital warts, but they are most effective when administered before being exposed to the virus. The CDC recommends everyone between the ages of 11 and 26 be vaccinated for HPV (Workowski & Bolan, 2015).

### Human Immunodeficiency Virus (HIV)

Human immunodeficiency virus (HIV) is the virus that causes Acquired Immune Deficiency Syndrome (AIDS). HIV is believed to have passed from chimpanzees to humans in West Central Africa in the early 1900s, then spread to the Caribbean (and other parts of the world) in the 1960s, and the United States in the 1970s. HIV came to the attention of doctors in the U.S. around 1980 when separate groups of gay men, Haitian immigrants, and intravenous drug users started dying from rare forms of skin cancer, fungal infections, and pneumonia. In

1984 French and U.S. teams of scientists discovered and named the underlying cause of their illnesses: HIV (Pepin, 2011; Quammen, 2015).

In the 1980s an HIV positive diagnosis was widely viewed as a death sentence and there was a great deal of fear, misinformation, and stigma associated with the disease. But since its discovery, research has revealed much about how HIV is transmitted and affects overall health, and many treatments have been developed. Today, HIV is a chronic, but serious, manageable illness comparable to diabetes. With early detection and appropriate treatment, those living with HIV can expect a near-normal life span (Samji et al., 2013).

HIV is transmitted when HIV-infected body fluids come into contact with another person's mucous membrane or damaged tissue, or are directly injected into the bloodstream (through intravenous drug use or blood transfusion). In infected people the HIV virus is found in blood, semen, pre-ejaculatory fluid (pre-cum), rectal mucus, vaginal secretions, and breast milk. Although HIV can be detected in other body fluids such as tears and saliva, contact with these fluids will not transmit the virus. Penetrative anal and vaginal sex (without condoms) are the riskiest sexual activities for transmitting or acquiring HIV. Multiple sexual partners, a history of STI infections, or a current infection with another STI are also associated with increased HIV risk. HIV specifically targets immune system cells that can be present in higher numbers to fight those STIs that trigger an immune system response (such as chlamydia, gonorrhea, and syphilis). Risk of acquiring HIV is two to four times higher if genital herpes sores are present (Freeman et al., 2006). Less common routes of infection are: congenitally (passed from an HIV-positive birth parent to infant during childbirth); being stuck with a needle/sharp object that came into contact with HIV-infected fluids; and receiving a blood transfusion (Carroll, 2016; Corinna, 2016).

Although most people experience flu-like symptoms 6–12 weeks after infection with the HIV virus, the disease usually has no other symptoms early on. However, during this acute phase of HIV infection, the amount of virus in the blood rises dramatically, increasing risk of transmission to others. An HIV-positive person may remain asymptomatic for as long as ten years, depending on their overall health and well-being. But gradually, over time, HIV hijacks the body's immune system, turning a type of white blood cell (CD4 T-cells) into factories that produce more HIV. CD4 T-cells help coordinate the body's immune response to infection. Eventually HIV so depletes the number of CD4 T-cells that the immune system is unable to defend against common bacteria, fungi, parasites, and viruses, which then cause illnesses rarely seen in healthy people (Carroll, 2014).

Acquired Immune Deficiency Syndrome (AIDS) is the term used to describe advanced HIV disease, characterized by a degraded immune system that struggles

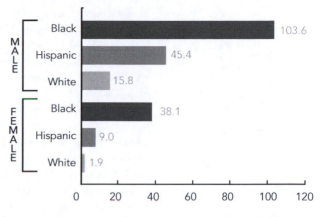

*Estimated rate of new HIV infections in U.S. Number of infections per 100,000 people (2010). Source: Adapted from original by U.S. Centers for Disease Control and Prevention, 2016.*

to fight off infections (that a healthy immune system easily defeats). It is these "opportunistic infections," not the HIV virus itself, that cause death from HIV infection. If left untreated, 95% of those infected with HIV will eventually develop AIDS-related illnesses and die (Carroll, 2016).

The CDC estimates that 1.2 million Americans are currently infected with HIV, and that one in eight infected people do not know they are infected. The number of new HIV diagnoses fell 19% between 2005 and 2015 but there were still nearly 40,000 new HIV diagnoses in 2015. In the United States, over 650,000 people have died of HIV/AIDS (CDC, 2016c, 2016d).

Gay and bisexual men; transgender women; teens and young adults; and African Americans and Latinos are most heavily burdened by HIV. Researchers estimate that as many as 15% of gay and bisexual men in the U.S. live with HIV infection, but rates are much higher in major U.S. cities and in both rural and urban areas of the South (Rosenberg et al., 2016). In the U.S. in 2015, gay and bisexual men accounted for 82% of all new diagnoses among men and 67% of all new diagnoses. Of these, 40% were African-American, 32% were White, and 23% were Latino. Although White MSM represent the largest HIV-infected subpopulation in the U.S., Latino and African-American MSM are over-represented (compared to their percentage of the U.S. population) among new HIV infections. By the end of 2011, 47% (311,087) of total U.S. AIDS deaths were gay and bisexual men (CDC, 2012, 2016c).

In 2016 the CDC predicted that, if current trends continue, half of all African-American (and a quarter of all Latino) MSM in the U.S. will be infected with HIV in their lifetime (Hess et al., 2016). However, stereotypes about African-American and Latino men's riskier sexual practices or numbers of sexual partners are not supported by research (Calabrese et al., 2013). HIV infection rates are likely higher among these men due to less access to STI testing and treatment services, higher rates of other STIs (that can increase likelihood of acquiring HIV), and lower rates of adherence to anti-retroviral treatment after HIV diagnosis. Minority community stigma surrounding same-sex behavior and beliefs that HIV/ AIDS is a "White people's disease" are also contributing factors. Together, this results in a greater number of undiagnosed and untreated HIV positive gay and bisexual men in African-American and Latino social and sexual networks. Because men of color are more likely to engage in sexual activity with men of the same race or ethnicity, their odds of encountering an HIV-positive partner, and acquiring or transmitting HIV, are increased (McCullom, 2016).

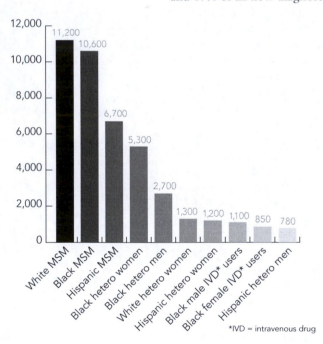

*IVD = intravenous drug

*U.S. population groups with the largest numbers of estimated new HIV infections (2010). Source: Adapted from original by U.S. Centers for Disease Control and Prevention, 2016.*

Sexual transmission of HIV between WSW is very difficult and rare, but WSW can become infected with HIV from IV drug use, prior male partners, and other routes of HIV transmission (Deol & Heath-Toby, 2009). HIV is one of the few STIs where data has been collected on transgender people. Several research studies suggest that 20%–25% of transgender women worldwide (including the U.S.) may be infected with HIV, but the number may be as high as 50% for African–American and Latina transgender women (Herbst et al., 2008; ODPHP, 2010a). In a recent study conducted by the National Center for Transgender Equality, transgender people reported living with HIV at more than four times (1.4%) the rate of the general population (.3%), with especially high rates among African–American (20%), Native American (4.6%), and Latina (44%) transgender women. This is likely due to employment discrimination and social marginalization, leading to poverty and elevated participation in the underground economy of sex and drug work (James et al., 2016). The number of HIV-infected transgender men appears to be significantly lower (Kenagy, 2002; Sevelius, 2009).

HIV/AIDS treatments are more effective if they are started soon after infection, so regular HIV testing is important for controlling the disease. HIV tests use small amounts of blood or saliva, or cell scrapings (from inside of the cheek). Some types of tests detect the HIV virus directly, while others can only detect HIV antibodies (the immune system's response to HIV). The body can take three weeks to six months to produce HIV antibodies; so testing soon after HIV exposure can produce false negative results. Blood-based lab tests detect HIV infection faster and with more accuracy than saliva or rapid tests. Positive tests are usually repeated to confirm results. If you feel you have been exposed to HIV but your test is negative, make sure the appropriate test is being used and get a follow up test three to six months later. If you believe you were *just exposed* to HIV, go immediately to an emergency room or public health clinic (like Planned Parenthood) and ask about post–exposure prophylaxis (PEP) (see box). HIV testing can be done in a doctor's office, public health office, or a campus or community health center. Costs are usually covered by healthcare insurance and free testing is often offered at public health clinics (Branson et al., 2014; Carroll, 2016).

Midwest rate: 8.2

Northeast rate: 14.2

West rate: 11.2

South rate: 18.5

*HIV diagnoses per 100,000 people (by region) (2014). From 2010–2014 rates decreased in Northeast and South but rose in West and Midwest. Source: Adapted from original by U.S. Centers for Disease Control and Prevention, 2016.*

Treatment for HIV/AIDS varies depending on the stage of the disease. Some treatments fight AIDS-related illnesses, while others combat the HIV virus itself. Improvements in antiretroviral drug therapies (ART) in the mid-1990s dramatically extended the life expectancy and improved the quality of life for those living with HIV. Where ART drugs once required 20–30 pills a day, some new drug combinations involve only one or two pills taken once a day. ART prevents HIV from using the body's CD4 T-cells to make copies of itself, thus lowering the amount of HIV in the bloodstream (the viral load) and leaving the immune system strong

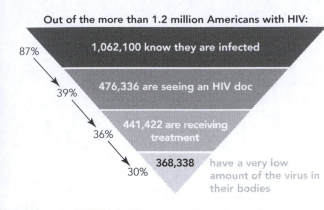

**Out of the more than 1.2 million Americans with HIV:**

87%  1,062,100 know they are infected

39%  476,336 are seeing an HIV doc

36%  441,422 are receiving treatment

30%  368,338  have a very low amount of the virus in their bodies

*Percentage of HIV-infected people in U.S. in select stages of care (2012). Source: Adapted from original created by U.S. Centers for Disease Control and Prevention, 2016.*

enough to fight off opportunistic infections. ART can reduce the amount of HIV in blood and other body fluids to undetectable levels, which several studies have shown makes it extremely unlikely, if not impossible, for an HIV-positive person to transmit the virus to sexual partners (Anglemyer et al., 2013; Rodger et al., 2016; Ryan 2017). For this reason, HIV testing and treatment can also represent forms of HIV prevention—a fact sometimes indicated by the term "TasP" (or, Treatment as Prevention) (Carroll, 2016; Workowski & Bolan, 2015).

However, ART drugs can cause serious side effects and can interact with other medications in unpredictable ways. They require blood tests every 3–6 months to monitor CD4 T-cell counts and viral load. Common side effects of ART include chronic diarrhea, lipodystrophy (shifts in distribution of body fat), and mood changes (including depression and anxiety). Long term, ART can also increase rates of osteoporosis, cardiovascular disease, diabetes, and high blood pressure. ART drugs also require near-perfect adherence to dosing schedules or their effectiveness can be reduced and drug-resistant strains of HIV may emerge. ART drugs can be very expensive but healthcare insurance, and government and pharmaceutical company assistance programs, may help reduce costs (Anderson-Minshall, 2016).

ART is not a cure for HIV and an HIV vaccine is probably many years away. HIV infection is a serious illness that entails a lifetime of medical monitoring and prescription drugs. An HIV-positive diagnosis can require permanent changes in sexual behaviors and affect relationships with existing or prospective sexual and romantic partners (Carroll, 2016; Corinna, 2016; PAGAA, 2016).

## STI Risk Groups and Testing Recommendations

Although STIs micro-organisms don't discriminate, certain LGBTQ+ groups are especially impacted by STIs: LGBTQ+ teens and young adults (aged 15–29); gay and bisexual men; LGBTQ+ Latinos and African Americans; and transgender people. All LGBTQ+ people can be at greater STI risk if they have multiple or casual sexual partners, favor specific sexual positions or roles (like receptive oral, vaginal, or anal sex), or do not practice safer sex (see below) consistently. Societal bi/trans/homophobia, stigma, and discrimination can contribute to behaviors that increase STI risk: drug and alcohol abuse; sex in exchange for drugs or money; and reluctance to be tested or treated. Internalized homophobia and stigma can lead to low self-esteem, which can make it more difficult to negotiate safe-sex practices with sexual partners, seek out STI testing, or adhere to treatments (CDC, 2016c; Jeffries, 2014; Workowski & Bolan, 2015). For these reasons, it is especially important for LGBTQ+ people to be regularly tested for STIs and undergo recommended treatment. This can require a frank discussion with a health professional about sexual anatomy, intimate relationships, and past and current sexual behavior.

When considering STI risks, testing, and treatment, it is important to remember that sexual anatomy and sexual behavior are more important factors than gender identity/expression and sexual orientation. A person who presents or identifies as a man may also possess a female-typical sexual anatomy (i.e. a vulva, vagina, cervix) that requires a specific kind of test (a Pap smear) to detect HPV-related cervical cancer. That same person's genitals may have been changed through hormone therapy or surgery, allowing penetration of a sexual partner's mouth, vagina, or anus, which can incur risk for other STIs. Surgically altered genitals may also affect how STI tests are conducted: from how urine is collected to how vaginal tissues are examined for STI symptoms. For anyone whose sexual anatomy does not align with their gender identity or gender expression in socially expected ways, gender-based STI testing and treatment recommendations may not be appropriate or adequate. Depending on individual anatomy, sexual behavior, and risk group membership, some LGBTQ+ people may require more frequent, comprehensive, or slightly different kinds of STI testing than is generally recommended (NCTE, 2012; ODPHP, 2010a; Palmisano, n.d.; Workowski & Bolan, 2015).

In addition to regular testing, those at high risk for HIV infection should talk to a health professional about PEP (post-exposure prophylaxis) and PrEP (pre-exposure prophylaxis) (see box). To locate an LGBTQ+ sensitive health professional search the Gay and Lesbian Medical Association's Provider Directory (www.glma.org) or the website of the World Professional Association for Transgender Health (www.wpath.org).

### Lesbians/Bisexual Women/WSW and WSWM

Although WSW are not considered a high-risk group for most STIs, most WSW have some lifetime history of sex with men that may have exposed them to a wide range of STIs (Bailey et al., 2003). Some research shows that WSWM are more likely than WSM to engage in a variety of high-risk sexual behaviors that can put them at greater STI risk (SAMHSA, 2012). Both WSW and WSWM can transmit STIs through (hand/mouth/genital) skin-to-skin contact, mucous membrane contact, vaginal fluids, rectal mucus, menstrual blood, and shared sex toys. Even if covered with condoms or gloves, hands, fingers, and sex toys can transmit STI microbes between sexual partners. WSW are especially at risk for bacterial vaginosis, chlamydia, herpes, and human papillomavirus (HPV). HPV can cause cervical cancer, but WSW are less likely to get routine gynecological screenings that would detect such cancers. The symptoms of some STIs can be mild or absent, but STIs can cause serious health problems, including infertility, so it is important to get tested regularly even if there are no symptoms. Sexually active WSW are recommended to discuss their sexual history with a health professional to determine the type and frequency of any STI testing. Anyone with a vagina, cervix, and uterus—but especially those over 30—should have annual gynecological exams that can detect many STI symptoms. Such exams often include tests (a Pap smear) that detect HPV and HPV-caused cervical cancer. HPV vaccination is also recommended for those under 26 (Bailey et al., 2004; Deol & Heath-Toby, 2009; Dolan & Davis, 2010; OWH, 2009; Workowski & Bolan, 2015).

### Gay and Bisexual Men/MSM and MSMW

MSM and MSMW are considered high risk groups for most STIs. Since the mid-1990s infection rates of chlamydia, syphilis, gonorrhea, and HIV have increased among MSM, especially Latino and African-American MSM (Barton et al., 2016). At the same time, use of condoms by MSM has declined dramatically (Paz-Bailey et al., 2016). Some research shows MSMW are *less* likely to engage in certain risky sexual behaviors (i.e. less anal sex, less receptive anal sex) but they have *higher* STI rates than MSW (though not as high as MSM) (ODPHP, 2010b; Rosenberger et al., 2011). Key risk factors (for all MSM) are higher numbers of sexual partners, multiple and/or casual sexual partners, riskier sexual behavior (sex while drunk or high, condomless anal sex, etc.), and already having another STI (Jeffries, 2014; SAMHSA, 2012). Regardless of how they identify, all MSM can transmit STIs through skin-to-skin contact, mucous membrane contact, and shared body fluids (semen, pre-ejaculatory fluid [pre-cum], rectal mucus, and blood). MSMW can also contract STIs from contact with vaginal fluids. Sexually active MSM/MSMW should be tested annually for HIV, syphilis, hepatitis, chlamydia, herpes, and gonorrhea (of the throat, urethra, and rectum). Those having multiple and/or casual sexual partners should be tested at 3–6 month intervals. Tests on urine and blood should be included, and on fluids collected by swab from the throat, urethra, and rectum (triple site testing). Vaccinations for hepatitis A and B, HPV, and influenza (the flu) are also recommended (Workowski & Bolan, 2015).

### Transgender People/Diverse Anatomies

Comparatively little is known about STI risks and infection rates among transgender people. However, because they can engage in the same sexual activities as everyone else (depending on anatomy, any medical transition, dysphoria, and sexual style/tastes), transgender people can potentially acquire and transmit STIs like anyone else. Some limited research shows that both transgender women and transgender men are at increased risk for HIV and other STIs. As with all LGBTQ+ STI risk groups, STI rates appear to be higher for transgender youth, African Americans and Latinos. Higher STI rates may be due to: increased sexual risk-taking; social stigma that can push transgender people into poverty and the underground economy of sex and drug work; and sharing of needles to inject illicit drugs, hormones, or cosmetic silicone. Transgender people may be less able to negotiate safer-sex practices (like condom use) with partners due to low self-esteem, a desire to have their gender identity affirmed, less access to accepting partners, and an imbalance of power between sexual partners. Unaddressed mental and physical health issues, physical abuse, social rejection, and lack of access to culturally competent or affirming healthcare providers may also contribute (Grant et al., 2011; Herbst et al., 2008; Kenagy & Hsieh, 2005; Nuttbrock et al., 2009; ODPHP, 2010a; Sevelius, 2009; Stephens, Bernstein, & Philip, 2011). Transgender people should discuss their sexual activities and histories, and any potential STI symptoms, with a culturally competent health professional to determine any necessary STI tests and treatments (Workowski & Bolan, 2015).

## Safer-Sex Practices

The only way to completely avoid STIs is to abstain from sexual activity that involves direct physical contact with sexual partners. Most people, however, engage in partnered contact sex at some point in their lives and this can put them at risk for STIs. Fortunately, it is possible to have an active sex life and reduce STI risks by engaging in safer-sex practices. However, it may be difficult for some LGBTQ+ people to practice safer sex and ask for it from partners due to lack of access to LGBTQ+-inclusive sex education, lack of sexual experience, poor sexual communication skills, absence of safer-sex materials that work with diverse anatomies, and low self-esteem related to internalized homophobia or transphobia (Corinna, 2016). Becoming informed and preparing in advance can go a long way to overcoming these hurdles. Every individual's "safer-sex toolkit" will look a little bit different. Here are some "tools" worth considering:

> *Get Tested, Get Treated.* Having one STI is a risk factor for acquiring others and many STIs get worse if left untreated. Even incurable STIs can be treated to minimize their impact on overall health and to reduce the likelihood of transmission to sexual partners. STI tests are simple, relatively painless, and easily performed in a doctor's office, community health clinic (like Planned Parenthood), or a campus or community health center. Testing is often free or low cost, covered by most healthcare plans as "preventative care," and may be confidential and anonymous. To find a free STI testing site near you, call 1–800–CDC–INFO or text your ZIP code to KNOWIT. Sign up for free testing reminder texts at www.WeAllTest.com (HIV.gov, 2018; Workowski & Bolan, 2015).

> *Communicate before Having Sex.* What are your STIs (if any)? When were you last tested? What are your safer-sex practices and expectations of partners? Frank sexual communication can feel awkward at first but it can also build trust and create intimacy, which enhances the pleasure of sex for many people. So think about your answers to these questions and plan to talk about them before getting caught up in "the moment." Corinna (2016) and Moon & diamond (2015) offer some excellent models for communicating about boundaries and STIs. Practicing with a trusted friend or health

professional can also be helpful. And remember, some STIs (i.e. herpes, chlamydia, HPV) are very common, so having an STI does not make someone "dirty" or a "slut." It only takes one time with one infected partner to get an STI (Corinna, 2016; Workowski & Bolan, 2015).

*Limit Number of Sex Partners.* Although it is possible to have many sexual partners and remain STI-free, having multiple casual sexual partners is associated with increased STI risk. This is because each sexual encounter increases the odds of coming into contact with STI micro-organisms from infected partners. Conversely, sexually monogamous relationships are not necessarily STI-risk free because one or more partners in a relationship may have acquired an STI from a prior partner. Safer-sex practices can help reduce STI risks, both for those with many lifetime sexual partners and those with only one partner who happens to have an STI (Corinna, 2016; Workowski & Bolan, 2015).

*Engage in Lower-risk Sexual Behaviors.* Not all sexual behaviors carry the same risk for STIs. There are many sexual activities with lower STI

## A "Yes" Is a "Yes"

Between 20% to 25% of women will survive rape or attempted rape in their lifetimes and one in six men are the survivors of childhood sexual abuse. LGBTQ+ people are not immune to sexual, relationship, and intimate partner violence. In fact, some research shows they are more likely to be raped, sexually assaulted, or sexually abused. Bisexual women and men, young LGBTQ+ people, and transgender women appear to be especially vulnerable to sexual violence. Any kind of sexual contact without the consent of all participants is a crime (sexual assault or rape). Consent means the enthusiastic, voluntary, and ongoing agreement to participate in a specific activity. It can be communicated verbally or non-verbally. Those under the influence of drugs or alcohol, or unconscious (or otherwise not able to communicate), are generally not viewed as able to consent to sexual activity (the absence of a "no" is not a "yes"!). Consent can be granted and withdrawn at any time before and during a sexual encounter and if consent is withdrawn sexually activity should stop. If at any time during a sexual encounter a partner appears to have "checked out" (dissociated), sexual activity should cease until consent is re-established. This is especially important for transgender partners for whom sexual contact with highly gendered body parts may contribute to dysphoria and dissociation. If there are sexual "red lines" you do not want to cross, make sure these are clearly communicated in advance to your partners. And, during sex, periodically "check in'" with partners to make sure consent is still being given. This need not be formal or awkward. A simple, "This good?" or "You, OK?" is an easy way to check in with partners and make sure consent is still being granted (Corinna, 2016).

risks: solo masturbation; sexting and cyber-sex; erotic rubbing or massage; mutual masturbation; oral, vaginal, or anal sex using a condom or dental dam (to minimize contact between skin, mucous membranes, and body fluids). Good hygiene may also help reduce STI risk, such as washing hands, genitals, and sex toys (before *and* after sex) and use of rectal enemas. Use a new condom and wash sex toys, hands and other body parts before switching between anal and vaginal play. Avoid oral sex if there are bleeding gums, mouth or lip sores, or a sore throat, and avoid brushing/flossing immediately prior to sex. Only engage in unprotected anal or vaginal penetration (without using condoms/gloves/dental dams) with partners who are regularly tested for STIs, limit their number of sexual partners, and honestly disclose their STI status (Corinna, 2016; Moon & diamond; Workowski & Bolan, 2015).

| **LOW** | Abstinence/celibacy<br>Fantasizing/sexting/cyber sex<br>Masturbation (solo)<br>Kissing (closed mouth)<br>Touching/fondling/massage (partnered)<br>BDSM (*no* broken skin or shared body fluids)<br>Kissing (open mouth) |
|---|---|
| **MID** | Masturbation (partnered)<br>Sex toy play (clean toys)<br>Oral sex*<br>Vaginal sex*<br>Anal sex*<br>    *with condoms/barriers; no shared body fluids* |
| **HIGH** | Oral sex°<br>Vaginal sex°<br>Anal sex°<br>BDSM (if broken skin/shared fluids/blood play)<br>    *°no condoms/barriers; shared body fluids* |

*The STI Risk Continuum. Different sexual behaviors carry different STI risks.*

*Use Condoms.* Used correctly and consistently for vaginal, oral, and anal sex, condoms can reduce STI risk by preventing contact between skin, mucous membranes, and body fluids. When used correctly and depending on the sexual activity, condoms are 75%–86% effective at preventing STIs. However, they only protect areas of skin covered by the condom, which may not protect against STIs spread through skin contact (HPV, herpes, syphilis, etc.). External or "male" condoms (designed to cover a penis) come in a variety of shapes, sizes, colors, and flavors. Non-latex condoms are available for those with latex allergies, but animal skin and "natural" condoms do not protect against viral STIs such as herpes, hepatitis, and HIV. Internal or "female" condoms (designed for insertion into the vagina) can also provide STI protection during vaginal or anal sex, although they are more difficult to use for anal sex than external condoms (Renzi et al., 2003). Wearing two external condoms or combining an external and internal condom carries a high risk of condom breakage due to friction between the two condoms. Condoms can also be used to cover sex toys, making them easier to clean and reducing risk of STI transmission. Reviews of condom sizes, fit, and features abound on the internet. Condoms are sold at grocery and drug stores, and online, and are often available free at campus and community health centers (Carroll, 2016; Corinna, 2016; Silverstein & Picano, 2006; Workowski & Bolan, 2015).

*Use Dental Dams and Gloves.* A dental dam is a square of latex, silicone, or nitrile that can be placed over the vagina, anus, or another erogenous zone.

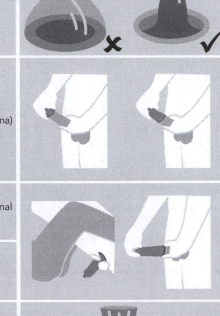

### Buy and Store
· choose latex or polyurethane condoms
· natural and lambskin don't protect against STIs
· store at room temp, away from heat/light/moisture

### Open
· check expiration date
· ensure package isn't damaged
· use hands to open, not teeth or scissors
· orient right side up
· right side up looks like a hat

### Roll to Base
· a drop of water- or silicone-based lube in tip increases sensitivity
· if uncircumcised, it might be more comfortable to pull foreskin back before rolling on condom
· roll on before penis touches partner's mouth or genital area (anus, vulva, vagina)
· pinch reservoir tip to leave room for semen
· unroll onto erect penis
· unroll fully to base of penis
· apply more lube to outside of penis (if desired)

### Use
· use a new one every time AND when switching between oral, anal, and vaginal sex
· have fun!

### After Fun
· before pulling out, hold tight to condom base
· carefully remove penis (w/condom) from mouth/anus/vagina
· avoid spilling semen on/in partner

### Dispose
· tie base of condom in knot
· throw in trash (not in toilet)

### Condom Tips
· wearing two condoms or using external ("male") condoms with internal ("female") condoms can cause breakage
· condoms & gloves can also be used to cover hands, fingers, and sex toys
· a cut up condom works as a dental dam and to cover atypical 'bits'
· condoms can clog drains or pipes so always throw in trash
· keep condoms on bedside table, or in purse/pocket when going out

*How to use an external or "male" condom.*

Dams allow oral sex with less risk of transmitting STIs from body fluids and mucous membranes. A drop of personal lube on the side touching the oral sex recipient's body increases sensitivity and pleasure. Users must take care that only one side of the dam is touched by each partner during oral sex. Wearing surgical gloves for vaginal and anal stimulation or penetration (with the hands or fingers) can reduce STI risk by limiting contact between skin, mucous membranes, and body fluids. Gloves can reduce the risk of cuts from sharp fingernails and can be cut up into a variety of shapes to create a dental dam or cover for uniquely shaped sex toys or diverse body parts (Hill-Meyer & Scarborough, 2014, Moon & diamond, 2014). Sometimes harder to find than condoms, dental dams and gloves are often sold at drug stores and online, and may be free at campus and community health centers (Corinna, 2016; Newman, 2004).

*Use Personal Lubricant.* Personal lubricants (lube) can increase sensitivity, and reduce friction during sex that might damage skin and allow STI microbes to pass between partners. A little lube on hands and fingers, inside a condom, or on the side of a dental dam touching a partner's body can greatly increase skin sensitivity and pleasure. Lube may be required for vaginal penetration and is usually required for anal penetration. Not all lubes are suitable for all sexual activities and some people are sensitive to common ingredients. Water-based lubes are the best all-around choice for a variety of sexual activities. Silicone-based lubes are extra slippery but can damage silicone toys and require a soap and water clean-up. Oil-based lubes (like Vaseline, cooking oils, baby oil, coconut oil) may be preferred for those with sensitive

## Preventing HIV: PEP and PrEP

After 2012, two new strategies emerged to prevent HIV infection: PEP and PrEP. Post-exposure prophylaxis (or PEP) is emergency medication for HIV-negative people that can help prevent infection *after* exposure to HIV. PEP is a month-long course of two or three anti-viral drugs. To be effective, PEP needs to be started no later than 72 hours (and preferably not later than 36 hours) after exposure. PEP can cause mild side effects (nausea, fatigue, headaches, diarrhea, vomiting, etc.) but can be up to 80% effective at preventing HIV infection. However, PEP does not prevent other STI infections and is not a replacement for safer-sex practices. PEP is covered by most health insurance and is offered at many emergency rooms and community/college health centers (GMHC, n.d.).

Pre-exposure prophylaxis (or PrEP) is the use of prescription drugs to reduce the risk of HIV infection *before* exposure to the HIV virus. There is currently one prescription drug approved for PrEP use: Truvada. Truvada is a once-a-day pill that blocks HIV's ability to reproduce in the body so, even if a person is exposed to HIV, it can prevent them from becoming infected with the virus. Truvada must be taken *before* HIV exposure and does not protect against other STIs. Although Truvada can cause some side effects, most are mild and disappear over time, but regular blood tests are required. Truvada is covered by most insurance plans and there are financial programs to help the uninsured access the drug. Research is ongoing, but early studies suggest that those who take Truvada every day can reduce their risk of HIV infection by over 90%. However, a very small number of HIV infections (with drug-resistant strains of the virus) have been reported by PrEP users (Knox et al., 2016). PrEP is recommended for anyone at high risk of HIV infection, as part of an overall HIV prevention toolkit that includes education, testing, treatment, and condom use (CDC, n.d.).

skin but they can damage latex condoms and dental dams, causing them to break during sex. Squeeze tubes, pumps, or single-use packets are a better choice over lube in tubs or pots—these can become contaminated with STI microbes. Include lube in your safer-sex toolkit next to your toys and condoms, gloves, and dental dams. A wide variety of lubes are sold at drug stores and online, and are often distributed free at community/campus health centers (Corinna, 2016; Moon and diamond, 2014).

*Avoid Sex while Drunk/High.* Having sex after using alcohol or drugs can impair judgment and lower inhibitions, making it more difficult to assert and respect boundaries, ensure a partner's consent, and practice safer sex. Having safer-sex materials prepared in advance (i.e. placing condoms, dental dams, and lube on a bedside table or bringing them in a small travel kit) may increase the likelihood of engaging in safer sex when drunk or high. Consider limiting sex while under the influence of drugs and alcohol to mutually monogamous, long-term, consenting partners who know and share their STI status (Corinna, 2016).

*Practice Sexual Harm Reduction.* Abstinence, monogamy, and condoms are not possible or preferred sexual practices for everyone wanting to reduce HIV risk. As a result some MSM have practiced "serosorting": only having condom-less sex with partners with the same HIV status (or, if HIV-positive, an undetectable viral load). Another strategy is "negotiated safety": only having unprotected sex within a monogamous relationship after both partners test negative for HIV and agree upon rules for managing risk during any sex outside their relationship. Others practice "strategic positioning": where HIV-positive partners elect to only "bottom" during oral and anal sex because these positions are less likely to put an HIV-negative "top" at risk. Sexual harm reduction requires frequent HIV testing and open communication between sexual partners. Unfortunately, many MSM assume they are HIV-negative even though they have never been tested. Due to stigma surrounding HIV, not all HIV-positive men are willing to disclose their HIV status to sexual partners in advance of having sex. Finally, unprotected sex still entails STI risks, including re-infection with different strains of HIV, which may be resistant to antiretroviral drugs. Sexual harm reduction strategies can reduce risk for HIV infection but not as much as using condoms, and they carry an increased risk for other STIs. For these reasons, public health officials do not recommend strategic harm reduction as the primary means of preventing STIs, including HIV (Workowski & Bolan, 2015).

## CONCLUSION

In 2016 president Barack Obama zeroed-out funding for abstinence-only sex "education" programs in his federal budget request to Congress (OMB, 2016). But even if such programs are defunded, many LGBTQ+ youth will still have little access to comprehensive, accurate, and affirming information about LGBTQ+

sex. Developing a healthy LGBTQ+ sexuality requires: becoming better informed about sexual anatomy and each body's unique capacity for pleasure; discovering one's preferred forms of sexual touch and sexual behavior; learning about the risks accompanying certain sexual activities; and, developing a personal strategy for managing these risks, which may include adopting safer-sex practices. Throughout this process, it is important to remember that LGBTQ+ sexual styles, behaviors, and health will differ from person to person. Because of individual differences, there can never be a "one size fits all" definition of what constitutes a healthy LGBTQ+ sexuality. But developing a healthy LGBTQ+ sexuality can be both a form of self-care and a way to care for the entire LGBTQ+ community.

## Learn More

### Readings

Bellwether, Mira. (2010). *Fucking trans women*, volume 1 [zine]. Lexington, KY: CreateSpace Independent Publishing Platform.

Corinna, H. (2016). *S.E.X.: The all-you-need-to-know sexuality guide to get you through your teens and twenties, second edition*. New York, NY: Da Capo.

Erickson-Roth, L., ed. (2014). *Trans bodies, trans selves: A resource for the transgender community*. Oxford, UK: Oxford University.

Gay, Bi, Queer Trans Men's Working Group. (2015). *PRIMED²: The back pocket guide for transmen & the men who dig them*. Toronto, ON: Gay Men's Sexual Health Alliance.

Human Rights Campaign & Whitman-Walker Health. (2016). *Safer sex for trans bodies*. Washington, D.C. HRC & WWH. Retrieved from www.hrc.org/resources/safer-sex-for-trans-bodies

Moon, A. and diamond, k. d. (2015). *Girl sex 101*. Lunatic Ink.

Newman, F. (2004). *The whole lesbian sex book: A passionate guide for the rest of us*, second edition. Jersey City, NJ: Cleis.

Page, M. M. (2013). *Brazen: Trans women safer sex guide*. Toronto, ON: The 519 Church Street Community Centre.

Silverstein, C. & Picano, F. (2006). *The joy of gay sex, revised and expanded*, third edition. New York, NY: William Morrow.

Terence Higgins Trust. (2012a). *TransMen: Sexual health, HIV and wellbeing—A guide for trans men*. London, UK: Terrence Higgins Trust.

Terence Higgins Trust. (2012b). *TransWomen: Sexual health, HIV and wellbeing—A guide for trans women*. London, UK: Terrence Higgins Trust.

Tetzlaff, K. (2015). *Patient's guide to transgender, trans, & gender diverse health*. Retrieved from https://ktetzlaff.com

Underwood, S. G. (2012). *Gay men and anal eroticism: Tops, bottoms, and versatiles*. New York: Routledge.

### Film/Video

*Note: LGBTQ+-inclusive educational videos and documentaries on sexual anatomy, behavior, and health are very difficult to find. Search YouTube and campus/local libraries for available options.*

Advocates for Youth, Answer and Youth Tech Health. (2016). *AMAZE: More info on sex ed. Less weird*. [YouTube channel]. Retrieved from https://www.youtube.com/c/amazeorg

Crash Course. (2015). *Reproductive system, parts 1–4*. [YouTube video]. Retrieved from https://www.youtube.com

Lipshutz, M., & Rosenblatt, R. (Directors). (2005). *The education of Shelby Knox: Sex, lies and education*. [Motion picture]. New York, NY: Incite.

Wein, D. (Director). (2010). *Sex positive*. [DVD]. United States: E1.

*Internet*

Down an' Dirty: www.downandirty.org
FS Magazine: www.fsmag.org.uk
Gay Men's Health Crisis: www.gmhc.org
GRUNT: www.grunt.org.au
Guttmacher Institute: www.guttmacher.org
Planned Parenthood: www.plannedparenthood.org
San Francisco AIDS Foundation: www.sfaf.org
Savage Lovecast: www.savagelovecast.com
Scarleteen: www.scarleteen.com
SIECUS: Sexuality Information and Education Council of the United States: www.siecus.org
U.S. Centers for Disease Control and Prevention—Lesbian, Gay, and Transgender Health: www.cdc.gov/lgbthealth
WPATH: World Professional Association for Transgender Health: www.wpath.org

# Note

1 The tone, content, and organization of this section on anatomy is heavily indebted to Corinna (2016).

# CHAPTER 4
# Together, Forever?
## *Relationships*

*Christine Smith and Joel A. Muraco*

*Parents of a gay son marching with PFLAG in Washington, D.C. Capital Pride Parade, June 12, 2010. Source: Photo by Tim Evanson/CC BY-SA 2.0 license. Image courtesy of Wikimedia Commons.*

In July of 2012 Mark Regnerus, a sociologist at the University of Texas, published a study reporting more negative outcomes for young adults whose parents had a same-sex relationship while they were growing up. The outcomes were especially negative for those who grew up with a mother who had a same-sex relationship, who were more likely to have been on welfare, arrested, or unemployed, less likely to be heterosexual, had higher rates of sexual coercion, and were more likely to be depressed (Regnerus, 2012). For many years, lesbians and gay men were considered to be bad parents solely because of their sexual orientation. They were forbidden by some states from fostering or adopting children, and those leaving a heterosexual relationship lost custody of their children because of their sexual orientation. Some laws have been changed, and barriers to adoption, fostering, and custody have decreased for lesbians and gay men. Sexual orientation is no longer always seen as a deviation that makes lesbians and gay men bad parents. Even though numerous studies have found that children of lesbian and gay parents fare no worse, and sometimes better, than children of heterosexual parents, Regnerus' research suggested that maybe the earlier beliefs were accurate (Manning, Fettro, & Lamidi, 2014; Stacey & Biblarz, 2001). Perhaps being gay, lesbian, or bisexual did have a negative impact on children. His article set off a media firestorm, with conservative outlets hailing the findings and progressive media condemning them (Gates et al., 2012; Oppenheimer, 2012).

This chapter discusses relationships in the lives of LGBTQ individuals, between parents and children, family members, romantic partners, and friends. In everyday use, the word "relationship" usually refers to romantic or sexual relationships with another person, a girl/boyfriend, partner, or spouse. However, social scientists—sociologists, psychologists, anthropologists—use the word to refer to a wide variety of social relationships formed over the course of a person's life, in different social situations and circumstances. The capacity to have relationships and the characteristics of those relationships are cumulative and lifelong. That is to say, people have relationships their entire lives and their ability to have them is developmental, with each new one informed by previous relationships. Social relationships are how humans seek to fulfill the need for intimacy with others. Intimate relationships are close, familiar, and usually loving and affectionate. As children, parents or parent-like figures fulfill the need for intimacy. Later, intimacy is fulfilled by friends and, eventually, romantic interests.

LGBTQ people have the same needs as cisgender and heterosexual people for intimacy, fulfilled through developmental social relationships. However, the shape and form of their relationships can be influenced by the larger social and cultural context, which can range from repressive to affirming, even celebratory. Internalized negative cultural messages, as with internalized transphobia and homophobia, can also affect LGBTQ social relationships. Because so many aspects of social relationships are governed by custom, rule, and law, these factors also play a role in the form, expression, and wider acceptance of LGBTQ social relationships. Romantic and sexual relationships, cohabitation, marriage, divorce, family forms, custody and adoption of children—all are affected by the social, cultural, and legal context of LGBTQ social relationships. Some LGBTQ people have enjoyed (limited) freedom to forge new and creative relationship forms—familial, romantic, or sexual—that fulfill unique individual needs for intimacy. These can both challenge and expand the definition of acceptable relationships in a heteronormative society, which helps explain why LGBTQ relationships have often been at the center of political conflicts, cultural controversies, and media attention, as they were with the Regnerus study.

This chapter surveys a wide variety of LGBTQ relationships across the lifespan. It begins with the concept of "attachment," to illustrate the cumulative nature of relationships and the influences within each developmental period. The chapter then turns to the ways parents and peers influence the development of relationships, especially in childhood. It then proceeds to describe relationships through adolescence into romantic and familial relationships, and ends with a discussion of relationships among LGBTQ elders. The chapter also touches on work relationships and the capacity to build relationships outside of the typical developmental path. The goal is to provide a broad perspective of the various capacities and implications of LGBTQ people's relationships over the course of their lives.

Much of the research on the relationships of gender and sexual minorities has focused on lesbians and gay men. Also, researchers have often assumed there are similarities between LGBTQ, and cisgender or heterosexual people's relationships. Or, that the relationships of lesbians and gay men are similar to those of bisexual, transgender, and queer people. Clearly, there is a need for more research in these areas. Throughout this chapter, acronyms like LGB and LGBT are used with care to denote only those identities included in the particular research study being discussed.

## ATTACHMENTS AND RELATIONSHIPS

Regardless of sexual orientation, the relationships formed over a person's life are based on the kinds of attachments and attachment style first developed in infancy, during which attachment is the close emotional bond between and infant and caregiver (King, 2017). These attachments are formed in direct response to the responsiveness of one's caregivers. If a caregiver was consistently present and addressing the needs of an infant, the infant will develop a secure attachment. A secure attachment is when a person views themselves as worthy of love and others as worthy of trust (Bowlby, 1973).

Attachment researchers have documented extensively how early attachment influences relationships for the rest of one's life. Early infant attachment strongly predicts self-reliance, effective peer relationships (including empathy and affective engagement), and positive relationships with teachers in preschoolers (Sroufe, 1983; Sroufe, Schork, Motti, Lawroski, & LaFreniere, 1984). Infant attachment quality and functioning in preschool is also associated with middle childhood relationships, including the ability to form close relationships and resolve conflict (Elicker, Englund, & Sroufe, 1992; Shulman, Elicker, & Sroufe, 1994). These peer relationships in middle childhood provide foundational experiences with relational skills such as positive expectancies about interactions with others, a context for learning reciprocity, and learning empathy (Collins & Sroufe, 1999).

Peer relationships remain most significant until the introduction of romantic relationships, which then take priority. Romantic relationships

## Locating a Culturally Competent Counselor

Although most LGBTQ people have good mental health and cope well with life's challenges, LGBTQ people are at greater risk for certain mental health problems—including bipolar disorder, depression, and anxiety—and mental health-related issues—such as drug and alcohol abuse, sexual risk taking, and attempted suicide. Societal stigma, discrimination, and minority stress contribute to LGBTQ mental health challenges (NAMI, 2016). Although LGBTQ have higher rates of use for mental health resources, finding an LGBTQ-friendly counselor can be difficult.

First, consider searching online directories of counselors. The Gay and Lesbian Medical Association (www.glma.org) and World Professional Association for Transgender Health (www.wpath.org) maintain active directories. Second, ask LGBTQ friends who they see or if they know an affirming therapist. After locating a potential counselor, it is important to determine whether they are a good fit for your needs. Some good interviewing questions are: "What is your training and experience working with LGBTQ clients?" and "Do you believe in 'reparative' therapy?" In addition to interview questions, a counselor's waiting room can tell a lot about their comfort working with LGBTQ clients. The Gay Lesbian Medical Association encourages LGBTQ-friendly providers to "post [a] rainbow flag, pink triangle, unisex bathroom signs, or other LGBT-friendly symbols or stickers" and "a non-discrimination statement stating that equal care will be provided to all patients, regardless of age, race, ethnicity, physical ability or attributes, religion, sexual orientation, or gender identity/expression" (GLMA, 2006, pp. 2–3).

Finding a transgender-affirming provider can be especially challenging. Although the "T" is part of being LGBTQ-affirming, many providers have limited to no understanding of the nuances of what it means to be a transgender-friendly therapist. Some transgender-friendly therapists call themselves "gender therapists" but not all do. Transgender specific questions to ask a therapist include: "Are you familiar with the latest version of the World Professional Association for Transgender Health (WPATH)'s Standards of Care (SOC)?"; "How many transgender youth have you worked with?"; "What is your policy around hormones?"; and, "How long do you require a client to be seen before you will provide a letter of support for gender affirmation surgery?"

*Abi Weissman*

continue to hone the skills acquired from parents and friends while also introducing new relational skills. These new relational skills may include practice with various sexual behaviors and the opportunity to deal with infidelity, breakups, and the emotions they invoke (Bouchey & Furman, 2003). Thus, relationships with parents and friends significantly influence social, emotional, and cognitive development, which will then influence one's romantic relationships.

Although most of the research on childhood emotional attachment has been conducted with heterosexual (or presumed heterosexual) participants, there is no reason to expect any differences in LGBTQ people's developmental trajectories or in the cumulative nature of their interpersonal relationships. Nevertheless, LGBTQ relationships can be affected by specific sexual and gendered behaviors and identities, and how those are received by the wider society.

## CHILDHOOD

Paradoxically, researchers and the general public often assume that children are both non-sexual *and* heterosexual. The notion that sexual identity and sexual orientation may develop prior to adolescence is a relatively recent development (Institute of Medicine, 2011). Parenting practices around gender and sexuality reveal how childhood is imbued with heteronormative ideals and practices that can penalize gender-non-conforming children—no matter their actual gender identity or sexual orientation. These practices may ultimately strain the parent-child relationship which, given the cumulative nature of relationships, can have negative repercussions for later relationships.

### "Doing" Gender

The need to adhere to society's gendered expectations is instilled in infancy and reinforced throughout childhood. Through interactions with their children, parents convey specific gendered expectations (Leaper, 2002; McHale, Crouter, & Whiteman, 2003; Ruble, Martin, & Berenbaum, 2006). Children then also police the gender behaviors of their peers (Robinson, 2005). For example, young girls may tell a young boy he is not allowed to sing a popular song by a female artist as it is a girl's song. Ultimately, as a result of gendered expectations from family, friends, and society in general, many children progressively adhere to gendered norms and expectations as they age. This is especially true for boys who, during adolescence, increasingly avoid displaying stereotypically feminine traits (McHale, Kim, Dotterer, Crouter, & Booth, 2009). As a consequence, boys show a drop in emotional expressiveness, while girls do not show a similar decline in instrumentality (McHale et al., 2009).

This steady process of gradual adherence to society's gender norms has been described as "doing gender" (West & Zimmerman, 1987). Rather than being innate, gender is something that people perform; something they "do" rather than something they "are." If a child is a boy, he is expected to do boy things, have specific interests, and behave in masculine ways. Children become active participants in the gendering process as early as two (Kane, 2006). Those who "do" gender in accordance with society's expectations are rewarded, while those who do not are punished. Gender-variant children (children who do not perform the gender associated with their biological sex) are often punished by parents, family members, teachers, and peers. Fathers' parenting practices appear to be more influenced by the gender of their children than are mothers' parenting practices, and both mothers and fathers appear to police sons' behaviors more than daughters' (Antill, 1987; Coltrane, & Adams, 1997; Maccoby, 1998). Fathers seem especially concerned with their sons' gender conformity. So much so that some mothers may invoke the threat of a father's wrath to police their son's gendered behavior (e.g., saying, "No you can't have that, your father wouldn't like it") (Kane, 2006, p. 171). But gender variance can be positive, because one is not limited by the roles and expectations associated with their biological sex. Some parents and others may encourage or embrace their child's gender expansiveness rather than limit it.

## Transgender Children

While many children exhibit gender-expansive or gender-variant behavior at some point during childhood, other children express a strong and persistent identification with a gender other than the one they were assigned at birth. This is the more common definition and understanding of the term "transgender." Most children are assumed—by parents, society, and child development researchers—to be cisgender. That is, that their gender identity will correspond to the gender they were labeled with or assigned at birth. Because the distinct concepts of gender and sexuality are often poorly understood by parents, caregivers, pediatricians, and the wider society, it may be assumed that a child's gender identity only emerges during adolescence as part of sexual maturation. Thus, when a child behaves or outright asserts a gender identity at odds with their labeling/assignment at birth, parents may alleviate their fears by viewing their child's behavior as a "phase" they will grow out of with time.

Parents of transgender children may struggle to come to terms with who their children are and may, even if well intentioned, cause psychological harm by rejecting or policing their child's gender expressions. While the parents of transgender children face many of the same issues as peers with gay- or lesbian-identified children, they can experience more difficulty and isolation. (Field & Mattson, 2016).

Specifically, parents of transgender children acknowledge difficulties with the physical changes their children undergo (if they decide to gender transition), the lack of transgender people represented in the media, the effect of the child's transition on their own identity, and the tensions involved with the child's successful transition in public settings. Some of these difficulties may be alleviated by recognizing some of the ways these parents are similar to parents of lesbian and gay children. Specifically, many parents of LGBTQ children grieve and mourn the loss of the imagined life they had for their child, as well as address fears of being a bad parent (Field & Mattson, 2016).

Clearly, parents play a crucial role in their children's lives and set the stage for future relationships. Unfortunately, the parent-child bond is often challenged when a child comes out as LGBTQ. However, not all children display gender variant behaviors, cause their parents to speculate about their sexual orientation, or realize their own feelings at such a young age. Indeed, many more are likely to come to such awareness only during or after adolescence.

## COMING OUT

It is during the adolescent years that, for many, a desire for intimacy (with a romantic other) and sexuality arise and prompt teenagers to begin dating. Adolescents are more likely than children to come out as LGBQ as they come to realize, and desire to share, their non-normative identity with those closest to them. Consistently lesbian and gay adolescents report that their relationships with their parents become more difficult around the time they come out (D'Augelli, Grossman, & Starks, 2005; Patterson, 2000). Perhaps unsurprisingly, supportive family environments can have long term positive effects on LGBTQ adolescents.

Coming out refers to the act of disclosing a minority or non-normative sexual or gender identity (those identities represented by the acronym LGBTQ) to friends, family, peers, and the wider society. The act of coming out to family is a very important psychological decision and is "perceived as an obstacle by the individual making the disclosure" (Perrin-Wallqvist & Lindblom, 2015, p. 468). Throughout the coming out process LGBTQ adolescents often feel a range of conflicting emotions that include: fear, confusion, vulnerability, empowerment, exhilaration, relief, pride, uncertainty, bravery, and affirmation (HRC, 2014). While there are numerous benefits to coming out, there are a few benefits that are particularly germane to relationships with family. Coming out can help LGBTQ people develop closer and more genuine relationships, reduce stress associated with hiding their true identity, and help build self-esteem through being known and loved for their whole selves (HRC, 2014).

Coming out can create stress for LGBTQ adolescents because it challenges the values, expectations, and boundaries of their families (Willoughby, Malik, & Lindahl, 2006). Coming out can be an important developmental milestone and a sign of psychological health (LaSala, 2000). After coming out to their parents, some lesbian and gay adolescents have said they feel whole, complete, and that they could now live fully (Perrin-Wallqvist & Lindblom, 2015). Yet, it may not be the best course of action for all LGBT adolescents (Green, 2000). When adolescents work up the courage to come out, family reaction can vary from withdrawal of support to acceptance (Heatherington & Lavner, 2008). Coming out is

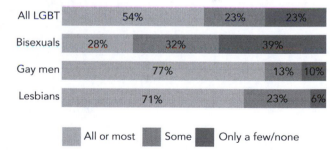

*Percent of LGBT people saying all or most of the important people in their life are aware that they are LGBT (2013). Source: Adapted from data collected by Pew Research Center.*

often a positive step for lesbian and gay adolescents and their relationship with their parents, but the stress associated with coming out can be similar to that experienced with depression (Russell, Toomey, Ryan, & Diaz, 2014). Some studies find that initial parental response to a child's coming out is negative (Robinson, Walters, & Skeen, 1989; Savin-Williams & Ream, 2003). LGB youth whose parents were rejecting report elevated levels of suicidal ideation and attempts, depression, drug use, and unprotected sex (Ryan, Huebner, Diaz, & Sanchez, 2009).

As others have speculated, parents' initial reaction may serve as a proxy for overall general support, attitude, and attachment to their children (Rothman, Sullivan, Keyes, & Boehmer, 2012). Rejecting parents may lose their child's trust, creating a barrier between parent and child. In some instances, parents disown their child, which helps account for an overrepresentation of LGBTQ youth in the homeless population. Indeed, homeless youth are more likely to be LGBT (Snyder et al., 2016). Researchers estimate that between 20% and 40% of all homeless youth are LGBT (Ray & Berger, 2007). Thankfully, not all families are rejecting and, given society's overall shift to acceptance of LGBTQ people, more families are accepting of their LGBTQ children than ever before (Pew Research Center, 2015).

It should be noted that the act of coming out is a concept that does not describe all LGBTQ adolescents' relationships with their families, especially for LGBTQ people of color, who are less likely to be out to their parents, while Latino youth disclose to fewer people in general (Grov, Bimbi, Nanin, & Parsons, 2006; Rosario, Schrimshaw, & Hunter, 2004). Further factors, such as social class, geographical location, and religious affiliation, among other characteristics, also impact the coming out experience. Lastly, while many begin to come out during their adolescent years, many wait until they are older, and regardless of when one comes out, the individual will find that coming out is a lifetime experience—having to potentially come out to every new person one meets.

## The Importance of Support

Supportive and accepting families increase a number of positive outcomes for their LGBTQ children, which in turn will help them foster healthier relationships across their lifespan. Not all parents' reactions to their child's sexual orientation disclosure are negative. In one study, two-thirds of LGB adolescents reported receiving social and emotional support from the parent to whom they first came out, that parent most often being their biological mother (Rothman et al., 2012). Indeed, numerous studies have found that family acceptance can have tremendously positive effects for LGBTQ adolescents. Specifically, family acceptance predicts greater self-esteem, social support, and general health status, while also buffering against depression, substance abuse, and risky sexual behavior (Ryan, Russell, Huebner, Diaz, & Sanchez, 2010).

Indeed, the benefits of family acceptance are multifaceted for LGBTQ adolescents. Family support has a positive effect on self-acceptance of one's sexual orientation and one's well-being while also being negatively associated with mental distress (Shilo & Savaya, 2011). Supportive and accepting parents help maintain the parent–child relationship, which has positive effects for LGBTQ adolescents. Positive parental attachment is associated with an older age of dating initiation (Starks, Newcomb, & Mustanski, 2015), which is likely to contribute to decreasing risky sexual behavior and substance use and abuse. Lastly, family support and acceptance protects LGBTQ adolescents from their own negative thoughts and feelings related to their sexual orientation, but not, unfortunately, from overt discrimination (Feinstein, Wadsworth, Davila, & Goldfried, 2014). Support groups for parents, such as PFLAG, can help strengthen parent-child or parent-adolescent or even parent-adult child relationships, which can have positive effects on other LGBTQ people's relationships.

---

### Parents and Friends of Lesbians and Gays (PFLAG)

Parents and Friends of Lesbians and Gays was founded in 1973 by Jeanne Manford, an elementary school teacher who had been advocating for gay rights after her son Morty was beaten while protesting a meeting of New York City politicians. Mrs. Manford started writing letters to the editor, giving radio and television interviews, and marching in parades to support her gay son. At the June 1972 Christopher Street Liberation Day Parade (what would now be called a Pride Parade) she carried a sign that read, "Parents of Gays Unite in Support for Our Children." The enthusiastic reception prompted her to start holding meetings for gay and lesbian-supportive parents, which eventually grew to become PFLAG. The first meeting was held in March 1973 in Greenwich Village, New York City. In the years following, PFLAG groups sprang up around the country. Organizations with similar names and purposes have been established in many other countries, including Canada and China. PFLAG's mission is to support families, allies, and people who are LGBTQ, educate about the unique issues and challenges facing LGBTQ people, and advocate for policies and laws that achieve full equality for LGBTQ people. The scope of the organization gradually expanded to include parents with bisexual and transgender children.

PFLAG offers the tools and resources families need to thrive and grow after a child comes out. Families that join PFLAG are often self-selecting, meaning that only more accepting and supportive families are likely to become involved in the organization. The challenge is reaching families who are rejecting of their LGBTQ adolescent to help parents mend their relationship with their child. Involvement in PFLAG often means that families come out as having an LGBTQ family member. Coming out as a family can illustrate to the LGBTQ family member that they are accepted and supported as well as help reduce the stigma surrounding LGBTQ identities (Goldfried & Goldfried, 2001).

## ADOLESCENT AND PEER RELATIONSHIPS

Coming out to family is just one realm wherein sexuality and/or gender expression affects relationships; another is within peer friendships. Although family relationships are established before peer relationships and the capacity to form and maintain peer relationships stems from familial relationships, LGBTQ people are more likely to come out to friends before family (Grov et al., 2006; Savin-Williams, 1998). Elementary school aged children report parents as their primary source of support, but by early and middle adolescence same-sex friends replace parents as the primary source of social support (Furman & Buhrmester, 1992). Just as attachment to parents is associated with self-esteem and life-satisfaction, so too is attachment to one's peers (Armsden & Greenberg, 1987). Therefore, coming out to peers carries with it the potential to be as stressful and as rewarding as coming out to parents. Similarly, the consequences of peer acceptance and rejection mirror those of family acceptance or rejection, although family support may be more salient and important than peer support (Mustanski, Newcomb, & Garofalo, 2011; Plöderl & Fartacek, 2005).

To understand the experience of LGBTQ adolescents and their peer relationships it is important to understand where they occur developmentally. Peer relationships become especially salient during early adolescence, when they eclipse family relationships (Brown & Braun, 2013; Brown & Larson, 2009). This increased importance, coupled with cognitive and social developments, can result in stress associated with fitting in and negative consequences of feeling rejected or being victimized (Rubin, Coplan, Chen, Buskirk, & Wojslawowicz, 2005; Steinberg, 2014).

## The School Context

School environments are key sites for the establishment and maintenance of LGBTQ peer relationships over the course of adolescence. Compulsory education laws require that children attend school for a predetermined amount of time, usually until the age of 18. As a result LGBTQ adolescents are legally required to attend school despite the fact that many schools are unsafe for LGBTQ people. Most LGBTQ adolescents experience discrimination at school (Kosciw, Greytak, Palmer, & Boesen, 2014), and 65% report often hearing homophobic remarks, 85% report being verbally harassed in the previous year, and 56% report experiencing discriminatory school policies and practices. Further, 30% of LGBT students missed at least one day of school within the previous month because they felt unsafe or uncomfortable. These experiences contribute to lower grade point averages, lower self-esteem, and less likelihood that LGBT students will plan to go to college (Kosciw et al., 2014).

Adolescents excel socially and academically when schools provide opportunities to engage actively and independently in their own learning within a supportive and warm climate (Grolnick & Raftery-Helmer, 2015; Gunn & Goldstein, 2017; Roeser, Eccles, & Sameroff, 2000). Yet, schools are often not fulfilling the needs of LGBTQ students (Kosciw et al., 2014). This failure on the part of the school likely strains relationships between LGBTQ students and their peers, even peers who may be supportive.

Thankfully, many schools have taken steps to transform unsupportive and hostile school climates for LGBTQ students and those who attend schools with Gay-Straight Alliances (GSAs), or safe spaces, report lower incidences of suicidal thoughts compared to LGBTQ students who do not (Hatzenbuehler, Birkett, Wagenen, & Meyer, 2014). Further, LGBT youth who have supportive peers report less loneliness compared to their unsupported peers (McConnell, Birkett, & Mustanski, 2015). For cisgender, heterosexual, and LGBTQ youth, GSAs create a context for developing positive attitudes about self and others, empower youth to critique and challenge dominant norms about gender and sexuality, increase feelings of safety at school, and find peer support and friendships (Herdt, Russell, Sweat, & Marzullo, 2007; Kosciw et al., 2014; Russell, Muraco, Subramaniam, & Laub, 2009).

## Bullying and Victimization

LGBTQ adolescents report an inordinate amount of discrimination and victimization at the hands of peers, family, or community members, which can affect their overall mental health (Hershberger & D'Augelli, 1995). One study found that one-quarter of LGBs had been or continued to be distressed regularly by their recollections of school bullying (Rivers, 2004). This same study found that these individuals were also more likely to suffer depression and to engage in riskier sexual behavior as they entered adulthood (Rivers, 2004). Lowered self-esteem and lowered school performance are often associated with bullying as well (Kowalski & Limber, 2013).

Many LGBTQ and heterosexual youth alike are targets of bullying because of their gender non-conformity. When bullies, victims, and bystanders were interviewed about why someone was bullied, they cited being different,

| LGBT Youth | Non-LGBT Youth |
| --- | --- |
| My parents/family not accepting 26% | Trouble with classes/exams/grades 22% |
| Trouble at school/Bullying 21% | College and career decisions 17% |
| Afraid to be out/open 18% | Finances/Paying for college/Getting a job 14% |
| Eating disorders/Self-harm/Depression/Suicide 14% | Family stress/pressure 10% |
| Generally being LGBT 12% | Life balance 8% |
| Trouble with classes 9% | General stress 5% |
| Lonely 7% | Want a boyfriend/girlfriend/Boy/girl problems 5% |
| Religion leading to lack of acceptance 6% | Family illness/death 3% |
| Problems in romantic relationship 6% | Problems with lack of friends/Social life 3% |
| Concerns about college/money for college 6% | Bipolar/Depression/Eating disorders/Anxiety 3% |
| Confused about sexuality 5% | Injuries 2% |
| Finding a partner/Accepting partner 5% | I don't have any difficult problems 2% |
| Drama 3% | Problems in romantic relationships 1% |
| Nobody to date 2% | Drugs/Drinking 1% |

*Biggest problems facing LGBT youth—in their own words. Source: Adapted using data collected by Human Rights Campaign.*

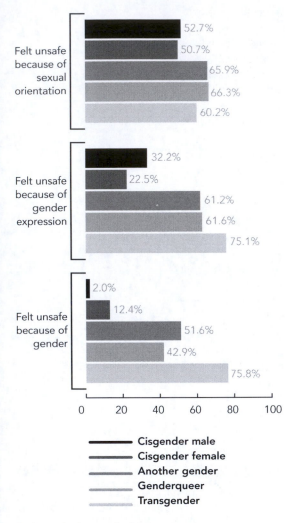

Felt unsafe because of sexual orientation
- 52.7%
- 50.7%
- 65.9%
- 66.3%
- 60.2%

Felt unsafe because of gender expression
- 32.2%
- 22.5%
- 61.2%
- 61.6%
- 75.1%

Felt unsafe because of gender
- 2.0%
- 12.4%
- 51.6%
- 42.9%
- 75.8%

0    20    40    60    80    100

— Cisgender male
— Cisgender female
— Another gender
— Genderqueer
— Transgender

*Feelings of safety at school by gender identity (2015). Source: GLSEN.*

the way someone talked, and the clothes they wore (Swearer & Cary, 2003). Bullying based on appearance or mannerisms, especially for LGBTQ youth, may result in increased internalized homophobia, which could hinder their ability to love and accept themselves. This, in turn, could make it more challenging to form meaningful and intimate relationships, especially as they reach developmental milestones associated with dating. Collectively, the negative effect of being ostracized and bullied because of actual or perceived sexual orientation has the potential to severely constrain the lives and relationships of LGBTQ individuals.

## DATING AND ROMANTIC RELATIONSHIPS

Much like cisgender and heterosexual people, dating is one way LGBTQ people practice and pursue romantic relationships (Savin-Williams, 2007). Whether it is an adolescent boy seeking his first boyfriend, a middle-aged transwoman who has recently transitioned, or an elderly widower seeking romantic connections again, looking for love can be exciting, terrifying, or difficult.

Although not all LGBTQ people are same-sex attracted, for those who are finding romantic and sexual partners often requires more effort and risk than searching for other-sex partners (Dube & Savin-Williams, 1999). Same-sex relationships are still stigmatized and seen as less authentic than other-sex romantic relationships (Frost, 2011). There are a number of risk factors affecting the development of same-sex romantic relationships, including homophobia, lack of a normative and legal template for same-sex couples, and lower levels of family support (Green, R., 2004). In fact, in a qualitative study of 40 committed same-sex couples of various ages only one-third perceived their family as supportive of their sexual orientation and as welcoming to their partner (Rostosky, Riggle, Gray, & Hatton, 2007).

Many LGBTQ people begin seeking romantic or sexual relationships in adolescence and young adulthood. LGB adolescents who are out are more likely to have had romantic relationships with same-sex partners, yet most LGB youth have engaged in heterosexual dating, whether out of curiosity or the desire to conform (Savin-Williams, 2007). Some LGB adolescents experience barriers to dating, such as peer harassment, lack of available partners, or lack of family support. A study of African-American bisexual and gay male adolescents also found that many had been sexually active with girls (Eyre, Milbrath, & Peacock, 2007). Many of the adolescent boys met their boyfriends through school, and reported courtships of several months before any sexual relationship began. Other research has found that young lesbians also often meet partners through school or networks of friends (Macapagal, Green, Rivera, & Mustanski, 2015).

## Unique Characteristics

While people may date at any age, older LGBT individuals may have barriers that impact dating, such as their own internalized homophobia (Suen, 2015). A study of single gay men aged 35 and over found that about 35% were seeking romantic partners (Hostetler, 2009). Many attributed their single status to stigma, discrimination, and a lack of positive role models. Research with similarly aged lesbians found that 11% were single (Rose & Zand, 2002).

The idea a person has about how a date proceeds is sometimes called a "dating script." Dating scripts are often based on heterosexual couples and tend to have heavily gendered role expectations (Klinkenberg & Rose, 1984). These scripts may not apply to same-sex dating. There is a common perception that same-sex relationships are structured by traditional heterosexual gender roles, with one partner playing the "feminine" or "woman's" role and the other playing the "masculine" or "man's" role. However, this stereotype is not supported by research on same-sex dating or partnered relationships (Bailey, Kim, Hills, & Linsenmeier, 1997; Smith & Stillman, 2002). In fact, some lesbians have asserted that what they felt was unique about lesbian dating was freedom from gender roles and an emphasis on friendship (Rose & Zand; 2002).

Committed relationships are generally beneficial. College students in romantic relationships tend to have better mental health than those not in a relationship (Braithwaite, Delevi, & Fincham, 2010). Married people have better psychological and physical health than those who are single (Robles, 2014; Robles & Kiecolt-Glaser, 2003; Wright, LeBlanc, & Lee Badgett, 2013). Married LGBT people had less psychological distress than those in same-sex couples who had a domestic partnership (Wright et al., 2013). For bisexual women, the benefits of being in a relationship may depend on the gender of the partner. Bisexual women in relationships with men report worse mental health and depression than bisexual women with female partners (Dyar, Feinstein, & London, 2014; Molina et al., 2015).

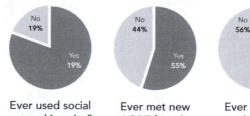

Ever used social networking site?

Ever met new LGBT friends online?

Ever revealed sexual orientation/ gender identity online?

Regularly discuss LGBT issues online?

Regardless of sexual orientation or gender, many want and seek out romantic partners for love, affection, and commitment. For sexual minorities in particular, romantic relationships may offer love and affirmation and a sense of well-being in a culture that does not often provide it. Regardless of sexual orientation, women

*Online behaviors of LGBT adults (2013). Source: Adapted using data collected by Pew Research Center.*

place more emphasis on potential romantic partners' personalities, whereas men tend to emphasize physical characteristics (Peplau & Fingerhut, 2007; Peplau & Spalding, 2000). Research also suggests that LGBT people are more likely than heterosexuals to have a partner of a different age, socioeconomic status, and race and ethnicity (Jepsen & Jepsen, 2002).

### Finding a Romantic Partner

Searching for partners using Internet websites and cell phone dating applications has increased for single people of all ages and sexual identities (Smith & Duggan, 2013). While some general dating sites have sections for "women seeking women" or "men seeking men," others specifically cater to same-sex attracted people, especially gay and bisexual men. The Internet provides privacy and a larger dating pool, which may especially appeal to those who are not out of the closet, live in less-than-supportive states or communities, and gender and sexual minorities generally (Potarca, Mills, & Neberich, 2015).

Like their heterosexual peers, LGBT individuals also use the Internet and networking sites at high rates to seek out social support, friendship, and sexual partners (Gudelunas, 2012). In fact, the majority of gay men in their study met their first sexual partner on the Internet (the second most common place was a gay venue such as a bar). LGB individuals are more likely than heterosexual individuals to use the Internet to seek romantic and sexual partners (Lever, Grov, Royce, & Gillespie, 2008). Unfortunately, no research has examined whether transgender individuals are more likely to use the Internet to seek out partners. There was a significant increase from 1993 to 2002 in usage of the Internet to meet first time sexual partners, suggesting that more and more LGBT folks may be accessing the Internet to search for partners (Bolding, Davis, Hart, Sherr, & Elford, 2007).

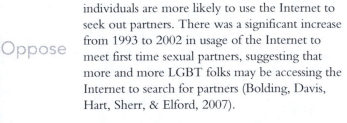

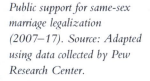

*Public support for same-sex marriage legalization (2007–17). Source: Adapted using data collected by Pew Research Center.*

### PARTNERED RELATIONSHIPS AND FAMILY FORMS

There are over 700,000 households headed by same-sex couples in the United States, with slightly more female than male same-sex couples (United States Census, 2014). About 16% of such couples were interracial (more than double that of married heterosexual couples). Same-sex couples were also more likely to have a Bachelor's Degree than heterosexual couples.

Lesbian and gay couples did not have access to state and federal marriage recognition until 2014–2015, and many still are denied social, legal, and family support (Kitzinger & Coyle, 1995; Kurdek, 2004; 2005). Romantic relationships may buffer against the stresses caused by being stigmatized; however, stigma can also create relationship stress (Peplau & Fingerhut, 2007). Stigma based on sexual orientation can affect the relationship satisfaction of same-sex couples, and discrimination and relationship stigma can negatively influence both transgender women and their male partners (Gamarel, Reisner, Laurenceau, Nemoto, Operario, 2014; Muraco, 2015). Further, some transgender people fear being rejected if they disclose their transgender identity to their partners (Iantaffi & Bockting, 2011).

Relationship quality and satisfaction appears to be similar among lesbian, gay male, and heterosexual couples (Kurdek, 2005; Roisman, Clausell, Holland, Fortuna, & Elieff, 2008). Although, some lesbian couples report higher levels of relationship satisfaction, less conflict, and more partner support than either heterosexual or gay male couples (Metz, Rosser, & Strapko, 1994; Meuwly, Feinstein, Davila, Nunez, & Bodenmann, 2013). Lesbian couples have also reported higher levels of intimacy than heterosexual and gay male couples (Kurdek, 1998). One factor that can influence relationship satisfaction for same-sex and other-sex partners is the social support of families and other important people in the lives of couples. Those couples with more support tend to be happier (Graham & Barnow, 2013).

One area of particular interest in research on lesbian and gay male relationships has been the issue of gender equality. Traditional relationship roles of men and women in heterosexual relationships are grounded in different expectations and inequality. Because both partners in a lesbian or gay relationship are of the same sex, partners typically do not play traditional gender roles. Gay male and lesbian couples are more likely to value equality in their relationships than are heterosexual couples (Kurdek, 2004). This is especially true for lesbian couples. Additionally, gay male and lesbian couples are more likely to divide household labor evenly (Kurdek, 2005; Kurdek, 2006; Goldberg, 2013). However, similar to heterosexual couples, factors such as education, income, and hours worked outside the home affected the division of household labor (Sutphin, 2010).

While many perceive monogamy or sexual exclusivity as the ideal relationship structure, other couples define their ideal relationship as one where partners are not sexually exclusive or ones that include multiple partners. Non-exclusive relationships are not unusual for gay men, bisexuals, and transgender people (Grov, Starks, Rendina, & Parsons, 2014; LaSala, 2004; Iantaffi & Bockting; 2011; Molina et al., 2015). When both members of a couple have agreed to non-monogamy, relationship satisfaction is similar to that of monogamous couples (LaSala, 2004). Some research has found that, compared to straight or gay/lesbian identified individuals, bi-identified individuals are less likely to see monogamy as enhancing a relationship and more likely to see it as a sacrifice in the relationship (Mark, Rosenkrantz, & Kerner, 2014). Because LGBTQ individuals do not have the specific norms for relationships that heterosexual couples do, they are more likely to create their own relationship structures that are free of traditional constraints. Without traditional role constraints, individuals and couples can create their own consensual relationships that work for them. For example, some LGBTQ people have sexual or romantic relationships with more than one person, but everyone involved is sexually exclusive. For others, they are exclusive with certain types of sex, non-exclusive with other kinds. Others have non-monogamous but asymmetrical and sexually exclusive relationships with more than one person.

Thus, LGBTQ romantic and sexual relationships, while similar to their heterosexual peers, can be more diverse. This diversity may exist, in part, in protest to heteronormativity and the notion that only monogamous heterosexual relationships are valuable and legitimate. However, despite this diversity, many LGBTQ individuals enter into long-term relationships, with many even marrying; however, freed from the shackles of heteronormative thinking, some LGBTQ people have creatively formed new and ever-evolving relationship structures with negotiated arrangements governing romance, commitment, and sex.

## RELATIONSHIP DISSOLUTION

Research done before legal marriage equality in the United States indicated that, in general, same-sex couples were more likely to break-up compared to heterosexual couples (Blumstein & Schwartz, 1983; Lau, 2012). In one study spanning five years, 7% of heterosexual married couples, 14% of gay couples and 16% of lesbian couples dissolved their relationship (Kurdek, 1998). These higher rates of relationship dissolution were at least in part because same-sex couples had fewer barriers to breaking-up than did heterosexual couples, especially no legal barriers (Kurdek, 1998, 2004). A comparison of the rates of "divorced" same-sex couples in registered partnerships and different-sex married couples in Norway and Sweden found that the divorce risk of gay male couples was 50% higher than for heterosexual couples, and the divorce risk of lesbian couples was about twice that of heterosexual couples (Andersson, Noack, Seierstad, & Weedon-Fekjaer, 2004). Risk factors such as age of partner and education level predicted the dissolution of relationships for both same-sex and heterosexual couples.

As same-sex couples become more visible and mainstream, this may lead to increased similarity to heterosexual couples in all aspects, including social structures that keep partners together. A more recent study comparing heterosexual married couples and married, or in marriage-like, same-sex relationships found little difference in break-up rates over the length of their respective relationships. Interestingly, both unmarried same-sex and heterosexual couples had higher break-up rates compared to *all* married couples, but unmarried same-sex couples were significantly *less* likely than heterosexual couples to break up in the long term (Rosenfeld, 2014).

Government-recognized same-sex marriage is a relatively recent phenomenon in the United States and in other countries. The first country to legally recognize same-sex marriages was the Netherlands in 2000, the U.S. only did so in 2015 (although some individual states recognized same-sex civil unions and marriages prior to that year). Thus, few divorce statistics are available for same-sex marriages. However, early research suggests that same-sex divorces occur at the same or slightly lower rate than in different-sex marriages. About 1.1% of same-sex couples divorce annually, compared to 2% for different-sex couples. Until recently, divorces of same-sex marriages have been hampered by state and country laws. Often, at least one spouse needed to reside in a state or county that recognized same-sex marriage in order to seek a divorce in that jurisdiction, which made it difficult to calculate divorce rates in some states (Lee Badgett & Herman, 2011).

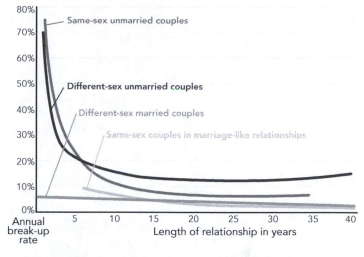

*Rates of relationship break-ups over time. Over the course of their relationships, married same-sex couples are no more likely to break up than married different-sex couples. Unmarried same-sex couples are less likely than different-sex couples to break up over time. Source: Adapted using data collected by Michael J. Rosenfeld, Stanford University.*

Married or not—when same-sex couples break up, lesbians and gay men are more likely to remain friends with former romantic partners (Swainson & Tasker, 2006; Weinstock, 2004). One study compared the attitudes of heterosexual males and females, gay men, and lesbians toward post-breakup connectedness and actual interactions with ex-partners (Harkless & Fowers, 2005). They found that both lesbians and gay men were more interested in keeping connections with their ex-partners and maintained more interactions and close ties with their ex-partners than were heterosexual women and men. The authors explain this phenomenon as motivated by a strong desire to maintain powerful bonds created during past relationships as a protection against surrounding homophobia and heterosexism. Thus, ex-partners may continue as friends and often serve in the support networks of many LGBTQ individuals.

## Violence in LGBT Relationships

Studies that have compared rates of relationship violence between same-sex and heterosexual couples generally find similar or higher rates among same-sex couples (Balsam, Rothblum, & Beauchaine, 2005; Drabble, Trocki, Hughes, Korcha, & Lown, 2013; Messinger, 2011). There are many reasons for higher levels of relationship violence within same-sex couples. Lesbians and gay men experience high rates of prejudice and discrimination and high rates of childhood abuse. They also report more feelings of disempowerment. As a result, lesbians and gay men are at increased risk of using and abusing alcohol. Collectively, these experiences, feelings, and the use of alcohol may result in attempts to

## Conflict and Communication in Same-Sex Relationships

All romantic couples, regardless of sexual orientation, struggle with various sources of stress and engage in conflict about similar topics, including finances, affection, sex, criticism, driving, and household chores (Kurdek, 2005). However, same-sex couples are often subject to additional stress sources beyond those of a different-sex couple, including stigmatization or marginalization, and fewer or unclear social norms surrounding their relationships. For example, while a different-sex couple may be quick to adopt traditional gender roles, a same-sex couple needs to divide these gendered roles between them (Toubia, 2014). They, in turn, may experience significant conflict in trying to decide which roles to take on and the perceived consequences.

These additional stress sources can make a same-sex couple ripe for conflict, which can cause a disruption in normal behaviors and, in turn, an increase in negative emotions (anger, fear, sadness, hurt, etc.). Therefore, the couple often experiences a decrease in relational satisfaction. Beyond affecting mental and relational health, conflict can also create physical health problems. For example, conflict is frequently linked to high blood pressure (Robles, Slatcher, Trombello, & McGinn, 2014), which can lead to numerous diseases, illnesses, and ailments.

The effects of such stress-inducing factors can be lessened through supportive social networks and effective conflict styles. First, social networks who are supportive of a couple are instrumental to a couple's relational satisfaction. Researchers have found many gay couples' social networks include many other gay individuals and couples (LeBlanc et al., 2015). Social support from within a marginalized community can help an individual or couple cope with the stress associated with potential stigmatization and marginalization (Frost & Meyer, 2012). In other words, because these individuals may have experienced similar stress or pressures, they may be better able to understand, relate to, and provide effective advice and information to same-sex individuals or couples.

Second, if conflict is handled successfully it can have less of a negative effect on the individual and the romantic relationship. Specifically, researchers suggest focusing on improving communication skills and effectively managing emotions. They found that, in comparison to different-sex couples, same-sex couples are more likely to begin conflict with a more positive tone and maintain a more constructive tone throughout the discussion (Gottman et al., 2003). The researchers speculated that same-sex couples were more likely to handle conflict in a positive manner because of a higher value on equality and fewer power and status differences within the couple than are found in a different-sex couple. And, same-sex couples are more likely than different-sex couples to seek out counseling to help improve their communication (Giammattei & Green, 2012). Even though same-sex couples may experience significant stress-inducing issues beyond different-sex couples, they are not destined for destructive conflict and/or break-ups.

*Elizabeth Ribarsky*

control those who expose vulnerabilities (Carvalho, Lewis, Derlega, Winstead, & Viggiano, 2011; Drabble et al., 2013; Fortunata & Kohn, 2003; McKenry, Serovich, Mason, & Mosack, 2006).

A study of LGB participants with ethnically diverse backgrounds found that bisexual women and men reported the lowest rates of perpetrating and receiving abuse (Turell, 2000). In that study, 92% of LGB Native Americans reported experiencing physical and emotional abuse. Women reported significantly higher levels of shaming, coercion, threat, and physical abuse. A more recent study that included both gay men and lesbians found lower rates of violence with about 17% of the sample reporting that they had been victims of same-sex partner violence and approximately 9% reporting that they had perpetrated violence against a same-sex partner in their lifetime (Carvalho et al., 2011).

While the previous studies were done with adult participants, a 2014 study examined dating violence in LGBT adolescents and found that LGBT youth reported high rates of physical, psychological, and cyber dating victimization and perpetration compared to heterosexual youth. Almost 89% of transgender youth in the study reported experiencing physical dating violence, while 58% reported perpetrating it (Dank, Lachman, Zweig, & Yahner, 2014).

Dating and partnering are both similar and distinctly different for LGBTQ individuals. In addition to many of the same stressors experienced by heterosexuals and cisgender people, LGBTQ people must navigate a society that does not necessarily value their sexual and romantic relationships.

## Unique Dimensions of IPV in Same-Sex Relationships

"Intimate partner violence" (IPV) is physical, verbal, emotional, economic, or sexual abuse by a romantic or sexual partner. Although IPV can occur in many kinds of relationships, there are some unique characteristics to IPV in same-sex relationships.

LGBTQ IPV can have unique dimensions: forced isolation from friends and family; coercion into unwanted sexual behavior, including forced, public, or unprotected sex; threats of outing to friends, family, or employers; undermining partners' gender or sexual identity; verbal assaults on gendered body parts or denial of access to objects that are central to sexual/gender-identity expression (for instance wigs, chest binders, etc.); threats to report immigration/citizenship status; and threats to reveal HIV status to police (in places where intentional HIV transmission is criminalized). IPV can result in long-term harm to physical and mental health, including low self-esteem, anxiety, depression, post-traumatic stress disorder (PTSD), suicidal ideation and suicide, engagement in risky sexual behavior, and drug and alcohol abuse.

LGBTQ IPV often goes unacknowledged, unreported, and unaddressed. This is due to legal definitions of IPV that don't include same-sex couples; fears of being "outed" if reporting IPV; the absence of LGBT-sensitive resources, shelters, or crisis centers; fears of homophobia from service

*(continued)*

*(continued)*

providers, healthcare workers, and law enforcement. Gender norms that associate dominance and independence with manliness may prevent or inhibit some bisexual, transgender, and gay men from reporting IPV, lest they appear to be less of "a man," thus confirming negative stereotypes about gender- and sexual-minority men. Heterosexist stereotypes about IPV (that only men perpetrate violence; that women's violence is not as bad as men's; etc.) can contribute to a reluctance to view LGBTQ relationship violence as wrong and potentially illegal. In small, close-knit LGBTQ communities, there may be a reluctance to report IPV out of a fear of losing chosen families or friendship networks, or of shedding a negative light on the LGBTQ community (Messinger, 2014; Brown & Herman, 2015).

*Michael J. Murphy*

## Family Forms

LGBT individuals may experience rejection or even violence from family members of origin because of their sexual orientation. Others may not be out to family because of their fears of negative outcomes (Savin-Williams & Ream, 2003). Some biological families may not be supportive or welcoming and, even when they are, they may not understand what it is to be gay in a stigmatizing culture. As a result, LGBT individuals have often formed "families of choice." LGBT people often have strong friendship networks to compensate for a lack of support or understanding by their biological families. A study of Belgian lesbians, gay men, and bisexuals found they were more likely to confide in friends, while heterosexual Belgians confided more in family members (DeWaele, Cox, Van den Berghe, & Vinke, 2011). Other research has found that young gay men often develop online networks to support them in coming out to families of origin (Etengoff & Daiute, 2015).

Families of choice are important for LGBTQ people throughout the course of their lives. As discussed earlier, lesbians and gay men are more likely to remain friendly with former partners. Aging LGBT individuals may find themselves caring for, or being cared for by, a strong supportive network of friends (Aronson, 1998; Cohen & Murray, 2007). Transgender people who feel part of a transgender community report a greater sense of well-being (Barr, Budge, & Adelson, 2016). A study of Black gay men in Toronto reported that they found connection and social and emotional support from the Black gay community (George et al., 2012).

It is clear that LGBTQ families of choice provide an important support that may be unique to LGBT culture. Yet, not all LGBT individuals receive the support they need. Because the LGBT community in many areas is predominantly White, LGBT individuals of color may not find the support they want or need. For example, Black lesbian couples reported that neither friends and family, nor gay and lesbian communities supported them, either as a couple or as a family headed by a Black lesbian couple (Glass & Few-Demo, 2013).

And a sample of gay Asian men in Canada reported mixed support in the gay community, with some finding it racist while others reported it as welcoming (Nakamura, Chan, & Fischer, 2013).

## Types of LGBTQ Families of Choice

LGBTQ children typically do not have LGBTQ parents and, thus, are unlikely to learn LGBTQ social practices and cultural rituals from their biological families. Also, some LGBTQ people are alienated from their biological kin, losing the kinds of support and community that families often provide. As a result, LGBTQ people have created a wide variety of alternative families—or "families of choice"—as sources of support, education, and community. LGBTQ families of choice may overlap, supplement, or completely replace biological families; and they may or may not replicate their titles (mom), roles (parent/child), or structures (Weston, 1997).

"Intergenerational families" or relationships, where older LGBTQ people (elders) mentor younger ones (gaybies; queerlings), are quite common. This type of family may consist of couples, small groups, or some combination of the two. They may arise through friendship networks (as when a group of older LGBTQ people "adopt" a younger LGBTQ person to support and mentor). Or, they may be the by-product of romantic or sexual relationships (as when young LGBTQ people find themselves part of an existing family of older LGBTQ people because they start dating one of its members). Finally, they may be formed intentionally through romantic or sexual relationships (as when LGBTQ people seek out partners who are significantly different in age). Importantly, there may or may not be romantic, sexual, or financial aspects to LGBTQ intergenerational families but, even if there are, these may not be explicit (Adam, 2000).

A "drag family" or "house" is formed by drag queens or kings to instruct and mentor young drag performers in the art of male or female impersonation for entertainment. (A similar kind of relationship can exist between older and younger transgender people, to mentor them in the nuances of gender expression during gender transition). Drag families may have a house "mother" or "father" and younger members may identify as "daughters" or "sons." More structured drag houses may compete against each other in elaborate "balls," where family members are judged on dancing, presentation, and personality (Labeija & Pendavis, 1992).

"Leather families" refer to chosen families between two or more members of the BDSM/leather community—some of which is LGBTQ-identified. Like other kinds of chosen families, LGBTQ leather families are grounded in a community organized around shared interests and activities that may or may not be romantic or sexual in nature. The term can refer to the larger community of BDSM/leather fetishists, close friends who are also BDSM/leather fetishists, cohabiting "households" of members with various roles

*(continued)*

*(continued)*

(dom/sub, master/slave, boy/daddy, etc.), and "back-patch" families that function as a kind of extended family with family trees, heraldic crests, and so on. Leather family titles, roles, and relationships (for instance "master" and "slave") may co-exist with romantic or sexual relationships with other partners who may or may not be part of the BDSM/leather community (Master Taíno, 2012).

"Polyamorous families" are negotiated sexual and/or romantic relationships between more than two people with the knowledge and consent of all involved. Terms such as "throuple" and "quad" have emerged to describe polyamorous relationships between three and four people. Ideally, "poly" families are characterized by a spirit of ethics, honesty, transparency, and mutual respect. They may be sexually exclusive or open (allowing sex outside the relationship). Although open relationships are common among gay male couples, polyamorous families are neither common nor exclusive to LGBTQ people. Few jurisdictions allow marriage or offer other kinds of legal recognition of polyamorous families (Shernoff, 2006).

*Michael J. Murphy*

## PARENTING

Beyond creating families of choice, increasingly same-sex couples are raising children. These families mirror traditional heterosexual families notwithstanding their more precarious position in society. Despite popular stereotypes, LGBTQ people are often parents, and a parent's gender expression, gender identity, and sexual orientation can influence the parent-child relationship. The 2014 U.S. Census American Community Survey Data reported over 17% of lesbian and gay male couples had children in the home, compared to 39% of married heterosexual couples and 41% of unmarried heterosexual couples. An estimated 37% of LGBT people have had a child at some point in their lives. The number of transgender individuals who are parents is estimated to be between one-quarter and one-half of all transgender individuals. Black and Latino/a couples are more likely to have children than White couples, and 41% of same-sex couples with children identify as people of color, and about half of all children living with same-sex couples are non-White (NBJC, 2012). LGB individuals are six times more likely to be foster parents and four times more likely to be adoptive parents than heterosexual couples (Gates, 2013).

In the past, most same-sex couples had their children in prior heterosexual relationships. In an attempt to conform to the demands of a heteronormative society or as a result of internalized homophobia, some gays and lesbians married different-sex partners and had families with children. Others were not fully aware of their same-sex attractions until after many years in opposite-sex relationships that may have produced children. Also, because many gay, lesbian, and bisexual people's first sexual encounters were with different-sex partners, they may also have children as a result of early sexual experiences that may not fully reflect their later sexual identities. Finally, some people's sexual orientations change over time, meaning that a person might have once (or later) identified as heterosexual and engaged in sexual behavior that produced children (Diamond, 2008; Hernandez, Schwenke, & Wilson, 2011; Higgins, 2002).

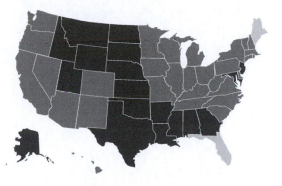

20%+ LGBT population raising children
16% - 19% LGBT population raising children
Under 15% LGBT population raising children

Today, more same-sex and transgender couples are having children within relationships with LGBTQ-identified partners, whether biologically or through adoption. This is partly owed to advancements in reproductive technologies and more socially progressive attitudes toward same-sex parent adoption.

*LGBT people raising children (2017). Source: Adapted from original by permission of Movement Advancement Project.*

While parenting can be stressful for any parent, LGBT parents may have additional stressors in that their right and ability to parent may be questioned, and legal barriers may prevent adoption or recognition of the non-biological parent (Patterson, 2013; Pyne, Bauer, & Bradley, 2015; Rye & Meany, 2010; Weiner & Zinner, 2015).

Contrary to the findings of the Regnerus study discussed at the beginning of this chapter, a large body of research demonstrates that children of same-sex parents are as well-adjusted as children of heterosexual parents and are no more likely to be LGBT than those raised by heterosexual parents (Patterson, 2006; Anderssen, Amlie, & Ytteroy, 2002; Bailey, Bobrow, Wolfe, & Mikach, 1995). In fact, adults who were raised by LGB parents indicate that they believed that, because of their parents, they were more open-minded and had more flexible ideas about gender and sexuality. They also felt some pressure to be heterosexual and to portray their family positively (Goldberg, 2007a). While as children they had a wide range of feelings about their parents' LGB status, as adults most children of LGB parents felt pride in their parents (Goldberg, 2007b).

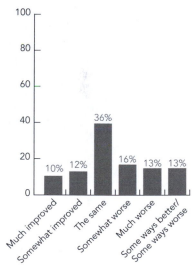

*How their gender identity impacted transgender parents' relationships with their children (2011). Source: Adapted from data collected by National Center for Transgender Equality.*

Research does suggest some parenting differences. Lesbian and gay parents share their household, parenting, and income-earning responsibilities more equally than do heterosexual couples (Biblarz & Stacey, 2010). Same-sex couples also report more compatibility with division of labor with the partner as co-parent, as well as more relationship satisfaction than heterosexual co-parenting couples. Gay fathers tend to show more warmth, higher levels of interaction, and more responsiveness than heterosexual fathers (Golumbok, Mellish, Tasker, & Lamb, 2014).

Less research has been done on transgender parents. A recent national study found that 38% of transgender respondents were parents (Grant, Mottet, Tanis, Harrison, & Herman, 2011). One study interviewed Canadian transgender fathers and mothers (Pyne, Bauer, & Bradley 2015). Many of the parents felt that being transgender had hurt or embarrassed their family. A number had lost custody or access to their child had been legally removed because they were transgender. Transgender parents often worry about how their trans status will impact their children (Haines, Ajayi, & Boyd, 2014). However, most transgender parents say that they have positive relationships with their children, including after gender transitioning (Gates, 2013).

## LGBT Youth with LGBT Parents

While children of LGBT parents appear no more likely to be LGB than children of heterosexual parents, some LGBT children do have LGBT parents, and those children have been called "second generation." Their experiences vary widely. For example, some experience subtle pressure not to be LGBT by their parents lest they confirm stereotypical beliefs that homosexuals expand their numbers by "recruiting" children. Only about half felt that their parents' LGBT identity affected their own. Many reported support and lack of fear of coming out to their parents because of their identity (Kuvalanka & Goldberg, 2009).

## WORK RELATIONSHIPS

Most adults spend substantial amounts of time at work and form relationships with co-workers. Many LGBT individuals may need to decide whether to disclose sexual orientation at work. Some research shows that disclosing a minority sexual or gender identity at work is related to higher job satisfaction (Drydakis, 2015; Griffith & Hebl, 2002). One study found that LGB employees who had not fully disclosed their sexual orientation were less satisfied with their job, more likely to say they would leave, engaged in less workplace participation, and had more workplace depression and anxiety (Ragins, Singh, & Cornwell, 2007). In a 2011 survey of transgender individuals about 50% were out as transgender at work (Grant et al., 2011). Because one may spend many hours with colleagues, needing to monitor and censor personal information can be very stressful and tiring.

However, disclosure of a minority sexual orientation is associated with workplace discrimination (Ragins & Cornwell, 2001). One study found 39.7% of sexual minorities had experienced sexual harassment in the past year, 76.9% experienced gender harassment (messages or treatment about failing to adhere to gender norms), and 66.4% experienced heterosexist harassment (hostile behaviors about perceived LGB identity) (Konik & Cortina, 2008). Being out at work may increase the likelihood of being a target of harassment, yet not disclosing is related to decreased job satisfaction (Waldo, 1999). About 26% of transgender workers in one survey lost their jobs due to their gender identity, with Black, multiracial, and Native American workers most likely to be impacted (Grant et al., 2011). In addition, 78% of transgender employees say they have been harassed at work, including 7% who were physically assaulted. Other research on transgender employees has also found high levels of job loss and harassment by supervisors and co-workers (Budge, Tebbe, & Howard, 2010).

Working for an employer perceived to be LGBT-supportive can be beneficial to LGBT employees. More supportive workplaces are related to increased disclosure, lower levels of harassment, and greater job satisfaction (Prati & Pietrantoni, 2014; Ragins & Cornwell, 2001). Those with more supportive employers and co-workers tend to have more positive experiences and experience less discrimination (Ruggs, Martinez, Hebl, & Law,

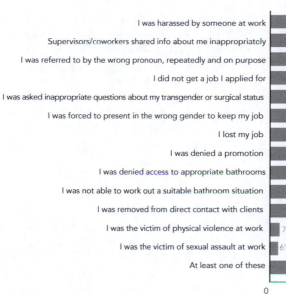

*Direct mistreatment and discrimination against transgender people in the workplace (2011). Source: Adapted from data collected by National Center for Transgender Equality.*

2015). In addition, having friendships at work with heterosexual and other LGB co-workers is associated with more affirmation and emotional support for LGB employees (Griffith & Hebl, 2002; Rumens, 2010, 2012).

One relationship that can be very important for workers' career success is that with a mentor. Mentors can provide career advice, feedback, social support, role modeling, and encouragement. Having a mentor is related to job satisfaction, career commitment, increased number of promotions, and increased salary (Allen, Eby, Poteet, Lentz, & Lima, 2004). The impact of having an LG mentor can be profound for LG workers. Those with LG mentors reported more job satisfaction and involvement, received more gay-specific career advice, reported more encouragement, and were more likely to see their mentor as a role model (Hebl, Tonidandel, & Ruggs, 2012). However, if individuals do not feel safe to be out at work, it is more difficult to find an LGBT mentor or mentee.

## THE LATER YEARS

There are an estimated 1.75 and 4 million LGBT Americans over the age of 60 (USHHS, 2014). LGBT individuals who are middle-aged or older may have come of age at a time when it was not as acceptable to be openly LGBT or receive affirmation for minority gender or sexual identities. In addition, some LGBT people do not come out until midlife or later. Lesbians tend to experience the milestones of a minority sexual identity later in life than do gay men (Floyd & Bakeman, 2006). A study of 73 lesbians who were at least 50 years old found that more than one in five (22%) reported being over 40 years of age when they first had sex with another woman (Tully, 1988). In a study of lesbians and gay men who came out between the ages of 30 to 60, 90% had been previously heterosexually married and most were parents.

While they felt that their coming out had disrupted many relationships, others saw their coming out as courageous. Many had suppressed their feelings of same-sex attraction since adolescence (Johnston & Jenkins, 2003).

There are various reasons why people come out later in life. One study of transwomen aged 50 and over found that their awareness of a dwindling time left to live was a catalyst for coming out (Fabbre, 2014). Other research has found that older lesbians and gay men came out because they met other LGBT individuals and were tired of "living a lie" (Johnston & Jenkins, 2003).

The experiences of LGBTQ elders are diverse and may in some ways parallel those of younger LGBTQ individuals, while in other ways be unique. A study of 1,200 LGBT Baby Boomers (born between 1946 and 1964) found that 61% were in a romantic relationship, 39% were single, and 33% lived alone. LGBT individuals in the sample were more likely than a heterosexual comparison group to rely on friends for support, encouragement, and in an emergency. While over 70% of lesbians and gay men reported being "mostly" or "completely" out, only 39% of transgender and 16% of bisexual individuals reported the same (Met Life, 2010). Slightly less than a quarter of bisexuals and 42% of transgender individuals indicated that their families were accepting. Over half of lesbian and gay men indicated their families were accepting of them.

## Coming Out Later in Life

Those who come out later may have had previous heterosexual relationships or marriages, and children from those relationships. Davies (2008) interviewed adult women whose mothers came out later in life. Most were not aware of their mother's lesbianism before they were told, and half reported becoming closer to their mother because of the disclosure. In LG parent-stepparent families, whose children were conceived through heterosexual relationships, some did not want to create stress for their children so they waited until they were adults to come out to them (Lynch & Murray, 2000).

## LGBT Grandparents

As more LGBT people become parents, the number of LGBT grandparents is also likely to grow. While there have long been LGBT grandparents and parents, those coming out today may have an easier time than in the past (Orel & Fruhauf, 2013). In a study of 16 lesbian and bisexual grandmothers, ten did not identify as lesbian or bisexual until their children were adults (Orel & Fruhauf, 2006), four had not come out to their children or grandchildren, and two were not out only to their grandchildren to honor their child's wishes. Those grandmothers who were not out reported more stress and felt more distant from their families. Coming out to grandchildren was easier when their adult child accepted their sexual orientation. Gay grandfathers were often encouraged by their adult children to come out to their grandchildren. They often said it was a positive experience, even easier than coming out to their own children (Fruhauf, Orel, & Jenkins, 2009).

## Caregiving

As LGBTQ people age, many will need additional caregiving or become caregivers themselves. Older LGBT people may be estranged from their families of origin, are less likely to have children, and are more likely to be single (SAGE n.d.). Families of choice, including intergenerational families, may provide caregiving (Grant, 2010). When asked about who they would prefer to care for them, older LGBT people often answer "partners" and "friends" more than "biological family" (Cahill, South, & Spade, 2000). In fact, one study found that 61% of caregivers of LGBT elders were friends of care recipients (Fredericksen–Goldsen, 2007).

Transgender elders are especially at risk for physical and mental health disparities, often with less access to support networks and resources. More than one in four state and local offices on aging say that older transgender adults would likely not be welcome at local providers of services to the elderly. Other research has found discrimination and abuse in long-term care facilities (NCTE, 2011).

Caregiving is not a new responsibility for many older LGBTQ individuals. Many gay men contracted HIV during the height of the HIV/AIDS crisis in the late 1980s. Many of these men are now aging with HIV, given the high incidence of infection among gay men 47–65 years old; some have been living with HIV for years. Thus, some aging gay and bisexual men may be caring for friends or partners who have HIV/AIDS. Gay-male caregivers themselves may *also* be living with HIV (Wright, Aneshensel, & LeBlanc, 2003). HIV positive people also experience higher rates of diabetes, bone weakness, and liver, kidney, and heart disease—all of which can complicate caring for HIV-positive LGBT elders. Some research on caregivers with HIV found higher levels of depression compared to caregivers without HIV (Land, Hudson, & Stiefel, 2003). When caregivers of partners with HIV perceive little social support for caregiving, they can feel highly burdened and experience high levels of suicidal thoughts (Rosengard & Folkman, 1997).

While many aging individuals prefer to remain in their own homes, not all can. Indeed, the reasons why LGBTQ elders enter care facilities is varied. Some LGBT elders may need more substantive care and enter long-term care facilities. Additionally, because they are less likely to have children and more likely to be single, many LGBT elders may enter into long-term care simply because there is no one else to take care of them. According to the National Resource Center on LGBT Aging (n.d.a, n.d.b), only 22% felt they could be open about their sexuality, 89% feared discrimination based on their

| | |
|---|---|
| 1. | Staying independent |
| 2. | Loss of partner |
| 3. | Financial stability |
| 4. | Isolation and loneliness |
| 5. | Going to a nursing home |
| 6. | Declining health |
| 7. | Affordable housing |
| 8. | Health insurance coverage |
| 9. | Not being able to drive |
| 10. | Needing help with personal care |

*Top ten concerns of older LGBT adults (2014). Source: Adapted from data collected by Elder Services of Worcester Area.*

LGBT status, and 43% reported experiencing mistreatment in their long-term care facility. An additional concern for those partnered is not being able to remain with their partner (Smith, McCaslin, Chang, Martinez, & McGrew, 2010).

Are these concerns justified? In an interview of nursing home residents, many felt there would be a range of responses and behaviors toward LGB residents, and many felt others would not approve (Donaldson, Asta, & Vacha-Haase, 2014). A majority of staff (68%) of one residential care facility reported that they would accept and respect LGB residents and not change care because of their sexual orientation (Villar, Serrat, Faba, & Celdran, 2015). Other research found long-term care nursing staff viewed same-sex sexual behavior among residents more negatively and less acceptable than different-sex activity (Hinrich & Vacha-Haase, 2010). As the number of LGBT seniors increases because of longevity and living openly, the need for LGBT-centered care will also increase.

## CONCLUSION

Relationships are lifelong and paramount to living a happy and healthy life. This chapter first established the developmental nature of relationships for all people before delving into the ways in which sexual orientation and gender expression uniquely influence relationships. From the ways in which one "does" gender as a child, to caregiving and grandparenting in the later years, sexual orientation and gender expression never stop influencing one's life and relationships. What LGBTQ people need most is acceptance, understanding, and support across all domains of life. In every domain examined, whether it be family, friends, work, or caregiving, LGBTQ people are happier and healthier when they feel safe, when they feel respected, and when they feel supported. When LGBTQ people are happy and healthy they are able to establish and maintain happy and healthy relationships. They are able to partner and parent more effectively. They excel in school and in the workplace. They are able to make the world better for the next generation.

## Learn More

### Readings

Biblarz, T. J., & Savci, E. (2010). Lesbian, gay, bisexual, and transgender families. *Journal of Marriage and Family*, *72*(3), 480–497.

James, S. E., Herman, J. L., Rankin, S., Keisling, M., Mottet, L., & Ana, M. (2016). *The report of the 2015 U.S. transgender survey*. Washington, DC: National Center for Transgender Equality.

Kosciw, J. G., Greytak, E. A., Giga, N. M., Villenas, C. & Danischewski, D. J. (2016). *The 2015 national school climate survey: The experiences of lesbian, gay, bisexual, transgender, and queer youth in our nation's schools*. New York: GLSEN.

Movement Advancement Project & Services and Advocacy for GLBT Elders (2016). *Understanding issues facing LGBT older adults*. Boulder, CO & Washington, D.C.: MAP & SAGE.

Movement Advancement Project, Family Equality Council, and Center for American Progress (2011). *All children matter: How legal and social inequalities hurt LGBT families.* Deniver, CO, Boston, MA, & Washington, D.C.: MAP, FEC, & CAP.

Nardi, P. M. (1999). *Gay men's friendships: Invincible communities.* University of Chicago.

Peplau, L. A., & Fingerhut, A. W. (2007). The close relationships of lesbians and gay men. *Annual Review of Psychology, 58*, 405–424.

Polikoff, N. D. (2008). *Beyond straight and gay marriage: Valuing all families under the law.* New York, NY: Beacon.

Savin-Williams, R. C. (1998). *"—and then I became gay": Young men's stories.* New York, NY: Psychology Press.

Savin-Williams, R. C. (2009). *The new gay teenager.* Cambridge, MA: Harvard University.

Stacey, J., & Biblarz, T. J. (2001). (How) does the sexual orientation of parents matter? *American Sociological Review, 66*(2), 159–183.

Weston, K. (1997). *Families we choose: Lesbians, gays, kinship.* New York, NY: Columbia University.

## Film/Video

Allen, P. (Director). (2005). *Family matters* [Documentary film]. Pasadena, Calif.: Intelecom, 2005.

Barbosa, P. (Director/Producer) & Lenoir, G. (Director). (2001). *De colores: Lesbian and Gay Latinos: Stories of strength, family and love* [Motion picture]. United States: WomanVision.

Chasnoff, D. (Director). (2000). *That's a family!* [Documentary film]. San Francisco, CA: GroundSpark.

Chasnoff, D. (Director). (2004). *One wedding and a . . . revolution* [DVD]. San Francisco, CA: Women's Educational Media.

Dong, A. (Director). (2004). *Stories from the war on homosexuality: Volume 2, Family fundamentals* [Documentary film]. New York, NY: Docurama/New Video Group.

Garner, K., Jhally, S., Kazlauskas, J., King, K., Rapp, A., Roberts, D., Rosenfeld, J. S., . . . Media Education Foundation (Producers). (2014). *Speak up!: Improving the lives of gay, lesbian, bi-sexual, transgender youth* [Streaming video]. Northampton, MA: Media Education Foundation.

Mosbacher, D., & Reid, F. (Producers). (1994). *Straight from the heart* [Motion picture]. United States: WomenVision.

Mulcahy, R. (Director). (2013). *Prayers for Bobby* [DVD]. A&E Home Video.

Regan, M. (Director). (2001). *No dumb questions* [Motion picture]. United States; Epiphany.

Seve, J. (Director). (2004). *Tying the knot* [Motion picture]. United States: Outcast Films.

Spadola, M. (Director). (2008). *Our house: Kids of gay and lesbian parents* [Documentary film]. New York, NY: Icarus /First Run.

Symons, J. (Director/Producer) & Sablosky, L. (Co-Producer). (2002). *Daddy & papa* [Motion picture]. United States: New Day Films.

## Internet

Bisexual Resource Center: biresource.org

Gay-Straight Alliance Network: gsanetwork.org

GSA Network: gsanetwork.org
Human Rights Campaign: www.hrc.org
It Gets Better Project: www.itgetsbetter.org
Movement Advance Project: www.lgbtmap.org
National LGBTQ Task Force: www.thetaskforce.org
PFLAG: www.pflag.org
Safe Schools Coalition: www.safeschoolscoalition.org
Services and Advocacy for GLBT Elders (SAGE): www.sageusa.org
The Trevor Project: www.thetrevorproject.org
TransParent: transparentusa.org

# CHAPTER 5
# Reading, Writing, Queering
## *Education*

*Elizabeth Dinkins and Patrick Englert*

*Marchers with GSA Network, San Francisco Pride Parade, June 30, 2013. Source: Photo by Quinn Dombrowski/CC BY-SA 2.0 license. Image courtesy of Flickr.*

I t's Valentine's Day and the students are abuzz with energy. They have just received the results of the MatchMaker™ personality survey, a fundraiser designed to pair students with others of the opposite sex, and an administrator comes to the class to remind everyone about the evening's dance. He announces that tickets are cheaper if purchased by the couple, explaining, "a couple can be just two friends, okay?" (Dinkins & Englert, 2016, p. 138).

This classroom interaction captures one way K–12 schools communicate heteronormative assumptions about their students (Sanders & Mathis, 2013). Students who identify as heterosexual are explicitly considered the norm, while students who identify as LGBTQ+ are limited and implicitly forced to display their relationships as "just friends." The message is clear: heterosexual students, their relationships and desires, are sanctioned in school and welcomed at extra-curricular events. LGBTQ+ students, on the other hand, are expected to censor their desires and are excluded from out-of-school social events, like the Valentine's Day dance mentioned above. How different might this interaction have been if both the MatchMaker™ game and the dance included options for same-sex couples? How could all students be included and feel welcomed?

Amidst the excitement and following the interruption the teacher quiets the classroom down and asks students to, "Face forward. This is a review." She begins by reviewing figurative language and notices two students not paying attention. She stops and looks at the two male students who are distracted. The students are talking and laughing—comparing the cuff bracelets they each wear on their forearm. The teacher moves to stand directly in front of the two students and interjects, "Alright. What are we? This is not bracelet class. I'm trying to teach you about figurative language and you are comparing his pink bracelet to his gold bracelet." The classroom responds in laughter, and one student whispers loud enough for others to hear, "Faggots." The teacher continues, "I didn't think that would ever happen—my class would get disturbed over who had the prettiest bracelet. I think the pink one is prettier. Put the bracelet away." Another student in the classroom intervenes, "Some girls say it's brave for a man to wear pink." The other students laugh, again. She closes the interaction and says, "We've got more things to do in this class besides compare that pink bracelet to his pretty little gold bracelet. So we'll get back to figurative language" (Dinkins & Englert, 2016, p.138).

Just as schools are often heteronormative in nature they can also perpetuate gender as a binary defined by sex—in which students must exist within cisnormative expectations, meaning they are expected to express gender as boy/man or girl/woman, depending upon the gender they were labeled or assigned at birth (Nelson, 2009). From the earliest stages of life gender expectations and stereotypes are engrained in each of us (Hill & Flom, 2007). As early as preschool, gender socialization makes children aware of the stigma and social pressures associated with gender binaries (Waxman, 2010). During this time, children begin making decisions about clothing, accessories, mannerisms, and interests, which are guided by gender stereotypes. These decisions are further supported through binaries ever present in society, such as: clothing stores divided into a boys' section, where blue- and red-colored clothing is found; and a girls' section filled with pink and purple clothing. The same is true with toys—dolls and toy ovens marketed to girls; trucks and action figures to boys.

Most K-12 school, college, and university environments and cultures expect students to be cisgender. That is, they are expected to outwardly present or express gender in a way that matches the gender they were assigned or labeled at birth (Grossman & D'Augelli, 2006). Students who are transgender or gender non-conforming may be at a disadvantage due to the gender-normative expectations of schools that may not allow for exploration or presentation of gender outside of a feminine/masculine binary (Toomey, McGuire, & Russell, 2012). Students' experiences in school are shaped by gender expectations or stereotypes and gender-normative school environments may not feel, and often are not, safe for transgender and gender non-conforming students. Bullying, physical and verbal harassment, mis-gendering (identifying a student by incorrect pronouns), stereotypes and gender expectations, and lack of gender inclusive bathrooms are just a few of the challenges faced by such students (McKay, Misra, & Lindquist, 2017; Smith & Payne, 2016). In the classroom interaction above two male students are shamed and called names for wearing colorful cuff bracelets, emphasizing the presence of heteronormative and cisnormative environmental expectations. This example demonstrates how one classroom failed to create a supportive environment for all students.

This chapter explores the role education plays in establishing, reinforcing, questioning, and dismantling school environments that marginalize LGBTQ+ and gender expansive students. It examines how the various levels of schools—the curricular level, the extra-curricular level, the role of educators, and the policy level—regard and behave toward LGBTQ+ identities through childhood, adolescence, and early adulthood. After establishing key terms and definitions, the chapter presents the ways in which education does and does not understand and support LGBTQ+ and gender expansive students. Next, the chapter presents models of LGBTQ+ student development throughout the educational process and the heteronormative nature of schooling. To examine the potential schools hold for challenging this heteronormative and cisnormative nature, the chapter shares the ways in which different facets of education support or marginalize LGBTQ+ and gender expansive individuals, including curricular and extra-curricular aspects, the ways in which some educators disrupt cisnorms and heteronorms, and the practices and policies that advocate for LGBTQ+ and gender expansive students.

## UNDERSTANDING TERMINOLOGY

This chapter uses the initialism "LGBTQ+" to refer to those who identify as lesbian (L), gay (G), bisexual (B), transgender (T), queer (Q), and questioning, fluid, or non-conforming to defined identities (+). This term is not meant to erase the distinction between those who identify as lesbian, gay, bisexual, transgender, queer, or questioning, but rather to be as inclusive as possible (Britzman, 1995; Honeychurch, 1996; Seidman, 2010). LGBTQ+ is also used in reference to social practices, behaviors, and beliefs associated with underrepresented genders and sexualities. To recognize the diversity within this initialism, the chapter uses individual initials when referring to specific identities included in research reports and studies. For example, when referring to the National School Climate Survey, the acronym LGBTQ is used because it reflects the identities used throughout the questions and results (Kosciw, Greytak, Giga, Villenas, & Danischewski, 2015).

This chapter also employs the word "queer," which refers to varying genders and sexualities and attempts to capture the possible social practices, behaviors, communities, and beliefs associated with this range. While "queer" has and still is used as an offensive and derogatory term by some, the word has been reclaimed by the LGBTQ+ community. Consistent with this reclamation, queer is used in this chapter to represent efforts to disrupt, challenge, or undermine cisgendered and heteronormative environments and the belief that these are the only possible ways of being sexual or gendered (Cohen, 1997; Dilley, 1999). For example, in kindergarten, students may be asked to think about what "family" means. Within many classroom conversations and assignments, the depiction of family is often heteronormative, including a mom and dad (Shema, 2014). A kindergarten teacher who thinks and teaches in ways that include LGBTQ+ perspectives may ask their students to consider family forms that include two moms, or two dads, or a transgender parent. This inclusive consideration queers heteronormative education by expanding what is meant by the word family and, by extension, can help create a more inclusive and welcome educational experience (Shema, 2014). Students, staff, faculty, and administrators who embrace queering as a way of thinking include LGBTQ+ perspectives as normal and transform what is possible within education.

## THE ROLE OF SCHOOLS

Schools are charged with providing students the experiences and environments that enhance their intellectual, civic, economic, and emotional potential (Elias, Zins, Graczyk, & Weissberg, 2003). The experience of school parallels student development, from reading first words to first dates, and from college entrance exams to first internships. At each developmental stage, educators strive to create environments in which students can grow and learn (hooks, 1994). Schools, however, do not operate in a vacuum. They are micro-societies that reflect and respond to their surrounding communities, and reproduce the societies they reflect (Russell, Kosciw, Horn, & Saewyc, 2010). Historically, schools, like societies, have not always offered equal opportunities to everyone. Students have been discriminated against due to race, gender, gender identity, religious identities, and sexual orientation. In the United States, some battles for civil rights and social justice have focused on equitable access to education, placing schools at the core of social change.

A major accomplishment of the black civil rights movement was the desegregation of public schools by the U.S. Supreme Court in the case *Brown v. Board of Education* (1954). In this case the Court ruled that "separate but equal" public schools were not equal at all and recognized the need for students to have access to the same resources—regardless of race. Title IX of the federal Education Amendments Act of 1972 (20 U.S.C. Â§1681 *et seq.*) prohibited discrimination based on sex in any federally funded educational institution or activity, from pre-kindergarten to college. In 2016 the U.S. Department of Education's Office of Civil Rights paired with the U.S. Department of Justice's Civil Rights Division and issued formal guidelines on how to protect gender identity and gender non-conforming students against discrimination in schools (Lhamon & Gupta, 2016). In 2017 the Trump administration rolled back protections for transgender students by withdrawing the federal guidelines. These examples demonstrate how schools have been and continue to be on the front line of social change in the United States.

Today, in states and communities across the country, advocates are fighting for the rights of LGBTQ+ students who do not have guaranteed access to safe and supportive learning environments (Kosciw, Greytak, Giga, Villenas, & Danischewski, 2015). A 2015 survey of LGBTQ-identified middle and high school students in the U.S. found that these students experience school as a hostile environment characterized by high rates of verbal harassment, discriminatory policies, and absences due to feeling unsafe, which led to lower grade point averages and lower self-esteem. School-based verbal and physical harassment may be more prevalent for gender non-conforming and out LGBTQ+ students because they have increased visibility and less control over their daily environments (McKay, Misra, & Lindquist, 2017). Classrooms, teachers, and classmates are generally not determined by students, making it difficult for LGBTQ+ students to select or create safe spaces. When schools took active steps to create welcoming and safe environments, LGBTQ students experienced more positive climates, increased academic success, and greater support for their identities (Kosciw et al., 2015).

A 2010 study focused on the experience of LGBTQ college and university students found "chilly" campus climates in which LGBTQ people were the least accepted among underrepresented groups on campus. Students reported feeling unsafe and unsupported on campus, as well as experiencing increased levels of harassment (Rankin, Weber, Blumenfield, & Frazer, 2010). The study linked negative experiences related to campus climate to whether or not a student persists to graduation. Students who have multiple underrepresented identities (e.g., a Latino transgender man), reported more hostile and unsupportive climates.

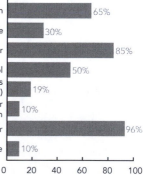

*The school experiences of today's LGBTQ youth (2014). Source: Adapted from data collected by GLSEN.*

While the experiences of LGBTQ+ college and university students can resemble those of K-12 students, colleges, and universities have also laid the foundation for supporting LGBTQ+ people and building support through activism. Research, policies, and practices that recognize and affirm LGBTQ+ students have developed on campuses across the United States (Renn, 2010). Because of their power and responsibility to shape student experiences, when schools, teachers, policies, and curricular and extra-curricular activities are supportive and inclusive of LGBTQ+ identities, schools become better places for LGBTQ+ students.

---

## Climate for LGBTQ Students in Colleges/Universities

In 2010 Campus Pride surveyed over 5,000 U.S. college and university students, faculty members, staff members, and administrators who identified as lesbian, gay, bisexual, transgender, questioning, or queer. It asked them about the climate for LGBTQ people on their campus.

LGBTQ college students were significantly more likely than cisgender/heterosexual peers to experience harassment, and seven times more likely to indicate the harassment was based on sexual identity. Those who identified as queer were significantly more likely to experience harassment than other sexual minority identities.

Compared to cisgender/heterosexual peers, LGBTQ college students were twice as likely to be targets of derogatory remarks, stared at, or singled out as an "authority" on LGBTQ issues due to their identity. Gay and bisexual males were most often the targets of derogatory remarks, while lesbians and bisexual women reported being deliberately ignored or socially excluded. Queer students were most often stared at or singled out as LGBTQ authorities.

About a third of transgender students reported harassment, but transmen were significantly less likely than transwomen and other gender non-conforming students to say harassment was based on their gender identity. Transwomen said they were deliberately ignored or socially excluded, isolated, or left out; transmen were most likely to be stared at, singled out as an authority on transgender issues, or socially excluded. About 80% of transgender students said poor treatment was due to their gender expression.

LGBTQ students of color were ten times more likely than white students to report racial profiling as a form of harassment. They also were more likely to report race as the basis for that harassment.

About two-thirds of LGBTQ students said they were uncomfortable on their college campus, in their academic department or campus workplace, and in the classroom.

LGBTQ students were much more likely than cisgender/heterosexual peers to perceive or observe harassment and to perceive that the harassment was based on sexual identity (Rankin et al., 2010).

---

## STUDENT DEVELOPMENT

Students enter educational institutions at varying stages of gender and sexual development. Accordingly, over the past two decades, educators and school administrators have incorporated different theories of sexual- and gender-identity development into their practice of educating and developing LGBTQ+ students. These theories partly result from a broader interest in gender and sexual development among researchers after 1970 (Bilodeau & Renn, 2005). The theories relevant to LGBTQ+ identity development tend to describe a set of common or shared experiences that individuals move through as their identity develops—a framework through which diverse individual LGBTQ+ experiences can be viewed in a similar way. (Cass, 1979; Fassinger, 1991; Savin-Williams, 1988). When applied in an educational environment, theories allow schools, teachers, and staff to better support, challenge, and serve LGBTQ+ students in and out of the classroom. However, the sample sizes of the research on which many of these theories are based were small and comprised predominately of white men, which may limit their usefulness for educators in describing LGBTQ+ gender and sexual identity development in diverse classroom settings (Ryan & Futterman, 1998).

## Cass Model

The Cass Model of Gay and Lesbian Identity Development was developed by Australian clinical psychologist Vivienne Cass in 1979. The Cass Model is a stage model, initially developed through work with adult males, as were most of the other stage models, such as Troiden's (1979 and 1988) Homosexual Identity Development Model, Fassinger's (1991) Model of Gay and Lesbian Identity Development, and Savin-Williams (1988) Gay Identity Development Model. These models do not attempt to provide a framework for bisexual identity and began to be created well before the word "pansexuality" emerged. They were also developed during a time when coming out generally occurred after adolescence. However, beginning in the 2000s, it became more common for LGBTQ+ people to publicly identify their sexuality and gender identity during middle or high school (Savin-Williams & Cohen, 2015).

The Cass Model is comprised of six stages and operates in a linear format, but allows for fluidity between the stages—meaning some stages may be revisited over time (Cass, 1979). This model can be used by educators and administrators

### Stage 1: Identity Confusion
· Recognition of emerging feelings, behaviors, experiences that challenge an individual to reflect and consider his/her/zir sexuality
· Unsure of what it means to be gay or lesbian

### Stage 2: Identity Comparison
· Begins to compare and explore heterosexual, gay, or lesbian identities
· Positive affiliation with the idea of being different
· May begin to grieve or struggle with letting go of ideals related to being heterosexual and begins to acknowledge challenges that may come with being gay or lesbian

### Stage 3: Identity Tolerance
· Accepts/tolerates the probability of being gay or lesbian & begins to connect with gay/lesbian culture through developing friendships, visiting bars, attending LGBTQ+ groups, etc.
· Identifies emotional, social, and sexual needs of being gay or lesbian

### Stage 4: Identity Acceptance
· Greater involvement in and acceptance of the gay/lesbian community
· Moving toward accepting gay or lesbian self-identity
· Increased frustration towards heterosexual community and intolerance of sexuality not being approved of or accepted by peers, family, and others

### Stage 5: Identity Pride
· The world is divided between gay/lesbian and heterosexual
· Disclosure of sexuality to family, colleagues, and peers
· Involvement in gay/lesbian culture

### Stage 6: Identity Synthesis
· Sexual identity is still core to the individual; however, it is not in the forefront of the individual's relationships & life
· Comes to terms with the role of allies and recognizes heterosexual support

*Cass Model of Gay and Lesbian Identity Formation. Source: Adapted from (Cass, 1979).*

for a generalized overview in framing and understanding the experiences and processes of lesbian and gay students during their time in educational settings. The first stage of the Cass model is Identity Confusion/Awareness, when a gay or lesbian person becomes aware of being different, perhaps recognizing that they display particular mannerisms or are attracted to the same gender. During this stage, a range of emotions can be experienced—fear, anxiety, anger, and denial. Educators may notice lesbian and gay students being made fun of or called names based on the students' peers identifying differences in appearance or mannerisms, making school an uncomfortable and sometimes unsafe environment for students.

Stage two, Identity Comparison, is when gay and lesbian people seek knowledge and compare sexual identities as a means to better understanding themselves and others. Educators have the opportunity to incorporate gay and lesbian history, LGBTQ+ characters in literature, and provide space for exploration and comparison, which promotes students' recognition of their sexuality.

Stage three is Identity Tolerance, when people acknowledge their sexuality as different but have not accepted or come to terms with the challenges that may be encountered. A student in this stage may begin to come out to trusted individuals and benefits from a supportive environment. For example, a lesbian college student who is struggling to come out to a straight roommate may feel less anxious about seeking support from an administrator or faculty who displays the Safe Zone sticker (see focus box on Safe Zone programs). In less supportive environments, LGBTQ+ students must consider regularly whom they will share their identity with and how they will go about doing so.

Stage four, Identity Acceptance, involves accepting one's sexual identity and beginning to engage in the LGBTQ+ community. This may include participating in a high-school Gay Straight Alliance (GSA) or becoming involved with the LGBTQ+ services office on campus. This involvement serves as a way to connect with other queer people, to learn about, and to become a part of the LGBTQ+ community.

In Stage five, Identity Pride, the individual becomes fully involved with the LGBTQ+ community, whether that is through continued involvement in clubs, dating a person of the same gender, or doing advocacy work. In this stage, gay and lesbian people may be frustrated by policies, practices, and people who fail to acknowledge and support LGBTQ+ people. School environments that affirm LGBTQ+ students' relationships and give voice to their needs are critical in this stage.

The sixth and final stage is Identity Synthesis, when the individual synthesizes their sexual identity with other aspects of self; for instance, a lesbian high school student who is out to peers and family and gets involved with a local youth group, ultimately connecting sexuality to faith. On a college campus, an example of this may be a gay male who is an education major. As he continues his school work he navigates what it might mean to be a gay educator. Each stage in the Cass Model is slightly different, emphasizing the complexities of coming out and developing one's identity.

## D'Augelli Model

Psychologist Anthony D'Augelli developed his Sexual Orientation and Gender Identity Development model in 1994. The D'Augelli Model allows for more fluidity, or ebb and flow, in how identity development occurs and recognizes that growth and development for gay and lesbian people occurs based on biological and environmental factors (1994). Whereas, stage models such as Cass' (1979) do not leave space for bisexual and transgender experiences because the focus is only on the linear progression of gay and lesbian people, D'Augelli's model has been used as a framework with which to understand the development of a broader range of LGBTQ+ identities. Based on the individual's place in life and the mediating circumstances surrounding their development, D'Augelli's model describes six independent identity processes. These do not necessarily occur in a particular order, but each process can be facilitated and supported by an individual's context or environment. Because young people spend a large proportion of their time in school, the educational environment becomes particularly important to LGBTQ+ student development. K-12 schools and college campus environments can affect whether a LGBTQ+ student feels safe or empowered to explore their identity.

The process of Exiting Heterosexuality includes identifying as lesbian, gay, or bisexual (LGB) and engaging in the ongoing act of disclosing a minority sexual identity to friends and family (coming out.) Because LGB students may not feel comfortable disclosing their sexual identity to family members, they may opt to disclose at school to trusted peers, teachers, or staff. The process Developing a Personal LGB Identity occurs through establishing connections and relationships with other LGBTQ+ people. Participation in extra-curricular organizations like student GSAs, or attending school social events where same-gender couples are explicitly included and welcomed can benefit students in this process.

The process Developing a Lesbian Gay Bisexual Social Identity involves creating an affirming social network that

| | | |
|---|---|---|
| **Exiting a Heterosexual Community** Identifying as LGB and beginning to come out to others | **Entering an LGB Community** Commitment to social and political action that empowers understanding and resistance to oppression | **Developing a Personal LGB Identity Status** Connections and relationships with the LGB community |
| **Developing an LGB Intimacy Status** Emotionally and intimately fulfilling LGB relationships | **Coming Out** | **Developing an LGB Social Identity** Affirming social network of LGB heterosexual allies |
| | **Claiming an Identity as an LGB Offspring** Coming out to family, peers, and colleagues and navigating their acceptance | |

*D'Augelli's LGB Identity Model. Source: Adapted from (D'Augelli, 1994).*

is comprised of LGBTQ+ friends and heterosexual allies, which necessitates a school climate in which heterosexual students include and advocate for their LGBTQ+ peers. An LGB person may find it affirming to walk into a classroom space or a professor's office and see a rainbow flag or equality sign. Similarly, policies or statements in syllabi that communicate inclusive classroom expectations around identity or language usage in the classroom may help students feel support.

Two processes are particularly focused on the process of coming out or sharing an LGB sexual identity. Exiting a Heterosexual Community and Claiming an Identity as an LGB Offspring, which is the process of coming out to parents or guardians and may extend to family members, friends, and colleagues, as they navigate their acceptance. Coming out is ongoing and may occur in different ways and times based on who the LGB person is sharing his or her identity with. Educators and administrators may play an integral role in assisting students through the coming out process. In K–12 settings educators and administrators are consulted by parents who reach out to seek support and resources on LGBTQ+ topics. In K–12 and on college campuses educators and administrators assist LGB students to navigate through the coming out process.

The process of Developing a Lesbian, Gay, or Bisexual Intimacy Status is associated with emotional and intimate relationships with other LGBTQ+ people. Developing emotional and intimate relationships in school can be difficult for LGB people. In K–12 education many schools do not have a GSA, which presents a challenge for students to identify other LGB people. Similarly, many colleges do not have a LGBTQ+ services office. LGBTQ+ student organizations serve an important role in connecting queer students to one another. In recent years dating and networking apps, such as Tinder and Grindr, have provided a social network for LGB people to connect and develop community. Lastly, Entering a Lesbian, Gay, or Bisexual Community involves developing a commitment to social and political action.

At every process level in D'Augelli's model, schools have the potential to offer powerful opportunities for LGBTQ+ students: the development of social networks, engagement as active citizens who advocate for themselves and others, and space for exploring complex and evolving identities. Since D'Augelli's model is not linear, the identity processes it describes serves as helpful checkpoints that mirror the fluidity of sexuality and allow individualized points through which to enter the model. For example, if a bisexual student is writing a research paper on the topic of pansexuality and is also organizing a protest on campus, it may be assumed that the student is Entering an LGB Community as the student is exhibiting their engagement with and immersion in the LGB community. However, it cannot be assumed that the student has Claimed an Identity as an LGB Offspring. A professor who is aware of this model would not share anything about a student's sexual identity with their parents. D'Augelli's model provides a framework to prompt reflection and engage in dialogue to better understand where an LGB person is in the sexual identity developmental process. D'Augelli's LGB identity model has also been adapted to serve as a framework for transgender and gender expansive people (Bilodeau & Renn, 2005).

## Layer Cake Model

The Layer Cake Model of Bisexual Identity Development was developed by four educational researchers who were interested in better understanding bisexuality, which they felt was less understood than homosexuality (Bleiberg,

Fertmann, Friedman, & Godino, 2005). The Layer Cake Model uses the metaphor of a slice of cake comprised of five layers—each layer supporting and pressing upon the previous layer's lessons, emotional impacts, and experiences that guide one's sexual identity.

The bottommost layer is Development of a Heterosexual Identity. In this layer, bisexual people are socialized and conditioned in a heteronormative context, which regards them as heterosexual. Students may arrive in the K–12 classroom with no experience of interacting with someone who is gay, lesbian, bisexual, or transgender. Similarly, a first-year college student may not have considered the fluidity of their sexuality until they are around peers who identify as non-heterosexual. These first experiences or interactions with the LGBTQ+ community begin to deconstruct the individual's context of a heterosexual world.

| | |
|---|---|
| **Layer 5** | Identification as Bisexual |
| **Layer 4** | Integration and Assimilation of Heterosexual and Homosexual Identities |
| **Layer 3** | Acceptance of Homosexual Attraction while Maintaining Heterosexual Identity |
| **Layer 2** | Experience Homosexual Thoughts, Feelings, or Behaviors |
| **Layer 1** | Development of a Heterosexual Identity |

*Layer Cake Model of Bisexual Identity Development. Source: Bleiberg, S., Fertmann, A., Friedman, A., Godino, C. (2005).*

In the next layer up, bisexual people begin to Experience Homosexual Thoughts, Feelings, and/or Behaviors. This layer is filled with reflection and the student may begin to question whether they are heterosexual, or what previous thoughts and interactions may mean about their sexual identity. A tension occurs between the concepts of being heterosexual and bisexual. A school's inclusion of opportunities for students to consider sexuality, in particular bisexuality, offers students interactions to explore how heterosexuality does not have to be the norm.

The middle layer is characterized by Acceptance of Homosexual Attraction while Maintaining Heterosexual Identity. Students in this category may feel there is not a comfortable identity for them. Identifying as heterosexual may be more comfortable, as bisexuality may not be recognized or supported by peers. Students may also not feel the pressure to come out as they may currently be dating a person of a different gender. Acceptance of homosexual attraction and heterosexual identity is challenging for students because bisexuality is often viewed as a phase or as a stepping stone to being gay or lesbian (Bleiberg et al., 2005).

The next layer up is Integration and Assimilation of Heterosexual and Homosexual Identities. This layer describes the time when students come to fully view themselves as bisexual. Students may begin to come out and share with close friends or family their identification as bisexual. This is also a time when bisexuals may experience frustration or anger due to being labeled as "confused" or "unsure" until they become more confident in their sexual identity.

The uppermost layer, Identification as Bisexual, occurs when bisexuals become comfortable with their sexual identity and define for themselves what a bisexual identity means. This layer is also where bisexual students experience sexual attraction on a case-by-case basis. For example, a high school senior who has dated a woman for two years and dates a man during her senior year, or a college student who dates men and women regularly based on individual attraction. This experience of sexual attraction may overlap with identities described as "pansexual," a term that describes those attracted to a wide range of genders, not just women or men. A person who identifies as bisexual is not necessarily pansexual, however the layer cake model could be adapted as a framework for exploring pansexual sexual identity development.

Bisexuality is a sexual identity that many educators and administrators may not fully understand, which can present challenges for bisexual students. For example, they may not feel supported by their school if their identity or experiences are not reflected in the school curriculum. The layer cake model recognizes the nuanced differences in identity development that bisexual people may experience and provides an approachable model through which educators and administrators can consider ways to incorporate bisexual identities into the school environment and curriculum.

## Transgender Emergence Model

The Transgender Emergence Model was created by counselor and social worker Arlene Istar Lev in response to the lack of a theoretical framework to guide work with transgender clients in therapy (Lev, 2004). The framework is comprised of six stages and is linear in structure, but allows for fluidity or movement between stages. This model was one of the first attempts to create a model to describe the transgender identity development process.

The first stage, Awareness, is usually marked by distress of some form as a transgender person comes to terms with the range of emotions that accompanies exploring gender identity. This awareness may occur at a young age. Many transgender people recognize the dissonance between their assigned gender and their gender identity as early as the preschool or primary school years (Vanderburgh, 2009). Transgender students may exhibit this through their selection of clothing, the books or toys they select to play with, or the ways in which they express themselves.

Stage two is Seeking Information and Reaching Out. In this stage, the transgender person seeks support and knowledge. An example might be a high school or college student who begins exploring feelings of disconnect with their assigned gender as a man and begins exploring femininity and living socially as a woman. Schools may support such students by offering resources such as: library and other informational resources; support groups through LGBTQ+ centers or student organizations; counselors and counseling centers; and health services.

The third stage is Disclosure to Significant Others—or coming out. A middle school or high school student may confide in a teacher or counselor before disclosing to friends or family. A prepubescent child may want to dress and act in a way that is consistent with their gender identity rather than the gender they were labeled or assigned at birth. Therefore, it is imperative that teachers and administrators are trained and prepared to support transgender students. College campuses have begun to offer training for faculty in regard to understanding name change requests and pronoun usage, and to create a supportive environment for transgender students.

Stages four and five are focused on Exploration of Identity and Self. They also include defining the scope, boundaries, or extent of any desired gender transition. For transgender and gender non-conforming people, gender transition may represent an ongoing, even lifelong, process that may or may not involve body modification, including medical therapies such as hormones or surgeries. For example, a 15-year-old high school student may begin stage four, but not consider stage five, which includes body modification, until years later (if ever). A fourth-grade student (who was assigned the gender of boy at birth) may enter into these stages by growing her hair longer and beginning to wear dresses and skirts to school. These gendered behaviors reflect efforts to explore the self and the limits of expressing gender in a way that is consistent with gender identity rather than assigned gender.

Stage six involves Acceptance of an Integrated and Synthesized Life and Gender Identity. Within this stage transgender students come to accept their gender identity even if their gender transition is ongoing. In this stage, a support network has been established and transgender people are able to navigate multiple environments within their daily life. An example of a transgender person who has reached stage six might be a transmasculine college student (assigned female at birth) who begins taking testosterone and undertakes chest reduction (top) surgery in order to live full time as a man.

One limitation of Lev's model is that it focuses solely on gender identity development. It does not offer a unified theory of sexual and gender identity development, even though these two aspects of identity are often intertwined and students may experience development of both simultaneously.

## Stage 1: Awareness
· This stage is often marked by distress as the person comes to terms with a range of emotions and thoughts

## Stage 2: Seeking Info/Reaching Out
· Outreach for support and knowledge regarding gender identity
· Connections are made to other transgender people to learn about their process and to discover additional supports

## Stage 3: Disclosure to Significant Others
· Disclosing one's transgender identity to significant people —partners, family, friends, etc.
· Developing additional support networks and navigating the challenges and responses of disclosure

## Stage 4: Exploration: Identity and Self-Labeling
· Exploring the numerous iterations of gender and becoming comfortable and owning the gender identity that is right for the individual

## Stage 5: Exploration: Transition Issues / Possible Body Modification
· Exploration of gender confirming interventions such as hormones, top or bottom surgery, and exploring specific expression of gender
· Self-advocating and the ability to navigate gender identity and expression as one, while also challenging the world to acknowledge and respect one's identity

## Stage 6: Integration: Acceptance and Post-Transition Issues
· Transitions begin and may be ongoing—hormones, hair removal, etc.
· Acceptance has been acknowledged and the individual is living life having integrated and synthesized their gender identity

*Transgender Emergence Model. Source: Adapted from (Lev, 2004).*

## THE HETERONORMATIVE STRUCTURE OF EDUCATION

Schools are organized into four interrelated levels. The curricular level consists of the content and information students experience as part of their learning and development. The classroom level consists of student and teacher interactions during the learning process. The co-curricular level includes the social organizations and supports schools offer students. The policy level is comprised of federal, state, and local legislation related to schools and education. At each level, schools impose gender and sexual norms on students: forms ask students (and parents) to identify as either female or male; students play on boys/men or girls/women sports teams; homecoming dances have kings and queens; and social events like Sadie Hawkins dances are organized around heterosexual attraction. These gendered and sexual educational practices are so common and widespread that they are rarely even noticed, much less questioned or changed.

When schools perpetuate these types of heteronormative environments, students are automatically considered heterosexual with limited binary gender expressions, and assumed to have heterosexual parents. Thus, the identities of LGBTQ+ students and their families are erased and their perspectives marginalized. When school culture challenges heteronormative expectations and behaviors, students are able to claim and develop LGBTQ+ identities, social practices, behaviors, and communities. Teachers, staff, and administrators have the greatest potential for positively impacting school culture for lesbian and gay students (Chesir-Teran, 2003). For example, curricula can include or exclude the work of LGBTQ+ people and history, and incorporate positive representations of gender-diverse families. Teachers can be open and supportive, or critical and hostile, of LGBTQ+ students. Co-curricular organizations may create safe spaces for LGBTQ+ students to express their identities, or they can make it difficult for those identities to be expressed. School policies may protect and create spaces for LGBTQ+ students, or discriminate and exclude them. Because every level in school supports a student's academic and social-emotional development, each plays a role in supporting (or oppressing) LGBTQ+ students (Elias et al., 2003).

## Curriculum

The word curriculum broadly refers to the educational experiences offered at every grade level, the goal of which is to foster student learning. Specifically, curriculum takes two forms: one is the formal curriculum, which consists of explicit and stated learning goals and experiences of students as they progress through academic grade levels and classes; the second is the hidden curriculum, which consists of unstated lessons and expectations that students experience as part of school and classroom interactions (Walton, 2005). The formal curriculum is visible and easy to identify. It is represented in the texts, events, and processes deemed worthy of study. For example, the decision to study Ernest Hemingway's *The Sun Also Rises* instead of (black gay writer) James Baldwin's *Giovanni's Room* silently communicates which texts belong (or don't belong) in the English classroom. Both novels tell stories of expatriates living abroad, but one is anchored in heterosexual love and desire while the other is anchored in same-gendered love and desire. The decision to study the New York City Draft demonstrations of 1863 but not the Stonewall Inn demonstrations of 1969 communicates messages about social action, institutional authority, and which protests left an important historical mark. A similar decision is made in life science classes when biological sex is discussed as causing gender, instead of teaching sex as biologically determined and gender as socially and culturally constructed. Decisions about what is included or excluded in curricula demonstrate what schools value as worthy of learning.

The hidden curriculum is subtle and harder to identify. It is communicated through cultural and procedural routines and practices that assume all students and their families are cisgender and heterosexual. These assumptions are communicated through visual and verbal messages that imply that all parents are either mothers or fathers, or when school dances only celebrate heterosexual couples and dating rituals. Behavioral expectations communicated to students may also privilege binary gender behaviors. For example, expectations that boys should not cry and girls should wear pink imply how students are expected to look and act according to cisgender norms. These implicit messages treat LBGTQ+ student behaviors and interactions as abnormal and can contribute to a hostile school environment. For example, when policies prohibit same-sex couples from holding hands in school hallways (but different-sex couples are permitted to), lesbian, gay, and bisexual students learn that their desires are not appropriate at school.

The hidden curriculum that permeates classroom and school climates can be revealed through a critical examination of who and what is valued by these policies, procedures, and assumptions. It is the intersection of the hidden and formal curriculum that communicates expectations and values about gender and sexuality. In this way, the curriculum (both formal and hidden) shapes school culture and how students experience education.

## QUEERING THE CURRICULUM

When schools decide what to teach and how to teach it, these decisions are made within the finite space of a school year broken into its corresponding units of study, semesters, and class periods. The curriculum is always partial because teachers and administrators must decide what to include within this limited space and time (Kumashiro, 2003). By recognizing this partiality, educators can critically examine who and what the curriculum represents and adjust their decisions to be inclusive of diverse genders and sexualities (Schmidt, 2015). Educators who include LGBTQ+ perspectives and reject assumptions of heterosexuality and cisgender binaries transform what is possible within education. These educators create learning spaces where all students are welcome. In these spaces, students are able to critically analyze the social practices, behaviors, and beliefs associated with sexuality and gender, then recognize and resist social structures and practices that oppress LGBTQ+ and other gender expansive identities (Abes & Kasch, 2007).

The content and experiences students encounter in schools and their classrooms act as windows, mirrors, and sliding glass doors (Bishop, 1990; Botelho & Rudman, 2009). Windows enable students to explore differences and look outside of themselves. Mirrors enable students to look inward and develop a deeper understanding of their own identities and potential. Sliding glass doors help students walk into the world outside of their own and share the intellectual and emotional experiences of others. Each of these opportunities depends on the degree to which students are able to look within or without. "Queering the curriculum" means destabilizing heterosexual identities as the norm, embracing the existence of multiple perspectives, and explicitly exploring the relationship between power and identity. When the windows, mirrors, and sliding glass doors open on to the perspectives and experiences of LGBTQ+ students, assumptions of heteronormativity are challenged and LGBTQ+ students are empowered.

Because decisions about the curriculum are made at the policy, school, and classroom levels, educators have multiple opportunities to design a curriculum that advocates for LGBTQ+ children, youth, and their families. At the elementary level, this opportunity includes expanding the understanding of gender and being inclusive of non-heterosexual families. At the secondary level, this opportunity includes explicit inclusion of LGBTQ+ identities and issues at every content level. At the collegiate level, this opportunity includes enriching classroom experiences with LGBTQ+ identities, issues, and experiences, while still striving to incorporate LGBTQ+ perspectives and identities fully into campus culture.

## Queering the Curriculum in Elementary Schools

Students begin to express their gender identity at an early age (Ehrensaft, 2013). Unfortunately, in most elementary school settings, gender expansive, gender creative, and transgender children are vulnerable. The majority of elementary school experiences are saturated with stereotypical, binary-gendered expectations that can create anxiety for students as early as the first days of kindergarten (Ryan, Patraw, & Bednar, 2013). Gender-complex education and gender-affirming education acknowledge the stereotypical gender binary, question the ways in which gender functions in a variety of settings, and communicate acceptance and support for gender creative, transgender, and gender non-conforming children (Rands, 2009; Ehrensaft, 2013). These approaches involve teaching students a variety of gender pronouns, explaining non-binary gender vocabulary, exploring the limitations of gender stereotypes, and the possibilities created when these are rejected. Research indicates that because young students can name stereotypical gender expectations and behaviors, they are also capable of exploring and disrupting these stereotypes in significant ways (Ryan, Patraw, & Bednar, 2013). In 2014 a seven-year old girl challenged gender stereotypes when she wrote a letter to the Lego Company asking why all the boy Lego people "went on adventures, worked, saved people and had jobs" while girl Lego people were depicted at home, on the beach, or shopping (Leggett, 2014, para.1). She wanted to know why the company did not produce more girl Lego people who were dressed for adventure and fun.

---

## Children's Literature for an LGBTQ+ Inclusive Classroom

Recent years have seen the publication of a host of children's books that are more inclusive of LGBTQ people and families. Some examples are:

- Hoffman, S., & Hoffman, I. (2014). *Jacob's new dress*. Park Ridge, IL: Albert Whitman & Company.
  A book that challenges what it means to be a boy. Jacob is a boy who loves playing dress-up and his favorite thing to wear is a dress. When he wants to wear a dress to school, his mom and dad have to decide what to do.
- Kilodavis, C., & DeSimone, S. (2010). *My princess boy*. New York, NY: Aladdin.
  The story of a boy who loves all things princess: pink, sparkles, and dancing. This book tells the story of how families and communities can support gender expansive children.
- Mujsch, R. (1980). *The Paper Bag Princess*. Toronto, CA: Annick Press.
  The story of a princess who has to save her fiancé from a dragon and demonstrates that it is more important to be brave and independent than pretty.
- Parnell, P., & Richardson, J. (2007). *And Tango makes three*. New York, NY: Simon and Schuster.
  The story of two male penguins, Roy and Silo, who live at the Central Park Zoo, and fall in love with each other. When the zookeeper notices the penguins want to start a family, Roy and Silo adopt an egg that needs to be nurtured.
- Oelschlager, V. (2010). *A tale of two daddies*. Akron, OH: VanitaBooks.
  The story of a girl explaining to her friend what life is like growing up with two dads. The question and answer structure of the book demonstrates how both dads share parenting responsibilities equally.
- Oelschlager, V. (2011). *A tale of two mommies*. Akron, OH: VanitaBooks.
  The story of a boy explaining to his two friends what life is like growing up with two moms. The question and answer structure of the book demonstrates how both moms share parenting responsibilities equally.
- Herthel, J., & Jennings, J. (2014). *I am Jazz*. New York, NY: Penguin.
  The biographical story of Jazz—a transgender girl who has always known she thought and felt like a girl, regardless of what her body looked like. The book defines what it means to be unique and transgendered and what it means to be loved and supported growing up.

Queering elementary school culture and curriculum means approaching gender as a content worthy of discussion and teaching by including gender as part of the formal curriculum. Students and teachers can explore gender by reading texts that display varied and non-stereotypical representations of gender, and by engaging students in discussions that challenge texts with stereotypical gender performances. These discussions provide time for students to explore the ways they feel limited by gender expectations, and how they would feel if they woke up with a different gender one day.

Because family is an important part of young students' lives, discussions and texts should explicitly include queerly-diverse families, and engage students to name and consider the range of family constellations (Shema, 2014). In terms of the hidden curriculum, elementary schools can abandon practices that divide students by boys and girls in favor of dividing them by birthdates or preferences. Teachers can refer to students using language that is gender inclusive (folks, y'all, and learners, instead of boys and girls or guys). Bulletin boards and school displays can be inclusive of queerly-diverse families and a spectrum of gender behaviors. Because young students develop understandings of themselves by making sense of their worlds, it is critical that elementary schools offer students windows and mirrors that expand beyond stereotypical gender representations and create affirming environments for students of all gender expressions to create and explore their identities.

## Queering the Curriculum in Secondary Schools

Students in middle- and high-school study discrete subjects, with their days divided between time in various classes. Each discipline-based curricular experience offers an opportunity for queering these subjects of study. Frequently, queering the curriculum in one class means embracing a cross-disciplinary experience. In this sense, queering the curriculum means crossing the artificial boundaries the school day creates between fields of study and embracing complexity and nuance as an inherent part of learning.

### *Mathematics*

Math is a subject that can be viewed as objective and devoid of social justice issues concerned with identity, inclusion, and power. Recently, however, some math teachers have focused on how math acts as a tool for exploring, understanding, and taking steps toward social justice (Gutstein, 2006; Rands, 2013).

Middle-school math teachers have used data from present and past National School Climate Surveys, which examine the experiences of LGBT students in schools, to teach students about statistics, fractions, ratio, and proportion, while also expanding their understanding of gender, school-based gender bias, and transphobia in schools (Rands, 2013). The lesson involved students examining the survey results focused on percentages and statistics about harassment of gender non-conforming students paired with statistics and percentages of how often peers intervened in response to this harassment. Once students understood the relationship between percentages and statistics reflecting instances of harassment and student intervention, they used a probability model to determine the likelihood of intervention in different numerical contexts. Following this numerical exploration, the lesson asked students to construct an action plan that encouraged peer intervention in response to harassment about gender expression. As the lesson proceeded from statistical understanding, to probability, to action, students used mathematical processes to examine the positive impact of students advocating for their peers.

This lesson shows how students can explore and manipulate data that focuses on making a positive social difference and rejects a victim-only perspective of transgender youth while acknowledging the prevalence of gender harassment in schools. It expands mathematical learning beyond the typical boundaries of a math classroom to embrace the ways in which numbers communicate understandings about the social world. In this example, mathematics enabled students to develop knowledge about math and the school experiences of transgender and gender non-conforming students, paired with the goal of developing a more socially just world.

## Science

Middle- and high-school life science and biology courses have the potential to create an overwhelmingly heteronormative view of the world that relies on outmoded ideas that biological sex is binary in form (i.e., that there are only two sexes: female and male). Sexual activity and behavior tend to appear in science education as part of discussions of reproduction, and sexual orientation tends to be presented in relation to HIV/AIDS (Bazzul & Sykes, 2011; Synder & Broadway, 2004). Biology, anatomy, and physiology lessons that ignore the diversity of animal and human sexual development (by presenting only female- and male-typical bodies) imply that society's gender binary (girl/boy; women/ man; feminine/masculine) is grounded in innate biological sex differences.

When presented this way science curricula ignore the complexity of the natural world (represented across species) and treat variation as a kind of abnormality instead of embracing inherent complexity and variation (Roughgarden, 2013; Bagemihl, 1999). Along with most science curricula, sex education in the United States, when present, has been reduced to a single purpose: to teach abstinence from sexual activity until marriage—a federally supported and funded approach prevalent for almost 20 years. Abstinence until marriage approaches have been criticized for promoting gender stereotypes, communicating religious ideals, focusing on heterosexual relationships, and failing to promote healthy decision making (Hall, Sales, Komro, & Santelli, 2016). This approach erases the experiences of LGBTQ+ youth, neglects their health needs, and further stigmatizes same-sex desires (Santelli, Ott, Lyon, Rogers, Summers, & Schleifer, 2006).

One way to disrupt the heteronormativity of science curricula would be for science teachers to include the topic of diverse sexual anatomies and sexual practices among humans and animals. There are South American male hummingbirds that display female coloration, fish and frogs that can change sex over the course of their lives, cases of intersexed deer, and male kangaroos with pouches (Roughgarden, 2013; Bagemihl, 1999). Humans are similarly diverse in their biological sexual traits and characteristics. Although facial hair is associated with maleness and masculinity, many women have visible facial hair. Similarly, some men have high-pitched voices even though that trait is associated with femaleness and femininity. Less visible is diversity in human sexual anatomy, including genitals and internal sexual organs. It has been estimated that approximately 1.7% of live births cannot be easily categorized as female or male on the basis of anatomy, hormones, or genetics/chromosomes (Fausto-Sterling, 2000). Science educators might also include a wider range of procreative and non-procreative sexual activities that are common among humans, including those between transgender and same-sex partners, as part of a comprehensive and inclusive sexual education program (Carroll, 2016).

Because science is also a profession, educators can queer the science curriculum by expanding and critiquing visual depictions of scientists. Images of scientists in popular culture and mass media tend to depict 'nerdy' men hovering over microscopes or data. These stereotypes perpetuate assumptions that only masculine bodies are fit to conduct science. Some scientists, in STEM (Science, Technology, Engineering, and Math) fields particularly, are working hard to change this image by recruiting women and girls into these fields, but the same push could be made for recruiting LGBTQ+ students to consider becoming future scientists. By expanding who and what is represented in the science curriculum, educators can embrace complex understandings of gender and sexuality found in the natural world and provide students with opportunities to question what is presented as "normal."

### English

Middle- and high-school English classes require students to learn about worlds—real and imagined; past, present, and future—through literary texts of all genres. Additionally, students are required to develop their writing skills through producing texts that communicate the significance of what they read, learn, and experience. When texts with LGBTQ+ authors, characters, and themes are part of the English classroom, windows, mirrors, and sliding glass doors offer students opportunities to explore the world and self. By teaching these texts in a manner that facilitates a connection between the complexities of diverse characters to the complexities of diverse students' lives, educators enable students to examine and potentially challenge representations of gender and sexual orientation. These texts also establish clear and positive associations of LGBTQ+ lives and offer opportunities to 'try on' different attitudes (Athanases, 1996; Ghiso, Campano, & Hall 2012; Greenbaum, 1994; Schall & Kauffman, 2003). Additionally, by including these texts as an explicit component of the English curriculum, teachers can affirm LGBTQ+ students by providing a sense of connection and vicarious experiences (Hughes-Hassel, Overberg, & Harris, 2013).

Because literature can offer rich and complicated characters in compelling and layered situations, these texts enable students to explore intersections of identity reflecting the human condition (Kumashiro, 2001). Literature captures the multidimensional nature of characters, developing them beyond their sexual or gender identities and practices. LGBTQ+ characters are family members, professionals, adolescents, and athletes with talents and cultures that extend beyond the LGBTQ+ aspects of their identities. In this way, both fiction and non-fiction literature, can provide rich representations for students to explore the intersections of LGBTQ+ and other identities. While a plethora of young adult literature contains LGBTQ+ characters and issues, texts frequently taught as part of a standards-based curriculum also offer these opportunities. Authors such as Emily Dickinson, Tennessee Williams, and Alice Walker (to name only a few) lived lives or wrote about characters with complex sexual attractions, behaviors, and desires having expansive and fluid gender identities and expressions. These authors are frequently studied in high-school English classrooms, opening a prime opportunity for students to consider the significant contributions of LGBTQ+ authors and texts to academic literary culture (Greenbaum, 1994).

Providing students with opportunities to consider themes, subtexts, and language that speaks to same-sex attraction or to gender-expansive perspectives may expand students' understanding of literary aesthetics beyond the politics of identity and representation. Family dynamics, love, belonging, power, and the complexities of the natural world are all examples of literary topics discussed in the English classroom that, when viewed through an LGBTQ+ lens, can open the door for literary interpretations that reject normative perspectives and create classroom climates embracing a range of voices. Additionally, examinations of how masculine and feminine are portrayed in literary characters and by authors offers students opportunities to disrupt gender expectations and see the spectrum of gender performances represented in literature.

Finally, teachers and students can learn to engage in "queer readings" of texts (Shlasko, 2005, p.130). This approach requires readers not only to identify and name LGBTQ+ or gender expansive elements presented in a text, but also to interpret texts based on alternative understandings. For example, instead of asking, "What's the text say and mean?" students might ask, "What *else* could this text mean?" and "What did I want to find or avoid finding in the text?" (Kumashiro, 2002). These questions push students to shift assumptions about gender and sexual orientation. For example, assuming characters are heterosexual may lead students to miss critical aspects of interpretations: How does the meaning of a character's words or actions shift if the character is gay or bisexual? How could small gestures, symbols, and interactions reflect queer or gender expansive desires and motivations? Asking and answering these questions require students to explore subtexts and ambiguities, and consider possible connections between the text and their lives. Embracing this process expands the English curriculum to include critically considering who and what is represented in texts and expanding the ways in which texts are interpreted—cultivating a dynamic approach to reading for meaning.

## History

History curricula have generally been driven by three educational goals: to help students understand the past; to develop the skills historians use to understand the world; to enable students to understand how historical narratives create interpretations of local, national, and global events (Schmidt, 2014). While different historians and history teachers may privilege one goal over the others, it is indisputable that the study of the past is always intertwined with the question of representation: what stories and whose stories shape history curricula? By discussing the range of sexual attractions, behaviors, and gender expressions, considered acceptable throughout time and cultures, history teachers help students understand gender as a social construction and sexual attraction as fluid and dynamic (Mayo & Sheppard, 2012). Including societies and cultures from the past that were not heteronormative or cisnormative as an explicit part of the history curricula affirms the lives of today's LGBTQ+ people and gender-expansive individuals.

The National Curriculum Standards for Social Studies requires students to study the "interaction among individuals, groups, and institutions" as well as "how people create, interact with, and change structures of power, authority, and governance" (NCSS, 2010). Many history courses address these standards through examining the evolution of constitutional amendments and the role of the Supreme Court in validating or invalidating regional judicial decisions. Expanding these examinations to include the relationship of the Defense of Marriage Act (DOMA) in 1996 to government recognition of same-sex marriage in 2015 via the fourteenth amendment enables students to track the path of civil rights legislation and creates an inclusive curriculum. This juxtaposition can help students explore the interplay between federal power, state power, and citizen action, while also explicitly including LGBTQ+ rights as civil rights encompassed in the constitution (Hess, 2009).

Studying the process to recognize same-sex marriage under the fourteenth amendment of the U.S. Constitution is just one example of several ways history can reflect LGBTQ+ experiences. History teachers have many opportunities to recognize the ways in which LGBTQ+ people and groups have organized around galvanizing ideas and goals. Others include examining the ways in which the 1966 Compton's Cafeteria riot was a catalyst of change for the transgender community of San Francisco and the effects of Stonewall on civil rights for lesbians and gay men. Studying the evolution of use of the pink triangle as an icon for gay people pushes students to think about the role of context in understanding symbols. The lives of Sylvia Rivera, Bayard Rustin, Harvey Milk, and Jane Addams could be studied to examine the civil rights accomplishments of LGBTQ+ individuals. Because the study of history is inextricable from the study of social change, the experience of gender and sexual minorities in the past can be an important part of the secondary and collegiate learning experience. A history curriculum without LGBTQ+ people, events, and themes perpetuates a heteronormative and cisnormative view of the world. It is also complicit in rejecting the experiences of LGBTQ+ students and perpetuating a heteronormative culture in a school.

## Emergence of LGBTQ Studies

LGBTQ studies is an area of teaching, research, and publishing that focuses on gender and sexual identities. As it is interdisciplinary, the field attracts scholars from a wide range of academic specialties, as well as independent scholars, archivists, and museum curators.

Institutionally, LGBTQ studies emerged in the years after Stonewall, primarily on the East and West Coasts of the U.S. The 1973 founding of the Gay Academic Union, which encouraged the teaching of "gay studies" throughout American education, stimulated the field's growth (D'Emilio, 1992). In the 1970s and 1980s at City College of San Francisco, a growing number of courses created the semblance of a program and in 1989 that school created the first Gay and Lesbian Studies department. In 1986 historian Martin Duberman mobilized colleagues to establish a Center for Lesbian and Gay Studies, which ultimately ended up at the City University of New York's Graduate School (CLAGS, 2003). Meanwhile, the medievalist John Boswell led the establishment of the Lesbian and Gay Studies Center at Yale University in 1987. After receiving a major donation in 2001, Yale developed a more comprehensive lesbian, gay, bisexual, and transgender studies program in 2007. In 2013 the University of Arizona launched the Transgender Studies Initiative, and in 2016 the University of Victoria established the first endowed Chair in Transgender Studies.

These examples illustrate the broader pattern of the field's development. Early course offerings developed into undergraduate certificates, degree concentrations, and major/minor degree programs; graduate certificates soon followed. Today, at least ten North American universities allow students to major in LGBTQ studies (or similarly-named majors) (Younger, 2016). The study of transgender people and issues is currently exploding in interest. For several decades, various professional associations organized caucuses and committees focusing on subfields, and further stand-alone institutes, libraries, archives, and community organizations added to the field's wider institutional base. The *Lesbian and Gay Studies Newsletter* of the Modern Language Association's Gay and Lesbian Caucus constituted one of the first scholarly serials (begun in 1974 as the *Gay Studies Newsletter*). Peer-reviewed academic journals followed, notably the *Journal of Homosexuality* (1976), *GLQ* (1993), *Journal of Bisexuality* (2000), and *Transgender Studies Quarterly* (2014).

During the 1970s and 1980s LGBTQ studies focused on identifying homosexuals who had been overlooked or intentionally erased within various academic disciplines, including literature, history, and art. This resulted in the recovery of many lost artists, writers, and historical figures to gay and lesbian history. But, starting in the 1980s, scholars began questioning some of the terms and categories they had used in their initial work. Heavily influenced by the English publication of Michel Foucault's book *The History of Sexuality* (1978), scholars began to think about sexuality not as an inherent biological or psychological trait, but as the result of power working through social institutions

*(continued)*

*(continued)*

and discourse (like language and visual representations). The field shifted from thinking about homosexuals and homosexuality as historical facts that needed to be identified, recovered, described, and analyzed. Rather, scholars began to consider how all sexuality was produced, managed, and policed in society. This shift is marked by the, so-called, essentialism vs. social constructivism debate. Essentialists argued that, because same-sex desire and sexual behavior exists throughout time and in every known culture, homosexuality and the homosexual are universal phenomena. Constructivists, on the other hand, cited evidence that sexualities and sexual identities vary historically and cross-culturally, arguing that homosexuality is not innate but socially constructed—produced in unique social, cultural, and historical contexts. Queer studies became an increasingly popular name for the field as it underwent this intellectual shift and developed a body of thought often described as queer theory (Jagose, 1996). The emergence of queer studies also facilitated a more inclusive study of sexual identities and behaviors, including more sophisticated thinking about bisexual behavior and the burgeoning sub-field of transgender studies (Ochs & Rowley, 2005; Stryker & Whittle, 2006).

*Donald L. Opitz*

## Queering Curriculum in Higher Education

College and university graduate students and professors are responsible for producing most of the research and writing about queer theory and LGBTQ+ issues in education. However, this work has not resulted in substantial curricular changes (Renn, 2010). Some schools have majors in LGBT or queer studies and, more commonly, gender or sexuality studies, but this is not the norm. Moreover, some institutions struggle to maintain these established majors (Seitz, 2009; Lindeman, 2013). Much like the way LGBTQ+ practices break heteronormative and cisnormative expectations of gender and sexuality, queer studies majors and programs require faculty and students to work across boundaries between subjects. The hierarchical organization of higher education, with departments and programs operating in isolation, creates challenges for teachers who wish to work across subject areas and create innovative approaches at the heart of queer studies (Renn, 2010). Still, some faculty traverse boundaries between fields such as the social sciences, sciences, humanities, and professional degree programs to teach and build knowledge about LGBTQ+ experiences, practices, and communities (Whitlock, 2010). At its most basic level, without crossing boundaries of formally established programs, queering the curriculum within higher education involves incorporating LGBTQ+ themes/concepts, people/events, and cultural representations into courses that have been void of these topics (Dilley, 1999).

The humanities—history, philosophy, art/art history, English, literary studies, music, theatre—have, and continue to be, academic disciplines in which

LGBTQ+ students are supported and curricula are rife with opportunities to critically analyze and explore the intersections of gender, sexuality, and culture (Linley, Renn, & Woodford, 2014). Following the tradition of English courses initiating the use of LGBTQ+ studies, faculty have created writing and literature courses that explore and disrupt norms of gender and sexuality. These courses use literature and rhetoric to explore the intersections of gender, sexuality, race, and class, to help students build critical understandings of language and narrative style along with literary and cultural interpretation (Alexander & Gibson, 2004; DiGrazia & Boucher, 2005; Lindemann, 2000).

The social sciences—psychology, sociology, anthropology, and social work—are disciplines in which students can explore the intersections of LGBTQ+ individuals and gender expansive identities with culture, social organizations, development, and public service. These disciplines lead their fields in developing and conducting research that identifies and challenges heteronormative and cisnormative policies and practices. This work promotes innovative paths to learning and research (Donelson & Rogers, 2004; Vicars, 2012). Multidisciplinary media courses enable students to investigate and produce stories about LGBTQ+ activism and politics expressed through a combination of investigative journalism, art, and film (Seitz, 2009). The disciplines with the least LGBTQ+ content are the sciences, technology, mathematics and engineering fields (Patridge, Barthelemy, & Rankin, 2014; Bilimoria & Stewart, 2009). Scholars working in these areas often present gender and sexuality as innate, biologically determined, and unchangeable, and many have not embraced the concepts of social construction or gender/sexual fluidity, unlike some scholars/teachers/researchers in the humanities and social sciences.

Some professional disciplines adhere to ethical expectations that also have an impact on curricula in higher education. For example, the National Association of Social Workers' *Standards and Indicators for Cultural Competence in Social Work Practice* (NASW, 2015a) calls for students in university social work programs to develop an appreciation and understanding of diverse identities, which include sexual orientation and gender expression. These standards require students to develop cultural knowledge about LGBTQ populations and cultural skills for communicating with and serving them. Additionally, NASW's National Committee on Lesbian, Gay, Bisexual, and Transgender Issues has published position statements advocating social workers to operate in ways that affirm LGBTQ individuals (NASW, 2015b). Because it is a practice standard for social work programs, social work faculty and administrators may be more mindful to ensure LGBTQ+ topics are included in the social work curriculum. As a result, social work students may be more familiar and comfortable with LGBTQ+ people and their issues and compassionate toward clients who may be disclosing or sharing a minority gender or sexual orientation.

Across college courses, however, the degree to which LGBTQ+ texts, issues, individuals, and events are incorporated into courses depends largely on the overall culture of the university, as well as faculty interests and knowledge. Thus, while colleges and universities offer the greatest opportunities for queering the curriculum, this has not occurred evenly across academic disciplines or courses.

While LGBTQ+ students can benefit when a curriculum is inclusive of their identities and experiences, queering the curriculum potentially benefits *all* students. The interactions and discussions that occur between students and teachers when expansive ideas about gender, sexuality, community, and culture are considered, enable students to develop critical understandings about the world (Ellsworth, 1989). When disciplines embrace a curriculum that includes LGBTQ+ individuals, gender expansive identities, queer ways in which to view the world, students develop a critical eye that challenges heteronormative and cisnormative assumptions. This practice demands that teachers and students embrace discomfort and acknowledge the contributions and experiences of LGBTQ+ individuals—all with the goal of deepening knowledge in every subject of study and at every grade level (Kumashiro, 2000).

## Queering Higher Education Beyond the Curriculum

The true queering of higher education has not occurred (Renn, 2010). While colleges and universities have entertained the concepts of queer theory, with some revising and changing higher education structures and cultures in regard to sexuality and gender, true change has yet to occur. Queering the higher-education curriculum is much more complicated than merely inserting LGBTQ+ concepts into the classroom because colleges and universities are complex organizational systems (Linley & Nguyen, 2015). Colleges and universities have adapted to accept the intellectual discussions about queer theory and to support LGBTQ+ scholarship without making a cultural shift to disrupt heteronormative practices and culture (Renn, 2010). Sexual and gender identities within higher education are viewed as a dichotomy in which heterosexuality and cisgender identities are assumed as normal and LGBTQ+ and gender-expansive identities are viewed as deviating from this norm (Fox, 2007).

Not surprisingly there are a several factors that directly contribute to the ways in which a campus can disrupt heteronormative and cisnormative culture and practices. The diversity and presence of LGBTQ+ faculty and administrators increase the chances of queer topics being incorporated into the curriculum in and outside of the classroom. On college and university campuses learning not only occurs in the traditional classroom, but also occurs in the residence halls, through organizational involvement, athletics, and throughout co-curricular involvement. The mission and campus climate of an institution influence the degree to which faculty and their courses reflect an LGBTQ+ curriculum. Lastly, peer-to-peer interaction plays a large role in the queering of college campuses (Nguyen et al., 2014). Students are primed and ready to learn and listen to one another. This peer to peer interaction becomes even more powerful when students receive training and development in how to engage in difficult dialogue and how to appreciate dissonance (Mezirow, 1997).

Due to recent progress in marriage equality, limited civil rights protections, and the increased presence of LGBTQ+ in popular culture and mass media, some groups have suggested that society—and particularly college and university campuses—are in a post–LGBTQ+ era (Linley & Nguyen, 2015; Sollender, 2011). This claim implies that LGBTQ+ individuals have moved into the mainstream, are no longer vulnerable to harassment, and no longer desire to claim their identities, communities, and cultures (Ng, 2013). While there have been advances for some LGBTQ+ people, a post LGBTQ+ era does not exist and therefore is problematic to the concept of queering the curriculum within higher education. If administration, faculty, staff, and students assume that harassment, bias, and prejudice are no longer occurring, and that the need to educate about gender and sexuality are no longer necessary, a substantial gap exists between assumption and reality.

## Safe Zone Allies Programs

Since the early 1990s, Safe Zone allies programs have proliferated across college campuses as a way to create more inclusive, supportive, and welcoming campus environments for sexual and gender minority (LGBTQIA+) students, staff, and faculty. A hallmark of these programs is the public identification of members by posting a Safe Zone sign on their office doors. Such signs offer visible support to sexual and gender minority students, an often-invisible population. The sign typically incorporates a rainbow and/or pink triangle with the words Safe Zone and a campus logo. These programs exist to help heterosexual and cisgender people on college campuses become better allies when confronting heterosexism, homophobia, and transphobia. The end result is increased conversations on these topics and an improved campus climate.

This emphasis requires skill development at workshop sessions that educate potential allies on topics relevant to sexual and gender minorities. Safe Zone workshops predominantly include heterosexual and cisgender students, staff, and faculty. Participation is usually voluntary, so self-selected individuals will be motivated to engage in the workshops. Workshops typically cover terminology, the coming out process, campus resources, sexuality across the lifespan, religion, transgender identities, and the intersection of multiple identities.

For there to be effective attitudinal change, facilitators do not use typical modes of learning, such as lectures or PowerPoint presentations. A constructivist pedagogy is employed that requires learners to actively engage in the material that models potential experiences. Workshops employ participatory activities that effectively meet workshop learning outcomes. All allies are taught that sexual orientation, biological sex, and gender identity are not binary concepts but a continuum (Poynter, 2016).

Through these workshops, Safe Zone members learn to become better allies to sexual and gender minorities. Ally development is a process of acquiring information and making meaning by employing three effective strategies: discussion, self-reflection, and perspective taking (Evans & Broido, 2005). Safe Zone programs ask participants to consider the process of how allies come to develop awareness, skills, and action. They also encourage an

*(continued)*

(continued)

*Typical sign posted by graduate of a university Safe Zone program. Source: Kerry John Poynter.*

increasing level of expertise that allows members to meet their developmental needs through ongoing educational interventions.

Allyship is neither an identity nor a one-time event. It is an ongoing pursuit of knowledge acquisition and skills development. As a campus' Safe Zone program matures, coordinators assess if it is meeting its stated goals by surveying membership, conducting climate assessments to gauge visibility of program signs, and consistently practicing facilitation skills with workshop facilitators. Coordinators of Safe Zone programs can leverage allies to enact inclusive policy change by using the Campus Pride Index (campusprideindex.org) and recommendations from The Consortium of Higher Education LGBT Resource Professionals (lgbtcampus.org).

*Kerry John Poynter*

## THE ROLE OF EDUCATORS IN SUPPORTING LGBTQ+ STUDENTS

It is clear that the majority of LGBTQ+ K-12 students report feeling unsafe at school because of their sexual orientation, and more than a third of these students report feeling unsafe because of their gender expression (Chesir-Teran, 2003; Kosciw, Greytak, Diaz, & Bartkiewicz, 2010; Kosciw et al., 2015). This lack of safety has remained consistent over the last decades despite the increased number of young people who express gender expansiveness or identify as LGBTQ+ (McKay, Misra, & Lindquist, 2017). LGBTQ+ youth also report that teachers and administrators have the potential to improve school climates. When LGBTQ students could identify more than ten supportive faculty or staff members, they reported feeling safer, more connected to their school, and had better attendance and higher grade point averages. LGBTQ students also reported feeling safe and supported when teachers and staff responded to reports of harassment or bullying. Responses included disciplining or contacting parents of the offending students, and providing educational experiences that focused on ending bullying and harassment in schools (Kosciw et al., 2015).

While teachers and staff have the power to make school a positive experience for LGBTQ+ students, they also face some challenges and obstacles. The heteronormativity that permeates school culture creates a system of rules, sometimes explicitly and sometimes implicitly, that may lead teachers to believe discussing LGBTQ+ topics is not allowed (Fredman, Schultz, & Hoffman, 2015). These rules fall along a continuum. On the most prohibitive end, teachers may believe that they are not allowed to talk about LGBTQ+ topics. On the most permissive end, teachers may believe that they are allowed to talk about LGBTQ+ topics as long as parents, administration, or community members agree. At a middle point, teachers may believe that talking about LGBTQ+ topics requires approval from some authority. Each of these perspectives reflects heteronormative values and communicates that LGBTQ+ topics are controversial or even dangerous for teachers, at K–12 and college levels, to approach. Additionally, even when teachers want to address LGBTQ+ topics in their classrooms, they feel unprepared to do so (Clark & Blackburn, 2009; Fredman, Schultz, & Hoffman, 2015). While many teacher education programs and professional development sessions focus on issues of diversity, it is common for diversity to have an overly broad definition that does not explicitly include LGBTQ+ identities (Castro & Sujak, 2014). When this happens, schools fall into a pattern of acknowledging and addressing racial and ethnic diversity, and the needs of students of color, while ignoring sexual and gender diversity, and the needs of LGBTQ+ students.

Supporting LGBTQ+ students in schools requires educators (and the systems that influence education) to question the status quo or to disrupt what is viewed or experienced as normal (Kumashiro, 2003). Additionally, this work requires educators to enable students to question the status quo and become co-creators of knowledge alongside educators. This disruption, by its nature, can be challenging and uncomfortable. It is possible that teachers with experience in negotiating the challenging issues of race, ethnicity, and class differences, may be more prepared to negotiate the challenges LGBTQ+ students face (Fredman, Schultz, & Hoffman, 2015; LeCompte, 2000). Teachers with experience and who are comfortable helping students grapple with topics of identity, representation, power, and society may be more prepared or comfortable helping students grapple with underrepresented gender and sexualities. These teachers can act as leaders that model and support other, less comfortable, teachers to embrace this level of disruption and understanding so that schools and classrooms become affirming, welcoming, and inclusive spaces for LGBTQ+ and gender expansive students.

Educators can prompt students to question the "normal" to understand how and why everyday practices and policies oppress, marginalize, or privilege majority and minority genders and sexualities. This questioning process requires self-reflection, intentionality, and discussion to build collaborative and ongoing understanding. This shift requires educators to enable students to share ideas and experiences, ask questions, and challenge each other's and the teacher's thinking (Dinkins & Englert, 2016). In this manner, educators can actively create a supportive space for student voices, a space for LGBTQ+ representations, and space to challenge the norm.

## EXTRA-CURRICULAR ORGANIZATIONS

Extra-curricular activities—activities that occur at school but are not part of the formal academic curriculum—are another way for schools to support LGBTQ+ students. When schools create a variety of "safe" spaces and visible support networks, LGBTQ+ students feel safer and more welcome, and are more likely to succeed academically at every level (Kosciw et al., 2015). Some extra-curricular efforts have included establishing GSAs and LGBT Offices/Centers, and recognizing the Day of Silence, National Coming Out Day, and the Transgender Day of Remembrance. These events, which are often organized and publicized by student-led groups like GSAs, are examples of how LGBTQ+ students and their allies can advocate for social justice through transformative practices that make visible the experiences of LGBTQ+ individuals.

### Gay Straight Alliances (GSAs)

GSAs were first established in California in 1998 by Carolyn Laub as a source of support for middle- and high-school students to counteract homophobia

*Gay-Straight Alliance bulletin board, Kent Place School, Summit NJ (2005). Source: Photo by Lauren Stokes, courtesy of Wikimedia Commons.*

and transphobia (GSA Network, 2016). The program established 40 clubs the first year but quickly grew to over 900 clubs throughout the state. In 2005 the National Association of GSA Networks was launched and 40 states are currently a part of the network. In 2016 the name of Gay Straight Alliances was changed to Genders and Sexualities Alliance Network to reflect the range of identities involved with the organizations across the United States. This change made explicit the mission of GSAs to accommodate the needs of LGBTQ+ students, their understandings and development of sexual orientation and gender expression. GSAs offer LGBTQ+ students support, opportunities for leadership, and social justice strategies to use in fighting for racial and gender justice. When home is not a safe or supportive space, GSAs can provide a support system for coming out, learning how to be an ally, and creating bully-free school environments. Because GSAs require some level of faculty sponsorship, their presence makes visible the faculty and staff LGBTQ+ allies who create safe spaces and offer support to LGBTQ+ students.

When schools have a GSA, LGBTQ+ students are less likely to experience verbal harassment associated with sexual orientation (i.e., hearing fag, dyke, or that's so gay), are less likely to experience gender-based harassment, and are more likely to report any such experiences to faculty and staff. When schools take pro-active steps to support LGBTQ+ students and their allies, these students experience positive educational results (Kosciw et al., 2015).

## Day of Silence

The Day of Silence began in 1996 at the University of Virginia (UVA). The day was created to raise awareness and take a stand against bullying as a part of an assignment in a class on non-violent protests. In 1997 UVA students launched a national campaign with over 100 schools involved in the effort. The Day of Silence is now sponsored by GLSEN and is an international day of advocacy and action against anti-LGBTQ+ harassment and bullying (GLSEN, 2016). The event occurs in April and takes place in over 10,000 middle-school, high-school, and college campuses. As an act of solidarity and social protest against injustice, participants spend the day adhering to a vow of silence that symbolizes the silencing, bullying, and harassment of LGBTQ+ students. Students will often wear t-shirts and buttons to explain why they are not speaking.

## Campus Pride Centers and Offices of Identity and Inclusion

Most college and university campuses have an office that focuses on diversity and inclusion—offering support for students, staff, and faculty from historically underrepresented groups. It is often the responsibility of this office to support LGBTQ+ students and, sometimes, staff and faculty. On other campuses, there are stand-alone LGBTQ resource offices. There are approximately 250 pride centers, which are specific offices with dedicated staff to offer programming and support for LGBTQ+ students and their allies (Campus Pride, 2016). Both diversity/inclusion and LGBTQ resource offices provide myriad resources and programs for LGBTQ+ people. In addition, these offices sometimes provide campus wide staff, faculty, and human resources education, policy creation and revision, and administrative advising responsibilities. Due to limited resources and capacity issues, a college or university may not have a pride center, in which case the LGBTQ+ students are responsible for creating safe zone training, planning educational programs, and ensuring that campus is a safe and welcoming climate for LGBTQ+ students.

LGBTQ+ student organizations may also be associated with these offices. Depending on the size of the institution, there may be specific organizations for different identity groups or one student organization that serves as a collective for all LGBTQ+ people on campus. At colleges and universities, student organizations and centers strive to be responsive to the needs of their particular student body with the common goal of educating all students about inclusivity and advocacy.

At the collegiate level, campus pride centers and LGBTQ+ student organizations offer space for LGBTQ+ students to come together to commemorate significant events. For example, students celebrated the landmark case legalizing gay marriage. Students on campus at a religiously affiliated small private liberal arts college celebrated with the campus community by giving out candy rings and encouraging the student body to "propose" why "#lovewins." In this way, the collegiate organizations and students actively participate in the greater national or global conversation about LGBTQ+ rights and experiences. These same communities that celebrate together also come together to mourn and process tragedy, such as the Pulse nightclub shooting in Orlando, Florida where 49 LGBTQ+ people were killed.

---

### Defunding of Campus Pride

The Pride Center at the University of Tennessee-Knoxville sent out a newsletter in early August 2015 to staff and faculty to raise awareness of gender neutral pronoun and name usage, in order to be more supportive of transgender and gender non-conforming students. Governor Bill Haslam and other members of the Tennessee government were displeased with the types of programs being funded through the Diversity office and Pride Center and as a result passed House Bill 2248 eliminating $445,000 from the University of Tennessee's Office of Diversity. The Pride Center was closed and LGBTQ+ students were without a space to learn, develop, and find support. As a public institution the administration had to carefully weigh how to support students and remain in a good space to lose no further funding. At the end of the spring semester the doors to the Pride Center were closed and students had no clearer sense of what would occur in the fall. Administrators met with LGBTQ+ students multiple times to offer support and to develop solutions. In fall 2016 the semester faculty came together to volunteer their time and keep the Pride Center doors open from 9am–9pm. While most educational programs have been cut, faculty are working in collaboration with students to ensure a space on campus is present.

---

## National Coming Out Day

National Coming Out Day takes place each year on October 11 and commemorates the 1987 National March on Washington, D.C., for Gay and Lesbian Rights (HRC, 2016a). It also celebrates the power of publicly identifying as LGBTQ+. An estimated one in two Americans has a close friend, relative, or co-worker who identifies as a lesbian or gay, while one in ten know someone who is transgender (HRC, 2016a). The more LGBTQ+

people a person knows the more likely they are to support equality and justice (Herek, 2009). Therefore, disclosing as a gender or sexual minority—coming out—is potentially a political act. On campuses, NCOD is celebrated in various ways, including sharing narratives of coming out, taking selfies coming out of a closet door and posting them to social media, and providing context to the diverse ways in which people come out based on their gender and sexual identity. These events are often student-created and student-centered, exemplifying the ways in which students explore identities and learn through participation in social movements (HRC, 2016a).

## Transgender Day of Remembrance

The Gay & Lesbian Alliance Against Defamation (GLAAD) is the national sponsor for the Transgender Day of Remembrance (TDOR), which occurs every November 20. The day was developed by Gwendolyn Ann Smith, who was a transgender advocate, as a way to commemorate Rita Hestor, a transgender woman who was murdered in 1998. TDOR is a designated day to remember the death of transgender people from violence and hate crimes. The day of remembrance acknowledges the premature loss of a life and provides a public forum to celebrate each life lost that year. TDOR is often a candlelight ceremony where the names of murdered transgender community members are read, songs are sung, moments of silence occur, and trans flags (light blue, pink, and white stripes) are placed in the ground to commemorate the loss from the community. TDOR also raises awareness in the greater community of the violence perpetrated against transgender people (GLAAD, 2016b).

## SCHOOL PRACTICES AND POLICIES

School practices and policies that fail to acknowledge LGBTQ+ students create and perpetuate a culture in which these students are rendered invisible, which creates negative impacts upon educational growth and personal development (Bailey, 2005; Sears, 2013). The ways that schools regard students as heterosexual and cisgender parallels the ways in which education refuses to support LGBTQ+ students, create inclusive environments, or challenge hetero- and cisnormative culture. By queering education practices and policies, schools can make LGBTQ+ students visible—making it challenging and problematic to erase their presence. Practices reflect the daily interactions, symbols, routines, and language that students encounter as central to the school experience, while policies reflect official plans and protocols for regular organizational operation. The degree to which practices and policies explicitly acknowledge and include LGBTQ+ students reflects the degree to which schools disrupt and reject heteronormative and cisnormative environments (Russell et al., 2010).

## Practices that Reject Heteronormativity and Cisnormativity

School buildings are awash with symbols and language that communicate which identities are accepted and visible. Signs declare traditional gender binaries for bathrooms and locker rooms. The plaques on these doors are easy for cisgendered students to forget. Students are supposed to know and feel that one gender expresses its gender by wearing pants, another does so by wearing dresses and skirts. Forms ask students to check boxes with limited options—male/female, boy/girl—assuming that all students fit into one of two boxes. Schools are also frequently organized around heterosexual social events, as in the case of the MatchMaker™ game referred to in the opening vignette to this chapter, with students only allowed to seek a 'match' to the gender that is often described as opposite, which denies the existence of same-sex attraction. Even the pronouns commonly used in schools fail to reflect the nuanced understandings that transgender students feel because they reflect the sex assigned at birth instead of the gender affiliation and names students prefer (Case & Meier, 2014). Each of these practices has to do with categorizing individuals within a binary and reflects the assumption that all students fit these categories even when the presence and experiences of some students stand as a direct contradiction to this assumption.

Schools can better include LGBTQ+ identities and experiences by adopting practices that use language that acknowledges gender and sexual minorities, as well as asking students to explain what and how they want to be recognized. Changing forms to include multiple or write-in options for gender identity provide students with an opportunity to select a non-binary option. Questioning the necessity of including gender identity on forms can reject the ways in which schools use gender to organize students. Changing language to be more inclusive via the use of transgender pronouns, or by embracing the use of 'they' as a gender-neutral pronoun. Beginning school years and semesters by asking students to provide the name they would like to be called (a standard practice, certainly) and the pronoun they prefer (a new practice), explicitly acknowledges that individuals have the right to be recognized in K-12 and college classrooms. Constructing and naming spaces that reject compulsory heterosexuality and cisgender gender presentation, and are explicitly welcoming and designed for

*Gender-neutral bathroom sign produced by Metro Trans Umbrella Group, St. Louis, MO. Source: Courtesy of Metro Trans Umbrella Group.*

LGBTQ+ students can also benefit students who feel pressured by gender stereotypes and are not comfortable with compulsory heterosexuality. Alternatively, when schools provide the GSA or Pride Center with a visible space in the heart of campus, the school communicates the importance and value of these students to the rest of the campus community. Finally, creating and following policies that allow students to use school facilities that align with their self-identified gender as opposed to the gender assigned at their birth. Each of these practices represents a change that visibly supports and acknowledges the needs of LGBTQ+ students.

## CONCLUSION

A fundamental right of every student is to learn in an environment that is safe, nurturing, and inclusive (hooks, 1994). While many K–12 schools and colleges are working to create positive environments for LGBTQ+ students, this goal has yet to be reached. Thus, K–12 schools and colleges either support and develop or marginalize and diminish the identities, experiences, and issues of LGBTQ+ students. Because schools are both catalysts for and symptoms of social change, educators have the opportunity to improve the school experiences of LGBTQ+ students. Taking advantage of this opportunity requires educators to understand the development of LGBTQ+ students, create and utilize LGBTQ+–based curricular opportunities, and facilitate extra-curricular opportunities for LGBTQ+ students. When these opportunities are embraced, schools become safe and welcoming spaces for LGBTQ+ students.

## Learn More

### Readings

Biegel, S. (2010). *The right to be out: Sexual orientation and gender identity in America's public schools*. Minneapolis, MN: University of Minnesota.

Emanuel, G. (2017, June 15). *Transgender teachers talk about their experiences at school* [Radio story]. Retrieved from www.npr.org/sections/ed/2017/06/15/531639614/transgender-teachers-talk-about-their-experiences-at-school

Gates, M. (2015, Sept. 18). What's it like to be gay at a historically black college? [Blog post]. *Huffington Post*. Retrieved from www.huffingtonpost.com/matthew-gates/what-its-like-to-be-gay-a_b_8159444.html

Hawley, J. C. (Ed.). (2015). *Expanding the circle: Creating an inclusive environment in higher education for LGBTQ students and studies*. Albany, NY: SUNY.

Jennings, K. (2015). *One teacher in ten in the new millennium: LGBT educators speak out about what's gotten better . . . and what hasn't*. Boston, MA: Beacon.

Lapointe, A. A. (2017). "It's not pans, it's people": Student and teacher perspectives on bisexuality and pansexuality. *Journal of Bisexuality, 17*(1), 88–107.

Macgillivray, I. K. (2014). *Gay-straight alliances: A handbook for students, educators, and parents*. New York, NY: Routledge.

Mayo, C. (2013). *LGBTQ youth and education: Policies and practices*. New York, NY: Teachers College.

Mayo, C. (2017). *Gay-Straight alliances and associations among youth in schools*. New York, NY: Palgrave Macmillan.

National Center for Transgender Equality. (2016, Nov. 3). *We stand with Gavin: The Supreme Court case and what it means* [Blog post]. Retrieved from www.transequality. org/blog/we-stand-with-gavin-the-supreme-court-case-and-what-it-means

Nutt, A.E. (2105) *Becoming Nicole: The transformation of an American family*. New York, NY: Random House.

Poynter, K. J. (Ed.) (2016). *Safe Zones: Training allies of LGBTQIA+ young adults*. Lanham, MD: Rowman & Littlefield.

Sadowski, M. (2016). *Safe is not enough: Better schools for LGBTQ students*. Cambridge, MA: Harvard Education.

### Film/Video

Brummel, B., & Sharp, G. (Directors). (2010). *Bullied: A student, a school, and a case that made history* [DVD]. Montgomery, AL: Southern Poverty Law Center.

Chasnoff, D., & Cohen, H. (Directors). (1996). *It's elementary: Talking about gay issues in school* [Motion picture]. United States: Women's Education Media.

Kazlauskas, J. (Director). (2002). *Speak up!: improving the lives of gay, lesbian, bi-sexual, transgender youth* [DVD]. Northampton, MA: Media Education Foundation.

Lipschutz, M., & Rosenblatt, R. (Directors & Producers). (2006). *The education of Shelby Knox* [DVD]. New York: Docurama.

Skurnik, J. (2016). *Creating gender inclusive schools* [DVD]. United States: New Day.

### Internet

Accredited Online Schools—LGBTQ Student Resources & Support: www.accreditedschoolsonline.org/resources/lgbtq-student-support

Campus Pride: www.campuspride.org

Consortium of Higher Education LGBT Resource Professionals: www.lgbtcampus.org

GLSEN: www.glsen.org

GSA Network: gsanetwork.org

It Gets Better Project: www.itgetsbetter.org

Midwest Bisexual Lesbian Gay Transgender Ally College Conference (MBLGTACC): sgdinstitute.org/mblgtacc

Safe Schools Coalition: safeschoolscoalition.org

The Point Foundation: pointfoundation.org

The Trevor Project: www.thetrevorproject.org

# CHAPTER 6
# We're Here! We're Queer!
## *Power, Politics, and Activism*

*George A. Waller*

*LGBTQ political buttons in the Smithsonian National Museum of American History, Washington D.C. (2015). Source: Photo by Erin Blasco/CC BY-SA 4.0 license. Image courtesy of Wikimedia Commons.*

Nancy Valverde, an 84-year-old lesbian, was assaulted by a Los Angeles police officer in the late 1950s while being arrested for "masquerading"—violating a law that criminalized women for wearing men's clothing and vice versa. She was handcuffed and kicked in the back by the policeman while being roughly escorted to the police car. Nearly every day when she left her barber school classes, a police car would be waiting for her outside ready to arrest her again. If she saw a police officer on the street, she would run and hide for fear of again being harassed, assaulted and arrested. After years of going to jail for daring to dress like a man, Valverde had had enough. She went to the local law library and researched masquerading laws, finding a case from 1950 where the California Supreme Court ruled that wearing clothes of the opposite sex could not be considered a crime. Valverde hired a lawyer and filed a suit against the Los Angeles Police Department. She won the suit, went on to graduate from barber school, and opened her own shop where she practiced her craft for over 25 years. Recently retired, Valverde says that she has endured continuous back pain stemming from that first kick in the back. Even now, her body tightens up when she sees a police officer (Compton, 2016).

Nancy Valverde's case demonstrates how oppression for LGBTQ people has been a function of discriminatory laws and actions by governing institutions and individuals. At the same time, it illustrates how resistance and action can change the laws and actions of those governing institutions and individuals. Valverde's legal activism in standing up to police harassment represents one way that LGBTQ people have responded to overt discrimination. Since the early twentieth century LGBTQ people in the United States have employed a wide range of tactics and strategies to secure basic rights and freedoms often taken for granted by other citizens. All of those strategies involve attempts to confront and change prevailing social and political norms that regulate what is acceptable in society. Some strategies have proven more successful than others. Often multiple strategies have been employed in combination to successfully break down barriers to LGBTQ equality. The problem for sexual and gender minorities is that the social and political institutions of the state that make and enforce norms of acceptable behavior are highly resistant to change and are unlikely to quickly and positively respond to challenge.

LGBTQ activist strategies generally fall into two broad camps: assimilationist and liberationist (Rimmerman, 2015). The assimilationist approach emphasizes a political strategy of working in and through existing social and political institutions and processes to accomplish change. An assimilationist strategy for achieving LGBTQ rights might be characterized as "let us in so that we might have a seat at the table where decisions are made." By contrast, liberationist strategies favor an approach that says, "let us show you a new way of thinking and seeing the world." For the liberationist it is not enough to merely have a seat at the table, since there is often a significant gap between mere access and real power. Rather than working to accomplish change in and through the existing system, the liberationist approach involves active efforts to transform social and political institutions in more fundamental ways; to shift from a purely legal and political approach to one that embraces an "outsider" activism that openly confronts and challenges the privileges of dominant groups and existing norms. Assimilationist strategies include efforts to influence the outcomes of elections for those who make the law, to influence

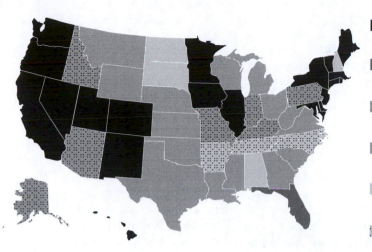

100% of state population is protected from employment discrimination based on gender identity (statewide protection)

50%–99% of state population is protected from employment discrimination based on gender identity through local ordinances

25%–49% of state population is protected from employment discrimination based on gender identity through local ordinances

1%–24% of state population is protected from employment discrimination based on gender identity through local ordinances

0% state population is protected from employment discrimination based on gender identity through local ordinances

State explicitly bans cities and counties from passing non-discrimination provisions

*State-level non-discrimination ordinances in the U.S. (2017). Source: Adapted from original by permission of Movement Advancement Project.*

implementation of the law by agencies of the state, and the interpretation and adjudication of law in courts. Liberationist strategies can involve direct action protests, marches, boycotts, and occasionally even physical violence.

Using the law to accomplish social change arises from a belief that legislation and court rulings can break barriers and eliminate policies and practices that discriminate. Therefore, one of the strategies employed by LGBTQ rights activists has been to change the law, either through legislative acts or through the courts. The assimilationist approach can provide an opportunity to challenge prevailing discrimination by appealing to values and principles ingrained in American social and political culture. By citing constitutional principles of equality and non-discrimination, as well as ideals of justice and fairness, while working in and through the existing institutions of American law and politics, the assimilationist approach can acquire a degree of legitimacy. If legislatures (local, state, and national) can be persuaded to change the law by extending civil rights to LGBTQ people, and if courts can be persuaded to uphold and apply values and ideals of equality and non-discrimination to LGBTQ people, then the larger society might come to accept those laws and rulings as legitimate and thereby change its attitudes and behaviors toward LGBTQ people.

## The Cis-Heteronormative State

The term state is used to describe the collective institutions of government and society that have the authority to make, implement, and enforce the rules that order, or govern, society. Institutions are "a relatively stable collection of practices and rules defining appropriate behavior for specific groups of actors in specific situations" (March & Olsen, 1998). Schools, workplaces, religious

*(continued)*

*(continued)*

organizations, and the family, are all social institutions. Law enforcement agencies, courts, legislatures, and political executives are examples of political institutions. Social institutions determine what normal, acceptable expressions of gender and sexuality are, while political institutions regulate and enforce those socially acceptable norms. In doing so, social and political institutions also bestow privilege on those who behave according to expectations of normalcy that reflect and reinforce the culture and values of groups in power. Those who openly identify or act in ways that do not conform to normative expectations may be deemed "deviant" and potentially subject to correction and punishment.

American society values and rewards behavior consistent with heteronormativity and heteropatriarchy. A heteronormative patriarchy (heteropatriarchy) is one in which the social and political institutions of the state work to build and maintain privilege and power for heterosexual, cisgender men. Conformity is enforced through "the attitudes, actions, and institutional practices that privilege heterosexuality and subordinate people on the basis of their gay, lesbian, bisexual, or transgender orientation." (Launius & Hassel, 2015). Those who openly display mannerisms and behaviors inconsistent with birth gender assignment or who deviate from the norm of heterosexual attraction and expression, face ridicule and ostracism. Early signs of gender or sexual non-conformity may be subject to medical and psychological treatment. Those who won't conform must be celibate, hide their sexual behavior, or risk punishment. Challenges to the power of heterosexual cisgender men to make the rules that govern society are scorned and often punished. LGBTQ people's identities, attractions, behaviors, claims on power, and fundamental assertion of the right to live a free, authentic, public life can threaten heteropatriarchy and may be subject to penalty.

Law enforcement agencies are an instrument of state power and, in heteropatriarchal societies, often enforce conformity by policing the gender expressions and sexual behaviors of LGBTQ people. Where same-sex sexual behavior is illegal, law enforcement implements and enforces the law by arresting those who violate it. Courts impose punishments as described under law, on those whose behavior is judged criminal. In this way, the criminal justice system becomes an instrument of heteropatriarchal state power wielded against those who challenge societal norms of gender and sexual identity and behavior.

## ASSIMILATIONIST ACTIVISM

### Non-Discrimination Ordinances

Early homophile organizations, like the Mattachine Society, pursued an assimilationist strategy of legal reforms that would protect gay and lesbian people from outright discrimination by law enforcement and courts in the 1950s. For example, the owner of San Francisco's Black Cat Bar sued the city for revoking his liquor license simply because his bar catered to a gay clientele. The California State Supreme Court ruled the revocation unlawful because the city had provided no evidence of any illegal or immoral conduct required to substantiate the revocation. Yet, that early legal victory failed to produce any widespread success at eliminating legal discrimination against gays and lesbians in California or elsewhere across the country during the remainder of the decade.

The 1960s ushered in a new social and political climate more conducive to LGBTQ organization and action. There was a great deal of optimism that courts and legislatures would become more receptive to efforts for civil rights for gays and lesbians. The U.S. Supreme Court signaled a more liberal orientation with rulings granting more widely available birth control (in 1965) and the legality of interracial marriage (in 1967). However, the language regarding privacy in those Court opinions did not extend to homosexuality, bisexuality or transsexuality. The Civil Rights Act of 1964 prohibited discrimination based on race, gender, religion, and ethnicity (but not sexual orientation) and provided legal remedies for those discriminated against in employment, housing, and public accommodations. In response to an increasingly vocal and organized gay and lesbian rights movement, a bill to amend the Civil Rights Act to include sexual orientation as a protected category was introduced in the Congress of the United States in 1974. That bill went nowhere when conservative Democrats and Republicans repeatedly blocked its movement through the legislative process. Failure to achieve this ambitious legislative goal, led many gay and lesbian rights organizations to pursue the passage of anti-discrimination measures at the local level. By concentrating organized political pressure in urban communities where gay and lesbian rights groups were now well established and mobilized, the goal of equal rights might be best achieved. Those efforts began to pay off.

By the late 1970s several dozen communities had adopted gay rights ordinances and policies. A major study of 28 cities and counties across the United States that had passed such ordinances before 1977, revealed that these were largely urban college communities; places where there were active and relatively large gay and lesbian rights organizations; places with more liberal and younger populations of students and a college faculty who were often in the vanguard of local rights movements or were sympathetic to its goals; and places where there was a general lack of organized opposition (Button, Rienzo, & Wald 1997).

In 1972 East Lansing, Michigan, became the first community in the United States to formally enact a policy that banned discrimination on the basis of sexual orientation. Contributing to that success was the Gay Liberation Movement (GLM), an officially recognized student group at Michigan State University. GLM had worked successfully to elect two city council candidates who publicly declared their support for gay rights and had formed a coalition with city civil rights organizations to propose to the East Lansing Human Relations Commission the inclusion of gender and sexual orientation as protected categories under the city's existing civil rights ordinance. Despite initial resistance from Commission members, intense lobbying and public attention campaigns by the GLM–led coalition secured the proposal's unanimous adoption. The full city council, under pressure from GLM and other civil rights groups, approved the proposed language with one dissenting vote (Button, Rienzo, & Wald 1997).

That scenario was typical of the drive for anti-discrimination ordinances in communities throughout the country where there were visible and active gay and lesbian rights and black civil rights coalitions. As in East Lansing, communities that adopted similar anti-discrimination laws saw little organized opposition. Where opposition did exist it came from individual officials in city and county government—insufficient to defeat a well-organized coalition of committed activists. The multi-community study from 1977 found that in the 14 communities that had passed an anti-discrimination policy or ordinance covering sexual orientation by formal council vote between 1972 and 1974, all but four did so with a unanimous, or near unanimous (only one dissenting council member) vote (Button, Rienzo, & Wald 1997). Also, since many of these same communities had already adopted ordinances consistent with the 1964 Civil Rights Act, proposing a mere amendment of existing civil rights ordinances proved to be more successful than advocating for a completely new policy. Linking gay and lesbian rights to rights already guaranteed for other minorities enhanced the legitimacy of what rights groups were seeking.

Those early victories were short-lived. By 1974 conservative religious-based opposition to gay and lesbian rights had begun to build. Gay rights ordinances (as they were called at the time) failed to win approval in a number of places that would have been thought to adopt them—proposals failed in Columbus, Ohio, and in Eugene, Oregon (both college communities with relatively liberal constituencies). Boulder, Colorado, passed a gay rights anti-discrimination policy in 1974 but that policy was later overturned by a two to one margin when conservative opponents mobilized voter opposition (Button, Rienzo, & Wald 1997).

The biggest victory for gay rights opponents came in 1977 when Dade County's (Miami, Florida) gay rights policy was repealed by voters following a well-organized effort led by the former Miss America and Florida Citrus Commission national spokesperson Anita Bryant, founder and principle spokesperson for the Save Our Children organization. Bryant's national reputation as a beauty queen and devout evangelical Christian garnered media attention, and financial resources from evangelical groups around the nation. The Save Our Children campaign argued that the Miami ordinance granted legitimacy to what it viewed as a religious abomination that encouraged homosexual behaviors and child molestation. One of the campaign's slogans was, "Homosexuals cannot reproduce, so they must recruit." Alan Rockway, a bisexual activist and psychologist who was co-author of the gay rights ordinance that had originally been adopted by a public vote in Miami-Dade County began to coordinate a nationwide "gaycott" of Florida orange juice in response to Bryant's Save Our Children campaign. The Florida Citrus Commission cancelled Bryant's million-dollar contract as a result (Stein, 2012).

*Button produced by opponents of Anita Bryant's homophobic "Save Our Children" campaign. Humor has been a frequent strategy used by LGBTQ activists (1977). Source: Photo by Moni3, courtesy of Wikimedia Commons.*

However, Bryant's organization gained allies from the Christian right, including the National Association of Evangelicals, Christian Cause, and even leaders of the YMCA and Kiwanis Club. It then successfully petitioned for a ballot measure to repeal the gay rights policy in Dade County. That well financed opposition coalition overwhelmed the much smaller Miami LGB coalition and the repeal passed easily, setting the stage for similar repeal efforts around the country. In places where repeals were successful, anti-discrimination policies were characterized as immoral and part of a national gay effort to recruit, molest children, and undermine "traditional" families (Bryant, 1977).

Despite backlash success, or perhaps because of it, gay and lesbian rights proponents responded to the opposition's attacks by presenting their cause more vigorously. The now-national campaign to roll back gay rights ordinances mobilized gays, lesbians, and bisexuals across the country to make a more persuasive case for civil rights. That paid off. California's statewide anti-gay referendum, known as Proposition 6, which would have allowed school boards to fire gay teachers, among other things, was resoundingly defeated in 1978. In a number of cities, including Hartford, Los Angeles, and Tucson reenergized gay rights groups successfully turned back attempts to block the passage of anti-discrimination ordinances and referenda. By 1979 gay rights advocates could claim significant progress on this front, despite setbacks suffered at the hands of opposition movements. Some 40 cities and counties in the United States had adopted and sustained policies that legally protected gays and lesbians from discrimination (Button, Rienzo, & Wald 1997).

Across the country bisexual rights advocacy groups, which were often aligned with the larger gay and lesbian community activists, achieved similar specific protections for the rights of bisexual people. In a number of cities bisexual organizations were instrumental in securing the passage of ordinances that included protections for bisexuals as well as gay men and lesbians. The Seattle Bisexual Women's Network and its partner group, The Seattle Bisexual Men's Network, worked tirelessly in 1988–1989 to testify before that city's governing bodies for the successful adoption of ordinances that specified non-discrimination against bisexual employees in city agencies and in city housing codes. In that same year members of Philadelphia-based Bi-Unity successfully lobbied the Mayor's Commission on Sexual Minorities to form a work group specifically devoted to the concerns and rights of bisexuals in that city (BiNet USA, 2016). Today, more than 30 cities and a handful of states have passed non-discrimination legislation that protects lesbians, gay men, and bisexuals. However, protections against discrimination on the basis of gender identity or gender expression, which would implicitly include many transgender people, are not nearly as common (Stryker, 2015).

Another success for non-discrimination protections came with the Supreme Court's 1996 decision in *Romer v. Evans*. In 1992 Colorado voters had approved an amendment to the Colorado state constitution (Amendment 2) that would have prevented any city, town, or county in the state from taking any legislative, executive, or judicial action to recognize homosexuals as a protected class. This would have made it illegal for any city, county, or the state to pass a

| Year | Case | Significance |
|------|------|-------------|
| 1958 | One, Inc. v. Olesen | Court ruled that speech "in favor of homosexuals" was not inherently obscene, effectively lifting a ban on books & magazines with lesbian & gay content. |
| 1985 | Rowland v. Mad River Local School District | Court refused to hear an appeal by a high-school guidance counselor fired because she told co-workers she was bisexual. |
| 1986 | Bowers v. Hardwick | Court held that a constitutional right of privacy does not apply to private, consensual, same-sex sexual activity ("sodomy"). Language in decision equated homosexual sex with adultery, incest, and other sexual crimes. |
| 1988 | Webster v. Doe & Carlucci v .Doe | Court held that Congress gave federal intelligence agencies special discretion to terminate employees for disclosing they were homosexual or had engaged in same-sex sexual activity. |
| 1989 | Price Waterhouse v. Hopkins | Court held that employment discrimination based on sex stereotypes (expectations about how persons of a certain sex should dress, behave, etc.) is unlawful sexual discrimination. |
| 1995 | Hurley v. Irish-American GLB Group of Boston | Court ruled that requiring St. Patrick's Day parade organizers to include LGB groups violated the organizers' free speech rights under the 1st Amendment to the U.S. Constitution. |
| 1996 | Romer v. Evans | Colorado's Amendment 2, prohibiting any state government entity from enacting or enforcing any law protecting or eliminating discrimination against homosexuals, was found to violate the Equal Protection clause of the 14th Amendment to the U.S. Constitution. |
| 1998 | Oncale v. Sundowner Offshore Services | Court found same-sex harassment in the workplace was sex discrimination under Title VII of the 1964 U.S. Civil Rights Act. |
| 2000 | Boy Scouts of America v. Dale | Court ruled that the Boy Scouts' 1st Amendment right to freedom of association allowed it to exclude homosexual scout leaders even where sexual orientation is included in a state's public accommodations law. |
| 2003 | Lawrence v. Texas | Court reversed decision in Bowers v. Hardwick (1986); ruled that private, consensual, adult, same-sex sexual activity is protected under the Due Process clause of the 14th Amendment. |
| 2013 | United States v. Windsor | Court held that Section 3 of the federal Defense of Marriage Act was an unconstitutional violation of the Equal Protection clause because there was no rational basis to support denial of federal benefits to married same-sex couples. |
| 2015 | Obergefell v. Hodges | Court ruled that denial of same-sex marriage licenses by states is an unconstitutional violation of the 14th Amendment. Same-sex marriages become legal across the nation. |
| 2017 | Gloucester County School Board v. G.G. | Case brought by transgender student denied access to school bathroom that corresponds to his gender identity was remanded to a lower court for rehearing. |

*LGBT-related U.S. Supreme Court cases and decisions.*

non–discrimination ordinance or adopt any policy protecting lesbians or gay men, and would have invalidated any existing ones. Evans, a gay man who worked for Denver's mayor, along with three Colorado municipalities, sued to block the amendment's enforcement. A state trial court issued a permanent injunction against the amendment, and the Colorado Supreme Court ruled that the amendment violated the U.S. Constitution's 14th Amendment: the equal protection clause. That ruling was appealed to the United States Supreme Court, which agreed with the Colorado Supreme Court. Colorado's Amendment 2 never went into effect (*Romer*, 1996).

## Overturning Sodomy Laws

One sustained focus of LGBTQ political activism has been state-level sodomy laws. These laws are a legal legacy of British colonialism in the Americas, outlawing a range of non–procreative sexual acts, including masturbation, anal sex, oral sex, and sex with animals. Although technically applicable to same-sex and other-sex sexual behavior, in practice sodomy laws were disproportionately enforced against men who had sex with men, especially during the middle decades of the twentieth century. By 1962 sodomy (variously defined) was a felony in every U.S. state and punishable by long imprisonment or hard labor—in Idaho the possible sentence was life imprisonment. After 1962 consensual sodomy became legal in some states but "soliciting" for sodomy was still a crime.

When police and prosecutors enforced sodomy laws, they often placed undercover police officers in public places—like parks, highway rest areas, and public restrooms—where men were known to "cruise" for male sexual partners. (For some men, sex in public spaces was exciting and desirable. For others, it was made necessary by the lack of other gay social spaces, like bars and nightclubs, and the risk of openly expressing same-sex desire in a homophobic society.) When an officer was approached for sex, he would make an arrest under a charge of "solicitation," "lewd solicitation," or "soliciting sodomy." In practice, prosecution of sodomy laws was intertwined with the prosecution of laws that also prohibited cross-dressing or public gatherings of homosexuals. Raids on gay bars, nightclubs, and bathhouses could subject attendees to any or all of these kinds of charges. Because the names of those arrested and prosecuted were often published in local newspapers, an arrest for solicitation or cross-dressing could cause loss of employment, eviction from housing, and loss of relationship with family members (Eskridge, 2008; D'Emilio, 1998). Today, police continue to target and entrap men seeking sex in parks, theaters, and public bathrooms—and newspapers and local TV stations occasionally publish the names and photographs of those arrested (Robbins, 2017; Branson-Potts & Queally, 2016).

The elimination of sodomy laws would have a liberating effect on the lives of anyone who engaged in same-sex sexual behavior because they would no longer fear persecution and prosecution. Yet, sodomy laws served a very important purpose for their supporters—they ensured that homosexuals would be viewed as deviant, unnatural, and immoral. Criminalizing same-sex sexual behavior legitimized and encouraged legal discrimination against lesbians, gay men, and bisexuals. Supporters of sodomy laws had a powerful public policy rationale for blocking gay rights proposals. Just as other types of criminal behavior resulted in the denial of basic rights and opportunities to those who engaged in them, criminalizing same-sexual activity would deny rights and opportunities to bisexuals and homosexuals.

In the United States, efforts to change laws criminalizing cross-dressing and same-sex activity were not common until homophile organizations emerged in the mid-twentieth century. Those efforts to challenge overt discrimination through legal action and to pass anti-discrimination laws illustrates the use of assimilationist strategies to achieve social and political change. Homophile groups, like the Mattachine Society, focused on legal challenges to police harassment. The first significant opportunity for action arrived in 1952 when one of Mattachine's founders, Dale Jennings, was arrested for allegedly engaging in "lewd solicitation" of an undercover police officer. Mattachine's leaders seized the opportunity to take action against police entrapment of gay men. The Citizen's Committee to Outlaw Entrapment was formed by Mattachine to publicize police practices and to raise funds for Jennings' defense. Victory came when Jennings' jury deadlocked on a verdict and charges were dropped. However, police across the country continued to raid countless gay and lesbian clubs and bars (Pierceson, 2016).

In 1961 Illinois became the first state to repeal its sodomy law. Prior to that every state had a sodomy law on its books. After Illinois' repeal, it was eight years before a second state (Connecticut) repealed its law. As a result of activism during the 1970s 22 states repealed their sodomy laws. Then, repeals slowed—during the 1980s Pennsylvania and Wisconsin were the only two states to repeal—before picking up in the 1990s. By 2003 only 13 states retained sodomy laws, six of which criminalized oral and anal sex *only* between same-sex partners (Mucciaroni, 2008). Those 13 states were among the most politically conservative states in the country, with sizable populations of religious conservatives who adamantly opposed decriminalizing same-sex sexual behavior. When the repeal of sodomy laws slowed in the 1980s political and religious conservatives had emerged as a powerful political force, especially within the Republican Party. It was in this politically conservative decade that the Supreme Court was asked in *Bowers v. Hardwick* (1986), to review the constitutionality of sodomy laws.

The central legal challenge to the legitimacy of sodomy laws in *Bowers* was that the government had violated the plaintiffs' fundamental right to privacy firmly established by the Supreme Court in *Griswold v. Connecticut* (1965). Michael Hardwick of Georgia was convicted in 1982 for engaging in consensual sex with another man in the privacy of his home, conduct that violated the state's sodomy law. *Bowers* reached the Supreme Court four years later, after lower courts had upheld the law. Hardwick's lawyers questioned whether the Georgia law interfered with adult decisions about private, consensual sexual activity. But, the Court majority ruled that the right to privacy established in *Griswold* was associated with marriage, procreation, and child rearing and therefore was not applicable to homosexual sex. Further, that majority stated that for a fundamental right to exist it had to be "implicit in the concept of ordered liberty" and "deeply rooted in history and tradition" (*Bowers*, 1986). Neither criterion was met in same-sex sexual behavior, according to the Court. Thus, the state of Georgia had a legal right to criminalize same-sex behavior. The decision infuriated gay and lesbian rights groups across the country, who redoubled their efforts by bringing continuous legal challenges to state sodomy laws.

In 2003, 17 years after its decision in *Bowers* the Court would reverse itself, to the delight of gay rights supporters. In *Lawrence v Texas* the central issue was "whether the petitioners (*Lawrence* et al.) were free as adults to engage in their private conduct as an exercise of their liberty under the Due Process clause of the 14th amendment." Mere moral disapproval, the Court said, did not give the state a rational and legitimate basis for criminalizing sexual behaviors. As long as there was no "injury to a person or abuse of an institution the law protects," government cannot set boundaries as to what kinds of intimate relationships

## LGBTQ People and Peace Movements

Since at least the 1940s many LGBTQ people have argued that participating effectively in the military had nothing to do with one's sexual orientation. At the same time, deep ties connect LGBTQ activism and peace activism. Furthermore, some contemporary thinkers argue that LGBTQ politics must be anti-militarist and that the community has little to gain from seeking equal access to military service.

The Women's Peace Party, founded in 1915 by Jane Addams and Carrie Chapman Catt, was one of the first anti-war organizations in the United States. Addams eschewed the confines of heterosexual marriage, but remained in constant contact with her "ever dear" Mary Rozet Smith for over 40 years. Catt married men twice, but lived her last 20 years with Mary Garrett Hay, alongside whom she was buried. When Addams and Catt traveled to Europe to form the Women's International League for Peace and Freedom, it was at the behest of the German feminists and lovers Anita Augspurg and Lida Gustava Heymann. Some accounts of early twentieth-century feminists reduce their work to the pursuit of suffrage, but many of these women identified unchecked patriarchal masculinity as central to militarization and lived in ways that actively defied expectations of conventional femininity and sexuality (Faderman, 1991).

Unfortunately, the feminist anti-militarist work begun during World War I was not able to prevent the outbreak of another world war in the 1940s. But during this same decade the political philosophy of non-violence spread globally and found a passionate adherent in a young, black, and gay activist named Bayard Rustin. From the earliest Freedom Rides to the historic March on Washington, Rustin was behind the scenes of most of the major events in the Civil Rights Movement, but the pacifist Fellowship of Reconciliation was where he gained the tools he would bring to that movement. Rustin often operated away from the cameras and did not receive as much credit as he was due, in large part owing to a 1953 arrest for having sex with another man that was used to shame and silence him. Rustin's politics turned rightward after the 1960s, but he remained a passionate advocate for what he believed in, arguing in 1986 that "The question of social change should be framed with the most vulnerable group in mind: gay people" (D'Emilio. 2003).

Even as many gay and lesbian organizations turned their focus toward equal access to the military in the 1990s, groups like ACT UP and Queer Nation embraced anti-militarism, notably interrupting the CBS evening news to shout "Fight AIDS, not Arabs" on the eve of the first U.S. war on Iraq. Following the demise of the military's gay ban, calls intensified to end the ban on transgender soldiers, but the militarization of LGBTQ identities remains controversial. As transgender legal scholar Dean Spade claims, "What makes sense for trans politics is to be aligned with anti-war and anti-military movements worldwide" because of the pervasive gendered violence present in the military and the harm done to LGBTQ people abroad by U.S. interventions (Geidner, 2013).

*Josh Cerretti*

adults may enter into (*Lawrence*, 2003). It was clear from the ruling in *Lawrence*, that the Court recognized the powerful negative impact of sodomy laws when it said, "the continuance of *Bowers* as precedent demeans the lives of homosexuals as persons and controls their destiny . . . the Nation's laws and traditions show an emerging awareness that liberty gives substantial protection to adult persons in deciding how to conduct their private lives in matters pertaining to sex" (*Lawrence*, 2003). The Supreme Court had now closed an important chapter in the history of LGBTQ rights. *Lawrence* meant that on this issue gay and lesbian rights advocates would achieve total success—not one of the sodomy laws from all 50 states remains legal today (even though many still remain on the books).

## Hate Crimes Legislation

Another accomplishment for LGBTQ assimilationist activism came with the passage of hate crimes legislation. Hate crime laws are intended to serve as deterrents to violent crimes against people based on race, gender, religion, disability, sexual orientation, or gender identity, and provide extra punishment for those convicted of hate-motivated crimes. Most of the hate crime laws that protect sexual and/or gender minorities have been adopted at state level. Currently 45 U.S. states have some kind of hate crimes law in which sexual orientation or gender expression is included as a motivating factor for the crime.

Anti-LGBTQ violence in the United States is not new, and while the incidence of hate crimes in general has been declining, hate crimes against LGBTQ people have remained steady, or even increased. A Human Rights Campaign 2009 report found that FBI statistics show that LGBTQ people are

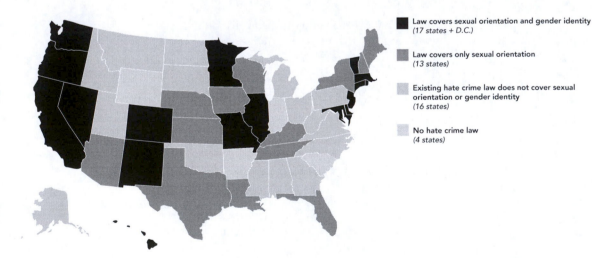

**Law covers sexual orientation and gender identity**
*(17 states + D.C.)*

**Law covers only sexual orientation**
*(13 states)*

**Existing hate crime law does not cover sexual orientation or gender identity**
*(16 states)*

**No hate crime law**
*(4 states)*

*State-level hate crimes laws in U.S. (2017). Source: Adapted from original by permission of Movement Advancement Project.*

disproportionately attacked relative to their estimated population size. In 2007 alone, the report found, 1,265 LGBTQ biased hate crimes were reported—a 6% increase on the previous year. That report also noted anecdotal evidence suggesting the actual number of LGBTQ biased hate crimes was undoubtedly much higher because many victims were unwilling to report them for fear of being outed and because of the failure of law enforcement agencies to identify attacks as hate crimes (Marzullo & Libman, 2009).

Some opponents of hate crime legislation object to what they believe is an attempt by government to regulate or criminalize thought or beliefs. Religious opponents of hate crimes laws claim that laws protecting LGBTQ people are intended to criminalize religious speech against a sexual behavior that some view as amoral or sinful. Supporters counter that hate crime laws penalize criminal actions not speech. (Pierceson, 2016)

Supporters of hate crime laws won a significant victory at the federal level with the passage of the Matthew Shepard and James Byrd, Jr., Hate Crimes Prevention Act of 2009. But, that law was enacted only after a long coalition campaign by racial, religious, and LGBTQ minority groups, and was expedited by the highly-publicized cases of James Byrd and Matthew Shepard, for whom the Act was named. Both Matthew Shepard (a young gay man) and James Byrd, Jr., (a black man), were viciously attacked and killed in 1998 by perpetrators whose attacks were clearly motivated by hateful bias.

The 2009 Act was not the first federal legislation to address hate crimes. In 1989 the Hate Crimes Statistics Act authorized the FBI to track hate crimes on the basis of sexual orientation, as well as race, ethnicity, and religion. In 1993 President Bill Clinton signed the Hate Crimes Sentencing Enhancement Act that allowed for enhanced penalties against any who committed race, ethnicity, religious, gender, or sexual orientation–biased hate crimes on federal property. Activists wanted legislation that went further and pushed for the introduction of a bill designed to extend hate crime sentencing beyond the boundaries of federal property. In 1997 that legislation was introduced with the public support of President Clinton, but the bill died in the House of Representatives in 1999 (Pierceson, 2016).

During the first six years of the George W. Bush administration, with Republican majorities in the U.S. Senate or House of Representatives (or both), attempts to re-introduce the bill failed. In 2006, when Democrats regained a congressional majority, the legislation was resurrected and included as part of a larger defense spending bill. President Bush threatened to veto the defense spending legislation unless the hate crimes provision was eliminated and, bowing to that threat, the hate crime language was removed. It would not be until the election of President Barack Obama, and a Democratic Congress in 2008, that the Shepard-Byrd Hate Crimes Prevention Act would become law.

## Military Service

Homophile groups of the World War II era, such as the George W. Henry Foundation and the Veteran's Benevolent Association, advocated for gay and lesbian rights by calling attention to the unjust treatment they experienced as

*Gravesite of U.S. Air Force Lt. Leonard Matlovich who fought for open inclusion of lesbians and gays in the U.S. military. Source: Photo by A. J. Lopp/CC BY 2.0 license. Image courtesy of Wikimedia Commons.*

military personnel during the war. U.S. military policy screened potential recruits to eliminate any who were psychologically profiled as suspected homosexuals and aggressively sought to identify and discharge any enlisted personnel suspected of being homosexual. Military policy effectively denied gay men and women the opportunity to serve their country and, for those convicted and discharged, denied them the benefits otherwise available to veterans in education, housing, and employment. In 1947 the U.S. State Department implemented a security policy that sought to identify and remove suspected homosexuals from the departments and agencies of the federal government. The 1952 U.S. Immigration and Nationality Act mandated the exclusion and deportation of non–citizen immigrants living in the U.S. determined to be "afflicted with psychopathic personality," made applicable to homosexuals by the American Psychiatric Association's classification of homosexuality as "sociopathic personality disturbance" in its *Diagnostic and Statistical Manual of Mental Disorders.*

In this post–war environment homophile groups made the U.S. military an early target of attention. Individual gay veterans were encouraged to challenge their discharges by appealing to military review boards. Gay veterans began to speak out about military discrimination and eventually convinced the U.S. House of Representatives to convene a special committee to study the issue of unfair treatment by the military. Despite some grudging acknowledgement of military discrimination, political opposition in the 1950s was fiercely entrenched and resulted in the adoption of even more stringent policies of anti–homosexual recruitment screening, discharge, and denial of benefits.

By the end of World War II the ban on homosexual service was part of the Uniform Code of Military Justice and if enlisted personnel were discovered to be homosexual it was grounds for immediate discharge. Air Force Technical Sergeant Leonard Matlovich was the first gay active-service member to purposely out himself to fight the ban on gays. His case was highly publicized and his photograph appeared on the cover of the September 8, 1975, issue of *TIME* magazine, making him a symbol for thousands of gay and lesbian service members.

During Matlovich's discharge hearing he was asked to sign a document pledging to never engage in same-sex sexual behavior or relationships again in exchange for being allowed to remain in the Air Force. Matlovich refused, and despite his strong performance evaluations, the discharge panel ruled him unfit for service. Matlovich successfully sued for reinstatement, and the Air Force was ordered to reinstate him. Instead, the Air Force offered Matlovich a financial settlement. Believing that the military would find another reason to discharge him if he re-entered, or that a new conservative Supreme Court would rule against him should the Air Force appeal the case, Matlovich accepted the settlement (Rimmerman, 2015).

Spurred on by the Matlovich case, the American Civil Liberties Union and the Lambda Legal Defense and Education Fund brought cases before the courts on behalf of men and women who were discharged from military service after their sexual orientations became known. *Hatheway v. Secretary of the Army* (1981) and *Beller v. Middendorf* (1980) are two cases that ended up before the United States Supreme Court. Hatheway was discharged from the Army after being convicted of sodomy; Beller was discharged after admitting that he had engaged in homosexual sex. The Supreme Court refused to hear either appeal and the discharges were allowed to stand.

In 1989 bisexual military veteran Cliff Arnesen testified before Congress on behalf of gay, lesbian, and bisexual veterans' issues. He was the first openly bisexual veteran ever to testify before Congress about veterans' issues in general, and the first veteran ever to testify specifically about LGB veterans' issues. His testimony, although it attracted some sympathy among members of Congress, did not result in legislative action (BiNet USA, 2016). It would not be until 1993 that the military policy of excluding gay men, lesbians, and bisexuals from military service would be altered with the Don't Ask, Don't Tell (DADT) policy.

Bill Clinton had announced, in his successful 1992 campaign for the presidency, his intention to end the U.S. military's ban on homosexuals. Although the move was popular among gay rights activists who supported Clinton's campaign, few political analysts thought he would move quickly on such a potentially explosive issue. When he did so, it was met with strong congressional and military opposition. Allowing openly gay men and lesbians to serve would undermine military morale and cohesiveness, it was argued.

After heated congressional debate, Clinton managed to gain support for, and signed into law, a compromise under which gays and lesbians could remain in the military if they did not openly declare their sexual orientation, a policy that became known as Don't Ask, Don't Tell. According to the law, homosexuals serving in the military could not talk about their sexual orientation and commanding officers were not allowed to question service members about it. Yet, military officers who were overwhelmingly opposed to that approach, used their authority under the act to ferret out homosexuals, despite the original intention to allow lesbians and gays to serve without fear of persecution if they kept their sexual orientation private. Most gays and lesbians in the military felt that the policy had the effect of shifting the burden of proof to the service member.

*Cover of U.S. Army's handbook on implementing "Don't Ask, Don't Tell" policy (Dignity & Respect: A Training Guide On Homosexual Policy (Washington, D.C.: U. S. Army, 2001). Source: Pritzker Military Library (Chicago, IL). Image courtesy of Wikimedia Commons.*

The policy's intention to "create a zone of privacy" did not work at all well. The number of discharges, which had declined steadily since 1982 under the old policy, began to rise again under DADT and peaked in 1998 (the highest point in ten years). By the 15-year anniversary of the law in 2008, more than 12,000 officers had been discharged from the military for refusing to hide their homosexuality (Rimmerman, 2015).

When Barack Obama became President in 2008 he pledged to overturn DADT to allow gay men and lesbians to serve openly in the military and directed the Pentagon to develop a plan to study the impact of that policy change. Although gay activists hoped that discharges would quickly end, they continued during Obama's first year in office, even while the Pentagon complied with the President's order to review DADT.

In 2010 the Pentagon announced it had commissioned a study, due to the President late that same year, that would determine how repeal would affect the military. While the study was underway, new measures were introduced to immediately relax the enforcement of DADT and make it more difficult for openly gay military service members to be expelled. The measures included permitting only high-ranking officers to oversee discharge proceedings and requiring higher standards for evidence presented in such cases (Rimmerman, 2015).

In May 2010 the U.S. House of Representatives and a U.S. Senate panel voted to allow the repeal of DADT, pending completion of the Pentagon study and certification by the President, the Secretary of Defense, and the Chairman of the Joint Chiefs of Staff that lifting the ban would not adversely affect military readiness.

On November 30, 2010, the Pentagon study concluded that repealing DADT would pose little risk to military effectiveness. The report revealed that militaries around the world that allowed open gay and lesbian service reported no detrimental impacts on military morale or readiness. Some 70% of service members surveyed by the Pentagon believed that ending the policy would have mixed, positive, or no impact (Daniel, 2010). A bill to officially repeal DADT was passed by both houses of Congress in mid-December and President Obama signed the bill on December 22, 2010.

While the ban on gay, lesbian and bisexual military service members had now been eliminated, that was not the case for transgender people. That ban would not be lifted until nearly five years later when, on June 30, 2016, the Secretary of Defense announced elimination of the ban on transgender military service. A study group assembled by the Defense Department had evaluated transgender service in militaries around the world and had once again concluded that concerns about military cohesiveness and readiness simply were not supported by empirical evidence. In those militaries where there was no transgender ban, there was ample evidence that transgendered personnel had served with honor and distinction and that other concerns about potential administrative and implementation problems were not problematic (Pollock & Minter, 2014).

## Marriage Equality

Same-sex marriage lawsuits began in the 1970s, when litigants unsuccessfully sought marriage licenses in Minnesota, Kentucky, and Washington state. Those bringing suit argued that they had a "fundamental right" to marry and demanded that any ban on same-sex marriage could only be legal if the state could prove that such bans met a "compelling state interest." But courts denied that a fundamental right to marry existed for gays and lesbians because marriage "by definition required a man and a woman" (*Baker v. Nelson* 1971). Litigants also argued that they were being denied equal protection under the law based on their sexual orientation, a violation of the 14th Amendment's equal protection clause. Courts also rejected this argument.

That was the case until the Hawaii Supreme Court ruled in *Baehr v. Lewin* (1993) that Hawaii's refusal to grant marriage licenses to same-sex couples might violate its constitutional non-discrimination clause. The Hawaii Supreme Court said that for the refusal to grant same-sex marriage licenses to be constitutional, the State would have to demonstrate that refusing to allow same-sex couples to marry met some rational and compelling purpose. That ruling put Hawaii on notice that its highest court was moving to declare that civil marriage licenses could not be withheld from same-sex couples.

Reaction to the court's decision was swift and negative. The Hawaii state legislature immediately amended state law stating that only heterosexual couples could receive marriage licenses, and opponents of gay marriage proposed a state constitutional amendment that would clarify the state legislature's right to define marriage. That proposed amendment would be placed on the ballot in a statewide referendum for voters to decide. Hawaii voters overwhelmingly approved the ballot measure in November 1998.

At the federal level, the U.S. Congress' consideration of the Defense of Marriage Act (DOMA) was a direct reaction to the Hawaii court's ruling. Debate in Congress took place in a political climate that was particularly unfriendly toward the idea of gay marriage. Public opinion polls that asked Americans to rank a list of interest groups on a favorability scale, saw gay men and lesbians consistently ranked near the bottom. Most surveys typically found more than 60% opposed to same-sex marriage (Button, Rienzo, & Wald 1997).

Given that larger political climate, the gay and lesbian rights movement had to decide how to move forward. The movement's task was to frame their agenda/issues in terms of fundamental fairness and to take its cases to courts that historically had been receptive to the extension of civil rights and generally opposed to legal discrimination unless necessary to meet a compelling state interest. At the same time, gay rights opponents understood that if they were successful in taking the issue outside of law courts to the court of public opinion, the debate would likely swing in their favor.

A coalition of conservative religious groups had promoted its Marriage Protection Resolution at a large political rally in Iowa in 1996 that was intentionally meant to coincide with the Iowa presidential caucuses. All the announced Republican presidential candidates signed the resolution. Same-sex marriage, the resolution said, offered proof of the danger of the "gay agenda" to adherents of conservative Christian ideology. But it also offered Republicans a political wedge issue to attract some voters who traditionally vote Democratic. President Clinton could be defined as an extremist if he supported the, so-called, gay agenda, or he could be estranged from an important political constituency by being forced to waver on LGBTQ issues—LGBTQ voters had supported Clinton in 1992 by overwhelming margins. President Clinton, in a re-election year, could not afford to alienate that key constituency, nor could he alienate the majority of Americans who opposed gay marriage (Rimmerman, 2015).

Clinton attempted to straddle the issue by expressing personal opposition to same-sex marriage while stating that he would sign a proposed Defense of Marriage Act if Congress passed it, and at the same time, saying that he thought the law was unnecessary and divisive. Three months after the Iowa rally, DOMA was introduced. The act denied recognition of same-sex marriages for federal purposes and declared that states were free to refuse recognition to same-sex marriages validly performed in other states. That second part was necessary since Article IV of the U.S. Constitution required that "full faith and credit" by all states be extended to legal judgments, licenses, and contracts validated in any other state. Supporters of the act argued that judicial decision-making was undemocratic—that activist liberal judges on the Hawaii Supreme Court had attempted to force homosexual marriage upon a Hawaiian public that overwhelmingly opposed gay marriage. They argued that the federal government had to prevent a single state from imposing its will on the other 49 to limit potential impact of the "full faith and credit" clause and that the words "marriage" and "spouse" appeared in hundreds of federal statutes and regulations, but without the clear definition the act would now provide. Finally, DOMA's sponsors argued that the moral understanding of the essential nature of the family was at stake and that decision-making on the question should be based on moral rather than civil rights grounds (Rimmerman, 2015).

DOMA opponents attacked the bill as politically designed to produce a wedge issue for conservative Republicans who lacked another issue to run on—the economy was in the midst of a boom cycle and the United States was not at war. DOMA opponents also argued that a marriage license did not grant moral approval any more than did a divorce decree and that the real basis for opposition to same-sex marriage was to grant a right to discriminate. The House of Representatives passed DOMA one month after it was introduced; the U.S. Senate approved it shortly thereafter and President Clinton signed it into law. The struggle would not end there however. LGBTQ activists were determined to press the issue forward in the courts.

By 1998, 26 states and Puerto Rico had banned same-sex marriages and 11 more states were in the process of considering such legislation. Many states introduced ballot referenda that defined marriage as exclusively between one man and one woman, which would embed such language in their state constitutions if passed. On the other hand, from 2003 to 2015 court decisions, state legislation, and popular referenda had legalized same-sex marriage to some degree in 38 states and the District of Columbia. And in 2013 the Supreme Court overturned a key provision of DOMA in *United States v. Windsor* because it singled out a specific class of persons for discrimination by refusing to treat their marriages equally under federal law, even though they were legal under state law. The ruling led to the federal government's recognition of same-sex marriage with entitlement to all federal marriage benefits. Beginning in July 2013, over 40 federal and state courts cited *Windsor* to strike down state bans on the legal recognition of same-sex marriage (Rimmerman, 2015).

On January 16, 2015, the U.S. Supreme Court agreed to simultaneously hear four cases from Ohio, Tennessee, Michigan, and Kentucky on appeal after the Sixth Circuit had earlier ruled that state bans on same-sex marriage were constitutional. Decided by the Court simultaneously under the heading of *Obergefell* (the Ohio case was named *Obergefell v. Hodges*) on June 26, 2015, the Court reversed the Sixth Circuit's upholding of state bans and declared that same-sex couples have the constitutional right to marry and to have their marriages recognized as legal throughout the country. Prior to *Obergefell*, same-sex marriage was legal to at least some degree in 38 states and the District of Columbia; after *Obergefell,* it was legal in every state.

*Scene outside U.S. Supreme Court building when* Obergefell v. Hodges *decision legalizing same-sex marriage was announced (June 26, 2015). Source: Photo by Ted Eytan / CC BY-SA 2.0 license. Image courtesy of Wikimedia Commons.*

Assimilationist activism was quite successful in bringing about legislative and legal changes that advanced the cause of LGBTQ rights. With the passage of anti-discrimination and hate crimes ordinances, the overturning of sodomy laws, the opening up of military service to LGBTQ folks, and the legalization of same-sex marriage, assimilationist activism produced significant results.

However, much of that success might well not have been achieved without the emergence of an equally vigorous and vocal liberationist strategy in the late 1960s.

## LIBERATIONIST ACTIVISM

Some in the LGBTQ rights movement criticized what they viewed as over-reliance on an assimilationist strategy involving legislative and legal efforts for change. They were skeptical of the ability of legal change to create real and lasting social change because, they said, too often the law is a tool of oppression rather than liberation. Law is more frequently used to deny rights and to reinforce discriminatory social norms than to break barriers and grant rights. Civil rights legislation, for example, to the extent that the law is approved by legislative majorities and upheld by courts, is filled with exemptions and loopholes, and is subject to limited legal interpretation that prevents its effective implementation and enforcement. Another criticism of the assimilationist approach was that the problem of LGBTQ discrimination and oppression could not be easily addressed and solved by focusing only on legislative and legal victories. Rather, the problem of LGBTQ discrimination occurred on multiple fronts (social, political, legal, economic, and religious) and would not be solved without working for solutions on all fronts—not just legal or political. Fighting for real change required not just a legislative and legal approach, but also a more visible and vocal effort to directly confront discrimination and oppression on all fronts through direct action sit-ins, boycotts, and mass public demonstrations. Those who argued for a liberationist strategy did not advocate abandoning legal and legislative action; instead they argued that assimilationist action needed to be supplemented with liberationist action.

### Stonewall

The importance of the Stonewall riots of 1969 for LGBTQ social and political liberationist activism cannot be overstated. Were it not for Stonewall it is difficult to imagine that the collective identity and consciousness first begun in the earlier homophile movement could have emerged as a liberationist social and political force. Without Stonewall the assimilationist strategy for attaining legal recognition of LGBTQ rights might never have been strengthened and transformed by the more confrontational liberationist movement that would emerge in the 1970s and 1980s. Indeed, without Stonewall, and the associated coming out phenomenon that followed, it is unlikely that the direct-action marches, "zaps!" and clashes with law enforcement that became part of LGBTQ liberationist activism in the following decades, would have become a central feature of the movement.

It is also certain that Stonewall created a broader and more inclusive activism among LGBTQ people across the country. Gay men, lesbians, bisexuals, and transgender people were present at Stonewall and came out to participate in the riots that ensued. Transgender "street queens" played an instrumental role in the riots when police attempted to arrest patrons of the club. Among those present were Sylvia Rivera and Marsha P. Johnson, who together founded STAR (Street Transvestite Action Revolutionaries) in 1970. Also in 1970, New York City drag activist Lee Brewster and heterosexual drag queen Bunny Eisenhower founded the Queens Liberation Front and began publication of the very political transgender-focused *Queens* newsletter (Stryker, 2015).

*The NAMES Project AIDS Memorial Quilt displayed on The National Mall, Washington, D.C. (October 9–11, 1992). 20,064 panels covered 13 acres. Source: The Names Project.*

In July of 1969 Brenda Howard, a bisexual woman, conceived and coordinated a one-month Stonewall Rebellion anniversary rally that would eventually become an annual march and celebration that spawned a host of annual Pride Parades around the United States and the world. By 1972 the National Bisexual Liberation Group had formed in New York City, and by 1975 there were more than 5,500 members in ten chapters across the United States who received *The Bisexual Expression*, a newsletter devoted to the interests of bisexuals, as well as wider LGBT issues (BiNet USA, 2016).

Stonewall demonstrated that LGBTQ people would openly and forcibly resist oppression by law enforcement and that resistance would transform the movement both in terms of numbers and strategy. The calls of homophile leaders for a more confrontational response to continuing oppression of the LGBTQ community, began to resonate strongly as public demonstrations of LGBTQ pride began occurring around the country. Before Stonewall there were fewer than 50 LGBTQ organizations around the United States. Four years after Stonewall that number had grown to more than 800 (Button, Rienzo, & Wald 1997). Those new organizations were more adamant and strident than the earlier homophile movement in stating their goals and utilizing confrontational tactics to supplement legislative and legal efforts to secure rights. Many who had stayed on the sidelines of the earlier homophile movement, felt compelled to fight back. Impatient and frustrated by the lack of significant progress through the largely assimilationist strategy of the homophile movement, these post-Stonewall activists became decidedly more confrontational.

This newfound energy, and a growing public awareness of an increasingly visible, active, nationwide LGBTQ presence after Stonewall, soon translated into some important victories. By 1973 the American Psychological Association had removed homosexuality from its classifications of mental illnesses, an action that signaled recognition of the legitimacy of gay and lesbian identity and was a challenge to institutionalized norms that defined homosexuality as an illness in need of treatment or correction. The United States Civil Service Commission eliminated its ban on gay and lesbian federal employment; the National Education Association amended its non-discrimination clause to include protection for sexual preference, and numerous states repealed their anti-sodomy laws (Button, Rienzo, & Wald 1997). Yet, despite those successes, the LGBTQ movement would face what might be seen as one of its most significant and difficult challenges with the AIDS crisis of the 1980s.

## Coming Out as an Activist Strategy

Coming out is a public statement of refusal to obey norms of acceptable sexual or gender identity and behavior. It is also a political act that challenges the legitimacy of state enforcement of hetero/cisgender normativity. Coming out means refusing to hide in "the closet," proclaiming the right to express one's gender/sexual identity openly, and to engage in sexual activity consistent with that identity, without fear of societal and institutional oppression. That is not easy to do. Societal and institutional resistance and backlash are likely since norms do not yield easily, and are fiercely resistant to calls for change. Therefore, there is considerable risk in the decision to come out—risk that brings with it the likelihood of having to face an angry and sometimes violent response from family and friends, and especially from a society that is intolerant and unaccepting of those who will not conform. Coming out is a political statement that challenges the legitimacy of laws and social norms that regulate acceptable gender/sexual identity and activity. Depending on personal resources, relative privilege or oppression, and the point in one's life in which it occurs, publicly identifying as LGBTQ and challenging those norms risks numerous negative consequences in areas of employment, housing, education, healthcare, family and other relationships, as well as physical safety and security. These risks may cause some to deny their own identity and sexuality, to see themselves as undeserving, sick, or sinful. That can, and too often does, lead to self-denial, self-imposed celibacy, refusal to come out, and, sadly, even self-destructive behavior—including suicide.

Coming out is not the same for all LGBTQ people. It is not the same for LGBTQ people of color as it is for LGBTQ whites; it is different for lesbians and gay men, bisexuals and transgender people; and it is different for those with wealth and other resources of privilege than for those without such resources. LGBTQ people of color face not only oppression for their sexual or gender identity, but the additional burden of oppression for being members of a minority population in a society that privileges white heterosexual people. A transgender person who is publicly viewed and treated as a cisgender woman or man (and not a transwoman or transman), may have their authenticity as a woman or man questioned if they come out as transgender. Lesbians, gay men, and bisexuals with the personal or financial resources that allow them to "disappear" into the dominant society or be insulated from the worst effects of societal homophobia, may pay a high cost for publicly identifying as LGB. Ironically, this can mean that those with the most to contribute to the cause of LGBTQ rights might be the least likely to be openly active in the effort to secure those rights.

## HIV/AIDS Activism

LGBTQ rights activists faced one of their greatest challenges with the HIV/AIDS crisis of the 1980s. Rather than relying solely on an assimilationist legislative and legal strategy to achieve their aims, LGBTQ activists adopted confrontational liberationist tactics when silence and unresponsiveness to the crisis became characteristic of American social and political institutions. Throughout the decade, rights activists battled stiff opposition from conservative religious groups who allied with the Republican party, while at the same time attempting to confront the frightening specter of AIDS. These developments mobilized LGBTQ political activists to form coalitions with emerging AIDS service organizations, other liberal activist groups, and eventually even medical professionals, to demand public attention and a government policy response to AIDS.

When Ronald Reagan became President in 1980, with overwhelming support from Christian conservatives, LGBTQ activists understood that they faced an unfriendly political environment. At almost the same time, early reports of a new disease that affected gay men circulated in the gay press in New York, San Francisco, and Los Angeles. Soon the U.S. Centers for Disease Control and Prevention published articles reporting that clusters of gay male patients in American cities suffered from weakened immune systems, rare cancers, and severe pneumonia that caused rapid deterioration and death. Medical professionals seemed unable to stop the quick progression of what appeared to be an incurable and deadly disease. Medical experts stressed that risk groups included heterosexuals and children, but most government officials, media commentators, and especially religious conservatives promoted the idea that this was a "gay disease." As reported cases soared, fear began to spread that this new disease was highly contagious and was spread through casual contact with anyone who began to exhibit symptoms. Hysteria and panic grew as many believed that casual contact with someone who had not yet even begun to manifest symptoms could cause one to contract the deadly disease (Rimmerman, 2015).

Even as medical research established that contact with infected bodily fluids, such as semen and blood, were the primary means by which the virus was transmitted, the vast majority of Americans continued to believe that the growing epidemic was "caused" by homosexuals. Gays, lesbians, and bisexuals were blamed for the health crisis and, some argued, should be isolated and shunned. Many Christian conservatives referred to AIDS as "God's punishment" for sinful and immoral sexual behavior and some even called for quarantine of all those infected with HIV/AIDS (Rimmerman, 2015).

As deaths from AIDS continued to rise and it became apparent that the disease was not confined to gay males but was also affecting hemophiliacs, intravenous drug users, blood transfusion recipients, and even children whose mothers had contracted the HIV virus during their pregnancies, demands for an aggressive policy response grew louder and more strident. LGBTQ movement spokespeople, in coalition with many in the medical profession, called on state and federal governments to fund care and treatment for people living with and suffering from AIDS, and to pass legislation that would increase funds for medical and pharmaceutical research to develop effective prevention and treatment drugs and to search for a cure.

However, with the increased power of the Republican Party and its Christian Right supporters, there was little substantive response to those demands. President Reagan did not even publicly acknowledge the existence of AIDS until 1987, after thousands had already died from AIDS-related illnesses and thousands more were living with, and suffering from, the disease.

It was in this unfriendly and unresponsive political environment that LGBTQ political culture changed in important ways. One of the most important developments was the active involvement and support in the fight against AIDS not just from gay male organizations, but from lesbian, bisexual, and transgender activists. Lesbian activists, in particular, became less separatist, responding to the crisis with commitment and compassion, even though their gay male counterparts were far more affected. The Blood Sisters of San Diego, for example, encouraged lesbians to donate blood for people with AIDS (PWA) when federal officials banned such donations from gay men (Stein, 2012). BiPOL, the first and oldest bisexual political organization formed in San Francisco and, as the AIDS epidemic spread, one of that group's most committed activists, Dr. David Lourea, persuaded the San Francisco Department of Public Health to recognize bisexual men in their official AIDS statistics. That was a significant accomplishment because prior to that health departments across the United States would only recognize gay men in their AIDS reports; since 1984 health care providers have recognized the existence of bisexual men and their need to be informed about the risks for contracting HIV and for prevention education (BiNet USA, 2016).

Transgender people involved in street prostitution and injection drug subcultures were among the hardest hit by the HIV/AIDS epidemic. As a result, AIDS activists worked to advance transgender awareness and activism. The response to AIDS required alliances between the different social groups affected by the epidemic—gay men, hemophiliacs, Haitians, sex workers, and intravenous drug users. Any effective response would have to address a variety of social problems, such as poverty and racism, that transcended narrow sexual or gender identities and that resonated within broader efforts for equality and justice (Stryker, 2015).

Transgender activists contributed time and energy to the cause and played active roles in AIDS service organizations and the promotion of safe sex practices.

LGBTQ people of color and a host of liberal political activists also joined the effort to care for those with AIDS and to demand a government response to the growing crisis. This coming together of LGBTQ subgroups was a critically important development. Working in unity and in coalition with other groups, including many medical professional organizations and well-established civil rights and liberal groups, would prove to be a necessary development for achieving an eventual policy response.

Assimilationist mobilization commenced in earnest in the immediate aftermath of the AIDS discovery. During the early 1980s that effort was undertaken by a number of new organizations, including the National Gay and Lesbian Task Force (1985), which emphasized grassroots community mobilization and local and national lobbying. The Human Rights Campaign Fund focused its efforts on lobbying federal officials and electoral support for candidates who pledged aggressive action to combat AIDS. LGBT legal advocacy groups, initially formed in the 1970s—including Gay and Lesbian Advocates and Defenders, Lambda Legal Defense, and National Gay Rights Advocates—redoubled their work to assist in AIDS-related legal causes. New bisexual and transgender groups, including BiPOL in San Francisco and the American Civil Liberties Union Transsexual Rights Committee, concentrated on political lobbying and electoral activism to encourage public policy action to deal with AIDS.

A National Lesbian and Gay Health Conference met for the first time in 1983 and a group of attendees who were AIDS victims announced the formation of the National Association of People with AIDS (PWA). They put out a statement that criticized media and public officials' references to people with AIDS as victims, calling for the "recognition of the rights of PWAs to have access to medical care and social services without discrimination, make informed decisions about research and treatment, enjoy full and satisfying sexual and emotional lives, have privacy and respect, and live and die with dignity" (Stein, 2012, p. 155). Because the nation's healthcare system had failed to effectively provide for the care and treatment of PWAs, AIDS service organizations were founded within LGBT communities. Among the largest and most effective of these service groups were Gay Men's Health Crisis (GMHC) in New York and the San Francisco AIDS Foundation.

## ACT UP

While all of these groups engaged in vigorous efforts to combat the effects of the AIDS crisis through political lobbying and electoral activism there was little success in gaining a governmental policy commitment to fight the epidemic. As the number of PWAs grew and deaths from AIDS continued to mount, government hesitation and silence became more infuriating. That unresponsiveness enraged LGBTQ activists who now called for more confrontational and liberationist tactics to force public attention and government action.

In 1986 the U.S. Department of Justice ruled that federal law did not prohibit employers from firing or refusing to hire people with AIDS. In California a

*Poster for ACT UP New York designed by the Silence=Death Project (ca. 1987). The inverted pink triangle has been a symbol of the gay rights movement since the 1970s. It invokes the colored cloth patches used to identify homosexual prisoners in Nazi concentration camps. Inverted, it turns an emblem of imprisonment and humiliation into an icon of solidarity and action. Source: Courtesy of Wellcome Collection (London), #LL0052822.*

referendum was placed on the ballot that would have authorized quarantines for PWAs, which was eventually defeated, but infuriated LGBTQ activists for even being on the ballot in the first place. Activists were especially angered when President Reagan only acknowledged the seriousness of the AIDS epidemic in 1987, and announced recommendations that the federal government focus its response on AIDS testing rather than treatment and prevention. As part of that recommendation, the federal government would mandate AIDS testing on prisoners and immigrants—with any aliens who tested HIV positive not allowed to enter the U.S. or to establish permanent residence without special permission (Stein, 2012).

Liberationist confrontation soon commenced. In March 1987, 300 New Yorkers formed ACT UP (AIDS Coalition to Unleash Power). That group's mission statement said that it was a "diverse, non-partisan group of individuals united in anger and committed to direct action to end the AIDS crisis" (Stein, 2012, p. 158). Soon thereafter, in major cities throughout the country, ACT UP groups formed. In New York ACT UP worked closely with a number of activist arts groups, like the Silence=Death Project and Gran Fury. Other activist LGBTQ groups, like Lesbian Avengers and Queer Nation, began to creatively call public attention to AIDS and to confront government inaction. ACT UP marchers disrupted traffic on Wall Street to protest "business as usual" while criticizing AIDS drug prices and the Food and Drug Administration's drug approval process. In June 1987 ACT UP sponsored demonstrations in Washington D.C. at the Third International Conference on AIDS and at the White House. Police wearing protective yellow rubber gloves arrested 64 marchers at the White House demonstration. This was one of the first times, but not the last, that police assigned to ACT UP protests arrived wearing yellow rubber gloves. That action infuriated AIDS activists across the country leading to the often-heard ACT UP chant, "Your gloves don't match your shoes! You'll see it on the news!" (Stein, 2012, p. 160).

In San Francisco, ACT UP marchers congregated around the regional headquarters of the pharmaceutical manufacturer of AZT (an early AIDS treatment drug) to demand more availability and lower prices. In April and May of 1988, 50 ACT UP groups around the country staged nine days of marches and demonstrations highlighting AIDS-related issues, including a march in New York that culminated with a gay and lesbian Kiss-In with Read My Lips posters that featured gay and lesbian couples kissing. At a Mets baseball game at Shea Stadium, 300 members of the Nine Days of Rage campaign distributed condoms and fliers that called on heterosexual men to take more responsibility for AIDS prevention. In January 1990, ACT UP activists in Los Angeles interrupted the Rose Parade with a large banner that read, "Emergency! Stop the Parade. 70,000 dead of AIDS!" Die-ins were staged at hospitals and medical clinics that refused treatment for PWAs. The invention and use of zaps! designed to publicly confront and embarrass elected officials became a mainstay of direct action.

Promotional material distributed by Houston chapter of Queer Nation (ca. 1990). Source: J. D. Doyle/Queer Music Heritage. Image courtesy of Wikimedia Commons.

These liberationist actions were undertaken to build a unified movement, to capture public awareness, and to motivate government policy action. Although not immediate, those public protests produced some desired results. The federal Food and Drug Administration sped up its drug approval process to expedite the development, testing, and availability of AIDS treatment drugs; pharmaceutical companies lowered drug prices for some treatments; the mass media improved its coverage of the AIDS epidemic by focusing attention on scientific and medical expertise and by illustrating the diversity of PWAs. The first major federal legislation to deal with AIDS would not become law until 1990, but it may not have been enacted at all without the aggressive direct-action tactics of ACT UP, Lesbian Avengers, and other activist groups.

### The Ryan White Comprehensive AIDS Resources Emergency Act

The first comprehensive legislation designed to deliver care and treatment to PWAs was The Ryan White Comprehensive AIDS Resources Emergency (CARE) Act. This legislation was made possible by events that broadened public awareness and understanding of the devastating impact of AIDs and about who was at risk for HIV infection. In addition to the visibility and public awareness advanced by LGBT liberationist tactics, the announcement in July of 1985 that Ryan White, a 13-year-old hemophiliac, had contracted AIDS through a blood transfusion captured widespread media and public attention. White was expelled from his school in Kokomo, Indiana, after fearful school parents pressured the school board to do so. Media reports featured medical professionals who attempted to calm those fears by pointing out that AIDS could not be contracted by simply being in the same room with a person with AIDS, but required contact with infected bodily fluids such as blood. However, while Ryan White became the touchstone for irrational fears about AIDS, media coverage would eventually result in some significant social learning about HIV/AIDS and its transmission. It had been previously believed to be a "gay disease" primarily affecting promiscuous gay men, but Ryan White's case showed that AIDS could affect people well outside of the gay community. As knowledge of HIV/AIDS transmission grew, prostitutes, intravenous drug users, medical workers who may have come into contact with blood from AIDS patients, and the children of mothers who had unknowingly harbored the HIV virus during their pregnancies, became part of the population of PWAs.

Greater public recognition of the potential extent of the epidemic provided an opportunity for federal lawmakers to consider an AIDS policy that would deliver care and treatment to PWAs such as medical workers, women, children, and hemophiliacs. Elected legislators could still remain publicly hostile toward PWAs who were perceived as undeserving, like gay men, sex workers and drug users, while working to enact legislation that would advance the care and treatment of AIDS patients. That provided political cover from attacks by religious conservatives who remained a strong political force into the early 1990s.

The Ryan White CARE Act was introduced into the Congress in 1989, one year after Ryan White had died at age 18 from AIDS-related illnesses. The Act provided federal funding for research and development of HIV/AIDS therapies with the eventual hope of developing a treatment protocol that would reduce the incidence of death and allow PWAs the possibility of living productive lives. The act would also expand federal funding for care and treatment facilities for PWAs.

When the Ryan White Act was introduced in Congress, Republican lawmakers immediately offered amendments to restrict benefits of the Act to only "deserving" populations of PWAs. Those amendments called for the mandatory HIV/AIDS testing of all prisoners, regardless of crime, a ban on the distribution of bleach to intravenous drug users to clean needles and syringes, and criminalization of the possible transmission of HIV by prostitutes and drug users. Senator Jesse Helms (R–NC) introduced an amendment that would have made it a crime to donate blood if an individual was a user of any intravenous drug or had engaged in prostitution. It went further to state that actual transmission of HIV did not have to occur for a person to be criminally charged (Donovan, 1993). This Helms amendment was defeated, but it paved the way for the Act's eventual compromise language that would restrict benefits to some populations of PWAs while imposing burdens on others.

Debate in the Senate illustrated how lawmakers sought to differentiate PWA populations. Donovan's analysis of 19 speeches by congressional lawmakers who supported passage of the Act shows that six of them were recounts of Ryan White's ordeal; five were stories of infants and young children who had contracted HIV; three were about women who had contracted AIDS from male sexual partners; two were about blood transfusion victims; one spoke about a heterosexual victim. Only one speech told the story of a gay man who had died of HIV/AIDS (Donovan, 1993).

Under the Act as passed and signed by President George H. W. Bush in 1990, intravenous drug users were prohibited from being given clean needles; prisoners convicted of sex-related crimes were required to undergo mandatory

HIV testing (but no treatment funds were provided for any prisoners found to be infected with HIV); and knowingly attempting to transmit HIV through unprotected sexual activity or blood donation became a felony. Furthermore, although nearly 90% of all AIDS cases were among gay and bisexual men, the Act required that 15% of all HIV care grants be set aside for women and children, with up to 10% set aside for hemophiliacs (Donovan, 1993). Ultimately, even with the set asides for women and children, the majority of care and treatment consisted of services delivered to gay and bisexual men. The Ryan White CARE Act has been amended to extend funding for HIV/AIDS treatment and care and has been reauthorized four times: in 1996, 2000, 2006, and 2009 (HRSA, 2016).

*National March on Washington for Lesbian and Gay Rights (October 14, 1979). Source: J. D. Doyle/Queer Music Heritage.*

## The Marches on Washington, D.C.

The largest national demonstration of LGBTQ direct activism occurred in 1987 with a march on Washington, D.C. Hundreds of thousands of LGBTQ activists and allies rallied in support of a policy response to the AIDS crisis. This, and subsequent LGBTQ rights marches in Washington, D.C., built on the legacy of the 1963 black civil rights march, featuring Martin Luther King, Jr.'s famous "I Have a Dream" speech and organized by Bayard Rustin, a black gay man. As part of the 1987 march, the NAMES Project AIDS Memorial Quilt, consisting of hundreds of panels sewn and quilted by family members and loved ones in memory of people who had died from AIDS, was displayed on the National Mall, vividly demonstrating the human devastation of HIV/AIDS and shaming the government's lack of response (see Image 6.6).

Marches on Washington became a semi-annual event, but not without some intra-LGBTQ movement conflict. In 1993 BiPOL mobilized a nationwide lobbying campaign for inclusion of a bisexual section in the march, which resulted in openly bisexual people taking key leadership roles in local and regional organizing for the event now called the March on Washington for Lesbian, Gay, and Bi Equal Rights and Liberation. For the first time bisexuals were included in the official title of the march, were allowed to march in a labeled contingent, and to give speeches at the culminating rally. The 1993 March signifies national recognition of bisexual issues and the grassroots power of bisexuals in the LGBTQ movement (BiNet USA, 2016).

The Millennium March on Washington for Equality was held on April 30, 2000, but only after some controversy. Human Rights Campaign (HRC), the nation's largest LGBTQ civil rights group, and Troy Perry of the Universal Fellowship of Metropolitan Community Churches, convened

*(continued)*

*(continued)*

an organizing committee without consulting grassroots LGBTQ groups around the country and announced that corporate sponsors had committed to financing the event. Many LGBT activists who were involved in the planning stages of previous marches reacted angrily to what they saw as a top-down, undemocratic, organizing structure. Criticism grew, and Perry and HRC agreed to changes that created a more diverse organizing committee to bring transgender activists and LGBTQ people of color into leadership positions. Those more inclusive efforts paid off when some 800,000 persons participated in the march to the National Mall.

Another LGBTQ march on Washington, held on National Coming Out Day (October 11, 2009), sought to build on renewed LGBTQ activism that had developed following approval of California's Proposition 8, which overturned the state's same-sex marriage law. LGBTQ leaders and supportive elected officials spoke in support of same-sex marriage, a federal employment non-discrimination bill (ENDA), and repeal of the military's DADT policy.

Thousands of LGBTQ people and their allies walked in the Equality March for Unity and Pride in Washington in June 2017. Scheduled close to the one-year anniversary of the shootings at Pulse nightclub in Orlando—the worst act of violence against LGBTQ people in U.S. history—the march highlighted issues of violence against LGBTQ people, LGBTQ immigrant rights, and disability rights (Chibbaro, 2017).

### Hate Crimes Direct Action

Much of the activism around hate crimes involved an assimilationist strategy of working in and through legislative institutions to ensure that LGBTQ people would be included in the language of hate crime laws. However, there were notable instances of more direct action that called attention to obvious and gruesome hate crimes perpetrated against LGBTQ people.

In September 1992 neo-Nazi skinheads threw a bomb into the Salem, Oregon apartment shared by Hattie Cohens, a black lesbian, and Brian Mock, a disabled gay white man. Cohens and Mock burned to death. The incident garnered no national media attention and only very limited local coverage. Lesbian Avengers was asked by the Anti-Violence Project in New York to participate in that city's annual Take Back the Night March and the group decided to highlight anti-LGBT violence by focusing attention on the Salem murders. The Avengers erected a shrine to Cohens and Mock, featuring their photos under a banner that read "Burned to Death for Being Who They Are," on a New York street corner where two lesbians had been viciously beaten a few months earlier. Members of Lesbian Avengers camped out on that corner for three days, handing out leaflets to passers-by highlighting instances of anti-LGBTQ violence around the country. Some in the group had also learned, from a colleague who had been a performer for Circus Amok—an LGBT activist art group—how to eat fire and they displayed that talent at the shrine and chanted, "Their fire will not consume us; we take it and make it our own" (Lesbian Avengers, 2016).

The horrific murder of Matthew Shepard in 1998 caused an outpouring of sympathy for his family, and gave national attention to the plight of young gay men who too often found themselves targets of hate crime violence. It also attracted the attention of members of the Westboro Baptist Church, a far-right fringe evangelical Christian congregation, who showed up at Shepard's funeral with signs reading "God Hates Fags," and "Matthew Shepard Burns in Hell." That same group pledged that they would show up to protest at the trials of the two young men who had beaten and murdered Matthew Shepard. With that announcement, one of Shepard's friends came up with the idea of forming a human chain of counter-protesters who would place themselves in front of the Westboro group dressed in white robes with large linen "angel wings." This silent, peaceful activism was designed to keep Westboro protesters almost completely out of sight of the Shepard family as they entered and exited the courthouse. That first action led to the creation of Angel Action, a group that, to this day, shows up to counter continuing Westboro protests at funerals and memorials for LGBTQ (and other) people across the country.

Transsexual Menace, a group of writers, artists, and transgender activists, was founded by Riki Wilchins in 1994 to provide an outlet for the outrage many transgender people felt following the brutal rape and murder of Brandon Teena, a transgender youth, and two of his friends in rural Nebraska. Those murders were depicted in the Academy Award winning film *Boys Don't Cry* (2000) and brought dramatic international attention to the serious problem of anti-transgender violence and hate crimes (Stryker, 2015). Transsexual Menace groups across the United States organized vigils for the victims of anti-trans violence and have held many community gatherings to organize transgendered people against oppression. For example, on October 4, 1995, transgender activists from around the U.S. (many of them wearing black Transsexual Menace t-shirts)

*Scene from* The Laramie Project *at Mary Institute and St. Louis Country Day School (St. Louis, MO) of the "Angel Action" to block protestors from view (2008). Source: Photo by Anthony Chivetta/CC BY 2.0 license. Image courtesy of Wikimedia Commons.*

demonstrated in front of the Washington D.C. mayor's office, handing out flyers to passers-by demanding a full investigation into the death of Tyra Hunter (a black D.C.-area transwoman) and calling for an end to what they said was a D.C. Fire Department cover-up. Hunter had been badly injured in a car accident and emergency services personnel began treating Tyra until they discovered that she had male genitals. EMTs then refused to continue treatment, opting instead to joke and laugh about it. Hunter later died in the emergency room. Following that event, Hunter's mother sued the city and was eventually awarded a $2.9 million settlement. The Washington D.C. Fire Department, also enacted a diversity and sensitivity training program, naming it after Tyra Hunter (Gay Men and Lesbians Opposing Violence, Inc. 1996).

Another example of direct action against hate crimes was the Pink Angels Anti-Violence Project. Founded in 1991 by Chicagoan Alyn Toler, the Pink Angels were modeled on the Guardian Angels, a non-police New York City group organized to patrol the city's subways to prevent violence. In Chicago, small, unarmed groups of Pink Angels wearing black berets and jackets patrolled LGBTQ neighborhoods on the city's north side. They intervened when they witnessed anti-gay violence, coordinated and shared information with police, trained citizens in self-defense, and encouraged them to report hate crimes. Their work was born of both anger over a spate of recent anti-gay violence and frustration at official police inaction. The organization consisted of lesbians, gays, bisexuals, heterosexuals, and people from a range of racial and ethnic backgrounds. Similar types of patrol organizations existed in New York, Boston, Seattle, San Francisco, and Houston (Terry, 1992; Baim, 2008; Hanhardt, 2013).

## Violence against Transgender People

In recent years violence against transgender women of color has hit a historic high. Studies have showed consistently that transgender people, especially transgender women of color, experience higher rates of violence compared to any other group of the population. According to the National Coalition of Anti-Violence Programs 2015 report, out of all the documented LGBTQ hate violence related homicides in 2014, 80% were people of color and 55% were transgender women, whereas transgender survivors of color were 6.2 times more likely to experience police violence (Ahmed, & Jindasurat, 2015). Transgender people are also more likely to be victims of sexual assault than cisgender people (Erickson-Schroth, 2014), and the lifetime intimate partner violence rate among this group is 35%, which is more than double that for gay and lesbian identifying individuals (Ard & Makadon, 2011). Although these numbers are daunting, the reality is much drearier. Since transgender people, and especially transgender women of color, are prone to experiencing violence at the hands of the police, most incidents of street and domestic violence go unreported.

The causes for such disproportionally high rates of violence can be found in the structural injustices transgender women experience on a daily basis. The *National Transgender Discrimination Survey* highlighted the social and institutional factors that shape the lives of transgender people and the additional risk that racial bias poses for transgender women of color in virtually every major area of life (Grant et al., 2011). Transgender people of color face overwhelming rates of harassment in school, which led to over one-fifth of the respondents to drop out. Unemployment rate among transgender people of color is over twice the rate of the national average and they are six times more likely to be living in extreme poverty than the U.S. general population.

The prevalence of physical and institutional violence against transgender women of color highlights the intersection of some of the entrenched biases in American culture: misogyny, racism, homophobia, and transphobia. Anything that proposes a threat to the dominant, heteronormative, white masculinity valued most in our society, is punished with excessive violence. Violence against women and the racial or sexual other is motivated by the desire to maintain the current order and serves the dual role of reaffirming the inferior identity of the victim and the superior position of the perpetrator (Perry, 2013).

Increased visibility of transgender people is only one step in eliminating violence that occurs at the intersections of racism, misogyny, and transphobia. Change to the status quo will be a slow process that involves the training of healthcare providers, educators, employers, and law enforcement officials on transgender issues.

*Helis Sikk*

## LGBTQ POLITICS: REMAINING CHALLENGES

In some regards, there has been steady progress toward equal protection from discrimination for LGBTQ Americans. But, significant progress does not mean there are not continuing challenges. Law enforcement agencies have taken significant steps to improve relationships with the LGBTQ community so that encounters with police do not become the harassing and violent confrontations experienced by Nancy Valverde. The New York City Police Department has formed an LGBTQ liaison unit to foster a positive working relationship with that city's large LGBTQ population. The FBI recently created an LGBTQ talent recruitment and retention program. In the words of FBI Inspector Vadim Thomas, a vocal champion of that program, "We're changing our culture, and we want members of the LGBT community among us . . . we want their talent. We want their drive" (Compton, 2016).

Despite those liaison and recruitment efforts, studies continue to show strains between law enforcement and LGBTQ communities. According to a recent report from the Williams Institute, nearly half of LGBTQ crime victims surveyed in 2013 reported police harassment or misconduct (Mallory, Hasenbush, & Sears, 2015). A separate 2014 study from the National Coalition of Anti-Violence Programs reported that more than 25% of the survivors of intimate partner violence experienced indifference or hostility from police officers (NCAVP, 2015). Meghan Maury, Director of the Criminal and Economic Justice Project for the National LGBTQ Task Force, states that part of the problem stems from ongoing racism, sexism, homophobia, and transphobia still commonplace in American society. Riding along with police officers, Maury has witnessed up close interactions between police officers and LGBTQ people. "When they roll up and stop a trans woman on the street, it's often because they're profiling her as a sex worker because she's trans, but the interaction between them is informed both by the fact that she's a black trans woman and by the fact that they think she's probably on drugs and probably engaged in some other kind of street crime" (Compton, 2016). Maury also notes that even police departments that have made significant steps to improve relations with LGBTQ communities and taken intentional measures to increase LGBTQ diversity within the ranks of their officers, have been at the center of controversy. The San Francisco Police Department, for example, faced extensive criticism when some of its officers were reported to have shared racist and homophobic text messages (Compton, 2016).

Despite progress at the local level, the U.S. Congress has yet to pass the long-sought Employment Non-Discrimination Act (ENDA), which would outlaw discrimination in employment, housing, and public accommodations on the basis of sexual orientation, and on gender and marital status. Originally introduced in 1974 as the Equality Act, the bill (in a variety of versions) has been stalled for decades. In 2014 a renewed attempt at passage led to Senate adoption of a version of the bill that included clear language that made sexual orientation and gender discrimination illegal in the workplace but did not extend those protections to public accommodations and housing. Furthermore, bowing to concerns from religious conservatives, the Senate bill contained language that allows religious organizations to be exempt from the requirement of protections. Under those exemptions, such organizations could continue to broadly discriminate on the basis of sexual orientation since the bill expressly forbids any affirmative action policies for sexual minorities and effectively prevents any legal employment discrimination claims against religious organizations. Even though that limited version of ENDA gained Senate passage in 2014, Republican resistance in the House of Representatives has again stalled the bill (Pierceson, 2016).

The notion of religious exemption from sexual orientation non-discrimination has gained traction in a number of U.S. states. As recently as 2016 a number of states considered legislation to allow private business owners to discriminate against LGBTQ people as a matter of religious conviction. So-called religious liberty statutes have been passed in 20 states and introduced in many others. The state legislature of Georgia, for example, passed the Free Exercise

Protection Act to ensure that pastors not be forced to perform same-sex marriages and that no one could be forced to attend one in violation of their religious convictions—thus protecting photographers, caterers, and florists from having to provide their services at same-sex marriages. The law would also allow faith-based organizations to refuse to provide services to LGBT people. Law professor Timothy Holbrook illustrates the impact of that language: "LGBT people can be denied services from such organizations, even ones that receive taxpayer money. A homeless trans adolescent would like to stay at a faith-based shelter? They'd have every right to turn them away" (Holbrook, 2016). Fortunately for LGBTQ rights advocates, Georgia Governor Nathan Deal vetoed the bill under intense pressure from LGBT and business lobbyists who warned of a national boycott of Georgia if he signed it into law.

In March 2015 Indiana Governor Mike Pence (elected U.S. Vice President in 2016) originally signed into law a Religious Freedom Restoration Act that allowed private businesses to deny service to openly LGBTQ people, if they opposed doing so on religious grounds. The conservative Christian group Advance America stated on its website that the Indiana law meant that "Christian bakers, florists, and photographers should not be punished for refusing to participate in a homosexual marriage" (Advance America, 2015). A national outcry from LGBTQ groups and others led to calls from national organizations, ranging from the NCAA to NASCAR, to repeal or amend the law to prevent obvious discrimination against LGBTQ people. Bowing to that pressure, in July 2016 Governor Pence signed a revised version of the law that banned "obvious discrimination." Controversy continues about what that means for LGBTQ rights in Indiana.

In North Carolina similar legislation became law, resulting in boycott threats from national organizations and corporations not to hold major events, conferences, or meetings in that state unless the law is revoked. Bruce Springsteen notably canceled a 2016 concert in Charlotte, NC, to protest the law. The NBA relocated its 2017 All Star game from its originally scheduled location in Charlotte to New Orleans. North Carolina's law contained additional language that requires transgender people to use only those public bathrooms and locker rooms that correspond to their birth gender assignment. Supporters claim that such a provision is necessary to protect the religious belief of those who deny the legitimacy of transgender identity. Opponents counter that argument by stating that it is irrational and impractical and nothing more than a thinly veiled attack on LGBTQ rights in general. In March 2017, following election of a Democratic governor and in reaction to the continuing backlash against the law, North Carolina repealed what had become known as the "bathroom bill" (Hanna, Park, & McLaughlin, 2017).

The integration of LGBTQ people in the U.S. military and the right of same-sex couples to legally marry are seen as major victories and testaments to the value of an assimilationist strategy for achieving change. Observers seek to explain those victories by pointing to social and cultural developments that created a political climate of support for progress on those fronts. The

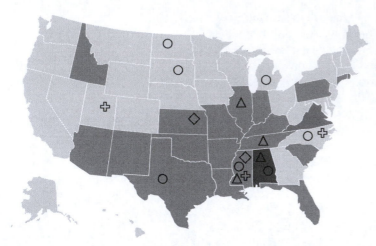

State has no broad religious exemption law
(29 states + D.C.)

State has statutory religious exemption laws
(20 states)

State has constitutional religious exemption laws
(1 state, Alabama)

○ State permits state-licensed child welfare agencies to refuse to place and provide services to children and families, including LGBT people and same-sex couples, if doing so conflicts with their religious beliefs
(7 states)

△ State has targeted religious exemption that permits medical professionals to decline to serve LGBT clients
(4 states)

◇ State has targeted religious exemption that permits faith-based organizations to deny services to married same-sex couples
(2 states)

✚ State had targeted religious exemption law that permits state and local officials to decline to marry couples of whose marriage they disapprove
(3 states)

*State-level religious exemption laws in the U.S. (2017). Source: Adapted from original by permission of Movement Advancement Project.*

phenomena of coming out, AIDS direct activism, and highly publicized anti-LGBT hate crimes, created more LGBT visibility, and fostered compassion and greater understanding for LGBT people in the American population. A more accepting and compassionate society creates a more favorable political environment for an assimilationist legislative and legal strategy for change. Other people view these accomplishments as resonating with conservative values and anti-government sensibilities. Privacy rights are part of traditional conservative ideology, as are "family values" that see marriage as a foundational institution for a "good society." Nurturing patriotism and nationalism through respect for, and service in, the military is consistent with conservative principles. Similarly, expanded opportunities for LGBTQ business entrepreneurship and marketing to tap LGBTQ buying power feeds into the traditional conservative promotion of corporate capitalism (Stein, 2012).

These observations have created divisions in the LGBTQ movement that may prove problematic as it begins to define a response to challenges that remain. Even as marriage was prioritized by many LGBTQ activists, there are others who allege that that goal was never a priority in the movement's early days but became one when a few movement leaders pushed for it. For critics within the movement, marriage was (and is) an oppressive heteronormative institution that was based on domesticity and monogamy. Some LGBTQ activists ask why government should privilege married couple relationships and not unmarried partners or even single people. Stein says that some ask why extending spousal healthcare benefits through same-sex marriage was part of the focus of attention rather than a campaign for universal access to healthcare whether married or not (Stein, 2012).

Yet, the reality is that same-sex marriage and military integration that dominated the attention and energy of contemporary LGBTQ activism have now been achieved. This leaves the LGBTQ movement to consider new priorities. Many call for a renewed comprehensive global campaign for HIV/AIDS prevention and treatment. In 2011 more than one million people in the United States were living with HIV infection; nearly 600,000 had died from AIDS-related illnesses (Stein, 2012). Around the world, millions more continue to die from AIDS. HIV/AIDS education programs, an important part of the original fight, have lagged as restrictions on sex education in many school districts have been adopted and the high cost of AIDS healthcare has put access to treatment and care out of reach for many HIV-positive people. Some say that the focus ought not to be just on HIV/AIDS, but on universal healthcare that would create access to healthcare for all Americans, regardless of sexual orientation or gender (Stein, 2012).

Other voices suggest that one of the most serious issues facing the LGBTQ movement is the high suicide rate among LGBTQ youth. A 2011 study of LGBTQ young people in Oregon found that LGBTQ teens were five times more likely to commit suicide than were heterosexual teens. The study also found that when schools adopted and enforced anti-bullying and anti-discrimination policies that specifically protected LGBTQ young people, the risk of attempted suicide dropped significantly (Welsh, 2011). This leads to calls for renewed efforts to convince school boards across the nation to adopt not just anti-bullying policies but also the inclusion of LGBTQ people, themes, and experiences in school curricula at all educational levels. This, of course, is not likely to be easily accomplished as there is ample evidence of continued organized opposition to any such efforts.

Another challenge for the LGBTQ movement involves building commitment to support the integration of bisexual and transgender people into the development of its goals. For much of the gay and lesbian rights movement's history, transgender people and their issues were not a central focus of activism. Some of that marginalization emerged from developing political ideologies within the gay and lesbian, feminist and progressive communities that viewed transgender people as reactionary in their cultural politics; as people who had a false sense of their own identity and who would rather change their bodies than change their minds (Stryker, 2015).

Much of what has been accomplished by the gay and lesbian rights movement has been focused on goals—such as marriage equality—that may not resonate very strongly with some transgender people. Many transgender people are more concerned about high levels of violence, unemployment, suicide, societal stigma and discrimination, and the prohibitive healthcare costs associated with medical treatment related to gender transition. Such costs are often seen as elective, and therefore not fully covered, if at all, by health insurance plans.

Whether, and how, the LGBTQ movement will address these and other transgender issues is an important open question. Because bisexuals have at times been faced with skepticism and outright marginalization from some gay men and lesbians who do not accept bisexuality as a legitimate sexual orientation, bisexuals have had to challenge that kind of biphobia with an intra movement activism. In 1990, for example, Bi PAC, a New York bisexual political action committee, engaged in a national letter-writing campaign to successfully persuade an educational institution to remove an offensive workshop it offered entitled "Bisexual Men: Fact or Fiction" (BiNet USA, 2016).

*U.S. Postal Service stamp depicting Harvey Milk (1930–1978), one of the first openly-gay elected officials in the United States. Issued May 22, 2014. Milk was assassinated while in office by a disgruntled former colleague on the San Francisco Board of Supervisors. Source: Photo by Catwalker, courtesy of Shutterstock.*

## CONCLUSION

As these internal challenges indicate, perhaps the most significant question for the future of the LGBTQ movement is whether it can continue to build and strengthen intra-movement unity and commitment to realistic goal-setting and effective action. There are disagreements about what issues should be prioritized. There are revisionist analyses as to whether what has been accomplished really amounts to substantive progress or whether it is just capitulation to a heteronormative society. Even if a set of goals is agreed upon, there are also differences of opinion about the most effective strategies for action; whether they should be assimilationist or liberationist, or some combination of both. The LGBTQ movement has always been one of somewhat fragmented and complex identities, facing a multitude of interrelated and simultaneously separate experiences of oppression and discrimination. But, as it faces the future, it will need to re-examine itself in a comprehensive and honest way to bring about its central focus—liberation from oppression and equality for all.

## Learn More

### Readings

Carter, D. (2005). *Stonewall: The riots that sparked the gay revolution*. New York, NY: Macmillan.

Chase, C. (1998). Hermaphrodites with attitude: Mapping the emergence of intersex political activism. *GLQ, 4*(2), 189–211.

Cogswell, K. (2014). *Eating fire: My life as a lesbian avenger*. Minneapolis, MN: University of Minnesota.

D'Emilio, J. (1998). *Sexual politics, sexual communities: The making of a homosexual minority in the United States, 1940–1970*, second edition. Chicago, IL: University of Chicago.

France, D. (2016). *How to survive a plague: The inside story of how citizens and science tamed AIDS*. New York, NY: Picador.

Jones, C. (2017). *When we rise: my life in the movement*. New York, NY: Hachette.

Pierceson, J. (2015). *Sexual minorities and politics: An introduction*. Lanham, MD: Rowman & Littlefield.

Stein, M. (2012). *Rethinking the gay and lesbian movement*. New York, NY: Routledge.

Stryker, S. (2008). *Transgender history*. Seattle, WA: Seal.

### Film/Video

Chasnoff, D. (2004) *One wedding and a revolution*. [Motion picture]. United States: Women's Educational Media.

Cowan, R., & Greenstreet, S., (Directors). (2010). *8: The Mormon proposition*. [DVD]. United States: David v. Goliath.

Davis, K. & Heilbroner, D. (Producers). (2010). *The American experience: Stonewall uprising*. [DVD] United States: PBS.

Dong, A. (Director/Producer). (1994). *Coming out under fire* [Motion picture]. United States: Deepfocus.

Dupre, J. (Producer) & McKenna, C. (Producer). (2004). *Out of the past: The struggle for gay and lesbian rights in America* [Motion picture]. United States: Zeitgeist.

Epstein, R. (Director) & Schmiechen, R. (Producer). (1984). *The times of Harvey Milk* [Motion picture]. United States: Black Sands.

France, D. (Director). (2012). *How to survive a plague.* [Motion picture]. United States: Public Square.

Hubbard, J. (Director). (2012). *United in anger: A history of ACT UP.* [Motion picture]. New York, NY: United in Anger.

Kates, N. (Director/Producer) & Singer, B. (Director/Producer). (2002). *Brother outsider: The life of Bayard Rustin* [Motion picture]. United States: California Newsreel.

Muska, S. (Director/Producer) & Olafsdttir, G (Director/Producer). (1998). *The Brandon Teena story* [Motion picture]. United States: Bless Bless.

Rix, J. (Director). (2012). *Lewd and lascivious.* [DVD] United States: Come True.

Seckinger, B. (Director). (2004). *Laramie inside out* [DVD]. United States: New Day.

Seve, J. (Director). (2004). *Tying the knot* [Motion picture]. United States: Outcast.

Silverman, V., & Stryker, S. (Directors). (2005). *Screaming queens: The riot at Compton's cafeteria* [DVD]. San Francisco: Frameline.

Weissman, D. & Weber, B. (Directors). (2012). *We were here: The AIDS years in San Francisco* [DVD]. United States: Weissman Projects.

Westmoreland, W. (Director) & Clements, A. (Producer). (2004). *Gay Republicans* [Motion picture]. United States: World of Wonder.

Zierling, A (Producer), & Dick, K. (Director). (2009). *Outrage* [Motion picture]. United States: Magnolia.

### Internet

ACT UP Oral History Project: actuporalhistory.org

Equality Federation: www.equalityfederation.org

Human Rights Campaign: www.hrc.org

Lambda Legal: www.lambdalegal.org

Lesbian Avengers Documentary Project: www.lesbianavengers.com

Movement Advancement Project: www.lgbtmap.org

National Center for Lesbian Rights: www.nclrights.org

National Center for Transgender Equality: www.transequality.org

National LGBTQ Task Force: www.thetaskforce.org

OutServe—Servicemembers Legal Defense Network: www.outserve-sldn.org

Sylvia Rivera Law Project: srlp.org

Transgender Law Center: transgenderlawcenter.org

Victory Fund: victoryfund.org

# CHAPTER 7
# Pop Out!
## *Mass Media and Popular Culture*

*Byron Lee*

*Wall-sized advertisement for Netflix series* Orange is the New Black *which included several transgender, lesbian, gay male, and bisexual characters (June 21, 2014). Source: Leonard Zhukovsky/Shutterstock.*

In 2015 LGBTQ activists and film critics lambasted the film *Stonewall*, a fictional retelling of the 1969 Stonewall Riots. The film told the story of fictional character, Danny Winters, a young, white man who leaves his conservative rural home, goes to New York City, and meets a group of LGBTQ people. Danny's sexual and romantic encounters, and experiences with homophobic police violence, lead to his interest in gay and lesbian activism. During a narrow escape from a police raid at the Stonewall Inn, Danny, enraged, throws a brick at the building and yells, "Gay Power!" After the film's trailer was released, film critics and LGBTQ activists quickly reacted to the emphasis on a cisgender, white male, over people of color, women, and transgender activists known to be at the Stonewall Riots. The film also revised historical accounts giving credit to the film's white protagonist for starting the Stonewall Riots by throwing the first brick. Some critics accused the film of "whitewashing," or the erasure of people of color from historical moments (Ginelle, 2015). Critics questioned how the Stonewall Riots, an important moment in LGBTQ history, was being remembered and represented in the film.

The critics' reaction raises several questions about LGBTQ communities and media. How are LGBTQ communities represented in mainstream media? Why are white gay men dominant in media representations of LGBTQ communities? Do the various LGBTQ communities have a single story and who gets to tell it? The controversy surrounding the film *Stonewall* hints at the important role mass media and popular culture play in shaping (and changing) public opinion about LGBTQ people—their experiences, struggles, communities, and civil rights. It also suggests that the issue of mass-media representation of LGBTQ people is far from simplistic or straightforward, no matter their producer's good intentions.

This chapter offers a brief overview of the representation of LGBTQ people in U.S-based media. It also considers the role of different media technologies—printed text, film and TV, and digital and mobile media—in helping LGBTQ people locate and form communities. Finally, and perhaps most importantly, this chapter aims to demonstrate how media technologies not only represent LGBTQ communities, but also provide new ways for LGBTQ communities to challenge society's ideas about gender and sexuality.

## LGBTQ MEDIA STEREOTYPES

A common approach to thinking about media is representation in content: who and what is included in the characters, themes, narrative, or storyline of a particular example of media like a film, video game, or comic book. As mass-media industries—print, film, and television—developed and expanded in the twentieth century, their content was regulated by governmental oversight, as well as by societal mores and pressures. Mass-media industries also enforced stereotypes, since their products reached a wide audience.

Stereotypes emerge from repeated images over time. Stereotypes succeed because the images are confirmed in different contexts, such as different mass-media forms and in social organizations such as education systems, churches, and community groups (Dyer, 1993). In the U.S. and Canada, common stereotypes of LGBTQ people include old theories that non-normative identities and behaviors come from psychological problems. Gender and sexuality are also conflated. Effeminate men (i.e., sissies, dandies) and masculine women (i.e., butches) serve as visual shorthand for gay men and lesbians, and similarly, gay men and lesbians are assumed to be feminine and masculine, respectively.

In order to counter these negative stereotypes, LGBTQ people have sought control of media representations by being the producers, the creators of media content. Their goal: incorporating negative stereotypes into a range of codes and characteristics of LGBTQ communities and lives.

## THE GAY PRESS

For most of the twentieth century, mainstream news media, when they bothered to report on LGBTQ people, offered an outside perspective, one that often depicted LGBTQ communities as problematic, odd groups in society. These mainstream news outlets frequently presented gays and lesbians as "perverts" (and in most of the twentieth century transgender people were assumed to be homosexuals and therefore included in this group), using tones that suggested that journalists were trying to expose and explain this group of people to "normal" society. Although smaller local newspapers in major cities, such as New York City's *Village Voice*, sometimes wrote non-demonizing stories about gays and lesbians, they were not dedicated to covering LGBTQ issues.

Looking to address this negative environment towards the LGBTQ community, early forms of the gay press didn't challenge stereotypes, as

*Daughters of Bilitis (NY) newsletter (Oct.–Nov. 1963). Source: Archives Center, Smithsonian National Museum of American History. CC BY-SA 2.0 license. Image courtesy of Flickr.*

they were mostly meant for other gays and lesbians. Instead, they sought to communicate with members of their own community. Starting in the 1950s as newsletters and political magazines of small social organizations, these early publications promoted early LGBTQ rights activist activities. Organizations such as the Mattachine Society and the Daughters of Bilitis each produced magazines (*One* and *The Ladder*, respectively). The newspaper, *The LA Advocate*, started in 1967 and eventually became a national magazine and renamed *The Advocate* in 1974 (Sender, 2004). By the 1970s several major cities had gay publications: *Bay Area Reporter* (San Francisco), *Philadelphia Gay News* (Philadelphia), *Gay Community News* (Boston), *Washington Blade* (Washington DC), *Windy City Times* (Chicago), *Dallas Voice* (Dallas), *Frontiers* (Los Angeles), and *Gay City News* (New York). Notably, in the 1970s and 1980s, most publications were run by white, gay men and gave less coverage to women. Several lesbian-specific newspapers were published in the 1970s, such as *Lesbian News* in Los Angeles, though most were short-lived. Many lesbian issues were also addressed in lesbian-friendly feminist publications, such as *off our backs* (Baim, 2012).

By being inherently biased, these outlets reported on and were sympathetic towards LGBTQ communities. The gay press covered LGBTQ political issues, such as the decriminalization of sodomy, the removal of homosexuality from the American Psychological Association's list of mental disorders, advocating for anti-discrimination laws and marriage equality. In the 1980s and 1990s the gay press was the main public source of information about HIV/AIDS, and in the 2000s and 2010s, gay press reporters were more likely to report on violence against transgender people. This was the case of Nizah Morris, a transgender woman who died in 2002 after interactions with Philadelphia Police. *Philadelphia Gay News* reporter Timothy Cwieck was credited for investigating the story and finding inconsistencies and anti-transgender bias in the police reports about Morris' death—an investigation that continued over ten years after Morris' death (Middleton, 2014). Their actions allowed for the slow erosion of queer stereotypes promulgated by mainstream outlets.

When not in control of its own media, the LGBTQ community also developed its own watchdog organizations to monitor how U.S.-based journalism represents LGBTQ communities, namely through two national organizations: Gay and Lesbian Alliance Against Defamation (GLAAD) and the National Lesbian and Gay Journalists Association (NLGJA). GLAAD monitors mainstream press coverage on LGBTQ communities, while the NLGJA helps journalists set and frame the agenda for LGBTQ issues. Both organizations also provide standards for language around transgender issues on their websites, including appropriate pronoun use and how to address changing slang terms. As the gay presses change and include online formats such as blogs and social media, and more LGBTQ-identified journalists are working in mainstream presses and covering LGBTQ issues, these organizations play an important role in maintaining quality reporting on LGBTQ communities (Nair, 2012).

## GLAAD and the GLAAD Media Awards

The media-monitoring organization GLAAD—Gay & Lesbian Alliance Against Defamation—was founded in 1985, a time when there were few flattering representations of LGBTQ people in news media, TV, or film. In addition to releasing reports assessing media content, GLAAD also provides resources and workshops to media producers, such as journalists and TV studios, helping them recognize and avoid stereotypical characters and narratives, and updating appropriate vocabulary for describing LGBTQ communities.

GLAAD gives the annual GLAAD Media Awards, which honor fair and accurate media representations of LGBTQ communities in mainstream media. The awards feature categories such as films, journalistic coverage, and fine arts. The awards are not, however, designed to award innovations in presenting LGBTQ content. Nominees are primarily selected from media already monitored by the organization. LGBTQ-identified media producers, independent filmmakers, and TV production companies, however, already have a mandate to tell LGBTQ stories honestly, and therefore are not regularly monitored by GLAAD. Media products from these producers, including independent films, must be nominated by people from outside the GLAAD Media Awards Nomination Committee.

GLAAD has been criticized for its focus on representation in mainstream media. GLAAD tends to emphasize "positive" portrayals of LGBTQ communities, ones that are not too disruptive to heterosexual society's values. While GLAAD has become an important organization for LGBTQ communities in media, its activities reflect current debates and tensions within LGBTQ communities regarding what it means to represent and support communities that do not fit into the mainstream.

## ADVERTISING AND THE GAY MARKET

While the gay press helped make LGBTQ communities publicly visible, advertising turned them into a recognizable market. Gay presses sold ad space to pay for printing costs, mostly to local businesses that were either gay-owned or catering to LGBTQ clientele. Early gay newspapers and magazines were produced primarily by and for men, and were mostly circulated through bathhouses and bars—primarily men's spaces. Gay men were also more likely to feel comfortable self-identifying as gay and respond to market research surveys. This caused a perception that the gay market was mostly male, more affluent, and more interested in issues of taste than other market segments, including lesbians. Gay men were also assumed to be in relationships without children or other dependents, leading to more disposable income. Thus, images in early gay press advertisements often depicted gay men as childless, stylish, globetrotting, lifestyle consumers (Branchik, 2002).

*The Greek alphabet letter "lambda," which is also a symbol in chemistry and physics for the complete exchange of energy, was chosen as a symbol for the lesbian and gay rights movement in 1970 by the New York Gay Activists Alliance. In December 1974, it was officially declared the international symbol for gay and lesbian rights by the International Gay Rights Congress in Edinburgh, Scotland.*

*The labrys, a symmetrical double-sided axe, was often associated with female divinities in ancient Greece and Rome. Since the 1970s it has been used by feminists and lesbians as a sign of female strength.*

Deemed a new, untapped market, gay and lesbian consumers were targeted in the late twentieth century through ads specifically for gay publications. However, they were not included in larger (i.e., mainstream) ad campaigns. For most mainstream audiences during the 1990s, gay men and lesbians were publicly visible, and largely associated with AIDS activism. Still, the overall social climate in the U.S. was homophobic, which explained why companies, fearing backlash, were hesitant to include LGBTQ people in their ads. For example, in 1994 the Swedish homegoods store IKEA produced a television ad that featured two men shopping for dining room furniture that only aired starting at 10 p.m. (after "family hours"). The two men, however, were clearly shown as a couple, and the American Family Association called for a boycott against IKEA (Horovitz, 1994).

An attempt to counter potential backlash as well as provide inclusion gave rise to "Gay Vague Advertising." Gay vague ads feature men or women together with language or visuals that could be interpreted as representing lesbian or gay male sexuality, but are open to other interpretations. In "Sunday Afternoon," a 1997 television commercial for the Volkswagen Golf, two men are driving and see an armchair on the street. They drive off with the armchair in the car. The driver makes a face indicating that he smells something unpleasant and the two share a look. The commercial ends with the armchair on a sidewalk as the two men drive away. The relationship between the men is never explained, nor is there dialogue between them. Their activity suggests cohabitation (getting furniture together), but the viewer does not know whether they are boyfriends, roommates, or just friends.

Using visual symbols and coded language provided a different strategy to target the gay market without showing non-heterosexual romantic couples or even using the words gay or lesbian. Symbols, such as the Lambda sign and the Labrys, were not known to non-LGBTQ audiences, and thus could reach an intended LGBTQ audience without offending those not in the know. Other recognizable symbols, such as the rainbow flag, allowed advertisers to reference LGBTQ communities without actually showing queer people (Guaracino, 2007). In 2003 the Greater Philadelphia Tourism Marketing Corporation (today named Visit Philadelphia) and the Philadelphia Gay Tourism Caucus released a print advertisement promoting the city of Philadelphia featuring an image of Betsy Ross. Instead of knitting the American flag, however, she knits a rainbow flag as a group of men (possibly the country's founders) look on. The mainstream press praised the ad's ability to cleverly incorporate LGBTQ symbols into Philadelphia's pre-existing tourism brand as a city that was central to the country's founding (Reed, 2004; Gelbart, 2003).

Gay vague and coded advertisements' cleverness did not satisfy everyone. Conservative groups suggested that the advertisements underestimated their intelligence, while some LGBTQ activists found the advertisements bland (Clinton, 2000). Thus, advertisements in the late 2000s and 2010s became more explicit, featuring lesbians and gay men holding hands, kissing, getting married, or embracing one another. A 2016 television ad for Zales, a jewelry company, briefly showed two women getting married. Even though this was just one of five couples featured in the 30-second ad, the conservative group One Million Moms (part of the American Family Association) called for a boycott of the company (Ciambriello, 2016). By this time in the U.S., however, LGBTQ rights were more accepted, and the call for the boycott had little effect (Behr, 2016).

The recent acceptance of LGBTQ people has created opportunities and visibility for transgender and gender fluid people. A few lifestyle ads for fashion, beauty, and fitness have included gender non-conforming and transgender models. Isis King, made famous by her 2008 appearance on *America's Next Top Model* in which she openly identified as transgender, regularly works as a runway model and in print media fashion photospreads and advertisements. Starting in 2011, models such as Andreja Pejić, Rain Dove, and Elliott Sailors were featured in both menswear and womenswear ad campaigns. In 2015 Aydian Dowling competed for a solo cover of *Men's Health*, and although he did not win, he was placed on the cover with the other five finalists, becoming the first transman to appear on the cover (Calderone, 2015).

*Advertisement promoting LGBTQ tourism to Philadelphia, PA. Source: Visit Philadelphia.*

Gender fluid people have also seen increased visibility. In 2016 both CoverGirl and Maybelline featured men in their campaigns: James Charles was announced as a "CoverBoy" for CoverGirl; and photos of Manny Gutierrez were featured on Maybelline's Instagram account. In both instances, however, the models still conform to normative standards of beauty. While Gutierrez sometimes maintains his facial hair, his photos are lit and framed like makeup glamor shots. Charles sometimes did not wear his visible septum piercing in non-social media-based ads, and kept his make-up style in line with the CoverGirl brand.

## Pinkwashing

The gay market has created a relationship between businesses and LGBTQ communities. Companies willing to purchase advertising in gay publications, and sponsor events such as Pride Parades and community fundraisers in the late twentieth century, are viewed as being in solidarity with LGBTQ communities. Major banks, retailers, and alcohol brands are often among such sponsors. These same companies, however, are critiqued for "pinkwashing" LGBTQ communities. Pinkwashing presents an image of LGBTQ communities as "respectable," matching the image of the status quo: white, cisgender men with disposable incomes. If they have families, they are nuclear families (i.e., two parents with children). Pinkwashing also refers to companies employing LGBTQ representation to win the favor of the gay market, despite their own policies not acknowledging and benefiting LGBTQ communities, including their own employees. Research has found that LGBTQ people acknowledge that companies marketing directly to gay and lesbian audiences are more likely to be LGBTQ-friendly, but they question how deeply this support runs (Gudelunas, 2011).

At its worst, pinkwashing commoditizes LGBTQ politics, suggesting that greater social support can be earned by participating in capitalism (i.e., by buying and selling goods and services) rather than challenging social, economic, and political systems that inherently put LGBTQ communities at risk. Pinkwashing suggests that LGBTQ communities can be part of mainstream society, while simultaneously maintaining that LGBTQ communities are different from the rest of society (Sender, 2004). Thus, the gay market can limit how society understands LGBTQ communities by creating demographic-based expectations of what makes up LGBTQ communities, that is, perpetuating stereotypes.

## COMIC BOOKS, STRIPS AND ZINES

While fine art and literature provide ways for some audiences to experience homoerotic imagery, comic art—in all its various forms—can reach different audiences. Starting in the latter half of the twentieth century, the advent of cheaper methods of printing and copying text (e.g., the photocopier) allowed LGBTQ people to publish and distribute their stories in new ways.

Comic zines with LGBTQ characters and content in the mid-twentieth century started as collections of strips from different artists. Collections published starting in the late 1960s—such as Robert Crumb's *Zap Comix*, Mary Wings' *Come Out Comix*, and Howard Cruse's *Gay Comix*—depicted LGBTQ relationships in ways this art form had rarely done before (Hall, 2012). These independently produced collections were relatively inexpensive to produce, allowing artists to produce works with greater freedom and less concern for audience size, financial investors, industry approval, sales numbers, or profits. Zine-style anthologies also allowed LGBTQ artists to tell their stories the ways that they wanted to, since other LGBTQ people were involved, even at the editorial level (Hall, 2012).

The emergence of gay presses in the 1960s and 1970s also created space for more traditional-style comics, such as political cartoons and serial comic strips, to address important LGBTQ issues. Homoerotic imagery in the graphic arts has an old history in Western culture, but one of the first self-consciously gay comic strips was *Harry Chess: That Man from A.U.N.T.I.E.*, which appeared in the Philadelphia homophile publication *Drum* on and off from 1965 to 1969. The strip later appeared through the 1970s in *Queen's Quarterly* (New York) and then the gay leather-porn magazine *Drummer* (San Francisco). *Harry Chess* parodied the 1964 spy-themed TV series, *The Man from U.N.C.L.E.* and other James Bond-like books and films, but with explicitly gay humor, male nudity, and sexual activity (Murphy, 2014). *Harry Chess* was the first of several sexually explicit gay comic strips and graphic arts that began in the mid-twentieth century with artists like Tom of Finland, Blade, George Quaintance, and Dom Orejudos (Murphy, 2003).

As gay presses stabilized in the 1980s, so could gay comics serials, many of which featured sexual situations, but were not necessarily meant to be pornographic. Howard Cruse's comic, *Wendel*, first appeared in *The Advocate* in 1983 (Hall, 2012). Alison Bechdel's *Dykes to Watch Out For* also started in 1983 in *Womanews*, and became more widely syndicated in 1985 (Yarow, 2010). By the 1990s there were enough alternative and gay presses printing LGBTQ comic strips, such as Eric Orner's *The Mostly Unfabulous Social Life of Ethan Green* and David Kelly's *Steven's Comics*, that artists could support themselves financially and focus on developing their art (Hall, 2012). These comics explored underreported LGBTQ social issues and debates, such as the government's Don't Ask, Don't Tell policy on lesbians and gay men in the military, the commercialization of Pride celebrations, and same-sex marriage equality (Hall, 2012; Shaw, 2009).

In fact, independently published comics are still largely where LGBTQ comic art can express anger over how LGBTQ communities are treated in society. Addressing the lack of action over AIDS, Robert Triptow's *Strip AIDS USA* took advantage of the medium to reach new audiences who needed more education about AIDS: "You can't get AIDS from reading this book. Instead, it could be part of a cure . . . for hysteria, the other AIDS epidemic" (Triptow, 1988). Today, comics also document changes in LGBTQ politics. Starting in 2001, Dylan Edwards published *Trannytoons*, which explored transgender issues. The title, however, is no longer used, as today the term tranny is considered offensive slang. Edwards still draws and writes about trans issues, such as in the anthology *Transposes*, but the shifts in terminology in his work show how comic art can respond to community standards.

Other comics, like those published by the Lesbian Cartoonists Network formed in 1991, challenged gender norms from a queer perspective, and also attempted to reclaim derogatory language (e.g., bitch, dyke, and queer) (Hall, 2012). The hero of Diane DiMassa's *Hothead Paisan: Homicidal Lesbian Terrorist* (series starting in 1991), was unapologetically angry at misogynistic men and society in general. She would sometimes violently confront oppressive men

*Announcement for first gay comic strip "Harry Chess: That Man from A.U.N.T.I.E." (Drum Magazine, 1965). Source: GLBT Historical Society (San Francisco). Image courtesy of Michael J. Murphy.*

(Hall, 2012). *Hothead Paisan* was critical of homophobia and not concerned about the politics of fitting in with the rest of society. *Hothead Paisan* also featured characters who were not cisgender, such as love-interest Daphne, who many readers assumed was transgender despite DiMassa's own claim that Daphne was merely ambiguous (DiMassa, 2004).

Mainstream comics, however, have been slow to include LGBTQ characters. Until 1989 mainstream comics were not permitted to publish characters or storylines with homosexual themes. The Comics Code Authority (CCA) was created during the 1950s, during the era of McCarthyism, when the U.S. government demonized communists and homosexuals (who were assumed to be communists). The CCA served as a moral editorial body, and functioned largely to limit content about sex, violence, and drugs (Hall, 2012). In the mid-1980s mainstream superhero comics began to feature more diverse characters, as audiences embraced more adult-oriented content, following DC's landmark series *The Dark Knight Returns*. Still, it was not until Marvel's *Alpha Flight #106*, published in 1992, that a main superhero (Northstar) came out. Other LGBT characters were usually temporary, supporting characters (Greyson, 2007).

Graphic novels in the 1990s included more LGBTQ characters, such as Howard Cruse's *Stuck Rubber Baby* and Judd Winick's *Pedro and Me*, and received broad acclaim (Hall, 2012). Graphic novels typically target more "mature" mainstream audiences, who were more likely to be receptive to honest and sincere portrayals of LGBTQ characters and issues. *Stuck Rubber Baby* (1995) told the story of a Southern gay man coming to terms with his homosexuality, and who connected with and supported the Civil Rights Movement. *Pedro and Me* (2000) was based on Winick's friendship with gay AIDS activist Pedro Zamora, which began on MTV's *The Real World: San Francisco*. Winick would later work for DC Comics' *Green Lantern*, in which he introduced the gay character Terry Berg, who came out and was later a victim of gay bashing (Greyson, 2007).

Meanwhile, mainstream newspaper comic strips, with a more conservative readership that includes children, featured only three openly gay characters up until 2000 (Dennis, 2012). Two of these characters appeared in *Doonesbury* (in 1976 and 1993), a comic known for its liberal content (Dennis, 2012). The third was Lawrence, a long-time supporting character in *For Better or For Worse,* a Canadian-based comic appearing in many U.S. papers about a suburban family. In 1993 Lawrence came out to his best friend Michael, one of the main characters. Forty newspapers refused to run the comic strip, and after one week, 19 newspapers canceled the comic completely (*For Better or Worse* website, www.fbofw.com, n.d.). Artist Lynn Johnston noted that response from LGBTQ communities was slow, probably because they were skeptical of whether she, a cisgender, heterosexual woman, would tell Lawrence's story sympathetically (*For Better or Worse* website, www.fbofw.com, n.d.).

Most recently, *Archie Comics*, which also targets a younger, pre-teen audience, introduced Kevin Keller, an openly gay high school student. Dan Parent, the artist, in a Reddit AMA (Ask Me Anything) (2013), noted that Keller's character was important because gay teens exist, and that people, including the characters of *Archie*, have sexuality (Parent, 2013).

## FILM

### Early LGBTQ Representations

While stereotypes can have negative cultural and political implications, they have sometimes been useful for LGBTQ people in film. The film industry in the early twentieth century was run under the studio-system, in which

---

## The Hays Film Production Code

Although lesbian and gay characters, themes, and romantic interests were quite common in early twentieth-century Hollywood film, after the 1920s they became less explicit due to the Motion Picture Production Code (the Hays Code). Named for Will Hays, who headed the Motion Picture Producers and Distributors of America (MPPDA) in the 1920s, and heavily influenced by conservative Catholic organizations, the Code was a series of content guidelines for Hollywood films. Film studios agreed to abide by the Code to avoid possible government censorship of films. From 1934 to 1961 the Code was vigorously enforced to protect the "sanctity of the institution of marriage and the home" (quoted in Eaklor, 2008, p. 65). Under the Code, scripts were submitted to the MPPDA for approval prior to film production, and all objectionable content was censored.

Nevertheless, gay, lesbian, and gender-variant characters and themes still appeared in Hollywood films produced under the Hays Code, just more covertly (Russo, 1987). Films based on other material that included homosexual characters or narratives were changed, such as 1947's *Crossfire*, which changed a narrative about homophobia to one of racism. If a character's homosexuality was suggested, the character died (often as punishment for whatever possibly made them homosexual). In Tennessee Williams' *Suddenly Last Summer* (1959), the MPPDA allowed the character Sebastian's gay behaviors to be suggested (i.e., he would look for men, but for a vague, unclear reason) but only because the film ends with Sebastian eaten by cannibals. Although the MPPDA permitted production of *The Children's Hour* (1961) and *Advise and Consent* (1962), which explicitly dealt with homosexuality, the homosexual characters died.

During the 1960s the power of Hollywood film studios over film content declined, causing the Hays Code to lose power. In the "New Hollywood" era of the 1960s and 1970s more power was given to individual directors and performers, limiting studio control over film production. In lieu of the Hays Code, the Motion Picture Association of America (MPAA) instituted a ratings system, which shifted the policing of film content, from before to after production. Today, the legacy of the Code can be seen in the MPAA ratings system. Films that deal frankly with sexuality are often given more severe ratings, and homosexual content is more harshly rated than similar heterosexual content.

a few major film studios (e.g., Warner Brothers, MGM, and 20th Century Fox) controlled the production, content, and distribution of film. Perhaps surprisingly, before 1930 it was not uncommon to find homosexual and gender-variant themes, story lines, and romances in Hollywood films. But between roughly 1930 and 1960, such depictions were less explicit, though not entirely absent. In much of early Hollywood cinema, stereotypes made lesbian and gay characters recognizable (Dyer, 1993). Film characters who might today be identified as lesbian or gay, were indicated by stereotypical, gender non-conforming behavior. Sissies, dandies, and butch women, regularly appeared as supporting characters in films prior to the 1950s, and such depictions were not always negative. After World War II American culture took a sexual- and gender-conservative turn, and the content of Hollywood films came under greater government scrutiny. Depictions of homosexuals took on a more sinister tone. Rather than friendly sidekicks, they were depicted as insane, murderers, traitors, or villains (Russo, 1987).

The first film permitted to openly depict homosexuality was 1961's *The Children's Hour*, the second Hollywood film directed by William Wyler based on a play of the same name. In the 1934 play by Lillian Hellman, two schoolteachers, Martha and Karen, are accused of being lesbians, and the accusation ruins their lives, including Karen's relationship with her boyfriend. The first film based on Helman's play, *These Three* (1936), followed the Hays Code, and changed the plot: Martha is accused of having a sexual affair with Karen's boyfriend. Even though Wyler was permitted to restore the lesbian plot in the 1961 film, actress Shirley MacLaine said that she, Wyler, and co-star Audrey Hepburn did not discuss lesbianism during the film's production (Russo, 1987). The film ultimately maintained the Hay's Code: admitting her lesbian feelings drives Martha (played by MacLaine) to suicide.

Throughout the 1960s most lesbian and gay characters in film were still troubled figures, afflicted with violent desires, loneliness, or insanity, following homophobic stereotypes designed to make mainstream audiences comfortable (Russo, 1987). Not all stereotypes, however, were so clearly negative. The meanings of stereotypes can be time-specific. Although *Boys in the Band* (1970) was one of the first films to feature almost all gay characters, at the time of its release, gay and lesbian activists criticized the film for showing negative stereotypes. The film, based on the successful, homonymous 1968 off-Broadway play, looked at the lives of closeted gay men, several of whom were unlikeable. Supporters of the 1950s and 1960s Homophile Movement disliked the play and film for showing "unrespectable" gay characters. When the film was released in 1970, after the 1969 Stonewall Riots, gay activists felt that the film's themes undermined the more radical and identity-affirming messages of the Gay Liberation Movement, even though life in the closet was still a reality for many gay men and lesbians. Today, however, critics view this film as representing a particular history, rather than an overall problematic representation gay men (Condon & Robey, 2011).

By 1968 the Hays Code had been replaced by the MPAA's rating system. New Hollywood was emerging: studios were losing control over production, and moral assessments of films took place after, not before, production, allowing more violence, profanity, and sexual behavior to appear in film. The 1970s saw a sexual revolution in U.S. society, and filmmakers began incorporating sexual behavior into storylines that dealt with the popular 1960s and 1970s concepts of free love and sexual freedom. Radley Metzger's *Score* (1974) portrayed an evening of bisexual swinging—the women pair up together for sex, as do the men—and starred Calvin Culver, who had appeared in gay porn under the name Casey Donovan.

Overall, however, negative stereotypical depictions of LGBTQ people still appeared in film. By the early 1980s several B-rated horror films featured psychotic killers who were lesbians (e.g., *Vampyres* [1974], *Shivers* [1975], and *Windows* [1980]), transgender (e.g., *Homicidal* [1961] and *Deranged: Confessions of a Necrophile* [1974]), or gay men (e.g., *Dressed to Kill* [1980] and *Deadly Blessing* [1981]). This trend eventually led to a backlash against director William Friedkin's non-horror film *Cruising* (1980). In the film, Al Pacino plays a policeman investigating a serial killer who murders gay men in the leather scene, and is revealed at the end to be the killer. Gay and lesbian activists, particularly in New York, protested against the film because it continued to show gay characters as perverts and killers (Russo, 1987).

In 1982, however, a few Hollywood films presented more positive portrayals of gay and lesbian characters and narratives. *Making Love* (gay men), *Personal Best* (bisexual women), *The World According to Garp* (transgender woman), and *Victor/Victoria* (gay men and drag performers) were lauded as examples of better representations of LGBTQ people. *Making Love* (1982) is notable because of the intense focus on gay male romantic feelings, rather than sexual desire or activity. In the film, a married man meets another man, confronts his attraction to men, comes out, and leaves his wife. The film was well received because the gay characters did not die or physically suffer, nor did the protagonist go back to his wife. Homosexual romance was finally allowed to succeed on screen. In 1986, *Desert Hearts*, directed by Donna Deitch, would also present a happy ending, but for a lesbian romance.

Not all "negative" portrayals of queer stereotypes, however, were unappreciated by queer audiences. During the late 1970s and 1980s, some B-rated movies, such as *Myra Breckinridge* (1970), presented exaggerated emotions and over-acting and gained cult followings, particularly from gay audiences. Filmmaker John Waters also presented a style that focused on and exaggerated the idea of filth. Waters' "Trash Trilogy"—*Pink Flamingos* (1972), *Female Trouble* (1974), and *Desperate*

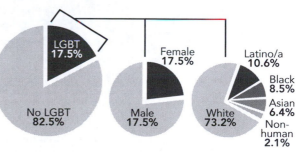

*The percentage of LGBT characters—broken out by gender and race—in major studio films released in 2015. Source: Adapted from data published by GLAAD, 2016.*

## Popular Music

LGBTQ people have been present in popular music, as producers, performers, and in song lyrics and content. Sometimes this presence was open; other times it was hidden; and at other times, performers/lyrics playfully or coyly straddled the line, which often contributed to their popularity.

Labeled "the most beautiful woman in the world," early-twentieth-century drag performer Julian Eltinge enthralled audiences in productions like *The Fascinating Widow* (1911); offered beauty and fashion tips for women in his *Eltinge* magazine; and promoted his own line of cosmetics and beauty products even as publicity materials emphasized his off-stage "normalcy" and masculinity. Broadway producer A. H. Woods built The Eltinge Theater (now the Empire Theater) in the performer's honor. During the Jazz Age, some lesbian and bisexual blues singers, like Gertrude "Ma" Rainey and Bessie Smith, sang of romantic, sexual, and social bonds between women in songs like "The Boy in the Boat" (1931) and "Prove It On Me Blues" (1928). Gladys Bentley wore short-cropped hair and a tuxedo as she tickled the ivories in Harlem's Clam House.

Some mid-twentieth-century gay male composers, like Cole Porter (*The Gay Divorcee, Anything Goes*) and Leonard Bernstein (*On the Town, West Side Story*), used double-entendre and playful innuendo in their lyrics and song titles. Classic examples are Porter's "Anything Goes," "Blow, Gabriel Blow," and "You're the Top!" and Bernstein's "Who Am I?" and "Glitter and Be Gay." However, the works never directly addressed homosexuality. Both were married to women who knew of and approved of their same-sex attractions and homosexuality. By the mid-1960s lyrics were occasionally more explicit, but performers had to hide their identities behind pseudonyms. Camp Records put out an album of parody songs called *The Queen is in the Closet* (1965), which included songs with titles like "Florence of Arabia" and "The Weekend of a Hairdresser." Camp Records also produced novelty singles such as "Stanley the Manly Transvestite" and "I'd Rather Fight that Swish." Lace Records produced *Love is a Drag—For Adult Listeners Only* (1965), an album of sincere renditions of songs like Gershwin's "The Man I Love" and Rodgers and Hart's "He's Funny That Way" (Doyle, 2012, n.d.).

The Gay Liberation Movement of the 1970s inspired some LGBT musicians to address sexuality more directly (Aston, 2016). Maxine Feldman's "Angry Atthis" was the first out lesbian song, and iconic singer-songwriter Laura Nyro would embrace lesbian themes in her work by the end of the decade. The bisexual protagonist of glam rocker David Bowie's "John, I'm Only Dancing" (1972) assures his male lover that, although he might be turned on by his female dance partner, there's nothing to worry about. Jobriath became the first openly gay rock musician to partner with a major label when he signed with Geffen Records. Singer-songwriter Steven Grossman's *Caravan Tonight* (1974) broke new ground as the first major-label artist to deal with gay themes in his lyrics, though Michael Cohen's *What Did You Expect? Songs About the Experience of Being Gay* appeared on Folkways in 1973 (Boucher, 2008). After stealing the spotlight as a standout member of San Francisco's Cockettes, disco diva and gender non-conformist Sylvester achieved international stardom with hits like "Mighty Real" and "Disco Heat." In many ways the quintessential 1970s disco band, Village People provided a musical map of the gay U.S. in songs like "Fire Island," "Go West," "San Francisco," and "In the Navy."

In the 1980s, erudite synth-pop icons The Pet Shop Boys continued the Porter-Bernstein tradition by using suggestive lyrics and homoerotic music videos, while Bronski Beat explored explicitly gay themes in songs like "Small Town Boy." Culture Club's Boy George and Dead or Alive's Pete Burns used the new medium of music video to broadcast their influential androgynous look, while Frankie Goes to Hollywood used homoerotic themes in the lyrics and music video of their 1983 hit "Relax." Lesbian women's music exploded in the 1980s, as artists like Ferron and Suede paved the way for Indigo Girls, Melissa Ethridge, and k. d. lang to achieve international acclaim, though none of these newer artists were out until the 1990s. And a number of gay men followed suit, including Rufus Wainwright, Antony Hegarty, Stephin Merritt, and Sam Smith.

Although cross-dressing, androgyny, and gender ambiguity are longtime themes for musical artists and in musical content, self-identified transgender musicians achieved unprecedented visibility in the twenty-first century. Rae Spoon, Baby Dee, and Conchita Wurst have garnered acclaim, while RuPaul and Big Frieda are household names. Joe Stevens, Naomi Brennett, Dalice Malice, and Skylar Kergil harness storytelling idioms of acoustic singer-songwriters to create songs about trans-specific issues. Other gender non-conforming artists Schmekel, Shawn Viagro, Little Waist, and Not Right celebrate their identities and politics using the raucous sounds of queercore punk and rock.

For decades, hip-hop has been dominated by heterosexual cisgender artists, but there has been a smattering of bisexual and homosexual artists (Homoground, N.D.). West Coast collective Rainbow Noise specializes in homo-hop, and their roster includes artists like OT, Stud, and Cee Smith. In 2012 UK artist Amplify Dot became the first female rapper to sign with a major label in that country, and her single "Outlaw" addresses homophobia, transphobia, and gender discrimination in hip-hop culture head on. And singer-songwriter-producer Frank Ocean made headlines when he came out in 2012.

*Matthew J. Jones*

*Living* (1977)—pushed the boundaries of film depictions and storylines by including scenes such as a couple having sex with a live chicken in the bed with them. Even Waters' more mainstream films, such as *Polyester* (1981) and *Hairspray* (1988), reflected this style and featured queer performers, in particular, the drag performer Divine (born Harris Glenn Milstead).

## New Queer Cinema and Increased Diversity

Independent filmmakers in the 1980s and early 1990s challenged LGBTQ stereotypes by experimenting with them, presenting queer perspectives that were angry and uninterested in mainstream society. In 1991 and 1992 a group of films with LGBTQ themes won awards at the Sundance Film Festival, the Toronto's Festival of Festivals, and the Amsterdam Gay and Lesbian Film Festival. Singled out were films like Jennie Livingston's documentary *Paris is Burning* (1990), Todd Kalin's *Swoon* (1992), Todd Haynes' *Poison* (1991), Gregg Araki's *The Living End* (1992), Gus Van Sant's *My Own Private Idaho* (1991), and Laurie Lynd's *R.S.V.P.* (1991). Labeled "New Queer Cinema" (NQC) by scholar B. Ruby Rich (1992), this group of films did not present "positive" images that countered stereotypes.

NQC films presented LGBTQ characters and stories without seeking understanding or sympathy from their audiences. LGBTQ characters' identities and motivations were not explained, nor did they follow conventional goals, such as marrying and having children. NQC was arguably a response to the social, cultural, and political conservatism of the 1980s, a time when U.S. politicians and mainstream society vilified homosexuals and turned away from the AIDS crisis (Aaron, 2004). Gay men in particular were treated as if they were already dead. For NQC filmmakers this was a cinematic challenge: knowledge of potentially imminent death became a part of life. In films like *The Living End* (1992), or *Swoon* (1992), characters do not treat death as a threat to life or love, nor do they try to survive in "good" society.

Films directly addressing HIV/AIDS show this difference of perspective. Hollywood films, such as *Longtime Companion* (1989) and *Philadelphia* (1993), featured sympathetic gay characters trying to describe and defend queer life to the non-gay characters. NQC films and subsequent independently produced films about HIV/AIDS, on the other hand, did not seek acceptance for gay men from mainstream society. Film adaptations of plays about AIDS, including *Jeffrey* (1995), *Love! Valor! Compassion!* (1995), *The Night Larry Kramer Kissed Me* (2000), and *Angels in America* (2003), presented more complex explorations of gay men's feelings of anxiety, joy, and anger associated with living during the AIDS crisis.

Most NQC films and other 1990s queer films that received distribution were made by and about gay white men. Even at the film festivals that screened NQC films in 1991 and 1992, films about women and people of color were appreciated by audiences, but not by financiers and distributors (Rich, 1992).

Later released films about lesbians, such as *Go Fish* (1994), *Bound* (1996), and *High Art* (1998), received critical acclaim from lesbian audiences, but less attention from mainstream and gay audiences. Recently, *Carol* (2015), based on the pulp lesbian novel *The Price of Salt* (1952), was lauded for its unsensational

---

### Evaluating Gender and Sexuality in Film

Alison Bechdel's popular comic strip, *Dykes to Watch Out For* (DTWOF), not only impacted LGBTQ literature, but also provided a popular way to examine gender in film. A 1985 strip, "The Rule," presented what is now known as the Bechdel–Wallace test. The test has become an easy way for gender theorists and popular feminist film critics to gauge how women are represented in film. A film passes the Bechdel–Wallace Test if it satisfies three criteria:

1.  There are more than two women in the film.
2.  The women must talk to each other.
3.  The conversation between the two women must be about something other than a man.

Inspired by the Bechdel–Wallace Test, and drawing from Vito Russo's criteria in *The Celluloid Closet* (1987), GLAAD created the Vito Russo Test to judge LGBTQ content in films. To pass the Vito Russo Test, the following must be true:

1.  The film contains a character that is identifiably lesbian, gay, bisexual, and/or transgender.
2.  That character must not be solely or predominantly defined by their sexual orientation or gender identity (i.e., they are comprised of the same sort of unique character traits commonly used to differentiate straight/non-transgender characters from one another).
3.  The LGBT character must be tied into the plot in such a way that their removal would have a significant effect, meaning they are not there simply to provide colorful commentary, urban authenticity, or set up a punchline. The character must matter.

Every year, GLAAD monitors major studio film releases and produces its Studio Responsibility Index, which reports the results of the Vito Russo Test. In 2015 only 17.5% (22) of films released by seven major studios featured LGBT characters. The report also broke down the gender and ethnic identities of these characters: 77% were male-identified (and mostly gay men, as opposed to transmen, or more masculine-appearing non-gender-conforming individuals); and most were white. Of these films, only 22% (8) passed the Vito Russo Test, suggesting that LGBTQ characters may be present, but are still underdeveloped, or not taken seriously.

visual style, and for avoiding stereotypical portrayals of butch or predatory women. *Carol*'s prominence and success, however, could be linked to its NQC filmmaker Todd Haynes, who had already garnered mainstream recognition from the films *Far From Heaven* (2002) and *I'm Not There* (2007), and the television miniseries *Mildred Pierce* (2011).

Most U.S. queer films in the twentieth century featured white gays and lesbians. Into the 2000s many gay and lesbian groups' politics focused on "fitting in." With the threat of HIV/AIDS diminishing, a major LGBTQ political battle was achieving marriage equality (the U.S. legalized same-sex marriages nationally in 2015). Films such as *The Broken Hearts Club* (2000) and *The Kids Are All Right* (2010) still presented the issues of predominantly white and middle- or upper-middle-class gays and lesbians who fit into conventional social norms and structures (e.g., friendships, forming partnerships, and having families with children). Racial diversity in LGBTQ films, however, is more complicated than simply having people of color appear on screen. Films such as *Boy Culture* (2007) and *The People I've Slept With* (2012) feature diverse casts, but racial tensions do not play a central role in the films' narratives.

In the 2000s several films featuring people of color emphasized cultural difference as the reason for issues with LGBTQ identity. Films such as *Saving Face* (2004), *East Side Story* (2006), *Mambo Italiano* (2003), *Under One Roof* (2002), and *Oy Vey! My Son is Gay!* (2009), showed gays and lesbians in immigrant communities, and their narratives focused on intergenerational differences, with older, straight generations taking issue with their younger, Americanized or American-born children being gay or lesbian. Coming out was shown to be more complicated for gays and lesbians of color because communities of color are assumed to be more homophobic and as viewing LGBTQ identity as white, urban, and North American.

Other films explore the intersections of sexuality and race in the U.S., but without immigration as the reason for cultural difference. Cheryl Dunye's *The Watermelon Woman* (1996) follows Cheryl's—the protagonist—research on an African-American actress who may have had a white lesbian lover. Cheryl, who is black, also begins a relationship with a white woman, which starts a conversation about for whom interracial relationships are a problem (Pick, 2004). Later films, such as *Noah's Arc: Jumping the Broom* (the 2008 sequel to the popular television series), *Pariah* (2011), and *Gun Hill Road* (2011), also feature queer people of color, and show how queer issues are different through non-white cultural perspectives.

While coming out is an important narrative in LGBTQ films, the act itself is not always the only factor affecting how queer characters acknowledge their identities. In 2016 two films, *Spa Night* (2016) and *Moonlight* (2016), dealt with young gay men of color growing up. *Spa Night* follows David, a young Korean American man, as he figures out his sexual desires, but more importantly, his struggle to find employment. Although David eventually acts on his desires, the film ends without a formal coming out moment. Similarly, *Moonlight*, winner of the 2017 Academy Award for Best Picture, follows three periods of life for Chiron, a shy, quiet, African-American person living in near poverty. Chiron's actions are shaped by his overall social situation, and more than only desire for another man.

In general, films with LGBTQ content produced by major studios and some non-LGBTQ independent filmmakers are usually produced with non-LGBTQ audiences in mind. The protagonists of films such as *The Wedding Banquet* (1993), *In & Out* (1997), *The Object of My Affection* (1998), *Philadelphia* (1993), *To Wong Foo, Thanks for Everything! Julie Newmar* (1995), and *The Birdcage* (1995), focus on their relationships with the straight people in their lives. Because of their larger intended audience and the perspective of their non-LGBTQ filmmakers, these films attempted to focus on the relatability of queer lives. When asked about *The Boys in the Band* (1970), which was written by and starred gay male actors, heterosexual director William Friedkin suggested that the film was about human problems, not simply problems faced by gay men (Russo, 1987).

More recently, *Brokeback Mountain* (2005) was heralded as a great achievement for being a widely distributed film that showed the romantic and sexual relationship between two masculine ranch hands, Ennis and Jack. Their relationship ends tragically with Jack's death, and Ennis is shown keeping Jack's shirt hung inside one of his own, granting the audience romantic and spiritual closure for the two characters. Director Ang Lee stated that the film was ultimately a romance story: "It's a great American love story, told in a way that felt as if it had never been done before" (quoted in Durbin, 2005). Critic Michael Mirasol (2011) noted that the film "cares much less about promoting gay rights than about telling the sad tale of two people who . . . just happen to be men."

## Documentary and Historical Nostalgia

Before the 1970s documentaries and journalist coverage depicted LGBTQ communities as a menace to U.S. society, such as CBS' 1967 television documentary, *The Homosexuals*. One of the first more positive documentaries about gays and lesbians was *Word is Out* (1977), which simply featured gays and lesbians telling their own stories, focusing on their everyday lives.

Documentary films made in the 1980s created more political and popular visibility of LGBTQ communities. *The Times of Harvey Milk* (1984) told the story of well-liked politician and activist Harvey Milk, bluntly labeling his assassination by Dan White on November 27, 1978, and White's acquittal, as acts of homophobia. *Paris is Burning* (1990) explored drag balls in New York City and the lives of queer black men. The film presented drag ball culture as a form of family and kinship, one that works (i.e., doing drag is work), and one that does not separate issues of gender identity, sexual identity, class, and race (Hilderbrand, 2013b).

Documentaries produced from the 2000s on further explored the diversity of LGBTQ communities. Films such as *Bear Nation* (2010), and *black./womyn.: Conversations with lesbians of African descent* (2008) gave voice to LGBTQ communities that were ignored in popular media. Other films, such as *Trembling Before G-d* (2001), *A Jihad for Love* (2008), *For the Bible Tells Me So* (2008), *Small Town Gay Bar* (2007), and *A Sinner in Mecca* (2015), addressed LGBTQ people with close ties to often homophobic communities, namely religious groups.

Recent documentaries connect LGBTQ history to contemporary civil rights and freedoms. Films such as *Stonewall Uprising* (2010), *Before Stonewall* (1985), *After Stonewall* (1999), and *Gay Pioneers* (2004) emphasize the idea that current rights are due to past activists' anger and bravery. *How to Survive a Plague* (2012) and *We Were Here* (2011) feature people retelling stories about life during the AIDS epidemic and what it means to survive. Other films challenge what is popularly remembered as LGBTQ history. Susan Stryker's *Screaming Queens: The Riot at Compton's Cafeteria* (2005) documented a 1966 riot started by transgender people in San Francisco, three years before the 1969 Stonewall Riots, and presented it as a story specifically about transgender people, not an overarching story about gay liberation.

LGBTQ historical dramas and biopics dramatize the lives of key people in LGBTQ movements (e.g., *Milk* [2008], *Dallas Buyers Club* [2013], *The Imitation Game* [2015], *Freeheld* [2015]), or use historical moments as the backdrop for fictional characters (e.g., *Stonewall* [2015]). Unlike documentaries, these films use fictional elements and characters, and often rely on nostalgia to create a cinematic narrative. Nostalgia, however, can lead to imprecise depictions of the past, including removing LGBTQ characters or narratives, such as the example of the whitewashing in *Stonewall* (2015) described at the beginning of this chapter.

Nostalgia can also omit LGBTQ narratives and characters themselves, in hopes of attracting broader, mainstream audiences. The UK-made film *Pride* (2014) told the story of a gay and lesbian activist organization that raised funds for the British coal miners' strike of the 1980s. The description used in the U.S. home media packaging, however, removed any mention of gay and lesbian identity in the description, and even removed an image of a protester's sign that read, "Lesbians and Gays Support the Miners." Director Matthew Warchus suggested that the studio's decision was likely to make the film a "universal" story, rather than labeling it as a "gay film" (Orley, 2015). Warchus' comments reflect a prominent issue for films with LGBTQ content: are films featuring LGBTQ protagonists and stories for LGBTQ audiences only? More than just LGBTQ audiences need to see diverse representations of LGBTQ communities in order to combat stereotypes. At the same time, however, erasing or minimizing LGBTQ identities from descriptions and narratives to trick audiences into watching films may suggest that LGBTQ content is less valuable to society.

## On Screen: Acting LGBTQ Lives

In film and TV LGBTQ visibility is not only marked by narratives and characters, but also by the real people whom audiences actually see. Hoping that LGBTQ narratives on screen also mean more opportunities for LGBTQ people, fans ask, "Who plays the parts of LGBTQ characters?" This question comes from two perspectives: first, who can "authentically" represent LGBTQ people? And second, are there employment opportunities for LGBTQ actors? Many non-LGBTQ-identified actors have played the roles of LGBTQ people. Even recently, starring roles in films such as *Brokeback*

## Celebrity Outing

In May 2016 actor Colton Haynes, known mostly for TV roles, confirmed that he was gay in an interview with *Entertainment Weekly*. Before this, Haynes had avoided discussing his sexual identity or romantic life, following the advice of his management and for his own comfort (Snetiker, 2016). Noah Galvin, out gay actor and star of the TV series *The Real O'Neals*, criticized Haynes for not really coming out of the closet; for not actually stating in a quote that he is gay (Jung, 2016). Galvin received backlash for his comments, including from Haynes, and later apologized (Stedman, 2016). Reactions to Galvin's interview centered on whether LGBTQ celebrities should be out to increase LGBTQ visibility, and the politics of coming out of the closet.

In the early and mid-twentieth century, many celebrities were actors, and the film studio system "protected" its stars. Studios often paid publications to prevent unflattering stories from appearing in the press. For some celebrities, evidence of their homosexuality did not emerge until after their careers or deaths (e.g., Greta Garbo). For others, being gay was an "open secret," but the studios suppressed stories about them, and other celebrities respected their secrets (e.g., George Cukor, Cary Grant, Rock Hudson).

Following Harvey Milk's political call for more gays and lesbians to come out to their friends and families in 1978, some members of the gay press called for gay and lesbian celebrities to publicly come out, or be outed. During the AIDS crisis in the 1980s many people distanced themselves from gays and lesbians, so celebrity support of gays and lesbians was seen as a political act. In 1985 author Armistead Maupin outed actor Rock Hudson—known for films such as *Pillow Talk* (1959). While some considered it a betrayal of his friend's trust, Maupin argued that mentioning Hudson's sexuality in a matter-of-fact way made it less sensational (Gale, 1999). Author and activist Michael Signorile advocated for outing celebrities in the 1990s, and his lead has been followed by journalists/writers such as Michael Rogers and Perez Hilton.

LGBTQ scholars and activists have mixed opinions about outing. Some argue that coming out is a personal decision, and that celebrities should be able to control whether and how they come out. Others support outing as a way to increase LGBTQ representation in public. Celebrities who stay silent about their sexual identities are perceived to be in the closet—hiding, and dishonest (Gross, 1993).

*Mountain* (2005), *Transamerica* (2005), *The Kids are All Right* (2010), *A Single Man* (2009), *Love is Strange* (2014), and *Carol* (2015), have been played by cisgender, heterosexual actors.

Addressing the first perspective, LGBTQ activists and critics worry about performers relying on stereotypical performances, such as the sissy gay man or butch lesbian (e.g., Lowder, 2013). Although this was historically an issue, there has been some positive change in how cis–heterosexual actors portray gay characters. The actors in the films mentioned above worked hard to avoid stereotypical performances. While playing LGBTQ characters, or "playing gay," could once damage mainstream acting careers, playing LGBTQ characters today can become opportunities for cisgender actors. Creating an authentic performance becomes an acting exercise that elevates actors to a status of "serious" actors. Heterosexual actors playing LGBTQ characters have won top acting awards: Tom Hanks in *Philadelphia* (1993); Charlize Theron in *Monster* (2003); Hilary Swank in *Boys Don't Cry* (1999); Sean Penn in *Milk* (2008); and Jared Leto in *Dallas Buyers Club* (2013).

The second perspective is about creating LGBTQ visibility by showing LGBTQ people on screen. Some critics argue that the acting exercise of performing a different identity only works for straight and cisgender actors, that audiences will be unable to see LGBTQ performers in non-LGBTQ roles (Setoodeh, 2010). This homophobic "worry" that audiences will feel uncomfortable watching LGBTQ performers "playing straight" assumes that LGBTQ performers cannot act as well as non-LGBTQ performers, and creates a system that prevents LGBTQ-identified actors from being considered for acting roles. Producers are also more likely to fund films if established actors appear in them, limiting filmmakers' abilities to create opportunities for LGBTQ actors (Lee Badgett & Herman, 2013).

## TELEVISION

Television today features more LGBTQ representation than film, and it brings content directly to audiences' homes. In part, the structure of television allows for this: content on television is controlled by the distributing channels, not all of which are accessible for free. There are more channels, many of which cater to specific types of audiences, including Here! TV and Logo, which are dedicated to producing and airing LGBTQ content. Television programming's multiple episode format permits more character and narrative development. However, this positive visibility has not always been the case.

Network and basic cable shows have a long history of including some LGBTQ content, but because these channels are free, or at a minimum cost, their audiences are wider, and often more conservative. While several network shows introduced minor LGBTQ characters, they were usually present only for single episodes or sporadic appearances. The first recurring (i.e., minor) gay character was Peter Panama, a flamboyant set designer, in the ABC show *The Corner Bar* (1972). *Soap* (1977–1981) also featured a main gay character,

Jodie Dallas (played by Billy Crystal), although he had affairs with both men and women on the show. On April 30, 1997, *Ellen* (1994–1998), starring Ellen Degeneres, became the first network television show in the U.S. with a gay or lesbian main character.

While *Ellen* was cancelled the season after the main character came out as a lesbian, it opened up the possibility for more network depictions of LGBTQ characters. *Will & Grace* debuted in 1998, and while it was critiqued for its polar representations of gay men (i.e., bland and normative Will alongside

---

## Gay and Lesbian Intimacy in Soap Opera

Daytime soap operas are known for their scandalous and borderline ridiculous storylines, yet restrained and conservative style and audiences. Soap operas featured LGBTQ characters on and off, starting in the late-twentieth century. Gay and lesbian characters usually had to come out to other characters, allowing them to explain their identities to viewers as well. These characters sometimes had love interests, but physical intimacy between individuals was limited. It was not until recently that gay and lesbian characters on soap operas could show affection with one another. The first lesbian kiss happened in 2003, on *All My Children*. The first kiss between two men was on *As the World Turns* in 2007.

While gay and lesbian characters were known to have sex, the sex scenes rarely appeared on screen, as they would have for heterosexual couples. For example, *As the World Turn*'s Luke Snyder and Noah Mayer (portrayed by Van Hansis and Jake Silbermann, respectively) were implied to have had sex in January 2009. The two are seen kissing in the bedroom, and then the scene cuts away. Their next scene shows them with their shirts off, suggesting that they had sex. *All My Children*'s Bianca Montgomery (portrayed by Sarah Livingstone), came out late in 2000, kissed another woman in 2003, and did not have sex until 2011—with Marissa Tasker (portrayed by Sarah Glendening). Similar to the scene between Luke and Noah, Bianca and Marissa are seen in a hotel room kissing on a bed while mostly clothed, the scene ends, and in the next scene, they are seen in the same room, but wearing bathrobes.

The first same-sex sex scene was shown on December 30, 2009, between *One Life to Live*'s Oliver Fish and Kyle Lewis (portrayed by Scott Evans and Brett Claywell, respectively). This scene followed soap opera conventions: even for heterosexual couples, sex in soap operas is filmed to emphasize intimacy, featuring close-ups of faces to highlight gazes and kissing, and hands caressing the body. For the scene between Oliver and Kyle, sex also involved close-ups of kissing, and then close-ups of lit candles with blurry bodies in the background, and ending with the two characters lying in bed with the covers pulled down just enough to show shirtless bodies.

the stereotypical sissy Jack), it garnered popular and critical success, and ran for eight seasons (Hilton-Morrow & Battles, 2015). With the success of *Will & Grace*, other networks have also attempted to build comedies around an LGBTQ character, such as *Some of My Best Friends* (2001), *Normal, Ohio* (2000), *The New Normal* (2012), *Partners* (2012), *The McCarthys* (2014–2015), and *The Real O'Neals* (2016–2017). These shows, however, often relied either on stereotypical humor, or storylines specifically about combating stereotypes, and have been canceled.

Ensemble cast shows featuring gay or lesbian main characters, such as *Thirtysomething* (1987–1991), *My So-Called Life* (1994–1995), *Buffy the Vampire Slayer* (1997–2003), *Happy Endings* (2011–2013), and *Glee* (2009–2015), have more successfully incorporated LGBTQ narratives, but without as much pressure to create only LGBTQ-focused content. In particular, *Modern Family* (2009-present) consistently features LGBTQ-related storylines, although it has been criticized for stereotypical characters (effeminate gay men), and for showing LGBTQ life as homonormative: the gay couple get married, adopt a child, and are comfortably middle class (with even wealthier family members) (Feiler, 2011; D'Addario, 2013).

Expanded cable and premium pay channels, such as HBO, Showtime, Starz, and Here! TV, can show more diverse content than network channels, but they are still confined by general FCC broadcasting standards and practices and the social mores of the times (Benshoff & Griffin, 2009, p. 341). In the 1980s HBO considered developing the book, *Tales of the City*, by Armistead Maupin, which prominently featured LGBTQ characters, but backed out because of the conservative political climate and the HIV/AIDS crisis. PBS eventually co-produced a miniseries based on the book with Channel 4 (UK-based) in 1994. PBS received so much backlash for the show's nudity, homosexuality, and swearing, that the publicly-funded station backed out of producing or distributing any sequels based on Maupin's books. This pushed production of the two sequels (*More Tales of the City* [1998] and *Further Tales of the City* [2001]) to Montreal, Canada, and they were distributed by Showtime. In 2017 digital subscription service Netflix announced that it would develop a new series based on Maupin's recent *Tales of the City* novels.

With increased mainstream acceptance in the 2000s, expanded cable and premium channels produced shows that centered on LGBTQ characters, where all of the protagonists were LGBTQ-identified. Shows such as *Queer as Folk* (2000–2005), *The L Word* (2004–2009), and *Noah's Arc* (2005–2007) explored LGBTQ issues with less explanation, since the characters in the shows were already out and primarily interacted with each other. More recently, HBO's *Looking* (2014–2015) focused on the lives of gay men, but received mixed reviews from critics because of what appeared to be a lack of diversity in the characters and narratives. Some critics disliked that the show's first season focused on the lives of white, cisgender gay men, ignoring the diversity of LGBTQ life in San Francisco—the show's location (Lang, 2013).

## "Reality" Television

Unscripted television, or "reality TV," allegedly presents authentic people on screen. Reality television may give the impression of truthful and authentic representations of queer identities, but producers are still trying to make good entertainment. In other words, even in reality television, performers are performing and shows are designed and edited to show certain types of narratives.

During the late-twentieth century, LGBTQ people could be found as subjects and guests on daytime talk shows. Especially popular during the late 1980s and the 1990s, shows such as *Donahue*, *The Oprah Winfrey Show*, *The Maury Show*, and *Ricki Lake*, featured episodes about LGBTQ people. These shows attempted to explain gender and sexual identity: the host and studio audience members could ask guests questions directly, and receive unfiltered responses. While the LGBTQ guests on the stage were often presented as freaks, they were in a forum where they could allegedly respond for themselves (Gamson, 1998). These shows also, however, became notorious for letting audience members ask questions that would otherwise seem inappropriate (Gamson, 1998).

As a sub-genre of documentaries, television docudramas create a sense of familiarity with the subjects by pacing their material over multiple episodes. In the 1973, 12-episode, docudrama *An American Family*, Lance Loud became one of the first gay characters on television when he came out to his family. Later, Pedro Zamora would star in MTV's *The Real World: San Francisco* (1994), already identifying as gay and open about being HIV-positive. Zamora's storylines dealt with his castmates' homophobia and misconceptions about HIV/AIDS. In most current docudramas, LGBTQ people (predominantly gay men) are supporting characters. In the Bravo *Real Housewives* franchise, even when some of the housewives have come out as bisexual or have had relationships with women, these relationships are usually not featured. For example, Kim Zolciak (*The Real Housewives of Atlanta*) and DJ Tracy Young dated in 2010, but this was never included in the show, in part at Young's request. The relationship also ended quickly, leading critics to speculate whether Zolciak was using her bisexual identity to gain press coverage (Voss, 2010; Reality Tea, 2010; Kregloe, 2010).

Although reality television is ostensibly more "authentic," docudramas complicate the idea of reality: by the 2010s audiences have become aware that while some of the reactions shown are unscripted, the situations and characters shown are not necessarily authentic. The structure of *The Real L Word* (2010–2012) combined the concepts of a *Real Housewives* show and Showtime's scripted *The L Word* (2004–2009). Critics found the show entertaining, but not a real documentary into lesbian lives (Goodman, 2010; Cauterucci, 2012). Similarly, Bravo's *The A-List* (2010–2011), emphasized conflicts between the stars. Caitlyn Jenner's *I Am Cait* (2015–2016), also faced scrutiny, as many saw it as a spin-off of the popular show, *Keeping Up with the Kardashians*. Ironically, the first season received mixed reviews in part because there was not enough drama for television (Hale, 2015). For the second season, Jenner was provided with several transgender activists as co-stars, offering different perspectives into transgender issues, notably debates about U.S. partisan politics. More successfully blending representation of LGBTQ issues with TV-style drama, *I Am Jazz* (started 2015) follows transgender teenager Jazz Jennings and her family (Poniewozik, 2015).

Lifestyle reality shows—home improvement, cooking, or makeover shows— have frequently featured gay and lesbian hosts or guests. With hosts, these shows

## Drag Performances in Media

In twentieth-century U.S. popular culture, drag, a form of crossdressing and performance, has often been depicted as a part of gay male culture. In film and television, drag queens (males who dress and perform as women) have often been conflated with gay men and positioned as the object of jokes.

In the film *To Wong Foo, Thanks for Everything! Julie Newmar* (1995) three drag queens drive cross-country and have a run-in with a sheriff who discovers they are not women when he attempts to sexually assault them. The queens get away, but their car breaks down in a small town where they befriend, and give makeovers to, the townspeople. The sheriff eventually finds them, but the townspeople, who are now dressed flamboyantly, defend their new friends. As in other mainstream films, *To Wong Foo* was not an accurate portrayal of drag queens: the queens stay in drag for almost the entire film and, ultimately, the film depicts drag queens as freaks. However, it did attempt to make gay men and drag queens accessible to a broader audience (Kohn, 2015).

Documentary films have been more careful to present drag cultures on their own, distinct from other aspects of the LGBTQ community. *Wigstock: The Movie* (1987; 1995), two documentary films about a New York City drag festival, featured performances, behind-the-scenes footage of rehearsals, and interviews with drag queens. *Gendernauts* (1999) and *Venus Boyz* (2002) documented the lives of drag king performers. *Paris is Burning* (1990) shed light on the family structures of drag "houses" in New York City's African-American drag ball scene. *Paris is Burning* also showcased vogueing, a dance-style further popularized in mainstream media by the iconic music video for Madonna's song *Vogue* (1990). *Kiki* (2016) examined more recent forms of ballroom culture in New York City, highlighting how ideas about gender fluidity have changed the look of the ballroom scene.

The TV series *RuPaul's Drag Race* (2009–) shows drag queens in a contest environment with challenges including photoshoots, joke telling, "throwing shade" (i.e., a form of insult), and lip synching to music. The host, RuPaul Andre Charles, and the contestants appear both in and out of drag, showing the process and work of transforming into a drag queen. The show's success suggests one way that queer-developed media with a queer point of view can reach mainstream audiences.

sometimes maintain the stereotype of queer people being arbiters of taste and fashion. In shows, such as *Queer Eye for the Straight Guy* (2003–2007), the hosts serve as cultural experts, capable of making over homes and people. While most lifestyle shows focus on the idea that hosts must exude personality, gay and lesbian hosts could be seen as stereotypical archetypes: stylish men with flair (e.g., Tim Gunn, Jeff Lewis, Brad Goreski, Ted Allen, Clinton Kelly), or tough lesbians (e.g., Anne Burrell, Cat Cora, Tabatha Coffey). Granted, in most of these shows, gender or sexual identity are not the hosts' primary qualifications; information about the hosts usually comes from interviews and press releases. As guests, queer people appear as ordinary members of society, and noticeably without comment or fanfare. Gay and lesbian people (often as couples) are regularly featured on HGTV's real estate and home improvement shows such as *House Hunters* and *House Hunters International*, and Food Network shows, such as *Worst Cooks in America* and *Chopped*.

Gay and bisexual identities have been used as gimmicks for romance-oriented competition shows. In 2003 Bravo produced *Boy Meets Boy*, a reality dating show similar to ABC's *The Bachelor*, in which participants competed for the affections of James Getzlaff. The competition, however, included a twist: only half of the suitors were gay. If James picked a gay suitor, he and the suitor would win a prize. If James picked a straight suitor, however, the suitor would win a prize. Viewers and critics disliked this twist for trivializing sexual identity, and the show was canceled after one season (Moylan, 2016). Similarly, MTV's *A Shot of Love with Tila Tequila* (2007–2008) had both men (straight) and women (lesbians) competing for a relationship with Tequila, who identified as bisexual. This show, however, used bisexuality more as a form of titillation; a way to keep the audience guessing the outcome. *Finding Prince Charming* (2016), another gay *Bachelor*-like program, also received mixed reviews. Critics noted that although the contestants represented a range of gay men in terms of race, body-type, and gendered mannerisms, the show came off as too contrived, and they anticipated that suitors selected to provide diversity/variety would be cut early (Hankinson, 2016).

## Online Viewing: Challenging Legacy Media Forms and Production

In legacy media—film, TV, and print—the issue of representation matters because communication is unidirectional: from media text to audience. Legacy media audiences also have fewer choices, since only certain films appear in theaters or are available in home-video format, newspaper editors choose the stories, and television channels limit their content. Digital formats and online distribution have made bringing LGBTQ content to consumers easier and faster. News can be posted online much more quickly than print. Advertising can also be more widespread, while simultaneously more targeted: online ads can be randomly selected, although through content tagging and algorithms applied to browser histories, consumers can receive more ads meant for LGBTQ audiences.

Online distribution, including through mobile media technologies, have also privatized access to LGBTQ content. Viewers do not need to go to a film festival, to the movie theater, or even a video rental store in hopes that the store will have LGBTQ titles. Streaming services changed film and television industries by providing consumers with a more direct channel to accessing content. Studios that distribute LGBTQ content, such as Wolfe Media and Here! TV, provide content through direct-subscription or Video On Demand (VOD). This form of distribution creates more opportunities for filmmakers to share their content and receive feedback through ratings and comments.

Large streaming services, such as Netflix, Amazon, and Hulu, have also become channels for LGBTQ content. Initially operating as cable television providers, these three services have also become studios, funding new TV-style content and films. While the programs are still rated, they are not subject to the same conditions and regulations as programs that appear on television networks. Shows such as *Orange is the New Black* (2013–) and *Sense8* (2016–2017) on Netflix, and *Transparent* (2014–) on Amazon prominently feature LGBTQ characters and have been critically acclaimed. These studios are also willing to take risks. Jill Soloway, the creator of *Transparent*, has openly discussed her efforts—with studio support—to hire transgender performers and writers (McDonald, 2015). This has meant giving people with less industry experience a chance in order to promote and produce more accurate representations of LGBTQ lives.

On a smaller, and more affordable scale, many filmmakers are also creating short films or web series, posted on sites such as YouTube or Vimeo, sometimes for free or for a small fee. While some sharing sites have some rules about sexual content (e.g., YouTube does not permit most nudity or hardcore sex), others (such as Vimeo) are less restrictive, allowing filmmakers to be more frank and honest in their work. This freedom also has encouraged more content about non-gay male—the LBTQ—communities: narratives about lesbians (*Between Women*, *Into Girls*, *The Chanticleer*), transgender people (*Her Story*, *Eden's Garden*, *Crave*) and bisexuals (*The Feels*) have received more notice as web series. This has also produced new channels through which young media professionals can have their work recognized and funded for further development. For example, in 2016 Noam Ash successfully raised enough money and interest to turn his web series, *My Gay Roommate* (2012–2014), into a television show (Nichols, 2016).

## PORNOGRAPHY

While pornography's general function, similar to erotica's, is to titillate and arouse its audience, it also teaches its audience about what kinds of bodies and acts can be sexy. With few or no social structures that model queer genders and sexualities, LGBTQ people may turn to pornography to learn about sex and explore their desires. Up until the 1980s gay and lesbian pornographic magazines and films were the main media texts depicting nude models, homosexual sex, and more positive narratives about and for gays and lesbians. Along with its limited view of LGBT sexuality, a major problem with pornography was about access.

In the twentieth century gay and lesbian pornography was difficult to access because of social mores defining sex as a private act not meant for documentation or distribution. What makes something pornographic is a moral and legal code that defines an erotic text/image as obscene. The definition is often left up to the courts to decide, and even then it changes over time. In *Jacobellis v. Ohio* (1964), Supreme Court Justice Potter Stewart famously stated, "I know it when I see it," as his test for obscene materials not protected by the First Amendment. Until the 1970s homosexuality was also socially unacceptable and depictions of homosexual acts were illegal.

A simple hierarchy of sexual obscenity in the U.S. can be briefly summarized in the following order (progressing in obscenity): nude figures (male chest < bare buttocks < breasts < genitals), nude people together and touching, oral sex, vaginal penetration, anal penetration, sex involving themes/kinks/props. Images of women were considered less obscene than images of men, and gay sex was more obscene than heterosexual sex or lesbian sex, making gay pornography harder to access than heterosexual pornography (Mitchell & Fitzgerald, 1998; Shamama, Leon, & Stabile, 2015). Because cisgender, heterosexual men are considered the main audience of pornography, this hierarchy mostly protected the desires of heterosexual male viewers. This moral hierarchy also established that men are supposed to look, not be looked at.

*Photographs of young, athletic, male nudes—like this ca. 1900 example—sidestepped obscenity laws with claims to be "artistic" or "physical culture" studies. In practice, they often enjoyed decades of underground circulation among bisexual and gay men. In the mid-twentieth century, publishers of physical culture (or "beefcake") magazines brought such images to an even wider audience of bi and gay men. Source: Wellcome Collection (London) #L0034531/CC BY 4.0 license.*

Men do appear in heterosexual pornography, but these performers serve as stand-ins for the viewer; they guide the viewer through experiencing sexual pleasure, with ejaculation as the climax. In gay male pornography, however, male performers serve as both the guides for the viewer and the objects of desire. In the 1940s and 1950s beefcake photography featured young, muscular men posing nude or nearly nude. Unlike physique photography, these photos were designed to admire the figure not as feats of muscular strength and work, but as sexual objects (Hooven, 1995). One pose that Bob Mizer (a beefcake photographer and the publisher of the beefcake magazine *Physique Pictorial* [1951–1990]) popularized was the male figure reclined with hands folded behind the head. With the body reclined, the pose still displayed some musculature, but from a more vulnerable position (Pronger, 1992). This style of posing became a standard in gay pornography, and is still used today. Gay pornographic films also challenge viewers to not assume gendered sex roles. Effeminate men can be the active partner, masculine acting men can be penetrated, and both are shown experiencing pleasure.

Although gay pornography changes the intended object of desire by featuring only men, men are still the intended audience. Lesbian pornography, however, is more complicated. A lot of commercially produced magazines and videos featuring women having sex with one another are produced by and for heterosexual men. These films and images—also known as pseudo-lesbian pornography—show women experiencing sexual pleasure in ways that are pleasurable for men to watch. Whether the women actually find the types of sex represented pleasurable is not the point. Pseudo-lesbian pornography shows women having sex with each other in the ways that heterosexual men fantasize it. The films focus on visuals of genitals and penetration (using sex toys), and a narrative that ends with some form of visible orgasm, mimicking heterosexual pornographic films. Most of the women in these films are hyper-feminine, and some also appear in heterosexual pornography. These films turn heterosexual male viewers into voyeurs, and simply increase the number of women for men to watch.

Displeased that pseudo-lesbian pornography's primary audience was heterosexual men, some lesbians in the 1970s and 1980s wanted to make pornography a tool to explore women's sexual pleasure. Susie Bright, Debi Sundahl, and Myrna Elana started the lesbian pornographic magazine *On Our Backs* (*OOB*) in 1984 to create porn by and for lesbians. Until 2006 *OOB* published articles, pornographic stories, and photospreads. *OOB*, and other subsequently published lesbian porn magazines, showed women enjoying sex with one another, and showed more variety in gendered bodies, featuring butch (masculine) and femme (feminine) women. Stories and photospreads also did not mimic heteronormative gender roles: butches were not simply replacements for men. Femmes could be paired together, as could butches. *OOB* was also known for including stories about and images of women engaging in BDSM, which some feminist critics identified as male-oriented and anti-woman.

Lesbian-produced pornographic films also challenge expected gender roles and sexual acts, namely not relying on penetration as the major activity. Scripts often include mention of emotions other than lust and desire. Some lesbian viewers, however, find that the focus on emotions, rather than sexual acts, renders the sex uninteresting to watch. In other words, many women's viewing practices come from first watching heterosexual or pseudo-lesbian pornography, and they respond sexually to seeing those pornographic conventions. Some lesbians and bisexual women also prefer to watch gay male pornography: it does not feature problematic representations of women, as found in straight pornography, and the male-oriented and styled representations of sex and desire can be familiar and arousing (Morrison & Tallack, 2005).

Like pseudo-lesbian pornography, many films featuring transgender women became niche, or fetish, markets for heterosexual male audiences. Films featuring transgender women having sex with cisgender men rose in popularity during the 1990s, coinciding with several mainstream films and television shows featuring transgender women, male crossdressers, and drag queens as "women with a surprise" (i.e., women with penises) (Escoffier, 2011). The women in these films mostly appear as receptive sexual partners, keeping the cisgender men as dominant partners. While these films are perhaps queer by virtue of featuring non-cisgender performers, the films also still feature gender norms that arouse straight men. The women have large breasts and are hyper-feminine, and the films feature close-ups of penetration and are filmed from the point of view of the male performer.

Starting in the 2000s transgender porn filmmakers and performers tried to move away from presenting transgender bodies as a form of fetish. These films, which often present a mixture of transgender and cisgender performers, do not explain the performers' bodies and preferences, nor do performers' gender presentations predict upcoming roles during sex. Buck Angel, a trans male pornographer, presents as hyper-masculine, often with the look of a biker. In his films, he performs with cisgender men, women, and other trans performers, presents himself as either dominant or submissive, and uses different sex toys with his partners as well as himself. Angel has also appeared in gay male porn, challenging what constitutes a male or masculine body.

*Adult film actor, producer, activist, and motivational speaker Buck Angel (2010). Source: Photo by Buck Angel/ CC BY-SA 3.0 license. Image courtesy Buck Angel Entertainment and Wikimedia Commons.*

## Race and Gay Pornography

LGBTQ pornography also reflects other significant forms of identity-based stereotypes in society, such as race. This is clearly seen in U.S.-produced gay pornography, in which most performers are white men. Men of color who appear are often presented in stereotypical ways. Filmmaker and scholar Richard Fung (1991) argued that gay pornography in the 1970s and 1980s reflected racism in society and other forms of media: "If we look at commercial gay sexual representation, . . . the images of men and male beauty are still of white men and white male beauty" (p. 149).

By the late 1980s, most U.S. porn studios featured similar looking men. Chuck Holmes, founder of Falcon Studios, a prominent gay porn studio, wanted performers who represented the "All-American" male: "clean-cut" men who were predominantly white, college-aged, muscular, blond haired, and without body hair. In early Falcon Studio films and other gay pornography studios, people of color were scarce. The few black performers performed as tops (the active role) with white men, matching stereotypical film images of black men being animalistic, sexually ravenous, and predatory.

Asian men in U.S.-based gay pornography are usually bottoms (the receptive role) to their white partners. Even as tops, however, their characters are often submissive (Nguyen, 2014). In *Fortune Nookie* (1998), white performer and "lawyer," Jacob Scott suggests that Asian performer, Brandon Lee have sex with him in lieu of paying lawyer's fees. Scott directs Lee to strip, then challenges him to have sex "like a man." During sex, Scott tells Lee what to do, and calls him, "boy." Lee ultimately fulfills Scott's demands and desires (Nguyen, 2014).

Pornography's race-related and racist imageries are constructed by filmmakers, and then interpreted and then possibly re-enacted by audiences (Fung, 1991; Han, 2015). Filmmakers, critics, academics, and performers have proposed several solutions. One method is to simply increase representation by producing or distributing more porn featuring people of color. Some porn distributors import pornography from other countries, such as Japan, Thailand, and Brazil. This approach, however, simply replicates the idea that the men of color are foreign and a niche market.

Another solution is to have more people of color in charge of the production process. PeterFever.com features mostly Asian men from the U.S., other men of color, and occasionally white men. Producer Peter Le is an adult model, and is aware of Asian male sexuality stereotypes seen in both gay and straight pornography (Smith, 2013). Studios such as PeterFever.com feature men doing different power roles, challenging stereotypical assumptions about the types of sexual activities men of color perform.

*The cast of season 8 of The Asiancy (Peter Fever Productions, 2014), an all-Asian gay pornography film series. Source: Peter Fever Productions.*

Digital media has facilitated a general increase in diversity in pornography. Since porn is cheaper to produce and distribute online, types of pornography that were previously considered underground or intended for niche markets are now easier to find and access. More user-generated, amateur pornography is also being produced and distributed. Webhosts such as Xtube, Pornotube, and Redtube mimic YouTube, by allowing people to upload videos of themselves on camera. Amateur content frequently features narratives, sexual acts, and bodies that are not found in studio-produced pornography. Video tags give users more control over how to label identities and activities.

# SOCIAL IMPACTS: PLAYING AND WORKING TOGETHER

## Creating Communities by Finding Films

Today, online media distributes most LGBTQ content in films, TV, and text. For producers, digital production and online distribution is cheaper and faster, and for LGBTQ audiences, new and mobile media technologies allow for more private and easy access to LGBTQ content. But before home and mobile media technologies existed, accessing LGBTQ content, particularly in films, was a method and reason to gather. Individuals found each other as fans of the same films, or created the LGBTQ content that they wanted to see.

For gay men, pornography created a particular form of public visibility, one that perhaps linked the public perception of gay men to a form of legally problematic sexual perversion. In the early twentieth century, erotic photographs depicting nudity and sexual activity were difficult to purchase, often from "special drawers in special rooms in special shops" (Waugh, 1996, p. 289). Early films, before the 1960s, were often shown in semi-private screenings at people's homes (Mitchell & Fitzgerald, 1998). Although pornography was usually viewed in private, shops that carried gay pornographic magazines and films created physical spaces where gay men could find one another. In the 1960s and 1970s, pornographic films were more widely distributed through XXX theaters, or in single-stall booths. These theaters became semi-public spaces for men to have sex—from mutual masturbation to intercourse (semi-public because these were businesses that technically could control who entered). Today, however, technology has created more private and mobile access to porn, which has eliminated, for a lot of people, the need for public venues, leading to the closure of many porn theaters and shops.

Though designed for a different purpose, LGBTQ film festivals, which started in the 1970s, also made LGBTQ content and people visible in public. While not all attendees were LGBTQ-identified, they were openly supporting LGBTQ content and filmmakers. For LGBTQ filmmakers festivals provide professional exposure, and opportunities to meet potential funders and distributors for their films. Frameline, the oldest exclusively LGBTQ film distributor, which started the Frameline Film Festival in 1977, often distributed films featured in its festival. Wolfe Video, another exclusively LGBTQ film distributor, founded in 1985, also works with festivals, as do other smaller distributors of independent films willing to include LGBTQ content, such as Strand Releasing and TLA Releasing.

Film festival planners often consider representation issues within LGBTQ communities. Since much of the queer content developed in the past 70 years has focused on gay men, film festival organizers often try to ensure that different groups within LGBTQ communities are represented, namely lesbians and transgender people. Some festivals (around the world, the U.S. included) even create quotas to ensure that the types of identity-based content, such as gender, sexual identity, and race, are more evenly represented (Magdalinou, Torneden, & Grillo, 2014).

Attempts to make different parts of LGBTQ communities evenly represented in film festivals are not always successful. Gender Reel held its first festival in 2011 in Philadelphia to address a lack of visibility of films dealing with transgender, gender non-conforming, and gender variant/queer experiences and issues. In addition to holding a "traditional" film festival, Gender Reel also holds mini-festivals as part of other events such as the Philadelphia Trans-Health Conference (June, 2016), and hosts online streaming of selected films when possible.

## The "It Gets Better" Project

In 2010 several teens in the U.S. committed suicide after being bullied for being or perceived as being gay. While LGBTQ teens suffer from higher rates of suicide than non-LGBTQ youth, the cases in 2010 received national press attention. In response, LGBTQ activist Dan Savage and his husband, Terry Miller, uploaded a video to YouTube, imploring LGBTQ teens to not commit suicide because "It Gets Better."

Soon after Savage posted his video, other YouTube users who were members of LGBTQ communities made similar videos, which Savage then turned into a campaign. The videos were eventually posted and archived through a central It Gets Better website and, in 2011, selected participants' stories were edited and published as a book. The narrative structure of the videos is simple: most videos tell personal stories, noting struggles with bullying because of LGBTQ identity, and then some form of resolution that leads to the advice to not commit suicide because "It Gets Better" (Savage, 2011).

As the campaign grew, video makers included celebrities—both LGBTQ and non-LGBTQ identified—and organizations. Several government officials, including then-U.S. President Barack Obama made videos, which was seen as part of a governmental response to what seemed like an increase in known cases of suicide related to LGBTQ-identity-based bullying. Organizations, such as professional sports teams and businesses, also made *It Gets Better* videos, which was sometimes a challenging task. Many of the videos associated with companies were spearheaded by employees who were LGBTQ-identified, not the companies themselves, and frequently required company approval. In other words, *It Gets Better* videos from companies and larger organizations had to be consistent with the organizations' own ideologies and mission statements, and people' stories were either lost or made less specific.

Conservative critics complained that the campaign promoted homosexuality and gender confusion (e.g., Hasson, 2011). Some LGBTQ critics argued that the campaign was too normative, particularly with Savage and Miller's example of "better" being a life with a monogamous partner, children, and financial stability (Goltz, 2013). Academic researchers, however, also found that many users defined the term better differently: better was more general and meant the possibility a life that was different from what was expected (West, Frischherz, Panther, & Brophy, 2013). Better simply means life, not death.

## User-Based Production and Social Networking

New media technologies have increased opportunities for forming queer communities. The cheaper production equipment and distribution channels of digital media can democratize media production: through writing blogs and produced video content LGBTQ people are sharing information with more ease. For those nervous or wary of being associated with the LGBTQ community in a public space like a gay bar, digital media permits direct communication with people anonymously, as in message boards and chat rooms (common in the 1990s and early 2000s), and today through different social media apps. Because LGBTQ people need to find one another on their own (i.e., they are not always introduced to each other through their families), being able to search independently online is important.

Social networking sites (SNS) not only facilitate communication, but they make interpersonal communication layered and more complex. By mixing different forms of communication (e.g., text, sound, and video), social networking sites such as Facebook, YouTube, Twitter, and Instagram allow for promotion of content, and they reframe modes of communication. Profile-based sites such as Facebook also become spaces for contesting identity categories. In 2014 Facebook created over 50 different options for "gender," providing users with more than "male," "female," and "other" (Weber, 2014). Some SNSs, such as Yik Yak and Whisper, allegedly keep user information suppressed, suggesting that users may share their thoughts and ideas anonymously. The gay blog *Queerty*, for example, regularly examines Whisper posts to see if people are anonymously sharing their experiences as LGBTQ people, or admitting to opinions about LGBTQ issues that might be unpopular in more mainstream forms of press, including the gay presses.

SNSs also offer queer people opportunities to describe their thoughts and themselves in their own terms. YouTube serves as the main platform for story-based campaigns, such as *It Gets Better*, or *I'm From Driftwood*. Tumblr, in particular, has been an important space for conversations about transgender issues. Tumblr's structure puts blog posts directly in conversation with one another publicly, making it easy for people to find information, and even join in with a community if they choose (Haimson, 2017). Unlike Facebook, Tumblr does not require authentication of identity—the use of "real" names and gender identity that correspond to one's birth certificate. This also allows for more anonymous participation: users who are not ready to come out publicly can explore ideas about gender identity with less fear about being found out.

## Personal Ads and Dating Apps

Because they have had fewer public methods and spaces safe from discrimination, LGBTQ people have relied on media technologies to find one another, especially for romantic and sexual encounters. In the second half of the twentieth century, LGBTQ people—predominantly men—frequently used newspaper personal ads to find one another. By the early 2000s newspaper published personal ads in print and online. Sites such as craigslist also replicated the newspaper personal advertisement format, only for free, without space constraints, and allowing photographs. There were also online-specific spaces such as message boards and chatrooms tailored to LGBTQ groups (Campbell, 2004).

## Women's Roller Derby

Women's flat track roller derby, which began in the early 2000s as a do-it-yourself, grassroots effort, has helped create an inclusive environment for women of different sexualities, gender expressions, body types, and social backgrounds (Finley, 2010). The Women's Flat Track Derby Association strictly prohibits discrimination based on sexuality or gender identity/expression. It also allows for transgender, gender non-conforming, and intersex athletes to participate, so long as the team is closely in line with their identity (WFTDA, 2014).

Since sexual minority and gender variant women continue to be discriminated against within sport and physical activity (e.g., sex-verification testing, focus on women athletes' appearance, or roles as wives and mothers), sports like roller derby challenge traditional gender and sexual norms that hold women back in sport and society as a whole.

Unlike mainstream sports in which women are often discouraged from being highly physical, roller derby celebrates aggression. Crashes and collisions between players are common, and many players view bruises or other injuries as a testament to their toughness (Finley, 2010).

Instead of a focus on body size, the strength and skill of players is emphasized. This has created an environment in which women of different body types feel accepted and valued (Carlson, 2010). Players often take on a derby persona through their style of dress (e.g., fishnet stockings, short shorts, fake [or real] bruises and tattoos) and derby name (e.g., Lady Pain). Through these performances, which mix elements of masculinity and femininity, the players reject heteronormative expectations for women's appearance and behavior (Carlson, 2010).

One popular derby ritual is that of taking on a derby wife. Although derby wives/marriages are often non-sexual, they question norms of heterosexuality by celebrating women's connections to other women (i.e., they do not need a man's support) and queering traditional marriage (Finley, 2010).

While derby can be seen as empowering for gender and sexual minority women, there are limits to its subversive potential. The do-it-yourself nature of the sport, for instance, places considerable financial and time demands on players, which can exclude women without such resources (Beaver, 2012). Also, the highly-sexual attire of derby players may be personally fulfilling, but it can send the message that derby is not a serious sport and that women's bodies—rather than their athletic skill—is the central feature of the sport (Parry, 2016).

*Julie Maier*

In the mid–2000s several social media sites focusing on gay and lesbian users, such as Gay.com and PlanetOut.com, were developed. Blending the personal advertisement with matchmaking services, social media sites had gay and lesbians create online profiles that provided more space and freedom to describe themselves than print newspaper personal ads, while simultaneously limiting identities to required fields and often drop-menu options. Websites allowed for more specific interests and intentions, such as men's sites Manhunt.com and Adam4Adam.com, which were known for casual sexual encounters. Lesbian online dating sites such as Superdyke.com, often emphasized the possibility of relationships for more than casual sex.

Grindr, a mobile social media application, launched for iPhones in 2009 and for Android devices in 2011. Using smartphone GPS technology, Grindr allows users to view profiles of other users based on live physical location (i.e., who is nearby). Grindr quickly rose to be a popular app for gay men, and soon became the inspiration for similar men's apps (Gudelunas, 2012), as well as mobile social media apps for other groups, such as HER, for women. Apps for heterosexual connections were later developed, such as Tinder and Bumble, although many LGBTQ people also use them. The apps simply focus on the gender of the users and their sought-after partners, whether men, women, or any. Interestingly, the apps for women, and the "straight" apps like Tinder are known more for dating, in contrast to the exclusively men's apps, which are known for casual sexual encounters (MacKee, 2016; Murray & Ankerson, 2016). Dating apps are also popular today in larger urban centers, where people may be moving in with fewer existing social networks—a social situation that mimics the lives of many LGBTQ people who leave their homes (often in smaller cities or towns) to find more people like themselves.

## Video Games

Video games and their connection to queer geek cultures are gaining visibility. While there are overlaps with popular culture spaces, such as Comic Conventions, video games are a more specific digital arena in which gender and sexualities play out.

Videogame culture has long been perceived as an arena reserved exclusively for teenage, cisgender, heterosexual males; however, women and LGBTQ-identified people have played for longer than people realized, and have more recently become acknowledged—both as players and in representation within the games themselves. As in other forms of media, representation is a major issue; historically, when the game's protagonist possessed a discernible gender, that gender was often male. As games have evolved, however, players have been given more diversity and control of the character or avatar they can use to navigate the game. In games where the player's avatar can be designed, having options such as gender and race can be simply fun, or, especially for women and LGBTQ players, something meaningful (Shaw, 2014). This wider variety of options finally addresses several issues mainstream players may not ever have thought about.

Until recently LGBTQ characters have occasionally appeared in video games, although often relegated to background characters, and usually based on stereotypes to make them explicitly queer, such as butch women or transgender prostitutes. Furthermore, role-playing games' narratives usually have rigid heteronormative expectations built into the storylines, such as flirtatious dialogue between characters, but only if they are in heterosexual couplings. Some games, however, have allowed for same-sex flirtations to take place. In the 2000s, games, such as *The Sims*, had unofficial ways for characters to have homosexual romances; and 2014's *Dragon Age: Inquisition* included a main playable character who was gay, though he did not have sex with the male non-player characters, as the straight male playable characters could with female non-player characters. Responses to these games have been mixed—some commenters question the need to announce and highlight LGBTQ characters and content (Baume, 2015). Again, many players are likely to be young, straight, white males, some of whom may be homophobic, others who may assume that LGBTQ representation is already established and normalized.

But there has been positive progress. For games that allow users to customize their avatars, players found ways to represent their own identities and impact how the games unfolded. Players' identities affected interactions with other characters in the games, and with other players in multi-player games (Shaw, 2014). In massively multiplayer online role-playing games, such as *EVE Online* or *World of Warcraft*, players sometimes experience the games differently by switching genders. Within these games, players also developed their own communities, and LGBTQ players often banded together. In *World of Warcraft*, the Stonewall Family Guild serves as an online space for LGBTQ players to meet up and form relationships, some of which extend offline.

Comics, gaming, and "nerd/geek-culture" enthusiasts frequently come together during conventions, and although large conventions such as San Diego's ComiCon may include LGBTQ-oriented activities, most are created by attendees themselves, which do not necessarily welcome all queer people. In contrast, queer-themed conventions prioritize making safer spaces for LGBTQ people, and they host panels that raise issues specific to LGBTQ players and game designers. GaymerX (which began in 2012) and Flame Con (a queer comic convention started in 2015) are organized by and for queer people. GaymerX draws in LGBTQ gaming fans and game developers, and focuses on promoting queer content and queer professionals. Flame Con is a queer comic convention, which includes discussions and participants interested in video games and queer geek culture. In 2016 Flame Con panels included, "Help! How Do I Write a Transgender or Non-Binary Character?", "Gaymers Webseries," "The Importance of Queer Erotica," and "Supergirl's Not Black!"—a panel "of all black and queer nerds . . . [exploring] the topic of cosplaying and the intersections of race, gender & sexual orientation." (That Jay Justice, 2016; Camacho, 2016). Like other conventions, queer convention attendees also participate in cosplay (costume play) parties, with more taking the opportunity to put queer twists on cosplay, often gender-flipping the costumes.

# CONCLUSION

Identifying LGBTQ content in media provides necessary validity to identities and relationships that are less publicly visible in mainstream society. Increased diversity of images can reduce the negative impact of stereotypes, and change how society sees LGBTQ communities. But queer media is more than just representing LGBTQ communities in media texts and products. Media technologies are communication tools that bring people together. This chapter ended with examples of how media technologies and products are the objects and facilitators of relationships between LGBTQ people. Media technologies simultaneously allow people to access LGBTQ content privately, and increase LGBTQ communities' public visibility. To borrow communication scholar Marshall McLuhan's phrase, "medium is the message," this chapter has demonstrated how the structures and technologies of the media industries have been integral to exploring and shaping LGBTQ communities. Media technologies are creating spaces and communication channels to help LGBTQ people connect and become socially and politically empowered.

## Learn More

### Readings

Aaron, M. (2004). *New queer cinema: A critical reader*. New Brunswick, NJ: Rutgers University.

Baim, T. (Ed.) (2012). *Gay press, gay power: The growth of LGBT community newspapers in America*. Chicago, IL: Prairie Avenue Productions and Windy City Media Group.

Benshoff, H. M., & Griffin, S. (2005). *Queer images: A history of gay and lesbian film in America*. Lanham, MD: Rowman & Littlefield.

Chasin, A. (2001). *Selling out: The gay and lesbian movement foes to market*. New York, NY: Palgrave Macmillan.

Escoffier, J. (2009). *Bigger than life: The history of gay porn cinema from beefcake to hardcore*. New York, NY: Running.

Hall, J. (2013). *No straight lines: Four decades of queer comics*. Seattle, WA: Fantagraphics.

Mayyasi, A. (2016, June 22). How Subarus came to be seen as cars for lesbians. *The Atlantic*. Retrieved from https://www.theatlantic.com/business/archive/2016/06/how-subarus-came-to-be-seen-as-cars-for-lesbians/488042/

Mercer, J. (2017). *Gay pornography: Representations of sexuality and masculinity*. New York, NY: I.B. Tauris.

Rich, B. R. (2013). *New queer cinema: The director's cut*. Durham, N.C.: Duke University.

Ruberg, B., & Shaw, A. (Eds.) (2017). *Queer game studies*. Minneapolis, MN: University of Minnesota.

Russo, V. (1987). *The celluloid closet (revised edition)*. New York, NY: Harper & Row.

Summers, C. (2004). *The queer encyclopedia of music, dance, and musical theatre*. Jersey City, NJ: Cleis.

Summers, C. (2005). *The queer encyclopedia of film and television*. Jersey City, NJ: Cleis.

Triptow, R. (1989). *Gay comics*. New York, NY: Plume.

Waugh, T. (2002). *Out/lines: Gay underground erotic graphics from before Stonewall*. Vancouver, BC: Arsenal Pulp.

Weiss, A. (1993). *Vampires and violets: Lesbians in film*. New York, NY: Penguin.

## Film/Video

Chisholm, C. (Director). (2016). *Pride denied: Homonationalism and the future of queer politics* [Documentary film]. Northampton, MA: Media Education Foundation.

Epstein, R., & Friedman, J. (Directors). (1996). *The celluloid closet* [DVD]. United States: HBO.

Fitzgerald, T. (Director). (1999). *Beefcake* [DVD]. United States: Strand Releasing.

Hinton, A. (Director). (2006). *Pick up the mic: The revolution of homo-hop* [DVD]. United States: Planet Janice.

Pohjola, I. (Director). (2003). *Daddy and the muscle academy* [DVD]. United States: Zeitgeist.

Schwarz, J. (Producer). (2011). *Vito [DVD]*. United States: First Run.

Sender, K., & Jhally, S. (Producers). (2006). *Further off the straight and narrow: New gay visibility on television, 1998–2006* [DVD]. Northampton, MA: Media Education Foundation.

Stabile, M. (2015). *Seed money: The Chuck Holmes story* [DVD]. United States: Breaking Glass.

## Internet

AdRespect (formerly The Commercial Closet): www.adrespect.org

GLAAD (Gay and Lesbian Alliance Against Defamation): www.glaad.org

Homoground—A Network of Queer Music and Media Creators: homoground.com

I'm From Driftwood—The LGBTQ Story Archive: www.imfromdriftwood.com

It Gets Better Project: www.itgetsbetter.org

NLGJA—The Association of LGBTQ Journalists: www.nlgja.org

Queer Music Heritage: www.queermusicheritage.com

Queer Music History 101: queermusicheritage.com/qmh101intro.html

# CHAPTER 8
# Signifying Queerness
## *Literature and Visual Art*

*Susan K. Thomas and William J. Simmons*

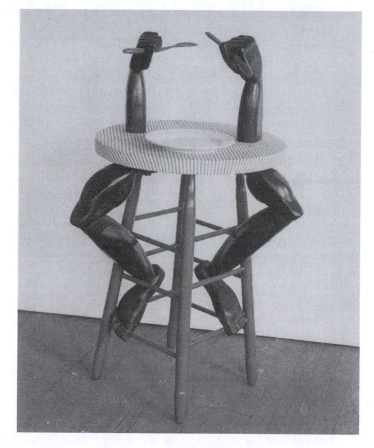

*Kate Millett,* Dinner for One, *1967, mixed media. Source: Estate of Kate Millett.*

From the earliest recorded history, words and images have been essential vehicles for human expression. Whether in the form of prehistoric fertility statuettes, Renaissance portraiture, modern poetry, or contemporary novels, literature and the visual arts have offered a means to transform the intangible into the tangible, which, in many ways, resembles LGBTQ experience. Through a focused process of introspection and articulation, the creation of art and literature allows personal traits such as gender identity and sexual orientation to be expressed and communicated to readers and viewers. But beyond individual expression, art and literature may also capture and record a society's collective sensibility about gender and sexuality—including minority gender identities and same-sex attractions—thus preserving it and making it available to future generations. As such, words and images can represent important resources for understanding the global history of gender variance and same-sex desire. The history of art and literature, alongside other forms of historical evidence, reveals that social attitudes about gender variance and same-sex desire have changed over time, with some societies being very accepting, even celebratory, while others being indifferent or repressive. It also shows that LGBTQ writers and artists persevered even in the most inhospitable familial, communal, or societal environments.

While it is not always possible to know if a writer or artist was same-sex attracted or gender variant, or identified as gay or transgender, art and literary historians have identified many, many texts and images with implicit or explicit themes of gender variance or same-sex desire. Some of these are now seen as essential to LGBTQ history, even though they may not have been viewed that way by their makers, or in the time or place where they were created. As such, it is not always easy to decide if such works or their makers should be characterized as gender non-conforming, homosexual, gay, etc. What, exactly, comprises LGBTQ history is a dynamic, evolving subject; so is the terminology used to describe it. This chapter is written from the perspective of the present day and describes art and literature that is now considered part of LGBTQ visual and literary history, therefore present-day terms are used to describe such works. The first half of the chapter describes major works, themes, and creators in LGBTQ literary history, with an emphasis on Europe and America, from antiquity through to the present day. The second half presents a similar overview of LGBTQ visual arts, such as painting, sculpture, photography, and related media.

## LITERATURE

There has not been a time that homoerotic literature has not existed beneath the larger umbrella of literature. Authors have used the genres of poetry, mythology, and prose to subtly (and at times, not so subtly) record their feelings and desires for same-sex lovers, or to live life as a different gender. Because of the persecution or opposition in many world cultures throughout history, queer individuals have turned to literature as a source of knowledge, validation, and comfort.

## Ancient Mythology and Classic Literature

Themes of love between members of the same sex exist in a variety of ancient texts throughout the world, drawing on heroic love between men who bond through the shared experience of battle. The affection between men often emerges through homoerotic undertones in these early works. The Ancient Greeks, and later the Romans, drew upon pederasty: romantic and sexual affection between older men and teenage boys.

The oldest surviving story is an Ancient Sumerian epic poem about a historical king who ruled the Mesopotamian city of Uruk in 2750 BCE. Written 1,000 years before Homer's *Iliad* or the Bible, *Gilgamesh* tells the story of a man who learns to temper his own emotions and actions, which turns him into a strong leader. The text also describes the friendship between the title character King Gilgamesh and Enkidu, a wild man who is tamed by a temple priestess. Although the poem does not explicitly state that Gilgamesh and Enkidu have a sexual relationship, the homoeroticism in the text is undeniable as the priestess Nikun tells Gilgamesh that after meeting Enkidu, "You will take him in your arms, embrace and caress him / The way a man caresses his wife" (Mitchell, 2004). While many literary critics have defined the relationship as homoerotic, historically, the text would have been a reflection of heroic love, a deep affection and respect between warriors.

Numerous mythologies and religious narratives include stories of romantic affection or sexuality between men or between male gods and men. There are also instances of divine action that results in a gender change. Critics often interpret these stories through a homoerotic lens, which may differ from the original culture's understanding of the stories. In classical mythology, the tradition of male lovers was credited to ancient Greek gods and heroes such as Zeus, Apollo, Poseidon, and Heracles (with Ganymede, Hyacinth, Nerites, and Hylas, respectively) to validate the tradition of pederasty, a same-sex relationship between an adult male and a pubescent or adolescent male, based on the consent of the boy. Pederasty was considered an educational institution in some cultures as the adult mentored the boy in that society's moral and cultural values (Freeman, 1999).

Although Homer (8th century BCE) did not portray the heroes Achilles and Patroclus as homosexual lovers in the *Iliad* (8th century BCE), later ancient authors, such as Aeschylus, presented the relationship as pederastic in *The Myrmidons*, writing of "our frequent kisses" and a "devout union of the thighs"

*The Sosias painter,* Achilles Binding the Wounds of Patroclus, *ca. 500 BCE, red-figure vase painting, Altes Museum (Berlin, Germany). Source: Photo by Bibi Saint-Pol. Image courtesy of Wikimedia Commons.*

(Crompton, 2003). Plato does the same in his work *Symposium* (385–370 BCE); Phaedrus cites Aeschylus and presents Achilles as an example of sacrificing oneself for a lover. *Symposium* also includes a creation myth that explains homosexuality and heterosexuality, and celebrates the pederastic tradition and erotic love between men (Woods, 1998).

In the *Symposium*, Aristophanes tells the creation myth to describe why people say that they feel whole when they have found their true love. He explains that in primal times, people had double bodies that looked like two people joined at the back, their faces and limbs turned away from each other. There were three sexes: the all-male, the all-female, and the androgynous, who were half male, half female. The people attempted to scale Olympus to set upon the gods. Zeus considered destroying them with thunderbolts, but not wanting to deprive himself of their devotions and offerings, cut them in half, separating the two bodies (Plato).

The tradition of pederasty in ancient Greece, and later the acceptance of limited homosexuality in ancient Rome, created an awareness of same-sex attraction between men and sex in ancient poetry. In the second of Virgil's *Eclogues* (1st century BCE), the shepherd Corydon proclaims his love for the boy Alexis. During the same century, some of Catullus's erotic poetry is directed at other men and his "Carmen 16" is considered to be one of the earliest examples of explicit sex acts between men (Woods, 1998).

Sappho (630/612–570 BCE) was a Greek lyric poet born on the island of Lesbos. (Lyric poetry is poetry meant to be read aloud accompanied by music played on a stringed instrument called a lyre.) Very little is known about Sappho's life, but her poetry was well-known and admired throughout much of antiquity. Subjects in Sappho's poetry vary. Some of her poems, such as "Fragment 16" and "Fragment 44," are lyric retellings of Homer epics (Rutherford, 1991). Several

*Group of Polygnotos,* Sappho (seated) reads one of her poems to a group of three student-friends, *ca. 440–430 BCE, red-figure vase painting, National Archaeological Museum (Athens, Greece), no. 1260. Source: Photo by Μαρσύας / CC BY-SA 2.5 license. Image courtesy of Wikimedia Commons.*

of her poems have themes of love, and would have been written to be performed as wedding poems, intended to be sung to the bride when she entered the nuptial chamber (Greene, 1996). Other poems appear to be odes from one woman to another, which has caused discussion regarding Sappho's sexuality and intentions within her work.

Sappho's sexual desire, whether for men or for women, has been debated for centuries. Today, she is a symbol of lesbianism and island where she lived (Lesbos) is the basis of the modern term lesbian. However, this has not always been so. In classic Athenian comedy Sappho was caricatured as a promiscuous heterosexual woman (Most, 1995). The first testimonia, or written documentation, that discuss Sappho's homoeroticism come from the Hellenistic period, but these ancient authors do not appear to have believed that Sappho had sexual relationships with other women (Rayor & Lardinois, 2014).

## Homosexuality and Biblical Allusions

The Judeo-Christian Bible has been used to both denounce and defend homosexuality. There are passages in the Old and New Testaments that appear to prohibit same-sex behavior, especially between men. Other passages describing romantic affection and homoeroticism between men have been interpreted as gay-themed and accepting of homosexuality.

In the latter half of the 20th century, scholars began to argue that the love between David and Jonathan reached further than platonic friendship. The story of David and Jonathan focuses on the close friendship that the two develop as youth after David has killed Goliath. "Now it came about when [David] had finished speaking to Saul, that the soul of Jonathan was knit to the soul of David, and Jonathan loved him as himself . . . Then Jonathan made a covenant with David because he loved him as himself" (1 Samuel 18, New JPS Translation). The traditional and mainstream interpretation of the relationship between the two men is platonic, an example of homosociality. The story of David and Jonathan is similar to that of Gilgamesh and Enkidu. Both relationships are between heroic and powerful men. Gilgamesh and David both have a love for the other man that is described as being stronger than that of a woman. Both Enkidu and Jonathan have untimely deaths. And both friendships can be read as homoerotic because of the close relationships that exist between the men as they put their love for each other above all else, even their love for women.

---

### Sodom and Gomorrah

The story of Sodom and Gomorrah is the best-known story in the Judeo-Christian Bible used to condemn homosexuality. The word sodomy, taken from Sodom, was coined by an English churchman to describe sex between men (Greenberg, 2004). The story is that God, knowing of the sin in Sodom, sent two angels disguised as men to the righteous man Lot, who welcomed the men, fed them and invited them to spend the night in his house. That night, the men of the city came to Lot's home and demanded he turn the visitors over to them so that they could have sex with them. Lot refused and offered his two virgin daughters instead. The men of the city once again insisted that Lot turn over his guests, but Lot again denied them. In the morning, the angels instructed Lot to take his family and flee the city, for God was going to destroy Sodom in fire and brimstone for its sins. Lot's family

*(continued)*

*(continued)*

was to take what they needed and flee to the hills without looking back. The family did as instructed but, as they fled, Lot's wife turned to look back at the destruction, only to be turned into a pillar of salt (Genesis 19:1–26, Tanakh).

Although the common perception is that the sin of Sodom was homosexuality, Jewish literature often rejects this reading (Greenberg, 2004). The text in the Book of Ezekiel cites Sodom's arrogance, and its inhospitality to both visitors and the poor, although the residents of the city had plenty to share (Ezekiel 16:49). Rabbinical scholars who authored the Talmud, a Jewish commentary on the oral Torah, describe the destruction of Sodom as the result of selfishness and an unwillingness to share their wealth with travelers (Tosefta Sotah 3:11–12).

Some biblical scholars argue that the use of the word *yada* (know), which is often used in the Hebrew bible to indicate carnal knowledge, reveals the intention of the men of Sodom to have same-sex relations with the angels. *Yada* is used in Genesis when Adam knew Eve, meaning that they had sexual intercourse (Genesis 4:1). If *yada* is translated as carnal knowledge, the implication is that the men of the city planned to rape the angels, a violent act of aggression that condemns the men of Sodom, not because it is same-sex rape, but because it is rape (Robinson, 2010). The rape of women would have been as abhorrent as homosexual rape. Additionally, the word *yada* exists in the Hebrew bible 900 times as meaning "to know" or "to interrogate," while "to know" as a euphemism for sexual intimacy is only used 13–14 times throughout the entire Hebrew scriptures (Hebrew frequency list, 2016). If this is the case, the men of Sodom sinned through their intent to interrogate the angels to learn their intentions and to avoid sharing personal wealth, which was inhospitable. Because Lot offered his two virgin daughters to the crowd in place of the angels, the translation of the word *yada* is more likely to be to know the angels sexually in the act of violent rape.

*Susan K. Thomas*

## The English Renaissance (15th–17th century CE)

The Renaissance was a cultural and artistic rebirth in Europe and England dating from the 14th century to the early 17th century. This period is often considered a cultural bridge between the Middle Ages and modern history. With the rediscovery of classical Greek philosophy, new thinking in Europe was reflected in art, architecture, politics, science, and literature. These changes in culture and art were reflected in England during the late 15th century. During the English Renaissance, gender divisions were substantial as women were considered inferior to men, and held subservient roles. Women were unable to hold property, and were expected to be under the safeguard of a male protector, either a husband or male family member, even when going out. Cross-dressing gave a woman a protection and independence that she did not otherwise possess by allowing her to leave the home and travel alone. However, cross-dressing was illegal for both men and women, as the Judeo-Christian Bible labeled it as a sin. Clergy delivered sermons against the practice during church services. The regulation of clothing produced and marked gender difference, although other cultural shifts were occurring. In the theater, cross-dressing was a necessity as women were not permitted to take the stage. Instead, young effeminate men often played the role of women. This was not a statement, but a comic tradition—playwrights often included the comic tradition of cross-dressing in their plays (Howard, 1988).

William Shakespeare (1564–1616) used the motif of cross-dressing as a subterfuge in seven of his plays by disguising women as men, and in all seven of those plays crossdressing both complicates and resolves the plot. This device creates a level of homoeroticism in the texts as the women often encounter their unknowing lovers while disguised as men, only later to reveal their true identities. In *As You Like It,* the character of Rosalind must disguise herself as a man, Ganymede, after being exiled from court. She flees with her friend, and daughter of the king, Celia, who is now disguised as a poor woman, to the Arcadian Forest of Arden, where they meet Orlando and his servant, Adam. Orlando is in love with Rosalind, and therefore is saddened at her exile. Rosalind is also in love with Orlando and, disguised as Ganymede, pretends to counsel Orlando to cure him of his love. Ganymede says that he will take Rosalind's place, and that he and Orlando can act out the relationship. Hilarity ensues when the young Phoebe falls in love with Ganymede (Rosalind). Over the course of the play, Ganymede convinces Orlando to promise to marry Rosalind. Ganymede then reveals himself as Rosalind to Orlando, and the two marry in the final scene of the play. The gender reversals in the story are of particular interest because Rosalind, who in Shakespeare's day would have been played by a boy, finds it necessary to impersonate a boy, who is then pursued by a young woman, who is played by a boy.

## 16th and 17th Century Europe

The period known as the Age of Enlightenment (1685–1815) permitted some challenge to traditional doctrines of society in Western Europe. Developments in industry allowed the production of consumer goods in greater quantities at lower prices, which encouraged the spread of books, pamphlets, and newspapers (Outram, 1995). With an increase in the dissemination of the printed word, literacy increased for both men and women (Darnton, 1985). In France, a waning of religious influence meant that the amount of literature about science and art increased (Petitfils, 2005). And while books were often too expensive for most to buy, readers accessed books through state-run libraries or by purchasing cheaply produced editions (Outram, 1995).

During this time, there was a renewed interest in the Classical era of Greece and Rome, allowing authors to allude to Greek mythological characters or to place their stories in Ancient Greece, where pederasty was common. Because the legal punishment for sodomy was death in some European countries and in England (and its colonies), it was dangerous to publish literature with overtly homosexual themes, which could result in an investigation of an author's personal life, potentially ruining their reputation and eliminating opportunities. Thus, authors often expressed homoerotic themes in coded language that only some readers would understand. This permitted authors to escape prosecution for obscenity and further investigation. Being too overt in writing would mean immediate suppression, as in the case of the text *Alcibiades the Schoolboy*, a satirical Italian dialogue published anonymously in 1652. The text, a written defense of homosexual sodomy and love between men, is set in ancient Athens. A teacher modeled after Socrates desperately wants to consummate the relationship with his student Alcibiades. He uses all the tactics of rhetoric and dishonesty at his disposal, arguing that Nature gave people sexual organs for their own pleasure, and that it would insult her to use them otherwise. Upon its publication, *Alcibiades* was suppressed for its explicit nature. Only ten copies of the text still survive. In 1888 an article revealed the author as Antonio Rocco, an Italian priest and philosophy teacher (Dynes, 1990). Had Rocco been discovered as the text's author in 1652, he would have been prosecuted for obscenity and, at the very least, imprisoned.

## 18th and 19th Century Europe and America

During the 18th and 19th centuries homosexual authors continued to protect themselves from prosecution under overbearing obscenity laws through the coding of texts, but others protected themselves by writing about heterosexual relationships through the woman's perspective, as in the case of John Cleland's (1709–1789) novel *Fanny Hill*, published in 1749.

Published in two installments, the erotic novel *Fanny Hill, or Memoirs of a Woman of Pleasure* is one of the most prosecuted and banned books in history. Written as a series of letters between Frances "Fanny" Hill, a former prostitute, and an unknown woman, it tells the story of Fanny's youth as a young girl coming to London and becoming a prostitute before marrying a man who does not care about her past. In November 1749, Cleland, the publishers, and the printer were arrested on obscenity charges as a result of the novel's content. Although its uncensored version was officially pulled from circulation, illegal copies were distributed, making *Fanny Hill* a best-selling novel until the 1970s (Sabor, 2004).

Contemporary critics described Cleland's novel as homoerotic due to the level of detail in Fanny's description of her sexual affairs, her obsession with penis size, and the two instances of homosexuality in the text (Robinson, 2006). These, as well as Cleland's lack of close friends and his unmarried status, have added to the supposition that he was homosexual. Additionally, his bitter falling out with his friend Thomas Cannon (1720–?), author of the 1749 pamphlet *Ancient and Modern Pederasty Investigated and Exemplify'd*, the earliest published defense of homosexuality in English, also led to this

*Cover of American edition of* The Life and Adventures Miss Fanny Hill *(ca. 1910). Source: Photo by Chick Bowen, courtesy of Wikimedia Commons.*

speculation regarding Cleland's sexuality (Gladfelder, 2012). Although none of the pamphlets have survived, a partial record of the contents exists in the publisher John Pulser's 1750 indictment for his part in the publication of the text. Cannon begins the pamphlet by half-heartedly denouncing the practice of pederasty (Gladfelder, 2007). The balance comprises an anthology of ancient Greek and Roman texts, complete with Cannon's own commentary supporting pederasty and homosexuality. The obscenity charges brought against Cannon were eventually dropped, and the pamphlet that brought such trouble has disappeared almost into obscurity.

During the second half of the 18th century, Gothic fiction became popular in both England and America, largely with female audiences, by combining horror, death, and at times romance. Homosexual authors of Gothic fiction, such Matthew Lewis's (1775–1818) *The Monk* (1795) and Charles Maturin's (1782–1842) *The Fatal Revenge* (1807), used one of Shakespeare's techniques to create homoerotic texts—writing a female character who disguises herself as a young man to gain access to the protagonist or to an all-male world that is excluding her. This plot device enabled the author to create a subject who becomes infatuated with a man, but permitted the author to safely avoid prosecution for obscenity through the reveal that the young man in the text is actually a woman in disguise, with whom the protagonist then falls in love.

While the Gothic novel grew in popularity, the Romantic movement gained momentum at the end of the 18th century and continued into the early 19th century. Romantic literature—which could allow men to express affection for each other in literature, often through the motif of ancient Greece and the use of pederasty—was an acceptable medium for depicting such affection. In 1805 Augustus, Duke of Saxe-Gotha-Altenburg (part of what is today Germany), published his novel *A Year in Arcadia: Kyllenion*, the earliest known novel to focus on an explicitly homosexual male love affair (Haggerty, 1995). The novel's setting is ancient Greece, and focuses on several couples falling in love, including a homosexual one (Béeche, 2013). Although the text is veiled as a close friendship, the homoeroticism is present, and even some of Duke August's contemporaries felt that his characters pushed the acceptable boundaries of male affection in literature (Jones, 2015).

*M. P. Rice,* Walt Whitman and his rebel soldier friend Peter Doyle *(ca. 1869).* Source: Bayley Collection, Ohio Wesleyan University. Image courtesy of Wikimedia Commons.

By the mid-19th century, literature in America was shifting between Transcendentalism (the omnipresent existence of the divine in all nature and humanity) and Realism (the authentic representation of reality). One of the best-known poets in American history, Walt Whitman (1819–1892), incorporated both in his work. His most popular collection of poetry, *Leaves of Grass*, was first published in 1855. The Calamus poems in *Leaves*

*William C. North,* Emily
Dickinson *(ca. 1846–47),
daguerreotype. Source: Archives
and Special Collections,
Amherst College (Amherst,
Mass.). Image courtesy of
Wikimedia Commons.*

*of Grass* celebrate and promote the "manly love of comrades" (Whitman, 1981 [1855]). Critics believe that these poems are Whitman's clearest expression in print of same-sex desire and attraction between men. He is believed to have had romantic and sexual relationships with several different men in his lifetime, but the only descriptions are by men who claimed to have had relationships with him.

Many scholars believe that American poet Emily Dickinson (1830–1886) was a lesbian, pointing to her relationship with sister-in-law Susan (Sue) Gilbert Dickinson. The poet lived much of her life as a recluse in a home next door to Sue Dickinson's home, allowing the two to see each other daily. Throughout their friendship Sue was supportive of Emily, who considered her not only a beloved friend, but also an influence, inspiration, and confidant (Martin, 2002b). Numerous poems and letters point to a close friendship between the two women, and Emily may have been in love with Sue, but there is no indication that the two had a romantic or sexual relationship.

In the later 19th century, Gothic fiction saw a resurgence with novels such as Sheridan Le Fanu's *Carmilla* (2009), Oscar Wilde's *The Picture of Dorian Gray* (1890), and Bram Stoker's *Dracula*. While both Le Fanu and Stoker were heterosexual, both *Carmilla* and *Dracula* openly approach homosexuality and homoeroticism, respectively. Critics have noted that *Carmilla* has influenced the portrayal of vampires in later fiction through its use of same-sex sensuality. In one passage, the protagonist Laura describes a night visitor from years before (Jøn, 2001). She describes the stranger's pretty face as she kneels next to the bed, her hands caressing her under the coverlet. The stranger moves into bed with her, comforting her. After Laura falls asleep, she is suddenly wakened by the "sensation as if two needles ran into my breast very deep at the same moment" (Le Fanu, 2009). What becomes notable about *Carmilla* is that Laura's predator is not a male vampire, but a female one, creating a level of homoeroticism that had not previously existed in the Gothic genre.

A similar homoeroticism marks Bram Stoker's *Dracula* (1897) through Dracula's pursuit of Jonathan Harker. In the text *Dracula*, Jonathan Harker has fallen asleep in an area outside of the safety of his room in Dracula's lair. As three female vampires converge and prepare to take Harker, Dracula appears and states firmly, "This man belongs to me!" (Stoker, 1997). Harker swoons and the scene ends. The following morning, Harker wakes with his clothes folded by his bedside, presumably by Dracula, and the reader is left to interpret what may have happened during their interaction. Other instances occur between the two that contribute to the homoeroticism within the novel (Stoker, 1997).

The intimacy of the vampire bite was further developed in the 20th century (Jøn, 2001). Homoerotic undertones in vampire literature exist through to the present day, and some contemporary scholars believe that people within the queer community identify strongly with vampires because the vampire's "experiences parallel those of the sexual outsider" (Keller, 2000). Vampires must be secretive, lest their true identity and passions are revealed. There is also the constant fear of discovery (Dyer, 1988).

Irish author Oscar Wilde's *The Picture of Dorian Gray* was published in novel form in 1891 after being published as a short story the previous year. The Gothic tale is the story of the title character, Dorian Gray, who makes a deal with the devil to remain forever young while his portrait ages. Reviewers of the novel criticized the text for its "decadence" and allusions to homosexuality (Ross, 2011). Although there is nothing overtly homosexual in the novel, it is homoerotic. Dorian Gray is described by his beauty, a trait often perceived as feminine. A homoerotic undertone surfaces when that beauty is recognized by other men. At the beginning of *Dorian Gray*, the artist Basil Hallward, paints Gray's portrait. Hallward is enamored of Gray's beauty, finding in him his ultimate muse. Over the course of the novel, a span of 18 years, Gray indulges himself by experimenting with the vices he has read about in a French novel. The implication is that these immoralities not only encompass alcohol and illicit drug use, but also sexual encounters with both men and women.

Four years later, in 1895, Oscar Wilde was arrested and charged with "sodomy" and "gross indecency" because of his affair with Lord Alfred Douglas, a younger man. Both men were found guilty and sentenced to two years' hard labor (Old Bailey Proceedings Online, 1895). The trial received worldwide attention, and was a bitter reminder to those with same-sex attractions that not only was sodomy considered unnatural, but that it was also a crime, although irregularly prosecuted.

*Napoleon Sarony,* Oscar Wilde, *ca. 1882, albumen print. Source: Library of Congress. Image courtesy of Wikimedia Commons.*

## Early 20th Century Europe and America

Gertrude Stein (1874–1946) was possibly the most famous lesbian author of the 20th century. Born in Pennsylvania, Stein spent much of her adult life as an expatriate in Paris. Living with her brother Leo, the two became avid collectors of modern art, and opened their home to avant-garde writers, authors, and musicians. Stein's sexuality was an open secret. She lived with her partner, Alice B. Toklas, from 1907 until Stein's death in 1946. While together, the two had close friendships with many well-known artists and authors, such as Pablo Picasso, Henri Matisse, Ernest Hemingway, Thornton Wilder, and Sherwood Anderson (Castle, 2003).

Much of Stein's writing was radically innovative as it incorporated repetition and word-play. She gained notoriety in the 1930s with the publication of *The Autobiography of Alice B. Toklas*, a memoir of Stein's early years in Paris. Several of her works had lesbian themes, including her short story "Miss Furr and Miss Skeen" (1922), which, like much of Stein's work, contains repetition and word-play throughout, specifically the word "gay," which is repeated at least 130 times. Stein was one of the first authors in the 20th century to use the word gay for homosexual, although it was a form of coding at that time since heterosexual readers would understand it to mean carefree or happy (Castle, 2003).

A contemporary of Stein, Willa Cather (1873–1947), was an American author who later critics speculate was lesbian. Many point to the years in her youth when she dressed in boy's clothing, wore her hair short, and preferred to be called William Cather, Jr. However, Cather understood that boys and men held special privileges in the world, and she likely longed for those privileges, but by her second semester at university Cather was dressing in women's clothing. As an adult, her longest relationships were with women, including Louise Pound, Isabelle McClung, and most notably, Edith Lewis, with whom Cather lived for 39 years. Literary scholars have identified homoeroticism, or same-sex desire, in two of Cather's novels, *One of Ours* (1922), which won the 1923 Pulitzer Prize in Literature, and *Death Comes for the Archbishop* (1927). Both novels are told from a male protagonist's point of view, which was uncommon for female authors at the time. Both texts also contain close friendships between men that are affectionate, although never sexual.

The Bloomsbury Group was an influential group of English writers, intellectuals, philosophers, and artists that began in 1912. The ten core members were Clive Bell, Vanessa Bell, Roger Fry, Duncan Grant, John Maynard Keynes, Desmond MacCarthy, Lytton Strachey, Leonard Woolf, and Virginia Woolf. The group were united by a belief in the importance of the arts. Their works and philosophical ideas influenced literature as well as modern attitudes toward feminism, pacifism, and sexuality. At least three of the men identified as gay—Duncan Grant, E.M. Forster, and Lytton Strachey—though Forster remained closeted to all but his close friends during his lifetime. Virginia Woolf (1882–1941) was the most famous of the Bloomsbury Group, at least to contemporary audiences. While already married, Woolf embarked on an affair with writer Vita Sackville-West in the early 1920s, which continued into the 1930s. In 1928 Woolf presented Sackville-West with *Orlando*, a novel about a man whose life spans three centuries and both sexes. Nigel Nicolson, Vita Sackville-West's son, described the novel as "the longest and most charming love letter in literature" (Blamires, 1983).

British author Radclyffe Hall (1880–1942) was at the height of her career when she decided to write the lesbian-themed novel *The Well of Loneliness* (1928). She was so determined that the text remain as she intended that prior to its publication she told her editor that she required complete commitment from the publisher as she would not allow even one word to be changed in the manuscript (Souhami, 1998). The narrative of the novel follows Stephen Gordon, a woman whose parents are expecting a boy when she is born, and christen her Stephen, which foreshadows her sexual identity. As she grows, Stephen develops crushes; first on girls and, later, women. After her father's untimely death, Stephen begins to dress in masculine clothes and falls in love with Mary, a woman who returns her feelings. The novel ends tragically when Stephen, who cannot keep her partner happy, pushes Mary into the arms of a man who has fallen in love with her, hoping that one of them can live happily.

*The Well of Loneliness* was published July 1928 to mixed reviews. Some critics thought the text was poorly structured. However, others praised the book for its sincerity and artistry. The book was the subject of an obscenity trial that resulted in a determination that the book was obscene and should be destroyed (Doan & Prosser, 2002). On appeal the verdict was upheld (Souhami, 1998). Initially, the novel faced the same outcome after its publication in the United States. In February 1929 courts deemed the book to be immoral. However, upon remand to the New York Court of Special Sessions, the book was determined not to be obscene (Taylor, 2001).

The Harlem Renaissance was a social, cultural, and artistic movement that began in the Harlem neighborhood of New York City near the end of the World War I and lasted until the middle of the 1930s. During this time it was known as the New Negro Movement, and was a resurgence of African-American arts. Several noted writers of the Harlem Renaissance were known to be gay or bisexual, including Richard Bruce Nugent (1906–1987), an openly gay writer and painter. His short story "Smoke, Lilies and Jade" in the November 1926 issue of *FIRE!!* is thought to be the first short story to be published on the theme of bisexuality. Contemporaries of Nugent during the Harlem Renaissance, Countee Cullen, Claude McKay, and Langston Hughes, were all successful writers who were closeted about their sexual identities.

The novel *Passing* (1929) by Nella Larsen (1891–1964), written and published during the Harlem Renaissance, has been recognized for its homoerotic subtext between the characters Irene and Clare because of Irene's appreciation of Clare's beauty. Additionally, Irene and her husband Brian have a sexless marriage and, while they do have children, they live as co-parents not as sexual partners (McDowell, 1986). The status of their marriage has

*Richard Bruce Nugent, Dancing Figures, ca. 1935, black ink and graphite on paper, Brooklyn Museum (New York, NY), acc. 2008.50.6. Source: Brooklyn Museum.*

caused both Irene and Brian to be interpreted as lesbian and gay respectively. Irene labels Brian as queer, and he often expresses a desire to go to Brazil, a country considered to be more tolerant of homosexuality in the 1920s. Both are considered indicators of Brian's sexuality. The text's primary theme is racial passing, but the metaphor expands to multiple levels, including sexual (Blackmore, 1992).

## Pulp Fiction

During the same period as the Harlem Renaissance in the early 1930s, the number of publishing houses catering to alternate texts began to expand. These presses published both heterosexual erotica and gay and lesbian texts. To circumvent censorship and legal prosecution, the publishers were cautious about how they marketed these publications. Panurge Press, founded by Esar Levine, was a mail-order company specializing in limited editions of erotica—some of it focused on same-sex desire and sexual activity. Although mail-order business made tracking a publisher more difficult, Levine was arrested several times, and once spent six months in prison after bail was not granted (Bronski, 2003).

These small publishers led the way for pulp fiction, the original novels published only in paperback form. Pulps were labeled as such because of the cheap wood-pulp paper on which they were printed, which was very economical for a small publishing house. The name became synonymous for books with eye-catching, often erotically suggestive, covers. Pulps were released in a variety of genres that included thrillers, romances, crime noir, westerns, science fiction, and horror. In the 1950s a larger number of lesbian-themed pulp novels were published than gay-themed pulps. These texts were often written by men and had an audience of both lesbians and straight men. The gay-themed texts were often considered more literary and less commercial than the lesbian publications (Bronski, 2003).

Tereska Torres's *Women's Barracks*, published in 1950, was the first pulp paperback to address a lesbian relationship. The book was a fictionalization of Torres's real-life experiences in the Free French Forces in London during World War II. The book sold four million copies and was selected by the House Select Committee on Current Pornographic Materials in 1952 as an example of how paperback books were promoting moral indecency. As a result, the Committee began to require publishers to conform to specific moral standards in the content and publicizing of books, or else face fines or imprisonment. While this initially affected how authors framed their work in pulp fiction, as the decade advanced publishers became bolder in printing material that might be deemed immoral (Stryker, 2001).

> By the 1960s more gay-themed than lesbian-themed pulp novels were being published. Beginning in 1957, obscenity laws began to change, allowing for more obviously gay material to be published without being prosecuted as obscene (Gunn and Harker, 2013). A number of renowned and respected gay authors began their careers writing for pulp fiction, such as Tennessee Williams, Gore Vidal, and Truman Capote (Stryker, 2001).
>
> *Susan K. Thomas*

## Post-World War II

Following World War II, more same-sex themed books were reaching bookshelves than ever before. American author Gore Vidal published *The City and the Pillar* in January 1948. The text is significant for being the first post-World War II text that has an openly gay character who is content and does not die tragically at the end of the novel (Stryker, 2001). Vidal also wrote the protagonist Jim to be an athletic, masculine man. The author was determined to challenge stereotypes of the gay man as a transvestite, lonely and bookish, or effeminate. He was determined to write the character as authentic and real (Vidal, 1995, xiii). Vidal was also very direct in his approach to the protagonist Jim's sexuality in the novel. The title of the text harkens back to the story of Sodom and Gomorrah, when Lot's wife turns to look back at the burning Sodom and is turned into a pillar of salt. Throughout Vidal's novel Jim is unable to stop thinking of a sexual encounter he had with his best friend, Bob, in high school. Jim's obsession with that encounter metaphorically freezes him so that he is unable to move on, resulting in disastrous consequences at the end of the text. Upon the release of *The City and the Pillar*, *The New York Times* refused to review the book, and every major newspaper or magazine refused to review any of Vidal's novels for the next six years (Vidal, 1995, xvi). The publication of the text was significant and led the way for the release of other gay-themed texts by authors such as Truman Capote and Charles Jackson.

In the same month as *The City and The Pillar*, Random House published Truman Capote's *Other Voices, Other Rooms*. The novel is in the style of the Southern Gothic, which uses common themes of deeply flawed, disturbing, or eccentric characters that may dabble in the occult, have ambivalent gender roles, are placed in decayed or derelict settings, grotesque situations, and other sinister events that often stem from poverty, alienation, crime, or violence (Merkel, 2008; Bloom, 2009). *Other Voices, Other Rooms*, while including openly gay characters differs from *The City and The Pillar* in that it does not include sex between men. This difference may explain the positive response to Capote's novel even before its publication.

Lesbian author Patricia Highsmith (1921–1995) published her second novel, *The Price of Salt*, in 1952; a story about the beginnings of a lesbian

*Cover of* The Price of Salt *by Claire Morgan (pseudonym of Patricia Highsmith) (Bantam Books, 1953). Painting by Barye Phillips. Source: Bantam Books/Penguin Random House.*

relationship in New York City in the 1940s. The book was initially published under the pseudonym Claire Morgan, as Highsmith feared that she would be forever labeled a lesbian author, which would overshadow her writing. The novel was considered groundbreaking for its time because of Highsmith's choice to end the novel with a happy ending, and for departing from the stereotypical characterization of lesbians (Carlston, 2015). Highsmith did not acknowledge authorship until the 1990 Bloomsbury re-release, retitled *Carol*. A film adaptation of *Carol* was released in 2015. Highsmith's novels *The Talented Mr. Ripley* (1955) and *Small g: A Summer Idyll* (1995) are also gay themed. The latter also mentions HIV, but not as a significant element in the plot or character development.

During the 1940s gay playwright Tennessee Williams (1911–1983) suddenly earned fame with *The Glass Menagerie (*1944). Critics consider Williams among the three foremost playwrights of 20th-century American drama, along with Eugene O'Neill and Arthur Miller (Bloom, 2009). Williams received the Pulitzer Prize for Drama for two of his plays, *A Streetcar Named Desire* (1947) in 1948 and *Cat on a Hot Tin Roof* (1955) in 1955. Both texts include references to Williams' life, including homosexuality, mental instability, and alcoholism, and both would be made into highly successful Hollywood films.

During this same period James Baldwin (1924–1987) published his second novel, *Giovanni's Room*, which had explicit gay and bisexual themes. Baldwin's first novel, *Go Tell It on the Mountain* (1953), which had a very subtle bisexual undercurrent, was widely accepted by African Americans, and Baldwin was considered the voice of a new generation. After reading *Giovanni's Room*, Baldwin's editor encouraged the author to burn the manuscript, arguing that a publisher would never be willing to accept a book with such an openly gay storyline, and that Baldwin's fans would never condone such a text. Critics, while not pleased with the explicit homosexuality in the text, were much kinder than anticipated (Levin, 1991). By 1963 Baldwin could publish the bisexual-themed novel *Another Country* with little issue.

Also during the 1950s, the Beat Generation was emerging in San Francisco. The central themes of the Beat culture are rejection of standard narrative values, the spiritual quest, exploration of American and Eastern religions, rejection of materialism, experimentation with psychedelic drugs, and sexual liberation and exploration (Charters, 2001). Among the best-known pieces of literature are Allen Ginsberg's "Howl" (1956), William S. Burroughs's *Naked Lunch* (1959), and Jack Kerouac's (1922–1969) *On the Road* (1957). Both Ginsberg and Burroughs identified as gay, and Kerouac engaged in same-sex relations during his life. "Howl" and *Naked Lunch* also became the focus of obscenity trials that ultimately helped to change obscenity laws in the United States (Charters, 2001; Morgan, 1988).

The poem "Howl" was written in 1955 and published in Allen Ginsberg's (1926–1997) collection *Howl and Other Poems* in 1956. "Howl" was considered controversial because of its numerous references to illicit drugs and sexual practices, both heterosexual and homosexual. At this time, a number of books that discussed sex were being banned, including *Lady Chatterley's Lover* (Raskin, 2004). Ginsberg's use of explicit language led to a trial on First Amendment issues after the publisher of the piece was brought up on charges for publishing pornography. The judge in the trial dismissed the charges, determining that the poem carried "redeeming social importance," thus setting an important legal precedent (Morgan, 2006).

William S. Burroughs' (1914–1997) *Naked Lunch* (1959) is a series of loosely connected vignettes that Burroughs said could be read in any order. The protagonist, William Lee, is a drug addict modeled after Burroughs, who was addicted to heroin, morphine, and several other drugs. The book was considered controversial for both its erotic subject matter and its harsh language, which Burroughs recognized and intended. The book was banned in Boston in 1962 for obscenity, but the Massachusetts Supreme Judicial Court reversed that decision (de Grazia, 1998). The Appeals Court found that the book did not violate obscenity statutes because it was believed to have some social value (Maynard & Miles, 1965).

The 1960s was a tumultuous period for the queer community, but with changing obscenity laws lesbian and gay authors could now publish without prosecution and were able to bring attention to the oppression faced by people in that community. Notably, Christopher Isherwood (1904–1986) published *A Single Man* (1964), which demonstrated the oppression that lesbian and gay people face. The protagonist loses his partner in a tragic car accident but is then shut out by his deceased lover's family and discouraged from attending the funeral, although the two had been together for years. *A Single Man* presents homosexuality as a human characteristic that deserves to be recognized and respected (Summers, 2015).

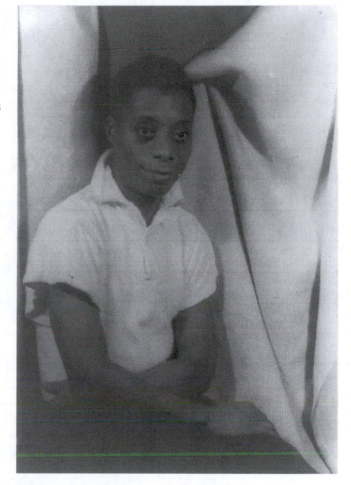

*Carl Van Vechten,* Portrait of James Baldwin, *Sept. 13, 1955, silver gelatin photographic print. Source: Courtesy of Van Vechten Collection, Library of Congress Prints and Photographs Division.*

## Post-Stonewall: 1970 and After

Following the 1969 Stonewall Riots, sexual minorities, now often publicly identifying as bisexual, gay, and lesbian enjoyed a renewed visibility in U.S.

society and mass media. Anything seemed possible as activist organizations were founded across the country in cities and on college campuses. This push in equal rights for lesbian and gay people was reflected in an increase in publications. With the shift in politics and obscenity laws, authors became even bolder in their texts, writing about openly affectionate same-sex characters. Lesbians often found it easier to publish than gay men during this period. Isabel Miller's *Patience & Sarah* (1971; the pen name of Alma Routsong, 1924–1996), Rita Mae Brown's *Rubyfruit Jungle* (1973), and Rosa Guy's (b. 1922) *Ruby* (1976) were published during the decade along with others. One of the common themes in 1970s lesbian and gay literature continued to be the lack of a happy ending, as in Brown's *Rubyfruit Jungle* when the protagonist moves to New York City to attend school and is forced to realize that, within the city, rubyfruit jungle (a metaphor for women's genitalia) is not as delicious or as varied as she had dreamed.

The late 1970s also saw some of the most provocative literature written by gay men to date. Larry Kramer's (b. 1935) *Faggots* (1978) and Andrew

---

## The Combahee River Collective Statement

The Combahee River Collective (CRC) was founded in 1974 in an attempt to create a feminist space for black women that also considered the intersectionality of class and sexuality (Marable and Leith, 516). While many African Americans belonged to and supported the National Organization of Women (NOW), its goals focused on improving the economic situation of middle- and upper-middle-class women (Harris, 2001). While many white women sought to leave the home to join the workforce, many black women had been required to work outside of their homes to support their families for decades.

The CRC began as the Boston chapter of the National Black Feminist Organization (NBFO), a black feminist organization that focused more closely on issues affecting black women. However, the members in the Boston chapter of NBFO were "more preoccupied with issues of sexual orientation and economic development" (Harris, 2001) than the main chapter of NBFO, which "aimed their activities at the more personal and practical level rather than at the political mainstream" (Harris, 2001). The Boston chapter, which became the Combahee River Collective, "came to define itself as anti-capitalist, socialist, and revolutionary" (Harris, 2001). Lesbian author and activist Barbara Smith wrote the statement with Demita Frazier and Beverly Smith, who divided the statement into four chapters: The Genesis of Contemporary Black Feminism; What We [CRC] Believe; Problems in Organizing Black Feminists; and Black Feminist Issues and Projects. Since the statement's publication and distribution, it has become a key influence on black feminism and on social theory about race.

*Susan K. Thomas*

Holleran's (b. 1944) *Dancer from the Dance* (1978) signaled a change in writing that was free from legal censorship. Both Kramer's and Holloran's novels focus on the gay party scene in New York City and on Fire Island, a summer resort destination near New York City. Kramer's text is a harsh parody of the casual sex and drugs that existed during the late 1970s as the protagonist attempts to find love in a culture that seems to emphasize casual sexual encounters. The book is sexually explicit in a way that would have led to its suppression just 15 years earlier.

Andrew Halloran's *Dancer from the Dance* is also the story of young men searching for love in an urban gay culture that emphasizes casual sex, partying, and drug use. Although Halloran's novel also exposes outsiders to certain parts of gay male culture in 1970s New York City and Fire Island, it is often considered to be less bitter than Kramer's novel. Instead, the book has been praised for its vivid imagery and lush language. Both texts are significant because of their authors' bold and explicit writing and their critiques of the gay community.

## The 1980s

The surge of publications in the 1970s continued into the 1980s, especially from women authors. African-American novelist Alice Walker's (b. 1944) 1982 novel *The Color Purple* won the 1983 Pulitzer Prize for Fiction and the 1983 National Book Award for Fiction. The epistolary novel is the coming of age story of a young African-American woman in rural Georgia, beginning in the 1930s. Young Celie is married off to an older widower who is both verbally and physically abusive. Through the course of the texts, Celie finds love with another woman, who helps Celie discover her own voice for the first time in her life. The novel's themes focus on the sisterhood of women, racism, and gender roles. *The Color Purple* has been listed as one of the 100 Most Frequently Banned Books by the American Library Association because of racism, harsh language, violence, physical abuse, and sexual content (100 notable books of the year, 2006). Although Walker has never made a public statement about sexual identification she has been romantically involved with both men and women.

During the 1970s and 1980s author Audre Lorde (1934–1992) published some of the most influential work in the women's rights movement as she examined the intersections of gender, race, and sexual identity. Her poetry expressed anger and outrage at civil and social injustices that she had observed and experienced throughout her life. Her best-known texts today are *Zami: A New Spelling of My Name* (1983), an autobiographical text, and *Sister Outsider: Essays and Speeches* (1984), a collection of Lorde's writings that draw upon her personal experiences of oppression, including sexism, heterosexism, racism, classism, and ageism.

The impact of HIV/AIDS on gay and bisexual men caused a shift in the content of literature during the late 1980s and the 1990s. Stories about the search for sex and love, and acceptance of one's sexual identity, gave way to tales of grief, loss, and survival in a time of political and social indifference to the

*K. Kendall,* Audre Lorde (Austin, TX, 1980)*, digital scan of a silver gelatin print. Source: Photo by K. Kendall/ CC BY 2.0 license. Image courtesy of Wikimedia Commons.*

HIV/AIDS epidemic. Numerous novels and memoirs were published in the 1980s and 1990s about the impact of HIV/AIDS on gay men. The earliest novels to mention the illness are Dorothy Bryant's *A Day in San Francisco* (1983) and Armistead Maupin's *Baby Cakes* (1984). However, Paul Reed's *Facing It* (1984) is often considered the first AIDS novel because the theme of the text is the epidemic, while Bryant's and Maupin's novels peripherally address the disease, which is present and affects the novel's characters, but is not the subject of the text (Reed, 1993).

Numerous memoirs also emerged from the 1980s and 1990s AIDS epidemics, documenting real-life witnessing of the disease from those who loved those living with and dying from AIDS. Paul Monette's *Borrowed Time: An AIDS Memoir* (1988) chronicles his partner Roger Horwitz's fight against and eventual death from AIDS. Abraham Verghese's *My Own Country: A Doctor's Story* (1994) traces Verghese's experience as a young infectious-disease physician in the mid-1980s in Johnson City, Tennessee, who begins to treat patients with the then-unknown disease. Out of necessity Verghese became the town's AIDS expert, and was often the only one at his patients' bedsides as they were abandoned by family and friends who were fearful or in denial. By the late 1990s more heterosexual-identified authors were including the theme of AIDS in their work, such as in Michael Cunningham's Pulitzer Prize winning novel *The Hours* (1999), whose character Richard Brown is dying of AIDS, and who is also the small thread tying much of the novel together.

## The 1990s

The number and kind of publications by or about gender and sexual minorities increased even further in the 1990s, expanding into the genres of romance, science fiction, and fantasy as many queer and allied authors published books with LGBTQ protagonists by large genre publishers throughout the decade. Melissa Scott's novels *Trouble and Her Friends* (1994), *Point of Hopes* (1995), co-written with Lisa Barnett, and *Shadow Man* (1995) explore ideas about sexuality and gender. *Trouble and Her Friends* was an early cyberpunk novel to feature a queer protagonist, while *Shadow Man* moved beyond the gender binary of male/female. Other authors, such as Rachel Pollack, Richard Bowes, Anne Harris, and Nicola Griffiths, created worlds in which queer protagonists were not only common, but also flourished.

Octavia E. Butler (1947–2006) is one of the best-known lesbian science fiction authors of the 20th and early 21st centuries. As an African American woman, one of her common themes was the intersection of cultures that often resulted in cross-species relationships and flexible views of sexuality and gender. In her novel *Fledgling* (2005), Butler writes of the vampiric Ina species and their emotional and sexual relationships with humans, both men and women. Butler also explores the intersection of species as the protagonist is 53-year-old Shori, who is part Ina and part human, and sexual relationships with humans (Nayar, 2011). These relationships are polyamorous, as the Ina are the primary partner of several male and female humans, who willingly allow the Ina to feed from them (Shaviro, 2013).

The science fiction novel *The Left Hand of Darkness* (1969), written by Ursula K. Le Guin (b. 1929), became immensely popular in 1970, winning both the Hugo and Nebula Awards for Best Novel (1970 Hugo awards; SFFWA, [n.d.]). The irrelevance of gender is one of the prominent themes in the text. Le Guin chose to eliminate gender "to find out what was left" (Cummins, 1990). This theme is most recognizable through the character Genly Ai, who begins the novel as masculine, but becomes more androgynous over the course of the novel as he becomes more patient and caring, and less rigidly rationalist (Cummins, 1990). In the novel, Ai visits the Gethen system, whose inhabitants are androgynous, a tactic that the author uses to examine gender relations in human society. In the Gethen culture, Ai is considered an oddity for his masculinity, which appears aggressive in relation to the passivity of the Gethenians (Reid, 2009). Ai is only able to bond with the Gethenians, primarily the character of Estraven, once he can accept the Gethenian's gender ambiguity. Some feminist theorists have criticized the novel for what they interpret as homophobia in the relationship between Estraven and Ai. There is an implied attraction between the two characters, but that aspect of their relationship is never physically explored. In a 1986 essay Le Guin acknowledged and apologized for the fact that the novel had presented heterosexuality as the norm on Gethen (White, 1999).

Leslie Feinberg (1949–2014), a transgender author and activist, wrote a handful of significant novels on themes of sexual orientation, gender non-conformity, and transgender politics. The groundbreaking 1993 novel *Stone Butch Blues* won both a Lambda Literary Award and an American Library Association Gay & Lesbian Book Award. The coming of age novel tells the story of Jess Goldberg, whose androgyny as a child creates problems for both her and her parents, and as she grows, she has difficulties fitting in. Throughout the book Jess discovers and accepts her gender differences and finally finds a voice to speak out against oppression. *Stone Butch Blues* was the first known novel published by a person identifying as transgender. In 2006 Feinberg published a second novel, *Drag King Blues*, which also had transgender and gay themes. Additionally,

Feinberg published several non-fiction books about transgender issues, including *Transgender Liberation: A Movement Whose Time Has Come* (1992) and *Trans Liberation: Beyond Pink or Blue* (1999).

## 21st Century

In the new millennium, LGBTQ themes and writers are appearing in more and more literary genres. Authors incorporate positive portrayals of LGBTQ protagonists into numerous genres, from romance, to historical fiction, to vampire detective fiction. Authors have also expanded into the graphic memoir, comics, and children's and young adult literature.

Lesbian cartoonist Alison Bechdel (b. 1960) was initially best known for her comic strip *Dykes to Watch Out For*, which ran from 1983 to 2008 and is one of the earliest ongoing depictions of lesbians in popular culture. However, Bechdel gained critical and commercial success in 2006 with the publication of her graphic memoir, *Fun Home*. The book chronicles her childhood and the years before and after her father's suspected suicide. The text focuses primarily on her relationship with her parents, especially her father, who Bechdel theorizes was also gay. *Fun Home* was named one of the top books of 2006 by *The New York Times* (100 notable books of the year, 2006), *The Times of London* (Gatti, 2006), and *Publishers Weekly* (The first annual *PW* comics week critic's poll, 2006). *Time* magazine named the book one of its top ten picks for 2006 (Grossman, 2007).

The late 20th and early 21st centuries have seen the publication of numerous memoirs and novels focused on gender identity. Trans author Kate Bornstein's *Gender Outlaw: On Men, Women, and the Rest of Us* (1994) describes hir transition from living as a man to a woman (Bornstein prefers the gender-neutral pronouns ze/hir). Following her medical and social transition to live as a woman, Bornstein realized that she still did not feel like she fit in, and realized that choosing a gender reflected society's gender binary, which requires people to identify according to the two available genders (Bornstein, 1994). She has since stated that she does not call herself a woman, and she knows that she is not a man (Bornstein, 2012). Trans activists Jennifer Finney Boylan and Janet Mock have both released memoirs describing their gender transitions and their work to expand the gender binary through their activism.

*Lane Rasberry,* Kate Bornstein at Babeland, Seattle, WA*, December 6, 2010. Source: Wikimedia Commons.*

In 2007 Jeffrey Eugenides published the novel *Middlesex*, a coming of age story about Calliope "Callie/Cal" Stephanides, an intersex person who is assigned female at birth. Callie is raised as a girl and is attracted to other girls. She only learns she is intersex after an accident, when tests determine that she has 5-Alpha Reductase Deficiency (5-ARD), a genetic condition that causes a genetically male-typical person to be born with genitals that appear to be female-typical. Although Callie was born with female genitalia, she also has male gonads, including internal testicles. Nature versus nurture and gender identity, and intersex status are two themes within the novel. Although raised as a girl, Cal quickly renounces his female gender upon learning he could have been raised a boy. In 2003, *Middlesex* was awarded the Pulitzer Prize for fiction (Fischer & Fischer, 2007).

## Children's and Young Adult Literature

Authors began publishing children's books with lesbian and gay themes in the 1980s. The first known gay storybook is *Jenny Lives with Eric and Martin* by Susanne Bösche, published in Denmark in 1981 and in England in 1983. The plot describes a few days in the life of Jenny, a five-year-old who lives with her father, Eric, and his boyfriend Martin. The book covers small stories such as Jenny, Eric, and Martin doing laundry together, and the preparation for a birthday party for Eric. Bösche explains that she wrote the book to help children recognize different family forms (Bösche, 2000). Similarly, Lesléa Newman (b. 1955) wrote *Heather Has Two Mommies* (1989) after speaking with a lesbian couple she knew with a child who commented that they could not find any children's books that reflected their family. The book is about a child, Heather, who is raised by her lesbian parents, Jane and Kate. The family unit is discussed simply and positively, as are other family situations in the book. Both *Jenny Lives with Eric and Martin* and *Heather Has Two Mommies* met with controversy upon publication, being both regulated in libraries and pulled from bookshelves. The American Library Association ranked Heather as the ninth most frequently challenged book in the United Stated during the 1990s (100 notable books of the year, 2016).

Since the 1980s, numerous LGBTQ storybooks have been published for children that reflect varying families and personal identities. Maurice Sendak's (1928–2012) *We Are All in the Dumps with Jack and Guy* (1993), Jeanne Arnold's *Amy Asks a Question: Grandma, What's a Lesbian?* (1996), Peter Parnell and Justin Richardson's *And Tango Makes Three* (2005), and Lesléa Newman's *Mommy, Mama, and Me* (2009) are just some of the titles that have been released about differing family forms. Other books have been published that reflect a diversity of gender and sexual identities, such as Linda de Haan and Stern Nijland's *King and King* (2003), Christine Baldacchino's *Morris Micklewhite and the Tangerine Dress* (2014), and Jazz Jennings's *I am Jazz* (2014).

The genre of young adult fiction has expanded immensely since the 1997 publication of J.K. Rowling's *Harry Potter and the Sorcerer's Stone*. The popularity of the Harry Potter series has inspired a new generation of readers as well as authors, who have released a variety of fiction in different genres from fantasy, to mystery fiction, to graphic novels. While the 20th century saw an increase in young adult fiction, hundreds of young adult LGBTQ novels have been published since 2000. While numerous texts still approach coming out, such as Perry Moore's *Hero* (2009) and Benjamin Alire Saenz's *Aristotle and Dante Discover the Secrets of the Universe* (2014), many other texts embrace situations that openly

LGBTQ young adults might face in their own lives, such as the quest for love in David Levithan's *Boy Meets Boy* (2005) or the still present danger of HIV/AIDS, as in J. H. Trumble's *Just Between* Us (2013).

Publishers have also released more young adult books about discovering gender identity. Alex Gino's *George* is the story of a pre-teen who was assigned male at birth, but identifies as female. George initially struggles to come out, but her best friend Kelly accepts her and supports her. Gino's text was a significant contribution to the genre of gender identity because it is written for an audience in Grades 4–6. Other novels, such as Jeff Garvin's debut novel *Symptoms of Being Human* (2016) embrace the theme of gender fluidity.

In the 21st century readers can expect the catalog of LGBTQ literature to expand as barriers that once blocked writers have been removed. The reading public has also become more accepting, and have embraced much of the work created within the queer community. Additionally, with the development of the internet, authors can now easily share writings through websites that promote publication and collaboration. The number of authors who self-publish has also increased substantially, which has continued to provide validation for writers not only for their work, but also for a wider range of sexual and gender identities. Authors are now able to reach audiences in ways that were never realized before, and in doing so, are helping reduce the ignorance that so heavily limited LGBTQ literature in the past.

## VISUAL ARTS

LGBTQ individuals around the world have contributed immensely to the visual arts: drawing, painting, sculpture, photography, and performance alike. For many, art has been an opportunity for expression where it has otherwise been denied. The visual arts—as a form of decoration, self-expression, worship, or political veneration—became increasingly important over the millennia, beginning long before modern times.

### Ancient and Medieval Art (before c. 1350)

The modern era (after c. 1500) is most often associated with investigations of gender and sexuality, these themes were present much earlier in the visual arts. While sexually explicit images do survive, they alternatively flourished and faced repression. Such depictions might be erotic or pornographic; they might also reflect political, social, religious, and ethical issues in the time they were created.

Masculinity was certainly valued in Ancient Egypt, as evidenced by the massive grandeur of the tombs and monuments to male (with a few exceptions) pharaohs. However, the Ancient Egyptians had a very complex and sophisticated understanding of gender. Queen Hatshepsut, for example, was often portrayed as a male pharaoh. Other depictions of pharaohs are androgynous, such as the *Colossal Figure of Akhenaten* (1352–1336 BCE), where the king does not at all look like traditional depictions of a pharaoh; his shoulders are narrow, his waist wide. Moreover, he has no genitalia, which reinforces the statue's androgynous presence. There are many theories as to why this might be the case, but it is possible that the pharaoh hoped to be represented in the manner of a multi-gendered, or androgynous god.

The secular states of ancient Greece and Rome, prior to the regulations placed upon sex by the institutionalization of Christianity, allowed for a variety of artistic depictions of same-sex desire, which became a cornerstone of Classical art, or the art at the height of Greco-Roman culture. One of the most famous literary works of classical antiquity, Plato's *The Symposium*, celebrates homosexual desire and, despite later restrictions on such behavior, the text has become central to Western philosophy. In ancient Greece there was a profusion of images of both homo-social bonding (that is, images that depict men socializing in erotic and non-erotic settings) and explicit same-sex intercourse. An example is *Achilles Binding the Wounds of Patroclus* (late 6th century), an image of masculine companionship, a type of quasi-sexual imagery that would remain a staple of Western art until the 18th century. Likewise, depictions of the lesbian poet Sappho, as on the painted pot *Sappho and Attendants* (c. 450 BCE), point to a world of same-sex desire and companionship, but not lesbian sex per se.

*Warren Cup (detail), Roman, 1st century CE, silver, British Museum (London, UK). Source: Photo by Sailko (Francesco Bini)/CC BY-SA 3.0 license. Image courtesy of Wikimedia Commons.*

Most famous among Greek depictions of male homosexuality in popular culture are images of pederasty, a sexual process of courtship and a means of intellectual and social stewardship, a form of sexual and intellectual companionship in which older men would court pubescent boys (up to the age of 17). Pederasty was often the subject of painted pottery, with the most commonly represented form of intercourse being intercrural sex—a non-penetrative form of sex that involves the rubbing of the penis between the thighs. There was no concept of pedophilia as understood today, and these relationships were not clandestine. In fact, they were woven into the fabric of Greek culture (Saslow, 1999). While pederasty did not feature as prominently in Roman society, there are instances of explicit sex between males, such as the Warren Cup (1st century)—a silver goblet depicting two scenes of anal sex between adult men and youths in a luxurious setting. Such drinking cups were intended as conversation pieces during dinner parties.

Homoeroticism in Greek and Roman art also took the form of representations of the athletic, youthful, subtly erotic male body. While these images are not explicitly "gay," as the term is understood today, Classical depictions of the male nude nevertheless became important to later gay male artists. This became more apparent beginning with Alexander the Great's reign (336–323 BCE). Changing notions of beauty prompted depictions of men who are slender and feminized, and depictions of Alexander often reveal a fashion for slimmer bodies and longer hair (Saslow, 1999). There are few surviving images of lesbianism in Roman art, and very few in Greek art (depictions of the lesbian poet Sappho being a prominent exception).

This shift can also be seen in depictions of the gods, such as with the *Apollo Belvedere* (c. 300 BCE), whose narrow waist and hairless body reflected a growing association of lightly muscled bodies with intellectualism, rather than the brutish muscularity associated with lower-class men and foreign people. The revival of a Greek and Roman style in art in the Renaissance would intensify this association between conventional masculine beauty and intellectual or artistic superiority. The *Barberini Faun* (c. 200 BCE) is another prime example that depicts a suggestive reclining male nude. But it is important to remember that such depictions could have appealed to women in a heterosexual sense, or to men in both a homosexual fashion and a merely masculine ideal of fitness and emotional fortitude. In this way, these works should not be viewed as purely homoerotic; they represented multiple desires—from the erotic to an urge to display artisanal skill by crafting a detailed, attractive body out of stone.

Dante and Virgil Meet the Sodomites in Hell, *in Guido da Pisa,* Commentary on Dante's Inferno, *ca. 1345 CE, painted manuscript.* Source: Wikimedia Commons.

The growth and influence of Christianity led to increased restrictions on non-procreative sexual behavior and related artistic representations. Images of homosexuality throughout the medieval era (5th to 15th century) in Western Europe depict same-sex behavior in the context of moral judgement and sin (Saslow 1999). Same-sex sexual behavior was increasingly termed sodomy and became a moral and spiritual transgression, as evidenced by illustrated manuscripts. Most famously, perhaps, Dante's *Divine Comedy* relegated male-male sex to the seventh circle of hell, which was illustrated in images such as *Dante and Virgil Meet the Sodomites (Inferno 15)* (c. 1345).

One notable exception is the phenomenon of tombs shared by men in the medieval period (Bray, 2003). While this was not commonplace, such burials were described using the Latin word *connubium,* which translates as marriage. This did not necessarily mean that the entombed men had a sexual relationship when alive but, rather, that there remained in the medieval period an interest in the companionship of men—whether it suggests sexual behavior or not. These burials were, in fact, blessed by the English church, and were understood as nonsexual friendships, but they are part of the cultural history of same-sex friendships that may or may not have been romantic or sexual.

## Renaissance and Baroque Art (c. 1350–1750)

As Europe rebuilt from the economic depression of the Middle Ages, there was an explosion of artistic and scientific inquiry that heralded the Renaissance as the beginning of what art historians call modernity, during which sculpture, painting, and drawing took on the status of a fine art, rather than a craft. During this period, artists begin identifying themselves as artists and exploring their identities through their work. The renewed focus on the nude—male and female—created a socially acceptable space (at least for male intellectuals and male artists) for viewing the naked body, even in religious contexts. There are increasing numbers of depictions of sensual and youthful bodies, following the ideal of Greco-Roman sculpture, and in many cases, this did reflect the sexual desires or attractions of the artist. There are many changes in this regard in the modern period (beginning with the late Renaissance) through to the 20th century, but from this point, art held an important role in self-expression and communication across lines of difference.

A variety of factors led to the explosion of artistic and scientific inquiry informing Renaissance art. European colonies in Africa, Asia, and the Americas created an influx of wealth, which also destabilized the rigid social hierarchies of the Middle Ages. Additionally, a rise in humanism (an interest in the affairs of human beings rather than the divine) began to challenge the power of the Catholic Church in Western Europe. There was a renewed interest in Classical art as a model for producing scientifically correct, beautiful human bodies. Finally, in 1450, Johannes Gutenberg created the printing press, which allowed for a wider dissemination of images beyond religious and aristocratic circles.

*Donato di Niccolò di Betto Bardi ("Donatello") (Italian, c.1386–1446 CE), David, ca. 1440 CE, bronze, Bargello Museum (Florence, Italy). Source: Photo by Rufus46/CC BY-SA 3.0 license. Image courtesy of Wikimedia Commons.*

## HIV/AIDS and the Performing Arts

As the devastating impact of HIV/AIDS on gay male communities started to become apparent in the early 1980s, a number of playwrights, musicians, and dancers responded through their work. In it, they memorialized the dead, addressed political and societal indifference, and captured the experiences of those who lived through the early years of the epidemic in the US (Román, 1998).

Though not the first HIV/AIDS-themed play, Larry Kramer's *The Normal Heart* (1985) is arguably one of the most famous. A thinly veiled autobiography, the play follows the experiences of a group of gay men, including the protagonist Ned Weeks, who create a community health center, confront an apathetic mayoral administration, and experience firsthand the destruction of bonds of friendship, romance, and community as HIV/AIDS grips New York City. Kramer's work epitomized the mixture of creative criticism and biographical storytelling that is a hallmark of much theater about HIV/AIDS including other works such as William Hoffman's *As Is* (1985) and Paula Vogel's farcical *The Baltimore Waltz* (1992). Tony Kushner's *Angels in America: A Fantasia on National Themes* (1993) is a monumental work comprising a sprawling cast of historical and fictitious characters whose destines are shaped by the epidemic.

Whereas theater leaves behind a script that can be performed again and again, dance performances often do not survive. Thus, the archive of videos by dancer Bill T. Jones and his lover Arnie Zane (1948–1988) is an invaluable collection. Their work *Still/Here* (1994) can be read as an allegory or metaphor for HIV/AIDS and Zane's experience of living with AIDS. John Bernd (1953–1988) explored the impact and politics of HIV/AIDS in works including *Surviving Love and Death* (1981), and Tracey Rhoades (1961–1993) confronted his own mortality in *Requiem* (1988). David Weissman's short film *Song from an Angel* (1988) put on display the emaciated body of a person with advanced HIV disease—in this case, Rodney Price—to resist the homophobic, pathological gaze of sensationalist news coverage of the epidemic (Gere, 2004).

Classical musicians and composers have likewise used their art to respond to HIV/AIDS. The most obvious examples of AIDS-themed works are texted songs. The *NAMES Project AIDS Quilt Songbook* is an open-ended collection to which composers donate their songs about AIDS that use the works of different poets, some of which are included in the anthology *Poets for Life: Seventy-Six Poets Respond to AIDS* (1992). Its patchwork format is meant to evoke the *NAMES Project AIDS Memorial Quilt*. American baritone William Parker (1943–1993) commissioned the first series of songs, which included submissions by William Bolcom, Fred Hersch, Ned Rome, and Libby Larsen. Abstract instrumental music has also been composed in response to HIV/AIDS. The most famous example is probably John Corigliano's *Symphony No. 1* (1990), which eulogizes one of the composer's friends in each of its four movements. Kristopher Jon Anthony's choral piece *When We No Longer Touch* (1993) eulogizes those lost to HIV/AIDS using poetry by Peter McWilliams. The ongoing series of

HIV/AIDS benefit concerts arranged by New York–based pianist Mimi Stern-Wolfe keep much of this repertoire alive into the present day.

Since the introduction of anti-retroviral drugs in 1996, the production of HIV/AIDS-themed performance artworks has slowed considerably (Attinello, 2006). Where tragedy once inspired artists to create, the luxury of a normal lifespan for people with HIV/AIDS and the vicissitudes of activist burnout have conspired to create conditions of "unforgetting" (Castiglia and Reed, 2012). Other artists have simply shifted the focus of their work and their energies on living with HIV.

*Matthew J. Jones*

In an iteration of the Renaissance centered on Rome (taking place slightly earlier and concurrently was the Northern European Renaissance, which encompassed the creative advances of the Germanic territories), there was a return to the androgynous beauty of the Classical and Hellenistic eras. A foundational image is Donatello's *David* (1430–1440), a bronze precursor to Michelangelo's more famous marble sculpture, in which the Biblical hero is portrayed as a slim aesthete rather than a brawny warrior. The cherubic boy stands daintily on the head of Goliath, whose masculine features imply a relative brutishness and foreign identity. It seems that David could not win a battle in his nakedness, but once again, this refers to the symbolism of intellectual beauty, that is, that well-crafted bodies recall moral and aesthetic virtue. Written records allow us to be more specific about the sexual practices of Renaissance artists onward. Donatello was indeed a homosexual, and it is likely that he was at work on his *David* at the same as Florentine officials were enacting laws against sodomy (Saslow, 1999).

Perhaps the most widely regarded artists of the period who were known to have had same-sex romantic or sexual relationships were Leonardo da Vinci and Michelangelo. While it is true that da Vinci continued the tradition of creating paintings and sculptures of young, androgynous men, such as his supple *Saint John the Baptist* (1515), it might be his most famous image that produces an interesting contemplation on homosexuality—the *Vitruvian Man* (1490). Though it is a small ink drawing, the image distills the simultaneously scientific, erotic, and aesthetic concern with male proportion and creates a formula for representing the ideal male body. In a similar vein, Michelangelo's *David* represents an attempt to depict the nude male body with mathematically precise, and hence "perfect," proportions. Artists of the Renaissance, drawing on Classical precedents, depicted lithe and hairless male bodies—a not-so-subtle feminization that was the contemporary ideal. This is not in itself homosexual, but it nevertheless reflects a cultural fascination on the part of male artists with the archetypal male body. An artistic obsession with the male form does not require homosexual activity, but it does suggest a widespread comfort with male intimacy. The artists of the Northern Renaissance, although they were not as committed to reviving Classical ideals, also engaged with body politics and sexuality in queer ways. A similar interest can be seen in the contemporaneous work of

German artist Albrecht Dürer (a major figure of the Northern Renaissance), whose *The Men's Bath* (c. 1496) illustrates a common arena of male fraternization, but because of a strategically placed faucet, could be interpreted as a homoerotic scene.

Another known bisexual artist Caravaggio (who has since become a modern gay icon) created work that was both part of high culture and vaguely pornographic. His work is filled with young men, many of whom were assistants or simply boys hired off the streets, who were inserted into mythological or religious scenes. Most important in a history of gay art might be Caravaggio's painting of Narcissus (1594–1596)—a mythological boy who was so beautiful that he fell in love with his own reflection. This meant that his pictures had a basis in erotic reality, rather than pure imagination. The boys in his paintings tend to be highly eroticized and sexualized—their boyish charm emphasized in such a way that it made his patrons very uncomfortable. The Catholic Church commissioned Caravaggio to paint *Saint Matthew and the Angel* (1602) but rejected the finished work, perhaps due to its intimate relationship between the saint and his androgynous companion (Saslow, 1999).

There were few women who could be artists in this period because of lack of access to artistic training. However, there were many images by male artists that might be interpreted as depicting lesbian relationships, such as Titian's *Diana and Actaeon* (1556–1559). Such images of Diana, Greek goddess of love, bathing with her nymphs, were often excuses for depicting several female nude figures, often bathing each other. Since most of the viewers of art in this period were men, it is hard to know how much these images of female intimacy were intended for male titillation or reflected an understanding of lesbianism as a unique identity.

*Anne-Louis Girodet de Roucy-Trioson ("Girodet") (French), The Sleep of Endymion (1791 CE), oil on canvas, Louvre Museum (Paris, France), inv. 4935. Source: Photo by Marie Lan Nguyen/CC BY-SA 3.0 license. Image courtesy Wikimedia Commons.*

## The 19th Century: Neoclassicism, Romanticism, Realism

The rising prominence of homosexual men in European upper-class and aristocratic circles in Europe allowed for the increasingly open admiration of male beauty in the 18th and 19th centuries. Johann Winckelmann, for instance, was a noted homosexual philosopher whose rhapsodic musings on the beauty of the *Apollo Belvedere* and other classical depictions of men created a renewed fad for Classical beauty. Winckelmann founded his art history on the masculine beauty of the *Apollo Belvedere*, which he exalted as history's most powerful artwork. Such nostalgia for Classical times paralleled the emergence of a discernibly homosexual identity in art history based on shared aesthetic and erotic ideals.

Jacques-Louis David was perhaps the most important of the neoclassical artists. His paintings revived classical themes not simply to valorize the past, but also to allude to contemporary events, a monumental shift of artistic self-awareness in the history of modern art. Indeed, his neoclassicism retains an element of the homoerotic. His *The Death of Socrates* (1787), for instance, portrays the famed philosopher not as an aging man, but rather as a muscular, smooth martyr. David himself was not homosexual, but his neoclassicism provided a fertile ground for such exploration.

Perhaps the most famous painting in this regard is Girodet's *The Sleep of Endymion* (1791), which has been frequently considered a depiction of same-sex desire, once again through allegory (Solomon-Godeau, 2005). Endymion was known to be among the most handsome subjects of Greek mythology, and Girodet depicts him with unabashed eroticism, and, in the Classical tradition, a notable feminization that places the male nude in between genders. The dappled lighting on Endymion's lightly muscled, lounging body, when combined with the voyeuristic fact that he is asleep, creates a distinctly sexual scene. Girodet, in his addition of erotics to traditionally classical subjects, became a foundational member of the artistic movement that has since been called Romanticism.

Some artists, however, rejected this style and opted instead for Realism, such as the renowned lesbian painter Rosa Bonheur. She was well known for painting animal scenes such as *The Horse Fair* (1852–1855), which, it has been speculated, contains a self-portrait of the artist dressed in men's clothes. Bonheur dressed as a man, which required an annual permit from the Parisian police, to have access to the exclusively male art world. At the same time, she had a public relationship with fellow artist Nathalie Micas. Some have argued that this was an early example of a butch-femme couple, with Bonheur taking on a masculine appearance and Micas occupying traditionally feminine roles. Bonheur also utilized the new medium of photography (invented in the 1830s) to create self-portraits in which she wears men's clothing. Another famous example of an early use of photography is Alice Austen's similar crossdressing in *Self-Portrait with Friends* (1891). Other depictions of crossdressing women are apparent in early

20th century Europe as a newly masculinized vision of the "New Woman" emerged, such as the lesbian painter Maud Hunt Squire's confident protagonist in *Munich Beer Garden* (1910).

*Rosa Bonheur (French, 1822–1899), The Horse Fair, 1852–55, oil on canvas, Metropolitan Museum of Art (New York, NY), acc. 87.25. Source: Metropolitan Museum of Art.*

Photography became an important, if fraught, tool for Realist artists' investigation of the body. The American Thomas Eakins, for example, used photographs of his nude male students in the process of creating sensual paintings. He sometimes painted himself into these compositions, emphasizing his own erotic

*Thomas Eakins (American, 1844–1916),* Eakins' Art Students Bathing *(1884), albumen silver photograph, J. Paul Getty Museum (Pacific Palisades, Calif.), no. 84.XM.811.1. Source: J. Paul Getty Museum Open Content Program.*

gaze. Eakins was fired from his teaching position at the Pennsylvania Academy of Fine Arts for removing the loincloth of a male model in front of female students, which the administration considered far too salacious. His contemporary Eadweard Muybridge used photography to bring scientific realism to the study of movement. He created series of photographs tracking the movement of nude male and female bodies to study the motion of muscles and bones. He could do so without much scrutiny, as his work was seen as a form of scientific investigation rather than art, but his pictures of wrestling male nudes and statuesque men nevertheless became a touchstone of a homosexual (or at least homosocial) imagery for many later gay male photographers.

Also working in this period was Harriet Hosmer, who was considered by many to be the greatest sculptor of the 19th century. She was an American expatriate in Rome, and her circle of friends and colleagues included many prominent artists and writers. Her longtime partner was Lady Ashburton, who she was with for 25 years. Much of Hosmer's sculpture focused explicitly on the subjugation of women by men (as she herself had often been as a woman in the male-dominated field of sculpture) as well as women occupying traditionally male roles (Cronin, 2009). For example, her *Zenobia in Chains* (c. 1859) depicts a queen from 3rd-century BCE Palmyra (near present day Syria) who had been captured by the Romans, which became incredibly famous, in part because of its overt (if problematic) feminist message of the patriarchal shackling of women. Hosmer was accused of utilizing male craftsmen to complete the sculpture, as many thought that a woman could not create a work of art of such strength and grace.

At the turn of the 20th century, artists took cues from earlier artists and movements to create art that explicitly spoke to the complexity of identity. Innovations in art corresponded with innovations in finding new ways to discuss gay and lesbian issues—explicitly and implicitly. At the same time, movements for gay rights in the 1950s and 1960s allowed for greater freedom for gay and lesbian artists. In the latter part of the century, "queer" became an operative term for LGBTQ artists. Today, the enormous amount of queer creativity in art has become a source of inspiration and debate in art history and in other disciplines.

## The 20th Century

### Mysticism and Abstraction

In the first half of the 20th century women made extraordinary strides in the development of modern art, as well as developing an understanding of sexuality in painting and photography. Despite histories of art that credit men with the creation of abstract art around 1900, it may have been a woman, Hilma af Klint, who did so. Klint was known to have relationships with women, and she spent much of her time in a women-only group of mystics who explored the relationship between art and mystic forces. Klint's quasi-spiritual abstractions provide a counterpoint to the very masculine, hard-edged abstractions by Wassily Kandinsky that have become more famous.

Another artist who worked in this woman-centric vein was Georgia O'Keeffe, who, though married to photographer Alfred Stieglitz, often had relationships with women. Henrietta Shore's *Cypress Trees, Point Lobos* (c. 1930) is also in this vein, depicting two voluptuous, intertwined trees that suggest a connection with a female-centered naturalism or spiritualism. Frida Kahlo's paintings, though they are more biographical, also connect to a sort of feminist/lesbian mysticism, this time in the context of Mexican traditions and symbolism. Kahlo's legendary affair with dancer Josephine Baker is always surprising to historians because of Kahlo's marriage to muralist Diego Rivera, but her paintings suggest that her sense of sexuality was beautifully in flux. Perhaps her most famous painting, *The Two Fridas* (1939), is both a double self-portrait and an allusion to same-sex desire, but also more generally the communion among women that was important to women artists in male-dominated artistic and intellectual worlds.

*Carl Van Vechten (American, 1880–1964),* Portrait of Diego Rivera and Frida (Kahlo) Rivera, *March 19, 1932, silver gelatin photograph. Source: Van Vechten Collection, Prints and Photographs Division, Library of Congress, repro. no. LC-USZ62-42516.*

### Dada and Hannah Höch

Other female artists in the early 20th century took a less autobiographical approach, but nevertheless suggested an increasing possibility for art to speak to different sexual experiences. Dada, a movement that swept through Europe and New York in the 1910s through the 1930s, aimed to combine politics and art in a way that had never been done before, often by lampooning political figures or making not-so-subtle *double entendres* to provoke humorous introspection. At the turn of the 20th century in Europe, photography and photomontage (a form of collage that incorporates photographs from magazines or newspapers) created unprecedented opportunities for the exploration of sexuality.

One of the inventors of Dada was Hannah Höch, whose longtime lover was a woman. Höch often dealt with sexual themes, though it is sometimes difficult to categorize them as lesbian (Lavin, 1993). At the very least, there is always a certain androgyny to Höch's work that was characteristic of a larger sexual

*Marcel Duchamp (French & American, 1887–1968), Fountain (1916–17), glazed ceramic. Source: Photo by Alfred Stieglitz published in* The Blind Man *2 (May 1917), 4. Image courtesy of Wikimedia Commons.*

permissiveness in Germany at the time. This is epitomized by the bi-gendered *Dompteuse (Tamer)* of 1930, in which the head of a female mannequin has been placed atop a prominently muscled male body. However, androgyny and female masculinity are not necessarily indicators of homosexuality and Höch did not identify as a lesbian.

Another foundational Dadaist was Marcel Duchamp, who often took on a female persona known as Rrose (or just Rose) Sélavy. When pronounced aloud Rrose Sélavy sounds like the French phrase "Eros, c'est la vie," meaning "Eros, that's life." (In Greek and Roman mythology, Eros [or Cupid] was the god of love.) Duchamp did not identify as gay, but much of his work explored sexual themes, as with his *Fountain* (1917). *Fountain* is simply a urinal turned on its side, but this was considered one of the most important moments in modern art. By presenting an object without changing it at all (other than rotating it), Duchamp asserted that anything could be art. That his chosen object was so closely associated with male genitalia and typically found in all-male spaces (men's rooms) that have long been notorious as sites of casual homosexual sex, implies that *Fountain* was intended to provoke more than observations about the state of modern plumbing. In late 19th and early 20th century Europe, the urinal was one of the most common places of queer sex and interaction, and Duchamp was no doubt aware of this space of homosocial/homosexual interaction. (Houlbrook, 2005).

## American Modernisms

*Paul Cadmus (American, 1904–1999), The Fleet's In, 1934, oil on canvas, Navy Art Gallery, Washington Navy Yard (Washington, D.C.). Source: U.S. Naval Historical Center and Wikimedia Commons.*

Modern art in the United States saw a number of painters and photographers who explored sexual themes in their work. Foremost among them was Marsden Hartley, an American painter and poet, whose work has only recently been understood in terms of his gay identity. Hartley moved to Berlin in 1913, partially to study with the great German painters, and also because the city had much to offer in terms of queer life. Hartley's *The Warriors* (1913) has become most emblematic of this sexual and artistic venture, with a host of men on horses with their bare buttocks turned toward us. In a series of related paintings composed of elements drawn from German military uniforms, Hartley mourned the Prussian officer Karl von Freyburg, the first great love of Hartley's life, who was killed in the first weeks of World War I. This new impulse toward autobiography also can be seen in the work of Paul Cadmus, whose lengthy career was marked by meticulously drawn, muscular male nudes and large paintings laden with social commentary—including explicit homosexual content.

Hartley and Cadmus were certainly important to three gay men who were associated with American Pop art—Jasper Johns, Robert Rauschenberg, and Andy Warhol. Johns and Rauschenberg were subject to closeting for their entire careers, as was the case for many other mid-century artists—men and women—despite the advances made in feminism and gay liberation. They were involved romantically, though this fact has been frequently silenced

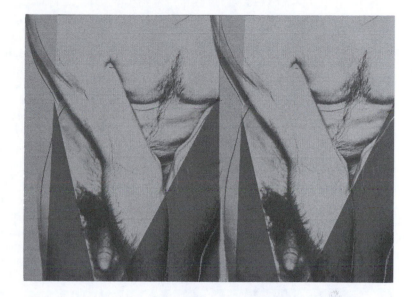

*Andy Warhol (American, 1928–1987),* Torso (Double), *ca. 1982, screenprint on paper. Source: © 2017 The Andy Warhol Foundation for the Visual Arts, Inc. / Artists Rights Society (ARS), New York.*

in academic art history (in fact, the art historian Jonathan D. Katz was removed from a conference at the Guggenheim Museum in New York for mentioning the relationship). However, Johns made frequent references to the gay poet Hart Crane, who killed himself after being beaten by male crewmembers on a steamship after making sexual advances to them. Johns's *Periscope (Hart Crane)* (1962) could be seen as an ode to Crane as a gay martyr. Rauschenberg likewise could be seen as discussing queer themes in works like *Bantam* (1954), which may be a subtle homage to his gayness because of the inclusion of an autographed picture of gay icon Judy Garland, among other potential queer codes (Katz, 1993). This closeting also applied to women. For example, the role of minimalist painter Agnes Martin's lesbianism in her work has been the subject of debate for decades (Schiff, 2012; Katz, 2011).

Andy Warhol, a contemporary of Johns and Rauschenberg, was out as a gay man, and created art that one could definitively say is "about" homosexuality, such as

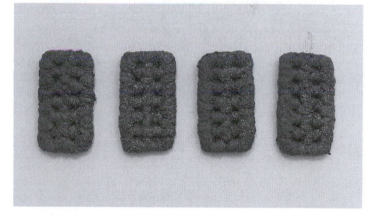

*Harmony Hammond (American, 1944–),* In Her Absence, *1981, mixed media. Source: Alexander Gray Associates, New York. © 2017 Harmony Hammond/Licensed by VAGA, New York.*

his iconic films *Blow Job* (1964) and *My Hustler* (1965), as well as his frequent nudes, anatomical pictures, and self-portraits in drag. Warhol's studio, called The Factory, was a place of sexual permissiveness that was central to the Downtown New York scene, which was a unique subculture that brought queer artists of all kinds together. His *Torso (Double)* (c. 1982) is an homage to the torsos of Classical and neo-Classical sculpture and simultaneously an example of Warhol's trailblazing gay pornographic imagery.

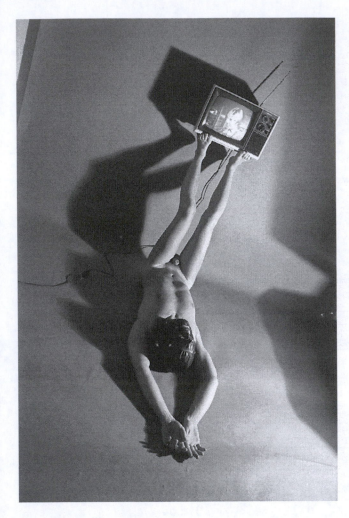

*Jimmy DeSana (American, 1949–1990), Television, 1978, silver gelatin photograph. Source: Jimmy DeSana Trust.*

## Feminism and Lesbian Art

A lesbian feminist identity also became more discernible in the visual arts. One of the most important Fluxus artists (a movement that combined music, art, and absurdist performance) was the lesbian feminist intellectual Kate Millett, who is best known for her landmark book *Sexual Politics* (1969). Millett is also a sculptor; her *Dinner for One* (1967), for example, is a mish-mash of body parts and objects that suggests a polymorphous sexuality. Other lesbian feminists, such as Harmony Hammond, combined the tenets of feminism with a developing interest in queer theory. Hammond uses repurposed materials like wood, rubber, hair, and rags to create complex sculptures. She also works with traditionally "feminine" art forms, like weaving, which illustrate the potential for a feminist revaluation of artistic modes that had been relegated to "craft" or "decoration." Hammond's *In Her Absence* (1981) may not represent actual bodies, but it nevertheless conveys a sense of longing for someone the artist has represented in abstract, mitochondrial forms.

Lesbian feminism in the arts, however, was seen by some to be a paradoxical statement. The painter Louise Fishman faced discrimination from mainstream feminists in 1960s and 1970s New York because of her lesbianism. Fishman's canvases have no subject matter per se, but nevertheless exhibit the heavy, active brushstrokes that have often been associated with male painters. For Fishman, this originated in her love of sports, which formed a central part of her self-image.

## The AIDS Crisis and Queer Activism

Artists' responses to HIV/AIDS were as diverse as the communities it affected. Many artists, such Keith Haring, and the collectives ACT UP (AIDS Coalition to Unleash Power) and Gran Fury, created art that mimicked the tactics of advertising to disseminate information about AIDS outside of the gallery and museum walls. In 1987 ACT UP activists began plastering the city with their now-famous *Silence = Death* posters, which repurposed the pink triangle—once used to mark homosexuals in the concentration camps of World War II—as a symbol of community resistance in the face of a national disregard for people with AIDS. In a similar community-building spirit, Haring's engaging, graphic prints, paintings, and murals depicted, in abstract terms, gay life in New York. His art became so woven into the fabric of the city that some of his public art projects remain prominent in the city as reminders of the ongoing presence of AIDS in queer communities.

Artists in other media also contributed to the ongoing discussion of AIDS. Photographers like Jimmy DeSana and Robert Mapplethorpe celebrated gay BDSM subcultures and heretofore unseen queer bodies. DeSana's *Television* (1978) is a comical and unsettling celebration of kinky sex, wherein a TV set becomes an unexpectedly erotic object. David Wojnarowicz and Derek Jarman created more expressly political photography and film, such as Jarman's homage to the eponymous Caravaggio in a 1986 film. Painters also took part in this activist aesthetic. Martin Wong, a gay Chinese-American painter, for instance, largely depicted people of color and the plight of the working class. Works like his *Mi Vida Loca* (1991), which depicts a large penis as if it were a Catholic icon, suggest a complex relationship between homosexuality and organized religion.

Other artists, such as the conceptual artist Felix Gonzalez-Torres, approached AIDS more metaphorically. His most famous works are his piles of wrapped candies, such as *"Untitled" (Portrait of Ross in L.A.)* (1991). Gonzalez-Torres and his partner, Ross Laycock, both died of AIDS-related illness, and some have argued that *"Untitled" (Portrait of Ross in L.A.)* was created as a conceptual performance of the body's fragility in the wake of the AIDS crisis. Museum-goers may take and eat a piece of the candy, which (literally) diminishes the work and recreates the "consumption" wrought by the AIDS virus, or, more generally, any kind of interpersonal loss (Hudson 2003). The candy may be replenished each night, or it could fully disappear over the course of an exhibition. While there are necessarily many interpretations available to *"Untitled" (Portrait of Ross in L.A.)*, it has nevertheless become a touchstone of a subtle, intellectual queer activism that influenced countless young artists. Another of Gonzalez-Torres's most important "portraits," *"Untitled" (Alice B Toklas' and Gertrude Stein's Grave, Paris)* (1992), depicts the grave of the famed lesbian writers, art patrons, and collectors who were buried together in Paris. One could understand this photograph as an homage to a previous generation of queer bohemian pioneers.

*Felix Gonzalez-Torres (Cuban-American, 1957–1996), "Untitled" (Alice B. Toklas' and Gertrude Stein's Grave, Paris), 1992, framed C-print, edition of 4, 1 AP. Source: © The Felix Gonzalez-Torres Foundation. Courtesy of Andrea Rosen Gallery, New York.*

*Nicole Eisenman (American, 1965–),* It Is So, *2014, oil on canvas. Source: Nicole Eisenman, Anton Kern Gallery (NY) and Susanne Vielmetter Los Angeles Projects.*

Censorship during the 1980s and into the present day continues to be a problem for artists hoping to discuss AIDS. The most famous case is the cancellation of a show of Mapplethorpe's work out of fear of loss of funding for the National Endowment for the Arts, which supported the show financially. A similar controversy erupted over Andres Serrano's *Piss Christ* (1987), which appears to depict a crucifix submerged in urine. Many felt that government funds should not be used to support art that was expressly gay, or deemed to be pornographic. This instance of censorship is one of many moments in the United States in which public and governmental opinion often took the form of homophobia.

## Contemporary Art (after 1990s)

After the body-centric queer art of the 1980s and early 1990s, there has been an increased interest in abstract art, as opposed to art that explicitly depicts LGBTQ life, as a vehicle for personal and community expression. For example, though Amy Sillman's paintings occasionally contain nods to real objects and people, they are largely abstract, multi-colored paintings that would not suggest anything about her own sexuality or the sexuality of her sitters. Her portraits like *N & O v3* (2006) reduce bodies to abstract shapes, but they are nevertheless part of a larger documentation of queer and straight artists alike in New York.

*Isaac Julien (British, 1960–),* Masquerade No. 3 *(Looking for Langston Vintage Series), 1989, Kodak Premier print / Diasec mounted on aluminum. Source: Isaac Julien, and Jessica, Silverman Gallery. © Isaac Julien.*

However, representational art has remained an important strategy. Many contemporary artists continue to use the human body as a central theme, also known as figuration. Nicole Eisenman and Celeste Dupuy-Spencer create surreal scenes of everyday life, wherein gender ambiguity is both celebrated and normalized, and is also combined with sophisticated art historical references. Eisenman's *It Is So* (2014), is an expressionistic ode to queer sexuality. Surrounding this couple, whose genders cannot be discerned, are literary and artistic references in the form of a stack of books—a copy of Homer's *The Iliad* and monographs about Dürer and Picasso. This mundane surrealism has also been used by Anthony Iacono to document the sexuality of everyday life, from somber BDSM scenes to subtly suggestive still lives. His painting-collage *Locked-in* (2015) implies some sort of sexual submission, but it does so only with a pile of fruit and a pair of bent knees. David Benjamin Sherry accomplishes a similar eroticism of the everyday, this time in the context of landscape photography drenched with disco colors. In an act of queering a gay male art history, Deborah Kass has appropriated the work of Andy Warhol in her self-portraits like *Yellow Deb* (2012), which reformulates Warhol's obsession with celebrities like Elizabeth Taylor, Marilyn Monroe, and Jackie Kennedy. Kass's partner Patricia Cronin has also continued this kind of queer figuration with *Memorial to a Marriage* (2002), a large-scale mortuary statue that depicts Cronin and Kass in a loving embrace.

Portraiture, an old genre, remains very important to LGBTQ artists. Lesbian feminist painter Clarity Haynes takes a documentary approach in her body-positive portraits of members of the LGBTQ community. In the Classical tradition of drawing and painting from nude models, Haynes celebrates all sexualities and body types with an intense realism. Other lesbian portraitists include JEB (Joan E. Biren), Gloria Longval, Catherine Opie, and Susan Fleisschmann. Using a more stylized approach, other artists producing portraiture— such as Ebony G. Patterson, Mickalene Thomas, and Ewan Atkinson—celebrate the beauty of the black body throughout the African Diaspora.

*Zachary Drucker (American, 1983–) and Rhys Ernst (American),* Relationship, #10 (Madam, in Eden I'm Adam), *C-print, 2009. Source: the artists and Luis De Jesus, Los Angeles.*

### Repurposing Photography and Video

Photography and video, with their increased availability via smartphones, has continued to be an important site of LGBTQ critique, performance, and creativity. Glenn Ligon's *Self Portrait Exaggerating My Black Features/Self Portrait*

*Exaggerating My White Features* (1998) features identical pictures of the artist, which calls to mind the arbitrary nature of gendered and racial stereotypes. Zackary Drucker's and Rhys Ernst's photography book *Relationship* (2016), for instance, documents their love affair as they transitioned genders. Their photographs are both sophisticated and humorous as they show themselves in the process of radically choosing their genders.

In a similar vein, K8 Hardy's Instagram performances and 2016 film *Outfitumentary* speak to a specifically femme lesbian point of view as Hardy chronicles her daily clothing choices. Hardy's contemporaries A. K. Burns and A. L. Steiner have also considered the expansiveness of lesbian creativity in their video installation *Community Action Center* (2010). Likewise, Martine Syms's and Isaac Julien's video performances and installations consider the complexities of race and sexuality. Julien's film *Looking for Langston* (1989) and its subsequent photographic series are an homage to the black gay identities of the Harlem Renaissance. Tommy Kha, a Southern gay photographer, also uses self-portraiture as a means of interrogating intersectionality. Photographs like Kha's *Home (I)* and *Home (II)* (2015) signal the ability of the photograph to speak to issues of regional identity in a queer, multinational context as Kha fades into the wall of his childhood home.

## Artistic Censorship

Censorship has plagued LGBTQ artists, especially with the intensification of homophobia in the wake of the AIDS crisis. Censors often demonstrate a curious fascination (if not obsession) with the visual art they attempt to censor and, ironically, their efforts often contribute to the awareness (and auction value) of censored works of art. Early in the 20th century, while employed by the Works Progress Administration, Paul Cadmus painted *The Fleet's In!* (1934), a highly eroticized depiction of Navy sailors, filled with prominent crotches and tight pants. The painting was removed from view after complaints from the Navy. In 1989 the Corcoran Gallery of Art in Washington, D.C., canceled an exhibition of work by Robert Mapplethorpe after an outcry emerged due to content that included nude black men and gay leathermen in BDSM clothing. Since the show was supported by funds from the National Endowment for the Arts (NEA), the cancelation of the exhibition brought into relief the role of public funding, free speech, and Reagan-era homophobia. Likewise, Andres Serrano's *Piss Christ* (1987), a photograph depicting a crucifix submerged in a jar of (what has been alleged to be) the artist's urine, was the subject of intense Congressional scrutiny after winning a visual arts award that was funded in part by the NEA. A 2007 Swedish exhibition of Serrano's photographs depicting nudity and sexual acts was vandalized by axe-wielding neo-Nazis. David Wojnarowicz's incomplete silent film *A Fire in My Belly* (c. 1986/7) was removed from an exhibition at the U.S. National Portrait Gallery in 2010 due to complaints from Republican politicians and the Catholic Church. The film contained a brief scene showing a crucifix crawling with ants. Although created prior to his diagnosis with HIV, the film is often seen as a response to the government's and church's lack of response to the HIV/AIDS crisis in the 1980s. Lesbian artist Alma Lopez's digital photograph *Our Lady* (1999), which reimagined the classic image of Our Lady of Guadalupe as a symbol of queer Chicana sexuality, was the subject of violent protests when it was exhibited in the U.S. and Europe. Michelle Handelman's video work *Dorian, A Cinematic Perfume* (2009), a queer re-presentation of Oscar Wilde's infamous novella *The Picture of Dorian Gray* (1890), was removed from a show at the Arthouse (Austin, TX) when one of the gallery's board members became "offended" by its content. The video was restored to the show but with limited screening times and a guard posted at the entrance to the screening room (Tyburczy, 2015; Meyer, 2002).

*William J. Simmons*

### Recent Debates

Contemporary art is a complex and exciting phenomenon, and the most important realization from studying art history is that art is not only a thing of the past. LGBTQ artists have drawn upon past issues while making their work speak to 21st century issues. A fertile area of inquiry in this regard is what has been called "cyber-queer" art, or art that deals with queer themes in the internet era, such as the work of Casey Jane Ellison, K8 Hardy, and Jacolby Satterwhite. All three artists utilize video as a central part of their practice, which makes their work easier to disseminate via YouTube, Twitter, and Instagram. Hardy, for example, uses Instagram to explore her daily sartorial rituals through a distinctly queer feminist lens. The 21st century is vastly diverse, and there are endless new avenues for the study of art and sexuality.

## CONCLUSION

Same-sex attraction and gender variance have long been a part of human literary and artistic expression. Prior to the modern period, they often appeared in literature and the visual arts. More recently, lesbian, gay, bisexual and transgender artists and writers became increasingly unafraid to explore gender variance and same-sex attraction in their work. The rich artistic and literary heritage that survives allows a greater appreciation of LGBTQ culture over time and across cultures.

## Learn more

### Readings

Fone, B. R. S. (2001). *The Columbia anthology of gay literature*. New York, NY: Columbia University.

Goods, G. (1999). *A history of gay literature: The male tradition*. New Haven, CT: Yale University.

Hammond, H. (2000). *Lesbian art in America: A contemporary history*. New York, NY: Rizzoli.

Jones, Sonya L. (1998). *Gay and lesbian literature since World War II: History and memory*. London, UK: Routledge.

Leavitt, D., & Mitchell, M. (Eds.) (1998). *Pages passed from hand to hand: The hidden tradition of homosexual literature in English from 1748 to 1914*. New York, NY: Mariner.

Lord, C., & Meyer, R. (2013). *Art and queer culture*. London, UK: Phaidon.

McCallum, E.L. & Tuhkanen, M. (2014). *The Cambridge history of gay and lesbian literature*. Cambridge, UK: Cambridge University.

Medd, J. ed. (2015). *The Cambridge companion to lesbian literature*. Cambridge, UK: Cambridge University.

Reed, C. (2011). *Art and homosexuality: A history of ideas*. Oxford, UK: Oxford University.

Saslow, J. (1999). *Pictures and passions: A history of homosexuality in the visual arts*. New York, NY: Viking Adult.

Summers, C. (2004). *The queer encyclopedia of the visual arts*. Jersey City, NJ: Cleis.

Summers, C. J. (Ed.) (1995). *The gay and lesbian literary heritage: A reader's companion to the writers and their works, from antiquity to the present*. New York, NY: Holt.

### Film/Video

Bailey, F, & Barbato, R. (Directors). (2016). *Mapplethorpe: Look at the pictures* [Documentary film]. United States: HBO.

Burns, R. (Director). (2006). *Andy Warhol: A Documentary Film* [Documentary film]. United States: PBS Paramount.

Griffin, A. G., & Parkerson, M. (1996). *A litany for survival: The life and work of Audre Lorde* [Television documentary]. United States: POV.

House, J. (Director). *Queer as art* [Television documentary]. London, UK: BBC Two.

Jarman, D. (Director). (2008). *Caravaggio* [Motion picture]. United States: Zeitgeist.

Julien, I. (Director). (1989). *Looking for Langston* [Motion picture]. London: British Film Institute.

Karpman, L., & Kroll-Rosenbaum, N. (Directors). (2014). *Regarding Susan Sontag* [Motion picture]. United States: Question Why.

Potter, S. (Director) (1996). *Orlando* [DVD]. United States: Sony Pictures Classics.

Schiller, G. (Director). (1996). *Paris was a woman* [Documentary film]. United States: Zeitgeist.

Taylor, F. (Director). (2007). *The polymath, or the life and opinions of Samuel R. Delany, gentleman* [Documentary film]. New York, NY: Maestro Media.

Thorsen, K. (Director). (1989). *James Baldwin: The price of the ticket* [Documentary film]. United States: PBS.

von Praunheim, R. (1990). *Silence = Death* [Documentary film]. New York: First Run.

Wright, R. (Director). (2014). *Hockney* [Documentary film]. United States: Film Movement.

Young, E. N. (Director). (2002). *The mind and times of Virginia Woolf* [Documentary film]. United States: Miramax and Paramount Pictures.

*Internet*

Art 21: art21.org

*Lambda Literary:* www.lambdaliterary.org

Leslie-Lohman Museum of Gay and Lesbian Art: www.leslielohman.org

Over the rainbow books: A book list from gay, lesbian, bisexual, and transgender round table. *American Library Association:* www.glbtrt.ala.org/overtherainbow

Queer Arts Resource: www.queer-arts.org

The 100 best lesbian and gay novels. *The Publishing Triangle:* www.publishingtriangle.org/100best.asp

# CHAPTER 9
# Getting Around
## *Globalization and Transnationalism*

*Evan Litwack*

*Man in Prague Pride parade (Aug. 15, 2015) holding sign that reads "Equal marriage does not cause global warming."*
*Source: Photo by WhiteHaven, courtesy of Shutterstock.*

Of all the political slogans to have emerged from the U.S. gay liberation movement of the 1970s—and, indeed, there were many—"We Are Everywhere" remains one of the most remarkable, if not also one of the most frequently memorialized. The phrase could be found plastered on street signs in major urban centers such as New York City and San Francisco; printed on homemade stickers placed furtively in public spaces ranging from restrooms to corporate boardrooms; and emblazoned across banners at marches and protests throughout the decade. This striking rallying cry allowed lesbians and gay men to express both outrage at ongoing homophobic oppression and collective pride in their increasingly visible community (Ghaziani, 2008).

In fact, for many activists "We Are Everywhere" seemed to perfectly capture a central paradox of gay and lesbian life in the post-Stonewall United States. For even as homosexuality was increasingly understood as a natural, and therefore omnipresent, variation of human sexuality, lesbians and gay men continued to live with the ongoing threat of state-sanctioned and everyday violence and invisibility (D'Emilio, 1983; Ordover, 2003). In the face of societal homophobia, activists deployed "We Are Everywhere" to demand the fundamental right of lesbians and gay men to live free of fear, shame, and persecution. In so doing, U.S. lesbian and gay activists of the 1970s used the term "everywhere" to invoke an image of a collective gay and lesbian "we" that was decidedly *global* in scope.

The notion that lesbians and gay men, along with bisexuals and transgender people, are everywhere may sound undeniable if not obvious. In the 40 some-odd years since "We Are Everywhere" first hit the streets of American cities, there has been an explosion in LGBTQ visibility around the globe. The evidence seems indisputable. One example is the proliferation of Pride parades, which now occur annually in over 200 locations during World Pride Month (Gay pride parades from around the world, 2014). Another is the recent emergence of international regulatory agencies and non-governmental organizations (NGOs), such as OutRight Action International and the International Lesbian, Gay, Bisexual, Trans and Intersex Association (ILGA), which serve to promote sexual orientation and gender identity-based human rights globally. There is now an enormous variety of LGBTQ-oriented websites, chat rooms, and social media dating apps that facilitate connections between sexual and gender dissidents across national borders. Who, then, could deny the assertion that queerness is now global?

It is frequently said that we live in an increasingly interconnected world. This means that we live in a world where ideas, images, bodies, and commodities regularly cross nation-state borders and, in the process, upset neat boundaries of cultural identity grounded in place. This sense—if not also the reality—of interconnectedness has undoubtedly transformed the ways that sexualities and genders are experienced, which has, in turn, raised some of the most important and challenging questions facing LGBTQ studies scholars today. How do sexualities and genders vary across cultures? If behaviors, acts, and bodies that *look* homosexual, bisexual, and transgender can be found mostly everywhere, does this mean that LGBTQ social identities are universally resonant? Does the application of Western models of LGBTQ identity to non-Western contexts impose Western attitudes about sex, sexuality, gender, and desire? What concepts can best help scholars, policy-makers, and activists understand the variety of ways in which sexual and gender variance are lived, experienced, and imagined in an increasingly interconnected world? These are some of the most pressing questions being posed by LGBTQ studies scholars today.

This chapter presents an overview of the relationship of sexuality and gender to globalization by examining lesbian, gay, bisexual, transgender, and queer identities from a transnational perspective. It looks at how global processes shape LGBTQ identities, practices, and experiences, and, in turn, how LGBTQ identities, practices, and experiences shape global processes. The first section offers a broad overview of the different ways that scholars have tried to make sense of same-sex sexuality and gender variance in a global frame. This means accounting for the prevalence of same-sex sexual behavior and gender non-conformity in different places in the world. It also requires thinking critically and historically about how identity categories such as gay, lesbian, bisexual, transgender, and queer are themselves embedded in the global circulation of ideas, images, people, and commodities. The second section engages ideas about sexual and gender difference as they emerge from the contexts of European and U.S. colonialism—ideas that continue to inform global dynamics to this day. The last section surveys three key areas of LGBTQ life that have been profoundly transformed by globalization: travel, tourism, and migration; HIV/AIDS; and international law and activism.

## LGBTQ STUDIES IN THE ERA OF GLOBALIZATION

### Defining Globalization and Transnationalism

The meaning and scope of the term globalization is the subject of disagreement. Although there are many (sometimes competing) definitions of globalization, it is possible to identify some common elements. Globalization is a term used by scholars, policy-makers, and activists to refer to the acceleration and intensification of interactions, geographic movements, and exchanges between peoples and across nations since the latter decades of the twentieth century (Appadurai, 1996; Massey, 2002; Tomlinson, 1999). The term is also used to explain the unprecedented way that previously distinct, and often distant, places have become newly connected by economic, technological, and cultural forces, such that it has become possible to imagine the world as an integrated whole (Robertson, 1992).

Global connections are not entirely new. Cross-cultural contact, convergence, and collision have been nearly consistent features of human civilization. Archaeologists regularly uncover evidence of ancient trade routes. In the Middle Ages, human migration, settlement, and trade between Africa, Asia, and Europe were regular occurrences. More recently, European contact with the Americas starting in the late 1400s contributed to an emerging understanding of the world as a single entity. Christopher Columbus' 1492 arrival in the Caribbean meant that for the first time in history humans could conceive of the globe as a single whole (Mendieta, 2001). The violent encounters that emerged from Western colonial expansion and the international slave economy, which reached a peak in the 1800s, created global economic, political, and cultural ties between peoples and across nations that continue to shape the unequal dynamics of power in the contemporary world. Although globalization is often presented as a wholly contemporary phenomenon, it is more accurate to say that contemporary global movements, exchanges, and processes are part of a much longer history of intercultural interaction set in motion by colonialism and slavery.

However, when the term globalization is used today, its historical roots are usually traced to the 1970s. This is partly because, in 1971, United States President Richard Nixon abandoned the Bretton Woods system, which had regulated international trade and monetary exchange after World War II (Harvey, 2007). One critical consequence of the collapse of Bretton Woods was the increased internationalization of trade and finance. This led to the increased power of intergovernmental financial organizations, such as the World Bank, the International Monetary Fund, and the World Trade Organization. Driven by new market pressures and technological innovations, the 1970s, 1980s, and 1990s also witnessed the exponential growth of multinational corporations that were no longer subject to strict national governmental oversight. The removal of barriers to free trade had a significant impact on global labor markets. Manufacturing industries swiftly moved production to cheaper and often more easily exploitable export processing zones (EPZs) in the Global South (Milberg & Amengual, 2008). At the same time, new international patterns of labor migration emerged, with many workers moving from former colonial peripheries in the Global South to wealthier metropolitan centers in the Global North (Munck, 2013).

This brief history reveals that globalization is partly an economic phenomenon. But it is in the arena of culture that these transformations are often most deeply felt, experienced, and understood. For as trade, financial investment, and workers crossed national borders, so did cultural products, beliefs, and ways of life. In different countries and geographic regions, more and more people seem to listen to the same music, watch the same television shows, and enjoy the same brands. Given this fact, a vocal cohort of scholars and activists argue that globalization is best understood as a process of cultural homogenization—in which previously distinct cultures begin to look, think, and act more and more alike (Berger, 2002). Sociologist George Ritzer (1993) famously dubbed the homogenizing effects of globalization "the McDonaldization of society." This phrase captures the way that one can now easily buy a Big Mac whether in a shopping mall in Tucson, Tokyo, or Tripoli. But Ritzer's concerns extended far beyond cheeseburgers and "special sauce." The term McDonaldization provides a way of thinking about globalization as a process through which distinct local and national cultures are gradually replaced by a unified and standardized global consumer culture. Seen this way, globalization is the effect of the spread of both U.S. cultural influence and U.S. corporate interest. It reflects the spread and triumph of U.S. capitalism through the global expansion of consumer markets. From this perspective, the global presence of U.S. brands such as McDonald's, Coca Cola, and Nike has contributed to a more homogenous world culture, such that globalization has become nearly synonymous with the Americanization of the world (Antonio & Bonanno, 2000).

In a similar vein, others argue that globalization's homogenizing effect represents a contemporary form of colonialism, or what former Ghanaian President Kwame Nkrumah (1965) first called "neocolonialism" (literally meaning "new colonialism"). In the period following World War II, a series of anti-colonial wars for national independence in Africa and Asia led to the gradual overthrow of European empires. Between 1945 and 1960 alone, three dozen new nation-states in Africa and Asia achieved either autonomy or full independence from European colonial powers. While European nation-states were no longer in formal political power, they retained control over formerly colonized countries through exploitative economic arrangements. Neocolonialism refers to a system of exploitation in which formerly colonizing nations continue to subordinate formerly colonized nations through unequal economic and cultural relationships (Young, 2001). Neocolonialism replaces direct military and political domination over colonized countries with largely indirect modes of economic exploitation and cultural control. Read in these terms, globalization is only the most recent stage in the long saga of European and U.S. colonial violence and domination.

While most scholars, policy-makers, and activists agree that globalization involves the dominance of Western powers, not all critics agree that globalization has had a homogenizing effect on global cultural life. In contrast, some argue that globalization has had the opposite effect: a massive proliferation or heterogenization of cultures (Appadurai, 1996; Pieterse, 2003). In this view, the intercultural connections fostered by globalization have led to the production of new, or hybrid, cultural forms born out of the recombination and reinvention of multiple local, national, and global cultural practices. An example is the prominence of relatively new languages such as Spanglish, in which migrant communities creatively combine Spanish and English languages into a new, hybrid form of linguistic expression. Another example is the popularity of *kwaito* in 1990s South Africa, a style of electronic music that fuses African samples with house music of the sort pioneered in the 1980s by gay Black disc jockeys in the U.S. Even McDonald's exhibits hybrid features. The appearance of Spicy Paneer Wraps in India, Rice McWraps in China, and Tabasco McWraps in Panama represent a fusion of multiple global, national, and local cultural forms. The concept of hybridity implies that local and national cultures, especially in the Global South, are not simply passive victims of all-powerful Western global forces (Kraidy, 2002). Hybridity demonstrates the complex ways that people actively negotiate, respond to, and resist the forces of globalization.

It is against the backdrop of these debates that the concept of transnationalism emerged as a framework for thinking about globalization and to refer to the movement of ideas, images, commodities, and people between or across national boundaries. Transnationalism refers specifically to the way those movements change the nature of ideas, images, commodities, people, and even nations themselves (Ong, 1999). A transnational perspective is used to understand the unstable, uneven, and multidirectional movements of ideas, images, commodities, and people across and between national borders. A transnational perspective avoids simple and easy generalizations about globalization by paying careful attention to the concrete relationships and interactions that shape people's lives in an increasingly interconnected world. It pays attention to both the inequalities that globalization sets in motion and the new potential avenues for social change that globalization makes possible. It is this attention to specificity and complexity that makes the transnational approach useful for understanding how globalization affects gender and sexual minorities across diverse geographical contexts.

## Desires and Identities across Borders

For some people, the initialism LGBTQ rolls off the tongue with ease. It may appear to simply describe a set of identities that are based on certain intertwined sexual and/or gender desires, expressions, or experiences. But looking at sexualities and genders from a transnational perspective reveals that there is no necessary correlation between LGBTQ identity categories and the people they might seem to describe. This is because identity categories such as lesbian, gay, bisexual, transgender, and queer are not transhistorical and transcultural constants. In other words, they are not eternal or universal identities that occur or make sense in all times and places. Rather, they are relatively recent and culturally specific ways of understanding the organization of desires, bodies, and communities. Therefore, a transnational approach to sexualities and genders thinks critically, carefully, and contextually about whether gender and sexual categories such as lesbian, homosexual, and transgender are relevant or applicable everywhere.

Rather than take the slogan We Are Everywhere as fact, a transnational approach to sexualities and genders instead asks the question, "Are 'we' everywhere?" For a long time, U.S. scholars largely presumed that the answer to this question was "yes." Much of the early scholarship on same-sex sexuality and gender variance in non-Western contexts emerged from the discipline of anthropology. Gilbert Herdt's 1984 study of the "Sambia" (a pseudonym) of Melanesia/Papua New Guinea remains one of the most well-known and influential of these now classic anthropological texts. Herdt's research concerned a practice among the Sambia in which boys ingest the semen of older men as a rite of passage into manhood. Semen is ingested following oral stimulation of the older man's penis, and is believed to bolster the masculinity of the boy-initiate. Herdt referred to this practice of semen ingestion as a form of "ritualized homosexuality," though he certainly did not mean to suggest that all

Sambia men are gay or bisexual.
Rather, what he concluded is
that homosexuality is a form
of behavior—an act, not an
identity—that can be discerned,
identified, and analyzed across
different cultural contexts,
despite the incredibly diverse
range of meanings attached to
homosexuality (Herdt, 1984).

Herdt's concept of ritualized
homosexuality caused much
debate within the discipline of
anthropology and beyond. Some
scholars worried that Herdt was

*Under globalization the world
is increasing interconnected.
Source: Photo by Muuraa.
Image courtesy of Shutterstock.*

condoning what to them looked like pedophilia or the sexual abuse of children
(Schiefenhövel, 1990). But beyond the rush to moralistic outcry, Herdt's study
also raised fundamental questions about the nature of sexuality and, specifically,
homosexuality as they manifest in different cultural contexts. Does genital activity
between people of the same sex necessarily constitute "homosexual" activity?
Do people need to identify as homosexual to be homosexual? Why even call
ritualized semen ingestion "sexual" in the first place if it has more to do with
initiating boys into manhood than with erotic desire or romantic attraction? Who
decides what counts as sexual and what doesn't (Franke, 1998)?

In response to Herdt's research, some critics argued that his decision to
label Sambia semen ingestion as both sexual and homosexual was deeply flawed
(Elliston, 1995). They argued that Herdt had failed to address the fact that what
counts as sexual varies across cultures. For even as Herdt had hoped to distinguish
the practices of Sambia boys and men from Western gay male sexual practices,
he still could not help but see in Sambia semen ingestion something that looked
overtly sexual and, more specifically, something that looked quite a bit like
male homosexual oral sex. In interpreting Sambia semen ingestion as (homo)
sexual critics claimed that Herdt had inadvertently imposed onto a non-Western
culture a series of distinctly Western assumptions about what constitutes sexuality
in general and homosexuality in particular. For this reason, critics argued that
Sambia man-boy semen practices should not be understood as a male homosexual
(or gay) sexual practice.

The debate about Sambia semen ingestion reflects a more general issue: the
imposition of assumptions about sexuality and gender from Western contexts
onto non-Western contexts. Consider, for example, the *lesbi* community of
Padang in West Sumatra, Indonesia. Reading quickly, one could mistake the
word *lesbi* for lesbian, which is the most prominent term used to describe female
homosexuals in U.S. culture. But *lesbi* are not lesbians (Blackwood, 2010). Even
though the word *lesbi* is linked etymologically to the English word lesbian, the
two terms do not have the same meaning. In Padang, *lesbi* is an identity marker
used to describe either two women who are involved romantically or a couple

## Globalization Terms

On most contemporary world maps, the earth is pictured as being divided by two imaginary lines. One line, the Prime Meridian, cuts the world in half longitudinally (vertically), dividing the world between Western and Eastern Hemispheres. The other line, the Equator, cuts the world in half latitudinally (horizontally), dividing the world between Northern and Southern Hemispheres. To say that these lines are imaginary indicates that the Prime Meridian and the Equator are not physically visible on the earth's surface. But it also suggests that these divisions are human inventions, created to order and organize how we imagine and understand the world. Maps do not simply portray the world as it is. Maps also *create* and *represent* our perceptions of the world. While world maps are often believed simply to depict the truth of our world geography, it is more accurate to say that maps reflect the perspectives and the biases of the cartographer, or map maker.

The establishment of the Prime Meridian and the Equator, along with the Western, Eastern, Northern, and Southern Hemispheres to which they give rise, is a product of European colonialism. European cartographers and geographers used these divisions to create, enact, and justify colonial programs in which "civilized" Westerners/Northerners could conquer, occupy, and "civilize" places and people in regions identified as "barbaric," "primitive," and "underdeveloped." For this reason, geographical terms, like Western, Eastern, Northern, and Southern, are not objective, neutral, or natural phenomena. Rather, they are socially produced categories that reflect and express historical and contemporary relations of power and authority. It is in this context that the terms Western and non-Western, Global South and Global North emerged as terms used by contemporary scholars, policy-makers, and activists to make sense of the complexities of world geography in the age of globalization.

The term Western is generally used as a shorthand for Europe, as well as for Europe's former settler colonies in North America, Australia, and New Zealand. Thus, Western does not necessarily refer to those countries that lie west of the Prime Meridian. For example, Gambia, in West Africa, is in the Western Hemisphere but is regularly described as a non-Western country. Australia is in the Eastern Hemisphere but is regularly described as Western. Western is less a geographical region than a group of places whose dominant political and cultural systems derive from Europe. There was no West prior to the onset of European colonialism in the 1400s. The West only made sense as a term in the context of the invention of its opposite: the non-West. As the negative prefix "non-" indicates, non-Western is commonly used to refer to all places, peoples, political systems, and cultural forms that are not part of the West. The non-West generally includes Central America, South America, Africa, Asia, the Pacific Islands, and sometimes Central and Eastern Europe. The term non-Western describes so many different places and people that its use can mask significant national and cultural differences. Use of the term non-Western can be problematic because it describes people for what they are not, rather than what they are. Even so, the term is used today to draw attention to how the world continues to be shaped and divided by the ongoing force of U.S. and European domination.

> The terms Global South and Global North are more recent inventions. They gained popularity after the end of the Cold War in 1991. These terms are generally used to refer to economic divisions between poor(er) nations (the Global South) and rich(er) nations (the Global North). The Global South is a metaphor used describe those regions of the world that have been most negatively impacted by global capitalism. This is the case even though the majority of people in the Global South live in the Northern Hemisphere. For example, India is in the Northern Hemisphere but is regularly described as being part of the Global South. The term Global South has been used increasingly by activists to create transnational activist networks to resist the worst forces of globalization.

in which one partner is masculine and the other feminine. *Lesbi* often use gender marked terms to describe themselves. The term *tomboi* is used by *lesbi* who identify as men, while their *girlfriends* identify as conventionally feminine. *Lesbi* identity is therefore significantly different from Western sex/gender categories like lesbian, transgender, or female masculinity. In fact, among *lesbi*, terms such as lesbian and transgender can be potentially offensive. To suggest that *lesbi* are "really" lesbians—merely a "local" variant of the universal phenomenon of female homosexuality—disrespects and disregards the right of *lesbi* to name and describe their own sexual and gendered identities and experiences.

The belief that sexuality and gender are experienced the same way globally or cross-culturally is sometimes referred to as the "universalizing approach" to sexual and gender identity. The universalizing approach starts with the premise that there are a set of standard or universal characteristics unique to same-sex desire, multiple-sex desire, and/or gender variance, regardless of historical or cultural context. From this perspective, non-normative sexualities and genders outside the West are essentially the same as lesbian, gay, bisexual, transgender, and queer ones. For advocates of the universalizing approach, when people fail to recognize that "We are Everywhere" they ultimately lose out on vital possibilities for cross-cultural community building, political organizing, and solidarity.

However, one significant problem with the universalizing approach is that it is quite frequently ethnocentric. Ethnocentrism refers to the inclination to view the entire world from the perspective of one's own culture. In the area of sexuality, an ethnocentric approach views all same-sex sexual activity, in any time and place, as homosexuality (Vance, 1991). For this reason, many LGBTQ studies scholars argue that the universalizing approach risks erasing or silencing those for whom terms such as homosexual, bisexual, or transgender do not accurately describe their identities, experiences, or understandings of gender and sexuality (Swarr & Nagar, 2003).

Problems with using universal terms to describe gender and sexual minorities are greater than mere language differences. Different ways of knowing and thinking about sex, sexuality, gender, desire, and romantic life are shaped by the cultural and national contexts out of which they arise (Binnie, 2004; Hemmings, 2007; Manalansan, 2003). One example is the metaphor of the "closet," which is commonly used in the United States to describe the need to hide a non-normative gender identity or sexual orientation from friends, family, and/or coworkers. To "come out of the closet" is to disclose a previously hidden sexual or gender identity. Thus, the closet also implies the conditions of visibility and invisibility, shame and acceptance, that surround gender and sexual minority lives in transphobic and homophobic societies. "Coming out" is often understood to be a, if not *the*, definitive transition in the life an LGBTQ person.

While the metaphor of the closet may seem global and universal, it is a relatively recent invention. It only gained popularity in the United States in the 1960s among lesbians and gay men (Chauncey, 1994). Since coming out is culturally and historically specific to the United States in the twentieth century, there is no reason to expect that it will be meaningful for sexual or gender minority communities throughout the world.

For example, many Filipino gay men in New York City view coming out as the preoccupation of white gay Americans (Manalansan, 2003). For these men, "the closet" is not a commonly used term nor a useful metaphor for their sexual identities and political struggles. This is because they do not understand their sexuality as a hidden secret in need of being revealed. This example suggests that coming out of the closet is not always a desired, necessary, or inevitable goal of struggles for sexual and gender justice. Such a view may in fact reflect a universalizing and ethnocentric vision of global sexual and gender liberation, one that is narrowly focused on the needs and desires of only certain mainstream U.S. LGBTQ communities. By contrast, a transnational approach to sexualities and genders strives to respect the needs and desires of various sexual and gender communities in all their complex particularities.

## Globalizing Sexuality and Gender

The intercultural encounters brought about by globalization produce new ways of thinking and classifying sexual and gender variance. As different ideas about sexual and gender identity—who we are, who or what we desire, and what our identities mean to us—travel across national and cultural borders, diverse systems of sexual and gendered meaning-making inevitably collide.

Consider, for example, contemporary Suriname in South America, where a growing class of educated Afro-Surinamese women increasingly identify as lesbian. These are women who may once have understood their sexual and spiritual relationships with women as "*mati* work." While the term *mati* means same-sex lover, it probably emerged from the Dutch word *maate*, meaning mate or shipmate. It refers historically and etymologically to women who survived together the Middle Passage epoch of the slave trade into the Americas (Tinsley, 2008). In contrast to lesbian, which refers to an identity (something one *is*), the *mati* work is generally understood by Afro-Surinamese women as an activity (something one *does*). While some women have now adopted the new identity label of lesbian, they have certainly not abandoned their *mati* sensibilities altogether. Many Afro-Surinamese lesbians continue to perform the kind of carework central to *mati* relationships, including nurturing emotional support, the raising of children, and cultivating sexual pleasure (Wekker, 1999, 2006).

In contemporary Mexico it is now increasingly common for urban masculine men who have sex with men to identify as gay or homosexual. This might not be especially surprising, were it not for the fact that, in Mexico, masculine, *activo* (active) sexual partners in male-male relationships have long been considered "normal" (that is, not homosexual). By contrast, *pasivo* (passive) or receptive sexual partners in male-male sexual relationships have long been considered effeminate or non-normatively masculine. This is largely due to their engagement in sexual behavior associated with femininity. The Mexican adoption of a system of sexual classification based on the gender of one's sexual object-choice (where men who are sexually attracted to other men are homosexual), rather than one organized around gender roles (where men who take the *activo* role as sexual penetrators are viewed as masculine and "normal" regardless of the sex of their sexual partners), did not happen overnight. The object-choice model of sexual classification first arrived in Mexico at the start of the twentieth century, when Mexican elites who had participated in European academic debates disseminated the model in their home country. Today, the object-choice model has spread to a much larger portion of the Mexican population (Carrillo, 2002).

Finally, consider the case of India, where a landmark 2013 Supreme Court ruling led to the legal recognition of "transgender" as an official third gender category. As a result of this decision, a wide variety of Indian gender and sexual identities—*hijras* (meaning roughly meaning third sex persons); *kothi* (meaning roughly meaning feminine male-assigned persons who may or may not identify as transwomen); and *dhurani* (meaning roughly feminine men who have sex with men and/or male sex workers)—have all been lumped together under a single demographic rubric (Dutta & Roy, 2014).

Each of these snapshots reflects the ways that globalization reshapes the lived experience of non-normative sexualities and genders in particular national contexts. As different ways of knowing and understanding sexuality and gender encounter one another, they are, in turn, transformed. How have scholars made sense of these transformations? Does the globalization of sexual and gender identities have a homogenizing effect on global sexual and gendered life? Are LGBTQ identities simply another set of Western exports—no different from McDonald's—that are now being imposed on people from every corner of the globe? Or has globalization had a heterogenizing effect on global sexual and gendered life, producing new and hybrid ways of knowing and understanding the organization of desires, bodies, and communities?

There are several major theories regarding the relationship of globalization to sexuality and gender. Some scholars argue that globalization is producing a homogenous "global gay" identity (Altman, 1997, 2001). Sometimes referred to as "the global gay thesis," this perspective suggests that the emergence of Western-style homosexuality outside the West is the primary consequence of a process of cultural diffusion, whereby ideas generated by a newly formed gay community spread quickly from the U.S. and Western Europe in the years following 1969, the year of the Stonewall riots in New York City. According to this view, globalization has set in motion a broadly unidirectional movement of gay images, narratives, systems of meaning, and modes of classification from Western to non-Western regions of the world. As a result, non-Western models of sexual and gender identity have been replaced by a Western model of LGBTQ identity. Thus, the increasing prevalence of self-identified gays and homosexuals in non-Western contexts reveals that sexual minorities across the world may now see themselves as members of the same relatively homogenous global gay community.

Other scholars contest the notion that globalization has produced a single Western-style global gay community (Blackwood, 2010; Martin, 1996; Oswin, 2006; Rofel, 1999). They point out that the global gay thesis hinges on the belief that a new universal gay identity has replaced many of the local "homosexualities" that existed prior to globalization. Critics of the global gay thesis take issue with this view, precisely because it imagines people outside the West as passive consumers of a Western sexual identity model, rather than active agents over the terms of their own sexual and gendered lives. Rather than ushering in a universal gay identity, these critics argue that globalization fuses and intermixes multiple ways of thinking about gender and sexuality. From this perspective, the globalization of sexuality and gender is not a homogenizing process; it is a heterogenizing one. It does not erase culturally specific, same-sex and gender non-conforming practices, identities, and experiences; it multiplies the diversity of same-sex and gender non-conforming practices, identities, and experiences globally. An example might be the shift from *mati* to lesbian discussed in the first snapshot above. The increasing popularity of lesbian self-identification in Suriname could suggest that a global Western-style lesbian identity has replaced the *mati* work altogether. Yet the enduring prevalence of *mati* practices indicates that this is far from the case. Different systems of sexual and gendered meaning and classification—some indigenous, some foreign—are everywhere undergoing ongoing processes of negotiation and change. New and emergent sexual and gender practices can be understood less as *either* purely Western or non-Western and more as *hybrid* forms produced in a shifting global landscape of intercultural encounter.

Critics of the global gay thesis also disagree with how the Stonewall riots are routinely identified as the singular origin of worldwide gay liberation. These critics suggest that the global gay argument imagines the West as the sole birthplace of modern, liberated, and politicized sexual identity. By contrast, non-Western societies are cast as traditional, primitive, or backward cultures that can only follow the forward-march of Western LGBTQ progress. Critics suggest that what emerges from the global gay thesis is a troubling binary opposition between an allegedly "modern" West, characterized by a penchant for sexual freedom, and an allegedly "traditional" and intolerant non-Western world (Grewal & Kaplan, 2001; Manalansan, 1995; Massad, 2002). This "liberated West" versus "repressed non-West" binary forcibly erases and ignores histories of and movements for social, sexual, and gender justice that do not center on European and U.S. history.

Consider, for example, the use of the term gay in Bangkok, Thailand, and Manila, The Philippines. Gay scenes in Bangkok and Manila emerged in the 1960s relatively independent of U.S. cultural influence, often years before the Stonewall riots (Jackson, 2001). Their existence shows that gayness is not solely a product of the West, nor is the prevalence of gay identity in Southeast Asia a wholly Western import. It is therefore both a historical error and an ethnocentric distortion to view the West as the singular locus and origin of "modern" gay sexual culture.

Another example is *tongzhi* identity in contemporary China. While the term *tongzhi* was once widely used as an amiable term of address to one's comrades in mid-twentieth century China, this original meaning has changed significantly. In the late 1980s the term was first repurposed by Hong Kong activists for the inaugural Lesbian and Gay Film Festival in Hong Kong as an umbrella term for sexual minorities (Coleman & Chou, 2000). In the past two decades, the popularity of *tongzhi* self-identification has increased dramatically, not only in Hong Kong but throughout Greater China (Wilson, 2006; Wong, 2010). The dissemination of *tongzhi* identity within China illustrates that sexual meanings, classifications, and identities under globalization do not simply travel from the West to "the Rest." The movements of sexual meanings, classifications, and identities within and across non-Western geographies constitute a common, though frequently ignored, component of globalization.

## COLONIALISM AND EMPIRE

Contemporary globalization is part of a much longer history of intercultural encounter that began with European colonialism in the 1400s. Contemporary world geography is an effect of European (and U.S.) colonial practices and policies that occurred over the course of the past five centuries. The construction of many of our contemporary ideas about sexuality and gender coincide with the epoch of colonialism (Mercer & Julien, 1988). The processes through which sexuality and gender have, historically, come to be understood as meaningful categories of social difference came about in the context of colonial rule. It is for this reason that revisiting the history of colonialism can aid in understanding the experiences of sexual and gender minorities in today's global world.

### Colonial Histories

Most broadly, colonialism refers to the process of settling territories, where one state controls and undermines the sovereignty, or political authority, of another people (Doyle, 1986). Unfolding across over five centuries of conquest in Africa, Asia, the Americas, and the Pacific, Western colonialism has been decidedly marked by a relentless and brutal quest for the control and extraction of indigenous resources, the exploitation of slave and native labor, the genocide and removal of indigenous peoples, the occupation of stolen lands, and the institutionalization of racist belief systems. Historians identify two main periods of colonialism. The first, which followed the Portuguese conquest of Ceuta, North Africa, in 1415 and the "discovery" of the Americas in 1492, extended approximately from the 1400s through to the 1700s. During this period, the Spanish, Portuguese, English, French, and Dutch settled colonies in what would come to be called North, Central, and South America. By 1750, the whole of South and Central America and half of North America were divided among these European powers.

The establishment of colonies in the "New World" depended upon the elimination and displacement of Indigenous peoples and nations. Frontier violence, massacres, the use of biological warfare (such as intentionally spreading smallpox), and the forced removal of Native peoples from their lands contributed to the massive destruction and depopulation of Indigenous America in the aftermath of 1492 (Stiffarm & Lane, 1992). Western colonial domination and settlement also extended to the Pacific. In the 1760s and 1770s, British Captain James Cook's voyages to the Pacific led to the British occupation of Australia, New Zealand, and Tasmania. Over the course of the next two centuries, France, Germany, and the United States would also occupy and colonize island nations in the Pacific. The occupation and colonization of the Americas and much of the Pacific continues to this day.

Slavery was the cornerstone of the economy that fueled European colonialism and the development of "New World" nation-states, such as the United States. At the heart of slavery was the slave trade, which involved the abduction and enslavement of approximately 12.5 million African people between 1500 and 1866 (Lovejoy, 1979). In 1860 the United States alone enslaved 3.9 million people of African descent, nearly 60% of the Western hemisphere's enslaved population (Mintz, 2011). Slave labor provided the agricultural base of Europe's economic wealth as well as the economic growth of the American colonies. Slavery also underpinned the social, political, and cultural systems that drew Europe, Africa, and the Americas together from the 1500s onward. For it was in the contexts of slavery and colonialism that race was invented as a defining category of social classification. Race is not a biological or natural given. Rather, the idea of race was created to justify enslavement, genocide, and exploitation. Race and racial difference were used to order, hierarchize, and secure the boundaries between the free and the enslaved, the colonizer and the colonized, the European and the non-European—between, in short, populations who are acknowledged as fully human and populations who are considered less than human. Race was—and continues to be—a central part of a worldview that rationalizes why freedom, rights, citizenship, and property are reserved for some populations and denied to others.

Historians argue that the second major period of colonialism took place in the late 1700s and the 1800s. In 1884 European powers met in Berlin to divide the African continent among themselves (Ndlovu-Gatsheni, 2015). At the Berlin Conference, Europeans converted over 1,000 political entities in Africa into 50 European colonies. This so-called "scramble for Africa" reveals Europe's complete disregard for African people's humanity, dignity, and sovereignty. One political consequence of the partition of Africa was that African people now found themselves locked into national boundaries that were decided by Europeans. By 1900 France and Britain occupied almost three-quarters of Africa, with Belgium, Italy, Portugal, and Spain also establishing colonies on the continent. By 1914 the entirety of Africa, with the exceptions of Ethiopia and Liberia, had been brought under violent colonial rule. Similar processes led to the establishment of colonial governments in the Middle East and Asia. Far from being over, colonialism continues to shape economies, cultures, and political systems in today's world. The United Nations (2016) currently identifies 17 non-self-governing territories, the majority of which are under the present jurisdiction of the United Kingdom and the United States.

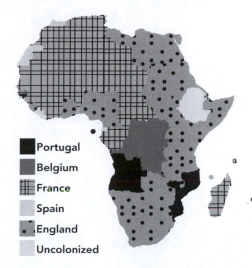

*At its height, European countries had colonies throughout the world. For example, at various times, territories in Africa were colonized by no less than 6 different European countries. Source: Adapted from original by Davius/CC SA-BY 3.0 license. Image courtesy of Wikimedia Commons.*

## Colonialism, Gender, and Sexuality

Sexuality and gender played central roles in the making of empires. For example, maps drawn by early European explorers frequently represented non-European lands as female and imagined exploration as an act of sexual conquest (McClintock, 1995; Pratt, 1992). Explorers also frequently circulated pornographic images of non-Western female nakedness. The equation of non-European "savage" lands with nudity and sexual promiscuity worked to construe the colonies as exotic spaces where Europeans could play out their innermost sexual desires (Garraway, 2005). For instance, since the time of Captain Cook's arrival in Tahiti, the Pacific Islands have been imagined as paradisiacal spaces of sexual freedom for Europeans (Wallace, 2003). Sexual violence, rape, and coerced intimacy were employed regularly by Europeans as weapons of domination and control (Deer, 2015; Nagel, 2003; Scully, 1995). In the context of slavery in the Americas, including the United States, rape and sexual violence against enslaved Black women served as tools of brutal dehumanization and as a means of ensuring the sexual reproduction of an enslaved labor force (Davis, 2003).

European colonizers were obsessed with studying and classifying the intimate practices and desires of the colonized. Knowledge about the West's racial and geographic "others" came to depend significantly on European ideas about the "unnatural" sexual desires and "abnormal" gendered expressions to which non-Europeans were allegedly predisposed (Aldrich, 2002; Hoad, 2000). Non-European populations were regularly (mis) represented by Europeans as pathologically and/or excessively sexual—as the complete opposite of traditional European middle-class heterosexual families (McClintock, 1995; Sharpley-Whiting, 1999; Stoler, 2002). These framings had direct material consequences. They were used by Europeans to justify the violence of colonialism as part of a benevolent "civilizing mission" to uplift and "save" allegedly primitive, animalistic, and sexually perverse non-Europeans from their "uncivilized" ways. Sexual and gendered discourse—the production of images, knowledges, and beliefs about sexuality and gender—thus offered a way for colonizers to distinguish themselves from the colonized, and to construct and reinforce racist beliefs about Western superiority and non-Western inferiority.

Even when same-sex sexual behavior or gender variance were not explicitly evident or discussed by colonizers, non-Europeans were still described and imagined as existing outside European understandings of what counted as "normal" sexuality and gender. In the Western colonial imagination, the non-Western woman came to be understood as everything that the Western woman was *not* (Gilman, 1985). The ideal of European white womanhood rested upon notions of purity, chastity, and domesticity. By contrast, the non-Western woman was imagined by Europeans to be precisely the opposite: prurient, immoral, and sexually available. The story of Saartjie Baartman is exemplary in this regard (Hobson, 2003). Baartman was a Khoisan woman from South Africa who was exhibited at freak shows (or human zoos as they were known at the time) in England and France during the early 1800s. Billed as the Venus Hottentot by her captors, Baartman was paraded on display for crowds who came to gawk at her buttocks, the size and shape of which were pathologized in Europe as a condition known as steatopygia (large buttocks). In Europe, Baartman's body became a symbol of African hypersexuality, first on the British stage, and then later in France where she was sold to animal trainers. After Baartman's death at the age of 26, she was dissected by scientists who stored her genitals and brain at The Museum of Natural History in Paris for 150 years. Baartman's tragic story reflects how the racial difference of colonized women served to violently exclude them from what was considered "normal" gender and sexuality by Europeans, regardless of their own sexual object-choices or senses of gendered selfhood. Racial difference was interpreted as a spectacle of gender and sexual difference which, in turn, justified the project of colonialism.

*George Catlin,* Wi-Jun-Jon, An Assinneboin Chief *from* Catlin's North American Indian Portfolio *(London: George Catlin and J. Adlard, 1844). Source: Courtesy of Wikimedia Commons/Bancroft Library, U.C. Berkeley.*

Even presumably "straight" non–Europeans were considered not quite "straight" enough by Europeans. Consider, for instance, a widely circulated description of Native American men by prominent eighteenth-century French naturalist Georges Louis Leclerc, Comte de Buffon, who wrote: "In the savage the organs of generation are feeble. He has no hair, no beard, no ardor for the female" (qtd. in Jefferson, 1997 [1785]). In Buffon's account, the Native male is understood to be insufficiently masculine—fundamentally lacking in both genital size and cross-gender sexual attraction. What narratives such as Buffon's reveal is that the attribution of "savage" status to colonized populations rested heavily on their purported failure to conform to dominant Western gender and sexual ideals. Indeed, colonial narratives were littered with representations of non–European men as feminized, perverse, and child-like. For example, during Spaniard Vasco Núñez de Balboa's 1513 imperial expedition to Panama, perceived sexual and gender transgression played a pivotal role in his gruesome decision to feed over 40 Panamanian men to his dogs (Goldberg, 1993). Spanish imperial accounts of Balboa's bloody expedition in the village of Quarequa repeatedly highlighted that the men were cross-dressers who cohabitated in sexual relationships. The significant amount of attention given to cross-dressing and sodomy worked not only to distinguish the "civilized" European from the "savage" Native, but also served to excuse the genocide of indigenous peoples.

Balboa läßt Indianer durch Bluthunde zerreißen. Nach einem Kupferstiche des 16. Jahrhunderts.

*Spanish conquistador Vasco Núñez de Balboa's war dogs killing indigenous Two-Spirit Panamanians (ca.1500 CE). Illustration by Theodor de Bry, from Rudolf Cronau, Amerika: Die Geschichte seiner Entdeckung von der ältesten bis auf die neueste Zeit (Leipzig: Abel Müller, 1892). Source: Image courtesy of New York Public Library Digital Collections.*

Balboa was not alone in tying Native Americans to gender and sexual abnormality. Early English, French, and Spanish encounters with Native peoples in North America frequently made reference to the category of the *berdache*. *Berdache* is a Persian-derived word meaning kept boy, male prostitute, prisoner, or simply, wound (Driskill, 2004; Jacobs, Thomas, & Lang, 1997; Morgensen, 2011). While the exact meaning of this derogatory term has shifted over the centuries, it has been deployed consistently by settlers to refer to Native gender and sexual practices that conflict with European binary gender and sexual norms. These include non-binary indigenous gender identities, such as Two-Spirit, which have no set European equivalents. From the perspective of the United States government, the figure of the *berdache* has long been viewed as a symptom of the widespread failure of Native peoples to conform to the moral standards of "modern" civilization. To this end, "civilizing" the so-called "savage"—making Native Americans fit for incorporation into the American polity—has often gone hand in hand with the active regulation and decimation of indigenous sexual and gender practices (Rifkin, 2011).

The enforcement of European sexual and gender norms among colonized populations was a key mechanism of colonial control. For example, prior to the British colonization of the Kingdom of Buganda (now part of Uganda in East Africa), intimate relations between the *kabaka* (king) and his male pages was a normal way of demonstrating political obedience to the Kingdom (Hoad, 2007). Archival evidence does not specify the exact nature of these intimate relations. Yet, when British Christian missionaries arrived in Buganda in the 1880s they deemed the relations between King Kabaka Mwanga and his pages an unnatural and sinful form of sexual behavior. After the missionaries converted some of the pages to Christianity, these pages refused to participate in Mwanga's so-called "unnatural vice." Their refusal culminated in Mwanga's execution of 30 pages in 1886. By recasting Bugandan political intimacies as both "sexual" and entirely "unnatural," European missionaries and colonizers shifted the pages' loyalty away from the King and toward the British crown. Their execution also served as justification among the British for the necessity of colonial rule. For it was this very event that led to intervention from the British government, which resulted in Buganda becoming a British Protectorate in 1894. By re-framing Bugandan male–male intimacies as a form of deviant sexuality, British powers could both dismantle existing African political practices and justify colonial occupation and subjugation.

The European attempt to link non-Europeans to sexual and gender perversion proliferated throughout the 1800s (Bleys, 1995). In his 1885 translation of *The Arabian Nights*, British explorer and ethnologist Sir Richard Francis Burton famously claimed the existence of what he called the "Sotadic zone." The Sotadic zone referred to a vast region in which the propensity for homosexuality was said to increase dramatically. In Burton's view, climate was understood as the decisive factor in causing homosexuality, and he located the Sotadic zone in a geographical band that comprised the Americas, Australia, Japan, China, the Pacific Islands, the Middle East, and the Mediterranean basin. The vast majority of neither Europe nor Africa appeared on Burton's list of homosexually inclined regions. Contemporary scholars speculate that it was Mwanga's execution of the pages in Buganda that had influenced Burton's belief that homosexuality does not exist in Africa (Rao, 2015). Burton believed that climate, and not race per se, was the primary cause of homosexuality. Yet his theory secured among Europeans a widespread belief in the superiority of racial whiteness by aligning Europe with "normal" heterosexuality.

The association between racial difference, colonized peoples, and sexual perversion reached new heights with the rise of sexology in Europe during the mid-1800s. Sexology is the scientific study of sexual life. In its original nineteenth-century form, sexology was especially concerned with the cause and classification of newly identified sexual perversions, which included homosexuality and bisexuality. While sexology was born in Europe, its identification of new sexual and gender identities developed in tandem with theories of racial difference emerging out of colonial encounters (Bleys, 1995). Sexologists frequently drew on ideas about racial difference in their attempts to comprehend and classify homosexuals and bisexuals. Key nineteenth-century treatises by leading sexologists Havelock Ellis and Richard von Krafft-Ebing drew peculiar analogies between

*Area described by Sir Richard Burton as the "Sotadic zone." Source: Adapted from original by Moo Guy/CC SA-BY 3.0 license. Image courtesy of Wikimedia Commons.*

the non-white body and the homosexual body (Hoad, 2000; Somerville, 2000). Sexologists believed that homosexuals had failed to develop their sexuality "correctly," which then impeded their ability to achieve "mature" and "civilized" humanity. Sexologists drew on the explicitly racial and colonial language of "primitiveness" to describe the homosexual as a fundamentally stunted or underdeveloped being. Ellis and Krafft-Ebing also drew on racial and colonial ideas to produce their accounts of bisexuality (Storr, 1997). For these sexologists, bisexuality was understood to be an original, primitive form of desire, to which all human beings are naturally predisposed. They argued that members of "civilized" European societies suppress or disavow their original bisexual impulse in order to cultivate a monosexual (heterosexual or homosexual) orientation. Bisexuality was believed to be far more prevalent among the so-called "underdeveloped races." If, according to nineteenth-century sexology, homosexuality was understood as a "primitive" failure to develop one's sexuality "correctly," then bisexuality was understood as a racially marked failure to develop at all.

The colonial origins of modern conceptions of sexuality and gender reveal the inextricable connections between racism, empire, and the construction of sexual and gender minority identity categories. The lasting legacy and contemporary reach of the histories described in this section offer a window onto the forms of inequality and violence that continue to shape experiences and understandings of sexuality, gender, and LGBTQ identities in today's global world.

## GEOGRAPHIES OF LABOR AND LEISURE

If globalization sets people, goods, images, and ideas on the move, then one of the primary mechanisms of globalization is travel. In today's world, LGBTQ people and other sexual and gender minorities travel across national borders for many reasons. Travel can be a leisure pursuit, as in the case of a vacation. At other times, however, people take flight under far less pleasant circumstances, as when leaving a country of origin to find work or to escape discrimination. LGBTQ travel has very different forms and motivations, which highlight the uneven experiences of LGBTQ mobility in the contemporary global world.

## LGBTQ Tourism

It has sometimes been said that LGBTQ people are natural travelers (Waitt & Markwell, 2014; Wesling, 2008). The desire to feel safe, find sexual partners, and meet like-minded people has often set LGBTQ people in motion, leaving their homes and families behind to find new lovers, communities, and families elsewhere. In the United States, in fact, travel guides were among the very first gay-themed publications ever to appear (Hilderbrand, 2013a). Since the 1960s, travel guides such as Bob Damron's longstanding *Address Book* (also known as the *Damron Guide*) have served as encyclopedic resources for LGBTQ travelers, highlighting bath houses, clubs, bars, and other sites of potential interest. Today, cities such as Palm Springs, Key West, Provincetown, and San Francisco in the U.S., and Ibiza (Spain), Berlin (Germany), Sydney (Australia), and San Paolo (Brazil) are all popular and well-known destinations for global LGBTQ tourists.

The massive size of the LGBTQ tourism industry offers some sense of the significant role that travel and tourism play in the lives of some LGBTQ people. It is currently estimated that the LGBTQ tourism industry has an annual economic impact of $65 billion in the United States alone (WTO, 2012). The Gay European Tourism Association (2016) values the LGBTQ travel market in Europe at €50 billion per year. Since the 1990s many major companies in the international travel and tourism industry have become aware of the hefty power of the so-called "pink dollar" (Southall & Fallon, 2011). Travel industry agents frequently describe the LGBTQ market as a "dream market." This is because LGBTQ people are often imagined to be DINKS (double income, no kids), who have large disposable incomes to spend on leisure time activities (Köllen & Lazar, 2012). Even though leisure travel is, in fact, available only to an elite minority of affluent LGBTQ people, travel companies still regularly court the LGBTQ market through niche marketing campaigns that target LGBTQ tourists. For instance, one well established travel agency publishes a regular periodical called *Out Around*, which is pitched as the first gay world travel guide (Hughes, 2006). Mainstream travel guides also now commonly include sections that list and describe attractions of potential interest to LGBTQ travelers. These are designed not only to direct travelers toward LGBTQ-friendly destinations, but also to garner the interest and the money of LGBTQ tourists.

With the appearance of a niche tourism market for LGBTQ travelers, it has now become possible not only to be an LGBTQ traveler, but to travel *as* LGBTQ (Puar, 2002). The LGBTQ tourism industry helps customers find LGBTQ-friendly hotels and destinations. It also sells and promotes group tours, cruises, and mass events such as circuit parties that cater specifically to an LGBTQ clientele. There is also an increasing segment of the LGBTQ international tourism industry that is geared specifically toward LGBTQ travelers with children (Gay European Tourism Association, 2016). Leading gay and lesbian cruise vacation companies—such as RSVP, Atlantis Events, Olivia Cruises, and Resorts—advertise their cruises as important sites for the creation of gay and lesbian community, while also promising the exotic pleasures of sun, sea, and, of course, sex. The international scope of these cruise lines is vast, as each of these major companies have cruises that dock on every populated continent.

*Sex districts, like Boyz Town in Pattaya, Thailand, cater to Western gay sex tourists. Source: Photo by Kantana/ CC0 1.0 license. Image courtesy of Wikimedia Commons.*

Although the LGBTQ commercial vacation industry is one of the most visible aspects of LGBTQ international travel, it is not the only means through which LGBTQ travel takes place. While many LGBTQ people have sex when they travel (with their partners, with other travelers, and with locals), other LGBTQ individuals practice and engage what has come to be known as sex tourism. Sex tourism refers to a travel experience during which sexual services from the local population provides either the impetus for travel or a significant component of the travel experience (Mullings, 1999). LGBTQ sex tourism, especially gay sex tourism, is a very lucrative industry that brings many gay people, primarily from the Global North, to international destinations elsewhere. Because the sex work upon which sex tourism depends is often illegal and takes place through informal underground economies, it is rather difficult to ascertain the precise frequency with which LGBTQ sex tourism takes place or the overall revenue that it generates. Yet research indicates that booming gay sex tourism industries exist throughout the world, with Brazil, the Dominican Republic, and Thailand serving as leading destinations for North American and Western European gay sex tourists (Padilla, 2007; Williams, 2013).

For example, in Rio de Janeiro, Brazil, *michês* cater to gay sex tourists from North America and Western Europe (Mitchell, 2010, 2011). *Michês* are heterosexually-identified Brazilian men who sell sexual services to male tourists. *Gringo* (foreigner)-*michê* relationships can take multiple forms. Some are one-time exchanges of sex for money, while other relationships can last for years. For some *gringos*, the attraction to *michês* are based on exoticizing and often deeply racialized fantasies about the "macho" Brazilian male sexual appetite. Others are driven by an earnest dream of forging long-term romantic relationships with *michês.* The unequal dynamics of race, class, and geography between *gringos* and *michês* suggest that gay sex tourism can reflect and enunciate larger global inequalities. At the same time, from the perspective of many working-class and poor Brazilian men, becoming a *michê* can be a source of upward mobility. It is a way of getting by and making do under intense economic pressures. Although the entrenched stigma attached to (male) sex work undoubtedly persists, male prostitution in Brazil is increasingly understood as a viable means of transitioning out of poverty.

## Global, Digital, Queer

Since the development of Internet technologies in the 1990s, LGBTQ people have used the Internet and other forms of digital media to forge cross-border and cross-cultural connections, commitments, and communities. The Internet has allowed some LGBTQ people to sustain preexisting relationships with LGBTQ friends, partners, comrades, and family members who live in distant geographical locations. The Internet has also aided in the production of new LGBTQ relationships and communities that cut across national borders. Transnational LGBTQ communities use digital media for a variety of purposes, including cybersex, community building, and activism.

In the mid-1990s gay and lesbian chat rooms were some of the first and most popular chat rooms on the Internet (Burke, 2004; Grov, 2014). They provide a relatively new channel of communication for sexual minorities in and across many different parts of the world. For example, some queer international migrants use chat rooms to keep in touch with family and friends in their countries of origin (Dhoest, 2016), or to connect with people who have had similar experiences of migration, mobility, and/or displacement (Atay, 2016).

Many transnational LGBTQ online communities are organized explicitly around sex, cybersex, and the sharing of pornography. Cybersex refers to the digitally mediated exchange of textual or visual data with the purpose of producing and/or providing sexual pleasure. Cybersex allows one to "hook up" with another person who lives far away or even across the world. Some LGBTQ cybersex practitioners note that they prefer the transnational sexual intimacies fostered through cybersex to IRL (in real life) sex. Cybersex can offer a certain degree of privacy, which provides some LGBTQ people, especially young LGBTQ people, with an opportunity to try out sexual practices and pleasures that they may not be able to explore IRL (Subrahmanyam & Smahel, 2010).

Other transnational LGBTQ digital communities have developed to raise awareness of LGBTQ concerns and to provide networks of support for LGBTQ people. One such community is Homan, an online support group for Iranian lesbians and gay men both in Iran and abroad (Valentine, 2006). Founded in Stockholm in 1991, Homan offers resources for gay and lesbian Iranians struggling with issues related to sexuality. The site provides an anonymous virtual forum for people to share information and advice. Homan's stated goal is to allow gay and lesbian Iranians in the diaspora to unite by addressing issues concerning gender and sexuality that are specific to their national and transnational communities. Homan also includes a robust guide to HIV/AIDS and sexual health.

Another increasingly visible form of LGBTQ international tourism is medical tourism and, in particular, gender confirmation surgical tourism (Aizura, 2010; Wilson, 2010). Since the early 2000s, Bangkok has often been hailed as the "Mecca" of gender confirmation surgery (GCS), a prime destination for people from North America, Europe, and Australia seeking GCS (Aizura, 2010; Mason, 2006). This is because of Thailand's unique approach to the medical and legal regulation of gender reassignment and reclassification. For the most part, North American, European, and Australian surgeons strictly enforce the World Professional Association for Transgender Health (WPATH) Standards of Care, which can make access to gender-affirming surgery difficult for many transgender people (Nicolazzo, Marine, & Galarte, 2015; Spade, 2004). The required medical documentation and psychiatric evaluations can take years to complete, and many candidates for GCS ultimately find themselves deemed ineligible for gender-affirming healthcare. In Thailand, by contrast, gender non-conformity is not generally understood through the pathologizing medical classifications of gender dysphoria and gender identity disorder. The rules and regulations for GCS are therefore far less stringent. Consequently, hundreds of North Americans, Europeans, and Australians now travel to Thailand for GCS each year.

Most of the patterns of LGBTQ international leisure tourism reflect the movement of LGBTQ tourists from the Global North to the Global South in search of pleasure and possibility. This trend illustrates that the celebratory language of the pink dollar effaces the fact that the vast majority of LGBTQ people, including those in the Global North, lack the economic and cultural resources required to engage in leisure mobility. For this reason, the LGBTQ tourism industry has been accused of selling and perpetuating a false image of an LGBTQ community that is homogenously wealthy, Western, and often white (Alexander, 2005; Puar, 2002).

The rather romanticized view of LGBTQ international tourism as inherently liberating can obscure the harm that LGBTQ tourists often enact against the people and places they encounter during their travels. LGBTQ international travel can reinforce exploitative consumer capitalist relations along with inequalities of race, class, and nation. For example, the Hawai'i Gay Liberation Program and National Community Relations Division of the American Friends Service Committee (AFSC) Hawai'i Area Program and Na Mamo O Hawai'i (a Kanaka Maoli and people of color LGBTQ activist organization) argue that LGBTQ tourism in Hawai'i perpetuates colonialism and undermines Native Hawaiian sovereignty (AFSC, 2002). They argue that LGBTQ tourism in Hawai'i appropriates and demeans Kanaka Maoli culture by promoting an exoticized and stereotypical image of Hawai'i and Hawaiians. LGBTQ tourism also destroys the islands' natural resources. LGBTQ tourists often fail to acknowledge the low-waged Native Hawaiian labor upon which their leisure depends. LGBTQ tourists frequently enjoy Hawai'i without thinking to give back to Native Hawaiians and their land. Therefore, these queer Hawaiian organizations ask that LGBTQ tourists join in solidarity with Kanaka Maoli by learning to travel to Hawai'i *differently*. They ask that LGBTQ tourists visit Hawai'i with the purpose of fighting for both Native Hawaiian sovereignty *and* LGBTQ liberation as intertwined freedom struggles.

## Migration, Mobility, and the Law

While leisure tourism is the world's largest growth industry, the majority of people who travel internationally in today's world do so for work or to survive in the face of difficult economic, political, and environmental circumstances. Members of this numerical majority are known as international migrants. According to the United Nations Educational, Scientific and Cultural Organization (UNESCO), an international migrant is defined as a person who lives in a different country than the one in which they were born and, in the process, acquires social ties to that country (2015). Since the 1960s the number of international migrations has more than doubled, with 76 million people migrating internationally in 1960 and 244 million in 2015. If these substantial numbers do not give immediate pause, it is well worth adding that these statistics include neither those people who cross national borders on a daily or weekly basis for work, nor do they account for undocumented migrants (Fourtier, 2014; UNPF, 2016).

Most LGBTQ migrants do not migrate internationally, but choose instead to move within their home countries. LGBTQ people migrate internationally for a wide variety of reasons. Although it is often assumed that the primary motivation for LGBTQ international migration is the desire to escape sexual and/or gender discrimination, it is important to highlight that many key catalysts for LGBTQ international migration maintain no explicit connections to sexuality and gender. The prospect of securing opportunities for work or education, the hope of reuniting with family or friends, and the promise of finding refuge in the aftermath of environmental or political displacement serve as some of the most pressing sociopolitical factors that contribute to LGBTQ international migration. However, for some LGBTQ international migrants, the decision to leave one's home country may be rooted far more firmly in matters of sexual and gender difference. The term sexual migration is sometimes used to describe LGBTQ international migration motivated, at least in part, by sexuality (Carrillo, 2004). This can occur for a range of reasons, including incentives linked to the maintenance of romantic relationships with foreign same-sex partners, the pursuit of unexplored or underexplored pleasures, and the need to flee one's country of origin due to fear of sexuality-based persecution.

Lesbians and gay men were officially banned from migrating to the United States for most of the twentieth century, though they did migrate to the U.S. during the years in which bans were in effect. Even so, lesbian and gay migrants were often forced to conceal their sexualities to ward off looming threats of persecution and deportation (Lee, 2015; Luibhéid, 2005). The legal origin of gay and lesbian exclusion in U.S. immigration policy remains unclear. One theory is that gay and lesbian exclusion is rooted in the 1917 addition of a psychopathic personality clause to U.S. immigration policy (Luibhéid, 2005). This clause barred so-called "constitutional psychopathic inferiors" from entering the country, including people with "abnormal" sexual instincts. Others argue that gay and lesbian exclusion began even earlier with the public charge or the moral turpitude provisions, which were introduced into American legal doctrine in 1882 and 1891 respectively (Canaday, 2009). These provisions forbade entry to migrants who were perceived to represent a burden to the national interest or to breach U.S. national moral codes of proper citizen conduct. While the precise legal principle used to justify homosexual exclusion is debatable, what is clear is that such exclusions have significantly defined the nature and experience of LGBTQ international mobility over the course of the twentieth century.

The modern iteration of the ban on gay and lesbian immigration to the United States took form in 1965, when the Immigration and Nationality Act explicitly barred "sexual deviates" from entering the U.S. (Luibhéid, 2005). It was not until 1990 that this ban was ultimately repealed. Shortly after, in 1994, lesbians and gay men were deemed eligible for claiming political asylum in the United States. Political asylum refers to the protection granted by a nation-state for a person who has left their country of origin due to their political beliefs or membership in an oppressed social group. Throughout the early 1990s, a series of precedent-setting legal cases in the Netherlands, Germany, and Canada came to the fore, in which individuals sought asylum because of their sexuality. One such case was *Re: Inaudi* in 1992, which granted an Argentinian man refugee status in Canada on the grounds that he would face violent persecution for his sexual orientation by the police were he to return to Argentina. As a result, it was argued that homosexuals constitute a "particular social group" who may experience violent persecution on the account of their membership in that group (Vagelos, 1993). While *Re: Inaudi* set a new standard for political asylum claims on the basis of sexual orientation in North America and elsewhere, cases that rule in favor of asylum-seeking plaintiffs are still exceedingly rare. For example, in 2009–2010, 98% to 99% of all sexual orientation-based asylum cases in the United Kingdom were rejected before even going to court (Lewis, 2014b).

While the ban on gay and lesbian immigration has been officially lifted, legal discrimination against gay and lesbian migrants persists. In general, national immigration policies tend to implicitly privilege middle- and upper-class heterosexual migrant families for inclusion into the nation. For instance, while most countries allow heterosexual citizens to sponsor their foreign spouses for national residency, only 19 countries currently allow homosexual citizens to sponsor their foreign spouses (Ho & Rolfe, 2011). In addition, having family in a country of destination tends to improve the likelihood that migrants will be deemed fit for citizenship. LGBTQ migrants often do not have family members in their country of destination and, when they do, these are frequently "chosen" or non-biological family members, who do not register or count as "family" in the eyes of the law.

Asylum seekers are subjected to a strict burden of proof to demonstrate that they are "really" gay or lesbian, and not simply making fraudulent claims to gain access to citizenship. This means that migrants must prove to immigration authorities that they have lived as an "out" gay or lesbian person in their nation of origin. This legal demand places the asylum seeker in a difficult double bind, as the inability to lead an "out" gay or lesbian life is sometimes precisely the primary motivation for leaving one's country of origin (Lewis, 2014b). In addition, courts frequently rely on visual criteria to adjudicate whether or not the asylum seeker is "really" a lesbian or gay man. These visual judgments depend substantially on stereotypical Western assumptions about gay and lesbian bodies and behaviors. National courts are more likely to grant asylum to gay men who present as effeminate, while denying asylum to gay men whose gender presentations fail to align with common gay stereotypes (Rodríguez, 2003). Similarly, lesbians seeking sexual orientation-based asylum have also reported that they feel pressured to present as more masculine to help prove their cases (Bennett & Thomas, 2013).

Another challenge facing asylum seekers involves the language used to discuss sexual and gender identity during legal proceedings. Courts regularly make use of culturally and nationally specific identity categories, such as "lesbian," "gay," and "homosexual." These are terms with which migrants themselves may not identify (Fassin & Salcedo, 2015). Thus, asylum seekers can be coerced into adopting U.S. sexual identity terms in order to prove they qualify for asylum.

Immigration authorities also frequently require that migrants verbally demonize their home countries. At the same time, migrants are expected to laud their countries of destination as utopian places free of violence and inequality. This reflects the way that sexual orientation-based asylum cases often rely on and promote a familiar binary opposition between the "liberated West" and the "repressive non-West." When the United States is framed as the progressive "savior" of non-Western "victims," the role of the U.S. in contributing to some of the conditions from which LGBTQ migrants flee can be obscured (Cantú, Luibhéid, & Stern, 2005). In other words, what is erased by the celebratory language of the "liberated West" are the ways that U.S. international economic and cultural domination produce and perpetuate global inequalities that can motivate LGBTQ international migration in the first place. For example, gay Pakistani migrant and legal scholar Saeed Rahman explains that he was required to denounce the entirety of Pakistani culture and celebrate how unique and wonderful the United States is in order to win his asylum case (Solomon, 2005). This demand for patriotic conformity can then make it difficult for queer immigrants to critique and voice dissent against forms of racial, class, gender, and sexual oppression experienced in the U.S. This includes forms of violence and discrimination enacted against queer immigrants by mainstream U.S. LGBTQ communities (Reddy & Syed, 1999).

As an important counter to these trends, LGBTQ migration scholars and activists work toward the collective empowerment of queer migrants. They contend that justice for queer migrants cannot settle on the achievement of legal citizenship for individual LGBTQ migrants as a final political goal. This is because individual legal decisions alone cannot challenge the patterns of harm that inform the operations of citizenship. The very idea of citizenship is an inherently exclusionary norm. It is a gatekeeping structure that distinguishes between people who are deemed worthy of protection (citizens) and those who are not (non-citizens). Given this fact, many LGBTQ scholars and activists recommend that the legal category of citizenship be vigorously critiqued, if not ultimately discarded, so as to allow for the collective survival and flourishing of marginalized LGBTQ people across national borders (Chávez, 2013; Reddy, 2010).

*Members of the Queer Undocumented Immigrant Project march in D.C. Capital Pride Parade, Washington, D.C. (June 7, 2014). Source: Photo by Tim Evanson/ CC BY-SA 2.0 license. Image courtesy of Wikimedia Commons.*

One recent example of queer migrant justice organizing is the Undocuqueer movement, a political movement led by undocumented LGBTQ immigrants. The term "undocuqueer" was coined in 2011 by Mexican-born/U.S.-based artist and activist Julio Salgado as a way of drawing attention to active LGBTQ leadership within organizing efforts for migrant justice (Beltrán, 2015). Undocuqueer activists seek to make LGBTQ voices central to struggles against anti-immigrant legislation and sentiment, while also making migrant voices central to struggles against anti-LGBTQ legislation and sentiment. At the same time, they actively challenge the legitimacy of national citizenship and national borders. They argue that citizenship should not serve as a necessary precondition for living a life worthy of dignity, respect, pleasure, and freedom.

## HIV/AIDS in Transnational Perspective

"AIDS does not discriminate" is a common refrain espoused by AIDS activists, policy-makers, and scientists alike. This popular expression serves as a reminder that no population or identity group is, biologically speaking, more predisposed to contracting the HIV virus than any other. The notion that AIDS does not discriminate is certainly true from an epidemiological standpoint. Yet the vastly uneven burden of HIV/AIDS across the globe demonstrates in no uncertain terms that social, economic, and political factors continue to foster and maintain global health disparities along the lines of nation, race, class, gender, and sexuality.

The Joint United Nations Programme on HIV/AIDS (2016) estimates that since 1981 approximately 35 million people have died from AIDS-related causes, with 1.1 million AIDS-related deaths in 2015 alone. Approximately 36.7 million people worldwide are living with HIV/AIDS today. Of the total number of people living with HIV/AIDS globally, there are approximately 5.1 million people living with HIV/AIDS in Asia and the Pacific, 19 million people living with HIV/AIDS in East and Southern Africa, 6.5 million people living with HIV/AIDS in West and Central Africa, 1.5 million people living with HIV/AIDS in Eastern Europe and Central Asia, 2.0 million people living with HIV/AIDS in Latin America and the Caribbean, 1.7 million people living with HIV/AIDS in North America, 830,000 people living with HIV/AIDS in Central and Western Europe, and 230,000 people living with HIV/AIDS in the Middle East and North Africa. As these numbers reveal, the clear majority of new HIV infections are identified in economically poor nations in the Global South. This fact reflects the way that HIV/AIDS augments already existing inequalities, including the polarization between economically rich and poor nations.

AIDS has often been understood as an unfortunate product of nature. Yet the story of the global HIV/AIDS pandemic is not one that has been shaped by biology alone. It is a life-and-death story about the impact of international social relations on health, mortality, and the burdens of disease. Rather than focusing exclusively on the biological and behavioral determinants of HIV/AIDS, a transnational LGBTQ studies approach to the pandemic seeks to understand the broader social, economic, and political contexts that shape the lived experiences of people living with HIV/AIDS in diverse global settings. A transnational approach also brings into focus the unequal social, economic, and political relations that structure and intensify HIV/AIDS-related disparities on an international scale. These inequalities include disproportionate rates of HIV transmission, uneven access to HIV medications (such as antiretroviral therapy [ART] and highly actively antiretroviral therapy [HAART]), and differential distributions of HIV/AIDS-related stigma and death.

The global AIDS pandemic reflects the experience of living in an increasingly interconnected world (Binnie, 2004; Warner, 1993). On the one hand, the transmission of HIV has been linked to the heightened movement of people and the breakdown of place-bound cultures introduced by globalization (Pray, Lemon, Mahmoud, & Knobler, 2006). On the other hand, the proliferation of international coalitions forged to combat HIV/AIDS also signals the way that the pandemic has mobilized activists, educators, and scientists to develop new practices of cross-border solidarity and connection. The biannual International AIDS Conference represents one international attempt at addressing the global pandemic. The First International AIDS Conference was held in Atlanta, Georgia in 1985. It was organized by HIV/AIDS professionals to present and share knowledge about the emerging epidemic, including its possible causes, modes of transmission, the nature of disease progression, and global epidemiological trends. In 2000 the Conference was held in Durban, South Africa, its first time in the Global South. Bringing an international cohort of scientists and policy-makers to the epicenter of the pandemic allowed many people living with HIV/AIDS to participate in an international conversation about HIV/AIDS. For instance, in his opening address at the Durban Conference, Judge Edwin Cameron of the High Court of South Africa charged pharmaceutical companies with imposing high prices that make it impossible for many people living with HIV/AIDS to access life-saving drugs (Cameron, 2000). While Cameron's damning indictment of the pharmaceutical industry was left largely unaddressed in Durban, this moment is taken by many commentators to represent an important turning point in the international response to the global HIV/AIDS pandemic.

AIDS activism at the grassroots-level has also fostered transnational networks of influence and exchange. For example, AIDS activists in Bangkok, Thailand, staged protests at the 2004 International AIDS Conference, which brought massive international media attention to the unethical and exploitative nature of HIV drugs trials running in Phnom Penh, Cambodia (Sandy, 2013). This drug trial had recruited HIV-negative sex workers in Phnom Penh, offering them three dollars per month as compensation for their participation. Recruited participants were given very little information about the drug and its potential side effects, nor were they offered medical or emotional care if they tested positive for HIV during the trial. The protests in Bangkok led to the end of the drug trial in Phnom Penh. This example demonstrates that grassroots AIDS activism has forced scientists and pharmaceutical companies to grapple with both the ethics of AIDS research and the political demands of transnational AIDS activist networks.

International statistical data on the impact of HIV/AIDS on sexual and gender minorities has been difficult for researchers to ascertain. There are two interlocking reasons for this. First, people tend to be reticent about discussing and disclosing information concerning sexual and gender practices that are frequently stigmatized. Second, it can be difficult to track and compile data about sexual and gender identity on a global scale. Because the meanings and definitions of sex, sexuality, gender, and identity vary considerably from place to place, HIV/AIDS researchers are tasked with the difficult challenge of interpreting and

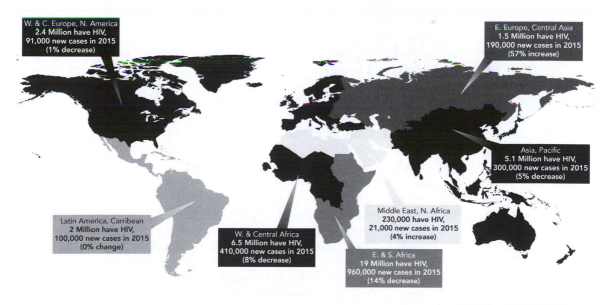

*Globally, HIV/AIDS is a major health problem (2016). Source: Adapted from data collected by AVERT.*

consolidating data samples that often conflict with one another and use dissimilar models of sexual and gender classification (Boyce, 2007; Meyer et al., 2010). One way biomedical experts have grappled with these challenges is by adopting new classificatory models that emphasize behavioral categories rather than identity labels. For example, the abbreviation MSM refers to men who have sex with men. By emphasizing men's sexual behaviors rather than their identities, MSM can address the sexual practices of men who do not necessarily identify with the culturally specific category of gay. While the move to address sexual behavior beyond a narrow model of Western gay identity has certainly benefited HIV/AIDS research, it has not always been able to adequately account for the diversity of global sexualities. This is partly because MSM takes the category of men as a universal category rather than one that is deeply inflected by cultural and national differences (Boellstorff, 2011). As a result, transwomen and gender non-conforming people who do not identify as men are often included in the MSM category. Misgendering can cause significant emotional as well as medical harm to affected communities.

MSM and transwomen are disproportionately affected by the global HIV/AIDS pandemic. Yet statistical research on rates of transmission and risk among MSM and transwomen vary dramatically in their results. The few existing epidemiological studies on trans people suggest that anywhere from 8% to 68% of the worldwide trans population is living with HIV/AIDS (WHO, 2011). Transmen have often been excluded from research studies entirely. This means that the sexual practices and behaviors of transmen have generally been overlooked in international HIV/AIDS policy efforts (Reisner & Murchison, 2016).

Statistical data draw important attention to the uneven international distribution of HIV/AIDS. But numbers alone cannot reveal the experiences and struggles of people living with HIV/AIDS. Nor can they show how popular ideas about the global AIDS pandemic circulate in and shape the global cultural imagination. To consider how the HIV/AIDS pandemic has been imagined in the arena of culture, it is useful to look to how popular discourses surrounding the global AIDS pandemic first took form in U.S. culture during the 1980s. In the United States, the original framing of HIV/AIDS focused on the *types* of people who seemed most to contract the virus, rather than the *ways* in which the virus is transmitted (Fee & Krieger, 1993). This meant that instead of studying risk-relevant behaviors, possibilities for risk-reduction, and the structural and institutional inequalities that make certain populations vulnerable to disease, epidemiologists tended to think about HIV/AIDS in terms of risk groups.

Risk groups refer to entire populations who are believed to be almost intrinsically or naturally at risk for contracting HIV. In 1983 the Center for Disease Control and Prevention (CDC) first identified four high-risk groups, who would soon come to be known colloquially as the 4-H Club, which included homosexual men, Haitians, heroin users, and hemophiliacs. This CDC report intensified both public fears of, and scientific misunderstandings about, already vulnerable communities. It naturalized and normalized a chain of negative associations between homosexuality, Blackness, addiction, AIDS, and death. In these terms, simply being homosexual or Haitian, for instance, seemed to be enough to explain—and explain away—the likelihood of infection. By imagining HIV/AIDS as a natural part of being a member of certain marginalized populations, the so-called "general population" (implicitly identified as white, heterosexual, gender-normative, middle-class U.S. citizens) could imagine itself as insulted from the impact of AIDS. At the same time the "general population" could place the burden of responsibility for HIV infection on already aggrieved communities.

As the pandemic escalated throughout the 1980s, U.S. journalists, scientists, and politicians devoted increased attention to the origin of the virus (Patton, 1990; Treichler, 1989). Although the desire to locate the geographic origin of HIV was perhaps a scientifically noble cause, the hunt to find an original vector of transmission often took a decidedly homophobic, racist, and xenophobic turn. Attempts to track down the original carrier of HIV (sometimes referred to as Patient Zero) resulted in the proliferation of all sorts of dubious and hysterical reports that blamed North American gay men, and Haitians and West Africans of all sexualities, for the global "outbreak" of infection. North American gay men were regularly portrayed in the U.S. media as sexually promiscuous. For this reason they were believed to be dangerous both to the health of others and to the health of the nation as a whole (Treichler, 1987).

In addition, racist mass media reports frequently cast West Africa as a barbaric and unregulated foreign space, where the primitive commingling of animals and humans facilitated the first transmission of HIV from the former to the latter. Haiti, too, was routinely claimed as the alleged origin of HIV/AIDS—a claim now thoroughly disputed by doctors and historians (Farmer, 1992). Haiti was framed as an especially potent threat to the U.S. in the popular U.S. media. It was imagined as the U.S.'s menacing neighbor, whose close proximity placed all Americans at unthinkable risk. These popular and medical narratives concerning the Haitian and/or African origin of AIDS were fueled by anti-Black sentiments and racialized stereotypes about Black people as biologically, sexually, and culturally deficient (McBride, 1991). Africa and Haiti figured so centrally in U.S. anxieties about the spread of AIDS that the story of AIDS was regularly framed as a story about the threat of foreigners, the risks of unchecked borders, and the dangers of globalization (Patton, 2002).

The panic surrounding both the alleged African origins of HIV and the alleged propensity of gay men to contract HIV converged in the mid-1980s. In 1984 sensational medical and media reports identified a young gay Canadian flight attendant named Gaëtan Dugas as North America's Patient Zero (Shilts, 1987). These reports suggested that Dugas had contracted HIV from an African man he had met in Europe, and then subsequently infected dozens of North American gay men in San Francisco, Los Angeles, and New York City. Recent biological research demonstrates definitively that Dugas could not possibly have been the original North American carrier of HIV (Doucleff, 2016). Nonetheless, Dugas proved an easy scapegoat for nearly three decades. As a sexually active gay man he was quickly framed as a promiscuous homosexual with an unstoppable sex drive and dubious moral compass (Wald, 2008). As a flight attendant, he was also seen as *geographically* promiscuous by trade, as his globetrotting profession required that he regularly cross borders and forge connections across the world. In the U.S. popular imagination, Dugas, like AIDS itself, came to symbolize the dangers of global mobility.

The false allegations against Dugas reflect the way that the desire to protect "normal" (white, heterosexual, gender-normative, middle-class, citizen) Americans from HIV/AIDS has consistently led to the stigmatization and punishment of racial, sexual, gendered, and national "outsiders" in the name of national security (Raimondo, 2003). In the 1980s and 1990s heightened homophobia led to a series of proposals to quarantine or even deport and strip U.S. gay men of their citizenship. Beginning in 1987, the United States began to bar entrance to HIV-positive immigrants. The ban was codified in law in 1993 with the Immigration and Nationality Act, which added HIV to an official list of communicable diseases of public health significance. In practice, this policy was only deployed selectively. It targeted immigrants from supposedly "dangerous" nations in the Caribbean and Africa, who were believed to potentially "contaminate" the U.S. national blood supply (Fairchild & Tynan, 1994). The ban on HIV-positive foreign nationals entering and residing in the U.S. was only lifted in 2010.

While a generic image of Africa has often served as an illusory site of blame and fear in the U.S. popular imagination of AIDS, the experience and response to AIDS across Africa varies widely. For example, Uganda has often received accolades from the international community for its response to the epidemic. This is largely due to the development and promotion of "zero grazing" campaigns by the Ugandan government and local NGOs (Green, Halperin, Natulya, & Hogle, 2006). These campaigns have sought to reduce HIV transmission by changing the sexual behavior of Ugandans through the promotion of faithfulness and partner reduction. Many international policy-makers consider Uganda to be an exemplary model for addressing AIDS in economically poor nations.

The Ugandan government's active role in HIV prevention is often contrasted to the South African government's response to the AIDS crisis. Former South African President Thabo Mbeki (1999–2008) notoriously questioned the scientific consensus that HIV is the cause of AIDS. Mbeki's denial of the causal connection between HIV and AIDS is referred to by South African AIDS activists as "denialism" (Wang, 2008). Mbeki's denialism stemmed from his controversial belief that AIDS is not the only, or the most significant, immune deficiency affecting South Africans. He argued that poverty, racism, capitalism, and Western (neo) colonialism cause AIDS. He suggested that equating HIV with the various social illnesses and inequalities affecting South Africans reinforced Western colonial stereotypes about African hypersexuality and incivility. Mbeki also argued that biomedical treatment, such as ARTs, served the neocolonial economic interests of the West, specifically those of multinational pharmaceutical companies.

Powerful grassroots AIDS activism in South Africa developed in response to Mbeki's denialism, though AIDS activism in South Africa had emerged well before Mbeki had entered office. AIDS was first identified in South Africa in 1982 and, as in the U.S., media reports cast HIV as a "gay plague" (Jochelson, 2001). Effective AIDS activism in South Africa was made possible due to the existence of a strong activist base that had developed in the context of the country's much longer history of anti-homophobia and anti-apartheid organizing. One decisive moment in the history of South African gay activism was the Raid in Forest Town. In 1966 police raided and arrested ten men at a party in Forest Town, a suburb of Johannesburg, for engaging in "obscene" sex acts. The Raid in Forest Town was followed by various threats by the government to institute anti-homosexual legislation. These threats, however, only strengthened both the visibility and the viability of gay community organizing. From 1948 through 1991, South Africa was legally a white supremacist apartheid state. Apartheid (meaning "separateness" in Afrikaans) was the official policy of racial segregation that dominated every aspect of social, political, and economic life in South Africa for nearly half a century. Apartheid policies violently enforced legal and systematic discrimination against South Africa's Black, coloured (mixed race), and Indian populations. The first free democratic election took place in 1994, which led to the 1996 creation of a new South African Constitution, the first in the world to prohibit discrimination on the basis of sex, gender, or sexual orientation.

AIDS activists in South Africa drew on the political legacies of militant anti-homophobia and anti-apartheid activism. One prominent South African AIDS activist organization is the Treatment Action Campaign (TAC), which was formed in 1998 in Cape Town. The TAC is now regularly considered to be the most impactful HIV/AIDS activist organization in the world (Mbali, 2013; Munro, 2012). The TAC first came together on the heels of tragedy. In 1998, HIV-positive activist Gugu Dlamini was murdered in the province of KwaZulu-Natal after publicly disclosing her serostatus. That very same year, an influential anti-apartheid activist, former political prisoner, and founding member of the National Coalition for Gay and Lesbian Equality named Simon Nkoli died of AIDS-related causes. In the wake of these AIDS-related deaths, Nkoli's comrade Zackie Achmat sought to forge a patient-driven movement led by people living with HIV/AIDS to ensure access to treatment for people living with HIV/AIDS. The result was the Treatment Action Campaign.

Since 1998 TAC's successes have been many. One important victory took place in 2001. Beginning in 1996, new HIV medications made it possible for many people, especially in the Global North, to live with HIV as a manageable chronic disease rather than an immediate death sentence. Despite the significance of this scientific breakthrough, pharmaceutical companies continued to keep the price of these medications extremely high, especially in countries in the Global South, such as South Africa. Pharmaceutical companies profit from HIV/AIDS-related suffering by maintaining monopoly rights to drugs that make them far too costly for poor people to buy. In 2001 the Pharmaceutical Manufacturers Association (PMA), a trade group representing the pharmaceutical industry, sued the South African government in an attempt to stop the passage of the Medicines and Related Substances Control Amendment No. 90, which would allow South Africa to import cheaper, generic versions of patented HIV medications. The TAC mobilized a domestic and international campaign to garner global political support for South Africa's right to import and manufacture cheaper, generic drugs. The PMA dropped the case as a result of TAC's organizing efforts and

*Treatment Action Campaign activists march on Parliament, Cape Town, South Africa (February 14, 2003). Source: Photo by Joe White. Courtesy of Treatment Action Campaign and Wikimedia Commons.*

TAC's activism ultimately helped provide many South Africans with access to affordable, life-saving medications (Mbali, 2013).

For members of the Treatment Action Campaign this important legal victory signaled not only a triumph for South African people living with HIV/AIDS, but a triumph for the nation as a whole. It demonstrated that the people of South Africa could stand up against global capitalism and, in the long tradition of anti-apartheid activism, regain sovereignty over their own economic and political needs. Thus, while TAC's primary mission is to provide access to treatment for affected communities, TAC activists emphasize that the AIDS pandemic does not exist in a vacuum. The TAC takes seriously the idea that the fight against AIDS, the fight against homophobia, the fight against racism, and the fight against capitalism are necessary and mutually connected struggles for freedom.

## Sexuality, Gender, and International Law

In 2011, U.S. Secretary of State Hillary Clinton famously marked the International Day of Human Rights by declaring that "gay rights are human rights and human rights are gay rights." Staged in the front of the United Nations Office at Geneva, Clinton's speech insisted that lesbian, gay, bisexual, and transgender human rights must serve as a central component of the international human rights agenda for the twenty-first century. Clinton's 2011 speech was one recent instance in a much longer history of international legal activism on behalf of LGBTQ human rights that has slowly unfolded since the latter half of the twentieth century.

The legal concept of an international human right is a relatively recent invention. In the aftermath of the atrocities of World War II, the newly formed United Nations adopted the Universal Declaration of Human Rights (UDHR) in 1948. This document has since served as the universal standard and adjudicating metric for establishing justice in the international community. According to the UN, a human right refers to a right that all humans have simply on the basis of their being human. The UDHR currently includes 30 articles, which range from the right to protection from torture, to the right to marriage, to the right to work.

The UDHR does not include an article that protects the rights of sexual and gender minorities. The UDHR's inattention to sexual and gender minorities can be broadly attributed to two interlocking factors. First, the prevalence of hostility toward sexual and gender minorities makes the prospect of coming to an international agreement regarding the human rights of sexual and gender minorities difficult to achieve. Second, understandings of sex, sexuality, gender, and identity vary considerably across cultural and national contexts, such that definitional clarity and consensus are difficult to reach on an international scale. Taken together, these factors point to the ongoing challenges faced by LGBTQ activists in the struggle to institutionalize international sexuality and gender-based human rights (Sanders, 1996).

The absence of international rights and protections for sexual and gender minorities has been actively challenged since at least the early 1990s. During the 1990s, there emerged a broad-based effort to extend international human rights to sexual (and later gender) minorities. While the UDHR largely disregards sexual and gender difference altogether, international LGBTQ human rights activists have made use of certain ambiguities in the document's language to set new legal precedents for addressing the human rights of sexual minorities. For example, a 1966 addendum to the UDHR called the International Covenant on Civil and Political Rights (ICCPR) added that all international human rights must be upheld regardless of a person's sex. The drafters of the treaty probably used the term sex to refer to the male/female binary, a distinction that does not explicitly suggest reference to sexuality or sexual orientation. Yet in *Toonen v. Australia* in 1994, an Australian court decided that the meaning of sex in the ICCPR is ultimately ambiguous and could therefore refer to sexual orientation (Conte & Burchill, 2009). This agenda-setting decision led to the overturning of sodomy laws in the Australian state of Tasmania. Sodomy laws are applied penal codes that criminalize specific sex acts, such as same-sex sex.

One especially vocal organization in the fight for the international human rights of sexual and gender minorities is the International Gay and Lesbian Human Rights Commission (IGLHRC), known since 2015 as OutRight Action International. The IGLHRC was founded in 1990 by activist Julie Dorf, following on the heels of the U.S.-based LGBTQ civil rights organization, the Human Rights Campaign (HRC) (Thoreson, 2014). OutRight Action International has since been committed to protecting and advancing the human rights of people subject to violence and discrimination on the basis of their sexual orientation, gender identity, and/or HIV status. It has invested much of its organizational energy into combating national sodomy laws, advocating for asylum seekers, and monitoring sexuality and gender-based human rights abuses throughout the world.

While OutRight Action International and similar organizations have been quite successful in overturning national sodomy laws (including early victories, for instance, in Cyprus and Russia), sodomy and same-sex sexual behavior between consenting adults continue to be criminalized in 76 countries worldwide (Bruce-Jones & Itaborahy, 2011). It is impossible to understand the history of sodomy laws outside of the historical contexts of colonialism. This is because half of the countries that currently criminalize sodomy inherited these laws under the rule of the British Empire (Han & O'Mahoney, 2014). As was discussed in the section of this chapter on colonialism and empire, colonizers frequently envisioned colonized peoples as sexually perverse. They believed that a "respectable" education in European morality was a central component of the colonizing mission. One such defining instance of colonial education was Section 377, which was first introduced by British lawmakers into the Indian Penal Code in 1860. Section 377 prohibited male–male sexual penetration. After 1860, the code quickly spread across the vast expanses of the British Empire, including to countries such as present-day Australia, Bangladesh, Bhutan, Botswana, Gambia, Ghana, Hong Kong, Kenya, Malaysia, Nigeria, Pakistan, Singapore, Sri Lanka, Tanzania, Uganda, Zambia, and Zimbabwe.

The implementation of sodomy laws under British imperial rule fortified in law a prohibition against same-sex sexual activity in more than one-third of the world. It also produced deep-rooted social barriers to decriminalizing sodomy today. In many countries, sodomy laws are still in effect long after the formal end of British colonial rule. Because sodomy laws so frequently find

Death penalty
Illegal
Legal

*Same-sex sexual activity is still criminalized throughout much of the world (2015). Source: Adapted from data collected by ILGA.*

their origins in British colonialism, many activists in former British colonies consider the overturning of sodomy laws a central part of the broader struggle for decolonization and self-determination. For example, Caribbean feminist M. Jacqui Alexander (2005) argues that fostering erotic autonomy and sexual agency is a necessary part of the work of decolonization. Practicing and cultivating non-normative desires and pleasures that have been outlawed by both colonial and postcolonial governments are crucial components of both personal transformation and widespread social change in formerly colonized societies.

A series of decisive United Nations-related initiatives have pushed international LGBTQ human rights agendas to the center of the mainstream political stage. The launch of the Yogyakarta Principles on the Application of Human Rights in Law in Relation to Sexual Orientation and Gender Identity in 2007 marks one key development toward the implementation of international LGBTQ human rights standards. Devised in Java, Indonesia, by a cohort of human rights experts, the Yogyakarta Principles seek to define the obligation of individual nation-states to protect and respect the human rights of all people. The Yogyakarta Principles have been rejected by the UN General Assembly on numerous occasions. Even so, their impact on global political sensibilities is nonetheless apparent. For example, in Nepal, the Principles have recently been used in court to successfully defend Nepal's *meti*, or third gender, community (Bochenek & Knight, 2012). The relative success of the Yogyakarta Principles can be explained, in part, by the modesty of their demands (Thoreson, 2009). For the Principles do not call for the international recognition of the human rights of sexual and gender minorities. Rather, they assert the need to protect the rights of *all people*, regardless of gender identity or sexual orientation. By emphasizing the rights of all people, and thus de-emphasizing sexual and gender non-conformity, the Principles draw attention away from a common conservative critique of civil and human rights law: that protecting oppressed communities grants those communities "special" rights and privileges at the expense of the "general population."

Conservative opposition has consistently sought to stifle efforts at institutionalizing international LGBTQ human rights policies. Throughout the 1990s and 2000s the Vatican played a key role in blocking a series of UN resolutions that included references to sexual orientation and gender identity (Fischlin & Nandorfy, 2007). In 1995, for instance, the Vatican declared that the word "gender" should be excluded from a UN resolution on the international status of women because it was argued that gender is a code word for homosexuality (Butler, 2004). This example shows that the mere mention of gender was enough to trigger a series of homophobic complaints. Similarly, in 2008, the Vatican led multinational opposition to a UN statement that sought to condemn violence on the basis of sexual orientation. The Vatican argued that the endorsement of this statement would lead to the worldwide imposition of same-sex marriage or contribute to the oppression of faith-based communities (Glatz, 2008).

Many of the most vocal and biting criticisms of international LGBTQ human rights activism actually emerge from sexual and gender minority communities themselves. These critics of LGBTQ human rights argue that international human rights frameworks demonstrate some of the most violently ethnocentric tendencies embedded in the universalizing approach (Massad, 2002; Morgan, 2000). As international human rights activists aim to implement a global standard for sexual and gender justice, they necessarily impose and apply narrow Western concepts of sexual and gender identity globally. In so doing, they confine sexual and gender minorities into managed categories that can be regulated by international governing bodies. LGBTQ human rights initiatives are thus often unable to address culturally and nationally specific forms of sexuality and gender, or culturally and nationally specific forms of inequality and oppression.

Similarly, other LGBTQ critics contend that the very categories of sexual orientation and gender identity—categories that are central to human rights initiatives such as the Yogyakarta Principles—are themselves Western inventions (Gross, 2007a; Katyal, 2002). Therefore, these categories may have little traction or importance in societies that are not organized around a primary distinction between heterosexuals and homosexuals. It is for this reason that international LGBTQ human rights agendas can be understood as mechanisms of globalization as a process of Western homogenization or neocolonialism.

These critiques of LGBTQ human rights serve as important correctives to the ethnic chauvinism that drives many prominent strands of international LGBTQ legal activism. Yet while many LGBTQ studies scholars and activists agree that international human rights frameworks can impose a dangerous universalizing approach to global sexualities and genders, others argue that there is also a danger in presuming that human rights are a solely Western invention and concern (Narayan, 1993). For these scholars and activists, queer critiques of international LGBTQ human rights can easily lead to inaccurate claims that cultures outside of the West lack systems for organizing claims to right and justice. They can also inaccurately presume that non-Western sexual and gender minorities lack any investment in pursuing recognition under international law.

Another related critique of international LGBTQ human rights frameworks involves the way that calls for LGBTQ human rights can be deeply implicated in the phenomenon that scholar Jasbir K. Puar (2007) has called "homonationalism." Homonationalism refers to the way that certain nations harness their averred tolerance for LGBTQ people to claim that they are more enlightened and civilized than other nations. The concept of homonationalism points to the way that the "acceptance" of LGBTQ people has now become an international measure of a nation's progress. By claiming to be more tolerant and accepting, certain nations can justify foreign wars and disparage other nations, cultures, and peoples. While homonationalist policies and practices are used for a variety of different ends, scholars and activists argue that homonationalism especially targets nations in the Middle East, Muslim-majority nations, and Muslim immigrants. For example, in the Netherlands, Muslim immigrants are required to pass a values test, which measures their views on homosexuality (Crouch, 2006). The Dutch government does not require Christian immigrants to take this test. This implies that from the perspective of the Dutch government Muslims are believed to be somehow intrinsically or naturally intolerant toward LGBTQ people. Here, one can see homonationalism at work, as religious hierarchies and racial inequalities are maintained in the name of securing LGBTQ rights. In short, homonationalism reveals how LGBTQ human rights can be used in the service of racism and (neo)colonialism.

Another example of homonationalism can be found in the case of Romanian sodomy laws (Stychin, 2003). Romania decriminalized homosexuality in 2002 following intense pressure from the European Union (EU). The EU argued that tolerance for homosexuality is a foundational criterion for entry into the EU. From the perspective of the EU, Romania's failure to comply with its "modern" moral standards meant that Romania was backward, premodern, and thus undeserving of the financial and political resources that EU membership would make available. Only by outlawing discrimination based on sexual orientation could Romania "prove" its modernity to the EU. At first glance, the decriminalization of homosexuality in Romania may appear to be nothing but an obvious victory for Romanian lesbians and gay men. But Romanian commentators note that this is far from the case. In fact, many Romanian gays and lesbians do not feel a sense of ownership over the legal reforms. They view the reforms as simply the imposition of Western European sensibilities. This example illustrates that tolerance for homosexuality is increasingly used in international relations as a means of distinguishing between "good" and "bad" countries, which allows Western nations to justify and further their own economic and cultural priorities.

Scholars and activists also draw attention to a specific homonationalist practice known as "pinkwashing." Pinkwashing refers to the way that certain nations market themselves as LGBTQ-friendly to divert attention away from their own human rights abuses (Puar, 2013; Schulman, 2012). Israel is one country that is well-known for its use of pinkwashing to promote an image of itself as a protector of LGBTQ rights and thereby draw attention away from its colonial occupation of Palestine and ongoing violence against Palestinians. Critics argue that Israel deploys pinkwashing strategies to present itself as both more modern and more Western than other nations in the Middle East. Other Middle Eastern nations are, in effect, framed as barbaric, homophobic, and backward. For this reason, Israel can gain the support of many LGBTQ people throughout the world who might otherwise align themselves with LGBTQ and non-LGBTQ Palestinians in their struggles for decolonization and self-determination.

Transnational LGBTQ studies scholars, activists, and policy-makers in the age of globalization must take care to nurture alliances across their multiple differences. At the same time, they must pay careful attention to how the differences between them shape their distinct relationships to power. Only by so doing can they begin to undo the systems of oppression and violence that permeate everyday practices of living, thinking, and organizing in today's global world.

*"Die-in" protest against "pinkwashing" during pride parade in Tel Aviv, Israel (June 15, 2014). Source: Photo by TMagen/CC BY-SA 3.0 license. Image courtesy of Wikimedia Commons.*

## CONCLUSION

Globalization has profoundly transformed the contours and conditions of sexual and gender minority lives. This chapter has shown that global connections across economies, cultures, and political systems frame how people understand and imagine the meanings of sexuality and gender today. By treating sexuality and gender as historical and cultural processes rather than transhistorical and transcultural constants, a transnational approach to LGBTQ identities insists on examining sexual and gender differences in terms of the complex and contextually specific networks of relations out of which they arise. As scholars, activists, policy-makers, and others continue to think about the impact of globalization on sexuality and gender, it is revealed that globalization shapes not only large-scale social and economic processes, but also our everyday intimacies, our desires, and our very sense of who we are.

## Learn More

*Readings*

Altman, D. (1997). Global gaze/global gays. *GLQ, 3*(4), 417–36.

Blackwood, E., & Wieringa, S. E. (Eds.). (1999). *Female desires: Same-sex relations and transgender practices across cultures.* New York, NY: Columbia University.

Bleys, R. (1995). *Geographies of perversion: Male-to-male sexual behavior outside the West and the ethnographic imagination, 1750–1918.* New York, NY: New York University.

Cruz-Malavé, J. C., & Manalansan, M. (Eds.). (2002). *Queer globalizations: Citizenship and the afterlife of colonialism*. New York, NY: New York University.

Ekine, S. & Abbas, H. (Eds.) (2013). *Queer Africa reader*. Dakar, Senegal: Pambazuka.

Levine, P. (2004). Sexuality, gender, and empire. In P. Levine (Ed.), *Gender and empire* (pp. 134–155). Oxford, UK: Oxford University.

Luibhéid, E. & L. Cantú (Eds.). (2005). *Queer migrations: Sexuality, U.S. citizenship, and border crossings* Minneapolis, MN: University of Minnesota.

Manalansan, M. (1995). In the shadows of Stonewall: Examining gay transnational politics and the diasporic dilemma. *GLQ, 2*(4), 425–438.

Padilla, M. (2007). *Caribbean pleasure industry: Tourism, sexuality, and AIDS in the Dominican Republic*. Chicago, IL: University of Chicago.

Povinelli, E., & Chauncey, G. (1999). Thinking sexuality transnationally: An introduction. *GLQ, 5*(4), 439–50.

Puar, J. K. (2002). Circuits of queer mobility: Tourism, travel, and globalization. *GLQ, 8*(1–2), 101–137.

Rupp, L. J. (2001). Toward a global history of same-sex sexuality. *Journal of the History of Sexuality, 10*(2), 287–302.

## Film/Video

Barbosa, P. (Director) & Lenoir, G. (Director). (2003). *I exist* [Motion picture]. United States: EyeBite.

Heymann, T. (Director). (2006). *Paper dolls*. [DVD]. United States and Canada: Strand.

Kwan, S. (Director). (1996). *Yang ± yin: Gender in Chinese cinema*. [Motion picture]. United Kingdom & Hong Kong: British Film Institute.

Lim, M. (1997). *Sambal Belacan in San Francisco*. [Motion picture]. San Francisco, CA: Women Make Movies.

Reddish, P. (Producer). (1994). *Guardians of the flutes* [Television documentary]. London, UK: BBC.

Santini, A., & Sickles, D. (Directors). (2014). *Mala mala*. [DVD]. United States: Strand.

Scagliotti, J. (Director). (2005). *Dangerous living: Coming out in the developing world*. [DVD]. United States: After Stonewall.

Sharma, P. (Director). (2007). *A jihad for love*. [DVD]. United States: First Run Features.

Spade, D. (2015). *Pinkwashing exposed: Seattle fights back!* [Video file]. Retrieved from https://pinkwashingexposed.net/2015/05/06/watch-pinkwashing-exposed-seattle-fights-back/

Von Wallstrom, J. (Director). (2016). *The pearl of Africa*. [DVD]. Uganda & Kenya: Rough Studio AB.

Wright, K. F. (Director). (2012). *Call me Kuchu* [DVD] United States: Cinedigm.

## Internet

Amnesty International: www.amnestyusa.org

Gay and Lesbian International Sport Association: www.glisa.org

Global Action for Trans Equality: transactivists.org

International Gay and Lesbian Travel Association: www.iglta.org

International Lesbian, Gay, Bisexual, Trans and Intersex Association: ilga.org

OutRight Action International: www.outrightinternational.org

Polaris Project: polarisproject.org/resources/sex-trafficking-and-lgbtq-youth

Rainbow Railroad: www.rainbowrailroad.ca

# Works Cited

100 notable books of the year. (2006). Sunday book review. *New York Times*. Retrieved from www.nytimes.com/ref/books/review/20061203notable-books.html

1970 Hugo awards. (n.d.). *The Hugo Awards*. Retrieved from www.thehugoawards.org/hugo-history/1970-hugo-awards/

Aaron, M. (2004). New Queer Cinema: An Introduction. In Aaron, M. (Ed.) *New queer cinema: A critical reader* (pp. 3–14). New Brunswick, NJ: Rutgers University.

Abad-Santos, A. (2017, June 20). Philadelphia's new, inclusive gay pride flag is making gay white men angry. *Vox*. Retrieved from www.vox.com/culture/2017/6/20/15821858/gay-pride-flag-philadelphia-fight-explained

Abes, E., & Kasch, D. (2007). Using queer theory to explore lesbian college students' multiple dimensions of identity. *Journal of College Student Development*, *48*(6), 619–636.

ACLU. (2012). *The cost of harassment: A fact sheet for lesbian, gay, bisexual, and transgender high school students*. New York, NY: American Civil Liberties Union.

Adam, B. D. (2000). Age preferences among gay and bisexual men. *GLQ*, *6*(3), 413–433.

Adams, H. E., Wright, L. W., & Lohr, B. A. (1996). Is homophobia associated with homosexual arousal? *Journal of Abnormal Psychology*, *105*(3), 440–445.

Advance America. (2015, March 29). Victory at the statehouse! *This Week with George Stephanopoulos* [TV program]. New York, NY: ABC News.

AFSC (American Friends Service Committee). (2002). AFSC Hawai'i gay liberation program: Activist materials addressing tourism. *GLQ*, *8*(1–2), 207–225.

Ahmed, O., & Jindasurat, C. (2015). *Hate violence against lesbian, gay, bisexual, transgender, queer and HIV-affected communities*. New York, NY: National Coalition of Anti-Violence Programs.

Aizura, A. Z. (2010). Feminine transformations: Gender reassignment surgical tourism in Thailand. *Medical Anthropology: Cross-Cultural Studies in Health and Illness*, *28*(4), 424–43.

Albelda, R., Lee Badgett, M. V., Schneebaum, A., & Gates, G. (2009). *Poverty in the lesbian, gay, and bisexual community*. Los Angeles, CA: The Williams Institute.

Aldrich, R. (2002). *Colonialism and homosexuality*. New York, NY & Abingdon, UK: Routledge.

Alexander, J., & Gibson, M. (2004). Queer composition(s): Queer theory in the writing classroom. *JAC 24*(1), 1–21.

Alexander, M. J. (2005). *Pedagogies of crossing: Meditations on feminism, sexual politics, memory, and the sacred*. Durham, NC: Duke University.

Allen, T. D., Eby, L. T., Poteet, M. L., Lentz, E., & Lima, L. (2004). Career benefits associated with mentoring protégés: A meta-analysis. *Journal of Applied Psychology*, *89*, 127–136.

Almaguer, T. (1991). Chicano men: A cartography of homosexual identity and behaviour, *Differences 3*(2), 75–99.

Altman, D. (1997). Global gaze/global gays. *GLQ, 3*(4), 417–436.

Altman, D. (2001). Rupture or continuity? The internationalization of gay identities. In J. C. Hawley (Ed.), *Postcolonial, queer: Theoretical intersections* (pp. 19–41). Albany: State University of New York.

Anderson, S. W. (1993, May 28). The rainbow flag. *GAZE (Minneapolis, MN), 191*, 25.

Anderson-Minshall, D. (2016). HIV side effects and the drugs that treat them. *Plus* (July/August): 24.

Anderssen, N., Amlie, C., & Ytteroy, E. A. (2002). Outcomes for children with lesbian and gay parents: A review of studies from 1978 to 2000. *Scandinavian Journal of Psychology, 43*, 335–351.

Andersson, G., Noack, T., Seierstad, A., & Weedon-Fekjaer, H. (2004). The demographics of same-sex "marriages" in Norway and Sweden. *Demography, 43*, 79–98.

Angier, N. (1999). *Woman: An intimate geography*. New York, NY: Anchor.

Anglemyer, A., Horvath, T., Rutherford, G., Baggaley, R., Egger, M., & Siegfried, N. (2013). Antiretroviral therapy for prevention of HIV transmission in HIV-discordant couples. *JAMA, 310*(15), 1619–1620.

Antill, J. K. (1987). Parents' belief and values about sex roles, sex differences, and sexuality. *Review of Personality and Social Psychology, 7*, 294–328.

Antonelli, P., & Fisher, M. M. (2015, June 17). MoMA acquires the rainbow flag. *Inside/out: A MoMA/MoMA PS1 blog*. Retrieved from www.moma.org/explore/inside_out/2015/06/17/moma-acquires-the-rainbow-flag/?utm_campaign=062615a&utm_medium=instagram&utm_source=social

Antonio, R. J., & Bonanno, A. (2000). A new global capitalism? From "Americanism and Fordism" to "Americanization-globalization." *American Studies, 41*(2–3), 33–77.

APA (American Psychiatric Association). (2013). *Diagnostic and statistical manual of mental disorders (DSM-5)*. Arlington, VA: American Psychiatric Publications.

APA Task Force on Appropriate Therapeutic Responses to Sexual Orientation. (2009). *Report of the American Psychological Association Task Force on Appropriate Therapeutic Responses to Sexual Orientation*. Washington, DC: American Psychological Association.

Appadurai, A. (1996). *Modernity at large: Cultural dimensions of globalization*. Minneapolis, MN: University of Minnesota.

Ard, K. L., & Makadon, H. J. (2011). Addressing intimate partner violence in lesbian, gay, bisexual, and transgender patients. *Journal of General Internal Medicine, 26*(8), 930–33.

Armsden, G. C., & Greenberg, M. R. (1987). The inventory of parent and peer attachment: Individual differences and their relationship to psychological well-being in adolescence. *Journal of Youth and Adolescence, 16*, 427–454.

Armstrong, E. A., & Crage, S. M. (2006). Movements and memory: The making of the Stonewall myth. *American Sociological Review, 71*(5), 724–751.

Aronson, J. (1998). Lesbians giving and receiving care: Stretching conceptualizations of caring and community. *Women's Studies International Forum, 21*, 505–519.

Arrington-Sanders, R., Harper, G. W., Morgan, A., Ogunbajo, A., Trent, M., & Fortenberry, J. D. (2015). The role of sexually explicit material in the sexual development of same-sex-attracted Black adolescent males. *Archives of Sexual Behavior, 44*(3), 597–608.

Asexual Awareness Week. (2012). What does 'asexual' mean?: A brief guide to asexuality for parents and family. Asexual Awareness Week.

Aston, M. (2016). *Breaking down the walls of heartache: How music came out*. London, UK: Constable.

Atay, A. (2016). Digital diasporic experiences in digital queer spaces. In M. Friedman & S. Schultermandl (Eds.) *Click and kin: Transnational identity and quick media* (pp. 139–48). Toronto, ON and Buffalo, NY: University of Toronto.

Athanases, S. (1996). A gay-themed lesson in an ethnic literature curriculum: Tenth graders' responses to "Dear Anita." *Harvard Educational Review, 66*(2), 231–257.

Attinello, P. (2006). Fever/fragile/fatigue: Music, AIDS, present, and . . . In N. Lerner, & J. Straus (Eds.), *Sounding off: Theorizing disability in music* (pp. 13–22.) New York, NY: Routledge.

Autostraddle.com. (2015, January 11). Ultimate lesbian sex survey (for lady types who sleep with lady types). Retrieved from www.autostraddle.com/announcing-the-ultimate-lesbian-sex-survey-for-lady-types-who-sleep-with-lady-types-271069/

*Baehr v. Lewin*, 852 P.2d 44, 74 Haw. 530, 74 Hawaii 530 (Court of Appeals 1993).

Bagemihl, B. (1999). *Biological exuberance: Animal homosexuality and natural diversity*. New York, NY: St. Martin's.

Bailey, J. M., Bobrow, D., Wolfe, M., & Mikach, S. (1995). Sexual orientation of adult sons of gay fathers. *Developmental Psychology, 31*(1), 124–129.

Bailey, J. M., Kim, P. Y., Hills, A., & Linsenmeier, J. A. W. (1997). Butch, femme, or straight acting? Partner preferences of gay men and lesbians. *Journal of Personality and Social Psychology, 73*(5), 960–973.

Bailey, J. M., Vasey, P. L., Diamond, L. M., Breedlove, S. M., Vilain, E., & Epprecht, M. (2016). Sexual orientation, controversy, and science. *Psychological Science in the Public Interest, 17*(2), 45–101.

Bailey, J. M., & Zucker, K. J. (1995). Childhood sex-typed behavior and sexual orientation: A conceptual analysis and quantitative review. *Developmental Psychology, 31*(1), 43.

Bailey, J. V., Farquhar, C., Owen, C., & Mangtani, P. (2004). Sexual transmitted infections in women who have sex with women. *Sexually Transmitted Infections, 80*(3), 244–246.

Bailey, J. V., Farquhar, C., Owen, C., & Whittaker, D. (2003). Sexual behavior of lesbians and bisexual women. *Sexually Transmitted Infections, 79*(2), 147–150.

Bailey, N. J. (2005). Let us not forget to support LGBT youth in middle school years. *Middle School Journal (J3), 37*(2), 31–35.

Baim, T. (2008). *Out and proud in Chicago: An overview of the city's gay community*. Evanston, IL: Agate Surrey.

Baim, T. (2012). The currency of the gay movement. In Baim, T. (Ed.), *Gay press, gay power: The growth of LGBT community newspapers in America*, (pp. 382–422). Chicago, IL: Prairie Avenue Productions and Windy City Media Group.

*Baker v. Nelson*, 191 N.W.2d 185, 291 Minn. 310, 291 Minn. 2d 310 (1971).

Baker, G. (2012, June 24). Gay Pride flag creator proud but humble (S. Grzanich, Interviewer, June 24) [Audio clip]. Retrieved from Chicago.cbslocal. com/2012/06/24/gay-pride-flag-creator-proud-but-humble/

Baker, P. (2004). *Fantabulosa: A dictionary of polari and gay slang*. London, UK: Bloomsbury.

Balsam, K. F., Rothblum, E. D., & Beauchaine, T. P. (2005). Victimization over the lifespan: A comparison of lesbian, bisexual, and heterosexual siblings. *Journal of Counseling and Clinical Psychology, 73*, 477–487.

Barr, S. M., Budge, S. L., & Adelson, J. L. (2016). Transgender community belongingness as a mediator between strength of transgender identity and well-being. *Journal of Counseling Psychology, 63*(1), 87–97.

Barton, J., Braxton, J., Davis, D. W., de Voux, A., Flagg, E. W., Grier, L., . . . & Llata, E. (2016). *Sexually transmitted disease surveillance 2015*. Atlanta, GA: U.S. Centers for Disease Control and Prevention.

Basler, C. (Ed.) (2001). *Abraham Lincoln: His speeches and writings*. Cambridge, MA: Perseus.

Bauer, R. (2014). *Queer BDSM intimacies: Critical consent and pushing boundaries*. London: Palgrave Macmillan.

Baum, J., Brill, S., Brown, J., Delpercio, A., Kahn, E., Kenney, L., & Nicoll, A. (n.d.) *Supporting and caring for our gender expansive youth: Lessons from the Human Rights Campaign's youth survey*. Washington, DC: Human Rights Campaign and Gender Spectrum.

Baume, M. (2015, July 13). Dorian of *Dragon Age: Inquisition*: Why gaming's 'breakout' gay character matters. *OUT*. Retrieved from www.out.com/popnography/2015/7/13/dorian-dragon-age-inquisition-why-gamings-breakout-gay-character-matters

Bazzul, J., & Sykes, H. (2011). The secret identity of a biology textbook: Straight and naturally sexed. *Cultural Studies of Science Education, 6*(2), 265–286.

Beaver, T. D. (2012). "By the skaters, for the skaters" The DIY ethos of the roller derby revival. *Journal of Sport & Social Issues, 36*(1), 25–49.

Béeche, A. E. (2013). *The Coburgs of Europe: The rise and fall of Queen Victoria and Prince Albert's European cousins*. Eurohistory.com.

Behr, U. (2016, December 7). One Million Moms don't frighten me. *Advocate*. Retrieved from www.advocate.com/commentary/2016/12/07/one-million-moms-dont-frighten-me

Bell, R. (1999). ABC of sexual health: Homosexual men and women. *British Medical Journal, 318*(7181), 452.

*Beller v. Middendorf*, 632 F.2d 788 (9th Cir. 1980).

Bellwether, M. (2010). *Fucking trans women, volume 1* [zine]. Lexington, KY: CreateSpace Independent Publishing Platform.

Beltrán, C. (2015). "Undocumented, unafraid, and unapologetic": DREAM activists, immigrant politics, and the queering of democracy. In D. Allen & J. S. Light (Eds.), *From voice to influence: Understanding citizenship in a digital age* (pp. 80–104). Chicago: University of Chicago.

Bennett, C., & Thomas, F. (2013). Seeking asylum in the UK: Lesbian perspectives. *Forced Migration Review, 42*, 26–28.

Benshoff, H. M. & Griffin, S. (2009). Sexualities on film since the sexual revolution. In *America on film: Representing race, class, gender, and sexuality at the movies*, second edition (pp. 329–355). Malden, MA: Wiley-Blackwell.

Berger, P. (2002). The cultural dynamics of globalization. In P. Berger & S. P. Huntington (Eds.), *Many globalizations: Cultural diversity in the contemporary world* (pp. 1–16). New York, NY: Oxford University.

Bergling, T. (2001). *Sissyphobia: Gay men and effeminate behavior*. New York, NY: Harrington Park.

Bernstein, M. (1997). Celebration and suppression: The strategic uses of identity by the lesbian and gay movement. *American Journal of Sociology, 103*(3): 531–556.

Bérubé, A. (1990). *Coming out under fire: The history of gay men and women in World War Two*. New York: Free Press.

Bhabha, H. (1984). Of mimicry and man: The ambivalence of colonial discourse. *October, 28*, 125–133.

Biblarz, T. J., & Stacey, J. (2010). How does the gender of parents matter? *Journal of Marriage and Family, 72*(1), 3–22.

Bilimoria, D., & Stewart, A. J. (2009). "Don't ask, don't tell": The academic climate for lesbian, gay, bisexual, and transgender faculty in science and engineering. *bili, 21*(2), 85–103.

Bilodeau, B. L., & Renn, K. A. (2005). Analysis of LGBT identity development models and implications for practice. In R. L. Sanlo (Ed.), *Sexual Orientation and Gender Identity: New Directions for Student Services*, *111*, 25–40.

BiNet USA. (2016). A brief history of the bisexual movement. Retrieved from www. binetusa.org/bihistory2.html

Binnie, J. (2004). *The globalization of sexuality*. London, UK: Sage.

Birke, L. (1992). In pursuit of difference: Scientific studies of women and men. In G. Kirkup, & L. S. Keller (Eds.), *Inventing women: Science, technology and gender* (pp. 81–102). London, UK: Open University.

Bishop, R. S. (1990). Mirrors, windows, and sliding glass doors. *Perspectives*, *6*(3), ix–xi.

Blackless, M., Charuvastra, A., Derryck, A., Fausto-Sterling, A., Lauzanne, K., & Lee, E. (2000). How sexually dimorphic are we? Review and synthesis. *American Journal of Human Biology, 12(2)*, 151–166.

Blackmore, D. (1992). 'That unreasonable restless feeling': The homosexual subtexts of Nella Larsen's *Passing*. *African American Review*, *26*(3): 475–484.

Blackwood, E. (2010). *Falling into the* lesbi *world: Desire and difference in Indonesia*. Honolulu, HI: University of Hawai'i.

Blamires, H. (1983). *A guide to twentieth century literature in English*. New York, NY: Routledge.

Bleiberg, S., Fertmann, A., Friedman, A. T., & Godino, C. (2005). The layer cake model of bisexual identity development: Clarifying preconceived notions. *Campus Activities Programming*, *37*(8), 53–58.

Bleys, R. (1995). *The geography of perversion: Male-to-male sexual behavior outside the West and the ethnographic imagination, 1750–1918*. New York, NY: New York University.

Bloom, H. (2009). *Tennessee Williams*. New York, NY: Chelsea House.

Blumstein, P., & Schwartz, P. (1983). *American couples: Money, work, sex*. New York, NY: William Morrow & Co.

Bochenek, M., & Knight, K. (2012). Establishing a third gender category in Nepal: Process and prognosis. *Emory International Law Review*, *26*, 11–41.

Boellstorff, T. (2011). But do not identify as gay: A proleptic genealogy of the MSM category. *Cultural Anthropology*, *26*(2), 287–312.

Bogaert, A. F. (2004). Asexuality: Prevalence and associated factors in a national probability sample. *Journal of Sex Research*, *41*(3), 279–287.

Bolding, G., Davis, M., Hart, G., Sherr, L., & Elford, J. (2007). Where young MSM meet their first sexual partner: The role of the internet. *AIDS and Behavior*, *11*(4), 522–525.

Bolin, A., & Whelehan, P. (2009). *Human sexuality: Biological, psychological, and cultural perspectives*. New York, NY: Routledge.

Bornstein, K. (1994). *Gender outlaw: On men, women, and the rest of us*. New York, NY: Routledge.

Bornstein, K. (2012). *A queer and pleasant danger: A memoir*. Boston, MA: Beacon.

Bornstein, K., & Bergman, S. B. (2010). *Gender outlaws: The next generation*. Seattle, WA: Seal.

Bösche, S. (2000). "Jenny, Eric, Martin. . .and Me." *The Guardian*. Retrieved from www. theguardian.com/books/2000/jan/31/booksforchildrenandteenagers.features11

Botelho, M. J., & Rudman, M. K. (2009). *Critical multicultural analysis of children's literature: Mirrors, windows, doors*. New York, NY: Routledge.

Boucher, C. (2008). Newly imagined audiences: Folkways gay and lesbian records. *Journal of Popular Music Studies*, *20*(2), 29–149.

Bouchey, H. A. & Furman, W. (2003). Dating and romantic experiences in adolescence. In G. R. Adams & M. D. Berzonsky (Eds.), *Blackwell handbook of adolescence* (pp. 313–329). Oxford, UK: Blackwell.

*Bowers v. Hardwick*, 478 U.S. 186, 106 S. Ct. 2841, 92 L. Ed. 2d 140 (1986).

Bowlby, J. (1973). *Attachment and loss. Vol. 2, separation*. New York, NY: Basic.

Boyce, P. (2007). "Conceiving *kothis*": Men who have sex with men in India and the cultural subject of HIV prevention. *Medical Anthropology, 26*(2), 175–203.

Boykin, K. (Ed.). (2012). *For colored boys who have considered suicide when the rainbow is still not enough: coming of age, coming out, and coming home*. New York, NY: Magnus.

Braithwaite, S. R., Delevi, R., & Fincham, F. D. (2010). Romantic relationships and the physical and mental health of college students. *Personal Relationships, 17*(1), 1–12.

Branchik, B. (2002). Out in the market: A history of the gay market segment in the United States. *Journal of Macromarketing, 22*(1), 86–97

Branson, B. M., Owen, S. M., Wesolowski, L. G., Bennett, B., Werner, B. G., Wroblewski, K. E., & Pentella, M. A. (2014). *Laboratory testing for the diagnosis of HIV infection: updated recommendations*. Atlanta, GA: U.S. Centers for Disease Control and Prevention.

Branson-Potts, H. (2016, February 16). Girl can wear "nobody knows I'm a lesbian" t-shirt at school. *Los Angeles Times*. Retrieved from www.latimes.com/local/lanow/la-me-ln-lesbian-shirt-lawsuit-20160217-story.html

Branson-Potts, H., & Queally, J. (2016, May 27). The handsome undercover cop smiles. Is he entrapping gay men or cleaning up a park? *Los Angeles Times*. Retrieved from www.latimes.com/local/lanow/la-me-gay-stings-police-20160527-snap-story.html

Braukman, S. (2004). Government and military witchhunts. In Marc Stein (Ed.), *Encyclopedia of Lesbian, Gay, Bisexual and Transgender history in America* (1st ed., vol. *1*, 464–468). New York: Charles Scribner's Sons.

Bray, A. (2003). *The friend*. Chicago, IL: University of Chicago.

Britzman, D. P. (1995). Is there a queer pedagogy? Or, stop reading straight. *Educational Theory, 45*(2), 151–165.

Bronski, M. (Ed.) (2003). *Pulp friction: Uncovering the golden age of gay male pulps*. New York, NY: St. Martin's Griffin.

Brotto, L. A., & Yule, M. (2017). Asexuality: Sexual orientation, paraphilia, sexual dysfunction, or none of the above?. *Archives of Sexual Behavior, 46*(3), 619–627.

*Brown v. Board of Education*, 347 U.S. 483 (1954).

Brown, B. B., & Braun, M. T. (2013). Peer relations. In C. Proctor & P. A. Linley (Eds.), *Research, applications, and interventions for children and adolescents: A positive psychology perspective* (pp. 149–164). New York, NY: Springer.

Brown, B. B., & Larson, J. (2009). Peer relationships in adolescence. In R. M. Lerner & L. Steinberg (Eds.), *Handbook of adolescent psychology, Vol 2: Contextual influences on adolescent development*, third edition (pp. 74–103). Hoboken, NJ: Wiley.

Brown, K. M. (1996). *Good wives, nasty wenches, and anxious patriarchs: Gender, race, and power in colonial Virginia*. Chapel Hill, NC: University of North Carolina.

Brown, T. N. T., & Herman, J. L. (2015). *Intimate partner violence and sexual abuse among LGBT people*. Los Angeles, CA: The Williams Institute.

Brown, T. N., Romero, A. P., & Gates, G. J. (2016). *Food insecurity and SNAP participation in the LGBT community*. Los Angeles, CA: The Williams Institute.

Bruce-Jones, E., & Itaborahy, L. C. (2011). State-sponsored homophobia: A world survey of laws criminalising same sex acts between consenting adults. *The International Lesbian, Gay, Bisexual, Trans, and Intersex Association*. Retrieved from www.lga.org/ilga/en/article/1161

Bryant, A. (1977). *The Anita Bryant story: The survival of our nation's families and the threat of militant homosexuality*. Old Tappan, NJ: Fleming H. Revell.

Budge, S. L., Tebbe, E. N., & Howard, K. A. S. (2010). The work experiences of transgender individuals: Negotiating the transition and career decision-making processes. *Journal of Counseling Psychology, 57*(4), 377–393.

Bullough, V. L. (2015). Homophobia. *GLBTQ Archive.com*. Retrieved from www.glbtqarchive.com/ssh/homophobia_S.pdf

Burke, S. S. (2004). In search of lesbian community in an electronic world. *CyberPsychology & Behavior, 3*(4), 591–604.

Burleson, W. (2014). *Bi America: Myths, truths, and struggles of an invisible community*. New York, NY: Routledge.

Burns, C. (2012). *The business of discrimination: The economic costs of discrimination and the financial benefits of gay and transgender equality in the workplace*. Retrieved from www.americanprogress.org/issues/lgbt/reports/2012/03/22/11234/the-costly-business-of-discrimination/

Butler, J. (2004). *Undoing gender*. New York, NY: Routledge.

Button, J. W., Rienzo, B. A., & Wald, K. D. (1997). *Private lives, public conflicts: Battles over gay rights in American communities*. Washington, DC: CQ Press.

Cahill, S., South, K., & Spade, J. (2000). *Outing age: Public policy issues affecting gay, lesbian, bisexual, transgender elders*. New York, NY: The Policy Institute of the National Gay and Lesbian Task Force Foundation.

Calabrese, S. K., Rosenberger, J. G., Schick, V. R., Novak, D. S., & Reece, M. (2013). An event-level comparison of risk-related sexual practices between black and other-race men who have sex with men: condoms, semen, lubricant, and rectal douching. *AIDS patient care and STDs, 27*(2), 77–84.

Calderone, A. (2015, October 15). Transgender activist Aydian Dowling loses *Men's Health* November cover competition but will appear on special edition cover. *People*. Retrieved from people.com/bodies/aydian-dowling-loses-mens-health-cover-competition/

Cameron, E. (2000). Breaking the silence. In *Opening remarks at International Conference on AIDS, Durban, South Africa, 13*(1).

Campbell, J. E. (2004). *Getting it on online: Cyberspace, gay male sexuality, and embodied identity*. New York, NY: Harrington Park.

Campus Pride. (2016). *Campus Pride Index*. Retrieved from www.campusprideindex.org/

Canaday, M. (2009). *The straight state: Sexuality and citizenship in twentieth-century America*. Princeton, NJ: Princeton University.

Cantú, L., Luibhéid, E., & Stern, A. M. (2005). Well-founded fear: Political asylum and the boundaries of sexual identity in the U.S.-Mexico borderlands. In E. Luibhéid & L. Cantú (Eds.), *Queer migrations: Sexuality, U.S. citizenship, and border crossings* (pp. 61–74). Minneapolis, MN: University of Minnesota.

CAP & MAP. (2014). *Paying an unfair price: The financial penalty for being LGBT in America*. Washington, DC and Denver, CO: Center for American Progress & Movement Advancement Project.

Carballo-Diéguez, A., Dolezal, C., Nieves, L., Díaz, F., Decena, C., & Balan, I. (2004). Looking for a tall, dark, macho man . . . sexual-role behaviour variations in Latino gay and bisexual men. *Culture, Health & Sexuality, 6*(2), 159–171.

Carlson, J. (2010). The female significant in all-women's amateur roller derby. *Sociology of Sport Journal, 27*(4), 428–440.

Carlston, E. G. (2015, November 22). Essay: Patricia Highsmith's *The Price of Salt*, the lesbian novel that's now a major motion picture. *National Book Review*. Retrieved from www.thenationalbookreview.com/features/2015/11/22/dlqvawdg1wjt1ls808mnk9y6e2xu3b

Carpenter, C. (2005). Self-reported sexual orientation and earnings: Evidence from California. *Industrial and labor relations review, 58*(2): 258–273.

Carrillo, H. (2002). *The night is young: Sexuality in Mexico in the time of AIDS.* Chicago, IL: University of Chicago.

Carrillo, H. (2004). Sexual migration, cross-cultural sexual encounters, and sexual health. *Sexuality Research & Social Policy, 1*(3), 58–70.

Carroll, J. (2016). *Sexuality now: Embracing diversity,* fourth edition. New York, NY: Wadsworth.

Cart, J., & Stanley, E. (1999, March 14). Rural life can be lonely, and risky, for gays. *Los Angeles Times.* Retrieved from http://articles.latimes.com/1999/mar/14/news/mn-17291

Carvalho, A. F., Lewis, R. J., Derlega, V. J., Winstead, B. A., & Viggiano, C. (2011). Internalized sexual minority stressors and same-sex intimate partner violence. *Journal of Family Violence, 26*(7), 501–509.

Case, K. A., & Meier, S. C. (2014). Developing allies to transgender and gender-nonconforming youth: Training for counselors and educators. *Journal of LGBT Youth, 11*(1), 62–82.

Cass, V. C. (1979). Homosexual identity formation: A theoretical model. *Journal of Homosexuality, 4*(3), 219–235.

Castiglia, C., & Reed, C. (2012). *If memory serves: Gay men, AIDS, and the promise of the queer past.* Minneapolis, MN: U of Minnesota.

Castro, I. E., & Sujak, M.C. (2014). "Why can't we learn about this?" Sexual minority students navigate the official and hidden curricular spaces of high school. *Education and Urban Society, 46*(4), 450–473.

Cauterucci, C. (2012, May 25). Reality bites: Why *The Real L Word* is bad for lesbians. *Huffington Post.* Retrieved from www.huffingtonpost.com/christina-cauterucci/real-l-word_b_1547206.html

CDC (U.S. Centers for Disease Control and Prevention). (2011). *Sexual identity, sex of sexual contacts, and health-risk behaviors among students in grades 9–12: Youth risk behavior surveillance.* Atlanta, GA: U.S. Centers for Disease Control and Prevention.

CDC. (2012). Estimated HIV incidence in the United States, 2007–2010. *HIV surveillance supplemental report, 17*(4), 1–26.

CDC. (2016b). *Viral hepatitis surveillance United States, 2014 (rev. Sept. 2016).* Atlanta, GA: U.S. Centers for Disease Control and Prevention.

CDC. (2016c). *HIV surveillance report; vol. 27. Diagnoses of HIV infection in the United States and dependent areas, 2015.* Atlanta, GA: U.S. Centers for Disease Control and Prevention.

CDC. (2016d). *CDC fact sheet: Today's HIV epidemic.* Atlanta, GA: U.S. Centers for Disease Control and Prevention.

CDC. (n.d.) PrEP facts. Retrieved from http://men.prepfacts.org/

Chandra, A., Copen, C. E., & Mosher, W. D. (2013). Sexual behavior, sexual attraction, and sexual identity in the United States: Data from the 2006–2010 National Survey of Family Growth. In A. K. Baumle (Ed.), *International handbook on the demography of sexuality* (pp. 45–66). Dordrecht, Netherlands: Springer Science+Business Media.

Chandra, A., Mosher, W. D., Copen, C., Sionean, C. (2011). Sexual behavior, sexual attraction, and sexual identity in the United States: Data from the 2006–2008 National Survey of Family Growth. *National health statistics reports, 36.* Hyattsville, MD: National Center for Health Statistics.

Charters, A. (2001). *Beat down to your soul: What was the beat generation?* New York, NY: Penguin.

Chase, C. (1998). Hermaphrodites with attitude: Mapping the emergence of intersex political activism. *GLQ, 4*(2), 189–211.

Chasin, A. (2000). *Selling out: The gay and lesbian movement goes to market.* New York, NY: St. Martin's.

Chauncey, G. (1994). *Gay New York: Gender, urban culture, and the making of the gay male world, 1890–1940.* New York, NY: Basic.

Chauncey, G. (2009). *Why marriage: The history shaping today's debate over gay equality.* New York, NY: Basic.

Chávez, K. (2013). *Queer migration politics: Activist rhetoric and coalitional possibilities.* Champaign-Urbana, IL: University of Illinois.

Chesir-Teran, D. (2003). Conceptualizing and addressing heterosexism in high schools: A setting-level approach. *American Journal of Community Psychology, 31*(3/4), 269–279.

Chibbaro, Jr., L. (2017, June 11). Our history of marching on Washington. *Washington Blade.* Retrieved from www.washingtonblade.com/2017/06/11/history-marching-washington/

Choi, S. K., & Meyer, I. H. (2016). *LGBT aging: A review of research findings, needs, and policy implications.* Los Angeles, CA: The Williams Institute.

Chung, C., Kim, A., Nguyen, Z., Ordona, T., & Stein, A. (1994). In our own way: A roundtable discussion. *Amerasia Journal, 20*(1), 137–147.

Ciambriello, R. (2016, November 28). Zales jewelers gets heat for putting a lesbian couple in its holiday ad. *Adweek.* Retrieved from www.adweek.com/creativity/zales-jewelers-gets-heat-putting-lesbian-couple-its-holiday-ad-174806/

CLAGS (Center for Lesbian & Gay Studies) (Eds.). (2003). *Queer ideas: The David R. Kessler Lectures in lesbian and gay studies.* New York, NY: Feminist Press at CUNY.

Clark, C. T., & Blackburn, M. V. (2009). Reading LGBT-themed literature with young people: What's possible? *English Journal, 98*(4), 25–32.

Clinton, H. (2011). Remarks in recognition of International Human Rights Day. Retrieved from www.state.gov/secretary/rm/2011/12/178368.htm

Clinton, K. (2000, September). Tastefully gay. *The Progressive, 64*(9), 14.

Cohen, C. J. (1997). Punks, bulldaggers, and welfare queens: The radical potential of queer politics? *Journal of Gay and Lesbian Studies, 3*(4), 437–465.

Cohen, H. L., & Murray, Y. (2007). Older lesbian and gay caregivers: Caring for families of choice and caring for families or origin. *Journal of Human Behavior in the Social Environment, 14,* 275–298.

Cohen, J. N., & Byers, E. S. (2014). Beyond lesbian bed death: Enhancing our understanding of the sexuality of sexual-minority women in relationships. *The Journal of Sex Research, 51*(8), 893–903.

Cohen, J. N., Byers, E. S., & Walsh, L. P. (2008). Factors influencing the sexual relationships of lesbians and gay men. *International Journal of Sexual Health, 20*(3), 162–176.

Coleman, E. J. & Chou, W-S. (2000). *Tongzhi: Politics of same-sex eroticism in Chinese societies.* Binghamton, NY: Haworth.

Colfax, G., Coates, T. J., Husnik, M. M. J., Huang, Y., Buchbinder, S., Koblin, B., . . . & EXPLORE Study Team. (2005). Longitudinal patterns of methamphetamine, popper (amyl nitrite), and cocaine use and high-risk sexual behavior among a cohort of San Francisco men who have sex with men. *Journal of Urban Health, 82*(1), i62–i70.

Colfax, G. N., Mansergh, G., Guzman, R., Vittinghoff, E., Marks, G., Rader, M., & Buchbinder, S. (2001). Drug use and sexual risk behavior among gay and bisexual men who attend circuit parties: a venue-based comparison. *JAIDS Journal of Acquired Immune Deficiency Syndromes, 28*(4), 373–379.

Collins, W. A., & Sroufe, L. A. (1999). Capacity for intimate relationships: A developmental construction. In W. Furman, B. B. Brown, & C. Feiring (Eds.), *The development of romantic relationships in adolescence* (pp. 125–147). New York, NY: Cambridge University.

Coltrane, S., & Adams, M. (1997). Children and gender. In T. E. Arendell (Ed.), *Understanding families, Vol. 9. Contemporary parenting: Challenges and issues* (pp. 219–253). Thousand Oaks, CA: Sage Publications.

Compton, J. (2016, October 25). After troubled history, law enforcement builds bridges with LGBTQ community. *NBC OUT.* Retrieved from www.nbcnews.com/feature/nbc-out/after-troubled-history-law-enforcement-builds-alliances-lgbtq-community-n671841

Comstock, G. D. (1996). *Unrepentant, self-affirming, practicing: Lesbian/bisexual/gay people within organized religion.* New York, NY: Continuum.

Condon, B. (Producer), & Robey (Director). (2011). *Making the boys* [Motion Picture] United States: First Run Features.

Conerly, G. (2000). Are you Black first or are you queer? In D. Constantine-Simms (Ed.), *The greatest taboo: Homosexuality in black communities* (pp. 7–23). Los Angeles, CA: Alyson.

Conte, A., & Burchill, R. (2009). *Defining civil and political rights: The jurisprudence of the United Nations Committee.* Surrey and Burlington, UK: Ashgate.

Copen, C. E., Chandra, A., & Febo-Vazquez, I. (2016). Sexual behavior, sexual attraction, and sexual orientation among adults aged 18–44 in the United States: Data from the 2011–2013 National Survey of Family Growth. *National health statistics reports,* (88), 1–14.

Corinna, H. (2016). *S.E.X.: The all-you-need-to-know sexuality guide to get you through your teens and twenties,* second edition. New York, NY: Da Capo Lifelong.

Cox, W. T., Devine, P. G., Bischmann, A. A., & Hyde, J. S. (2016). Inferences about sexual orientation: The roles of stereotypes, faces, and the gaydar myth. *Journal of Sex Research, 53*(2), 157–171.

Crenshaw, K. (1991). Mapping the margins: Intersectionality, identity politics, and violence against women of color. *Stanford Law Review, 43*(6), 1241–1299.

Crompton, L. (1976). Homosexuals and the death penalty in colonial America. *Journal of Homosexuality, 1*(3), 277–293.

Crompton, L. (2003). *Homosexuality and civilization.* Cambridge, MA: Harvard University.

Cronin, P. (2009). *Harriet Hosmer: Lost and found: A catalogue raisonné.* Milan, Italy: Charta.

Crouch, G. (2006, March 16). Dutch immigration kit offers a revealing view. *New York Times.* Retrieved from www.nytimes.com/2006/03/16/world/europe/16iht-dutch-5852942.html

Cummins, E. (1990). *Understanding Ursula K. Le Guin.* Columbia, SC: University of South Carolina.

Cunningham, M., Pergamit, M., Astone, N., & Luna, J. (2014). *Homeless LGBTQ+ youth.* Washington, DC: Urban Institute.

D'Addario, D. (2013, September 24). *Modern Family* is a class-blind fantasy world. *Salon.* Retrieved from www.salon.com/2013/09/24/modern_family_is_a_class_blind_fantasy_world/

D'Augelli, A. R. (1994). Identity development and sexual orientation: Toward a model of lesbian, gay, and bisexual development. In E. J. Trickett, R. J. Watts, and D. Birman (Eds.) *Human diversity: Perspectives on people in context.* San Francisco: Jossey-Bass.

D'Augelli, A. R., Grossman, A. H., & Starks, M. T. (2005). Parents' awareness of lesbian, gay, and bisexual youths' sexual orientation. *Journal of Marriage and Family, 67*(2), 474–482.

D'Emilio, J. (1983). *Sexual politics, sexual communities*. Chicago, IL: University of Chicago.

D'Emilio, J. (1992). Inaugurating the first lesbian and gay studies department. In *Making trouble: Essays on gay history, politics, and the university*, 155–159. New York, NY: Routledge.

D'Emilio, J. (1998). *Sexual politics, sexual communities: The making of a homosexual minority in the United States, 1940–1970*, second edition. Chicago, IL: University of Chicago.

D'Emilio, J. (2003). *Lost prophet: The life and times of Bayard Rustin*. New York, NY: Free Press.

D'Emilio, J., & Freedman, E. (1997). *Intimate matters: A history of sexuality in America*. Chicago: University of Chicago.

Daniel, L. (2010, November 30). Repeal of "Don't Ask, Don't Tell" offers few risks, report finds. *Armed Forces Press Service*. Washington, DC: United States Department of Defense.

Dank, M., Lachman, P., Zweig, J. M., & Yahner, J. (2014). Dating violence experiences of lesbian, gay, bisexual and transgender youth. *Journal of Youth and Adolescence, 43*(5), 846–858.

Darnton, R. (1985). *The literary underground of the old regime*. Cambridge, MA: Harvard University.

Davies, K. (2008). Adult daughters whose mothers come out later in life: What is the psychosocial impact? *Journal of Lesbian Studies, 12*(2–3), 55–263.

Davis, A. (1998). *Blues legacies and black feminism: Gertrude "Ma" Rainey, Bessie Smith, and Billie Holiday*. New York, NY: Pantheon.

Davis, A. D. (2003). Slavery and the roots of sexual harassment. In C. MacKinnon & R. B. Siegel (Eds.), *Directions in sexual harassment law* (pp. 457–78). New Haven, CT: Yale

Davis, C. M., Yarber, W. L., & Bauserman, R. (1998). *Handbook of sexuality-related measures*. Thousand Oaks, CA: Sage.

De Grazia, A. (1998, Fall). Ed de Grazia: Allen Ginsberg, Norman Mailer, Barney Rosset: Their struggles against censorship recalled. *Cardozo life*. New York, NY: Yeshiva University.

Deer, S. (2015). *The beginning and end of rape: Confronting sexual violence in Native America*. Minneapolis, MN: University of Minnesota.

DeMarco, J. (1983). Gay racism. In M. J. Smith (Ed.), *Black men/White men: A gay anthology* (pp. 109–118). San Francisco: Gay Sunshine.

Dennis, J. P. (2012). Gay content in newspaper comics. *The Journal of American Culture, 35*(4), 304–314.

Deol, A. K. & Heath-Toby, A. (2009). *HIV risk for lesbians, bisexuals & other women who have sex with women*. New York, NY: Gay Men's Health Crisis.

DeWaele, A., Cox, N., Van den Berghe, W., & Vinke, J. (2011). Families of choice? Exploring the supportive networks of lesbians, gay men, and bisexuals. *Journal of Applied Social Psychology, 41*(2), 312–331.

Dhoest, A. (2016). Feeling (dis)connected: Diasporic LGBTQs and digital media. *International Journal of E-Politics, 7*(3), 1–14.

Diamond, L. M. (2008). *Sexual fluidity*. Cambridge, MA: Harvard University.

Diamond, L. M., & Rosky, C. J. (2016). Scrutinizing immutability: Research on sexual orientation and U.S. legal advocacy for sexual minorities. *The Journal of Sex Research, 53*(4–5), 363–391.

DiGrazia, J., & Boucher, M. (2005). Writing inqueeries: Bodies, queer theory, and an experimental writing class. *Composition Studies, 33*(2), 25–44.

Dilley, P. (1999). Queer theory: Under construction. *QSE: International Journal of Qualitative Studies in Education, 12*(5), 457–472.

DiMassa, D. (2004). Letter from Diane DiMassa. *Eminism.org*. Retrieved from http://eminism.org/michigan/20040700-dimassa.txt

Dinkins, E. & Englert P. (2016) "You don't have to think about it in that way": Deconstructing teacher assumptions about LGBTIQ students. In *Queering classrooms: Personal narratives and educational practice to support LGBTQ youth in schools* (pp. 127–144). Charlotte, NC: Information Age.

Doan, L. & Prosser, J. (Eds.) (2002). *Palatable poison: Critical perspectives on* The Well of Loneliness. New York, NY: Columbia University.

Dodge, B., Reece, M., Herbenick, D., Schick, V., Sanders, S. A., & Fortenberry, J. D. (2010). Sexual health among US Black and Hispanic men and women: A nationally representative study. *The Journal of Sexual Medicine, 7*(s5), 330–345.

Dodge, B., Schnarrs, P. W., Reece, M., Martinez, O., Goncalves, G., Malebranche, D., . . . & Fortenberry, J. D. (2013). Sexual behaviors and experiences among behaviorally bisexual men in the Midwestern United States. *Archives of Sexual Behavior, 42*(2), 247–256.

Doidge, N. (2007). *The brain that changes itself: Stories of personal triumph from the frontiers of brain science.* New York, NY: Viking.

Dolan, K. & Davis, P.W. (2010). Lesbian women and sexually transmitted infections. In M. Stombler, D. M. Baunach, E. O. Burgess, D. Donnelly, W. Simonds, & E. J. Windsor (Eds.). *Sex matters: The sex & society reader* (pp. 36–37). Boston: Allyn & Bacon.

Donaldson, W. V., Asta, E. L., & Vacha-Haase, T. (2014). Attitudes of heterosexual assisted living residents toward gay and lesbian peers. *Clinical Gerontologist: The Journal of Aging and Mental Health, 37*(2), 167–189.

Donelson, R., & Rogers, T. (2004). Negotiating a research protocol for studying school-based gay and lesbian issues. *Theory Into Practice, 43*(2), 128–135.

Donovan, M. C. (1993). The politics of deservedness: The Ryan White Act and the social constructions of people with AIDS. *Review of Policy Research, 12*(3/4), 3–29.

Doucleff, M. (2016, October 26) Researchers clear 'Patient Zero' from AIDS origin story. *National Public Radio*. Retrieved from www.npr.org/sections/health-shots/2016/10/26/498876985/mystery-solved-how-hiv-came-to-the-u-s

Downs, J. (2016). *Stand by me: The forgotten history of gay liberation.* New York, NY: Basic.

Doyle, M. W. (1986). *Empires.* Ithaca, NY: Cornell University.

Drabble, L., Trocki, K. F., Hughes, T. L., Korda, R. A., & Lown, A. E. (2013). Sexual orientation differences in the relationship between victimization and hazardous drinking among women in the National Alcohol Survey. *Psychology of Addictive Behaviors, 27*(3), 639–648.

Dreger, A. D. (1998). "Ambiguous sex"—or ambivalent medicine?: Ethical issues in the treatment of intersexuality. *Hastings Center Report, 28*(3), 24–35.

Dreger, A. D. (2000). *Hermaphrodites and the medical invention of sex.* Cambridge, MA: Harvard University.

Driskill, Q-L. (2004). Stolen from our bodies: First Nations two-spirits/queers and the journey to a sovereign erotic. *Studies in American Indian Literatures, 16*(2), 50–64.

Drydakis, N. (2015). Effect of sexual orientation on job satisfaction: Evidence from Greece. *Industrial Relations: A Journal of Economy and Society, 54*(1), 162–187.

Dube, E. M. & Savin-Williams, R. C. (1999). Sexual identity development among ethnic sexual-minority male youths. *Developmental Psychology, 35*(6), 1389–1398.

Duberman, M. (1990). Writhing bedfellows in antebellum South Carolina: Historical interpretation and the politics of evidence. In Duberman, M., Vicinus, M., & Chauncey, G. (Eds.), *Hidden from history: Reclaiming the gay and lesbian past* (pp. 153–168). New York, NY: Meridian.

Durbin, K. (2005, September 4). Cowboys in love . . . with each other. *New York Times*. Retrieved from www.nytimes.com/2005/09/04/movies/cowboys-in-love-with-each-other.html

Durso, L. E., & Gates, G. J. (2013). Best practices: collecting and analyzing data on sexual minorities. In Baumle, A. (Ed.), *International handbook on the demography of sexuality* (pp. 21–42). Dordrecht, Netherlands: Springer Science+Business Media.

Dutta, A., & Roy, R. (2014). Decolonizing transgender in India: Some reflections. *TSQ: Transgender Studies Quarterly, 1*(3), 320–337.

Dyar, C., Feinstein, B. A., & London, B. (2014). Dimensions of sexual identity and minority stress among bisexual women: the role of partner gender. *Psychology of Sexual Orientation and Gender Diversity, 1*(4), 441–451.

Dyer, R. (1988). Children of the night: Vampirism as homosexuality, homosexuality as vampirism. In Susannah Radstone (Ed.), *Sweet dreams: Sexuality, gender, and popular fiction*. London, UK: Lawrence & Wishart.

Dyer, R. (1993). *The matter of images: Essays on representations*. London, UK: Routledge

Dynes, W. R. (1990). L'Alcibiade, fanciullo a scola. *Encyclopedia of homosexuality*. New York, NY: Garland Publishers.

Eaklor, V. L. (2008). *Queer America: A GLBT history of the twentieth century*. Westport, CT: Greenwood.

Eaklor, V. (2011). *Queer America: A people's GLBT history of the United States*. New York, NY: The New Press.

Ehrensaft, D. (2013) "The Gender affirmative model: what we know and what we aim to learn." Hidalgo, M.A., Ehrensaft, D. Tishelman, A.C., Clark, L.F., Garofalo, R., Rosenthal, S.M., Spack, N.P., & Olson, J., *Human Development, 56*: 285–290.

Eisner, S. (2013). *Bi: Notes for a bisexual revolution*. Seattle, WA: Seal.

Elia, J. P., & Eliason, M. J. (2010). Dangerous omissions: Abstinence-only-until-marriage school-based sexuality education and the betrayal of LGBTQ youth. *American Journal of Sexuality Education, 5*(1), 17–35.

Elias, M. J., Zins, J. E., Graczyk, P. A., & Weissberg, R. P. (2003). Implementation, sustainability, and scaling up of social-emotional and academic innovations in public schools. *School Psychology Review, 32*(3), 303–319.

Elicker, J., Englund, M., & Sroufe, L. A. (1992). Predicting peer competence and peer relationships in childhood from early parent-child relationships. In R. Parke & G. Ladd (Eds.), *Family-peer relationships: Models of linkage* (pp. 77–106). Hillsdale, NJ: Erlbaum.

Elliston, D. (1995). Erotic anthropology: "Ritualized homosexuality" in Melanesia and beyond. *American Ethnologist, 22*(4), 848–867.

Ellsworth, E. (1989). Why doesn't this feel empowering? Working through the repressive myths of critical pedagogy. *Harvard Educational Review, 59*(3), 297–325.

Erickson-Schroth, L. (2013). Update on the biology of transgender identity. *Journal of Gay & Lesbian Mental Health, 17*(2), 150–174.

Erickson-Schroth, L. (Ed.). (2014). *Trans bodies, trans selves: A resource for the transgender community*. Oxford, UK: Oxford University.

Escoffier, J. (2011). Imagining the she/male: Pornography and the transsexualization of the heterosexual male. *Studies in Gender and Sexuality, 12*(4), 268–281.

Eskridge, Jr., W. J. (2008). *Dishonorable passions: Sodomy laws in America, 1861–2003*. New York, NY: Viking.

Espin, O. M. (1984). Cultural and historical influences on sexuality in Hispanic/Latin women: Implications for psychotherapy. In C. S. Vance (Ed.), *Pleasure and danger: Exploring female sexuality* (pp. 149–163). Boston, MA: Routledge and Kegan Paul.

Etengoff, C., & Daiute, C. (2015). Online coming-out communications between gay men and their religious family allies: A family of choice and origin perspective. *Journal of GLBT Family Studies, 11*(3), 278–304.

Evans, N. J., & Broido, E. M. (2005). Encouraging the development of social justice attitudes and actions in heterosexual student. *New Directions for Student Services, 2005*(110), 43–54.

Eyre, S. L., Milbrath, C., & Peacock, B. (2007). Romantic relationship trajectories of African American gay/bisexual adolescents. *Journal of Adolescent Research, 22*(2), 177–131.

Fabbre, V. D. (2014). Gender transitions later in life: The significance of time in queer aging. *Journal of Gerontological Social Work, 57*(2–4), 161–175.

Faderman, L. (1981). *Surpassing the love of men: Romantic friendship and love between women from the renaissance to the present.* New York, NY: William Morrow.

Faderman, L. (1991). *Odd girls and twilight lovers: A history of lesbian life in twentieth-century America.* New York, NY: Penguin.

Faderman, L., & Timmons, S. (2006). *Gay L. A.: A history of sexual outlaws, power politics, and lipstick lesbians.* New York, NY: Basic.

Fairchild, A. L., & Tynan, E. A. (1994). Policies of containment: Immigration in the era of AIDS. *American Journal of Public Health, 84*(12), 2011–2022.

Farmer, P. (1992). *AIDS and accusation: Haiti and the geography of blame.* Berkeley, CA: University of California.

Fassin, E., & Salcedo, M. (2015). Becoming gay? Immigration policies and the truth of sexual identity. *Archives of Sexual Behavior, 44*(5), 1117–1125.

Fassinger, R. E. (1991). The hidden minority: Issues and challenges in working with lesbian women and gay men. *Counseling Psychologist, 19*(2), 157–176.

Fausto-Sterling, A. (1993). The five sexes. *The Sciences, 33*(2), 20–25.

Fausto-Sterling, A. (2000). *Sexing the body: Gender politics and the construction of sexuality.* New York, NY: Basic.

Fausto-Sterling, A. (2012). *Sex/gender: Biology in a social world.* New York, NY: Routledge.

*Federal Education Amendments Act*, 20 U.S.C. Â§1681 et seq., (1972).

Fee, E., & Krieger, N. (1993). Understanding AIDS: Historical interpretations and the limits of biomedical individualism. *American Journal of Public Health, 83*(1), 1477–1486.

Feiler, B. (2011, January 21). What *Modern Family* says about modern families. *New York Times.* Retrieved from www.nytimes.com/2011/01/23/fashion/23THISLIFE.html

Feinstein, B. A., Wadsworth, L. P., Davila, J., & Goldfried, M. R. (2014). Do parental acceptance and family support moderate associations between dimensions of minority stress and depressive symptoms among lesbians and gay men? *Professional Psychology: Research and Practice, 45*(4), 239.

Fidas, D., & Cooper, L. (2014). *The cost of the closet and the rewards of inclusion: Why the workplace environment for LGBT people matters to employers.* Washington, DC: Human Rights Campaign.

Field, T. L., & Mattson, G. (2016). Parenting transgender children in PFLAG. *Journal of GLBT Family Studies, 12*(5), 413–429.

Fine, C. (2010). *Delusions of gender: How our minds, society, and neurosexism create difference.* New York, NY: W. W. Norton.

Finley, N. J. (2010). Skating femininity: Gender maneuvering in women's roller derby. *Journal of Contemporary Ethnography, 39*(4), 359–387.

Fischer, H. D., & Fischer, E. J. (Eds.). (2007). *Chronicle of the Pulitzer Prizes for Fiction: Discussions, decisions and documents* (vol. *21*). Boston: K. G. Saur.

Fischlin, D., & Nandorfy, M. (2007). *The concise guide to global human rights*. Montreal, ON: Black Rose.

Flores, A. R., Herman, J. L., Gates, G. J., & Brown, T. N. T. (2016). *How many adults identify as transgender in the United States?* Los Angeles, CA: The Williams Institute.

Floyd, F. J., & Bakeman, R. (2006). Coming-out across the life course: Implications of age and historical context. *Archives of Sexual Behavior, 35*(3), 287–297.

Fortunata, B., & Kohn, C. S. (2003). Demographic, psychosocial, and personality characteristics of lesbian batterers. *Violence and Victims, 18*(5), 557.

Foucault, M. (1978). *The history of sexuality, volume 1: An introduction*, tr. Robert Hurley. New York, NY: Pantheon.

Fourtier, A-M. (2014). Migration studies. In R. Adley, D. Bissell, K. Hannam, P. Merriman, & M. Sheller (Eds.), *The Routledge handbook of mobilities* (pp. 64–73). New York, NY & London, UK: Routledge.

Fox, C. (2007). From transaction to transformation: (En)Countering white heteronormativity in "safe spaces." *College English, 69*(5), 496–511.

France, D. (2007, June 17). The science of gaydar. *New York*. Retrieved from http://nymag.com/news/features/33520/

Franke, K. (1998). Putting sex to work. *University of Denver Law Review, 75*, 1139–1180.

Fredman, A. J., Schultz, N. J., & Hoffman, M. F. (2015). "You're moving a frickin' big ship": The challenges of addressing LGBTQ topics in public schools. *Education and Urban Society, 47*(1), 56–85.

Freeman, C. (1999). *The Greek achievement: The foundation of the Western world*. London, UK: Allen Lane.

Freeman, E. E., Weiss, H. A., Glynn, J. R., Cross, P. L., Whitworth, J. A., & Hayes, R. J. (2006). Herpes simplex virus 2 infection increases HIV acquisition in men and women: systematic review and meta-analysis of longitudinal studies. *AIDS, 20*(1), 73–83.

Freud, S., & Strachey, J. ([1905]1975). *Three essays on the theory of sexuality*. New York, NY: Basic.

Frost, D. M. (2011). Stigma and intimacy in same-sex relationships: A narrative approach. *Journal of Family Psychology, 25*(1), 1–10.

Frost, D. M., & Meyer, I. H. (2012). Measuring community connectedness among diverse sexual minority populations. *Journal of Sex Research, 49*(1), 36–49.

Fruhauf, C. A., Orel, N. A., & Jenkins, D. A. (2009). The coming-out process of gay grandfathers: Perceptions of their adult children's influence. *Journal of LGBT Family Studies, 5*(1–2), 99–118.

Frye, M. (1983). *The politics of reality: Essays in feminist theory*. Berkeley, CA: Crossing.

Fung, R. (1991). Looking for my penis: The eroticized Asian in gay video porn. In Bad Object-choices (Eds.), *How do I look? Queer film & video* (pp. 145–168). Seattle, WA: Bay.

Fur, G. (2007). Weibe-town and the Delawares-as-women: Gender-crossing and same-sex relations in eighteenth-century northeastern indian culture. In Foster, T. (Ed.), *Long before Stonewall: Histories of same-sex sexuality in early America* (pp. 32–50). New York, NY: New York University.

Furman, W., & Buhrmester, D. (1992). Age and sex differences in perceptions of networks of personal relationships, *Child Development, 63*(1), 103–115.

Gale, P. (1999). *Armistead Maupin*. Bath, UK: Absolute.

Gallo, M. M. (2006). *Different daughters: A history of the Daughters of Bilitis and the rise of the Lesbian Rights Movement*. Seattle, WA: Seal.

Gamarel, K. E., Reisner, S. L., Laurenceau, J., Nemoto, T., & Operario, D. (2014). Gender minority stress, mental health, and relationship quality: A dyadic investigation of transgender women and their cisgender male partners. *Journal of Family Psychology*, *28*(4), 437–447.

Gamson, J. (1998). *Freaks talk back: Tabloid talk shows and sexual nonconformity*. Chicago, IL: University of Chicago.

Garber, E. (1988). Gladys Bentley: The bulldagger who sang the blues. *out/look: National lesbian and gay quarterly*, *1*(1), 52–61.

Garraway, D. L. (2005). *The libertine colony: Creolization in the early French Caribbean*. Durham, NC: Duke University.

Gates, G. J. (2011). *How many people are lesbian, gay, bisexual and transgender?* Los Angeles, CA: The Williams Institute.

Gates, G. J. (2013). *LGBT parenting in the United States*. Los Angeles, CA: The Williams Institute.

Gates, G. J. (2017). In U.S., more adults identifying as LGBT. *Gallup*. Retrieved from www.gallup.com/poll/201731/lgbt-identification-rises.aspx

Gates, G. J., & Newport, F. (2012). Special report: 3.4% of U.S. adults identify as LGBT. *Gallup*. Retrieved from www.gallup.com/poll/158066/special-report-adults-identify-lgbt.aspx

Gates, G. J., et al. (2012). Letter to the editors and advisory editors of *Social Science Research*. *Social Science Research*, *41*(6), 1350–1351.

Gatti, T. (2006). The 10 best books of 2006. *Times* [London]. Retrieved from www.thetimes.co.uk/

Gay European Tourism Association. (2016). Retrieved from www.geta-europe.org

Gay Men and Lesbians Opposing Violence, Inc. (1996, August 1). *Homophobia in the District of Columbia Fire Department*. Retrieved from www.glaa.org/archive/a996/glovfire.shtml.

Gay pride parades from around the world. (2014, June 29). *TIME*. Retrieved from http://time.com/2938635/gay-pride-parades-from-around-the-world/

Geidner, C. (September 9, 2013). Meet the trans scholar fighting against the campaign for out trans military service. *Buzzfeed*. Retrieved from www.buzzfeed.com/chrisgeidner/meet-the-trans-scholar-fighting-against-the-campaign-for-out?utm_term=.abagxXd7m#.boe8W1qm2

Gelbart, M. (2003, November 14). New tourism ads: Come out and visit. *Philadelphia Inquirer*. Retrieved from LexisNexis, October 14, 2008.

George, C., Adam, B. D., Read, S. E., Husbands, W. C., Remis, R. S., Makoroka, L., & Rourke, S. B. (2012). The MaBwana Black men's study: community and belonging in the lives of African, Caribbean and other Black gay men in Toronto. *Culture, health & sexuality*, *14*(5), 549–562.

Gere, D. (2004). *How to make dances in an epidemic: Tracking choreography in the age of AIDS*. Madison, WI: University of Wisconsin.

Ghaziani, A. (2008). The dividends of dissent: How conflict and culture work in lesbian and gay marches on Washington. Chicago, IL: University of Chicago.

Ghiso, M. P., Campano, G., & Hall, T. (2012). Braided histories and experiences in literature for children and adolescents. *Journal of Children's Literature*, *38*(2), 14–22.

Giammattei, S. V., & Green, R. J. (2012). LGBT couple and family therapy. In J. J. Bigner, & J. L. Wetchler (Eds.). *Handbook of LGBT-affirmative couple and family therapy*, (pp. 1–22). New York, NY: Routledge.

Gilman, S. (1985). Black bodies, white bodies: Toward an iconography of female sexuality in late nineteenth century art, medicine, and literature. *Critical Inquiry*, *12*(1), 205–42.

Ginelle, L. (2015, September 24). The new *Stonewall* film is just as whitewashed as we feared. *Bitch*. Retrieved from www.bitchmedia.org/article/new-stonewall-film-just-whitewashed-we-feared

GLAAD (Gay and Lesbian Alliance Against Defamation). (2016a). *GLAAD media reference guide*, tenth edition. New York & Los Angeles: GLAAD.

GLAAD. (2016b). Transgender Day of Remembrance. Retrieved from www.glaad.org/tdor

Gladfelder, H. (2007). In search of lost texts: Thomas Cannon's Ancient and Modern Pederasty Investigated and Exemplify'd. *Eighteenth-Century Life*, *31*(1), 22–38.

Gladfelder, H. (2012). *Fanny Hill in Bombay: The making and unmaking of John Cleland*. Baltimore, MD: John Hopkins University.

Glass, V. Q., & Few-Demo, A. L. (2013). Complexities of informal social support arrangements for Black lesbian couples. *Family Relations*, *62*, 714–726.

Glatz, C. (2008, December 2). Vatican makes clear its opposition to U.N. homosexuality declaration. *Catholic News Service*. Retrieved from https://stjosephgv.nyc/news/vatican-makes-clear-its-opposition-to-un-homosexuality-declaration

Glick, S. N., Feng, Q., Popov, V., Koutsky, L. A., & Golden, M. R. (2013). High rates of incident and prevalent anal human papillomavirus infection among young men who have sex with men. *The Journal of Infectious Diseases*, *209*(3), 369–376.

GLMA. (2006). *Guidelines for the care of lesbian, gay, bisexual, and transgender clients*. San Francisco, CA: Gay and Lesbian Medical Association.

GLSEN. (2016). Day of Silence. Retrieved from www.glsen.org/day-of-silence

GMHC (Gay Men's Health Crisis). (n.d.) Quick facts about PEP & PrEP. Retrieved from www.gmhc.org/prevent-hiv/pep-and-prep#whatispep

Godbeer, R. (2007). The cry of Sodom: Discourse, intercourse, and desire in colonial New England. In T. Foster (Ed.), *Long before Stonewall: Histories of same-sex sexuality in early America* (pp. 81–113). New York, NY: New York University.

Golash-Boza, T. M. (2016). *Race & racisms: A critical approach, brief edition*. Oxford, UK: Oxford University.

Goldberg, A. E. (2007a). (How) does it make a difference? Perspectives of adults with lesbian, gay, and bisexual parents. *American Journal of Orthopsychiatry*, *77*(4), 550–562.

Goldberg, A. E. (2007b). Talking about family: Disclosure practices of adults raised by lesbian, gay, and bisexual parents. *Journal of Family Issues*, *28*(1), 100–131.

Goldberg, J. (1993). Sodomy in the New World: Anthropologies old and new. In Warner, M. (Ed.), *Fear of a queer planet* (pp. 3–18). Minneapolis, MN: University of Minnesota.

Goldberg, N. G. (2009). *The impact of inequality for same-sex partners in employer-sponsored retirement plans*. Los Angeles, CA: The Williams Institute.

Goldfried, M. R., & Goldfried, A. P. (2001). The importance of parental support in the lives of gay, lesbian, and bisexual individuals. *Journal of Clinical Psychology*, *57*(5), 681–693.

Goldstone, S., Palefsky, J. M., Giuliano, A. R., Moreira, E. D., Aranda, C., Jessen, H., . . . & Marshall, J. B. (2011). Prevalence of and risk factors for human papillomavirus (HPV) infection among HIV-seronegative men who have sex with men. *Journal of Infectious Diseases*, *203*(1), 66–74.

Goltz, D. B. (2013). It Gets Better: Queer futures, critical frustrations, and radical potentials. *Critical Studies in Media Communication*, *30*(2), 135–151.

Golumbok, S., Mellish, L., Tasker, F., & Lamb, M. E. (2014). Adoptive gay father families: Parent–child relationships and children's psychological adjustment. *Child Development*, *85*(2), 457–478.

Goodman, T. (2010, June 18). TV Review: *The Real L Word* on Showtime. *San Francisco Gate*. Retrieved from www.sfgate.com/news/article/TV-review-The-Real-L-Word-on-Showtime-3184929.php

Gorman, B. K., Denney, J. T., Dowdy, H., & Medeiros, R. A. (2015). A new piece of the puzzle: sexual orientation, gender, and physical health status. *Demography*, *52*(4), 1357–1382.

Gottman, J. M., Levenson, R. W., Swanson, C., Swanson, K., Tyson, R., & Yoshimoto, D. (2003). Observing gay, lesbian and heterosexual couples' relationships: Mathematical modeling of conflict interaction. *Journal of Homosexuality, 45*(1), 65–91.

Gottschalk, L., & Newton, J. (2009). Rural homophobia: Not really gay. *Gay and Lesbian Issues and Psychology Review, 5*(3), 153–159.

Graham, J. M., & Barnow, Z. B. (2013). Stress and social support in gay, lesbian, and heterosexual couples: Direct effects and buffering models. *Journal of Family Psychology, 27*(4), 569–578.

Grant, J. M. (2010). *Outing age 2010: Public policy issues affecting, lesbian, gay bisexual and transgender elders.* Washington, DC: National Gay and Lesbian Taskforce Policy Institute.

Grant, J. M., Mottet, L. A., Tanis J., Harrison, J., & Herman, J. L., & Keisling, M. (2011) *Injustice at every turn: A report of the National Transgender Discrimination Survey.* Washington, DC: National Center for Transgender Equality and National Gay and Lesbian Task Force, 2011.

Graves, K. L. (2009). *And they were wonderful teachers: Florida's purge of gay and lesbian teacher*s. Champaign, IL: University of Illinois.

Green, C., Halperin, D. T., Natulya, V., & Hogle, J. A. (2006). Uganda's HIV prevention success: The role of sexual behavior change and the national response. *AIDS and Behavior, 10*(4), 335–346.

Green, J. (2004). *Becoming a visible man.* Nashville, TN: Vanderbilt University.

Green, J. (2010). Sex and the trans man. In M. Stombler, D. M. Baunach, E. O. Burgess, D. Donnelly, W. Simonds, & E. J. Windsor (Eds.). *Sex matters: The sex & society reader* (pp. 24–26). Boston: Allyn & Bacon.

Green, R. (2000). Lesbians, gay men, and their parents: A critique of LaSala and the prevailing clinical "wisdom." *Family Process, 39*(2), 257–266.

Green, R. (2004). Risk and resilience in lesbian and gay couples: Comment on Solomon, Rothblum, and Balsam (2004). *Journal of Family Psychology, 18*(2), 290–292.

Greenbaum, V. (1994). Literature out of the closet: Bringing gay and lesbian texts and subtexts out in high school English. *The English Journal, 83*(5), 71–74.

Greenberg, D. F. (1990). *The construction of homosexuality.* Chicago, IL: University of Chicago.

Greenberg, S. (2004). *Wrestling with God & men: Homosexuality in the Jewish tradition.* Madison, WI: University of Wisconsin.

Greene, E. (1996). *Reading Sappho: Contemporary approaches.* Berkeley, CA: University of California.

Grewal, I., & Kaplan, C. (2001). Global identities: Theorizing transnational studies of sexuality. *GLQ, 7*(4), 663–679.

Grey, J. A., Robinson, B. B. E., Coleman, E., & Bockting, W. O. (2013). A systematic review of instruments that measure attitudes toward homosexual men. *Journal of Sex Research, 50*(3–4), 329–352.

Greyson, D. (2007). GLBTQ content in comics/graphic novels for teens. *Collection Building, 26*(4), 130–134.

Griffith, K. H., & Hebl, M. R. (2002). The disclosure dilemma for gay men and lesbians: "Coming out" at work. *Journal of Applied Psychology, 87*(6), 1191–1199.

Grimes, W. (2017.) George Weinberg dies at 87; Coined 'homophobia' after seeing fear of gays. *New York Times.* Retrieved from www.nytimes.com/2017/03/22/us/george-weinberg-dead-coined-homophobia.html

Grolnick, W. S., & Raftery-Helmer, J. N. (2015). Contexts supporting self-regulated learning at school transitions. In T. Cleary (Ed.), *Self-regulated learning interventions with at-risk youth: Enhancing adaptability, performance, and well-being* (pp. 251–276). Washington, DC: American Psychological Association.

Gross, A. (2007a). Queer theory and international human rights law: Does each person have a sexual orientation?. In *Proceedings of the Annual Meeting (American Society of International Law)* (Vol. *101*, pp. 129–132). Cambridge, UK: American Society of International Law and Cambridge University.

Gross, J. (2007b, October 9). Aging and gay, and facing prejudice in twilight. *New York Times*. Retrieved from www.nytimes.com/2007/10/09/us/09aged.html

Gross, L. (1993). *Contested closets: The politics and ethics of outing.* Minneapolis, MN: University of Minnesota.

Grossman, A. H., & D'Augelli, A. R. (2006). Transgender youth: Invisible and vulnerable. *Journal of Homosexuality, 51*(1), 111–128.

Grossman, A. H., & D'Augelli, A. R. (2007). Transgender youth and life-threatening behaviors. *Suicide and Life-threatening Behavior, 37*(5), 527–537.

Grossman, A. H., D'Augelli, A. R., & O'Connell, T. S. (2001). Being lesbian, gay, bisexual, and 60 or older in North America. *Journal of Gay & Lesbian Social Services, 13*(4), 23–40.

Grossman, L. (2007). 10 best books. *TIME.* Retrieved from http://content.time.com/time/arts/article/0,8599,1578073,00.html

Grov, C. (2014). Gay and bisexual men's use of the internet: Research from the 1990s through 2013. *Journal of Sex Research, 51*(4), 390–409.

Grov, C., Bimbi, D. S., Nanin, J. E., & Parsons, J. T. (2006). Race, ethnicity, and generational factors associated with the coming-out process among gay, lesbian, and bisexual individuals. *Journal of Sex Research, 43*(2), 115–121.

Grov, C., Starks, T. J., Rendina, H. J., & Parsons, J. (2014). Rules about casual sex partners, relationship satisfaction, and HIV risk to partnered gay and bisexual men. *Journal of Sex & Marital Therapy, 40*(2), 105–122.

GSA Network. (2016). Our approach. Retrieved from: https://gsanetwork.org/about-us

Guaracino, J. (2007). *Gay and lesbian tourism: The essential guide for marketing.* Oxford, UK: Elsevier.

Gudelunas, D. (2011). Consumer myths and the gay men and women who believe them: A qualitative look at movements and markets. *Psychology & Marketing, 28*(1), 53–68.

Gudelunas, D. (2012). There's an app for that: The uses and gratifications of online social networks for gay men. *Sexuality & Culture, 16*(4), 347–365.

Gunn, D. W., & Harker, J. (2013). *1960s gay pulp fiction.* Amherst, MA: University of Massachusetts.

Gunn, J. F., & Goldstein, S. E. (2017). Bullying and suicidal behavior during adolescence: A developmental perspective. *Adolescent Research Review, 2*(2), 77–97.

Gutiérrez, R. A. (2010). A history of Latina/o sexualities. In Asencio, M. (Ed.), *Latina/o sexualities: Probing powers, passions, practices, and policies* (pp. 13–37). New Brunswick, NJ: Rutgers University.

Gutmann, M. C., & Vigoya, M. V. (2005). Masculinities in Latin America. In M. Kimmel, J. Hearn, & R. W. Connell (Eds.), *Handbook of studies on men and masculinities* (pp. 114–128). Thousand Oaks, CA: Sage.

Gutstein, E. (2006). *Reading and writing the world with mathematics: Toward a pedagogy for social justice.* New York, NY: Routledge.

Haggerty, G. E. (1995). Gothicism. In C. J. Summers (Ed.), *The gay and lesbian literary heritage: A reader's companion to the writers and their works, from antiquity to the present*. New York, NY: Holt.

Haimson, O. (2017, March). Opportunities and challenges for transgender people in digital spaces. Paper presented at the Conference Workshop on Vulnerable Communities in the Digital Age, in Wuhan, China.

Haines, B. A., Ajayi, A. A., & Boyd, H. (2014). Making trans parents visible: Intersectionality of trans and parenting identities. *Feminism & Psychology, 24*(2), 238–247.

Halberstam, J. (1998). *Female masculinity*. Durham, N.C.: Duke University.

Hale, C. J. (1997). Leatherdyke boys and their daddies: How to have sex without women or men. *Social Text*, (52/53), 223–236.

Hale, M. (2015, July 22). Review: In *'I Am Cait,'* Caitlyn Jenner documents a changing self. *New York Times*. Retrieved from www.nytimes.com/2015/07/24/arts/television/review-in-i-am-cait-caitlyn-jenner-documents-a-changing-self.html

Hall, J. (Ed.) (2012). *No straight lines: Four decades of queer comics*. Seattle, WA: Fantagraphics.

Hall, K. S., Sales, J. M., Komro, K. A., & Santelli, J. (2016). The state of sex education in the United States. *Journal of Adolescent Health, 58*(6), 595–597.

Han, C. S. (2006). Geisha of a different kind: Gay Asian men and the gendering of sexual identity. *Sexuality and Culture, 10*(3), 3–28.

Han, C. W. (2015). *Geisha of a different kind: Race and sexuality in Gaysian America*. New York, NY: New York University.

Han, E., & O'Mahoney, J. (2014). British colonialism and the criminalization of homosexuality. *Cambridge Review of International Affairs, 27*(2), 268–288.

Hanhardt, C. B. (2013). *Safe space: Gay neighborhood history and the politics of violence*. Durham, NC: Duke University.

Hankinson, B. (2016, September 9). *'Finding Prince Charming'* is looking for love in the most boring places [RECAP]. *Towleroad.com*. Retrieved from www.towleroad.com/2016/09/finding-prince-charming-recap/

Hankivsky, O. (2014). *Intersectionality 101*. Vancouver, BC: The Institute for Intersectionality Research & Policy, Simon Fraser University.

Hanna, J., Park, M., & McLaughlin, E. C. (2017, March 30) North Carolina repeals 'bathroom bill.' *CNN*. Retrieved from www.cnn.com/2017/03/30/politics/north-carolina-hb2-agreement/index.html

Hansen, K. V. (1995). "No kisses is like youres": An erotic friendship between two African-American women during the mid-nineteenth century. *Gender and History, 7*(1), 153–182.

Harris, D. (2001). From the Kennedy Commission to the Combahee Collective. In B. Collier Thomas, et al. (Eds.), *Sisters in the struggle: African-American women in the Civil Rights-Black Power Movement* (pp. 280–305). New York, NY: New York University.

Harvey, D. (2007). *A brief history of neoliberalism*. New York, NY: Oxford University.

Hasenbush, A., Flores, A., Kastanis, A., Sears, B., & Gates, G. (2014). *The LGBT divide: A data portrait of LGBT people in the Midwestern, Mountain & Southern states*. Los Angeles, CA: The Williams Institute.

Hasson, M. R. (2011, July 29). It Gets Better—The youth campaign that makes everything worse. *Mercatornet*. Retrieved from www.mercatornet.com/articles/view/it_gets_better_-_the_youth_campaign_that_makes_everything_worse/

Hatzenbuehler, M. L., Birkett, M., Wagenen, A. V., & Meyer, I. H. (2014). Protective school climates and reduced risk for suicide ideation in sexual minority youths. *American Journal of Public Health, 104*(2), 279–286.

Heatherington, L., & Lavner, J. A. (2008). Coming to terms with coming out: Review and recommendations for family-systems-focused research. *Journal of Family Psychology, 22*(3), 329–343.

Hebl, M. R., Tonidandel S., & Ruggs, E. N. (2012). The impact of like-mentors for gay/lesbian employees. *Human Performance, 25*(1), 52–71.

Hebrew frequency list (2016). *Teach me Hebrew.* Retrieved from www.teachmehebrew.com/hebrew-frequency-list.html.

Hemmings, C. (2007). What's in a name? Bisexuality, transnational sexuality studies, and western colonial legacies. *The International Journal of Human Rights, 11*(1–2), 13–32.

Hennen, P. (2008). *Faeries, bears, and leathermen: Men in community queering the masculine.* Chicago, IL: University of Chicago.

Herbenick, D., Reece, M., Schick, V., & Sanders, S. A. (2014). Erect penile length and circumference dimensions of 1,661 sexually active men in the United States. *The Journal of Sexual Medicine, 11*(1), 93–101.

Herbenick, D., Reece, M., Schick, V., Sanders, S. A., Dodge, B., & Fortenberry, J. D. (2010). Sexual behavior in the United States: results from a national probability sample of men and women ages 14–94. *The Journal of Sexual Medicine, 7*(s5), 255–265.

Herbst, J. H., Jacobs, E. D., Finlayson, T. J., McKleroy, V. S., Neumann, M. S., Crepaz, N., & HIV/AIDS Prevention Research Synthesis Team. (2008). Estimating HIV prevalence and risk behaviors of transgender persons in the United States: a systematic review. *AIDS and Behavior, 12*(1), 1–17.

Herdt, G. (1984). *Ritualized homosexuality in Melanesia.* Berkeley, CA: University of California.

Herdt, G., Russell, S. T., Sweat, J., & Marzullo, M. (2007). Sexual inequality, youth empowerment, and the GSA: A community study in California. In N. Tenuis & G. Herdt (Eds.), *Sexual Inequalities* (pp. 233–252). Berkeley, CA: University of California.

Herek, G. (n.d.) Facts about homosexuality and child molestation. Retrieved from http://facultysites.dss.ucdavis.edu/~gmherek/rainbow/html/facts_molestation.html

Herek, G. M. (2009). Sexual stigma and sexual prejudice in the United States: A conceptual framework. In D. A. Hope (Ed.), *Contemporary perspectives on lesbian, gay and bisexual identities: The 54th Nebraska Symposium on Motivation* (pp. 65–111). New York, NY: Springer.

Hernandez, B. C., Schwenke, N. J., & Wilson, C. M. (2011). Spouses in mixed-orientation marriage: A 20-year review of empirical studies. *Journal of Marital and Family Therapy, 37*(3), 307–318.

Hershberger, S. L., & D'Augelli, A. R. (1995). The impact of victimization on the mental health and suicidality of lesbian, gay, and bisexual youths. *Developmental Psychology, 31*(1), 65–74.

Hess, D. (2009). Teaching about same-sex marriage as a policy and constitutional issue. *Social Education, 73*(7), 344–349.

Hess, K., Hu, X., Lansky, A., Mermin, J., & Hall, H. I. (2016, February). Estimating the lifetime risk of a diagnosis of HIV infection in the United States [conference paper]. Conference on Retroviruses and Opportunistic Infections (Boston,).

Higgins, D. J. (2002). Gay men from heterosexual marriages: Attitudes, behaviors, childhood experiences, and reasons for marriage. *Journal of Homosexuality, 42*(4), 15–34.

Hilderbrand, L. (2013a). A suitcase full of Vaseline, or travels in the 1970s gay world. *Journal of the History of Sexuality, 22*(3), 373–402.

Hilderbrand, L. (2013b). *Paris is burning.* Vancouver, BC: Arsenal Pulp.

Hill-Meyer, T., & Scarborough, D. (2014). Sexuality. In L. Erickson-Schroth (Ed.), *Trans bodies, trans selves: A resource for the transgender community* (pp. 355–389). Oxford, UK: Oxford University.

Hill, S. E., & Flom, R. (2007). 18- and 24-month-olds' discrimination of gender-consistent and inconsistent activities. *Infant Behavior and Development*, *30*(1), 168–173.

Hillman, B. L. (2011). 'The most profoundly revolutionary act a homosexual can engage in': Drag and the politics of gender presentation in the San Francisco Gay Liberation Movement, 1964–1972. *Journal of the History of Homosexuality*, *20*(1), 153–181.

Hilton-Morrow, W., & Battles, K. (2015). *Sexual identities and the media: An introduction*. New York, NY: Routledge.

Hinrich, K. L. M., & Vacha-Haase, T. (2010). Staff perceptions of same-gender sexual contacts in long-term care facilities. *Journal of Homosexuality*, *57*(6), 776–789.

HIV.gov. (2018). Who should get tested? Retrieved from https://www.hiv.gov/hiv-basics/hiv-testing/learn-about-hiv-testing/who-should-get-tested

Ho, S. I., & Rolfe, M. E. (2011). Same-sex partner immigration and the civil rights frame: A comparative study of Australia, Israel, and the USA. *International Journal of Comparative Sociology*, *52*(5), 390–412.

Hoad, N. (2000). Arrested development or the queerness of savages: Resisting evolutionary narratives of difference. *Postcolonial Studies*, *3*(2), 133–158.

Hoad, N. (2007). *African intimacies: Race, homosexuality, and globalization*. Minneapolis, MN: University of Minnesota.

Hobson, J. (2003). The 'batty' politic: Toward an aesthetic of the black female body. *Hypatia*, *18*(4), 87–105.

Holbrook, T. (2016). Georgia religious freedom law threatens LGBT rights. *CNN*. Retrieved from www.cnn.com/2016/03/28/

Homoground: A network of queer music and media creators. (n.d.) Retrieved from http://homoground.com/

Honeychurch, K. G. (1996). Researching dissident subjectivities: Queering the ground of theory and practice. *Harvard Educational Review*, *66*(2), 339–355.

hooks, b. (1994). *Teaching to transgress: Education as the practice of freedom*. New York, NY: Routledge.

Hooven, F. V. (1995). *Beefcake: The muscle magazines of America 1950–1970*. Berlin, Germany: Taschen.

Horovitz, B. (1994, April 5). TV commercial featuring gay couple creates a Madison Avenue uproar. *Los Angeles Times*. Retrieved from http://articles.latimes.com/1994-04-05/business/fi-42403_1_madison-avenue

Horvath, K. J., Iantaffi, A., Swinburne-Romine, R., & Bockting, W. (2014). A comparison of mental health, substance use, and sexual risk behaviors between rural and non-rural transgender persons. *Journal of Homosexuality*, *61*(8), 1117–1130.

Hostetler, A. J. (2009). Single by choice? Assessing and understanding voluntary singlehood among gay men. *Journal of Homosexuality*, *56*(4), 499–531.

Houlbrook, M. (2005). *Queer London: Perils and pleasures in the sexual metropolis, 1918–1957*. Chicago, IL: University of Chicago.

Howard, J. E. (1988). Crossdressing, the theatre, and gender struggle in early modern England. *Shakespeare Quarterly*, *39*(4), 418–440.

HRC (Human Rights Campaign). (2014). *A resource guide to coming out*. Retrieved from http://hrc-assets.s3-website-us-east-1.amazonaws.com//files/assets/resources/resource_guide_april_2014.pdf

HRC. (2016a). National Coming Out Day. Retrieved from: www.hrc.org/resources/national-coming-out-day

HRC. (2016b). Statewide employment laws & policies. Retrieved from www.hrc.org/state_maps

HRC. (n.d.) Growing up LGBT in America: HRC youth survey report key findings. Washington, DC: Human Rights Campaign.

HRSA (Health Resources & Services Administration). (2016, October). Ryan White and global HIV/AIDS programs. Retrieved from https://hab.hrsa.gov/about-ryan-white-hivaids-program/ryan-white-hivaids-program-legislation.

HRW (Human Rights Watch). (2017). *"I want to be like nature made me": Medically unnecessary surgeries on children in the U.S.* New York, NY: Human Rights Watch.

Hudson, S. (2003). Beauty and the status of contemporary criticism. *October, 104,* 115–130.

Hughes-Hassell, S., Overberg, E., & Harris, S. (2013). Lesbian, gay, bisexual, transgender, and questioning (LGBTQ)-themed literature for teens: Are school libraries providing Adequate collections? *School Library Media Research, 16,* 1–18.

Hughes, H. L. (2006). *Pink tourism: Holidays of gay men and lesbians.* Wallingford, UK: CABI.

Hussain, P. (1993). Class action: Bringing economic diversity to the gay and lesbian movement. In A. Gluckman & B. Reed (Eds.), *Homo economics: Capitalism, community, and lesbian and gay life* (pp. 241–249). New York, NY: Routledge.

Iantaffi, A., & Bockting, W. O. (2011). Views from both sides of the bridge? Gender, sexual legitimacy, and transgender people's experiences of relationships. *Culture, Health, & Sexuality, 13*(3), 355–370.

Iasenza, S. (2002). Beyond "lesbian bed death": The passion and play in lesbian relationships. *Journal of Lesbian Studies, 6*(1), 111–120.

Ingraham, C. (2002). Heterosexuality: It's just not natural. In D. Richardson & S. Seidman (Eds.), *Handbook of lesbian and gay studies* (pp. 73–82). London, UK: Sage.

Institute of Medicine (2011). *The health of lesbian, gay, bisexual, and transgender people: Building a foundation for better understanding.* Committee on Lesbian, Gay, Bisexual, and Transgender Health Issues and Research Gaps and Opportunities. Washington, DC: National Academies.

Jackson, P. A. (2001). Pre-gay, post-gay: Thai perspectives on proliferating gender/sex diversity in Asia. In G. Sullivan & P. A. Jackson (Eds.), *Gay and lesbian Asia: Culture, identity, community* (pp. 1–25). Binghamton, NY: Harrington Park.

Jacobs, S. E., Thomas, W., & Lang, S. (1997). *Two-spirit peoples: Native American gender identity, sexuality, and spirituality.* Champaign-Urbana, IL: University of Illinois.

Jagose, A. (1996). *Queer theory: An introduction.* New York, NY: New York University.

James, S. E., Herman, J. L., Rankin, S., Keisling, M., Mottet, L., & Ana, M. (2016). *The report of the 2015 U.S. transgender survey.* Washington, DC: National Center for Transgender Equality.

Jefferson, T. (1997 [1785]). *Notes on the state of Virginia.* New York, NY: Penguin Classics.

Jeffries, W. L. (2014). Beyond the bisexual bridge: sexual health among US men who have sex with men and women. *American Journal of Preventive Medicine, 47*(3), 320–329.

Jepsen, L. K., & Jepsen, C. A. (2002). An empirical analysis of the matching patterns of same-sex and opposite-sex couples. *Demography, 39*(3), 435–453.

Jochelson, K. (2001). *The colour of disease: Syphilis and racism in South Africa, 1880–1950.* Basingstoke, UK & New York, NY: Palgrave.

Johnson, A. (2005). *The gender knot: Unraveling our patriarchal legacy.* Philadelphia, PA: Temple University.

Johnson, D. K. (2004a) *The lavender scare: The Cold War persecution of gays and lesbians in the Federal Government.* Chicago: University of Chicago.

Johnson, O. S. (2004b). *The sexual spectrum: Exploring human diversity.* Vancouver, B.C.: Raincoast.

Johnson, S. L. (2000). *Roaring camp: The social world of the California gold rush*. New York, NY: W. W. Norton.

Johnston, L. B., & Jenkins, D. (2003). Coming out in mid-adulthood. *Journal of Gay and Lesbian Social Services, 16*(2), 19–42.

Joint United Nations Programme on HIV/AIDS. (2016) *Fact sheet 2016*. Retrieved from www.unaids.org/en/resources/fact-sheet

Jøn, A. A. (2001). From Nosferatu to Von Carstein: Shifts in the portrayal of vampires. *Australian Folklore, 16*, 97–106.

Jones, J. W. (2015). German and Austrian literature: nineteenth and twentieth centuries. *GLBTQ Archive.com*. Retrieved from www.glbtqarchive.com.

Jordan-Young, R. M. (2010). *Brain storm: The flaws in the science of sex difference*. Cambridge, MA: Harvard University.

Jung, E. A. (2016, June 9). Noah Galvin has nothing to hide. *Vulture*. Retrieved from www.vulture.com/2016/06/noah-galvin-has-nothing-to-hide.html

Ka'ahumanu, L., & Hutchins, L. (1991). *Bi any other name: Bisexual people speak out*. Los Angeles, CA: Alyson.

Kane, E. W. (2006). "No way my boys are going to be like that!" Parents' responses to children's gender nonconformity. *Gender & Society, 20*(2), 149–176.

Kaplan, M. B. (1997). *Sexual justice: Democratic citizenship and the politics of desire*. New York, NY: Routledge.

Katyal, S. (2002). Exporting identity. *Yale Journal of Law and Feminism, 14*, 98–176.

Katz, J. (2014, January 20). The birth of the queer t-shirt. *Newsweek*. Retrieved from www.newsweek.com/birth-queer-t-shirt-226598

Katz, J. D. (1993). The art of code: Jasper Johns and Robert Rauschenberg. In W. Chadwick & I. Courtivron, (Eds.), *Significant others: Creativity and intimate partnership* (pp. 193–208). London, UK: Thames and Hudson.

Katz, J. D. (2011) Agnes Martin and the Sexuality of Abstraction. In L. Cooke, & K. Kelly (Eds.) *Agnes Martin* (pp. 93–121). New York, NY and New Haven, CT: Dia Foundation and Yale University.

Katz, J. N. (1992). *Gay American history: Lesbians and gay men in the U.S.A*. New York, NY: Plume.

Katz, J. N. (1997). "Homosexual" and "heterosexual:" Questioning the terms. In M. Duberman (Ed.), *A Queer world: The Center for Lesbian and Gay Studies reader* (pp. 177–180). New York, NY: New York University.

Kazyak, E. (2012). Midwest or lesbian? Gender, rurality, and sexuality. *Gender & Society, 26*(6), 825–848.

Keller, J. R. (2000). *Ann Rice and sexual politics: The early novels*. Jefferson, NC: McFarland.

Kenagy, G. P. (2002). HIV among transgendered people. *AIDS Care, 14*(1), 127–134.

Kenagy, G. P., & Hsieh, C. M. (2005). The risk less known: Female-to-male transgender persons' vulnerability to HIV infection. *AIDS Care, 17*(2), 195–207.

Kennedy, E. L., & Davis, M. D. (1993). *Boots of leather, slippers of gold: The history of a lesbian community*. New York, NY: Routledge.

Kessler, S. (1998). *Lessons from the intersexed*. New Brunswick, NJ: Rutgers University.

Kessler, S. J., & McKenna, W. (1978). *Gender: An ethnomethodological approach*. Chicago, IL: University of Chicago.

Khazan, O., & Berman, R. (2016). How syphilis came roaring back. *The Atlantic*. Retrieved from www.theatlantic.com/health/archive/2016/06/how-syphilis-came-roaring-back/488375/

King, L. A. (2017). *The science of psychology*, fourth edition. New York, NY: McGraw-Hill.

Kinsey, A. C., Pomeroy, W. B., Martin, C. E., & Sloan, S. (1948). *Sexual behavior in the human male.* Bloomington, IN: Indiana University.

Klein, F., Sepekoff, B., & Wolf, T. J. (1985). Sexual orientation: A multi-variable dynamic process. *Journal of Homosexuality, 11*(1–2), 35–49.

Klinkenberg D., & Rose, S. (1994). Dating scripts of gay men and lesbians. *Journal of Homosexuality, 26*(4), 23–25.

Knopp, L. (1997). Gentrification and gay neighborhood formation in New Orleans. In A. Gluckman & B. Reed (Eds.), *Homo economics: Capitalism, community, and lesbian and gay life* (pp. 45–59). New York, NY: Routledge.

Knox, D. C., Tan, D. H., Harrigan, P. R., & Anderson, P. L. (2016, February). HIV-1 infection with multiclass resistance despite preexposure prophylaxis (PrEP) [Conference paper]. *Conference on Retroviruses and Opportunistic Infections.* Retrieved from www.croiconference.org/sessions/hiv-1-infection-multiclass-resistance-despite-preexposure-prophylaxis-prep

Kohn, M. (2015, August 13). Op-ed: The amazing story behind *To Wong Foo. The Advocate.* Retrieved from www.advocate.com/commentary/2015/08/13/op-ed-amazing-story-behind-wong-foo

Köllen, T. & Lazar, S. (2012). Gay tourism in Budapest: An exploratory study on gay tourists' motivational patterns for traveling to Budapest. *American Journal of Tourism Management, 1*(3), 64–68.

Komisaruk, B., Beyer-Flores, C., & Whipple, B. (2006). *The science of orgasm.* Baltimore, MD: Johns Hopkins University.

Konik, J., & Cortina, L. M. (2008). Policing gender at work: Intersections of harassment based on sex and sexuality. *Social Justice Research, 21*(3), 313–337.

Kosciw, J. G., Greytak, E. A., Diaz, E. M., & Bartkiewicz, M. J. (2010). *The 2009 National School Climate Survey: The experiences of lesbian, gay, bisexual, and transgender youth in our nation's schools.* Washington, DC: Gay, Lesbian and Straight Education Network.

Kosciw, J. G., Greytak, E. A., Giga, N. M., Villenas, C. V., & Danischewski, D. J. (2015). *The 2015 National School Climate Survey: The experiences of lesbian, gay, bisexual, transgender, and queer youth in our nation's schools.* Washington, DC: Gay, Lesbian and Straight Education Network.

Kosciw, J. G., Greytak, E. A., Palmer, N. A., & Boesen, M. J. (2014). *The 2013 National School Climate Survey: The experiences of lesbian, gay, bisexual and transgender youth in our nation's schools.* Washington, DC: Gay, Lesbian and Straight Education Network.

Kost, K., & Henshaw, S. (2013). *U.S. teenage pregnancies, births and abortions, 2010: National and state trends by age, race, and ethnicity.* New York, NY: Guttmacher Institute.

Kowalski, R. M., & Limber, S. P. (2013). Psychological, physical, and academic correlates of cyberbullying and traditional bullying. *Journal of Adolescent Health, 53*(1), 13–20.

Kraidy, M. (2002). Hybridity in cultural globalization. *Communication Theory, 12*(3), 316–339.

Kregloe, K. (2010, October 5). *"The Real Housewives of Atlanta"* mini-cap: "*New Attitude.*" *AfterEllen.com.* Retrieved from www.afterellen.com/tv/79856-the-real-housewives-of-atlanta-mini-cap-new-attitude

Kubicek, K., Carpineto, J., McDavitt, B., Weiss, G., & Kipke, M. D. (2011). Use and perceptions of the internet for sexual information and partners: a study of young men who have sex with men. *Archives of Sexual Behavior, 40*(4), 803–816.

Kulick, D. (1997). The gender of Brazilian transgendered prostitutes. *American Anthropologist, 99*(3), 574–585.

Kumashiro, K. (2000). Toward a theory of anti-oppressive education. *Review of Educational Research, 70*(1), 25–53.

Kumashiro, K. (2001). "Posts" perspectives on anti-oppressive education in social studies, English, mathematics, and science classrooms. *Educational Researcher, 30*(3), 3–12.

Kumashiro, K. (2002). *Troubling Education: Queer activism and anti-oppressive pedagogy.* New York, NY: Routledge.

Kumashiro, K. (2003). Queer ideals in education. *Journal of Homosexuality, 45*(2–4), 365–367.

Kurdek, L. A. (1998). Relationship outcomes and their predictors: Longitudinal evidence from heterosexual married, gay cohabiting, and lesbian cohabiting couples. *Journal of Marriage and the Family, 60*, 553–568. doi:10.2307/353528

Kurdek, L. A. (2004). Are gay and lesbian cohabiting couples really different from heterosexual married couples? *Journal of Marriage and Family, 66*, 880–900.

Kurdek, L. A. (2005). What do we know about gay and lesbian couples?. *Current Directions in Psychological Science, 14*(5), 251–254.

Kurdek, L. A. (2006). Differences in partners from heterosexual, gay, and lesbian cohabitating couples. *Journal of Marriage and Family, 68*, 509–528.

Kurtz, S. P. (1999). Butterflies under cover: Cuban and Puerto Rican gay masculinities in Miami. *The Journal of Men's Studies, 7*(3), 371–390.

Kuvalanka, K. A., & Goldberg, A. E. (2009). "'Second generation' voices." Queer youth with lesbian/bisexual mothers. *Journal of Youth and Adolescence, 38*(7), 904–919.

Labeija, P., & Pendavis, K. (Producers). (1992). *Paris is burning [videorecording].* United States: Buena Vista Home Entertainment.

Lancaster, R. N. (1988). Subject honor and object shame: The construction of male homosexuality and stigma in Nicaragua. *Ethnology, 27*(2), 111–125.

Lang, N. (2013, November 15). HBO's 'Looking' looks awfully white. *Los Angeles Times.* Retrieved from http://articles.latimes.com/2013/nov/15/news/la-ol-hbo-looking-gay-men-diversity-20131115

LaSala, M. C. (2000). Lesbians, gay men, and their family: Family therapy for the coming-out crisis. *Family Process, 39*(1), 67–81.

LaSala, M. C. (2004). Extradyadic sex and gay male couples: Comparing monogamous and nonmonogamous relationships. *Families in Society, 85*(3), *405–412.*

Land, H., Hudson, S. M., & Steifel, B. (2003). Stress and depression among HIV-positive and HIV-negative gay and bisexual AIDS caregivers. *AIDS and Behavior, 7*, 41–53.

Lau, C. Q. (2012). The stability of same-sex cohabitation, different-sex cohabitation, and marriage. *Journal of Marriage & Family, 74*, 973–988.

Launius, C., & Hassel, H. (2015). *Threshold concepts in Women's and Gender Studies: Ways of seeing, thinking, and knowing.* New York, NY: Routledge.

Lavin, M. (1993). *Cut with the kitchen knife: The Weimar photomontages of Hannah Höch.* New Haven, CT: Yale University.

*Lawrence v. Texas,* 539 U.S. 558, 123 S. Ct. 2472, 156 L. Ed. 2d 508 (2003).

Le Coney, C., & Trodd, Z. (2009). Reagan's rainbow rodeos: queer challenges to the cowboy dreams of eighties America. *Canadian Review of American Studies, 39*(2), 163–183.

Leaper, C. (2002). Parenting girls and boys. In M. Bornstein (Ed.), *Handbook of parenting* (Vol. *1*, pp. 189–225). Mahwah, NJ: Erlbaum.

LeBlanc, A. J., Frost, D. M., Alston-Stepnitz, E., Bauermeister, J., Stephenson, R., Woodyatt, C. R., & de Vries, B. (2015). Similar others in same-sex couples' social networks. *Journal of Homosexuality, 62*(11), 1599–1610.

LeCompte, M. D. (2000). Standing for just and right decisions: The long, slow path to school safety. *Education and Urban Society, 32*(3), 413–29.

Lee, A. (2015). Sexual deviants need not apply: LGBTQ oppression in the 1965 immigration amendments. In G. J. Chin & R. C. Villazor (Eds.), *The Immigration and Nationality Act of 1965: Legislating a new America* (pp. 258–272). New York, NY: Cambridge University.

Lee Badgett, M. V. (1997). Beyond biased samples: Challenging the myths on the economic status of lesbians and gay men. In A. Gluckman & B. Reed (Eds.), *Homo economics: Capitalism, community, and lesbian and gay life* (pp. 65–72). New York, NY: Routledge.

Lee Badgett, M. V. (2009). *Best practices for asking questions about sexual orientation on surveys.* Los Angeles, CA: The Williams Institute.

Lee Badgett, M. V., Durso, L. E., & Schneebaum, A. (2013). *New patterns of poverty in the lesbian, gay, and bisexual community.* Los Angeles, CA: The Williams Institute.

Lee Badgett, M. V., & Herman, J. L. (2011). *Patterns of relationship recognition by same-sex couples in the United States.* Los Angeles, CA: The Williams Institute.

Lee Badgett, M. V., & Herman, J. L. (2013). *Sexual orientation & gender identity diversity in entertainment: Experiences & perspectives of SAG-AFTRA members.* Los Angeles, CA: The Williams Institute.

Lee Badgett, M. V., & King, M. C. (1997). Lesbian and gay occupational strategies. In A. Gluckman, & B. Reed (Eds.), *Homo economics: Capitalism, community, and lesbian and gay life* (pp. 73–85). New York, NY: Routledge.

Lee Badgett, M. V., Lau, H., Sears, B., & Ho, D. (2007). *Bias in the workplace: Consistent evidence of sexual orientation and gender identity discrimination.* Los Angeles, CA: The Williams Institute.

Le Fanu, S. (2009). *Carmilla.* Richmond, VA: Valancourt.

Leggett, T. (2014, February 1). Lego just got told off by a 7-year-old girl. *BuzzFeed.* Retrieved from www.buzzfeed.com/tabathaleggett/lego-just-got-told-off-by-a-7-year-old-girl?utm_term=.xy1AvjW5xy#.gtNGdENv3Z

Leong, R. (Ed.) (1995). *Asian American sexualities: Dimensions of the gay and lesbian experience.* New York, NY: Routledge.

Lesbian Avengers. (2016). *Lesbian Avengers: A brief history.* Retrieved from www.lesbianavengers.com/about/history.shtml

Lev, A. I. (2004). *Transgender emergence: Therapeutic guidelines for working with gender variant people and their families.* New York, NY: Haworth.

LeVay, S. (2016). *Gay, straight, and the reason why: The science of sexual orientation.* New York, NY: Oxford University.

Lever, J., Grov, C., Royce, T., & Gillespie, B. J. (2008). Searching for love in all the "write" places: Exploring internet personals use by sexual orientation, gender, and age. *International Journal of Sexual Health, 20*(4), 233–246.

Levin, J. (1991). *The gay novel in America.* New York, NY: Garland.

Lewis, A. (2014a, March 19). The growth of gay retirement homes. *BBC News.* Retrieved from www.bbc.com/news/magazine-26554710

Lewis, R. A. (2014b). "Gay? Prove it": The politics of queer anti-deportation activism. *Sexualities, 17*(8), 958–975.

Lhamon, C. E., & Gupta, V. (2016). *Dear colleague letter on transgender students.* Washington DC: U.S. Department of Justice, Civil Rights Division & U.S. Department of Education, Office for Civil Rights.

Lick, D. J., & Johnson, K. L. (2015). Intersecting race and gender cues are associated with perceptions of gay men's preferred sexual roles. *Archives of sexual behavior, 44*(5), 1471–1481.

Lindemann, M. (2000). Who's afraid of the big bad witch?: Queer studies in American literature. *American Literary History*, *12*(4), 757–770.

Lindemann, M. (2013). Building (and rebuilding) LGBT studies at the University of Maryland. *Feminist Studies*, *39*(2), 507–511.

Linley, J. L., & Nguyen, D. J. (2015). LGBTQ Experiences in Curricular Contexts. *New Directions for Student Services*, *2015*(152), 41–53.

Linley, J. L., Renn, K. A., & Woodford, M. (2014). *Examining the academic microsystems of successful LGBT STEM majors*. Paper presented at the annual meeting of the American Educational Research Association, Philadelphia, PA.

Lorber, J. (1995). *Paradoxes of gender*. New Haven, CT: Yale University.

Lovejoy, P. (1979). *Transformations of slavery: A history of slavery in Africa*. Cambridge, UK: Cambridge University.

Lowder, J. B. (2013, June 6). The curious case of gayface. *Slate*. Retrieved from www.slate.com/articles/arts/culturebox/2013/06/straight_actors_in_gay_roles_is_gayface_ok.html

Luibhéid, E. (2005). Introduction: Queering migration and citizenship. In E. Luibhéid & L. Cantú (Eds.), *Queer migrations: Sexuality, U.S. citizenship, and border crossings* (pp. ix–xlvi). Minneapolis: University of Minnesota.

Lussana, S. (2016). *My brother slaves: Friendship, masculinity, and resistance in the American south*. Lexington, KY: The University Press of Kentucky.

Lynch, J. M., & Murray, K. (2000). For the love of the children: The coming out process for lesbian and gay parents and stepparents. *Journal of Homosexuality*, *39*(1), 1–24.

Macapagal, K., Green, G. J., Rivera, Z., & Mustanski, B. (2015). "The best is always yet to come": Relationship stages and processes among young LGBT couples. *Journal of Family Psychology*, *29*(3), 309–320.

Maccoby, E. E. (1998). *The two sexes: Growing up apart, coming together*. Cambridge, MA: Harvard University.

Machalek, D. A., Grulich, A. E., Jin, F., Templeton, D. J., & Poynten, I. M. (2012). The epidemiology and natural history of anal human papillomavirus infection in men who have sex with men. *Sexual health*, *9*(6), 527–537.

MacKee, F. (2016). Social media in gay London: Tinder as an alternative to hook-up apps. *Social Media+ Society*, *2*(3), 1–10.

Magdalinou, C., & Torneden, S. (Producers & Directors), & Grillo, A. (Director). (2014). *Acting Out: 25 Years of Queer Film & Community in Hamburg* [Documentary Film]. Germany: Aye Aye Film.

Mallory, C., Hasenbush, A., & Sears, B. (2015). *Discrimination and harassment by law enforcement officers in the LGBT community*. Los Angeles, CA: The Williams Institute.

Manalansan, M. (1995). In the shadows of Stonewall: Examining gay transnational politics and the diasporic dilemma. *GLQ*, *2*(4), 425–438.

Manalansan, M. (2003). *Global divas: Filipino gay men in the diaspora*. Durham, NC: Duke University.

Manley, E., Levitt, H., & Mosher, C. (2007). Understanding the bear movement in gay male culture: redefining masculinity. *Journal of Homosexuality*, *53*(4), 89–112.

Mann, J. (2010). Bear culture 101 (no prerequisite). *The Gay & Lesbian Review Worldwide*, *17*(5), 22.

Manning, W. D., Fettro, M. N., & Lamidi, E. (2014). Child well-being in same-sex parent families: Review of research prepared for American Sociological Association Amicus Brief. *Population Research and Policy Review*, *33*(4), 485–502.

MAP. (2016). *Invisible minority: The disparities facing bisexual people and how to remedy them*. Denver, CO: Movement Advancement Project.

Marable, M., & Mullings, L. (Eds.). (2000). Introduction. *Let nobody turn us around: Voices of resistance, reform and renewal*. Lanham, MD: Rowman & Littlefield.

March, J. G., & Olsen, J. P. (1998). The institutional dynamics of international political orders. *International Organization, 52*(4), 943–969.

Mark, K., Rosenkrantz, D., & Kerner, I. (2014). "Bi" ing into monogamy: Attitudes toward monogamy in a sample of bisexual-identified adults. *Psychology of Sexual Orientation and Gender Diversity, 1*(3), 263–269.

Marple, L. (2005). Rural queers? The loss of the rural in queer. *Canadian Woman Studies, 24*(2/3): 71–74.

Marrazzo, J. M., Koutsky, L. A., Stine, K. L., Kuypers, J. M., Grubert, T. A., Galloway, D. A., . . . & Handsfield, H. H. (1998). Genital human papillomavirus infection in women who have sex with women. *Journal of Infectious Diseases, 178*(6), 1604–1609.

Marrazzo, J. M., Stine, K., & Wald, A. (2003). Prevalence and risk factors for infection with herpes simplex virus type-1 and-2 among lesbians. *Sexually Transmitted Diseases, 30*(12), 890–895.

Martin, F. (1996). Fran Martin responds to Dennis Altman. *Australian Humanities Review, 2* (July–September).

Martin, W. (2002b). *The Cambridge companion to Emily Dickinson*. Cambridge, UK: Cambridge University.

Marzullo, M. A., & Libman, A. J. (2009). Research overview: Hate crimes and violence against lesbian, gay, bisexual and transgender people. Washington DC: Human Rights Campaign Foundation.

Mason, M. (2006, August 23). Bangkok a mecca for sex-change surgeries. *Washington Post*. Retrieved from www.washingtonpost.com/wp-dyn/AR2006082301222_pf.html

Massad, J. A. (2002). Re-orienting desire: The Gay International and the Arab world. *Public Culture, 14*(2), 461–485.

Massey, D. (2002). Globalisation: What does it mean for geography? *Geography, 87*(4), 293–296.

Master Taíno. (2012). Leather Families. *House of Decorum*. Retrieved from http://houseofdecorum.org/writings/leather-families-by-master-taino/

Matthews, A. K., Tartaro, J., & Hughes, T. L. (2002). A comparative study of lesbian and heterosexual women in committed relationships. *Journal of Lesbian Studies, 7*(1), 101–114.

Maynard, J. & Miles, B. (1965, June). The Boston trial of *Naked Lunch*. *Evergreen Review, 9*(36), n.p.

Mayo Jr., J. B., & Sheppard, M. (2012). New social learning from two spirit Native Americans. *The Journal of Social Studies Research, 36*(3), 263–282.

Mbali, M. (2013). *South African AIDS activism and global health politics*. London, UK: Palgrave Macmillan.

McBride, D. (1991). *From TB to AIDS: Epidemics among urban blacks since 1900*. Albany, NY: State University of New York.

McBride, K. R., & Fortenberry, J. D. (2010). Heterosexual anal sexuality and anal sex behaviors: a review. *Journal of Sex Research, 47*(2–3), 123–136.

McClintock, A. (1995). *Imperial leather: Race, gender, and sexuality in the colonial conquest*. New York, NY and Abingdon, UK: Routledge.

McConnell, E. A., Birkett, M. A., & Mustanski, B. (2015). Typologies of social support and associations with mental health outcomes among LGBT youth. *LGBT Health, 2*(1), 55–61.

McCullom, R. (2016). Perfect storm. *The Advocate #1085* (June/July), 42–45.

McDonald, S. N. (2015, December 7). Jill Soloway couldn't find any TV writers with a 'trans-feminine' perspective so she trained her own. *Washington Post*. Retrieved from www.washingtonpost.com/news/arts-and-entertainment/wp/2015/12/07/transparent-creator-jill-soloway-couldnt-find-any-tv-writers-with-a-trans-feminine-perspective-so-she-trained-her-own/?utm_term=.fe80ffe7f641

McDowell, D. E. (Ed.). (1986). Introduction. In Nella Larsen, *Quicksand and Passing*. New Brunswick, NJ: Rutgers University.

McHale, S. M., Crouter, A. C., & Whiteman, S. D. (2003). The family contexts of gender development in childhood and adolescence. *Social Development*, *12*(1), 125–148.

McHale, S. M., Kim, J. Y., Dotterer, A. M., Crouter, A. C., & Booth, A. (2009). The development of gendered interests and personality qualities from middle childhood through adolescence: A biosocial analysis. *Child Development*, *80*(2), 482–495.

McIntosh, P. (1988). White privilege: Unpacking the invisible knapsack. In Paula Rothenberg (Ed.), *Race, class, and gender in the United States: An integrated study*, fifth edition (pp. 163–168). New York, NY: Worth.

McKay, T., Misra, S., & Lindquist, C. (2017). *Violence and LGBTQ+ communities: What do we know, and what do we need to know?* Research Triangle Park, NC: RTI International.

McKenry, P. C., Serovich, J. M., Mason, T. L., & Mosack, K. (2006). Perpetration of gay and lesbian partner violence: A disempowerment perspective. *Journal of Family Violence*, *21*(4), 233–243.

Mendieta, E. (2001). Society's religion: The rise of social theory, globalization, and the invention of religion. In D. N. Hopkins, L. A. Lorentzen, E. Mendieta, & D. Batstone (Eds.), *Religions/globalizations: Theories and cases* (pp. 46–65). Durham, NC: Duke University.

Mercer, K., & Julien, I. (1988). Race, sexual politics and Black masculinity: A dossier. In R. Chapman & B. Rutherford (Eds.), *Male order: Unwrapping masculinity* (pp. 97–164). London, UK: Lawrence & Wishart.

Merkel, J. (2008). *Writing against the odds: The south's cultural and literary struggle against progress and modernity*. Munich, Germany: Grin Verlag.

Messinger, A. M. (2011). Invisible victims: Same-sex IPV in the National Violence Against Women Survey. *Journal of Interpersonal Violence*, *26*, 2228–2243.

Messinger, A. M. (2014). Marking 35 years of research on same-sex intimate partner violence: Lessons and new directions. In *Handbook of LGBT communities, crime, and justice* (pp. 65–85). New York, NY: Springer.

Met Life (2010). *Still out, still aging: The Met Life study of lesbian, gay, bisexual and transgender baby boomers*. New York, NY and San Francisco, CA: MetLife Mature Market Institute and The American Society on Aging.

Metz, M. E., Rosser, B. R. S., & Strapko, N. (1994). Differences in conflict resolution styles among heterosexual, gay, and lesbian couples. *Journal of Sex Research*, *31*, 293–308.

Meuwly, N., Feinstein, B. A., Davila, J., Nunez, D., C., & Bodenmann, G. (2013). Relationship quality among Swiss women in opposite-sex versus same-sex romantic relationships. *Swiss Journal of Psychology*, *72*, 229–233.

Meyer, R. (2002). *Outlaw representation: censorship & homosexuality in twentieth-century American art*. Oxford, UK: Oxford University.

Meyer, W., Costenbader, E. C., Zule, W. A., Otiashvili, D., & Kirtadze, I. (2010). "We are ordinary men": MSM identity categories in Tbilisi, Georgia. *Culture, Health & Sexuality*, *12*(8), 955–971.

Meyerowitz, J. (2004). *How sex changed: A history of transsexuality in the United States.* Cambridge, MA: Harvard University.

Mezirow, J. (1997). Transformative learning: Theory to practice. In P. Cranton (Ed.), *New directions for adult and continuing education: No. 74. Transformative learning in action: Insights from practice* (pp. 5–12). San Francisco, CA: Jossey-Bass.

Middleton, J. (2014, April 18). *Philly Gay News* reporter wins award for trans homicide coverage. *Philadelphia Magazine.* Retrieved from www.phillymag.com/g-philly/2014/04/18/philly-gay-news-reporter-wins-award-trans-homicide-coverage/

Milberg, W., & M. Amengual. (2008). Economic development and working conditions in export processing zones: A survey of trends. *International Labour Office.* Geneva, Switzerland: ILO.

Miller, N. (1995). *Out of the past: Gay and lesbian history from 1869 to the present.* New York, NY: Vintage.

Miller, N. (2002). *Sex-Crime Panic: A Journey to the Paranoid Heart of the 1950s.* Los Angeles: Alyson Books.

Mintz, S. (2011). American slavery in comparative perspective. *The Gilder Lehrman Institute of American History.* Retrieved from www.gilderlehrman.org/history-by-era/originsslavery/resources/american-slavery-comparative-perspective

Mirasol, M. (2011, July 1). A great love story: "Brokeback Mountain." *RogerEbert.com.* Retrieved from www.rogerebert.com/far-flung-correspondents/a-great-love-story-brokeback-mountain

Mitchell, G. (2010). Fare tales and fairy tails: How gay sex tourism is shaping the Brazilian dream. *Wagadu, 8*(Fall) 93–114.

Mitchell, G. (2011). TurboConsumers™ in paradise: Tourism, civil rights, and Brazil's gay sex industry. *American Ethnologist, 38*(4), 666–682.

Mitchell, S. (2004). *Gilgamesh: A new English version.* New York, NY: Free Press.

Mitchell, S. (Producer), & Fitzgerald, T. (Producer & Director). (1998) *Beefcake* [Motion Picture]. Canada: Strand Releasing.

Mock, S. E., & Eibach, R. P. (2012). Stability and change in sexual orientation identity over a 10-year period in adulthood. *Archives of Sexual Behavior, 41*(3), 641–648.

Molina, Y., Marquez, J. H., Logan, D. E., Leeson, C. J., Balsam, K. F., & Kaysen, D. L. (2015). Current intimate relationship status, depression, and alcohol use among bisexual women: the mediating roles of bisexual-specific minority stressors. *Sex Roles, 73*(1–2), 43–57.

Moon, A., & diamond, k. d. (2015). *Girl sex 101.* Lunatic Ink.

Morgan, B. (Ed). (2006). *Howl on trial: The battle for free expression.* San Francisco, CA: City Lights.

Morgan, T. (1988). *Literary outlaw.* New York, NY: Avon.

Morgan, W. (2000). Queering international human rights law. In C. Stychin & D. Herman (Eds.), *Law and sexuality: The global arena* (pp. 208–225). Minneapolis, MN: University of Minnesota.

Morgensen, S. (2011). *Spaces between us: Queer settler colonialism and indigenous decolonization.* Minneapolis, MN: University of Minnesota.

Morris, B. (1999). *Eden built by Eves: The culture of women's music festivals.* New York, NY: Alyson.

Morrison, T., & Tallack, D. (2005). Lesbian and bisexual women's interpretations of lesbian and ersatz lesbian pornography. *Sexuality & Culture, 9*(2), 3–30.

Most, G. W. (1995). Reflecting Sappho. *Bulletin of the Institute of Classical Studies, 40*(1), 15–38.

Moylan, B. (2016, July 12). *Finding Prince Charming*: the 'first gay dating show' on American television. *Guardian*. Retrieved from www.theguardian.com/tv-and-radio/2016/jul/12/finding-prince-charming-first-gay-dating-show

Mucciaroni, G. (2008). *Same sex, different politics: Success and failures in the struggle over gay rights*. Chicago, IL: University of Chicago.

Mullings, B. (1999). Globalization, tourism, and the international sex trade. In K. Kempadoo (Ed.), *Sun, sex, and gold: Tourist sex work in the Caribbean* (pp. 51–80). Lanham, MD: Rowman & Littlefield.

Munck, R. (2013). Labor migration and worker organization, Global North and Global South. In I. Ness & P. Bellwood (Eds.), *The encyclopedia of global human migration* (pp.198–235). Malden, MA: Wiley-Blackwell.

Munro, B. M. (2012). *South Africa and the dream of love to come: Queer sexuality and the struggle for freedom*. Minneapolis, MN: University of Minnesota.

Munt, S., & Smyth, C. (Eds.). (1998). *Butch/femme: Inside lesbian gender*. London, UK: Cassell.

Muraco, J. A. (2015). *Minority stress in the lives of gay and lesbian couples* (unpublished doctoral dissertation). The University of Arizona, Tucson, AZ.

Murphy, M. (2003). Zap! Pow! Out!: Twentieth century queer comics. *Neureuther Book Collection Essay Competition Paper 17*. St. Louis, MO: Washington University in St. Louis Libraries. Retrieved from http://openscholarship.wustl.edu/nbcec/17

Murphy, M. J. (2014, March–April). The lives and times of Harry Chess. *The gay and lesbian review, 21*(2), 22–24.

Murray, S., & Ankerson, M. S. (2016). Lez takes time: Designing lesbian contact in geosocial networking apps. *Critical Studies in Media Communication, 33*(1), 53–69.

Mustanski, B., Newcomb, M. E., & Garofalo, R. (2011). Mental health of lesbian, gay, and bisexual youth: A developmental resiliency perspective. *Journal of Gay & Lesbian Social Services, 23*(2), 204–225.

Nagel, J. (2003). *Race, ethnicity, and sexuality: Intimate intersections and forbidden frontiers*. New York, NY: Oxford University.

Nair, Y. (2012). Do we still need gay news media? In T. Baim (Ed.), *Gay press, gay power: The growth of LGBT community newspapers in America* (pp. 433–437). Chicago, IL: Prairie Avenue Productions and Windy City Media Group.

Nakamura, N., Chan, E., & Fischer, B. (2013). "Hard to crack": Experiences of community integration among first- and second-generation Asian MSM in Canada. *Cultural Diversity and Ethnic Minority Psychology, 19*(3), 248–256.

NAMI (National Alliance on Mental Illness). (2016). LGBTQ mental health. Retrieved from www.nami.org/Find-Support/LGBTQ

Narayan, U. (1993). What do rights have to do with it?: Reflections on what distinguishes "traditional nonwestern" frameworks from contemporary rights-based systems. *Journal of Social Philosophy, 24*(2), 168–199.

NASW. (2015a). Standards and indicators for cultural competence in social work practice. Washington, DC: National Association of Social Workers.

NASW. (2015b). Sexual orientation change efforts (SOCE) and conversion therapy for lesbians, gay men, bisexuals, and transgender persons. Washington, DC: National Association of Social Workers.

National Resource Center on LGBT Aging (n.d.a). *Identifying and assisting LGBT elder abuse clients: A guide for abuse professionals*. Retrieved from www.lgbtagingcenter.org/resources/pdfs/Assisting_LGBT_Elder_Abuse_clients.pdf

National Resource Center on LGBT Aging (n.d.b). *LGBT older adults in long-term care facilities*. Retrieved from www.lgbtagingcenter.org/resources/pdfs/NSCLC_LGBT_report.pdf

Nayar, P. K. (2011). Vampirism and posthumanism in Octavia Butler's *Fledgling*. *Notes on Contemporary Literature, 41*(2), 6–10.

NBJC (National Black Justice Coalition). (2012). *LGBT families of color: Facts at a glance*. Retrieved from www.nbjc.org/sites/default/files/lgbt-families-of-color-facts-at-a-glance.pdf

NCAVP (National Coalition of Anti-Violence Programs). (2015). *Lesbian, gay, bisexual, transgender, queer, and HIV-affected hate violence in 2014*. New York, NY: New York City Anti-Violence Project.

NCSS (National Council for the Social Studies). (2010). *National Curriculum Standards for Social Studies: A Framework for Teaching, Learning, and Assessment*. Silver Spring, MD: NCSS.

NCTE. (2011). *A blueprint for transgender equality: Improving the lives of trans older adults*. Washington, DC: National Center for Transgender Equality.

NCTE. (2012). *Transgender sexual and reproductive health: Unmet needs and barriers to care*. Washington, DC: National Center for Transgender Equality.

Ndlovu-Gatsheni, S. J. (2015). Genealogies of coloniality and implications for Africa's development. *African Development, 40*(3), 13–40.

Near, H. (1990). *Fire in the rain. . .singer in the storm: An autobiography*. New York, NY: William Morrow.

Nelson, C. D. (2009). *Sexual identities in English language education*. New York, NY: Routledge.

Nero, C. (2005). Why are gay ghettos White? In P. Johnson & M. G. Henderson (Eds.), *Black queer studies: A critical anthology* (pp. 228–245). Durham, NC: Duke University.

Nestle, J. (Ed.). (1992). *The persistent desire: A butch-femme reader*. Boston, MA: Alyson Publications.

Nestle, J., Howell, C., & Wilchins, R. A. (Eds.). (2002). *Genderqueer: Voices from beyond the sexual binary*. Los Angeles, CA: Alyson.

Newman, D. M. (2007). Identities and inequalities: Exploring the intersections of race, class, gender, and sexuality. Boston, MA: McGraw Hill.

Newman, F. (2004). *The whole lesbian sex book: A passionate guide for the rest of us*, second edition. Jersey City, NJ: Cleis.

Newport, F., & Gates, G. J. (2015). San Francisco metro area ranks highest in LGBT percentage. *Gallup*. Retrieved from http://news.gallup.com/poll/182051/san-francisco-metro-area-ranks-highest-lgbt-percentage.aspx?utm_source=Social%20Issues&utm_medium=newsfeed&utm_campaign=tiles

Ng, E. (2013). A "Post-Gay" era? Media gaystreaming, homonormativity, and the politics of LGBT integration. *Communication, Culture & Critique, 6*(2), 258–283.

NGLCC. (2015). National Gay and Lesbian Chamber of Commerce. Retrieved from https://nglcc.org/

Nguyen, D. J., Gonyo, C. P., Secrist, S. M., Long, L. D., Brazelton, G. B., & Renn, K. R. (2014, November). *Peers as sources of support to LGBTQ+ college students*. Paper presented at the Association for the Study of Higher Education, Washington DC.

Nguyen, T. H. (2014). *A view from the bottom: Asian American masculinity and sexual representation*. Durham, NC: Duke University.

Nichols, J. M. (2016, September 20). Beloved web series '*My Gay Roommate*' to return as comedy pilot. *HuffPost*. Retrieved from www.huffingtonpost.com/entry/my-gay-roommate-tv-pilot_us_57e02a85e4b04a1497b5d66c

Nichols, M. (2004). Lesbian sexuality/female sexuality: Rethinking 'lesbian bed death'. *Sexual and Relationship Therapy, 19*(4), 363–371.

Nicolazzo, Z., Marine, S. B., & Galarte, F. J. (2015). Introduction. *TSQ: Transgender Studies Quarterly, 2*(3), 367–375.

Nkrumah, K. (1965). *Neo-colonialism: The last stage of imperialism.* London, UK: Thomas Nelson & Sons.

Nuttbrock, L., Hwahng, S., Bockting, W., Rosenblum, A., Mason, M., Macri, M., & Becker, J. (2009). Lifetime risk factors for HIV/STI infections among male-to-female transgender persons. *Journal of Acquired Immune Deficiency Syndromes, 52*(3), 417.

Nyitray, A. G., da Silva, R. J. C., Baggio, M. L., Lu, B., Smith, D., Abrahamsen, M., . . . & Giuliano, A. R. (2011). Age-specific prevalence of and risk factors for anal human papillomavirus (HPV) among men who have sex with women and men who have sex with men: the HPV in men (HIM) study. *Journal of Infectious Diseases, 203*(1), 49–57.

O'Mara, M. (2012). The correlation of sexual frequency and relationship satisfaction among lesbians. (Unpublished Doctoral Dissertation). The American Academy of Clinical Sexologists, Orlando, FL.

Obear, K. (1991). Homophobia. In N. J. Evans, & V. A. Wall (Eds.), *Beyond tolerance: Gays, lesbians, and bisexuals on campus* (pp. 39–66). Alexandria, VA: American Association for Counseling and Development.

*Obergefell v. Hodges*, 135 S. Ct. 2071, 576 U.S., 191 L. Ed. 2d 953 (2015).

Ochs, R., & Rowley, S. E. (Eds.) (2005). *Getting bi: Voices of bisexuals around the world.* Boston, MA: Bisexual Resource Center.

ODPHP. (2010a). *Healthy people 2020 transgender health fact sheet.* Washington, DC: Office of Disease Prevention and Health Promotion.

ODPHP. (2010b). *Healthy people 2020 bisexual health fact sheet.* Washington, DC: Office of Disease Prevention and Health Promotion.

Old Bailey Proceedings Online. (1895, May). Trial of OSCAR FINGAL O'FFLAHARTIE WILLS WILDE (40) ALFRED WATERHOUSE SOMERSET TAYLOR (33) (t18950520-425). Retrieved from www.oldbaileyonline.org, version 7.2.

OMB. (2016). *Budget of the U.S. government: Fiscal year 2017.* Washington, DC: Office of Management and Budget.

Omi, M., & Winant, H. (2014). *Racial formation in the United States*, third edition. New York, NY: Routledge.

Ong, A. (1999). *Flexible citizenship: The cultural logics of transnationality.* Durham, NC: Duke University.

Oppenheimer, M. (2012, October 12). Sociologist's paper raises questions on role of faith in scholarship. *New York Times.* Retrieved from www.nytimes.com/2012/10/13/us/mark-regnerus-and-the-role-of-faith-in-academics.html

Ordover, N. (2003). *American eugenics: Race, queer anatomy, and the science of nationalism.* Minneapolis, MN: University of Minnesota.

Orel, N. A., & Fruhauf, C. A. (2006). Lesbian and bisexual grandmothers' perceptions of the grandparent-grandchild relationship. *Journal of GLBT Family Studies, 2*(1), 43–70.

Orel, N., & Fruhauf, C. A. (2013). Lesbian, gay, bisexual, and transgender grandparents. In A. E. Goldberg and K. R. Allen (Eds*.), LGBT parent families: Innovations in research and implications for practice* (pp. 177–192). New York, NY: Springer Science+Business Media.

Orley, E. (2015, January 5). The story behind the controversial *"Pride"* DVD cover. *BuzzFeed.* Retrieved from www.buzzfeed.com/emilyorley/the-story-behind-the-controversial-pride-dvd-cover?utm_term=.sfKNZ5Jop#.jud9PpMVQ

Oswald, R. F., & Culton, L. S. (2003). Under the rainbow: Rural gay life and its relevance for family providers. *Family Relations, 52*(1), 72–81.

Oswin, N. (2006). Decentering queer globalization: Diffusion and the 'global gay.' *Environment and Planning D: Society and Space, 24*(5), 777–790.

Outram, D. (1995). *The enlightenment.* Cambridge, UK: Cambridge University.

OWH. (2009). *FAQ: Lesbian and bisexual health.* Washington: Office of Women's Health, U.S. Department of Health and Human Services.

Owusu-Edusei, Jr., K., Chesson, H. W., Gift, T. L., Tao, G., Mahajan, R., Ocfemia, M. C. B., & Kent, C. K. (2013). The estimated direct medical cost of selected sexually transmitted infections in the United States, 2008. *Sexually Transmitted Diseases, 40*(3), 197–201.

Pachankis, J. E., Eldahan, A. I., & Golub, S. A. (2016). New to New York: ecological and psychological predictors of health among recently arrived young adult gay and bisexual urban migrants. *Annals of Behavioral Medicine, 50*(5), 692–703.

Padilla, M. (2007). *Caribbean pleasure industry: Tourism, sexuality, and AIDS in the Dominican Republic.* Chicago, IL: University of Chicago.

PAGAA (Panel on Antiretroviral Guidelines for Adults and Adolescents). (2016). *Guidelines for the use of antiretroviral agents in HIV-1-infected adults and adolescents.* Washington, DC: U.S. Department of Health and Human Services.

Palefsky, J. M. (2010). Human papillomavirus–related disease in men: not just a women's issue. *Journal of Adolescent Health, 46*(4), S12–S19.

Palmisano, B. (n.d.). *Safer sex for trans bodies.* Washington, DC: Whitman–Walker Health and Human Rights Campaign.

Parent, D. (2013, March 19). I am Dan Parent, comic book artist for Archie Comics and creator of Archie's first gay character, Kevin Keller – AMA. Retrieved from www.reddit.com/r/IAmA/comments/1alpop/i_am_dan_parent_comic_book_artist_for_archie/

Parry, D. C. (2016). "Skankalicious": Erotic capital in women's flat track roller derby. *Leisure Sciences, 38*(4), 295–314.

Paternoster, R. (1991). *Capital punishment in America.* New York: Lexington Books.

Patridge, E. V., Barthelemy, R. S., & Rankin, S. R. (2014). Factors impacting the academic climate for LGBQ STEM faculty. *Journal of Women and Minorities in Science and Engineering, 20*(1), 75–98.

Patterson, C. J. (2000). Family relationships of lesbians and gay men. *Journal of Marriage and Family, 62*(4), 1052–1069.

Patterson, C. J. (2006). Children of lesbian and gay parents. *Current Directions in Psychological Science, 15,* 241–244.

Patterson, C. J. (2013). Children of lesbian and gay parents: Psychology, law, and policy. *Psychology of Sexual Orientation and Gender Diversity, 1,* 27–34.

Patton, C. (1990). Inventing "African AIDS." *New Formations, 10*(spring), 25–39.

Patton, C. (2002). *Globalizing AIDS.* Minneapolis, MN: University of Minnesota.

Paz-Bailey, G., Mendoza, M., Finlayson, T., Wejnert, C., Le, B., Rose, C., Raymond, H. F., Prejean, J., & NHBS Study Group. (2016). Trends in condom use among men who have sex with men in the united states: the role of antiretroviral therapy and sero-adaptive strategies. *AIDS, 30*(12):1985–1990.

Penney, J. (2013). Eminently visible: The role of t-shirts in gay and lesbian public advocacy and community building. *Popular Communication, 11*(4), 289–302.

Pepin, J. (2011). *The origins of AIDS.* Cambridge: Cambridge University.

Peplau, L., & Fingerhut, A. W. (2007). The close relationships of lesbian and gay men. *Annual Review of Psychology, 58,* 405–424.

Peplau, L., & Spalding, L. R. (2000). The close relationships of lesbians, gay men, and bisexuals. In C. Hendrick, & S. S. Hendrick (Eds.), *Close relationships: A sourcebook* (pp. 111–123). Thousand Oaks, CA: Sage.

Perrin-Wallqvist, R., & Lindblom, J. (2015). Coming out as gay: A phenomenological study about adolescents disclosing their homosexuality to their parents. *Social Behavior and Personality*, *43*(3), 467–480.

Perry, B. (2001). *In the name of hate: Understanding hate crimes*. New York, NY: Routledge.

Perry, B. (2013). 'Doing' gender and 'doing' gender inappropriately: Violence against women, gay men, and lesbians. In Abbey L. Ferber, Kimberly Holcomb, & Tre Wentling (Eds.), *Sex, Gender, and Sexuality: The New Basics* (pp. 323–329). New York, NY: Oxford University.

Petitfils, J. (2005). *Louis XVI*. Paris, France: Perrin.

Pew Research Center. (2013). A survey of LGBT Americans: The LGBT population and its sub-groups. Retrieved from www.pewsocialtrends.org/2013/06/13/a-survey-of-lgbt-americans/#the-lgbt- population-and-its-sub-groups

Pew Research Center. (2015). Support for same-sex marriage at record high, but key segments remain opposed. Retrieved from www.people-press.org/2015/06/08/section-2-knowing-gays-and-lesbians-religious-conflicts-beliefs-about-homosexuality/#reactions-to-a-gay-child.

Pick, A. (2004). New queer cinema and lesbian films. In M. Aaron (Ed.), *New queer cinema: A critical reader* (pp. 103–118). New Brunswick, NJ: Rutgers University.

Pierceson, J. (2016). *Sexual minorities and politics: An introduction*. Lanham, MD: Rowman & Littlefield.

Pieterse, J. (2003). *Globalization and culture: Global mélange*. Lanham, MD: Rowman & Littlefield.

Pingel, E. S., Thomas, L., Harmell, C., & Bauermeister, J. A. (2013). Creating comprehensive, youth centered, culturally appropriate sex education: what do young gay, bisexual, and questioning men want? *Sexuality Research and Social Policy*, *10*(4), 293–301.

Plato (2014). *Symposium*. (B. Jowett, Trans.). Retrieved from https://ebooks.adelaide.edu.au/p/plato/p71sy/symposium.html

Plöderl, M., & Fartacek, R. (2005). Suicidality and associated risk factors among lesbian, gay, and bisexual compared to heterosexual Austrian adults. *Suicide and Life-Threatening Behavior*, *35*(6), 661–670.

Polikoff, N. D. (2008). *Beyond (straight and gay) marriage: Valuing all families under the law*. Boston, MA: Beacon.

Pollock, G. S., & Minter, S. (2014). *Report of the Planning Commission on Transgender Military Service*. Retrieved from www.palmcenter.org/publication/report-of-the-planning-commission-on-training-military-service/

Poniewozik, J. (2015, July 15). Review: An extraordinary, ordinary girlhood in TLC's *I Am Jazz*. *TIME*. Retrieved from http://time.com/3957689/review-i-am-jazz-tlc-transgender/

Potarca, G., Mills, M., & Neberich, W. (2015). Relationship preferences among gay and lesbian online daters: Individual and contextual differences. *Journal of Marriage and Family*, *77*(2), 523–541.

Povinelli, E., & Chauncey, G. (1999). Thinking sexuality transnationally: An introduction. *GLQ*, *5*(4), 439–50.

Poynter, K. J. (Ed.) (2016). *Safe zones: Training allies of LGBTQIA+ young adults*. Lanham, MD: Rowman & Littlefield.

Prati, G., & Pietrantoni, L. (2014). Coming out and job satisfaction: A moderated mediation model. *The Career Development Quarterly*, *62*(4), 358–371.

Pratt, M. L. (1992). *Imperial eyes: Travel writing and transculturation*. New York, NY & Abingdon, UK: Routledge.

Prause, N., & Graham, C. A. (2007). Asexuality: Classification and characterization. *Archives of Sexual Behavior, 36*(3), 341–356.

Pray, L., Lemon, S., Mahmoud, A., & Knobler, S. (Eds.). (2006). *The impact of globalization on infectious disease emergence and control: Exploring the consequences and opportunities, workshop summary—Forum on microbial threats.* Washington, DC: National Academies.

Prieur, A. (1998). *Mema's house, Mexico City: On transvestites, queens, and machos.* Chicago, IL: University of Chicago.

Pronger, B. (1992). *The arena of masculinity: Sports, homosexuality, and the meaning of sex.* Toronto, ON: University of Toronto.

Puar, J. K. (2002). Circuits of queer mobility: Tourism, travel, and globalization. *GLQ, 8*(1–2), 101–37.

Puar, J. K. (2007). *Terrorist assemblages: Homonationalism in queer times.* Durham, NC: Duke University.

Puar, J. K. (2013). Rethinking homonationalism. *International Journal of Middle East Studies, 45*(2), 336–339.

Pyne, J., Bauer, G., & Bradley, K. (2015). Transphobia and other stressor impacting trans parents. *Journal of GLBT Family Studies, 11*(2), 107–126.

Quammen, D. (2015) *The chimp and the river: How AIDS emerged from an African forest.* New York, NY: W.W. Norton.

Ragins, B. R., & Cornwell, J. M. (2001). Pink triangles: Antecedents and consequences of perceived workplace discrimination against gay and lesbian employees. *Journal of Applied Psychology, 86*(6), 1244–1261.

Ragins, B. R., Singh, R., & Cornwell, J. M. (2007). Making the invisible visible: fear and disclosure of sexual orientation at work. *Journal of Applied Psychology, 92*(4), 1103–1118.

Raimondo, M. (2003). "Corralling the virus": Migratory sexualities and the "spread of AIDS" in the US media. *Environment and Planning D, 21*(4), 389–407.

Rands, K. (2009). Considering transgender people in education: A gender–complex approach. *Journal of Teacher Education. 60*(4). 419–431.

Rands, K. (2013). Supporting transgender and gender–nonconforming youth through teaching mathematics for social justice. *Journal of LGBT Youth, 10*(1–2), 106–126.

Rankin, S., Weber, G., Blumenfeld, W., & Frazer, S. (2010). *The state of education for lesbian, gay, bisexual & trangender people.* Charlotte, N.C: Campus Pride.

Rao, R. (2015). Re-membering Mwanga: Same-sex intimacy, memory and belonging in postcolonial Uganda. *Journal of East African Studies, 9*(1), 1–19.

Raskin, J. *American scream: Allen Ginsberg's "Howl" and the making of the Beat Generation.* Berkeley, CA: University of California.

Ray, N., & Berger, C. (2007). *Lesbian, gay, bisexual, and transgender youth: An epidemic of homelessness.* Washington, DC: National Gay and Lesbian Task Force Policy Institute.

Rayor, D. & Lardinois, A. (2014). *Sappho: A new edition of the complete works.* Cambridge, UK: Cambridge University.

Reality Tea. (2010, April 20). Kim Zolciak's ex-girlfriend DJ Tracy Young dishes on their relationship. *Reality Tea.* Retrieved from www.realitytea.com/2010/04/20/kim-zolciaks-ex-girlfriend-dj-tracy-young-dishes-on-their-relationship/

Reddy, C. (2010). *Freedom with violence: Race, sexuality, and the U.S. state.* Durham, NC: Duke University.

Reddy, C., & Syed, J. (1999). "I left my country for this?!" *Trikone, 14*(4): 8–9.

Reed, J. (2004, January 25). Outbound: Philadelphia's friendly face. *Boston Globe.* Retrieved from LexisNexis, November 8, 2009.

Reed, P. (1993). Early AIDs fiction. In. J. L. Pastore (Ed.), *Confronting AIDS through literature: The responsibilities of representation* (pp. 91–94). Urbana, IL: University of Illinois.

Regnerus, M. (2012). How different are the adult children of parents who have same-sex relationships? Findings from the New Family Structures Study. *Social Science Research*, *41*(4), 752–770.

Reid, R. A. (Ed.) (2009). *Women in science fiction and fantasy*. Westport, CT: Greenwood.

Reis, E. (2007). Divergence or disorder?: The politics of naming intersex. *Perspectives in Biology and Medicine*, *50*(4), 535–543.

Reis, E. (2009). *Bodies in doubt: An American history of intersex*. Baltimore, MD: Johns Hopkins University.

Reisner, S. L., & Murchison, G. R. (2016). A global research synthesis of HIV and STI behavioural risks in female-to-male transgender adults. *Global Public Health*, *11*(7–8), 866–887.

Renn, K. A. (2010). LGBT and Queer research in higher education: The state and status of the field. *Educational Researcher*, *39*(2), 132–141.

Renzetti, C., Curran, D. J., & Maier, S. L. (2012). *Women, men and society*, sixth edition. Boston, MA: Pearson.

Renzi, C., Tabet, S. R., Stucky, J. A., Eaton, N., Coletti, A. S., Surawicz, C. M., . . . & Celum, C. L. (2003). Safety and acceptability of the RealityTM condom for anal sex among men who have sex with men. *AIDS*, *17*(5), 727–731.

Rich, B. R. (1992). New Queer Cinema. *Sight and Sound*, *2*(5), 30–34.

Rifkin, M. (2011). *When did Indians become straight?: Kinship, the history of sexuality, and Native sovereignty*. New York, NY: Oxford University.

Rimmerman, C. A. (2015). *The lesbian and gay movements: Assimilation or liberation*, second edition. Boulder, CO: Westview.

Ritzer, G. (1993). *The McDonaldization of society*. London, UK: Sage.

Rivers, I. (2004). Recollections of bullying at school and their long-term implications for lesbians, gay men, and bisexuals. *Crisis*, *25*(4), 169–175.

Robbins, S. (2017, June 2). 18 men arrested in four-day sex sting at Volusia parks. *Dayton* [Florida] *News-Journal*. Retrieved from www.news-journalonline.com/news/20170603/18-men-arrested-in-four-day-sex-sting-at-volusia-parks

Robertson, R. (1992). *Globalization: Social theory and global culture*. London, UK: Sage.

Robinson, B. E., Walters, L. H., & Skeen, P. (1989). Response of parents to learning that their child is homosexual and concern over AIDS: A national study. *Journal of Homosexuality*, *18*(1–2), 59–80.

Robinson, D. M. (2006). *Closeted writing and lesbian and gay literature: Classical, early modern, eighteenth century*. Surrey, UK: Ashgate.

Robinson, K. H. (2005). 'Queerying' gender: Heteronormativity in early childhood education. *Australian Journal of Early Childhood*, *30*(2), 19–28.

Robinson, V. G. (2010, December 8). Homosexuality in Sodom and Gamorrah. *Onfaith*. Retrieved from www.onfaith.co/onfaith/2010/12/08/homosexuality-in-sodom-and-gomorrah/9051

Robles, T. F. (2014). Marital quality and health: Implications for marriage in the 21st century. *Current Directions in Psychological Science*, *23*(6), 427–432.

Robles, T. F., & Kiecolt-Glaser, J. K. (2003). The physiology of marriage: Pathways to health. *Physiology & Behavior*, *79*(3), 409–416

Robles, T. F., Slatcher, R. B., Trombello, J. M., & McGinn, M. M. (2014). Marital quality and health: A meta-analytic review. *Psychological Bulletin*, *140*(1), 140–187.

Rodger, A. J., Cambiano, V., Bruun, T., Vernazza, P., Collins, S., Van Lunzen, J., . . . & Asboe, D. (2016). Sexual activity without condoms and risk of HIV transmission in serodifferent couples when the HIV-positive partner is using suppressive antiretroviral therapy. *JAMA, 316*(2), 171–181.

Rodríguez, J. M. (2003). *Queer Latinidad: Identity practices, discursive spaces.* New York, NY: New York University.

Roeser, R. W., Eccles, J. S., & Sameroff, A. J. (2000). School as context of early adolescents' academic and social-emotional development: A summary of research findings. *The Elementary School Journal, 100*(5), 443–471.

Roisman, G. I., Clausell, E., Holland, A., Fortuna, K., & Elieff, C. (2008). Adult romantic relationships as contexts of human development: A multimethod comparison of same-sex couples with opposite-sex dating, engaged, and married dyads. *Developmental Psychology, 44*, 91–101.

Rofel, L. (1999). Qualities of desire: Imagining gay identities in China. *GLQ, 5*(4), 451–74.

Román, D. (1998). *Acts of intervention: Performance, gay culture, and AIDS.* Bloomington, IN: Indiana University.

*Romer v. Evans*, 517 U.S. 620, 116 S. Ct. 1620, 134 L. Ed. 2d 855 (1996).

Rosario, M., Schrimshaw, E. W., & Hunger, H. (2004). Ethnic/racial differences in the coming-out process of lesbian, gay, and bisexual youths: A comparison of sexual identity development over time. *Cultural Diversity and Ethnic Minority Psychology, 10*(3), 215–228.

Roscoe, W. & Hay, H. (Eds.) (1996). *Radically gay: Gay liberation in the words of its founder.* Boston: Beacon.

Rose, S. M., & Zand, D. (2002). Lesbian dating and courtship from young adulthood to midlife. *Journal of Lesbian Studies, 6*(1), 85–109.

Rosenberg, E. S., Grey, J. A., Sanchez, T. H., & Sullivan, P. S. (2016). Rates of prevalent HIV infection, prevalent diagnoses, and new diagnoses among men who have sex with men in US states, metropolitan statistical areas, and counties, 2012–2013. *JMIR Public Health and Surveillance, 2*(1), e22.

Rosenberger, J. G., Reece, M., Schick, V., Herbenick, D., Novak, D. S., Van Der Pol, B., & Fortenberry, J. D. (2011). Sexual behaviors and situational characteristics of most recent male-partnered sexual event among gay and bisexually identified men in the United States. *The Journal of Sexual Medicine, 8*(11), 3040–3050.

Rosenfeld, M. J. (2014). Couple longevity in the era of same-sex marriage in the United States. *Journal of Marriage and Family, 76*, 905–918.

Rosengard, C., & Folkman, S. (1997). Suicide ideation, bereavement, HIV serostatus, and psychosocial variables in partners of men with HIV. *AIDS Care, 9*, 373–384

Ross, A. (2011). Deceptive picture: How Oscar Wilde painted over "Dorian Gray." *New Yorker.* Retrieved from www.newyorker.com/magazine/2011/08/08/deceptive-picture.

Rostosky, S., Riggle, E. B., Gray, B. E., & Hatton, R. L. (2007). Minority stress experiences in committed same-sex couple relationships. *Professional Psychology: Research and Practice, 38*(4), 392–400.

Rothman, E. F., Sullivan, M., Keyes, S., & Boehmer, U. (2012). Parents' supportive reactions to sexual orientation disclosure associated with better health: Results from a population-based survey of LGB adults in Massachusetts. *Journal of Homosexuality, 59*(2), 186–200.

Roughgarden, J. (2013). *Evolution's rainbow: Diversity, gender, and sexuality in nature and people,* third edition. Berkeley, CA: University of California.

Roy, S. (1998). Curry queens and other spices. In D. L. Eng & A. Y. Hom (Eds.), *Q & A: Queer in Asian America* (pp. 256–263). Philadelphia, PA: Temple University.

Rubin, K. H., Coplan, R., Chen, X., Buskirk, A. A., & Wojslawowicz, J. C. (2005). Peer relationships in childhood. In T. P. Gullotta & M. Bloom (Eds.), *Encyclopedia of primary prevention and health promotion*, second edition (pp. 808–812). New York, NY: Springer.

Ruble, D. N., Martin, C. L., & Berenbaum, S. A. (2006). Gender development. In W. Damon, & R. M. Lerner (Series Eds.) & N. Eisenberg (Vol. Ed.), *Handbook of child psychology: Vol. 3. Social, emotional, and personality development*, sixth edition (pp. 858–932). Hoboken, NJ: Wiley.

Rudder, C. (2014). *Dataclysm: Love, sex, race, and identity—what our online lives tell us about our offline selves*. New York, NY: Crown.

Ruggs, E. N., Martinez, L. R., Hebl, M. R., & Law, C. L. (2015). Workplace "trans"-actions: How organizations, coworkers, and individual openness influence perceived gender identity discrimination. *Psychology of Sexual Orientation and Gender Diversity*, *2*(4), 404–412.

Rumens, N. (2010). Firm friends: Exploring the supportive components of gay men's workplace friendships. *The Sociological Review*, *58*(1), 135–155.

Rumens, N. (2012). Queering cross-sex friendships: An analysis of gay and bisexual men's workplace friendships with heterosexual women. *Human Relations*, *65*(8), 955–978.

Rupp, L. (1999). *A desired past: A short history of same-sex love in America*. Chicago: University of Chicago.

Rupp, L. J. (2001). Toward a global history of same-sex sexuality. *Journal of the History of Sexuality*, *10*(2), 287–302.

Russell, S. T., Kosciw, J., Horn, S., & Saewyc, E. (2010). Social policy report: Safe schools policy for LGBTQ students. *Sharing Child and Youth Development Knowledge*, *24*(4), 1–12.

Russell, S. T., Muraco, A., Subramaniam, A., & Laub, C. (2009). Youth empowerment and high school gay-straight alliances. *Journal of Youth and Adolescence*, *38*(7), 891–903.

Russell, S. T., Toomey, R. B., Ryan, C., & Diaz, R. M. (2014). Being out at school: The implications for school victimization and young adult adjustment. *American Journal of Orthopsychiatry*, *84*(6), 635–343.

Russo, V. (1987). *The celluloid closet*, revised edition. New York, NY: Harper & Row.

Rutherford, R. (1991). *Classical literature: A concise history*. Hoboken, NJ: Wiley-Blackwell.

Ryan, B. (2017, July 25). Yet another study finds no HIV transmissions when viral load is undetectable. *POZ*. Retrieved from www.poz.com/article/second-study-finds-hiv-transmissions-viral-load-undetectable_IAS

Ryan, C. L., Patraw, J. M., & Bednar, M. (2013). Discussing princess boys and pregnant men: Teaching about gender diversity and transgender experiences within an elementary school curriculum, *Journal of LGBT Youth*, *10*(1–2), 83–105.

Ryan, C., & Futterman, D. (1998). *Lesbian and gay youth: Care and counseling*. New York, NY: Columbia University.

Ryan, C., Huebner, D., Diaz, R. M., & Sanchez, J. (2009). Family rejection as a predictor of negative health outcomes in White and Latino lesbian, gay, and bisexual young adults. *Pediatrics*, *123*(1), 346–352.

Ryan, C., Russell, S. T., Huebner, D., Diaz, R., & Sanchez, J. (2010). Family acceptance in adolescence and the health of LGBT young adults. *Journal of Child and Adolescent Psychiatric Nursing*, *23*(4), 205–213.

Rye, B. J., & Meany, G. J. (2010). Self-defense, sexism, and etiological beliefs: Predictors of attitudes toward gay and lesbian parenting. *Journal of GLBT Family Studies*, *6*(1), 1–24.

Sabor, P. (2004). John Cleland. In H.C.G. Matthew and Brian Harrison, (Eds.) *The dictionary of national biography*, volume 12. London, UK: Oxford University.

SAGE (Services and Advocacy for GLBT Elders). (n.d.). Discrimination. Retrieved from www.sageusa.org/issues/general.cfm

SAGE & MAP. (2010). *Improving the lives of LGBT older adults.* Denver, CO and New York, NY: Movement Advancement Project & Services and Advocacy for GLBT Elders.

SAGE & NCTE. (2012). *Improving the lives of transgender older adults: Recommendations for policy and practice.* New York, NY and Washington, DC: Services and Advocacy for GLBT Elders and National Center for Transgender Equality.

Said, E. (1978). *Orientalism.* New York, NY: Pantheon.

Salama, S., Boitrelle, F., Gauquelin, A., Malagrida, L., Thiounn, N., & Desvaux, P. (2015). Nature and origin of "squirting" in female sexuality. *The Journal of Sexual Medicine, 12*(3), 661–666.

SAMHSA. (2012). *Top health issues for LGBT populations information & resource kit.* HHS Publication No. (SMA) 12–4684. Rockville, MD: Substance Abuse and Mental Health Services Administration.

Samji, H., Cescon, A., Hogg, R. S., Modur, S. P., Althoff, K. N., Buchacz, K., . . . & Justice, A. (2013). Closing the gap: increases in life expectancy among treated HIV-positive individuals in the United States and Canada. *PLOS One, 8*(12), e81355.

Sanders, A. M., & Mathis, J. B. (2013). Gay and lesbian literature in the classroom: Can gay themes overcome heteronormativity? *Journal of Praxis in Multicultural Education, 7*(1), 1–18.

Sanders, D. (1996). Getting lesbian and gay issues on the international human rights agenda. *Human Rights Quarterly, 18*(1), 67–106.

Sandfort, T. G., & Dodge, B. (2008). ". . . and then there was the down low": Introduction to black and Latino male bisexualities. *Archives of Sexual Behavior, 37*(5), 675–682.

Sandilands, C. (2002). Lesbian separatist communities and the experience of nature: Toward a queer ecology. *Organization & Environment, 15*(2), 131–163.

Sandy, L. (2013). International agendas and sex worker rights in Cambodia. In M. Ford (Ed.), *Social activism in Southeast Asia* (pp. 154–169). London, UK & New York, NY: Routledge.

Santelli, J., Ott, M.A., Lyon, M., Rogers, J., Summers, D., Schleifer, R. (2006). Abstinence and abstinence-only education: A review of U.S. policies and programs. *Journal of Adolescent Health. 38*(1), 72–81.

Saslow, J. M. (1999). *Pictures and passions: A history of homosexuality in the visual arts.* New York, NY: Viking.

Satterwhite, C. L., Torrone, E., Meites, E., Dunne, E. F., Mahajan, R., Ocfemia, M. C. B., . . . & Weinstock, H. (2013). Sexually transmitted infections among US women and men: prevalence and incidence estimates, 2008. *Sexually Transmitted Diseases, 40*(3), 187–193.

Savage, D. (2011). Introduction. In D. Savage & T. Miller (Eds.), *It gets better: Coming out, overcoming bullying, and creating a life worth living* (pp. 1–8). New York, NY: Dutton.

Savin-Williams, R. C. (1988). Theoretical perspectives accounting for adolescent homosexuality. *Journal of Adolescent Health, 9*(6). 95–104.

Savin-Williams, R. C. (1997). *"—and then I became gay": Young men's stories.* New York, NY: Routledge.

Savin-Williams, R. C. (1998). Parental reactions to their child's disclosure of a gay/lesbian identity. *Family Relations, 47*(1), 7–13.

Savin-Williams, R. C. (2007). Dating and romantic relationships among gay, lesbian, and bisexual youth. In S. J. Ferguson (Ed.), *Shifting the center: Understanding contemporary families* (pp. 163–175). New York: McGraw-Hill.

Savin-Williams, R. C. (2009). How many gays are there? It depends. In D. A. Hope (Ed.), *Contemporary perspectives on lesbian, gay, and bisexual identities* (pp. 5–41). New York: Springer.

Savin-Williams, R. C., & Cohen, K. M. (2015). Developmental trajectories and milestones of lesbian, gay, and bisexual young people. *International Review of Psychiatry*, *27*(5), 357–366.

Savin-Williams, R. C., & Ream, G. L. (2003). Sex variations in the disclosure to parents of same-sex attractions. *Journal of Family Psychology*, *17*(3), 429–438.

Savin-Williams, R. C., & Ream, G. L. (2007). Prevalence and stability of sexual orientation components during adolescence and young adulthood. *Archives of Sexual Behavior*, *36*(3), 385–394.

Savin-Williams, R. C., & Vrangalova, Z. (2013). Mostly heterosexual as a distinct sexual orientation group: A systematic review of the empirical evidence. *Developmental Review*, *33*(1), 58–88.

Sbicca, J. (2012). Eco-queer movement (s): Challenging heteronormative space through (re) imagining nature and food. *European Journal of Ecopsychology*, *3*(1), 33–52.

Schall, J., & Kauffmann, G. (2003). Exploring literature with gay and lesbian characters in the elementary school. *Journal of Children's Literature*, *29*(1), 36–45.

Schiefenhövel, W. (1990). Ritualized adult-male/adolescent-male sexual behavior in Melanesia: An anthropological and ethnological perspective. In J. R. Feierman (Ed.), *Pedophilia: Biosocial dimensions* (pp. 394–421). New York: Springer-Verlag.

Schiff, K. (2012). Agnes Martin, under new auspices. *Art Journal*, *71*(3), 121–125.

Schlanger, Z. (2014, July 10). Where teens were abused in the name of God. *Newsweek*. Retrieved from www.newsweek.com/where-american-teens-abused-name-god-258182

Schmidt, S. J. (2014). Civil rights continued: How history positions young people to contemplate sexuality (in)justice. *Equity & Excellence in Education*, *47*(3), 353–369.

Schmidt, S. J. (2015). A queer arrangement of school: using spatiality to understand inequity. *Journal of Curriculum studies*, *47*(2), 253–273.

Schnarrs, P. W., Rosenberger, J. G., Schick, V. R., Novak, D. S., Herbenick, D., & Reece, M. (2012). Gay and bisexual Latino men's sexual health and behaviors: a national online sample. *International Journal of Men's Health*, *11*(1), 22–36.

Schulman, S. (2012). *Israel/Palestine and the queer international*. Durham, NC: Duke University.

Schwartz, P., & Rutter, V. (1998). *The gender of sexuality*. Landham, MD: Rowman & Littlefield.

Scully, P. (1995). Rape, race, and colonial culture: The sexual politics of identity in the nineteenth century Cape Colony, South Africa. *The American Historical Review*, *100*(2), 335–359.

Sears, B., & Mallory, C. (2011). *Documented evidence of employment discrimination & its effects on LGBT people*. Los Angeles, CA: The Williams Institute.

Sears, J. T. (2013). *Growing older: Perspectives on LGBT aging*. New York: Routledge.

Sedgwick, E. K. (1990). *Epistemology of the closet*. Berkeley, CA: University of California.

Seidman, S. (2010). *The social construction of sexuality*. New York, NY: W. W. Norton.

Seitz, D. (2009). Interdisciplinarity, local studies, and identity-building. *Change*, *41*(2) 57–58.

Sell, R. L. (1997). Defining and measuring sexual orientation: A review. *Archives of Sexual Behavior*, *26*(6), 643–658.

Sender, K. (2004). *Business, not politics*. New York, NY: Columbia University.

Setoodeh, R. (2010, May 9). From *Glee* to Sean Hayes: Gay actors play straight. *Newsweek*. Retrieved from www.newsweek.com/glee-sean-hayes-gay-actors-play-straight-70225

Sevelius, J. (2009). "There's no pamphlet for the kind of sex I have": HIV-related risk factors and protective behaviors among transgender men who have sex with nontransgender men. *Journal of the Association of Nurses in AIDS Care*, *20*(5), 398–410.

SFFWA (Science Fiction & Fantasy Writers of America). (n.d.) Nebula Award winners. Retrieved from www.sfwa.org/nebula-award-winners-1965-2000/

Shamama, J., Leon, B. (Producers), & Stabile, M. (Producer & Director). (2015). *Seed money: The Chuck Holmes story* [Motion Picture]. USA: Breaking Glass Pictures.

Shapiro, L. (2015, March 28). 'Nail salons are more regulated': A gay survivor takes on the 'troubled teen' industry. *Huffington Post*. Retrieved from www.huffingtonpost.com/2015/03/28/troubled-teen-programs_n_6957646.html

Sharpley-Whiting, T. D. (1999). *Black Venus: Sexualized savages, primal fears, and primitive narratives in French*. Durham, NC: Duke University.

Shaviro, S. (2013). Exceeding the human: Power and vulnerability in Octavia Butler's fiction. In R. J. Holden, & N. Shawl (Eds.) *Strange matings: Science fiction, feminism, African American voices, and Octavia E. Butler* (pp. 221–232). Seattle, WA: Aqueduct.

Shaw, A. (2009). Women on women: Lesbian identity, lesbian community, and lesbian comics. *Journal of Lesbian Studies*, *13*(1), 88–97.

Shaw, A. (2014). *Gaming at the edge: Sexuality and gender at the margins of gamer culture*. Minneapolis, MN: University of Minnesota.

Shema, A. (2014). Troubling "Family": How primary grade teachers negotiate hegemonic discourses of family. In K. Becker, E. Miller, N. Reid, B. Smith, & M. Sorensen (Eds.), *Collective unravelings of the hegemonic web: Movement, place, and story*. Charlotte, NC: Information Age Publishing.

Shernoff, M. (2006). Negotiated nonmonogamy and male couples. *Family Process*, *45*(4), 407–418.

Shilo, G., & Savaya, R. (2011). Effects of family and friend support on LGB youths' mental health and sexual orientation milestones. *Family Relations*, *60*(3), 318–330.

Shilts, R. (1987). *And the band played on: Politics, people, and the AIDS epidemic*. New York, NY: St. Martin's.

Shlasko, G. D. (2005). Queer (v.) pedagogy. *Equity & Excellence in Education*, *38*(2), 123–134.

Shulman, S., Elicker, J., & Sroufe, L. A. (1994). Stages of friendship growth in preadolescence as related to attachment history. *Journal of Social and Personal Relationships*, *11*(3), 341–361.

SIECUS (Sexuality Information and Education Council of the United States). (2014). *Support comprehensive sex education & adolescent sexual health promotion*. Washington DC: Sexuality Information and Education Council of the United States.

Silva, T. (2017). Bud-sex: Constructing normative masculinity among rural straight men that have sex with men. *Gender & Society*, *31*(1), 51–73.

Silverstein, C., & Picano, F. (2006). *The joy of gay sex, revised and expanded*, third edition. New York, NY: William Morrow.

Singh, D., Fine, D. N., & Marrazzo, J. M. (2011). Chlamydia trachomatis infection among women reporting sexual activity with women screened in family planning clinics in the Pacific Northwest, 1997 to 2005. *American Journal of Public Health*, *101*(7), 1284–1290.

Smith M. J., & Payne, E. (2016) Binaries and biology: Conversations with elementary education professionals after professional development on supporting transgender students, *The Educational Forum*, *80*(1), 34–47.

Smith-Rosenberg, C. (1989). Discourses of Sexuality and Subjectivity: The New Woman, 1870–1936. In M. Duberman, M. Vicinus, & G. Chauncey, Jr. (Eds.), *Hidden From History: Reclaiming the Gay & Lesbian Past* (pp. 264–280). New York: New American Library.

Smith, A. W., & Duggan, M. (2013). *Online Dating & Relationships*. Washington, DC: Pew Research Center's Internet and American Life Project.

Smith, C. A., & Stillman, S. (2002). Butch/femme in the personal advertisements of lesbians. *Journal of Lesbian Studies*, *6*(1), 45–51.

Smith, J. (2013, December 16). Interview: Peter Le. *TimeOut Beijing*. Retrieved from www.timeoutbeijing.com/features/Feature/25918/Interview-Peter-Le.html

Smith, L. A., McCaslin, R., Chang, J., Martinez, P., & McGrew, P. (2010). Assessing the needs of older gay, lesbian, bisexual, and transgender people: A service-learning and agency partnership approach. *Journal of Gerontological Social Work*, *53*(5), 387–401.

Sneticker, M. (2016, May 5). Colton Haynes gets honest about life after '*Arrow*'. *Entertainment Weekly*. Retrieved from http://ew.com/article/2016/05/05/colton-haynes-interview/

Snyder, S. M., Hartinger-Saunders, R., Brezina, T., Beck, E., Wright, E. R., Forge, N., & Bride, B. E. (2016). Homeless youth, strain, and justice system involvement: An application of general strain theory. *Children and Youth Services Review*, *62*, 90–96.

Snyder, V. L., & Broadway, F. S. (2004). Queering high school biology textbooks. *Journal of Research in Science Technology*, *41*(6), 617–636.

Sollender, J. (2011, August 12). Are we entering a post-gay era? *Rage*. Retrieved from www.ragemonthly.com/2011/08/12/are-we-entering-a-post-gay-era-2/

Solomon-Godeau, A. (2005). Is Endymion gay? Historical interpretation and sexual identities. In S. Bellenger (Ed.) *Girodet 1767–1824* (pp. 81–95). Paris, France: Gallimard.

Solomon, A. (2005). Trans/migrant: Christina Madrazo's all-American story. In E. Luibhéid & L. Cantú (Ed.), *Queer migrations: Sexuality, U.S. citizenship, and border crossings* (pp. 3–29). Minneapolis, MN: University of Minnesota.

Somerville, S. (2000). *Queering the color line: Race and the invention of homosexuality in American culture*. Durham, NC: Duke University.

Souhami, D. (1998). *The trials of Radclyffe Hall*. London, UK: Harper Collins.

Southall, C., & Fallon, P. (2011). LGBT tourism. In P. Robinson, S. Heitmann, and P. U. C. Dieke (Eds.), *Research themes for tourism* (pp. 218–232). Wallingford, UK: CABI.

Spade, D. (2004). Resisting medicine/remodeling gender. *Berkeley Women's Law Journal*, *15*, 15–37.

Springate, M. (Ed.) (2016). *LGBTQ America: A theme study of lesbian, gay, bisexual, transgender, and queer history*. Washington, DC: U.S. National Park Service.

Sroufe, L. S. (1983). Infant–caregiver attachment & patterns of adaption in preschool: The roots of maladaptation & competence. In M. Perlmutter (Ed.), Minnesota Symposium in Child Psychology (Vol. *16*, pp. 41–83). Hillsdale, NJ: Erlbaum.

Sroufe, L. A., Schork, E., Motti, E., Lawroski, N., & LaFreniere, P. (1984). The role of affect in social competence. In C. Izard, J. Kagan, & R. Zajonc (Eds.), *Emotion cognition and behavior* (pp. 289–318). New York, NY: Plenum.

Stacey, J., & Biblarz, T. J. (2001). (How) does the sexual orientation of parents matter? *American Sociological Review*, *66*(2), 159–183.

Stanger-Hall, K. F., & Hall, D. W. (2011). Abstinence-only education and teen pregnancy rates: why we need comprehensive sex education in the US. *PLOS One*, *6*(10), e24658.

Starks, T. J., Newcomb, M. E., & Mustanski, B. (2015). A longitudinal study of interpersonal relationships among lesbian, gay, and bisexual adolescents and young adults: Mediational pathways from attachment to romantic relationship quality. *Archives of Sexual Behavior, 44*(7), 1821–1831.

Stedman, A. (2016, June 9). Colton Haynes calls Noah Galvin diss 'frankly embarrassing on his part.' *Variety*. Retrieved from http://variety.com/2016/tv/news/colton-haynes-noah-galvin-lgbt-1201792777/

Stein, M. (2012). *Rethinking the gay and lesbian movement*. New York, NY: Routledge.

Steinberg, L. (2014). Cognitive Transitions. In L. Steinberg (Ed.), *Adolescence*, eleventh edition (pp. 42–68). New York: McGraw Hill.

Steinem, G. (1999 [2007]). Supremacy crimes. In V. Taylor, N. Whittier, and L. J. Rupp (Eds.), *Feminist Frontiers*, seventh edition (pp. 428–430). New York, NY: McGraw-Hill.

Stephens, S. C., Bernstein, K. T., & Philip, S. S. (2011). Male to female and female to male transgender persons have different sexual risk behaviors yet similar rates of STDs and HIV. *AIDS and Behavior, 15*(3), 683–686.

Stiffarm, L. A., & Lane, P. (1992). The demography of Native North America: A question of American Indian survival. In M. A. Jaimes (Ed.), *The state of Native America: Genocide, colonization, and resistance*. (pp. 23–54). Boston, MA: South End.

Stoker, B. (1997). *Dracula*. New York, NY: W.W. Norton.

Stoler, A. L. (2002). *Carnal knowledge and imperial power: Race and the intimate in colonial rule*. Berkeley, CA: University of California.

Storms, M. D. (1980). Theories of sexual orientation. *Journal of Personality and Social Psychology, 38*(5), 783–792.

Storr, M. (1997). The sexual reproduction of "race": Bisexuality, history, and racialization. In P. Davidson, J. Eadie, C. Hemmings, A. Kaloski, & M. Storr (Eds.), *The bisexual imaginary: Representation, identity, and desire* (pp. 73–88). London, UK & Washington, DC: Cassell.

Stryker, S. (2001). *Queer pulp*. San Francisco, CA: Chronicle.

Stryker, S. (2008). *Transgender history*. Seattle, WA: Seal.

Stryker, S. (2015). Transgender activism. *GLBTQ Archive.com*. Retrieved from www.glbtqarchive.com

Stryker, S., & Whittle, S. (Eds.) (2006). *The transgender studies reader*. New York, NY: Routledge.

Stychin, C. F. (2003). *Governing sexuality: The changing politics of citizenship and law reform*. Oxford, UK & Portland, OR: Hart.

Subrahmanyam, K., & Smahel, D. (2010). *Digital youth: The role of media in development*. New York, NY: Springer.

Suen, Y. T. (2015). To date or not to date, that is the question: Older single gay men's concerns about dating. *Sexual and Relationship Therapy, 30*(1), 143–155.

Summers, C. J. (2015). Isherwood, Christopher (1904–1986): Isherwood's masterpiece, *A Single Man*. *GLBTQ Archive.com*. Retrieved from www.glbtqarchive.com.

Sutphin, S. T. (2010). Social exchange theory and the division of labor in same-sex couples. *Marriage & Family Review, 46*, 191–206.

Swainson, M., & Tasker, F. (2006). Genograms redrawn: Lesbian couples define their family. In J. J. Bigner (Ed.), *An introduction to GLBT family studies* (pp. 89–115). New York: Haworth.

Swarr, A. L., & R. Nagar. (2003). Dismantling assumptions: Interrogating "lesbian" struggles for identity and survival in India. *Signs, 29*(2), 491–516.

Swearer, S. M., & Cary, P. T. (2003). Perceptions and attitudes toward bullying in middle school youth: A developmental examination across the bully/victim continuum. *Journal of Applied School Psychology, 19*(2), 63–79.

Takagi, D. Y. (1996). Maiden voyage: Excursion into sexuality and identity politics in Asian America. In R. Leong (Ed.), *Asian American sexualities: Dimensions of the gay &*

*lesbian experience* (pp. 21–35). New York, NY: Routledge.

Taylor, A. (1997). A queer geography. In A. Medhurst & S. Munt (Eds.), *Lesbian and gay studies: A critical introduction* (pp. 3–19). London, UK: Cassell.

Taylor, B. S., Chiasson, M. A., Scheinmann, R., Hirshfield, S., Humberstone, M., Remien, R. H., . . . & Wong, T. (2012). Results from two online surveys comparing sexual risk behaviors in Hispanic, Black, and White men who have sex with men. *AIDS and Behavior, 16*(3), 644–652.

Taylor, L. A. (2001). 'I made up my mind to get it': The American trial of *The Well of Loneliness*, New York City, 1928–29. *Journal of the History of Sexuality, 10*(2), 250–286.

Teich, N. (2012). *Transgender 101: A simple guide to a complex issue*. New York, NY: Columbia University.

Terry, D. (1992, April 7). 'Pink Angels' battle anti-gay crime. *New York Times*. Retrieved from www.nytimes.com/1992/04/07/us/pink-angels-battle-anti-gay-crime.html

Terry, J. (1999). *An American obsession: Science, medicine, and homosexuality in modern society*. Chicago, IL: University of Chicago.

Tetzlaff, K. (2015). Patient's guide to transgender, trans, & gender diverse health. *Katja Tetzlaff: Illustrator. Educator. Activist*. Retrieved from https://ktetzlaff.com

That Jay Justice. (2016, August 13). Flame Con is back! [Tumblr post]. Retrieved from http://thatjayjustice.tumblr.com/post/148887325924/flame-con-is-back-new-york-citys-first-lgbtqia

The first annual *PW* comics week critic's poll (2006). *Publishers Weekly*. Retrieved from www.publishersweekly.com/pw/by-topic/industry-news/comics/article/12081-the-first-annual-pw-comics-week-critic-s-poll.html

Thompson, M. (Ed.). (1991). *Leatherfolk: Radical sex, people, politics, and practice*. Los Angeles, CA: Alyson.

Thongthiraj, T. T. (1994). Toward a struggle against invisibility: Love between women in Thailand. *Amerasia Journal, 20*(1), 45–58.

Thoreau, H. D. (1907). *Friendship: An essay*. Boston, MA: Alfred Bartlett.

Thoreson, R. R. (2009). Queering human rights: The Yogyakarta Principles and the norm that dare not speak its name. *Journal of Human Rights, 8*(4), 323–339.

Thoreson, R. R. (2014). *Transnational LGBT activism: Working for sexual rights worldwide*. Minneapolis, MN: University of Minnesota.

Tinsley, O. N. (2008). Black Atlantic, queer Atlantic: Queer imaginings of the Middle Passage. *GLQ, 14*(2–3), 191–215.

Tomlinson, J. (1999). *Globalization and culture*. Chicago, IL: University of Chicago.

Toomey, R. B., McGuire, J. K., Russell, S. T. (2012). Heteronormativity, school climates, and perceived safety for gender nonconforming peers. *Journal of Adolescence, 35*(1), 187–196.

Tosefta Sotah 3:11–12. Talmud. *On1Foot: Jewish texts for social justice*. Retrieved from www.on1foot.org/text/tosefta-sotah-311-12.

Toubia, B. (2014). Gender role conflict, role division, and the gay relational experience. *Journal of Systemic Therapies, 33*(4), 15–23.

Treichler, P. (1987). AIDS, homophobia, and biomedical discourse: An epidemic of signification. *October, 43*, 31–70.

Treichler, P. (1989). AIDS and HIV infection in the Third Word: A First World chronicle. In B. Kruger & P. Mariani (Eds.), *Discussions in contemporary culture: Remaking history* (pp. 31–86). Seattle, WA: Bay.

Trenholm, C., Devaney, B., Fortson, K., Quay, L., Wheeler, J., Clark, M. (2007). *Impacts of four Title V, section 510 abstinence education programs (final report)*. Princeton, NJ:

Mathematica Policy Research.

Triptow, R. (1988). Introduction. In *Strip AIDS USA* (p. 4). San Francisco, CA: Last Gasp.

Troiden, R. R. (1979). Becoming homosexual: A model of gay identity acquisition. *Psychiatry, 42*(4), 362–373.

Troiden, R. R. (1988). Homosexual identity development. *Journal of Adolescent Health Care, 9*(2), 105–113.

Tsang, D. C. (1994). Notes on queer 'n'Asian virtual sex. *Amerasia Journal, 20*(1), 117–128.

Tully, C. (1988). Caregiving: What do midlife lesbians view as important? *Journal of Gay and Lesbian Psychotherapy, 1*(1), 87–103

Turell, S. (2000). A descriptive analysis for same-sex relationship violence for a diverse sample. *Journal of Family Violence, 15*(3), 281–293.

Tyburczy, J. (Curator). (2015). *Irreverent: A celebration of censorship* [Museum exhibition]. Chicago, IL: Leslie Lohman Museum of Gay and Lesbian Art.

Ulrichs, K. H. (1994). *The riddle of "man-manly love": The pioneering work on male homosexuality.* Buffalo, NY: Prometheus.

Underwood, S. G. (2003). *Gay men and anal eroticism: Tops, bottoms, and versatiles.* New York, NY: Routledge.

UNESCO (United Nations Educational, Scientific and Cultural Organization). (2015). Migrant/migration. Retrieved from www.unesco.org/new/en/social-and-human-sciences/themes/international-migration/glossary/migrant

United Nations. (2016). The United Nations and decolonization: Non-self-governing territories. Retrieved from www.un.org/en/decolonization/nonselfgovterritories.shtml

United States Census (2014). Characteristics of same-sex couple households: 2014. *American Community Survey.* Retrieved from www.census.gov/hhes/samesex/

*United States v. Windsor,* 133 S. Ct. 2675, 570 U.S. 12, 186 L. Ed. 2d 808 (2013).

UNPF (United Nations Population Fund). (2016). Migration. Retrieved from www.unfpa.org/migration

USHHS (U.S. Department of Health and Human Services). (2014). Administration for community living. Retrieved from www.aoa.gov/AoA_programs/Tools_Resources/diversity.aspx#LGBT

Vagelos, E. (1993). The social group that dare not speak its name: Should homosexuals constitute a particular social group for the purposes of obtaining refugee status? Comment on *Re: Inaudi. Fordham Law Review, 17*(1), 227–276.

Valentine, G. (2006). Globalizing intimacy: The role of information and communication technologies in maintaining and creating relationships. *Women's Studies Quarterly, 34*(1–2), 365–93.

Vance, C. (1991). Anthropology rediscovers sexuality: A theoretical comment. *Social Science and Medicine, 33*(8), 875–884.

Vanderburgh, R. (2009). Appropriate therapeutic care for families with pre-pubescent transgender/gender-dissonant children. *Child & Adolescent Social Work Journal, 26*(2), 135–154.

Veale, D., Miles, S., Bramley, S., Muir, G., & Hodsoll, J. (2015). Am I normal? A systematic review and construction of nomograms for flaccid and erect penis length and circumference in up to 15,521 men. *BJU International, 115*(6), 978–986.

Vicars, M. (2012). Towards a rhizomatic methodology: How queer. In S. R. Steinberg & G. S. Cannella (Eds.) *Critical qualitative research reader* (pp. 468–478). New York: Peter Lang.

Vidal, G. (1995). *The city and the pillar and seven early stories.* New York, NY: Random

House.

Villar, F., Serrat, R., Faba, J., & Celdran, M. (2015). Staff reactions toward lesbian, gay, or bisexual (LGB) people living in residential aged care facilities (RACFs) who actively disclose their sexual orientation. *Journal of Homosexuality, 62*(8), 1126–1143.

Villicana, A. J., Delucio, K., & Biernat, M. (2016). "Coming out" among gay Latino and gay White men: implications of verbal disclosure for well-being. *Self and Identity, 15*(4), 468–487.

Voss, B. (2010, March, 11). The truth about Tracy and Kim. *Advocate.* Retrieved from www.advocate.com/arts-entertainment/music/2010/03/11/truth-about-tracy-and-kim

Vrangalova, Z., & Savin-Williams, R. C. (2012). Mostly heterosexual and mostly gay/lesbian: Evidence for new sexual orientation identities. *Archives of Sexual Behavior, 41*(1), 85–101.

Waitt, G., & Markwell, K. (2014). *Gay tourism: Culture and context.* New York, NY & London, UK: Routledge.

Wald, P. (2008). *Contagious: Cultures, carriers, and the outbreak narrative.* Durham, NC: Duke University.

Waldo, C. R. (1999). Working in a majority context: A structural model of heterosexism as minority stress in the workplace. *Journal of Counseling Psychology, 46*(2), 218–232.

Wallace, L. (2003). *Sexual encounters: Pacific texts, modern sexualities.* Ithaca, NY: Cornell University.

Walters, S. D. (2003). *All the rage: The story of gay visibility in America.* Chicago, IL: University of Chicago.

Walton, G. (2005). The hidden curriculum in schools: Implications for lesbian, gay, bisexual, transgender, and queer youth. *Alternate Routes, 21*, 18–39.

Wang, J. (2008). AIDS denialism and 'the humanization of the African.' *Race & Class, 49*(3), 1–18.

Ward, J. (2015). *Not gay: Sex between straight white men.* New York, NY: NYU.

Warner, M. (1991). Introduction: Fear of a queer planet. *Social Text, 9*(4 [29]): 3–17.

Warner, M. (1993). Introduction. In M. Warner (Ed.), *Fear of a queer planet* (pp. vii–xxxi). Minneapolis, MN: University of Minnesota.

Warner, M. (2000). *The trouble with normal: Sex, politics, and the ethics of queer life.* Cambridge, MA: Harvard University.

Waugh, T. (1996). *Hard to imagine: Gay male eroticism in photography and film from their beginnings to Stonewall.* New York, NY: Columbia University.

Waxman, S. R. (2010). Names will never hurt me? Naming and the development of racial and gender categories in preschool-aged children. *European Journal of Social Psychology, 40*(4), 593–610.

Weber, P. (2014, February 21). Confused by all the new Facebook genders? Here's what they mean [blog post]. *Slate: Lexicon blog.* Retrieved from www.slate.com/blogs/lexicon_valley/2014/02/21/gender_facebook_now_has_56_categories_to_choose_from_including_cisgender.html

Weiner, B. A., & Zinner, L. (2015). Attitudes toward straight, gay male, and transgender parenting. *Journal of Homosexuality, 62*(3), 327–339.

Weinstock, J. (2004). Lesbian FLEX-ibility: Friend and/or family connections among lesbian ex-lovers. In J S. Weinstock and E. D. Rothblum (Eds.), *Lesbian ex-lovers: The really long-term relationships* (pp. 193–238). Binghamton, NY: Harrington Park.

Wekker, G. (1999). What's identity got to do with it? Rethinking identity in light of the *mati* work in Suriname. In E. Blackwood & S. E. Wieringa (Eds.), *Female desires: Same-sex relations and transgender practices across cultures* (pp. 119–138). New York, NY: Columbia University.

Wekker, G. (2006). *The politics of passion: Women's sexual culture in the Afro-Surinamese diaspora*. New York, NY: Columbia University.

Welsh, J. (2011, April 11). Homosexual teen suicide rates raised in bad environments. Retrieved from www.livescience.com/13755-homosexual-lgb-teen-suicide-rates-environments.html

Wesling, M. (2008). Why queer diaspora? *Feminist Review, 90*(1), 30–47.

West, C., & Zimmerman, D. H. (1987). Doing gender. *Gender & Society, 1*(2), 125–151.

West, I., Frischherz, M., Panther, A., & Brophy, R. (2013). Queer worldmaking in the "It Gets Better" Campaign. *QED, 1*(1), 49–85.

Weston, K. (1997). *Families we choose: Lesbians, gays, kinship*. New York, NY: Columbia University.

WFTDA. (2014). Women's Flat Track Derby Association Gender Statement. Retrieved from https://wftda.com/wftda/gender-statement

White, D. R. (1999). *Dancing with dragons: Ursula K. Le Guin and the critics*. Columbia, SC: Camden House.

Whitlock, R. U. (2010). Getting queer: Teacher education, gender studies, and the cross-disciplinary quest for queer pedagogies. *Issues in Teacher Education, 19*(2) 81–104.

Whitman, W. (1981) *Leaves of grass*. New York, NY: Penguin.

WHO (World Health Organization). (2011). Transgender people. Retrieved from www.who.int/hiv/topics/transgender/about/en

Wienke, C., & Hill, G. J. (2013). Does place of residence matter? Rural–urban differences and the wellbeing of gay men and lesbians. *Journal of Homosexuality, 60*(9), 1256–1279.

Wilchins, R. (2011). *Queer theory, gender theory: An instant primer*. Los Angeles, CA: Alyson.

Wilchins, R., & Taylor, T. (2006). *50 under 30: Masculinity and the war on America's youth—A human rights report*. Washington, DC: GenderPAC.

Williams, E. L. (2013). *Sex tourism in Bahia: Ambiguous entanglements*. Champaign-Urbana, IL: University of Illinois.

Williams, W. (1986). *The spirit and the flesh: Sexual diversity in American indian cultures*. Boston: Beacon.

Willoughby, B. L. B., Malik, N. M., & Lindahl, K. M. (2006). Parental reactions to their sons' sexual orientation disclosure: The role of family cohesion, adaptability, and parenting style. *Psychology of Men & Masculinity, 7*, 14–26.

Wilson, A. (2006). Queering Asia. *Intersections: Gender, History and Culture in the Asian Context, 14*(3), n.p.

Wilson, A. (2010). Medical tourism in Thailand. In A. Ong & N. N. Chen (Eds.), *Asia biotech: Ethics and communities of fate* (pp. 118–143). Durham, NC: Duke University.

Wilton, J. (2012). Putting a number on it: The risk from an exposure to HIV. *Prevention in Focus*. Retrieved from www.catie.ca/en/pif/summer-2012/putting-number-it-risk-exposure-hiv

Witeck, B. (2013). *America's LGBT 2013 buying power estimated at $830 billion*. Washington, DC: Witeck Communications.

Wolfson, E. (2007). *Why marriage matters: America, equality, and gay people's right to marry*. New York, NY: Simon and Schuster.

Wong, D. (2010). Hybridization and the emergence of "gay" identities in Hong Kong and China. *Visual Anthropology, 24*(1–2): 152–70.

Woods, G. (1998). *A history of gay literature: The male tradition*. New Haven, CT: Yale University.

Workowski, K. A., & Bolan, G. A. (2015). Sexually transmitted diseases treatment guidelines (2015). *Reproductive Endocrinology, 24*, 51–56.

Wright, L. K. (1997). A concise history of self-identifying bears. In L. K. Wright (Ed.), *The bear book: Readings in the history and evolution of a gay male subculture* (pp. 29–38).

New York: Harrington Park.

Wright, R. G., LeBlanc, A. J., & Lee Badgett, M. V. (2013). Same-sex legal marriage and psychological well-being: Findings from the California Health Interview Survey. *American Journal of Public Health*, *103*(2), 339–346.

Wright, T. (2000). Gay organizations, NGOs, and the globalization of sexual identity: The case of Bolivia. *Journal of Latin American Anthropology*, *5*(2), 89–111.

WTO (World Tourism Organization). (2012). *Global report on LGBT tourism*. Retrieved from www.e-unwto.org/doi/pdf/10.18111//9789284414581

Xu, F., Sternberg, M. R., & Markowitz, L. E. (2010a). Men who have sex with men in the United States: demographic and behavioral characteristics and prevalence of HIV and HSV-2 infection: results from National Health and Nutrition Examination Survey 2001–2006. *Sexually Transmitted Diseases*, *37*(6), 399–405.

Xu, F., Sternberg, M. R., & Markowitz, L. E. (2010b). Women who have sex with women in the United States: Prevalence, sexual behavior and prevalence of herpes simplex virus type 2 infection—Results from National Health and Nutrition Examination Survey 2001–2006. *Sexually Transmitted Diseases*, *37*(7), 407–413.

Yarow, D. (2010). Gay and lesbian themes. In M. K. Booker (Ed.), *Encyclopedia of Comic Books and Graphic Novels, Volume 1: A-L* (pp. 245–251). Santa Barbara, CA: Greenwood.

Young, R. J. C. (2001). *Postcolonialism: An historical introduction*. Oxford, UK: Blackwell.

Young, R. M., & Meyer, I. H. (2005). The trouble with "MSM" and "WSW": Erasure of the sexual-minority person in public health discourse. *American Journal of Public Health*, *95*(7), 1144–1149.

Younger, J. G. (2016). University LGBT/Queer programs. Retrieved from www.people.ku.edu/~jyounger/lgbtqprogs.html

Zeglin, R. J. (2015). Assessing the role of masculinity in the transmission of HIV: a systematic review to inform HIV risk reduction counseling interventions for men who have sex with men. *Archives of Sexual Behavior*, *44*(7), 1979–1990.

# About the Contributors

## ABOUT THE EDITOR

**Michael J. Murphy**, PhD, is Associate Professor of Gender and Sexuality Studies at the University of Illinois Springfield, where he has taught since 2009. He holds degrees in the history of art, and women's/gender/sexuality studies, from the University of Iowa and Washington University in St. Louis. Since 2005 he has taught numerous courses in women's/gender studies, critical men's/masculinity studies, and LGBTQ+/sexuality studies. He is the author of many encyclopedia and journal articles, and other publications, including *Activities for Teaching Gender and Sexuality in the University Classroom*, Michael J. Murphy and Elizabeth Ribarsky, eds. (Lanham, MD: Rowman & Littlefield Education, 2013). He lives with his husband in St. Louis, Missouri.

## ABOUT THE ILLUSTRATOR

**Brytton Bjorngaard** is an Assistant Professor of Digital Media at the University of Illinois Springfield. She holds an MFA in Graphic Design from Iowa State University and a BA in Graphic Design from Saint Mary's University of Minnesota. She is a freelance graphic designer, working primarily for non-profit organizations in the Springfield, Illinois area, including the Enos Park Neighborhood Improvement Association, Springfield Art Association, Shelterbelt Press, and Compass for Kids.

## ABOUT THE CHAPTER AND FOCUS BOX AUTHORS

**Josh Cerretti** is an Assistant Professor in the Department of History and Program in Women, Gender, and Sexuality Studies at Western Washington University. He received his PhD in Global Gender Studies from SUNY University at Buffalo and his MA in Gender & Peacebuilding from the UN University for Peace. His research on militarizing sexuality in the post-Cold War United States has appeared in Radical History Review and Gender & History.

**Elizabeth Dinkins** is an Associate Professor in the School of Education at Bellarmine University in Louisville, Kentucky. Her work has focused on LGBTQ issues and identities in classroom instruction, the use of young adult literature, and approaches to teacher development and school-wide literacy. Her articles have been published in *Middle Grades Research Journal*; *Sex Education: Sexuality, Society, and Learning*; and *English Journal*. She's also been a contributing author to *Queering Classrooms: Personal Narratives and Education Practices to Support LGBTQ Youth in Schools* and *Developing Contemporary Literacies through Sports: A Guide for the English Classroom*. She strives to produce scholarship that humanizes and empowers the youth and communities. Previously, she taught English language arts and coordinated school-wide literacy instruction in an urban middle school.

**Shaun Edmonds** is a PhD candidate in Kinesiology at the University of Maryland specializing in Physical Cultural Studies. His interests include sexuality, physical activity, body politics, subcultures, and virtual spaces.

**Patrick Englert** is the Assistant Vice President for Student Affairs at Bellarmine University in Louisville, Kentucky where he oversees the areas of identity and inclusion, career development, service and leadership, and student activities. He is currently working on completing his dissertation which is a qualitative case study entitled, *Experiences Explored through the Prism: Out Gay and Lesbian Pathways to Presidency*. His research interests focus on LGBTQ+ topics surrounding higher education and critical inquiry of sexuality and gender. He has had articles published in the *AHEPPP Journal* and *Sex Education Journal*. Patrick has worked as a university administrator for nearly 15 years as well as teaching as an adjunct instructor for nine years. He has taken his passion for working with college students in the diverse setting of higher education and focused on infusing a critical approach in his work with students and the community.

**Christianne Anastasia Gadd**, PhD, is a Teaching Assistant Professor in the College of Sciences, Health, and the Liberal Arts at Thomas Jefferson University in Philadelphia whose research interests include media representations of LGBT individuals and issues, gender-based discourses in the LGBT community, and American popular culture more broadly. Her current project explores the role of early gay publications like *The Advocate* in the mainstreaming of gay, lesbian, and bisexual identities in the late twentieth-century United States.

**Eric Nolan Gonzaba** is a doctoral candidate in History at George Mason University. He won a 2016 National Council on Public History prize for his digital archive *Wearing Gay History*. His work has been supported through fellowships from the University of Pennsylvania and the Point Foundation.

**Andrew Gurza** is a Disability Awareness Consultant who strives to "do disability with a twist" in his work, which seeks to explore how the lived experience of disability feels as it interplays with intersectional communities. He has presented across North America on sex and disability as a Queer Crippled man. His written work has been highlighted in *Out Magazine*, *The Advocate*, and *Huffington Post*. He is also host of *Doing "It" With a Twist*, a podcast that explores the realities of sex and disability.

**Matthew J. Jones** received his doctorate in Critical & Comparative Studies of Music in 2014 from The University of Virginia. His work explores the intersections of music, sexuality, illness, and social justice with essays in *The Journal of Popular Music Studies*, *The Journal of the Society for American Music*, and *Women and Music*. He is currently completing a biography of AIDS activist and songwriter Michael Callen and a second book about music and the AIDS epidemic.

**Byron Lee**'s research examines public communications about sexual identities. He has published work on gay tourism advertising, and masculinities in gay pornography. His research also looks at media and public memory. He has previously taught in the Critical Writing Program at the University of Pennsylvania, and in the School of Media and Communication at Temple University. He holds a PhD in Mass Media and Communication from Temple University, and a Master's Degree in Women's Studies from Canada's Simon Fraser University.

**Evan Litwack** is a doctoral student in the Department of Communication at the University of North Carolina, Chapel Hill. He is currently working on a dissertation that concerns the history and theory of sexuality under and in the wake of U.S. slavery.

**Julie Maier** is a PhD Candidate in Kinesiology (Physical Cultural Studies focus) at the University of Maryland. Her research interests center on how normative health discourses and practices affect women's—and other marginalized groups'—well-being. She is particularly interested in the development of programming aimed at creating more meaningful, pleasurable, and empowering physical activity experiences for different groups of women (e.g. those who are queer, living with mental illness, etc.).

**Bonnie J. Morris** is a women's studies professor and historian, an archivist/scholar of the women's music movement. She is the author of 15 books, including three Lambda Literary Finalists (*Eden Built By Eves*, *Girl Reel*, *Revenge of the Women's Studies Professor*) and the critical feminist texts *Women's History for Beginners* and *The Disappearing L*. Her recent exhibit on women's music at the Library of Congress broke new ground, showcasing lesbian albums. She is an historical consultant to the Smithsonian Institute, the AP U.S. History exam, Disney Animation, the State Department's International Visitor program, the Global Women's Institute, and Pacifica Radio Archives.

**Joel A. Muraco**, PhD, is an online lecturer in Human Development at the University of Wisconsin–Green Bay and Human Development and Family Studies at The Pennsylvania State University. His research primarily focuses on the intersection of sexual identity and romantic relationships. He teaches courses in human sexuality and sexual identities.

**Donald L. Opitz** is Associate Professor in the School for New Learning, DePaul University, Chicago. A member of the faculty advisory board of DePaul's

LGBTQ Studies Program and affiliated scholar of the Department of History, his teaching and research interests include topics within the history of science, women's and gender studies, and LGBTQ studies. He is lead editor of *Domesticity in the Making of Modern Science* (Palgrave Macmillan, 2016).

**Kerry John Poynter** has over 20 years of experience working with gender and sexual minority students in higher education at a number of institutions including Columbia University, Duke University, New York University, and Western Michigan University. Among his experiences he has managed a 2500 sq. ft. LGBTQIA+ location; coordinated four LGBTQIA+ Safe Space Ally Programs; and empowered students through peer education. His work with Lavender Graduation ceremonies was cited by *Instinct Magazine* as the best of LGBTQ offerings on college campuses. He is the editor and author of *Safe Zones: Training Allies of LGBTQIA+ Young Adults* (Rowman & Littlefield Publishers, 2017) and has articles that appear in *About Campus*, *The Journal of LGBT Youth*, *The New Directions in Student Services* series, and *The Journal of Baccalaureate Social Work*. Since 2010, he has served as the Director of the Gender & Sexuality Student Services Office at the University of Illinois Springfield where he also served as the Interim Director of the Diversity Center for two years.

**Elizabeth Ribarsky** (PhD, University of Nebraska-Lincoln) is an associate professor in the Communication Department at the University of Illinois Springfield. She teaches courses in interpersonal communication and focuses her research on communication and identity within romantic relationships. Elizabeth has presented numerous papers and panels at regional and national conferences and co-edited (with Michael J. Murphy) *Activities for Teaching Gender and Sexuality in the University Classroom* (Rowman & Littlefield Education, 2013).

**Helis Sikk** is a Postdoctoral Fellow at the Smithsonian and a Visiting Assistant Professor in the Gender, Sexuality, and Women's Studies Program at The College of William and Mary. Her research takes a feral multidisciplinary approach to explore the relationships between queerness, affect, the built environment, communities, media and visual cultures.

**William J. Simmons** received his BA in art history and LGBTQ studies at Harvard University. He is a Provost's Fellow in the Humanities in the art history PhD program of the University of Southern California and a Mellon Fellow in Women's History at the New-York Historical Society.

**Christine Smith** is Associate Professor of Psychology, Human Development, and Women's and Gender Studies at the University of Wisconsin-Green Bay. A social psychologist by training, she has taught courses on LGBT lives and experiences as well as courses on sexuality and the psychology of women and gender. She has written extensively on romantic relationships and in the area of fat studies.

**Daniel B. Stewart**, MS, is a doctoral candidate in Social Work at Saint Louis University. He holds degrees in Psychology and Gerontology from Saint Louis University and the University of Missouri–St. Louis, respectively. He oversees SAGE (Services and Advocacy of GLBT Elders) of PROMO Fund, a Missouri statewide affiliate. In addition, he presents to organizations across the state on LGBTQ topics including: cultural sensitivity, LGBTQ and aging, and an introduction to the Trans experience.

**Susan K. Thomas** earned her PhD in English from The University of Kansas in 2012. She is currently an Assistant Researcher at KU's Assessment & Achievement Institute and an independent scholar. Her current research interests are the intersections of race and sexuality and the marginalization of fetish communities within the LGBTQ communities.

**George A. Waller** is Assistant Professor of Political Science at the University of Wisconsin-Fox Valley (one of the two year colleges in the University of Wisconsin System). He teaches all Political Science courses offered at UW-Fox Valley, and also teaches courses in the Gender, Sexuality, and Women's Studies Program including: *Introduction to Gender, Sexuality, and Women's Studies* (GSW 101) and *Sex, Power, and Public Policy* (POL/GSW 231). Professor Waller obtained his BA from Marquette University and his MA from the University of North Dakota. He did PhD work (ABD) at the University of Wisconsin-Milwaukee. Research interests include LGBTQ politics, public policy, and political behavior. Waller is currently researching the resurgence of authoritarianism in American and world politics.

**Abigail "Abi" Weissman**, PsyD (PSY 27497; pronouns: she, her, hers), is a feminist and LGBTQIQ- affirming, multiculturally-competent, California clinical psychologist who provides psychotherapy, training, supervision, and consultation, in San Diego County. She is Co-Chair of the San Diego Psychological Association (SDPA)'s LGBT Committee and been elected as a Member at Large on the SDPA's Board of Directors. She holds an MA in Human Sexuality studies and a Doctorate and MA in Clinical Psychology.

# Index

Note: Bold page numbers denote illustrations.